Emily Mupinga

Quantitative Research in Education

Intermediate & Advanced Methods

DIMITER M. DIMITROV

George Mason University

New York

Published by Whittier Publications, Inc.

Oceanside, NY 11572

Tel: 1-800-897-TEXT (8398)

516-432-8120

Cover Design: Zheko Aleksiev

ISBN 978-1-57604-301-1

Printed in the United States of America

1 0 9 8 7 6 5 4 3 2 1

Contents

Chapter 5
BASIC RESEARCH DESIGNS 53

PART III UNIVARIATE DATA ANALYSIS 65

Chapter 6
REVIEW OF INTRODUCTORY STATISTICS 67

Chapter 14

ONE-FACTOR ANALYSIS OF VARIANCE 217

Chapter 15

TWO- AND THREE-FACTOR ANOVA 241

PREFACE

This book offers a comprehensive presentation of quantitative research design and statistical methods in the context of education and related fields. The text is intended primarily for use by students who take intermediate and advanced quantitative research courses as a part of their graduate degree program, but it can be a useful resource for researchers in education, counseling, rehabilitation, psychology, sociology, social work, and human development as well.

The main purpose of this book is to provide the readers with an in-depth conceptual and methodological understanding of intermediate and advanced quantitative research methods, as well as the skills necessary to apply such methods using SPSS and to interpret the results. This is achieved by building layers of context-based understanding of research concepts and methods, their statistical translation, methodological principles, computer-based data analysis, presentation of the results in APA style format, and contextual interpretations. The text allows people who experience difficulties with analytic representations of statistical concepts to capitalize on conceptual understanding and still be able to master the research tools necessary for their work on theses, dissertations, and professional research.

While there are many excellent introductory books on research design and statistics in education and the social sciences, most books at the intermediate and advanced levels tend to be either too technical and mathematical or too simplistic. Typically, claiming to have an "applied orientation," such books are dominated by presentations of SPSS dialog boxes and printouts at the expense of theoretical and methodological rigor. To bridge the gap between these extremes, this book attempts to provide a balance between conceptual meaning and its statistical translation by developing understanding and application skills in a spiral exposure to quantitative concepts and methods. For example, the comparison of groups on variables of interest is addressed in a sequence from univariate cases of *t*-tests, nonparametric methods, and analysis of variance (ANOVA) to scenarios illustrating the use of multivariate analysis of variance (MANOVA) and structural equation modeling (SEM). As another example, the concept of validity is addressed in the framework of measurement, research design, and structural equation modeling. Particular attention is devoted to potential problems associated with violation of assumptions, common misconceptions (e.g., conducting MANOVA versus separate ANOVAs), effect sizes, confidence intervals, and sample size. The book is organized in four parts comprising 24 chapters. Each chapter ends with a summary and study questions.

Part I [*Measurement in Educational Research*] consists of three chapters. Chapter 1 presents variables and measurement scales in the context of education. The focus is on the nature of measurement in education, types of variables, types of scales and their transformations, permissible arithmetic operations with scale values, summation symbols, and basic rules of summation. Chapter 2 introduces the classical model of reliability of scores, types of reliability, and reliability of composite scores. Chapter 3 deals with the concept of validity for measurement instruments (e.g., tests, questionnaires, or inventories) and types of validity (content-related validity, criterion-related validity, and construct-related validity).

Part II [*Research Design*] consists of two chapters. Chapter 4 deals with research problems, hypotheses, and types of quantitative research: nonexperimental research, experimental research, and threats to internal and external validity. Chapter 5 presents pre-experimental and true experimental research designs that involve quantitative methods of data analysis. The focus is primarily on conceptual understanding and methodological principles underlying the application of such designs in educational research.

Part III [*Univariate Statistics in Educational Research*] consists of fourteen chapters. The first five of these chapters (6, 7, 8, 9, and 10) cover introductory statistics and prepare the ground for understanding and practical applications of intermediate statistics in educational research. The next six chapters (11 through 16) provide intermediate treatment of correlation, regression, and analysis of variance (ANOVA) including some nonparametric methods. The last three chapters in this section (17, 18, and 19) provide more advanced treatment of multiple regression, analysis of variance, and the relations between them.

Part IV [*Multivariate Statistics in Educational Research*] consists of five chapters. This part covers the topics of logistic regression, multivariate analysis of variance (MANOVA), exploratory factor analysis, confirmatory factor analysis, and elements of structural equation modeling (SEM). The analytic framework of these topics is simplified and tailored to conceptual understanding, computer-aided applications, and interpretations in the context of educational research.

Supplements

Data sets for computer-based applications in examples using SPSS can be downloaded from the online supplement to this book [http://cehd.gmu.edu/book/dimitrov]. This supplement provides also (a) answers to the study questions for each chapter, (b) addendum to some topics discussed in the book, (c) syntax for confirmatory factor analysis, path analysis, and group comparison on latent variables in the framework of major computer programs — LISREL, AMOS, EQS, and M*plus* [used for illustrations in Chapters 23 and 24], and (d) additional references (books, articles, and online products) related to the content of this book.

Acknowledgments

I would like to acknowledge the assistance of my graduate research assistant, Jill Lammert, who provided valuable editorial comments and suggestions throughout the writing of this book. I also appreciate the feedback and encouragement of colleagues from different universities as well as graduate students who used draft chapters of this book in quantitative research courses that they took with me in the Graduate School of Education at George Mason University.

Dimiter M. Dimitrov

MEASUREMENT *in* EDUCATION

CHAPTER 1

VARIABLES AND MEASUREMENT SCALES

Contrary to common belief, *science* is not just about discovering new facts and adding them to a body of knowledge. The basic goal of science is to provide general theoretical explanations of natural phenomena. Important steps in the process of building, revising, or extending theory are *explanation*, *understanding*, *prediction*, and *control*. As Kerlinger (1986, p. 9) noted, this is because of the definition and nature of theory:

> **A theory is a set of interrelated constructs (concepts), definitions, and propositions that present a systematic view of phenomena by specifying relations among variables, with the purpose of explaining and predicting the phenomena.**

A researcher may want to "explain" (or "predict") the academic performance of students from a set of variables such as gender, socioeconomic status, test anxiety, self-esteem, motivation, verbal skills, and numeric skills. A scientific approach to such explanation would require that the selection of these "predictors" of students' academic performance be guided by some theoretical model of school success. Even better, the researcher may test hypotheses about the presumed predictive relationships using two (or more) "rival" models of school success. An important condition for reaching valid interpretations and conclusions from testing hypotheses is collecting accurate measures (data) for the variables involved in the hypothesized relations. The researcher must, therefore, clearly understand the nature of the study variables and the properties of their measurement scales.

1.1 Variables in Educational Research

In general, a **variable** is any characteristic of a person (or an object) that may vary across persons or across different time points. A person's weight, for example, is a variable with different values for different people, although some people may weigh the same. This variable can also take on different values at different points in time, such as when obtaining repeated measurements for one person (say, every month during a one-year period to monitor the effect of a weight-loss treatment). Most often, the capital letters X, Y, and Z (in italics) are used to denote variables. If a study involves many variables, we can use one capital letter with subscripts to denote different variables. For example, if an education study is about the prediction of college success for freshmen from their high school grade-point average (GPA), SAT score, and number of advanced placement (AP) courses taken, we can use Y to denote the variable being predicted (Y = college success) and X, with subscripts, to name the variables used as predictors: X_1 = GPA, X_2 = SAT score, X_3 = number of AP courses.

As will be discussed below, variables can also be described (or classified) according to their nature, different characteristics, and scale of measurement — for example, *observable* versus *unobservable* (hidden, latent) variables or *continuous* versus *discrete* variables. We also use lowercase letters in italics (e.g., *a, b, c, d* or others) to stand for **constants** (numbers that remain the same throughout an analysis).

1.1.1 Observable versus Latent Variables

Variables which can be measured directly are referred to in behavioral research as **observable variables**. In the education study cited above, for example, the observable variables would be the students' *gender*, *ethnicity*, *age*, *weight*, *height*, *grade level*, *socioeconomic status*, *number of AP courses taken*, and *GPA*. Variables such as *intelligence*, *attitude toward education*, *motivation*, *anxiety*, *verbal ability*, and *math ability*, on the other hand, are not directly observable and are therefore referred to as **latent** (unobservable, hidden) **variables** or **constructs**. Typically, a construct is given an operational definition which specifies which observed variables are considered to be measurable indicators of the construct. For instance, measurable indicators of anxiety can include the person's responses to items on an anxiety test, the person's heartbeat and skin responses, or [his or her reactions to] some experimental manipulations. Hereafter, the terms *latent variable* and *construct* will be used interchangeably.

It is important to note that the operational definition for a construct should be based on a specific theory and, therefore, the validity of the measurable indicators of the construct will depend on the level of correctness of this theory. For example, if a theory of creativity assumes, among other things, that people who can provide different approaches to the solution of a given problem are more creative, then the number of approaches to solving individual problems (or tasks) can be used as an indicator of creativity. If, however, this theory is proven wrong, then the person's score on this indicator cannot be used for valid assessment of creativity. We will learn more about validation and measurement of constructs in Chapters 3 and 23.

1.1.2 Continuous versus Discrete Variables

Another distinction that must be made related to variables involved in a research study is that between continuous and discrete variables. **Continuous variables** are those that can take any possible value within a specific numeric interval. For example, the height of the students in a middle school population is a continuous variable since it can take any value within an interval on the scale; (usually rounded to the nearest inch or tenth of an inch). All variables associated with *distance*, *weight*, and *temperature* are continuous in nature. Other examples of continuous variables are the student's age, time on task involvement in a classroom observation, and proficiency in a subject area such as math, science, and reading. All latent variables (constructs) involved in educational research are continuous in nature — e.g., academic achievement, motivation, anxiety, depression, and attitude (e.g., toward school, religion, or racial groups).

Discrete variables can only take separate values (say, integer numbers). The measurement of a discrete variable usually involves counting or enumeration of "how many times" something has occurred. Counting variables are, for example, the number of spelling errors in a writing sample or the number of successful shots (points) by individual players in a basketball game. Thus, while the measurement of a continuous variable relates to the question "How much?," the measurement of a discrete variable relates to the question "How many?"

NOTE [1.1] It may be confusing that values of continuous variables are reported as "discrete" values. This is because the values of a continuous variable are usually rounded. Take, for example, a weekly weather report on temperature (in Fahrenheit): 45°, 48°, 45°, 58°, 52°, 47°, 51° — values of the continuous variable *temperature* look like "discrete" because they are rounded to the nearest integer. As another example, GPA scores rounded to the nearest hundredth (e.g., 3.52, 3.37, 4.00, etc.) also look like "discrete" values, but they represent a continuous variable (*academic achievement*).

1.2 Scales of Measurement

1.2.1 What is Measurement?

We can think of **measurement** as a process that involves three components — an *object of measurement*, a *set of numbers*, and a *system of rules* that serve to assign numbers to magnitudes of the variable being measured. The object of measurement can be an observable variable (e.g., height, age, or grade level in school) or a latent variable (e.g., motivation, verbal ability, or attitude). Any latent variable can be viewed as a "hidden" continuum (dimension) with magnitudes increasing in a given direction (say, from left to right if the continuum is represented with a straight line – see Figure 1.1). As discussed earlier (1.1.1), a latent variable in education is usually defined with observable indicators (e.g., test items). The person's total score on these indicators is the number assigned to the "hidden" magnitude for this person on the continuum of the latent variable.

In this chapter, the term "magnitude" will indicate the location of a person on the continuum of a latent variable, whereas the "number assigned to a magnitude" will stand for the person's "score" on observable indicator(s) of this latent variable (e.g., test items). Related to this, we will also distinguish "distance between magnitudes" from "difference between numbers."

Let's say, for example, that we measure reading comprehension of middle school students using a test of 20 binary items (1 = correct, 0 = incorrect). These items serve as observable indicators of the latent variable reading comprehension. The student's total test score is the number assigned to the actual magnitude of reading comprehension for this student. Graphically, this is illustrated in Figure 1.1, where M_1, M_2, M_3, and M_4 stand for the actual (yet, practically "hidden") magnitudes on the continuum of reading comprehension of four students, Mitch, Christi, Peter, and Jill, and the numbers (total test scores) associated with these magnitudes are 10, 12, 17, and 19, respectively. With 21 binary items, there are 21 "discrete" integer numbers (possible test scores: 0, 1, 2, ..., 19, 20) that can be assigned to magnitudes of the continuous variable reading comprehension. The explanation of this "paradox" is that each number must be viewed as a midpoint of a *score interval*, so that all score intervals together cover with no "gap" a continuous interval on the number line. There are 21 such intervals in this case: (-0.5, 0.5) with a midpoint of 0, (0.5, 1.5) with a midpoint of 1, and so on, up to the interval (19.5, 20.5) with a midpoint of 20.

Figure 1.1 *Measurement of a latent variable (reading comprehension)*

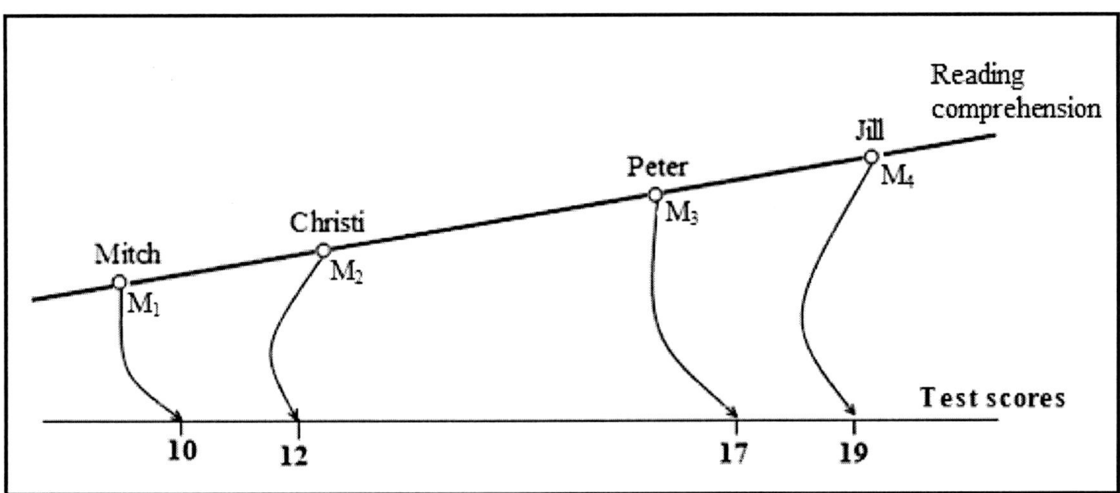

1.2.2 Nominal Scale

A **nominal scale** is used to classify persons (or objects) into mutually exclusive categories, say, by gender, ethnicity, professional occupation, etc. The numbers on a nominal scale serve only as "names" of such categories, hence the name of this scale; (in Latin, "nome" means "name"). It is important to emphasize that nominal scale numbers do not reflect "magnitudes" of the classification variable. For example, if we use the nominal scale "1 = male, 2 = female" to label gender groups, this does not mean that 1 and 2 are numeric values assigned to different gender "magnitudes." Thus, the nominal scale is not a true measurement scale because we cannot place individuals in any sort of (increasing or decreasing) order based on their nominal classification. Taking this into account, nominal scales are useful for the purposes of coding and analysis of educational data.

1.2.3 Ordinal Scale

An **ordinal scale** is one in which the magnitudes of the variable (trait, property) being measured are ordered in the same way as the numbers assigned to these magnitudes. For example, Figure 1.1 illustrates an ordinal scale of measurement since the students' actual magnitudes of reading comprehension (M_1, M_2, M_3, and M_4) increase in the same order as their scores (10, 12, 17, and 19, respectively). We can also say that, with an ordinal scale, for any two individuals the higher score will be assigned to the person who has *more* of the variable (trait) being measured. However, the ordinal scale does not show *by how much* the two individuals differ on this variable. In other words, an ordinal scale provides information about the order of individuals, in terms of their actual magnitudes on the variable being measured, but not about the distances between such magnitudes. In a beauty contest, for example, if the ordinal scale values of 1, 2, and 3 indicate first, second, and third place, thus specifying which of the contestants is "more beautiful," the equal differences $2 - 1 = 3 - 2$ do not necessarily mean that the actual "beauty difference" between the first and second contestants is the same as that between the second and third contestants.

1.2.4 Interval Scale

An **interval scale** provides information about the order and the distances between actual magnitudes of the variable being measured. Specifically, equal distances between magnitudes on the variable being measured will result in equal differences between the scores assigned to these magnitudes with an interval scale. To illustrate, let's look again at the latent magnitudes of reading comprehension provided in Figure 1.1. If we assume that the latent distance between Mitch and Mary in reading comprehension is the same as that between Peter and Jill (that is, $M_2 - M_1 = M_4 - M_3$), then this is an interval scale since the difference between the scores assigned to Mitch and Mary is the same as the score difference between Peter and Jill ($12 - 10 = 19 - 17$).

It is important to note, however, that the interval scale has an *arbitrary zero point*. In other words, when "zero" is assigned to a given magnitude of a variable measured on an interval scale, this does not necessarily mean that this magnitude is actually "missing" (that is, that there is no magnitude at all). For example, the measurement of temperature is an interval scale, but if at a given moment the temperature is "zero degrees" (in Fahrenheit or Celsius) this does not mean that there is no temperature at all at this moment. The *zero* (origin) of an interval scale is conventional and can be "moved" (up or down) using an appropriate linear transformation. For example, the formula used for transformation from Celsius to Fahrenheit is: $F = (9/5)C + 32$, where C and F stand for temperature readings in Celsius and Fahrenheit, respectively. Thus, if C

= 0, then $F = 32$ (that is, 0° in Celsius corresponds to 32° in Fahrenheit). Note also that, because the *zero* (origin) of an interval scale is arbitrary and does not indicate absence of the trait being measured, the ratio of two numbers on an interval scale does not provide information about the *ratio* of the trait magnitudes that correspond to these two numbers. For example, if the temperature readings in two consecutive days were, say, 60°F on Tuesday and 30°F on Wednesday, we cannot say that "on Tuesday was twice as hot as on Wednesday." We can only say that the temperature on Wednesday was 30°F lower than that on Tuesday (or "the temperature dropped by 30°F").

1.2.5 Ratio Scale

A **ratio scale** provides information about the *ratio* between magnitudes of the variable being measured, in addition to the information that this scale provides about the order of such magnitudes and distances between them. The zero (origin) of a ratio scale is naturally "fixed," that is, "zero" indicates absence of the property being measured. For example, "zero distance" between two points on a straight line indicates that there is no distance between these two points (which is the case when two points perfectly coincide). Also, the origin of all ratio scales for distance measurement is the same (e.g., "zero" inches and "zero" centimeters indicate the same thing — absence of distance). As a reminder, this is *not* the case with interval scales — for example, 0°C and 0°F stand for different magnitudes of temperature and do not indicate absence of temperature. Further, let's assume that the property being measured on a ratio scale is *length* of objects. If two objects are 50 feet and 25 feet long, respectively, we can say that "the first object is *twice as long* as the second object." Unfortunately, it is not possible to measure latent variables in education (or in other behavioral fields) on a ratio scale. Therefore, we cannot say, for example, that "Mary is twice as creative as John" if Mary has 100 points and John has 50 points on a test of creativity. The best we can hope is that latent variables in education are measured on interval (or close to interval) scales.

1.2.6 Scale Transformations and Operations

In this section, the terms "transformation and "operation" have different meanings when related to scale numbers. Specifically, *transformation of numbers* means that each number is submitted to the same mathematical transformation (e.g., formula). For example, we can transform the numeric values (say, 2, 3, 5, and 10) of a variable X using the transformation $Y = X + 10$ (that is, "adding 10" to each number) thus obtaining a new set of numbers: 12, 13, 15, and 20. Instead, carrying out an *operation with numbers* means that these numbers are submitted to an arithmetic operation (addition, subtraction, multiplication, or division). For example, the arithmetic operation "addition" is used with numbers to calculate their sum $(2 + 3 + 5 + 10 = 20)$.

Of particular interest in this chapter are **linear transformations**. Specifically, given the values of a variable X, the general form of a linear transformation of X is:

$$Y = bX + a, \qquad (1)$$

where b is a constant, called the *slope*, a is a constant called the *intercept*. The values of the "new" variable, Y, are obtained by multiplying each value of X by the slope, b, and adding the intercept, a. The slope, b, can be any number different from zero ($b \neq 0$) and the intercept, a, can be any number (including zero). For example, (a) $Y = 0.5X + 10$ is a linear transformation of X, with $b = 0.5$ and $a = 10$, (b) $Y = 1.5X$ is a linear transformation of X, with $b = 1.5$ and $a = 0$, and

(c) $Y = X - 5$ is a linear transformation of X, with $b = 1$ and $a = -5$. To illustrate, if the values of a variable X: 2, 4, and 10 are on an interval scale, the transformation $Y = 0.5X + 10$ produces new values, Y: 11, 12, and 15, which are also on an interval scale.

For any linear transformation of X, the dots with coordinates X values (on the horizontal axis) and the transformed Y values (on the vertical axis) fall on a straight line, hence the name "linear transformation." The slope, b, determines the steepness of the line, whereas the intercept, a, shows where the line intersects with the vertical axis, Y; (hence the term 'intercept" for a). More information in this regard is provided later in this book [Chapter 10, Section 10.2.3]. All transformations with the same slope will produce parallel straight lines, the location of which is determined by their intercepts.

1.2.6.1 Nominal scale. Any transformation of numbers that label different categories in a nominal scale is permissible, as long as the resulting new numbers are also different. To illustrate, let's say that we have the nominal scale "1 = White, 2 = Black, and 3 = Asian" for three racial groups. We can, for example, *subtract one* from each of the original numbers, thus obtaining the nominal scale: "0 = White, 1 = Black, and 2 = Asian." It should be noted, however, that arithmetic operations with numbers that label nominal categories is meaningless. For example, if "1 = male, 2 = female" is a nominal scale for gender groups, it does not make any sense to add, subtract, or average these two numbers.

1.2.6.2 Ordinal scale. Any transformation to an ordinal scale that preserves the order of the scores originally obtained with this scale is permissible. For example, let's assume that 1, 2, and 3 are ordinal scale numbers that stand for first, second, and third place assigned to three students based on their ranking by popularity among other students. If we square these numbers, the resulting numbers (1, 4, and 9) are in the same order and, therefore, they also form an ordinal scale. However, it is not permissible to perform arithmetic operations with these numbers. For example, calculating the arithmetic mean of ordinal numbers (e.g., ranks) for a group of individuals in an attempt to provide an "average rank" for this group would be meaningless. This is because, as noted earlier (see 1.2.3), equal differences between ordinal scale numbers (e.g., ranks) do not necessarily represent equal distances between the corresponding magnitudes of the variable being measured — such distances remain unknown in ordinal scales.

1.2.6.3 Interval scale. If the numbers on an interval scale are changed by using a linear transformation, the resulting numbers will also be on an interval scale. That is, linear transformations maintain the interval scale. For example, the formula $F = (9/5)C + 32$, which is used to transform temperature readings from Celsius to Fahrenheit, is a linear transformation (*slope* = 9/5, *intercept* = 32). For instance, suppose that 5°, 10°, 20°, and 25° are temperature readings in Celsius. By replacing these numbers for C in the formula for transformation from Celsius to Fahrenheit, we obtain 41°, 50°, 68°, and 77° on the Fahrenheit scale. As we can see, equal differences between numbers on the Celsius scale (10° – 5° = 25° – 20°) result in equal differences between their corresponding numbers on the Fahrenheit scale (50° – 41° = 77° – 68°). Because of this property, arithmetic operations with interval scale numbers are permissible. So, given the temperature readings 5°, 10°, 20°, and 25° (in Celsius), we can compute the average temperature: (5° + 10° + 20° + 25°)/4 = 15°. Thus, arithmetic operations are permissible for interval scale numbers, but not for ordinal scale numbers.

NOTE [1.2] In many scenarios of assessment in education (e.g., traditional teacher-made tests), it is unlikely that the scale is (even close to) interval. Therefore, arithmetic operations with scores in such cases (e.g., calculation of *mean* and *standard deviation*) may produce misleading results. Interval (or close to interval) scales can be obtained with appropriate data transformations, which are usually performed with the development of standardized tests.

1.2.6.4 Ratio scale. If we multiply (or divide) each of the numbers on a ratio scale by a (non-zero) constant, the resulting new numbers will also be on a ratio scale. For example, since one inch is approximately 2.5 centimeters, we can transform the length of an object given in inches (L_{inch}) to its equivalent length in centimeters (L_{cm}) by using the transformation: $L_{inch} = 2.5L_{cm}$. It is now easy to see that the ratio of any two numbers in inches is the same as the ratio of their corresponding numbers in centimeters. [*Check*: take the ratio 'two inches to three inches,' 2/3, and calculate the ratio of corresponding numbers in centimeters.] This, of course, is true for any ratio scale. That is, multiplication (or division) of ratio scale numbers by a non-zero constant maintains the ratio scale. In addition, arithmetic operations with a set of ratio scale numbers are permissible (e.g., we can calculate statistics such *mean* and *standard deviation* for numbers obtained with a ratio scale). As noted earlier, typical ratio scales are those that measure distance (e.g., height of people or length of objects), weight, age, time, and counting (e.g., number of spelling errors). Unfortunately, it is not possible to develop ratio scales for latent variables (e.g., academic achievement, motivation, anxiety, depression, and self-esteem), although such variables are of major interest in education.

1.2.7 Scaling of Individual Items

Instruments for assessment in education and related fields consist of a number of individual items. The scale for examinees' responses on each item depends on the response format of the item. A *Binary scale* (1 = correct, 0 = incorrect) is typical for multiple-choice test items. A *Likert-type rating scale* is widely used with questionnaire items, say, on a 3-point scale (e.g., 1 = Never, 2 = Rarely, 3 = Always) or a 5-point scale (e.g., 1 = Strongly disagree, 2 = Disagree, 3 = Uncertain, 4 = Agree, 5 = Strongly agree). When the instrument measures several constructs (domains), the items related to different constructs may have different response formats or all of the items may be on the same scale. For example, the *Disruptive Behavior Rating Scale (DBRS*; Erford, 1993) measures disruptive behaviors of children aged 5-10 years. It assesses symptoms associated with four different domains (distractibility, impulsive-hyperactivity, oppositional behavior, and antisocial conduct), but all items are answered on a 4-point Likert-type rating scale for the frequency of a displayed behavior: 0 = Rarely/Hardly Ever, 1 = Occasionally, 2 = Frequently, and 3 = Most of the time.

Since the overall assessment with an instrument is based on the respondent's scores on all items, the measurement quality of the total (composite) score is of particular interest. An important task in this regard is to obtain (at least close to) interval scales through the development of instruments for assessment of constructs in education and related fields (e.g., reading comprehension, mathematics proficiency, motivation, behavior, self-esteem, anxiety, etc.). As already noted, it is difficult (if not impossible) to measure such constructs on a ratio scale [a *ratio-like* scale for latent variables (constructs) can be obtained with some advanced measurement models (e.g., Rasch, 1960), but their discussion is beyond the scope of this book.]

1.3 Symbols and Rules for Summation of Variables

1.3.1 Symbolic Notations

As noted earlier, italicized capital letters (most frequently, *X*, *Y*, and *Z*) are used to denote variables. For example, if we study the relationship between *age* and *memory*, *X* may stand for age and *Y*, for memory. Table 1.1 provides hypothetical numeric values of *X* and *Y* for a small sample of five people ($n = 5$). The values of X represent the persons' age (in years), while the Y values represent their scores on a memory test.

Table 1.1 *Age (in years) and memory test scores*

Person's ID	*Name*	*Age (X)*	*Memory (Y)*
1	John	12	32
2	Mary	16	42
3	Mitch	22	50
4	Kristine	35	46
5	Tony	65	30

Subscripts--italicized lowercase letters such as *i*, *j*, *k*, *l*, or *m*--are used for symbolic notation of numeric values ("observations") of a variable being measured. With the data in Table 1.1, for example, X_i stands for the *i*th observation on X, and Y_i, for the *i*th observation on Y; ($i = 1, 2, \ldots, 5$). Specifically, using the person's identification number (ID), the X values (age in years) are: $X_1 = 12$, $X_2 = 16$, $X_3 = 22$, $X_4 = 35$, and $X_5 = 65$. Likewise, the Y values are: $Y_1 = 32$, $Y_2 = 42$, $Y_3 = 50$, $Y_4 = 46$, and $Y_5 = 30$. We can also represent the sum of X and Y values for each person in a symbolic form as follows: $(X_1 + Y_1)$, $(X_2 + Y_2)$, $(X_3 + Y_3)$, $(X_4 + Y_4)$, $(X_5 + Y_5)$.

1.3.2 Summation Operator

The capital Greek letter Σ (*sigma*) is used to symbolize *summation* of variable values. For example, the sum of all X values in Table 1.1 can be represented as follows:

$$\sum_{i=1}^{5} X_i = X_1 + X_2 + X_3 + X_4 + X_5 = 12 + 16 + 22 + 35 + 65 = 150.$$

[*Check*: Do the same for the sum of all Y values in Table 1.1] In the general case of n observations on a variable X, the symbol $\sum_{i=1}^{n} X_i$ stands for "the sum of all X values starting from X_1 and ending with X_n." We can use only ΣX_i, provided that the range of the index i is already known.

Some basic **summation rules** follow.

Rule 1. The sum of a constant, c, multiplied by each value of a variable, X_i, equals the sum of all values multiplied by the constant. That is,

$$\sum_{i=1}^{n} cX_i = c\sum_{i=1}^{n} X_i \qquad \textbf{(1.1)}$$

For example, if we multiply each X value in Table 1.1 by 10, the sum of the resulting five products can be calculated by using equation (1.1) as follows:

$$\sum_{i=1}^{5} 10X_i = 10\sum_{i=1}^{5} X_i = (10)(150) = 1500.$$

Rule 2. The summation over the sum of two (or more) variables is the same as adding their individual sums. With two variables, this rule can be presented as follows:

$$\sum_{i=1}^{n}(X_i + Y_i) = \sum_{i=1}^{n} X_i + \sum_{i=1}^{n} Y_i. \qquad \textbf{(1.2)}$$

For example, if we add the X and Y values for each person in Table 1.1, the summation over the resulting five sums can be performed using equation (1.2):

$$\sum_{i=1}^{5}(X_i + Y_i) = \sum_{i=1}^{5} X_i + \sum_{i=1}^{5} Y_i = 150 + 200 = 350.$$

Rule 3. If a variable X has n values and a constant, c, is added to each of them, the summation over the resulting sums ($X_i + c$) equals the sum of all X values plus n times the constant.

$$\sum_{i=1}^{n}(X_i + c) = \sum_{i=1}^{n} X_i + nc. \qquad \textbf{(1.3)}$$

For example, if we add 10 to each X value in Table 1.1, the summation over the resulting five sums, using equation (1.3), is

$$\sum_{i=1}^{5}(X_i + 10) = \sum_{i=1}^{5} X_i + (5)(10) = 150 + 50 = 200.$$

[*Check*: Do the same, assuming that 10 is added to each Y value in Table 1.1]

Equation 1.3 also holds when the constant c is a negative number. To illustrate, let's first calculate the *mean* of all X values in Table 1.1 (i.e., the "average age" of all five persons). Given that the sum of all X values is 150, the mean for the group of five people is: $\overline{X} = 150/5 = 50$. If we subtract the mean from each X value, the sum of the resulting differences, referred to as the "sum of deviations about the mean," can be calculated by using equation 1.3 with a negative constant (c = -50):

$$\sum_{i=1}^{5}(X_i - \overline{X}) = \sum_{i=1}^{5}(X_i - 50) = \sum_{i=1}^{5} X_i - (5)(50) = 150 - 150 = 0.$$

In fact, it is always true that the sum of deviations about the mean equals zero. However, this is *not* true for the "sum of squared deviations about the mean" [Check this for X in Table 1.1].

1.4 Summary

Understanding the nature of variables and the properties of their measurement scales is crucial for obtaining accurate results and valid interpretations in the context of educational research and practice. A bulleted summary of concepts and highlights provided in this chapter follows:

- A **variable** is any characteristic of a person (or an object) that may take on different values across different persons or across different time points for the same person.

• **Observable variables** can be measured directly — for example, a student's *gender*, *age*, *grade level*, *height*, and *weight*.

• **Latent variables**, referred to also as **constructs**, are "hidden" (unobservable) in nature — for example, a student's *intelligence*, *academic achievement*, *verbal ability*, *attitude*, *motivation*, *anxiety*, *depression*, *locus of control*, and *self-esteem*.

• **Continuous variables** can take any possible value within a specific numeric interval — for example, *age*, *height*, *weight*, and all latent variables (e.g., intelligence, academic achievement, motivation, etc.).

• **Discrete variables** take only separate (clearly distinguishable from one another) numeric values — they usually involve *counting* or *enumeration* (e.g., number of spelling errors in a writing test, number of push-ups in a physical education test, etc.).

• When measures of a continuous variable are reported like "discrete" values (rounded, say, to the nearest integer), each such value should be viewed as a midpoint of a numeric interval, so that all adjacent numeric intervals cover (with no "gap") some continuous part on the numeric line. Thus, if four grade scores (1, 2, 3, and 4) are used to assess students on a continuous variable (e.g., verbal ability), the *score* of 2, for example, must be viewed as a *score interval* (from 1.5 to 2.5), and 2 is the midpoint of this interval.

• **Measurement** is a process that involves three components — an *object of measurement*, a *set of numbers*, and a *system of rules* that serve to assign numbers to magnitudes of the variable being measured.

• A **nominal scale** is used to classify persons (or objects) into mutually exclusive categories (e.g., by gender, ethnicity, or professional occupation). Numbers in a nominal scale serve only as "names" (labels) of nominal categories. Therefore, arithmetic operations with such numbers (e.g., calculating their *mean*) are meaningless.

• An **ordinal scale** is one in which the magnitudes of the variable being measured are ordered in the same way as the numbers assigned to these magnitudes. Any transformation of ordinal numbers that preserves their original order is permissible, but arithmetic operations (e.g., calculating their mean) are not allowed. An example of ordinal scales are ranking numbers assigned to participants in, say, a beauty contest.

• An **interval scale** is one in which equal distances between magnitudes on the variable being measured result in equal differences between the numbers assigned to these magnitudes. The *zero* (origin) of an interval scale is arbitrary and can be moved up or down by means of a linear transformation. Zero on an interval scale does not indicate absence of the variable (trait) being measured; (e.g., "zero degrees" in Fahrenheit or Celsius does not mean that there is no temperature). Any linear transformation ($Y = bX + a$) on a variable X measured on an interval scale produces a variable, Y, which is also measured on an interval scale — that is, linear transformations maintain interval scales. Also, arithmetic operations with interval scale values (e.g., calculation of their *mean*) are permissible. In the education, interval scales (or close to interval scales) are usually obtained through the development of standardized tests.

• A **ratio scale** is one in which the proportion of any two magnitudes on the variable being measured equals the proportion of the two numbers assigned to these magnitudes. The *zero* (origin) of any ratio indicates absence of the trait being measured (e.g., "zero distance" indicates the lack of distance). Any scale that measures *distance* or *weight* is a ratio scale. Only linear transformations with an intercept of zero ($Y = bX$) are permissible with a ratio scale.

- **Summation operator:** $\sum_{i=1}^{n} X_i = X_1 + X_2 + \ldots + X_n$.

- **Summation rules:**

  Rule 1. $\sum_{i=1}^{n} cX_i = c\sum_{i=1}^{n} X_i$

  Rule 2. $\sum_{i=1}^{n} (X_i + Y_i) = \sum_{i=1}^{n} X_i + \sum_{i=1}^{n} Y_i$.

  Rule 3. $\sum_{i=1}^{n} (X_i + c) = \sum_{i=1}^{n} X_i + nc$.

1.5 Study Questions

1. If equal differences between scores for any two pairs of examinees on a standardized anxiety test correspond to equal distances between the actual anxiety magnitudes that the scores represent, the measurement scale is:

(a) ordinal **(b)** interval **(c)** ratio **(d)** all of the above.

2. Check (√) all appropriate boxes for the measurement scale in the following table [*Hint*: Each scalc has thc characteristics of its lower level scales.]

	Type of Scale			
Variable	**Nominal**	**Ordinal**	**Interval**	**Ratio**
Gender (1 = male, 2 = female)				
Temperature (in F° or C°)				
Age (in years)				
Level of disability (1 = mild, 2 = severe)				
Math proficiency (scores on a standar-dized proficiency test)				
Beauty contest ranks (1st, 2nd, 3rd place)				
Ethnicity (1 = White, 2 = Asian, 3 = African-American, 4 = Latino, 5 = Other)				

3. Check (√) two appropriate boxes for each variable in the table that follows.

Variable	**Observed**	**Latent**	**Discrete**	**Continuous**
Age				
Attitude				
Gender				
Verbal skills				
Motivation				
Academic achievement				
Ethnicity				
Number of spelling errors				
Anxiety				

4. If runners on a track team took 1st, 2nd, and 6th place in an athletic competition, is it appropriate to compute (1 + 2 + 6)/3 = 3 and say that, on average, this team took 3rd place in that competition? Explain your answer.

5. If John and Mary have 20 and 40 points, respectively, on a reading test, is it appropriate to say that Mary is twice as proficient as John in reading? Explain your answer.

6. Which type of scale would use the categories *low*, *average*, and *high* to classify people by level of performance?

(a) nominal, **(b)** ordinal, **(c)** interval, **(d)** ratio, **(e)** all of the above.

8. Provide the developed form of the symbolic summation:

(a) $\sum_{i=1}^{4}(X_i + 7)$; **(b)** $\sum_{i=1}^{5}(Y_i - 5)$; **(c)** $\sum_{i=1}^{10}5X_i$; **(d)** $\sum_{i=1}^{4}(X_i + 10)^2$.

9. Present the sum using the summation symbol, Σ:

(a) $X_1 + X_2 + X_3 + X_4 + X_5 + X_6 + X_7 + X_8 + X_9 + X_{10}$.

(b) $(X_1 - 5)^2 + (X_2 - 5)^2 + (X_3 - 5)^2 + (X_4 - 5)^2 + (X_5 - 5)^2$.

10. Calculate the sum with the *X* and *Y* values in Table 1.1

(a) $\sum_{i=1}^{5}100Y_i$; **(b)** $\sum_{i=1}^{5}(Y_i - X_i)$; **(c)** $\sum_{i=1}^{5}10(X_i + Y_i)$; **(d)** $\sum_{i=1}^{5}(Y_i + 100)$.

[*Hint*: Use the summation rules provided with equations 1.1, 1.2, and 1.3.]

CHAPTER 2

RELIABILITY

2.1 What is Reliability?

Measurements in education, other behavioral sciences, and even physical measurements, are not completely accurate and consistent. For example, although the height of a person remains constant throughout repeated measurements using the same scale within a short period of time (say, 20 minutes), the observed values would be scattered around this constant due to imperfection in the visual acuity of the individual(s) performing the repeated measurements. It is even less likely that the scores of students on a given test (e.g., on reading proficiency or anxiety) are "error free." When a person takes a test, there is always some error involved due to his or her emotional, physical and/or psychological state of mind (e.g., mood or fatigue) and/or due to external conditions (e.g., noise) that may randomly occur during the measurement process. The *instrument of measurement* (tests, inventories, or raters) may also affect the accuracy of the scores. For example, it is unlikely that the scores of an examinee on two different forms of a reading comprehension test would be equal. Also, different scores are likely to be assigned to a student when different teachers evaluate, say, his or her specific behavioral characteristics. In another scenario, if a group of persons takes the same test twice within a short period of time, one can expect the rank order of their scores on the two test administrations to be somewhat similar, but not exactly the same. In other words, one can expect a relatively high, yet not perfect, positive correlation of test-retest scores for the group of examinees. Inconsistency may occur also in different criterion-referenced classifications of students (e.g., *mastery/non-mastery* of content knowledge) based on the subjective judgments of raters (e.g., teachers or school counselors).

In measurement parlance, the higher the accuracy and consistency of measurement scores, the higher their reliability. The **reliability** of measurements indicates the degree to which they are *accurate*, *consistent*, and *replicable* when (a) different people conduct the measurement, (b) using different instruments that purport to measure the same trait (e.g., proficiency, ability, attitude, anxiety), and (c) there is incidental variation in measurement conditions (e.g., lighting, seating, temperature). That is, the reliability of scores shows the degree to which they are "free" of random error. Most importantly, the reliability of scores is a necessary condition for their valid interpretations and data-driven decisions in education and other fields [we will learn more about *validity* in the next chapter].

> **NOTE [2.1]** *Reliability* refers to the measurement data (scores) obtained with an instrument, NOT to the instrument itself. Tests cannot be accurate, stable, or unstable, but observations (scores) can. Therefore, any reference to reliability of a test should be interpreted to mean the reliability of the measurement data derived from a test.

2.2. Classical Concept of Reliability

2.2.1 True Score

A fundamental assumption in the classical treatment of *reliability* is that the observed score, *X*, that a person receives on a test is affected by random error, referred to as *error of measurement* (*E*). Thus, if we subtract the random error from the observed score, $X - E$, we will obtain the person's "true" score, *T*, on this particular test. In other words, the observed score, *X*, that a person may receive on a single test administration consists of two components — the true score, *T*, and the error of measurement, *E*. That is,

$$X = T + E. \qquad \textbf{(2.1)}$$

To further explain the meaning of a *true score*, imagine that a person takes a standardized math test each day for, say, 100 days in a row. The person would likely obtain a number of different observed scores over these 100 test administrations. The mean of all observed scores would represent an approximation of the person's true score, *T*, on this math test. In general, a person's **true score** is the mean of the theoretical distribution of scores that would be observed in repeated independent measurements using the same test. Clearly, the true score, *T*, is a hypothetical concept because it is not practically possible to test the same person infinity times in independent repeated measurements, given that each testing could influence the subsequent testing (e.g., due to "carry over" effects of practice or memory).

NOTE [2.2] A person's **true score** is not a "crystal ball" value for the actual location of this person on a continuum of the trait (or ability) being measured. This is because the true score depends on the difficulty of the test and, therefore, will vary across tests with different levels of difficulty. Thus, a person with a given ability in, say, math will have different true scores on math tests with different levels of difficulty. Estimates of the person's actual ability (or trait) level, regardless of test difficulty, are provided by item response theory (IRT) models which are beyond the scope of this book.

2.2.2 Definition of Reliability

Equation 2.1 represents the classical assumption that any *observed score* (*X*) consists of a *true score* (*T*) and *error of measurement* (*E*). Because errors are random, it is assumed that they do not correlate with the true scores (i.e., $r_{TE} = 0$). Indeed, there is no reason to expect that persons with higher true scores would have systematically larger (or smaller) measurement errors than persons with lower true scores. Under this assumption, the following is true for the *variances* of observed scores, true scores, and errors for a population of test-takers:

$$\sigma_X^2 = \sigma_T^2 + \sigma_E^2. \qquad \textbf{(2.2)}$$

Thus, the *observed score variance*, σ_X^2, is the sum of *true score variance*, σ_T^2, and *error variance*, σ_E^2. Given this, *the reliability of scores* (denoted r_{XX}) *indicates what proportion of the observed score variance is true score variance.* The analytic form of this definition is

$$r_{XX} = \frac{\sigma_T^2}{\sigma_X^2}. \tag{2.3}$$

NOTE [2.3] The notation for reliability, r_{XX}, stems from the definition that reliability is the correlation between the observed scores on two *parallel tests* — tests with equal true scores and equal error variances for every population of persons.

The definition of reliability implies that r_{XX} takes values from 0.00 to 1.00. The closer r_{XX} is to 1.00, the higher the reliability and, conversely, the closer r_{XX} to zero, the lower the reliability. *Perfect reliability* (r_{XX} = 1.00) can theoretically occur when the total observed score variance equals the true score variance ($\sigma_X^2 = \sigma_T^2$) or, equivalently, when the error variance equals zero ($\sigma_E^2 = 0$). In general, a r_{XX} of .90 (or higher) is desirable for achievement tests and a r_{XX} of .75 (or higher) is good for inventories that measure more stable traits such as self-esteem.

2.2.3 Standard Error of Measurement (SEM)

The classical treatment of reliability also assumes that (a) the distribution of observed scores that a person may obtain under repeated independent administrations of the same test is *normal* and (b) the standard deviation of this normal distribution, referred to as the *standard error of measurement* (*SEM*), is the same for all persons taking the test. Figure 2.1 represents a hypothetical normal distribution of observed scores for a person with a true score of 20 on a specific test. The mean of the distribution is the person's true score (T = 20) and the standard deviation is the standard error of measurement (SEM = 2).

Figure 2.1. *Theoretical distribution of observed scores for one person over repeated independent measurements using the same test*

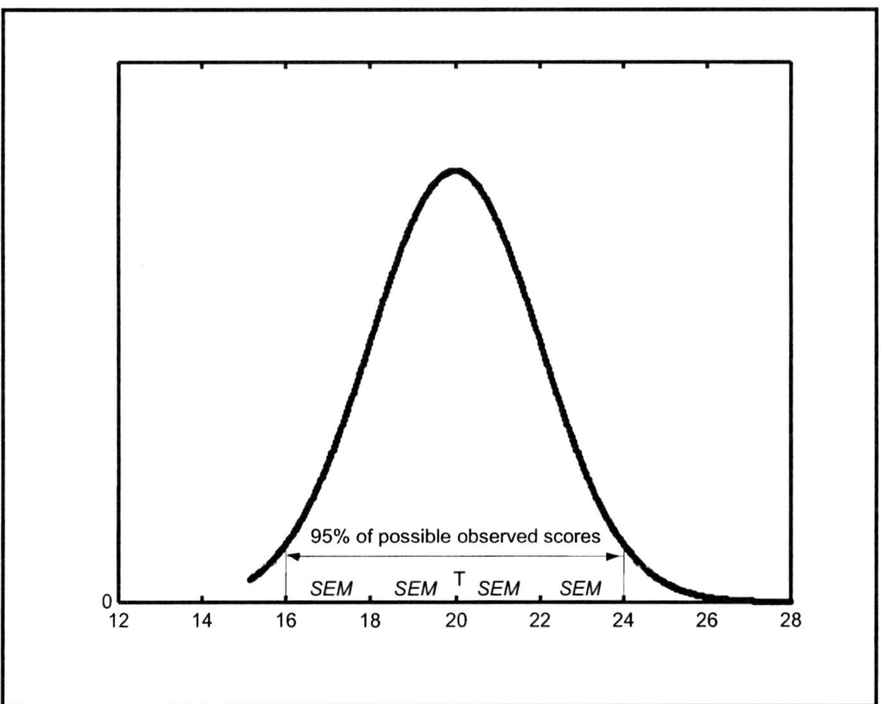

Based on the statistical properties of normal distributions, about 95% of the scores fall in the interval between two standard deviations below the mean, $T - 2(SEM)$, and two standard deviations above the mean, $T + 2(SEM)$ (in Figure 2.1, this is the interval from 16 to 24). This property can be used to construct (approximately) a 95% **confidence interval** of a person's true score, T, given this person's observed score, X. Specifically, in 95% of the cases, the true score of a person with an observed score X will fall in the interval from $X - 2(SEM)$ to $X + 2(SEM)$. [*Check*: With $SEM = 2$, the (approximate) 95% confidence interval for the true score of a person with an observed score of 17 ($X = 17$), is from 13 to 21.] Clearly, a smaller *SEM* will produce smaller confidence intervals for the person's true score, thus improving the accuracy of measurement.

Because the *SEM* is inversely related to the accuracy of measurement, low SEM indicates high reliability. If the reliability, r_{XX}, and the standard deviation of the observed scores, σ_X, are given, we can calculate the *SEM* using the formula:

$$SEM = \sigma_X \sqrt{1 - r_{XX}}\,. \tag{2.4}$$

[*Check*: If the reliability is .80 and the standard deviation of the persons' observed scores is 10, the standard error of measurement is: $SEM = (10)\sqrt{1-.80} = 4.47$]

> **NOTE [2.4]** Although the reliability coefficient is a unitless number between 0 and 1, conveniently used to report reliability in empirical studies, the *SEM* relates directly to the meaning of the test's scale of measurement (e.g., number-right score), deviation IQ score, T-score, or z-score) and is, therefore, more useful for score interpretations.

2.3 Types of Reliability

The reliability of test scores for a population of examinees shows what proportion of the variance in the observed scores is true score variance (see Equation 2.3). In empirical research, however, true scores cannot be directly determined. Therefore, the reliability is typically estimated by coefficients of internal consistency, test-retest, alternate forms, and other types of reliability estimates discussed in the measurement literature. It is important to emphasize that different types of reliability relate to different sources of measurement error and, contrary to common misconceptions, are generally not interchangeable.

2.3.1 Internal Consistency Reliability

Internal consistency estimates of reliability are based on the average correlation among items within a test in a single administration of this test. A widely known method for determining internal consistency of test scores yields a *split-half reliability* estimate. With this method, the test is split into two halves—for example, by assigning the odd-numbered test items to one half and the even-numbered test items to the other half [this is particularly appropriate when the items are presented in order of increasing difficulty]. If r_{12} is the Pearson correlation between the scores on the two test halves, the reliability for the whole test is estimated using the *Spearman-Brown Prophecy formula*:

$$r_{XX} = \frac{2r_{12}}{1+r_{12}} \tag{2.5}$$

For example, if the correlation between the two test halves is 0.7, the split-half reliability estimate is: $r_{XX} = 2(0.7)/(1+0.7) = 0.82$. A general premise is that, with all other things being equal, the more items on a test, the more reliable the test scores will be.

The Spearman-Brown Prophecy formula assumes that the two halves of the test are *parallel* (i.e., they have equal true scores and equal error variances). When there are indications that the test halves are not parallel, the internal consistency of the scores for the whole test can be estimated with Cronbach's *coefficient α* (*alpha*) using the formula (Cronbach, 1951):

$$\alpha = \frac{n}{n-1}\left[1 - \frac{\sum \mathrm{VAR}(X_i)}{\mathrm{VAR}(X)}\right] \tag{2.6}$$

where: n is the number of test items,
X_i is the observed score on the ith test item,
$\mathrm{VAR}(X_i)$ is the variance of X_i; (the summation, Σ, is for $i = 1, 2, \ldots, n$),
X is the observed score for the whole test (i.e., $X = X_1 + X_2 + \ldots + X_n$),
$\mathrm{VAR}(X)$ is the variance of X.

Equation 2.6 is simply an extension of the two-component formula (Equation 2.5) to the case of two or more test components. In general, each item is viewed as a test component and can be scored on a binary scale (1 = correct, 0 = incorrect) or on a Likert-type scale (e.g., 1= Strongly disagree, 2 = Disagree, 3 = Uncertain, 4 = Agree, 5 = Strongly agree).

NOTE [2.5] Cronbach's *alpha* is an **accurate** estimate of the internal consistency reliability of test scores **if** the test components (e.g., test items) satisfy two assumptions: (a) there is no correlation among errors associated with item scores, and (b) the items are essentially *tau-equivalent* (i.e., they measure the same trait and their true scores have equal variances). When the latter is not true, Cronbach's alpha **underestimates** the reliability. If, however, there are items with correlated errors, Cronbach's alpha **overestimates** the reliability. Correlated errors may occur, for example, when different items relate to a common piece of test information (e.g., same graph) or when tests are presented in a speeded fashion.

2.3.2 Test-Retest Reliability

When educators want to assess the extent to which people respond consistently to the same test or questionnaire administered on different occasions, this is a matter of *test-retest reliability* (or *stability*) of test scores. **Test-retest reliability** is estimated by calculating the correlation between the observed scores of the same participants taking the same test on two separate occasions. The resulting correlation coefficient is also referred to as the *coefficient of stability*, because the primary source of measurement error is lack of stability over time.

The major problem with test-retest reliability estimates is the potential for carry-over effects between the two test administrations. Re-administrations of a test within a short period of time (e.g., a few days or even a couple of weeks) may produce carry-over effects due to memory and/or practice. For example, students who take a math or vocabulary test may look up some answers they were unsure of after the first administration of the test, thus changing their true knowledge of the content measured by the test. Or, if an individual learns a lot about math between the first and second administration of a math achievement test, the scores of this individual may vary substantially. Indeed, if the construct being measured varies over time (e.g., cognitive skills, depression), a long period of time between the two administrations of the instrument may produce score changes due to biological maturation, cognitive development, experience, and/or mood shifts. Thus, test-retest reliability estimates are most appropriate for measurements of traits that are stable over the period of time between the two test administrations (e.g., visual acuity, personality, and work values).

NOTE [2.6] *Test-retest reliability* and *internal consistency* are independent concepts. They are affected by different sources of error and, therefore, it may happen that measures with low internal consistency have high temporal stability and vice versa.

2.3.3 Alternate Forms Reliability

If two versions of an instrument (test or questionnaire) have very similar observed score means, variances, and correlations with other measures, they are referred to as *alternate forms* of the instrument. In fact, any decent attempt to construct parallel tests is expected to result in alternate test forms, as it is practically impossible to obtain perfectly parallel tests (i.e., with equal true scores and equal error variances). Alternate forms are usually easier to develop for instruments that measure ability/aptitude or proficiency in specific academic subjects than for instruments that measure constructs such as personality, motivation, and anxiety.

Alternate form reliability is a measure of the consistency of scores obtained from the administration of alternate test forms to the same group of individuals. The correlation between observed scores on two alternate test forms provides an estimate of the reliability of either one of the alternate forms. Just like the test-retest reliability coefficients, the estimates of alternate form reliability are subject to carry-over (practice) effects, but to a lesser degree because the persons are not tested twice on the same items. A recommended rule-of-thumb is to have a 2-week time period between administrations of alternate test forms.

Whenever possible, it is better to obtain both internal consistency coefficients and alternate forms correlations for a test. If the correlation between alternate forms is much lower than the internal consistency coefficient (e.g., a difference of 0.20 or more), this might be due to (a) differences in content, (b) subjectivity of scoring, and/or (c) changes in the trait being measured over the time period between the administrations of alternate forms. When scores on alternate forms of an instrument are assigned by raters (e.g., teachers or counselors), scoring errors due to subjectivity can be reduced by training the raters how to use the instrument and providing clear guidelines for scoring the traits being measured.

2.3.4 Criterion-Referenced Reliability

Criterion-referenced measurements show how the examinees' performance compares to a specific criterion. In education, the criterion is usually some specific performance objective such as "knowing how to solve simple algebra equations." Most teacher-made tests are criterion-referenced because the teacher is more interested in how well students master the coursework (criterion-referenced) rather than how students compare to other students (norm-referenced). Likewise, counselors frequently want to know whether or not a client has "enough" of a mental disorder (e.g., depression) to warrant a diagnosis.

When the results of criterion-referenced measurements are used for classifications related to mastery or nonmastery of the criterion, the reliability of such classifications is often referred to as **classification consistency**. This type of reliability shows the consistency with which classifications are made, either by the same test administered on two occasions or by alternate test forms.

Two widely known indices of classification consistency are (a) P_o—the observed proportion of consistent classifications, and (b) Cohen's κ (*kappa*)—the proportion of nonrandom consistent classifications. Let's examine Table 2.1, in which the entries are proportions of persons classified as masters or nonmasters by two alternate forms of a criterion-referenced test (Form A and Form B). The marginal proportions are: $P_{A1} = p_{11} + p_{10}$, $P_{A0} = p_{01} + p_{00}$, $P_{B1} = p_{11} + p_{01}$, and $P_{B0} = p_{10} + p_{00}$. The observed proportion of consistent classifications (masters or nonmasters) is:

$$P_o = p_{11} + p_{00} \tag{2.7}$$

Table 2.1 *Mastery-Nonmastery Classification Table*

		Form B		
		Master	Nonmaster	
Form A	Master	p_{11}	p_{10}	P_{A1}
	Nonmaster	p_{01}	p_{00}	P_{A0}
		P_{B1}	P_{B0}	

It should be noted that the observed proportion of correct classifications, P_o, can be "inflated" because part of P_o may occur by chance. Cohen's *kappa* takes into account the proportion of consistent classifications that is theoretically expected to occur by chance, P_e, and provides a ratio of nonrandom consistent classifications (Cohen, 1960):

$$\kappa = \frac{P_o - P_e}{1 - P_e}, \tag{2.8}$$

where P_e is obtained by summing the cross-products of marginal proportions in Table 2.1, that is: $P_e = P_{A1}P_{B1} + P_{A0}P_{B0}$. The numerator ($P_o - P_e$) is the proportion of nonrandom consistent classifications being detected, whereas the denominator ($1 - P_e$) is the maximum proportion of nonrandom consistent classifications that may occur. Thus, Cohen's *kappa* shows what proportion of the maximum possible nonrandom consistent classifications is found with the data.

EXAMPLE 2.1 Assume that we want to know how well a teacher-made test in math compares to the "pass-fail" classification produced by a state proficiency test in math for 9th grade students in a given school. Let's say that, using the student records on the two math tests (Form A and Form B), we can assign the following specific values to the respective proportions in Table 2.1: $p_{11} = 0.4$, $p_{10} = 0.2$, $p_{01} = 0.1$, and $p_{00} = 0.3$. The marginal proportions are: $P_{A1} = 0.4 + 0.2 = 0.6$, $P_{A0} = 0.1 + 0.3 = 0.4$, $P_{B1} = 0.4 + 0.1 = 0.5$, and $P_{B0} = 0.2 + 0.3 = 0.5$. These results are presented in Table 2.2.

Table 2.2 *Classification table for "pass-fail" on a math proficiency test*

		Form B: State Proficiency Test		
		Pass	Fail	
Form A: Teacher-Made Test	Pass	0.4	0.2	$P_{A1} = 0.6$
	Fail	0.1	0.3	$P_{A0} = 0.4$
		$P_{B1} = 0.5$	$P_{B0} = 0.5$	

The observed proportion of consistent classifications is $P_o = 0.4 + 0.3 = 0.7$. The proportion of consistent classifications that may occur by chance is: $P_e = (0.6)(0.5) + (0.4)(0.5) = 0.50$. Using Formula 2.8, Cohen's *kappa*: $\kappa = (0.7 - 0.50)/(1 - 0.50) = .20/.50 = .40$. Thus, the initially obtained 70% of observed consistent classifications ($P_o = 0.7$) is reduced to 40% consistent classifications after controlling for those that may occur by chance. Because *kappa* provides "conservative" estimations of consistency, it is reasonable to report in this case that the classification consistency is between .40 and .70 (i.e., between κ and P_o).

2.3.5 Interrater Reliability

The chances of measurement error increase when the scores are based on subjective judgments of raters (e.g. experts, judges). This may occur, for example, with portfolio assessments or "pass-fail" decisions where raters (e.g., teachers) are the "instrument" of assessment. In situations of rater-based scoring, it is important to estimate the degree to which the scores are unduly affected by subjective judgments of the raters. Such estimation is provided by coefficients of **interrater reliability,** referred to also as coefficients of *interrater agreement.*

Frequently used measures of interrater reliability are the Pearson correlation coefficients; the observed proportion of consistent classifications, P_o; and Cohen's *kappa* coefficient. When more than two categories are used by two raters to classify persons (or their products), one can still use Equations 2.7 and 2.8, but P_o and P_e should be calculated with a contingency table for the respective number of categories. For example, let two raters (A and B) classify student portfolios in three performance categories (e.g., 1 = low, 2 = medium, and 3 = high). Let also p_{11}, p_{22}, and p_{33} denote the proportion of consistent classifications in categories 1 (low), 2 (medium), and 3 (high), respectively. The marginal proportions for rater A are denoted P_{A1}, P_{A2}, and P_{A3}, while those for rater B are P_{B1}, P_{B2}, and P_{B3}, across categories 1, 2, and 3, respectively. We can now calculate Cohen's *kappa* using Equation 2.8, with $P_o = p_{11} + p_{22} + p_{33}$ and $P_e = P_{A1}P_{B1} + P_{A2}P_{B2} + P_{A3}P_{B3}$.

In another scenario, if two raters independently score student portfolios, for example, the Pearson correlation coefficient for the two sets of scores can be used as an estimate of interrater agreement. The higher the correlation coefficient, the lower the error variance due to scorer differences, and thus the higher the interrater agreement.

NOTE [2.7] The principle behind improving reliability is *to maximize the variance of relevant individual differences and minimize the error variance.* Researchers can do this by (1) writing items clearly, (2) providing complete and understandable test instructions, (3) administering the instrument under prescribed conditions, (4) reducing subjectivity in scoring, (5) training raters and providing them with clear scoring instructions, (6) using heterogeneous respondent samples to increase the variance of observed scores, and (7) increasing the length of the test by adding items which are (ideally) parallel to those that are already in the test.

2.4 Reliability of Composite Scores

In many situations, scores from two or more scales are combined into *composite scores* to measure and interpret a more general dimension (e.g., trait, ability, or proficiency) related to these scales. Composite scores are often used with test batteries for aptitude, achievement, intelligence, or depression, as well as with local school measurements such as performance and portfolio assessments. One frequently reported composite score, for example, is the sum of verbal and quantitative scores on the *Graduate Record Examination* (GRE). Although the composite score may be simply the sum of several scale scores, its reliability is usually not simply a calculation of the mean of the reliabilities for the scales being combined. The estimation of reliability for composite scores is addressed here for (a) the sum of two scale scores, (b) the difference of two scale scores (e.g., *gain* score for pretest to posttest), or (c) the sum of three or more scale scores.

2.4.1 Reliability of Sum of Scores

As already mentioned, the overall GRE assessment is based on a composite score which represents the examinee's combined performance on the verbal and quantitative sections of the test (i.e., composite score = verbal score + quantitative score). The reliability of the composite score, however, is not just the sum of the reliabilities of the verbal and quantitative parts. In general, if Y is a composite score obtained by adding together the scores of two scales, X_1 and X_2 (that is, $Y = X_1 + X_2$), the *reliability of the sum of two scores*, r_{YY}, can be estimated as

$$r_{YY} = 1 - \frac{(1 - r_{11})VAR(X_1) + (1 - r_{22})VAR(X_2)}{VAR(Y)} \quad \textbf{(2.9)}$$

where VAR(X_1), VAR(X_2), and VAR (Y) stand for the variances of X_1, X_2, and Y, respectively, whereas r_{11} and r_{22} are reliability estimates of X_1 and X_2, respectively.

NOTE [2.8] Although not explicitly shown in Equation 2.9, a correlation between X_1 and X_2 affects the reliability of the composite score. When X_1 and X_2 do not correlate ($r_{12} = 0$), the reliability of their sum ($Y = X_1 + X_2$) is simply the average of their reliabilities:

$$r_{YY} = (r_{11} + r_{22})/2.$$

EXAMPLE 2.2 In a study on parental support for school children, two separate domains (constructs) were found to underlie the parents' responses on a survey with 20 items on a 4-point Likert-type rating scale (1 = Never, 2 = Rarely, 3 = Often, 4 = Always). The score variance on the first domain, related to financial support, was 1.38 and the Cronbach's *alpha* estimate of internal consistency reliability was .51. For the second domain, related to academic support (e.g., help with homework assignments), the score variance was 1.42 and the Cronbach's *alpha* estimate of internal consistency reliability was .94. The variance of the sum of the respondents' scores on these two domains (constructs) was 2.66.

The translation of this information to the notations used in Equation 2.9 is as follows: X_1 = *financial support*, X_2 = *academic support*, $Y = X_1 + X_2$ (*composite score*), $r_{11} = .51$, VAR(X_1) = 1.38, $r_{22} = .94$, VAR(X_2) = 1.42, and VAR(Y) = 2.66. Thus, replacing these values in Equation 2.9, the reliability of the composite score is

$$r_{YY} = 1 - \frac{(1-.51)(1.38) + (1-.94)(1.42)}{2.66} = .714.$$

As you may notice, the reliability of the composite score (.714) is very close to the mean of the reliabilities of the two domains: (.51 + .94)/2 = .72. As can be expected, this is due to the lack of correlation between X_1 and X_2, which in this case was equal to -.05 (not statistically significant for the sample of 60 observations in example) — see NOTE [2.8].

When the scores that are combined into a composite score come from scales with different units of measurement (e.g., 3-point and 5-point Likert-type scales), it is appropriate to present them on a common scale —e.g., by converting them into standard scores (z- scores) before being summed. Then Equation 2.9 translates into a simpler form:

$$r_{YY} = 1 - \frac{2 - (r_{11} + r_{22})}{VAR(Z_{12})}, \qquad \textbf{(2.10)}$$

where VAR(Z_{12}) is the variance of the sum of the z-scores of X_1 and X_2 ($Z_{12} = z_1 + z_2$) and, as before, r_{11} and r_{22} are reliability estimates of X_1 and X_2, respectively.

Equations 2.9 and 2.10 can be readily extended for cases where the composite score is a sum of more than two scale scores (e.g., Nunnally & Bernstein, 1994). For the sum of three scores, for example, the reliability of the composite score $Y = X_1 + X_2 + X_3$ can be estimated by extending Equation 2.10 as follows:

$$r_{YY} = 1 - \frac{3 - (r_{11} + r_{22} + r_{33})}{VAR(Z_{123})}, \qquad \textbf{(2.11)}$$

where VAR(Z_{123}) is the variance of the sum of the standard (z-) scores for X_1, X_2, and X_3, and r_{11}, r_{22}, and r_{33} are the reliabilities for X_1, X_2, and X_3, respectively.

2.4.2 Reliability of Difference of Scores

Frequently educational researchers attempt to assess the effect of a specific "treatment" (program or intervention) targeting *change* in, say, students' academic performance, behavior, or mental health. The quality of such assessments depends, among other things, on the reliability of the *score difference* (or *gain score*) from pretest to posttest measurements on the targeted variable for the sample of treatment participants. Technically, the difference $Y = X_2 - X_1$ is a composite score of the sum $Y = X_2 + (-X_1)$; (e.g., X_1 = pretest score, X_2 = posttest score, and Y = gain score). Therefore, the reliability of the difference score (Y) can be estimated with Equation 2.9. Equation 2.10 (the z-score version of Equation 2.9) also works, but this time VAR(Z_{12}) is the variance of the difference between the z-scores of X_2 and X_1 (i.e., $Z_{12} = z_2 - z_1$).

NOTE [2.9] The use of difference (gain) scores in measurement of pretest to posttest change has been criticized because of the (generally false) assertion that the difference between scores is less reliable than the scores themselves (Cronbach & Furby, 1970). This assertion is true **only if** the pretest scores and the posttest scores have equal variances and equal reliability. When this is not the case, the reliability of the gain score is reasonably high (Zimmerman & Williams, 1982). Therefore, without ignoring the caution urged by some authors, researchers should not always discard gain scores and should be aware when gain scores are useful.

2.5 Reliability Estimation with SPSS

2.5.1 Calculation of Cronbach's *alpha*

The calculation of Cronbach's *alpha* for internal consistency reliability using SPSS is illustrated here for the responses of 20 teachers on four survey questions (Q1, Q2, Q3, and Q4) on a 5-point Likert-type rating scale (left panel in Table 2.3). The right panel in Table 2.3 provides an edited SPSS output for reliability statistics (Cronbach's *alpha*) and item-total statistics.

Table 2.3 *SPSS data and edited output for Cronbach's alpha of four survey items*

TABLE2_3.sav [DataSet1] - SPSS Data Edito

File Edit View Data Transform Analyze

20 :

	Q1	Q2	Q3	Q4
1	2	4	4	2
2	5	5	5	1
3	1	1	3	1
4	1	1	3	1
5	3	4	4	2
6	2	1	2	1
7	4	3	5	1
8	3	3	5	1
9	4	3	5	1
10	4	3	4	1
11	2	3	4	1
12	2	4	3	1
13	5	5	4	2
14	2	3	3	1
15	2	3	4	2
16	2	4	4	2
17	5	5	5	1
18	1	1	3	1
19	1	1	3	1
20	4	3	3	1

Reliability Statistics

Cronbach's Alpha	N of Items
.775	4

Item-Total Statistics

	Corrected Item-Total Correlation	Cronbach's Alpha if Item Deleted
Q1: Insufficient plan time	.715	.650
Q2: Insufficient equipment	.820	.567
Q3: Insufficient class time	.689	.681
Q4: Limited curriculum design knowledge	.225	.849

If question Q4 is deleted from the survey, Cronbach's alpha will increase to .849.

The SPSS output (right panel in Table 2.3) is obtained by using the following steps:

1. Click **Analyze**, click **Scale**, and click **Reliability Analysis**.
2. In the dialog box that appears, select all questions (Q1, Q2, Q3, and Q4) and then click ► to move them into the **Items** box.
3. Click **Statistics**. In the box that appears, move the cursor in the upper left panel (**Statistics for**) and select **Scale if item deleted**.
4. Click **Continue** and then click **OK.**

The Cronbach's *alpha* (.775) is provided in the **Reliability Statistics** table. For space consideration, only two columns of the table **Item-Total Statistics** are shown here — the column "Corrected Item-Total Correlation," which shows the correlation between the score on a particular item (survey question) and the total score on the survey, and the column "Cronbach's alpha if Item Deleted" which shows the value of Cronbach's alpha after a particular item is deleted. Clearly, item Q4 is not consistent with what the other three items measure as its elimination would result in an increase of *alpha* to .849.

2.5.2 Calculation of Cohen's *kappa* in SPSS

The calculation of Cohen's κ (*kappa*) using SPSS is illustrated in Table 2.4 for the classification of 20 portfolios into three categories (1 = Poor, 2 = Satisfactory, and 3 = Good) by two raters (A and B). The edited SPSS printout (right panel in Table 2.4) is obtained as follows:

1. Click **Analyze**, click **Descriptive Statistics**, and click **Crosstabs**.
2. In the dialog box that shows up, select **Rater A** and click ► to move this rater into the box **Row(s).** Then select **Rater B** and click ► to move this rater into the box **Column(s)**.
3. Click **Statistics**. In the box that shows up, select **Kappa**.
4. Click **Continue** and then click **OK.**

In this example, Cohen's *kappa* (.524) is statistically significant at the .05 level ($p < .05$).

Table 2.4 *SPSS data and edited output for Cohen's kappa*

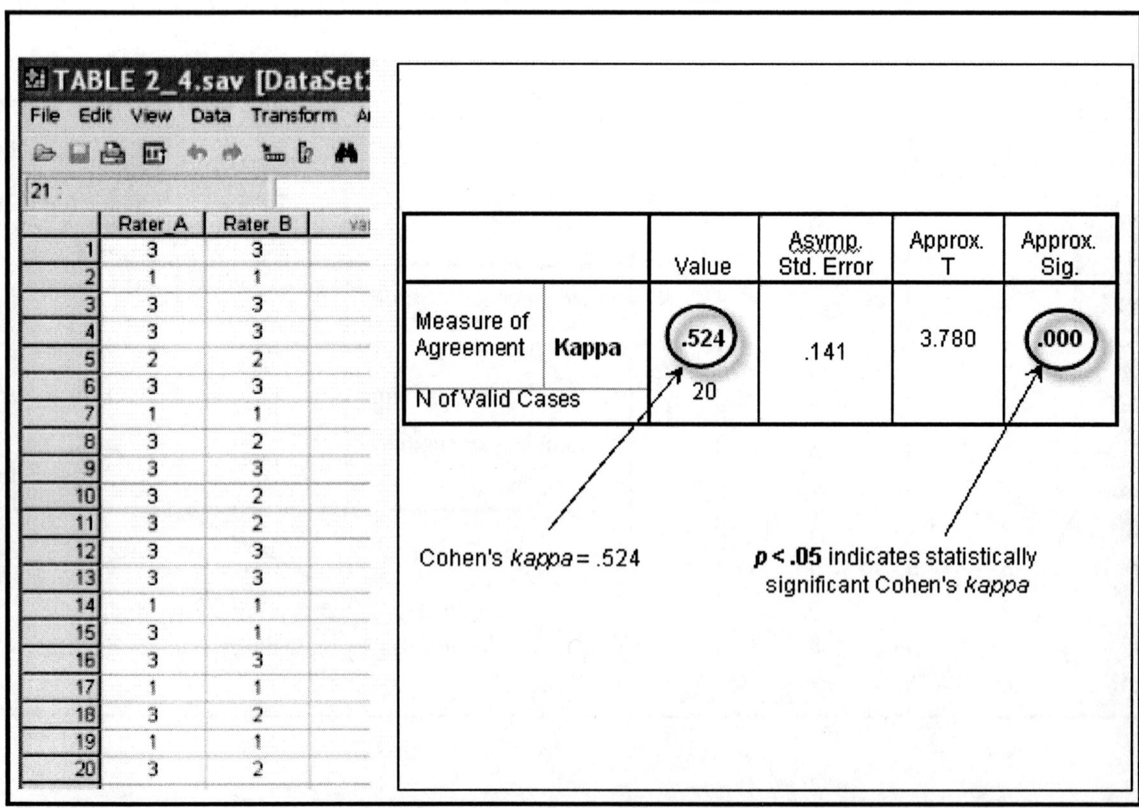

TABLE 2_4.sav [DataSet

File Edit View Data Transform

	Rater_A	Rater_B
1	3	3
2	1	1
3	3	3
4	3	3
5	2	2
6	3	3
7	1	1
8	3	2
9	3	3
10	3	2
11	3	2
12	3	3
13	3	3
14	1	1
15	3	1
16	3	3
17	1	1
18	3	2
19	1	1
20	3	2

		Value	Asymp. Std. Error	Approx. T	Approx. Sig.
Measure of Agreement	Kappa	.524	.141	3.780	.000
N of Valid Cases		20			

Cohen's *kappa* = .524

$p < .05$ indicates statistically significant Cohen's *kappa*

2.6 Summary

This chapter presented classical concepts of score reliability, types of reliability, reliability of composite scores, and calculation of reliability estimates using SPSS. A bulleted summary of concepts and highlights provided in this chapter follows:

- **Reliability** of scores indicates the degree to which they are *accurate*, *consistent*, and *replicable* when (a) there is incidental variation in measurement conditions—internal (e.g., examinee's mood or fatigue) or external (e.g., noise, temperature, or lighting), (b) different people conduct the measurement, and (c) different instruments that purport to measure the same trait are used.
- **Reliability** refers to measurement data (scores) obtained with an instrument, NOT to the instrument itself.
- A fundamental assumption in the classical model of measurement is that any *observed score* (*X*) consists of a *true score* (*T*) and *error of measurement* (*E*): $\boldsymbol{X = T + E}$.
- A person's **true score** is the mean of the theoretical distribution of scores that would be observed in repeated independent measurements of that person using the same test.
- Under the classical model of measurement, the **reliability of scores** indicates what proportion of the observed score variance is true score variance: $r_{XX} = \sigma_T^2 / \sigma_X^2$.
- The classical model of measurement also assumes that (a) the distribution of observed scores that a person may obtain under repeated independent administrations of the same test is *normal*, and (b) the standard deviation of this normal distribution, called the **standard error of measurement** (*SEM*), is the same for all persons taking the test.
- Given a person's observed score, *X*, and the standard error of measurement, *SEM*, the (approximate) **95% confidence interval** for the true score of this person is from *X* - 2 *SEM* to *X* + 2 *SEM*.
- **Internal consistency** estimates of reliability are based on the average correlation among items within a test in a single administration of this test. Thus, the *internal consistency reliability* shows the degree to which all test items measure the same trait. **Cronbach's *alpha*** is a widely used estimate of internal consistency reliability. It is a coefficient between 0 and 1; (the closer to 1, the higher the reliability). Typically, Cronbach's *alpha* does not exceed the actual value of reliability, but in case of correlated errors among items, Cronbach's *alpha* may largely overestimate reliability.
- **Test-retest reliability** is estimated by the Pearson correlation coefficient between the observed scores of the same people taking the same test twice. A short period of time (e.g., a few days or even a couple of weeks) between the two administrations of the test may produce carry-over effects due to memory and/or practice. Conversely, if the construct being measured varies over time (e.g., cognitive skills, depression), a long period of time between the two administrations of the instrument may produce score changes due to biological maturation, cognitive development, experience, and/or mood shifts.
- **Test-retest reliability** and **internal consistency reliability** are independent concepts. They are affected by different sources of error and, therefore, it is possible that measures with low internal consistency have high temporal stability and vice versa.
- **Alternate form reliability** is a measure of the consistency of scores on alternate test forms administered to the same group of individuals. The correlation between observed scores on two alternate test forms provides an estimate of the reliability of either one of the alternate forms. Just like with test-retest reliability, the estimates of alternate form reliability are subject to carry-

over (practice) effects, but to a lesser degree. A 2-week time period between administrations of alternate test forms is recommended.

• **Criterion-referenced reliability** (or **classification consistency**) indicates the consistency with which classifications of persons (or their products) are made, either by the same test administered on two occasions or by alternate test forms. Classifications are made with respect to a specific criterion (e.g., *mastery-nonmastery* of math content). Two widely known indices of classification consistency are (a) P_o, the observed proportion of consistent classifications, and (b) Cohen's κ (*kappa*), the proportion of nonrandom consistent classifications.

• In situations of rater-based scoring, it is important to estimate the degree to which the scores are unduly affected by subjective judgments of the raters. Such estimation is provided by coefficients of **interrater reliability** (or **interrater agreement**). Frequently used measures of interrater reliability are the Pearson correlation coefficient; the observed proportion of consistent classifications, P_0; and Cohen's *kappa* coefficient.

• Sometimes, scores from two or more scales are combined into **composite scores** to measure and interpret a more general dimension (e.g., trait or ability) related to these scales. Equations 2.9-2.11 are used to estimate reliability of composite scores.

2.7 Study Questions

1. *Reliability* indicates the degree to which scores are

(a) objective, **(b)** free of random error, **(c)** free of systematic error, **(d)** subjective.

2. If 80% of the observed score variance on a test is a true score variance, the reliability of the test scores is

(a) 80% **(b)** .20 **(c)** .50 **(d)** 20%, **(e)** .80 **(f)** none of the above

3. If a person's observed score on a test is 22 and the *SEM* = 2.5, we can be about 95% confident that the true score of this person on the test will fall between which two scores?

(a) 22 and 24.5, **(b)** 19.5 and 22, **(c)** 20 and 24, **(d)** 17 and 27,

(e) none of the above.

4. If the standard deviation of the observed scores is 10 and their reliability is .90, the *standard error of measurement* (rounded to the nearest hundredth) is

(a) 3.10 **(b)** 9.49 **(c)** 5.00, **(d)** 5.16 **(e)** none of the above.

5. Under what condition may Cronbach's coefficient *alpha* overestimate the actual value of the internal consistency reliability?

6. Carry-over effects (e.g., due to practice) may occur with which type of reliability?

(a) internal consistency, **(b)** test-retest, **(c)** alternate forms, **(d)** criterion-referenced

7. Suppose that Y is the sum of the respondent's scores on two scales of a survey, X_1 *attitude toward school* and X_2 = *motivation for academic success*; ($Y = X_1 + X_2$). Estimate the reliability of the composite score, Y, given that the reliability of X_1 and X_2 are .72 and .80, respectively, and the variances of X_1, X_2, and Y are 22.10, 18.00, and 28.50, respectively. [*Hint*: see Equation 2.9.]

CHAPTER 3

VALIDITY

3.1 What is Validity?

While reliability of scores deals with their accuracy and consistency, **validity** has to do with whether an instrument (e.g., test or questionnaire) measures what it purports to measure. As shown later in this chapter, reliability is a necessary, albeit not sufficient, condition for validity. That is, high reliability of test scores does not guarantee validity, but represents an important condition for valid interpretation of test scores. As Cronbach (1971) noted, "One validates not a test, but an *interpretation of data arising from a specified procedure*" (p. 447). Take, for example, the students' scores on a test that consists of items on arithmetic computations. An example of invalid interpretation of these scores would be to make inferences from them about the students' "mathematics ability," because the test measures computational skills, not mathematics ability. On the other hand, a valid interpretation of these test scores would be to say that the score differences reflect meaningful differences in computational skills of the students. Likewise, a valid anxiety test must generate scores that reflect meaningful differences in anxiety among persons taking the test. Recall from Chapter 1 (Section 1.1.1) that latent variables such as anxiety, math ability, reading comprehension, etc., represent theoretical **constructs**. The items of a test are observable indicators of the construct that underlies the examinees' responses on these items.

Historically, there are three major stages in the development of validity models: (1) *criterion-based model* (Cronbach & Gleser, 1965) in which validity of measures is viewed as the degree to which these measures are consistent with (or "predict") the measures on a specific "criterion," (2) *construct-based model* (Cronbach & Meehl, 1955) which considers three different types of validity—content validity, criterion validity, and construct validity—and (3) *unified construct-based model of validity* (Messick, 1989, 1995). A comprehensive review of the history of validity can be found, for example, in Kane (2001).

Under the **criterion-based model**, the validity of test scores was depicted as the degree to which these scores were accurate representations of the values of a specified *criterion.* A major drawback of the criterion-based conception of validity is that (a) it is too limited and does not capture some basic (e.g., content-related) aspects of validity and (b) it is not possible to identify criterion measures is some domains. While the **construct-based model** of validity does a better job in this regard, it's major problem is that content validity, criterion validity, and construct validity are depicted as different types of validity. This can mislead test users to believe that these three "types of validity" are comparable or, even worse, that they are equivalent and, thus, collecting evidence for any of them is sufficient to label a test as valid. Messick (1995) argued that the different kinds of inferences from test scores require different kinds of evidence, not different kinds of validity.

The **unified construct-based model of validity** is based on a definition of validity provided by Messick (1989): "Validity is an integrated evaluative judgment of the degree to which empirical evidence and theoretical rationales support the *adequacy* and *appropriateness* of *inferences* and *actions* based on test scores or other modes of assessment" (p. 13). This definition is also reflected in the recent *Standards for Educational and Psychological Testing* (AERA, APA,

& NCME, 1999), where it is stated that "validity refers to the degree to which evidence and theory support the interpretation of test scores entailed by proposed uses of tests" (p. 9). This conception of validity represents a *unified construct-based model of validity*, by providing a comprehensive view that integrates content-related and criterion-related evidence into a unified framework of construct validity and empirical evaluation of the meaning and consequences of measurement. Messick (1995) noted that "the measure is viewed as just one of an extensible set of indicators of the construct. Convergent empirical relationships reflecting communality among such indicators are taken to imply the operation of the construct to the degree that discriminant evidence discounts the intrusion of alternative constructs as plausible rival hypotheses."

A comprehensive **definition of the construct** under validation allows one to identify the behavioral boundaries of the construct, differentiate the construct from other (similar or dissimilar) constructs, and specify relationships between the construct and other constructs. For example, the construct measured by the reading comprehension section on the verbal part of a large-scale standardized test is defined as "one's ability to reason with words in solving problems," and it is expected that "reasoning effectively in a verbal medium depends primarily on ability to discern, comprehend, and analyze relationships among words or groups of words and within larger units of discourse such as sentences and written passages" (Educational Testing Service, 1998). Typically, the core definition of a construct is embedded into a more general theory and then refined and operationalized in the context of the theory and practice in which inferences and decisions are to be made based on assessment scores.

Based on the adopted construct definition, instrument developers should build a detailed **construct model** that specifies (a) the internal structure of the construct — i.e., its componential structure, (b) the external relationships of the construct to other constructs, (c) potential types of indicators (item formats) for measuring behaviors that are relevant to assessing individuals on the construct, and (d) construct-related processes — e.g., causal impacts that the construct is expected to have on specific behavior(s). Messick (1995) specifies six aspects of the unified conception of construct validity — content, substantive, structural, generalizability, external, and consequential aspects. A brief description of these six aspects is provided in the next section.

3.2 Aspects of Construct Validity

3.2.1 Content Aspect of Validity

The *content aspect* of validity includes evidence of content relevance, representativeness, and technical quality (Messick, 1995). This definition is interpreted with some variations in different assessment contexts. In employment assessment, for example, evidence of content validity is provided when the assessment includes a representative sample of tasks, behaviors, knowledge, skills, abilities, or other characteristics necessary to perform the job. Evidence of content validity is usually gathered through job analysis. In educational assessment, evidence of content validity is gathered primarily through curriculum analysis and inquiry into the nature of knowledge, skills, and other characteristics targeted with the assessment.

Initial evidence of the content aspect of validity is usually established through subjective judgments of experts and/or examinees regarding whether the test content is relevant to the purpose of the test; [sometimes this is referred to as "face validity"]. A more rigorous procedure is to develop a logical design of test items in order to cover all the important aspects of the targeted content domain — such a design is organized in a two-way (*content area* x *test objective*) table. Experts judgments regarding readability and suitability of the items in the assessment instrument should also be documented in collecting evidence about the content aspect of validity.

3.2.2 Substantive Aspect of Validity

The *substantive aspect* of validity refers to theoretical rationales for the observed consistencies in test responses, including process models of task performance along with empirical evidence that the theoretical processes are actually engaged by respondents in the assessment tasks (Messick, 1995). The substantive aspect addresses the need for empirical evidence of response consistencies or performance regularities reflective of domain processes. Evidence about the substantive aspect of validity can be collected through cognitive modeling of the examinees' response processes, observations of behaviors exhibited by the examinees when answering the items, analysis of scale functioning, consistency between expected and empirical item difficulties, and other relevant procedures.

Specifically, identification and modeling of cognitive processes that underlie the persons' responses on the items of the instrument can be done by using existing theory and empirical research on cognitive processes related to the construct of interest, "think aloud" protocols or retrospective reflections through which examinees explain the reasoning they have employed in responding to each item, experts judgments, and/or other sources of relevant information. When such techniques yield the identification of cognitive processes that also exist in the processing model of the construct, this provides a strong support to the substantive aspect of validity. Documentation of relationships between observable behaviors of examinees when answering the items and their responses on these items can also support the substantive aspect of validity. Example of such observable behaviors are eye movements, time of accomplishing specific subtasks, note taking, graphics, computations, etc.

Yet another piece of evidence related to the substantive aspect of validity is provided when the observed responses of examinees on items are consistent with the intended response characteristics of these items as targeted by the item developers. With multiple-choice items, for example, a typical expectation is that (a) response options that are incorrect (distractors) for an item will be equally "attractive" to examinees who don't know the correct answer of that item, and (b) each distractor should "attract" more examinees at the lower level of ability than examinees at the higher level of the ability that is measured by the test.

3.2.3 Structural Aspect of Validity

As described by Messick (1995), the *structural aspect of validity* appraises the fidelity of the scoring structure to the structure of the construct domain at issue. Messick (1995) emphasizes that "the theory of the construct domain should guide not only the selection or construction of relevance assessment tasks but also the rational development of construct-based scoring criteria and rubrics" (p. 746). He defines *structural fidelity* as a property of the construct-based scoring model under which "the internal structure of the assessment (i.e., interrelations among the scored aspects of task and subtask performance) should be consistent with what is known about the internal structure of the construct domain" (p. 746).

Typically, evidence of the structural aspect of validity is sought by correlational and measurement consistency between the targeted constructs and their indicators (test items). This is done primarily through the use of factor analysis. An exploratory factor analysis (EFA) is used when the instrument developers do not have enough theoretical or empirical information to hypothesize how many constructs (factors) underlie the initial set of items and which items form which factor. Therefore, EFA is typically used earlier in the process of scale development and construct validation. A confirmatory factor analysis (CFA) is used in later phases of scale validation after the underlying structure has been established on prior empirical and/or theoretical grounds. Thus, CFA is employed when the goal is to test the validity of a hypothesized model of constructs (factors) and their relationships with a set of observable variables (items, indicators). Factor analysis (EFA, CFA, or both) are widely used and play a key role in the process of development and structural validation of instruments in education, psychology, and other behavioral fields. Methodological and technical aspects of factor analysis are presented later in this book (see Chapters 22 and 23).

3.2.4 Generalizability Aspect of Validity

The *generalizability aspect of validity* examines the extent to which score properties and interpretations generalize to and across population groups, settings, and tasks, including validity generalization of test criterion relationships (Messick, 1995). To collect evidence related to the generalizability aspect of validity means to identify the boundaries of the meaning of the scores across tasks and contexts. Typical procedures for collecting such evidence deal with testing for invariance of targeted constructs across groups and/or time points, item bias, consistency of predictions across groups, contextual stability, and reliability.

Specifically, testing for *invariance* of a construct across population groups is used to provide evidence that the properties and interpretations of test scores are generalizable across these groups; [this topic is addressed in Chapter 24, Section 24.2.2.2]. The presence of *item bias* is a serious threat to the generalizability aspect of validity. By definition, item bias occurs when respondents at the same level of the construct being measured (e.g., reading comprehension) differ in their responses because they belong to different groups — e.g., majority versus minority groups. For narrative texts, for example, cultural differences are the most likely source of irrelevant difficulty for students with limited English proficiency. This is because although the narrative genre is universal, narration varies across cultures in terms of types used, their function, their content, thematic emphasis, structural organization, and style (e.g., Westby, 1994).

The consistency of the relationship between the targeted construct and an external criterion across population groups also provides support to the generalizability aspect of validity. The respective correlation coefficient is called the *predictive validity coefficient* when the criterion is a future "behavior" of the examinees — e.g., using *SAT* scores to predict the future performance (college GPA) of college applicants. Under the unified construct-based model of validity (Messick, 1995), changes of the predictive validity coefficient across groups is referred to as *differential prediction.* The lack of differential prediction provides support to the generalizability aspect of validity. Studies of differential prediction typically examine group differences in linear regression slopes or intercepts for predicting criterion scores from scores of the test under validation; [the topic of linear regression is addressed in Chapters 10 and 13].

Evidence in support to the generalizability aspect of validity is provided also in the presence of *contextual stability* — that is, when the test scores are (a) stable across contexts of administration of the assessment instrument — e.g., when the test is administered in paper-based and computer-based format — and (b) relate to external criteria in a consistent manner across contexts of decision-making — e.g., when the test is used to predict attitude toward school and attitude toward academic achievement.

Further, as described in Chapter 2, the *reliability* of test scores indicates the degree to which they are accurate, consistent, and replicable when different people conduct the measurement, different instruments that purport to measure the same trait are being used, and there is incidental variation in measurement. Thus, the reliability of test scores is a necessary condition for their valid interpretations and generalization across samples of items, time points, raters, testing conditions. It is also important to note that the *predictive validity coefficient* of a test *X* regarding an external criterion, *Y*, does not exceed the square root of the reliability coefficient of *X* (r_{XX}). That is: $r_{XY} \leq \sqrt{r_{XX}}$. Indeed, Equation 2.3 (in Chapter 2) shows that the reliability coefficient can be represented as the squared correlation between true and observed scores: $r_{XX} = r_{XT}^2$. Or, equivalently, $r_{XT} = \sqrt{r_{XX}}$. But, in general, the correlation between observed scores, *X*, and other observed scores, *Y*, does not exceed the correlation between the observed *X* scores and their true values, *T*, that is: $r_{XY} \leq r_{XT}$. It follows then that: $r_{XY} \leq \sqrt{r_{XX}}$. Clearly, the predictive validity coefficient of a test *X*, r_{XY}, cannot reach high values unless the reliability of *X*, r_{XX}, is sufficiently high. In other words, high reliability is a necessary condition for high predictive validity of a test.

3.2.5 External Aspect of Validity

The *external aspect of validity* includes convergent and discriminant evidence from multitrait-multimethod comparisons, as well as evidence of criterion relevance and applied utility (Messick, 1995). The convergent evidence indicates a correspondence between measures of the same construct, whereas the discriminant evidence indicates a distinctness from measures of other constructs. As noted earlier, the operational definition of a construct is based on a specific theory and, therefore, the validity of the measurable indicators of the construct depends on the correctness of this theory. For example, if we adopt Rosenberg's (1965) theoretical argument that a student's level of "self-esteem" is positively related to participation in school activities, high positive correlation between students' scores on Rosenberg's self-esteem scale and measures of their involvement in school activities will provide convergent evidence of the external aspect of validity for the self-esteem scale.

Convergent evidence of the external aspect of validity is commonly established by correlating the scores on the test that (supposedly) measures the construct under validation with scores on other test(s) that measure the same construct or very similar constructs. High correlations provide evidence of convergent validity. For example, a newly developed verbal ability test can be assessed for convergent validity by calculating the correlation between examinees' scores on this test and their scores on the verbal section of the *SAT*.

Discriminant evidence of the external aspect of validity is supported when low correlations exist between examinees' scores on the test and their scores on constructs unrelated to the construct under validation. For example, the discriminant validity of a newly-developed verbal ability test will be supported by low correlations between examinees' scores on this test and their scores on the quantitative section of the SAT.

A **multitrait-multimethod (MTMM)** approach to collecting convergent and discriminant evidence can be used when two or more traits (constructs) are measured by two or more methods. This is commonly performed using a *multitrait-multimethod matrix*, which is a two-way display of the correlations between a person's scores on each trait as measured by each method. Table 3.1 illustrates such a matrix for an example in which two traits (*motivation* and *anxiety*) of high school students are measured by two different methods (a *questionnaire* and *school counselor evaluations*). The questionnaire scores come from student responses and the counselor scores are derived from evaluations provided by school counselors. In the MTMM matrix (Table 3.1), the correlation values of 1.00 in the main diagonal (shaded cells) are replaced by estimates of reliability for the scores on each trait as measured by each method. These estimates must be sufficiently large to warrant confidence in the interpretation of results with the MTMM matrix.

Table 3.1 *Multitrait-multimethod matrix for two traits (motivation and anxiety) measured by two methods (Questionnaire and Counselor Evaluations)*

	Motivation (Questionnaire)	**Anxiety** (Questionnaire)	**Motivation** (Counselor)	**Anxiety** (Counselor)
Motivation (Questionnaire)	**.82**	.22	.80	.12
Anxiety (Questionnaire)		**.86**	.15	.77
Motivation (Counselor)			**.84**	.27
Anxiety (Counselor)				**.80**

For simplicity, only the correlation coefficients above the main diagonal are presented in Table 3.1 because they are equal to their symmetrically located counterparts below the main diagonal of the matrix. In general, the correlation coefficients in a MTMM matrix provide both convergent and discriminant evidence, as well as information about possible method bias. Specifically, *convergent evidence* is demonstrated by high correlations between scores on the same trait obtained with different methods. *Discriminant evidence* is supported by low correlations between scores on different traits, especially when the same method is used. A *method bias* is detected if correlations between scores on different traits are higher when using the same method compared to when using different methods to measure these traits.

The correlation coefficients in Table 3.1 provide both convergent and discriminant evidence of the external aspect of validity. Specifically, the high correlation between scores obtained with two different methods (questionnaire and counselor) on the same trait (.80 for motivation, and .77 for anxiety) provides convergent evidence. At the same time, discriminant evidence is provided by the low correlations between scores on different traits (motivation and anxiety) measured with the same method (.22 and .27) or different methods (.12 and .15). There is, however, a possibility of *method bias*, as indicated by the fact that the correlations between scores on two different traits measured by the same method (.22 and .27) are higher than those when the traits are measured by different methods (.12 and .15).

3.2.6 Consequential Aspect of Validity

As described by Messick (1995), the *consequential aspect of validity* appraises the value implications of score interpretations as a basis for action as well as the actual and potential consequences of test use, especially in regard to sources of invalidity related to issues of bias, fairness, and distributive justice. Both short-term and long-term consequences (positive and/or negative) should be evaluated in searching evidence to support this aspect of validity. It is particularly important to make sure that negative consequences have not resulted from drawbacks of the assessment such as (a) *construct underrepresentation* — the assessment is too narrow and fails to measure important dimensions or facets of the construct, and/or (b) *construct-irrelevant variance* — the assessment allows for variance generated by sources unrelated to the target construct (e.g., item bias).

3.3 Summary

This chapter presented the concept of validity and different aspects of validity under the **unified construct-based model of validity.** A bulleted summary of concepts and highlights provided in this chapter follows:

• In general terms, **validity** has to do with whether an instrument measures what it purports to measure. Historically, there are three major stages in the treatment of validity: (a) *criterion-based model,* in which validity of measures is viewed as the degree to which these measures are consistent with (or "predict") the measures on a specific "criterion," (b) *construct-based model,* which considers three different types of validity—content validity, criterion validity, and construct validity—, and (c) *unified construct-based model of validity* based on the definition that "**validity** is an integrated evaluative judgment of the degree to which empirical evidence and theoretical rationales support the *adequacy* and *appropriateness* of *inferences* and *actions* based on test scores or other modes of assessment" (Mesick, 1989, 1995).

• The **content aspect** of validity includes evidence of content relevance, representativeness, and technical quality.

• The **substantive aspect** of validity refers to theoretical rationales for the observed consistencies in test responses, including process models of task performance along with empirical evidence that the theoretical processes are actually engaged by respondents in the assessment tasks.

• The **structural aspect** of validity appraises the fidelity of the scoring structure to the structure of the construct domain at issue.

• The **generalizability aspect** of validity examines the extent to which score properties and interpretations generalize to and across population groups, settings, and tasks, including validity generalization of test criterion relationships.

• The **external aspect** of validity includes convergent and discriminant evidence as well as evidence of criterion relevance and applied utility. *Convergent evidence* is established by high correlations between the scores on the test designed to measure the construct and scores on other tests that measure the same construct or very similar constructs. *Discriminant evidence* is established by low correlations between the examinees' scores on the test and their scores on constructs unrelated to the construct under validation. When two or more traits (constructs) are measured by two or more methods, the correlation coefficients in a *multitrait-multimethod matrix* are examined for convergent evidence, discriminant evidence, and method bias.

• The **consequential aspect** of validity appraises the value implications of score interpretations as a basis for action as well as the actual and potential consequences of test use, especially in regard to sources of invalidity related to issues of bias, fairness, and distributive justice.

3.4 Study Questions

1. If all items on a test deal with grammar rules, do score differences on this test reflect meaningful differences in reading comprehension? [Relate your explanation to *validity*.]
2. What is the major drawback of the criterion-related model of validity?
3. What is the major drawback of the construct-based model of validity?
4. What is the definition of validity under the unified construct-based model as provided by Messick (1989)?

5. What is the role of a comprehensive definition of a construct in the process of validating the construct?

6. A logical (*content area* x *test objective*) design and experts judgments regarding readability and suitability of the items in an assessment instrument are documented to collect evidence about which validity aspect?

(a) substantive aspect, **(b)** structural aspect, **(c)** external aspect, **(d)** none of the above.

7. Documenting "think aloud" protocols or retrospective reflections through which examinees explain the reasoning they have employed in responding to each item is used to support which validity aspect?

(a) substantive aspect, **(b)** structural aspect, **(c)** external aspect, **(d)** none of the above.

8. Factor analysis (exploratory and/or confirmatory) is employed to collect evidence regarding which validity aspect?

(a) substantive aspect, **(b)** structural aspect, **(c)** external aspect, **(d)** none of the above.

9. If the reliability of test scores is .81, the predictive validity coefficient of this test in regard to any criterion cannot be larger than which value?

(a) .30, **(b)** .50 **(c)** .81, **(d)** .90, **(e)** none of the above.

10. Contextual stability and reliability relate to which aspect of validity?

(a) content aspect, **(b)** structural aspect, **(c)** generalizability aspect,
(d) consequential aspect, **(e)** none of the above.

11. Drawbacks in the assessment measures such as *construct underrepresentation* and *construct-irrelevant variance* threaten which aspect of validity?

(a) content aspect, **(b)** structural aspect, **(c)** generalizability aspect,
(d) consequential aspect, **(e)** none of the above.

12. Two traits (**A** and **B**) are measured by two tests: a test of multiple-choice items (MCI) and a test of "True-False" items. Given the *multitrait-multimethod* matrix below, provide comments on (a) convergent evidence, (b) discriminant evidence, and (c) method bias.

	Trait A (MCI)	**Trait B** (MCI)	**Trait A** (True-False)	**Trait B** (True-False)
Trait A (MCI)	**.90**	.12	.82	.10
Trait B (MCI)		**.89**	.11	.79
Trait A (True-False)			**.87**	.12
Trait B (True-False)				**.85**

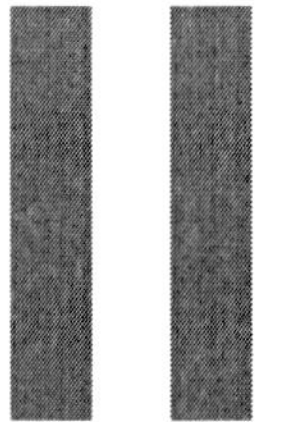

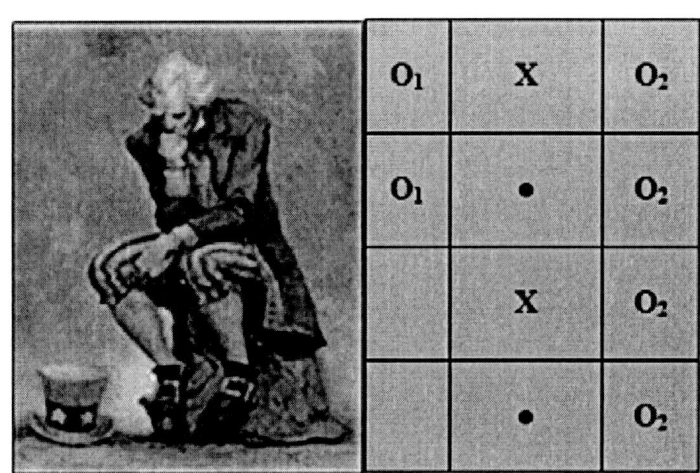

RESEARCH DESIGN

CHAPTER 4

QUANTITATIVE RESEARCH

As noted at the beginning of this book, the basic goal of *science* is to provide general theoretical explanations of natural phenomena. Important steps in the process of building, revising, or extending a theory are *explanation*, *understanding*, *prediction*, and *control*. Scientific explanations and predictions of phenomena are guided by a theoretical model (or, even better, "rival" models) of the phenomena and involve testing hypotheses about presumed relationships among variables identified with the model(s). Concepts and principles related to the nature of such variables, measurement scales, reliability of scores, and validity of interpretations were addressed in Part I of this book.

The methodological framework for the content in Part II is in line with the definition of *scientific research* provided by Kerlinger (1986, p. 10):

> **Scientific research is systematic, controlled, empirical, and critical investigation of natural phenomena guided by theory and hypotheses about the presumed relations among such phenomena.**

According to this definition, scientific research is organized in a (systematic and controlled) way that rules out alternative explanations, thus providing researchers with critical confidence in the research outcomes. Also, scientific research is *empirical*, which means that researchers must always put any subjective belief, expectation, and/or hypothesis to a test and base their conclusions on the test results.

Major steps in conducting empirical research are (a) identification of a problem in the area of interest, (b) statement of the general purpose of the study, (c) statement of the research question(s) and related hypotheses, (d) description of the research design and procedures, (d) data analysis, and (e) interpretation of the results and generalization of the findings. More details on the different components of these steps (e.g., assumptions and limitations) are provided with related discussions and illustrations throughout the book.

4.1 Research Questions and Hypotheses

A clear statement of research questions (or problems) and related hypotheses to be tested is of critical importance to research in education and other behavioral fields. There are three basic characteristics (criteria) of a good empirical/quantitative research question. Namely, the question *must* (a) ask about a specific relation between two (or more) variables, (b) be stated explicitly and unambiguously in question form, and (c) imply possibilities of empirical testing.

Let's take, for example, the following research question: "**What are the effects of socioeconomic status and motivation on students' academic achievement?**" Assuming that the student population has already been specified, this question clearly satisfies the criteria of a good research question. First, the question is about specific relations among three variables — *socioeconomic status*, *motivation*, and *academic achievement*. Second, it is stated clearly and explicitly in question form. Third, the question implies possibilities of empirical testing — e.g., using methods of regression analysis or structural equation modeling (discussed in Parts III and IV). This, however, is not the case with the question, "**Do private schools provide better education than public schools?**" Although there is an attempt to investigate a relation (comparing private schools versus public schools), the general concept of "better education" does not specify measurable variables and does not provide options for empirical testing of this relation.

Once the research question is established, the researcher may formulate a specific hypothesis (or "rival" hypotheses) about the relations between variables outlined in the question. A **hypothesis** is a statement about the relation between two or more variables. To illustrate, let's look again at the research question about the effects of socioeconomic status and motivation on academic achievement. Based on existing theoretical and/or empirical knowledge, the researcher may formulate one or more hypotheses about the expected relations ("effects") between the variables identified by this question. For example, two specific (and plausible) models of such "effects" are depicted in Figure 4.1, thus generating two "rival" hypotheses: First, "*motivation mediates the effect of socioeconomic status on academic achievement*" (Figure 4.1a.), and, second, "*socioeconomic status and motivation have independent effects on academic achievement*" (Figure 4.1b.).

Figure 4.1. *Two "rival" hypotheses about the effects of motivation and socioeconomic status on academic achievement*

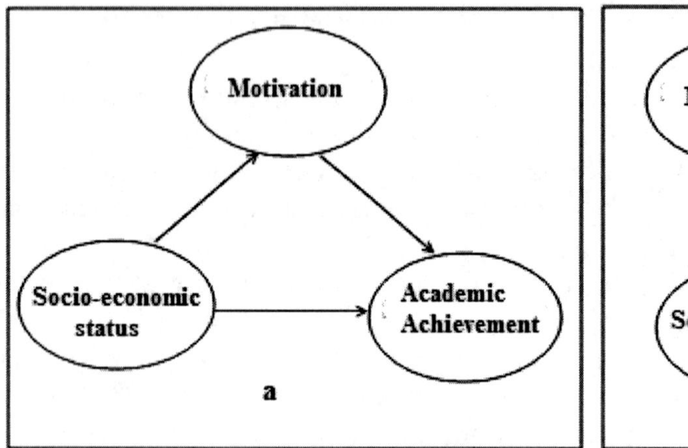

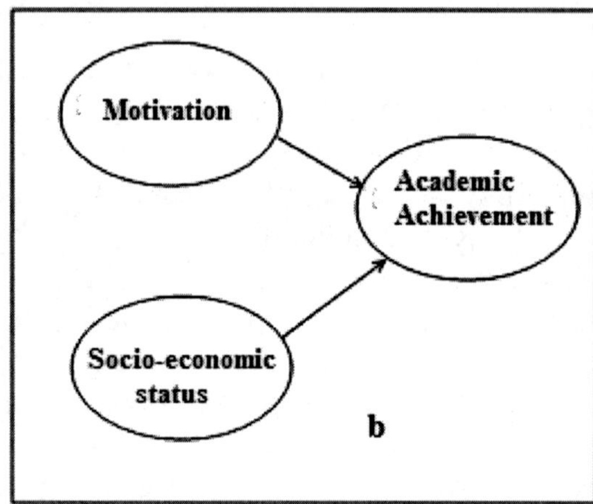

NOTE [4.1] Attention must be paid to problems related to **generality, specificity**, and **value questions** (or statements) which do not represent research questions (or hypotheses). Here are some hints in this regard.

- Research questions and hypotheses that are **too general** and/or **vague** are NOT amenable to testing and, thus, must be avoided.
- Research questions and hypotheses that are **too specific** are NOT recommended either because, although much easier to test, they tend leave out important variables and relations. Too much specificity produces trivial hypotheses and limits the scope of generalization.
- **Value (or judgment) questions or statements** are NOT scientific research questions or hypotheses. Words such as "best," "better," "should," etc. are typical examples of this. For instance, "What is the *best* way to improve student learning?" is not a good research question. Likewise, "Computerized education is *better* than traditional teaching" is not a research hypothesis that can be empirically tested using quantitative methods.

4.2 Types of Quantitative Research

There are two major types of quantitative research — experimental and nonexperimental research. **Experimental research** is classified as *true experimental*, *quasi-experimental*, and *single-case* research. **Nonexperimental research** includes *descriptive*, *correlational*, *causal-comparative* (*ex post facto*), and *meta-analysis* research. A brief description of these types of quantitative research is provided here, whereas basic research designs are provided in Chapter 5.

4.2.1 Nonexperimental Research

4.2.1.1 *Descriptive research*

Descriptive research, referred to also as **survey research,** is intended to provide systematic and accurate description(s) of characteristics for a population of interest. This is done primarily by using surveys with study samples drawn from a population. In this context, *survey* is a generic term for mail questionnaires, personal interviews, and panel (or telephone) sessions. Survey research has been developed as a branch of social scientific research with the main purpose of studying relations among sociological and psychological variables such as people's demographic characteristics, opinions, beliefs, preferences, practices, attitudes, and behavior.

Survey research is also widely used in educational research and evaluation. The endless opportunities provided by the internet are flourishing into an industry of online survey development, analyses, and reports. As an example, Webfeedback™ is a web-based system specializing in developing customized surveys for education and other fields (http://www.webfeedback.com). The education surveys available from this system include (1) *School Climate Survey* — principals give an annual school climate survey to parents, teachers and/or students to assess their satisfaction with school goals, programs and activities. The survey results are used for on-going school planning and program improvement; (2) *Classroom Climate Survey* — teachers give this survey to students several times during the year to assess the classroom learning climate and the impact of their classroom environment on student learning. The teacher and students use the information to make immediate improvements in the classroom to better meet the learning needs of the students; and (3) *District Services Survey* — district office administrators give an annual survey to school-level administrators to assess the effectiveness of district programs and services to schools. Survey questions usually cover curriculum and instruction, human resource and technology services to schools. District departments use the information to make improvements in their services and programs to schools.

Descriptive research is commonly classified in terms of how many times a sample of persons is surveyed (cross-sectional or longitudinal surveys) and how the data are collected (self-reports or observations). A **cross-sectional survey** involves a one-time data collection — for example, a survey conducted in 2007 to investigate differences in attitude toward religion among people from different age groups (say, 80 years old, 50 years old, 30 years old, and 20 years old). A **longitudinal survey** involves collecting data repeatedly (two or more times) on the same subjects with the purpose of measuring changes over time on the variables and relations of interest. For example, the findings of the ***Early Head Start Research and Evaluation (EHSRE) Study, 1996-2001*, are based, among other things, on longitudinal** ratings of children's behaviors by their parents, and parents' self-reports of their own behaviors, attitudes, and circumstances (http://www.childcareresearch.org). **A combination of cross-sectional and longitudinal surveys, referred to as a cohort-sequential survey, is also possible by starting a new longitudinal "cohort" at different time points of the study assessments.**

In terms of how the data are collected, **self-reports** require individuals to respond to statements and/or questions about themselves (or other people). For example, "The curriculum must be oriented toward success on proficiency tests" can be a statement included on a survey for teachers. Typically, a survey consists of (a) demographic information, (b) standardized questions/statements (Yes/No or Likert-type scale), and (c) free responses. Unlike self-reports, an **observation study** does not require individuals to provide responses to questions and/or statements. Instead, data on predetermined behavior of the participants are collected through observations by the researcher. Of course, both self-reports and observations can be employed in a descriptive study. Of particular importance is that the survey items (questions, statements) be clear and unambiguous. It is important to **avoid** (a) jargon; (b) words like "several" or "typically" — be specific; (c) controversial, embarrassing, and/or touchy questions to which respondents may not reply honestly or at all; (d) leading questions such as "Do you agree that …"; and (e) unwarranted assumptions— for example, the question "How many hours, on average, do the students in your school spend per day in the computer lab?" assumes that the school has a computer lab.

4.2.1.2 ***Correlational research***

The general purpose of **correlational research** is to study relationships between variables and/or use such relationships to make predictions regarding variable scores. Correlational research is widely used in education — for example, asking questions such as, "Is anxiety related to test performance?" or "Do high school GPA, number of advanced placement (AP) courses, and SAT score predict college GPA?" Correlational studies typically investigate how a set of variables relates to (explains or predicts) a particular variable of interest — most often, a *construct* such as achievement, proficiency, anxiety, or mental health. The variable which is explained (or predicted) is referred to as the **dependent variable** (or **criterion**), whereas the variables used as predictors are referred to as **independent variables**. Usually, the letter Y denotes the dependent variable, whereas X stands for an independent variable (or X_1, X_2, …, when there are two or more independent variables). Variables such as gender and ethnicity are *always* independent variables, whereas variables such as achievement and proficiency are primarily used as dependent variables in educational research. However, most variables (e.g., anxiety or motivation) can be dependent or independent variables, depending on the specific research question.

Most correlational methods assume that there is a **linear relationship** between the variables being studied; that is, plotting the persons' scores on two variables will result in a straight line. The Pearson correlation coefficient, which is most frequently used in correlational research, is meaningful only under this assumption. An example of a **curvilinear** relationship would be that between "age" and "physical strength" (e.g., number of push-ups) for persons in a large age interval (say, from 5 to 85 years). However, over this interval one can detect a positive linear relationship for the age group, say, up to 30 years old, and a negative linear relationship for the age group above 30 years old. Details and illustrations of correlational methods and testing are provided in Chapter 10.

NOTE [4.2] It is important to emphasize that **correlation does not mean causation**. That is, the presence of a high correlation between two variables does not necessarily mean that one variable "causes" the other variable. However, strong correlations may lead to the generation of hypotheses about possible causal effects that can be further examined in causal-comparative or experimental studies. Testing "rival" hypotheses can be particularly useful. For example, knowledge about the correlations among socioeconomic status, motivation, and academic achievement of students may lead to testing hypotheses such as those depicted in Figure 4.1.

4.2.1.3 *Ex post facto research*

Ex post facto ("after the fact") research is conducted to investigate cause-and-effect relationships by analyzing data on events that have taken place in the past. With this approach, both the effect and the presumed cause have already occurred and are being studied in retrospect. That is, the researcher is interested in some "effects" and examines data by going "back to the future" to seek out possible causes. It is referred to also as **causal-comparative research.** Here are two examples of ex post facto research:

- To identify factors leading to aggressive behavior of students by analyzing data collected from school records and family "history."
- To study the "effects" of gender and ethnicity on changes in students' performance in math and science by examining archival data from the *National Educational Longitudinal Study of 1988* (NELS, 1988, http://nces.ed.gov/surveys/nels88.)

It is important to emphasize that in these, or any other, examples of ex post facto studies the researcher has no control over the data. That is, the researcher cannot manipulate the independent variables through random assignment of subjects to treatment groups because the subjects are already in (predetermined) groups. Therefore, it would be more appropriate to interpret ex post facto findings as *relationships*, rather than "causal effects," among variables. On the other hand, ex post facto research can be useful when (a) the independent variables cannot be controlled by the researcher or (b) manipulation of independent variables is possible, but it may be unethical, impractical, or costly. For example, in a study of factors contributing to lung cancer, it would be unethical and hazardous for the participants if the researcher attempted to control for variables related to smoking and tobacco use.

Just like correlational research (see NOTE [4.2]), ex post facto research cannot prove "cause-and-effect" relations, but can lead to the generation of hypotheses that are worth testing later with true experimental designs through manipulation of independent variables. This can be of both theoretical and practical benefit because true experimental studies are costly (in time, money, and effort) and, therefore, are worth pursuing only when there is a good reason for doing so. Of course, as alluded to earlier, ex post facto research has its unique role in educational studies when the variables of interest *cannot* or *should not* be manipulated in experimental studies.

4.2.1.4 *Meta-analysis research*

Meta-analysis refers to an approach of integrating and analyzing the quantitative results from different studies on the same research topic. This approach is particularly useful when the results reported by different studies are dissimilar thus providing a confusing picture about the phenomenon of interest. For example, if the research topic relates to "gender differences in math performance of middle school students," a meta-analytic study would examine as many published studies as possible on this topic with the purpose of integrating the statistical results on gender differences in math for the target population. This is done by comparing the **"effect sizes" (ES)** across the different studies. The effect size for the difference between the sample means on a variable being measured for two groups (say, *experimental* and *control*) was introduced by Glass (1977) and the formula is as follows:

$$ES = \frac{\overline{X}_E - \overline{X}_C}{S_C}, \qquad \textbf{(4.1)}$$

where $\overline{X}_E$ and $\overline{X}_C$ are the sample means for the scores of experimental and control groups, respectively, and S_C is the standard deviation of scores for the control group. In this context, the effect size measures the average *superiority* (or *inferiority*, if negative) of the experimental group relative to the control group. According to a conventional classification provided by Cohen (1988), this effect size can be considered (a) *small* if $ES = .20$, (b) *medium* if $ES = .50$, and (c) *large* if $ES = .80$; (for absolute values of *ES*).

Meta-analysis is widely used in educational research and has proven its usefulness in guiding data-driven decisions about teaching, learning, and policy making. For example, Kulik, Kulik, and Cohen (1979) have used meta-analysis to integrate findings from 75 published studies of Keller's (1968) personalized system of instruction. Another study (Cohen, Kulik, & Kulik, 1982) provided a meta-analysis of findings from 65 independent evaluations of school tutoring programs and showed that these programs had positive effects on the participants' academic performance and attitudes toward the subject matter. Perhaps the most consistent large-scale analysis of effect sizes and their meta-analytic integration is reported with evaluations of the *Tennessee K-3 Class Size Study* known also as the *Student-Teacher Achievement Ratio* (STAR) project — a large-scale, four-year, experimental study of reduced class size (http://www.heros-inc.org/star.htm). Among numerous findings related to this study, it was concluded that "*the results of Project STAR show clearly that average pupil performance in the primary years can be increased (with reduced class size) by approximately one-fourth to one-third of a standard deviation without the introduction of new materials or curricula and without retraining the teachers*" (Finn, Fulton, Zaharias, & Nye, 1989). It was also reported that "*the effect size for minority was about double that for majority*" (Mosteller, 1995).

Most arguments in published criticisms of meta-analysis seem (unduly) related to meta-analytic studies with poor planning and technical problems, rather than to the essence of contemporary meta-analysis. In any case, researchers must be aware of potential problems and pitfalls in conducting meta-analyses. To list a few:

- Including studies with obvious methodological flaws can hurt the validity of meta-analytic findings.
- As meta-analysis is based on published studies, effect sizes in unpublished work (e.g., doctoral dissertations) are not taken into account.
- An "apples and oranges" effect may occur when combining results from studies that differ a great deal in conditions, populations, criteria, or assessment instruments.
- The accuracy of meta-analytic estimates can be negatively affected by a poor match of curriculum with outcome measures and/or sizeable differences in reliability or variances of scores across study samples used in the meta-analysis.

NOTE [4.3] Most potential problems are reduced (if not eliminated) with the contemporary methods of meta-analysis (see, e.g., Hedges, 1981; Hunter, Schmidt, & Jackson, 1982). Although less often, meta-analysis of effect sizes for *correlations* or *differences between proportions*, as well as *multivariate effect sizes*, is also used in educational research. Such effect sizes and their calculation are presented in Parts III and IV of this book.

4.2.2 Experimental Research

4.2.2.1 *True experimental research*

True experimental research is conducted with the purpose of testing hypotheses about *possible causal effects* by manipulating independent variable(s) believed to produce such effects and controlling for all other relevant variables. Independent variables frequently manipulated in educational research include, among others, *method of instruction* (e.g., computer-based versus traditional teaching), *class size* (e.g., small versus large), or *type of assessment* (e.g., standardized tests versus portfolios). True experimental research is derived from the fundamental principle of "systematic control" required in scientific inquiry. An independent variable in this type of research is also referred to as a *treatment variable*, *causal variable*, or *experimental variable*. The variable upon which the manipulation of independent variable(s) is expected to produce "effects" is called the *dependent variable*, or the *criterion* or *outcome variable*. If a true experimental study is conducted to investigate the effect of class-size on student achievement, the independent variable is "class size" and the dependent variable is "student achievement." The *Tennessee K-3 Class Size Study* (see the previous section, 4.2.1.4) is an example of a true experimental large-scale educational study. Here is an excerpt from an annotated description of this study [http://www.heros-inc.org/classsizeresearch.htm]:

> The research started with an experimental group consisted of 105 first grade students divided into seven classes of 15 students each. A blind control group was selected comprising 105 students drawn from 35 elementary schools, demographically matched with the experimental group according to five pre-established criteria: (a) sex, (b) race, (c) economic status, (d) date of birth within 45 days, and (e) total pre-reading raw score within four points on the California Achievement Test Level 10. The statistical analysis of pre- and post-test results indicated that the experimental group consistently achieved better results than either control group. The only intervening variable was the reduction of class size from 1:25 to 1:15. Therefore, it was concluded that reducing class size to 1:15 has a positive effect on student reading and math outcomes.

While manipulating the independent variable(s), true experimental research controls all other relevant variables — that is, variables that may also impact the outcome, thus producing "confounding" effects and making it difficult (if not impossible) to conclude to what degree, if at all, the outcome effects are due to the treatment. With the purpose of such "control," the true experimental research requires that (a) the study participants are randomly selected from a well-defined population, (b) these participants are then randomly assigned to groups, and (c) the groups are randomly assigned to treatment conditions. This three-step process is called **full randomization** in assigning participants to treatment groups. The main characteristics of the true experimental research are:

- *Manipulation of the independent variable(s).* The researcher creates conditions to be studied, referred to as "levels" of the independent variable. For example, if the independent variable in a study is *reinforcement*, the researcher may create, say, two levels of this variable — "reinforcement" (experimental group) versus "no reinforcement" (control group).
- *Fully randomized assignment of participants to treatment groups.* The purpose of the random assignment of subjects to conditions is to equate the participants on the dependent variable before the experimental treatment begins; (that is, to avoid "selection bias" that may affect the validity of the study results).

• *Controlling for possible confounding variables.* The researcher must hold constant, as much as practically possible, variables that are different from the independent and dependent variables, but that may also impact the results on the dependent variable, such as possible exposure to a similar type of treatment in another classroom — for example, when investigating the effects of one teaching method on student's reading test scores.

True experimental research in education is difficult to conduct for a variety of reasons (e.g., time, money, effort, and ethical issues). With the exception of largely funded state or national studies (such as the aforementioned *Tennessee K-3 Class Size Study*), true experimental studies in education are usually short in time span. This makes it difficult to detect sizable (or any) treatment effects, even if such effects may exist, since the participants are exposed to treatments only for a short period of time. When differences are found to exist, educational researchers must still be careful not rush to conclusions regarding "cause" and "effect," even in well designed true experimental studies. It is more realistic to base research inferences on results from testing "rival" hypotheses about possible causal relations. Moreover, causation is a controversial topic at philosophical, methodological, and technical levels (e.g., Asher, 1976; Cook & Campbell, 1979; Cronbach, 1982; Grossman & Mackenzie, 2005; Maxwell, 2004; Nash, 2005; Rubin, 1974; Scott, 2007; West & Anderson, 1976).

4.2.2.2 *Quasi-experimental research*

As already noted, the conditions for conducting true experimental research are difficult to meet in educational settings. Very often, for example, educational studies are conducted with intact groups (e.g., school classes) and, thus, even if such groups are randomly assigned to treatments, the condition for full randomization is not in place. In general, when an experimental study is lacking some characteristics of true experimental research, it is referred to as a **quasi-experimental study**.

It is important to emphasize that a quasi-experimental study must be planned with every effort made to meet the conditions of true experimental research as much as possible within the existing restrictions on full experimental control. For example, given the restriction on full randomization with intact groups, the researcher must employ all available tools to control for other sources of experimental "contamination." One such tool can be a statistical procedure called "analysis of covariance" (ANCOVA), which is used to control for preexisting differences among intact groups on a variable (covariate) that also relates to the dependent variable. Typical examples in this regard are quasi-experimental studies that employ "pretest-posttest" design.

4.2.2.3 *Single-case research*

A **single-case research** involves an in-depth study of a single "case" which can be a single person, group, institution, or culture. This type of research, also referred to as **single-subject research**, can take the form of (a) a *single-case study*, in a natural (uncontrolled) environment, or (b) a *single-case experiment*, in a more controlled environment — e.g., to investigate the way a subject responds over time in a controlled exposure of this subject to a treatment. Single-case experiments relate primarily to the work of psychologists, counselors, and social workers—but they are also quite often used in research in the field of special education (e.g., Yin, 1993). Case studies in education may investigate, for example, a single teacher in a classroom (e.g., Wood, Cobb, & Yaekel, 1991); development of teaching materials based on case studies (e.g., Kreber, 2001; see also http://www.materials.ac.uk/guides/casestudies.asp); or entire educational systems — (e.g., *To Sum It Up: Case Studies of Education in Germany, Japan, and the United States* (http://www.ed.gov/pubs/SumItUp/index.html).

4.2.3 Internal and External Validity in Experimental Research

There are two major questions that must be addressed with any experimental research. The first question, which relates to the **internal validity** of the research, asks if the study results are due only to the manipulation of the independent variables, or whether there are also some confounding effects produced by insufficient (or lack of) control in the experimental design. The second question, which deals with the **externally validity** of the study, asks if the results are generalizable to persons, contexts, or measurement instruments beyond the specific settings and/or circumstances of the experimental study.

These two types of experimental validity are related, and both are very important for the value and quality of the study findings. However, the researcher must be aware of the "catch-22" that occurs in attempts to maximize both the internal and external validity in an experimental study (Gay & Airsian, p. 372). Specifically:

> Maximizing internal validity requires the use of very rigid controls over participants and conditions, similar to a laboratory-like environment. However, the more a research situation is narrowed and controlled, the less realistic and generalizable it becomes. A study can contribute little to educational practice if there is no assurance that a technique in a highly controlled setting will also be effective in a less controlled classroom setting. On the other hand, the more natural the experimental setting becomes, the more difficult it is to control extraneous variables.

To achieve a good balance between control of experimental conditions and generalizability of results over populations and settings, the researcher must be aware of factors that may threaten the internal and external validity of experimental studies.

4.2.3.1 *Threats to Internal Validity*

Traditionally, the literature on experimental research refers to eight factors identified in a classic paper by Campbell and Stanley (1963) as potential threats to the internal validity of an experimental design: *history*, *maturation*, *pretesting*, *measuring instruments*, *statistical regression*, *differential selection*, *experimental mortality*, and *interaction among factors*. The researcher must be aware that the results obtained within the specific settings of the study can be, partially or entirely, due to confounding effects produced by the presence of some of these factors.

- **History**. This threat to internal validity may occur when the study participants experience an event during the time period of the study that may influence their responses on the dependent variable of interest. Such an event (contemporary "history") may take place within or outside of the experimental setting of the study. For example, suppose that the study "treatment" consists of sessions on religious prejudice and in the meantime the tragic event of "September 11, 2001" occurs. Clearly, one can expect that the post-treatment responses of the study participants on a survey about religious prejudice will be affected by this event thus "confounding" the actual results due to the treatment.
- **Maturation**. When the time span of an experimental study is relatively long, the results can be confounded by effects due to, say, biological or cognitive maturation of the participants during that period of time. For example, when investigating students' problem solving skills, the results of a long-term study may be affected by the natural process of cognitive development that children experience as they mature.
- **Pretesting**. Experimental studies often involve pretesting — testing the participants on the dependent variable of interest before the experimental treatment takes place. While pretesting may give the researcher a better idea of the participants' starting points, thereby allowing for improved experimental control, it may also affect the posttest measures on the dependant variable.

This can happen, for example, when participants memorize facts or subsequently pay increased attention to the material being tested.

• **Measuring instruments**. Changes in the measurement instruments used to collect experimental data can affect the accuracy of scores, thus distorting the real picture of treatment effects. As we already know from the discussion on reliability (Chapter 2), the accuracy of scores varies across instruments of measurement — e.g., standardized tests, rater evaluations, teacher grading, or self-reports. As such, it is important to have a clear idea of the differences among instruments when interpreting results.

• **Statistical regression**. The effect of "statistical regression" typically occurs with experimental studies in which the participants are selected based on their extreme scores observed prior to treatment. At posttest measurements, participants with initially high scores tend to score lower, whereas those with initially low scores tend to score higher. This effect, referred to as "regression toward the mean," occurs primarily because the initially observed extreme scores include relatively large (positive or negative) random error that will probably not be as large with replicated measures. For example, we cannot expect people who have "won big" (or, conversely, those who have "lost big") gambling to continue to do so over an entire month in Las Vegas. In the context of educational experimental studies, the regression toward the mean effect from pre- to post-treatment measures may also distort the picture about treatment outcomes.

• **Differential selection**. In studies that involve control and experimental groups, pretest differences between these groups on the dependent variable (or some "covariate") will carry over as group differences on the posttest. This can affect the internal validity of the study because it is not known to what degree the post group differences are due to the experimental treatment (e.g., new teaching strategy). Methods for statistical control of differential selection are addressed in Parts III and IV of this book.

• **Experimental mortality**. This type of threat to internal validity, also referred to as **attrition**, may occur when some participants drop out of one of the groups during the experimental study. Typically, this is not a random process. In a study on student achievement with control and experimental groups, for example, low achieving participants are more likely to drop out of the experimental group — say, for fear that they may "jeopardize" the experiment or because they cannot "catch up" with the rest of the group. Evidently, this will affect the results of the experimental study, even if the two groups were equated (matched) on relevant characteristics prior to the experimental treatment.

• **Interaction among factors**. Some of the aforementioned factors threatening interval validity may occur in interaction, thus producing additional confounding effects on the results of the experimental study. For example, an interaction of *differential selection* and *maturation* may occur when the participants in the experimental group are volunteers and they are more "mature" (or more motivated) than the nonvolunteers in the control group. Clearly, such interaction of "self-selection" and "maturation" will threaten the internal validity of the study.

4.2.3.2 *Threats to external validity*

While *internal validity* deals with the legitimacy of the study findings within the specific settings of an experimental study, *external validity* shows whether these findings are generalizable to other subject populations, treatment settings, and/or measurement instruments. The researcher can enhance external validity prior to the experimental study through careful planning and development of an appropriate experimental design. Clearly, the sample used in the experimental study must be representative of the population to which the study findings are expected to generalize. For example, if the target population of an experimental study are all students in a given demographic region, the study sample must represent this population sufficiently well on characteristics such as location (rural, urban, suburban), ethnic group composition, school district characteristics (location, number of schools, school size, etc.), and other categories that are relevant to the context and goals of the study. The random selection of sample units from the target population is an essential condition for the sample to be representative. This topic will be addressed in more detail in Chapter 5.

Awareness of potential threats to external validity is of critical importance to the success of the study. Factors traditionally reported as threatening the external validity of an experimental study are (a) *interaction effects of selection biases with experimental treatment*, (b) a *reactive effect of pretesting*, (c) *reactive effects of experimental procedures*, and (d) *multiple-treatment interference*.

• **Interaction of selection biases with experimental treatment.** This threat to external validity typically relates to situations in which the experimental treatment is more effective for participants with particular characteristics; therefore, the findings are not generalizable (do not hold) for the entire population. Let's assume, for example, that a large school district decides to study the implementation of a new approach to teaching and learning science based on computer simulations. If the treatment is conducted with students from a school with a well equipped computer lab and experience in using education technology, the treatment results will probably not be the same as for schools that lack such resources and experience. Thus, the interaction between a "selection bias" in favor of students who are experienced with computer-based technology and the "experimental treatment" (using such technology) prevents the researcher from generalizing the study findings over the entire population of students in this school district.

• **Reactive effect of pretesting**. When the participants in an experiment take a pretest, they become aware of and sensitive to issues targeted by the treatment. Because of this, their post-treatment results may not be generalizable over a population of students who have not been pretested. This type of threat to external validity is referred to as the *reactive* (or *interaction*) *effect of pretesting*. Assume, for example, that the experiment is a program intervention targeting changes in students' attitudes toward the use of drugs and alcohol. A survey conducted prior to the intervention could sensitize the participants to this issue; therefore, the intervention effects may not hold to the same degree for the entire population of students who, under normal circumstances, would not have been exposed to the pre-intervention survey (or other "pretesting" procedures).

• **Reactive effects of experimental procedures**. The participants in experiments usually "react" to the presence of observers and experimental procedures (e.g., audio- or video-recording) and, consequently, may alter their normal behavior. Such reactive effects make it difficult to generalize the experimental findings over subjects (e.g., students and/or teachers) who are exposed to the treatment in normal settings. For example, when the experiment involves an intensive student-teacher interaction, student participation in class sessions that are videotaped could be much higher than that in regular class sessions that are not videotaped, even when the same teaching method is used in both settings.

• **Multiple-treatment interference**. When the participants in an experiment are exposed over time to two or more treatments (or variations of the same treatment), the effect of the second (and any following treatment) might be confounded with "residual effects" from its preceding treatment(s). The overall outcome of the treatments will depend, among other things, on the sequence in which they were introduced. Thus, the results obtained with a particular sequence of treatments are not necessarily generalizable over subjects who are exposed to the same treatments, but in different order. For example, if subjects are exposed to three types of mental health therapy during the day (taking medication in the morning, exercising at noon, and listening to classical music in the evening), their scores on a mental health test can be generalizable only over subjects exposed to the same sequence of treatments.

4.3 Summary

- **Scientific research** is systematic, controlled, empirical, and critical investigation of natural phenomena guided by theory and hypotheses about the presumed relations among such phenomena.

- **Major steps in conducting empirical research** are (a) identification of a problem in the area of interest, (b) statement of the general purpose of the study, (c) statement of the research question(s) and related hypotheses, (d) description of the research design and procedures, (d) data analysis, and (e) interpretation of the results and generalization of the findings.

- A **hypothesis** is a statement about the relation between two or more variables.

- Research questions and hypotheses that are **too general** and/or **vague** are NOT amenable to testing and, thus, must be avoided.

- Research questions and hypotheses that are **too specific** are NOT recommended either because, although much easier to test, they tend leave out important variables and relations. Too much specificity produces trivial hypotheses and limits the scope of generalization.

- **Value (or judgment) questions or statements** are NOT scientific research questions or hypotheses.

- **Descriptive research**, referred to also as **survey research,** is intended to provide systematic and accurate description(s) of characteristics for a population of interest. This is done mainly by using surveys with study samples drawn from a population.

- The purpose of **correlational research** is to study relationships between variables and use such relationships to make predictions regarding variable scores. Keep in mind that **correlation does not mean causation**.

- **Ex post facto** research is conducted to investigate cause-and-effect relationships by analyzing data on events that have taken place in the past.

- **Meta-analysis** is a statistical approach to integrating and analyzing the quantitative results from different studies on the same research topic.

- **True experimental research** is conducted with the purpose of testing hypotheses about *possible causal effects* by manipulating independent variable(s) believed to produce such effects and controlling for all other relevant variables.

- **Full randomization** is achieved when (a) the study participants are randomly selected from a well-defined population, (b) the participants are then randomly assigned to groups, and (c) the groups are randomly assigned to treatment conditions.

- The **main characteristics of the true experimental research** are (a) manipulation of the independent variable(s), (b) fully randomized assignment of participants to treatment groups, and (c) controlling for possible confounding variables.

- When an experimental study is lacking some characteristic(s) of true experimental research, it is referred to as a **quasi-experimental study**. A quasi-experimental study must be planned with every effort made to meet the conditions of true experimental research as much as possible within the existing restrictions on full experimental control.

- A **single-case research** involves an in-depth study of a single "case" which can be a single person, group, institution, or culture.
- The **internal validity** question is whether the study results are due only to the manipulation of the independent variables, or whether there are also some confounding effects produced by insufficient control in the experimental design.
- The **external validity** question is whether the results are generalizable to persons, contexts, or measurement instruments beyond the specific settings and/or circumstances of the experimental study.
- **Threats to internal validity** — history, maturation, pretesting, measuring instruments, statistical regression (toward the mean), differential selection, experimental mortality, and interaction among such factors (e.g., interaction between differential selection and maturation).
- **Threats to external validity** — interaction of selection biases with experimental treatment, reactive effect of pretesting, and multiple-treatment interference.

4.4 Study Questions

1. What are the characteristics of scientific research?
2. What are the major steps in conducting empirical research?
3. What is the main limitation of research questions that are too specific?
4. What is the main limitation of research questions that are too general?
5. Suppose you have found correlation between socio-economic status (SES) and academic achievement of students. Does this mean that SES has a causal impact on academic achievement?
6. What is the role of correlational analysis in subsequent investigations of causal relations?
7. What is an ex post facto research?
8. What is the purpose of true experimental research?
9. What is a fully randomized design?
10. What are the main characteristics of true experimental research?
11. A study design that involves randomly selected intact groups (e.g., classrooms) is

    (a) true experimental, **(b)** single-case, **(c)** quasi-experimental, **(d)** meta-analytic.
12. What is the internal validity question?
13. What is the external validity question?
14. (True or false?) The more a research situation is narrowed and controlled in an attempt to increase the internal validity, the more realistic and generalizable are the results.
15. What are the threats to internal validity?
16. What are the threats to external validity?

17. Research conducted to investigate cause-and-effect relationships by analyzing data on events that have taken place in the past is called

(a) descriptive research, **(b)** meta-analysis, **(c)** ex-post facto research, **(d)** history

18. A school with a well equipped computer lab and experience in using education technology is involved in an experiment targeting to improve the results in math education through the use of computers. What validity threat is likely to occur in this experimental study?

19. What type of validity threat is likely to occur in a long-term study on children's metacognition about reading? [*Note*: Research has shown that what children know about the goals, tasks, and strategies of reading can influence how well they plan and monitor their own reading.]

CHAPTER 5

BASIC RESEARCH DESIGNS

The research designs described in this chapter are grouped into three categories — pre-experimental, true experimental, and quasi-experimental designs. The **pre-experimental designs** do NOT possess the two key characteristics (*randomization* and *control*) of true experimental research described in Chapter 4. The **true experimental designs** involve both randomization and control, while the **quasi-experimental designs** involve control, but not randomization. The following notational system is used to depict research designs:

R random assignment
O observations (data collected, say, at pretest and posttest time points)
X treatment condition; (X_1, X_2, X_3, …, etc., stand for different treatments)
• control condition (lack of treatment **X**)
Group **E** — group of study participants submitted to the treatment condition, **X**
Group **C** — group of study participants submitted to the control condition, **•**

With some variations, this notational system is largely adopted in the research literature (e.g., Cook & Campbell, 1979). The observations, **O**, represent data for the study sample (e.g., test scores). When such data are collected at different time points, **O** is used with subscripts. For example, $\mathbf{O_1}$ and $\mathbf{O_2}$ stand for data collected at Time 1 (e.g., pretest) and Time 2 (e.g., posttest), respectively. If the study involves two or more treatments (or different variations of one treatment), **X** is used with subscripts: $\mathbf{X_1}$, $\mathbf{X_2}$, $\mathbf{X_3}$, …, etc. The groups submitted to different treatment conditions (e.g., different "experimental" groups) are then denoted as follows: E_1, E_2, E_3, …, etc.

It should be also noted that the "control condition" (•) means that this is not the treatment condition of interest, **X**, but it does not mean that "nothing is happening." For example, if **X** denotes a "new method of teaching" (experimental treatment), then • will denote a "traditional method of teaching" (non-experimental treatment).

5.1 Pre-experimental Designs

As alluded to earlier, the designs referred to here as "pre-experimental" designs, do not possess two important characteristics of true experimental research: randomization and control. With awareness of the threats to internal validity that such designs may bring, they can be used to provide some useful information in pre-experimental piloting of experimental studies.

5.1.1 One Group Posttest-Only Design

With the **one group posttest-only design** (a) the selection of study participants is *non-random*, (b) all participants are assigned to a single treatment, and (c) all observations are made after the treatment. This design is represented in Figure 5.1

Figure 5.1 *One group posttest-only design*

Treatment Condition	Group Label	Treatment	Posttest
Experimental	**E**	**X**	**O**

The lack of pretesting has both positive and negative implications for internal validity in this design. On one hand, there is no threat to internal validity associated with pretesting procedures, but, on the other hand, it is difficult to determine whether changes in the variable of interest have occurred. Further, even if such changes are detected, the lack of a control group makes it difficult to know whether the changes were due to the treatment, **X**, or to some other (confounding) variable(s). Somewhat valid conclusions in this regard can be reached *only if* the researcher knows sufficiently well the pre-treatment status of the participants on the variable of interest (say, from existing records). The one group posttest-only design can be useful in preliminary stages of developing ideas, questions, and planning the study, but not in reaching valid finalized conclusions about treatment effects.

5.1.2 One Group Pretest-Posttest Design

With the **one group pretest-posttest design** (a) the selection of study participants is *nonrandom*, (b) all participants are assigned to a single treatment, and (c) observations are made before and after the treatment. This design is represented in Figure 5.2.

Figure 5.2 *One group pretest-posttest design*

Treatment Condition	Group Label	Pretest	Treatment	Posttest
Experimental	**E**	$\mathbf{O_1}$	**X**	$\mathbf{O_2}$

The one group pretest-posttest design makes it possible to examine changes in the dependent variable from pretest to posttest observations. However, the lack of a control group is an obstacle in reaching valid conclusions about the possible cause(s) of such changes. That is, as with the previous design (5.1.1), it is not known whether the changes are causally related to the treatment, **X**, or to some other variable(s). Although it allows the researcher to measure pretest-posttest changes, the pretest-posttest design also opens the door to some threats to internal validity that are not associated with the one group posttest-only design (5.1.1) — e.g., *pretesting procedures*, *statistical regression toward the mean*, and *history* (see 4.2.3).

5.1.3 Nonrandomized Control Group Posttest-Only Design

With the **nonrandomized control group posttest-only design** (a) the selection of study participants is *nonrandom*, (b) there are two treatment groups, but the study participants are not assigned randomly to each group, and (c) only posttest observations are collected for each group. This design is represented in Figure 5.3.

Figure 5.3 *Nonrandomized control group posttest-only design*

Treatment Condition	Group Label	Treatment	Posttest
Experimental	**E**	**X**	**O**
Control	**C**	•	**O**

The lack of pretesting has both positive and negative implications for internal validity in this design. As mentioned above (5.1.1., 5.1.2) while there is no threat to internal validity associated with pretesting procedures, it is difficult to determine whether some changes in the dependent variable have occurred as a result of the treatment.

5.2 True Experimental Designs

The two research designs presented in this section are referred to as **true experimental designs** because they possess the key characteristics of true experimental research — randomization and control.

5.2.1 Randomized Pretest-Posttest Control Group Design

With the **randomized pretest-posttest control group design** (a) the study participants are selected by random sampling from the target population, (b) the selected sample is randomly split into two groups, (c) each group is randomly assigned to one treatment condition (experimental or control), and (d) observations on the dependent variable are collected before and after the treatment administration. As a reminder, the first three conditions, (a), (b), and (c), together are referred to as *complete randomization.* This design is represented in Figure 5.4.

Figure 5.4 *Randomized pretest-posttest control group design*

Type of Assignment	Treatment Condition	Group Label	Pretest	Treatment	Posttest
R	**Experimental**	**E**	O_1	**X**	O_2
R	**Control**	**C**	O_1	•	O_2

The randomized pretest-posttest control group design allows for the examination of treatment effects from different perspectives. For example, the researcher may compare the experimental and control groups on pretest-posttest changes ("gain" scores), as well as on the posttest performance of the two groups assuming that they have an "equal start" on the pretest. This can be achieved, for example, by using statistical methods known as "Analysis of variancc (ANOVA) on gain scores," and "Analysis of covariance" (ANCOVA) discussed later in this book.

The characteristics of this design (complete randomization and use of a control group) guard against numerous threats to internal validity — *selection bias*, *history*, *maturation*, *statistical regression toward the mean*, *history*, etc. However, the external validity is still jeopardized because the pretesting may sensitize the study participants to issues relevant to the treatment conditions, thus making it difficult to generalize the study results from the sample to the population.

The randomized pretest-posttest control group design can be extended to include additional variations on the independent variable (treatment conditions). For example, Figure 5.5 depicts the design for a study which involves two experimental conditions (**E_1** and **E_2**) and one control condition, **C**.

Figure 5.5 *Extended randomized pretest-posttest control group design*

Type of Assignment	Treatment Condition	Group Label	Pretest	Treatment	Posttest
R	**Experimental**	**E_1**	**O_1**	**X_1**	**O_2**
R	**Experimental**	**E_2**	**O_1**	**X_2**	**O_2**
R	**Control**	**C**	**O_1**	•	**O_2**

This design allows the researcher to make valid inferences about different aspects of the treatment effects in terms of pretest-posttest changes and/or posttest outcomes controlling for pretest differences. For example, one can investigate (a) the differential effects of the two experimental conditions, (b) the effect of each experimental condition compared to the control condition, and (c) the joint effect of the two experimental conditions versus the effect of the control condition.

5.2.2 Randomized Solomon Four-Group Design

With the **randomized Solomon four-group design** (a) the study participants are selected by random sampling, (b) the selected sample is then randomly divided into four groups, (c) by random assignment, two of the groups are assigned to the experimental condition and two groups to the control condition, (d) all four groups take a posttest, and (e) by random assignment, one of the two experimental groups and one of the two control groups take a pretest. This design is shown in Figure 5.6.

Just like the randomized pretest-posttest control group design, the randomized Solomon four-group design guards against internal validity threats. There are, however, additional advantages of this design. First, this design overcomes the external validity problem related to pretesting. This is because observations are taken for each condition (experimental and control) and for groups *with* and *without* pretesting, thus eliminating the interaction effect of pretesting and treatment. Second, unlike any other design, the randomized Solomon four-group design makes it possible to evaluate, not only to guard against, the "magnitude" of threats to the internal validity.

For example, there are four factors that may contribute to the score difference from pretest to posttest for the first experimental group (say, $\Delta E_1 = \mathbf{O_2} - \mathbf{O_1}$): *treatment* **X**, *pretesting*, *history*, and *maturation*. At the same time, the factors that may contribute to the pretest-posttest score difference for the first control group (say, $\Delta C_1 = \mathbf{O_2} - \mathbf{O_1}$) are *pretesting*, *history*, and *maturation* (treatment **X** is not assigned to this group). Therefore, the difference between ΔE_1 and ΔC_1 ($\Delta E_1 - \Delta C_1$) can serve as a measure of the effect of treatment **X**. Also, the factors that may contribute to the posttest scores, O_2, of the second experimental group, $\mathbf{E_2}$, are: *treatment* **X**, *history*, and *maturation*. It follows then that, by subtracting O_2 for this group from ΔE_1, one can evaluate the effect of *pretesting*.

Figure 5.6 *Randomized Solomon four-group design*

Type of Assignment	Treatment Condition	Group Label	Pretest	Treatment	Posttest
R	**Experimental**	$\mathbf{E_1}$	$\mathbf{O_1}$	**X**	$\mathbf{O_2}$
R	**Control**	$\mathbf{C_1}$	$\mathbf{O_1}$	•	$\mathbf{O_2}$
R	**Experimental**	$\mathbf{E_2}$		**X**	$\mathbf{O_2}$
R	**Control**	$\mathbf{C_2}$		•	$\mathbf{O_2}$

NOTE [5.1]: Despite its important advantages, the randomized Solomon four-group design is still underrepresented in published educational research. Researchers seem to pass up the opportunity to use this design even when it is relatively easy to do so. For example, when the more frequently-used randomized pretest-posttest control group design (5.2.1) is employed with a relatively large sample, this sample can be randomly divided into four groups and then implement the randomized Solomon four-group design.

5.2.3 Randomized Control-Group Posttest Only Design

With the **randomized control-group posttest only design** (a) the study participants are randomly selected from the target population, (b) the selected sample is randomly split into two groups, (c) each group is then randomly assigned to one treatment condition, and (d) data on the dependent variable are collected only after the treatment administration (see Figure 5.7).

Figure 5.7 Randomized control-group posttest only design

Type of Assignment	Treatment Condition	Group Label	Treatment	Posttest
R	**Experimental**	$\mathbf{E_1}$	$\mathbf{X_1}$	$\mathbf{O_2}$
R	**Control**	**C**	**•**	$\mathbf{O_2}$

Due to random assignment of subjects to treatment conditions, this design provides much better control over possible sources of validity threats compared to the nonrandomized control-group posttest only design (5.1.3). Also, this design is better than the randomized pretest-posttest control group design (5.2.1) in terms of control for validity threats from pretesting. However, the lack of pretesting makes it difficult to measure the effect produced by the experimental treatment (say, in pretest-posttest changes). Overall, the randomized control-group posttest only design provides rigorous control over validity treats and can be particularly useful when pretest data are difficult, or expensive, to collect.

5.3 Quasi-Experimental Designs

While true experimental designs are highly desirable for guarding against threats to internal and external validity, their practical implementation is not always possible. In a large-scale educational study, for example, it would be extremely difficult to randomly assign students to experimental and control conditions due to the intact nature of school units, policy regulations, high-stake educational and social implications, and associated the costs (time, money, and efforts). Among the few exceptions in this regard is the *Tennessee K-3 Class Size Study* (see http://www.heros-inc.org/star.htm).

When use of a true experimental design is not an option, attempts to provide reasonable control over validity threats result in designs referred to as **quasi-experimental designs.** Although there are numerous quasi-experimental designs (e.g., Cook & Campbell, 1979), briefly described here are some frequently occurring scenarios of such designs in educational research. Typical examples involve "intact" groups such as schools, or intact classes within schools.

5.3.1 Nonrandomized Pretest-Posttest Control Group Design

With the **nonrandomized pretest-posttest control group design,** (a) the study groups are "intact" units, so there is no random assignment of subjects to groups, (b) each intact group is randomly assigned to one (experimental or control) treatment condition, and (c) observations on the dependent variable are collected before and after the treatment administration. The only difference between this design and the "randomized pretest-posttest design" (5.2.1) is that the *nonrandomized pretest-posttest design* does not involve random assignment of subjects to groups; [with both experimental designs each group is randomly assigned to one treatment condition—experimental or control]). The diagram for this design is shown in Figure 5.8.

Possible *selection bias* is probably the most serious threat to internal validity with this design. One way to alleviate this problem is to select the intact groups by *matching* them prior to treatment on characteristics that may unduly affect their posttest results. Such characteristics can be, for example, group size, ethnic composition, socioeconomic status, group scores on the pretest, or other "proxies" to the dependent variable. Suppose, for example, that the nonrandomized pretest-posttest design is a realistic choice in an experimental study that involves a new approach to teaching high school science (say, by using computer simulations of science phenomena). Given the sampling restriction in this case (i.e., random assignment of students to groups is not an option), the researcher must assign *intact* high school classes to experimental and control conditions. To guard against selection bias, the researcher may use a "matching" strategy— that is, to select intact classes that are as similar as possible on characteristics that may contribute to their posttest performance on a science test. Such characteristics include, for instance, previous performance of the intact classes on state assessments in science, as well their school-based experience using computers in classroom sessions. If there is a sufficiently large pool of intact classes, the researcher may just randomly select as many classes as needed and then randomly assign each of them to one of the two treatment conditions.

Figure 5.8 *Nonrandomized pretest-posttest control group design*

Type of Assignment	Treatment Condition	Group Label	Pretest	Treatment	Posttest
Intact Group	**Experimental**	**E**	O_1	**X**	O_2
Intact Group	**Control**	**C**	O_1	•	O_2

An approach to matching treatment groups that is gaining serious attention in behavioral and medical research is referred to as *propensity score matching* (Rosenbaum & Rubin, 1983). Under this approach, the "propensity" score of a person is defined by the probability with which this person can be assigned to a specific treatment group. This probability is predicted from a set of characteristics that may affect the dependent variable of the experimental study. The statistical method of prediction, referred to as *logistic regression*, is discussed in Chapter 20.

NOTE [5.2] Although the nonrandomized pretest-posttest control group design is not as good as its randomized counterpart (5.2.1) in guarding against validity threats, it preserves the natural settings of the intact groups (e.g., classrooms) during the experimental treatment. Therefore, subjects' awareness that they are participating in an experiment is much lower with intact groups than with random groups that operate in "artificial" experimental settings. Thus, the nonrandomized pretest-posttest design decreases the *reactive effects of experimental procedures*. Additionally, the use of intact groups lowers the chances for another threat to the external validity: *interaction of group selection and treatment*. This is particularly true when a variety of intact groups are selected from different settings.

5.3.2 One Group Time-Series Design

With the **one group time-series design** (a) the selection of subjects is *nonrandom*, (b) there is no control group — all subjects are assigned to a single experimental treatment, and (c) multiple observations are collected before and after the treatment using the same procedure at equal time intervals. This design is know also as a *single group interrupted time-series design*, with "interrupted" indicating that the treatment should be *distinctive* (i.e., different) to the existing practice and environment. The diagram of the one group time-series design for the case of four pretest and posttest observations is shown in Figure 5.9.

Figure 5.9 One group time-series design

Treatment Condition	Group Label	Pretest	Treatment	Posttest
Experimental	**E**	**O_1, O_2, O_3, O_4**	**X**	**O_5, O_6, O_7, O_8**

The repeated pretests and repeated posttests with this design provide control over possible threats to internal validity, except for *contemporary history* — i.e., events other than the experimental treatment may still affect the posttest measures. Threats to external validity may occur when (a) the repetitive pretests affect the subjects in a way that they are no longer representative of the target population, (b) the subjects are volunteers, or (c) most (if not all) subjects have some special characteristics that are not typical for the target population.

5.3.3 Control Group Time-Series Design

The **control group time-series design** is obtained from the one group time-series design (5.3.2) by adding a control group with multiple pretest and posttests observations. The diagram for this design is shown in Figure 5.10.

Figure 5.10 *Control group time-series design*

Treatment Condition	Group Label	Pretest	Treatment	Posttest
Experimental	**E**	**O_1, O_2, O_3, O_4**	**X**	**O_5, O_6, O_7, O_8**
Control	**C**	**O_1, O_2, O_3, O_4**	•	**O_5, O_6, O_7, O_8**

The control group time-series design provides even better control over validity threats, including *contemporary history*, compared to the one group time-series design. Of course, "perfect" control over factors such as *contemporary history*, *maturation*, *pretesting*, and *statistical regression toward the mean* is hardly possible with this (or any other) design. There are, however, design modifications that can enhance control over these validity threats. One example of this is a design in which (a) several (say, four) groups are assigned to the experimental treatment, **X**, (b) all groups take a single pretest at the same time, and (c) all groups take a single posttest, but at different time points (e.g., two months apart). Then, the same number of control groups, with the same pretest and posttest pattern, is added to complete the design.

The use of time-series designs in educational research is still limited, due primarily to the need for a large number of observations in order to conduct rigorous statistical estimations with such designs — e.g., 25 pretest and 25 posttest observations (Glass, 1977). However, this can be done, for example, with repetitive classroom observations in a study on "student-teacher interaction." In another scenario, the researcher may use a post-hoc approach going back to existing records on, say, student behaviors, at numerous time points before and after the implementation of some school regulation. In general, the use of time-series designs, even with a smaller number of observations, can provide useful information about "short-term" and "long-term" treatment effects — e.g., through the analysis of individual pretest and posttest trajectories. Such differential in time effects are usually "masked" with designs that involve only one-time pretest and posttest data collection.

Additional research designs, among which factorial designs and regression designs, will be addressed together with their analytical presentation and computer-aided applications later in this book.

5.4 Summary

This chapter describes three categories of research design — pre-experimental, true experimental, and quasi-experimental designs. The **pre-experimental designs** do not possess the two key characteristics of true experimental research (*randomization* and *control*), but **true experimental designs** do. **Quasi-experimental designs** involve control, but not randomization. Bulleted here are basic concepts and features of pre-experimental, true experimental, and quasi-experimental designs.

5.4.1 Pre-experimental Designs

- **One group posttest-only design:** (a) the selection of study participants is *nonrandom*, (b) all participants are assigned to a single treatment, and (c) all observations are made after the treatment. This design does not guard against validity threats.

- **One group pretest-posttest design:** (a) the selection of study participants is *nonrandom*, (b) all participants are assigned to a single treatment, and (c) observations are made before and after the treatment. This design controls for *differential selection* and *experimental mortality* of subjects, assuming that the pretest and posttest observations come from the same subjects. However, the design does not guard against other threats to internal or external validity.

- **Nonrandomized Control Group Posttest-Only Design:** (a) the selection of study participants is *nonrandom*, (b) there are two treatment groups, but the subjects are not assigned randomly to each group, and (c) only posttest observations are collected for each group. The control group makes it possible to differentiate an experimental "effect," but the lack of randomization makes it difficult to determine what part (if not all) of this effect is due to pre-treatment differences between the experimental and control groups.

5.4.2 True Experimental Designs

- **Randomized Pretest-Posttest Control Group Design:** (a) the subjects are selected at random, (b) the sample is randomly split into two groups, (c) each group is randomly assigned to one treatment condition (experimental or control), and (d) observations are collected before and after the treatment. This design controls for all threats to internal validity, but caution is needed with external validity threats, particularly with possible *pretesting effects*.

• **Randomized Solomon Four-Group Design:** (a) the subjects are selected at random, (b) the sample is randomly divided into four groups, (c) by random assignment, two groups are assigned to the experimental condition and two groups to the control condition, (d) all four groups take a posttest, and (e) by random assignment, one of the two experimental groups and one of the two control groups take a pretest. This design controls for all threats to internal validity, but caution is needed with external validity threats. Compared to the randomized pretest-posttest control group design (5.2.1), the randomized Solomon four-group design provides better control for *pretesting*. It also makes it possible to evaluate the "magnitude" of effects due to the *experimental treatment* or to sources of internal invalidity — *contemporary history*, *maturation*, *pretesting*, etc.

• **Randomized Control Group Posttest-Only Design:** (a) the subjects are selected at random, (b) the sample is randomly split into two groups, (c) each group is randomly assigned to one treatment condition (experimental or control), and (d) both pretest and posttest observations are made. This design provides rigorous control over validity treats and can be particularly useful when pretest data are difficult, or expensive, to collect. The lack of pretesting makes it difficult to measure the effect produced by the experimental treatment (say, in pretest-posttest changes).

5.4.3 Quasi-Experimental Designs

• **Nonrandomized Pretest-Posttest Control Group Design:** (a) the study groups are "intact" units (e.g., school classes), (b) each intact group is randomly assigned to one treatment condition (experimental or control), and (c) both pretest and posttest observations are made. *Selection bias* is the most serious threat to internal validity with this design. This problem can be addressed by *matching* the experimental and control groups prior to treatment on characteristics that may affect their posttest results. Along with direct matching of subjects to such characteristics, one can use *propensity score matching*. Under this approach, the "propensity" score of a person is defined by the probability with which this person can be assigned to a specific treatment group.

• **One Group Time-Series Design:** (a) the selection of subjects is *nonrandom*, (b) all subjects are assigned to the experimental treatment, and (c) multiple observations are collected before and after the treatment using the same procedure at equal time intervals. This design controls for threats to internal validity, except for *contemporary history*. Threats to external validity may occur when the pretests affect the subjects in a way that they are no longer representative of the target population, when the subjects are volunteers, or when the subjects have some special characteristics that are not typical for the target population.

• **Control Group Time-Series Design:** This design is obtained from the one group time-series design by adding a control group with multiple pretest and posttests observations. The control group time-series design controls for internal validity threats, including *contemporary history*, but still allows for possible threats to external validity such as *interaction between the experimental treatment and selection or pretesting.*

• Time-series designs require a relatively large number of observations for rigorous statistical estimations (e.g., 25 pretest and 25 posttest observations). In educational research this can be achieved, for example, with multiple classroom observations or by using existing records prior to and after the treatment. In general, even with smaller number of observations, the time-series design can provide useful information about "short-term" and "long-term" treatment effects — information that often remains “hidden" with designs that involve only one-time pretest and posttest data collection.

5.5 Study Questions

1. Which research designs allow the researcher to evaluate changes in the dependent variable that have occurred during the experimental treatment:

- **a.** one group posttest-only design
- **b.** one group pretest-posttest design
- **c.** randomized pretest-posttest control group design
- **d.** randomized control-group posttest only design
- **e.** one group time-series design
- **f.** none of the above

2. Which research designs allow the researcher to attribute changes in the dependent variable to the experimental treatment:

- **a.** one group pretest-posttest design
- **b.** randomized control-group posttest only design
- **c.** randomized pretest-posttest control group design
- **d.** randomized Solomon four group design
- **e.** control group time-series design
- **f.** all of the above

3. Which research designs guard against *differential selection* (or *selection bias*):

- **a.** nonrandomized pretest-posttest control group design
- **b.** one group pretest-posttest design
- **c.** control group time-series design
- **d.** randomized pretest-posttest control group design
- **e.** randomized Solomon four group design
- **f.** none of the above

4. Which research designs control for effects from reactive experimental procedures:

- **a.** randomized Solomon four group design
- **b.** randomized control-group posttest only design
- **c.** control group time-series design
- **d.** one group pretest-posttest design
- **e.** randomized pretest-posttest control group design
- **f.** none of the above.

5. What is *propensity score matching*?

Explain: ____

6. What are the disadvantages and advantages of the nonrandomized pretest-posttest control group design compared to the randomized pretest-posttest control group design?

Explain: ____

7. Which design makes it possible to evaluate the "magnitude" of effects due to the experimental treatment or to sources of internal invalidity?

a. control group time-series design
b. randomized control-group posttest only design
c. randomized Solomon four group design
d. one group pretest-posttest design
e. randomized pretest-posttest control group design
f. none of the above.

8. Which design is in place under the following conditions: (a) the study participants are randomly selected from the target population, (b) the selected sample is randomly split into two groups, (c) each group is then randomly assigned to one treatment condition, and (d) data on the dependent variable are collected only after the treatment administration.

a. nonrandomized pretest-posttest control group design
b. one group pretest-posttest design
c. control group time-series design
d. randomized pretest-posttest control group design
e. randomized Solomon four group design
f. none of the above.

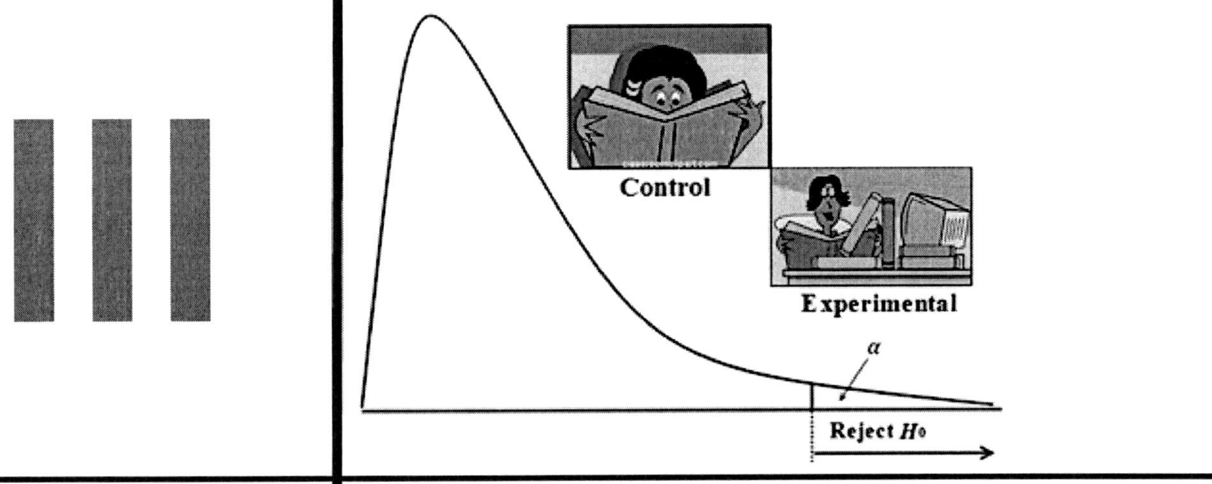

UNIVARIATE DATA ANALYSIS

CHAPTER 6

REVIEW OF INTRODUCTORY STATISTICS

6.1 Organizing and Graphing Data

6.1.1 Frequency Table

The development of a frequency table is the first step in organizing and graphic data. To illustrate this process, the scores of 30 students on a 4-point scale that measures *attitude toward science* are given with the SPSS data spreadsheet in Figure 6.1 (left panel). The SPSS output with the frequency table for these data is also shown in Figure 6.1 (right panel). The entries in the columns **Percent** and **Valid Percent** are the same because there are no missing data.

Figure 6.1 *Data and SPSS output of their frequency distribution table*

Survey Data.sav [DataS...

File Edit View Data Transform Analyze
Graphs Utilities Add-ons Window Help

2 :

	X	var	var	va
1	1			
2	4			
3	3			
4	3			
5	2			
6	2			
7	2			
8	3			
9	3			
10	3			
11	3			
12	4			
13	3			
14	3			
15	3			
16	2			
17	3			
18	4			
19	4			
20	3			
21	3			
22	3			
23	2			
24	4			
25	4			
26	2			
27	3			
28	2			
29	3			
30	3			

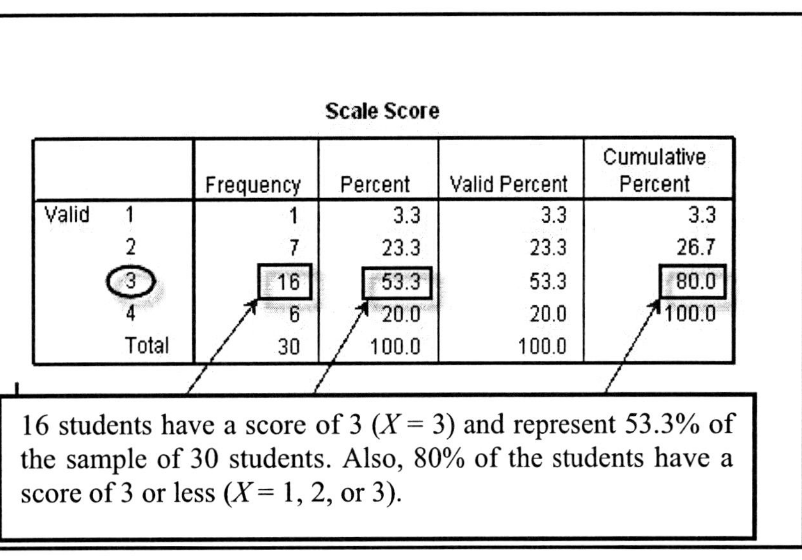

Scale Score

		Frequency	Percent	Valid Percent	Cumulative Percent
Valid	1	1	3.3	3.3	3.3
	2	7	23.3	23.3	26.7
	3	16	53.3	53.3	80.0
	4	6	20.0	20.0	100.0
	Total	30	100.0	100.0	

16 students have a score of 3 ($X = 3$) and represent 53.3% of the sample of 30 students. Also, 80% of the students have a score of 3 or less ($X = 1, 2,$ or 3).

Note. Given that the 4-point scale measures a continuous variable (*attitude*), each score must be viewed as a midpoint of a score interval, so that all four score intervals cover, without "gaps," an interval on the number line from 0.5 to 4.5. Thus, the frequency of 16 for the score of 3 actually means that there are 16 scores that fall between 2.5 and 3.5 (the score interval for 3). Also, the cumulative information that "80% of the students score at or lower than 3" can be translated as "80% of the students score lower than 3.5."

6.1.2 Basic Distribution Graphs

For the data in Figure 6.1 (left panel), the **histogram** in Figure 6.2 shows the frequency distribution by percent of students across the score intervals, whereas Figure 6.3, referred to as a **cumulative frequency distribution**, shows the *cumulative percentage* of students across these intervals. As noted earlier, 53.3% of the students score between 2.5 and 3.5 (the score interval for 3), whereas 80% of them score lower than 3.5 — that is, 80% of the students fall within the score interval 1, 2, or 3.

Figure 6.2 *Histogram for the data in Figure 6.1*

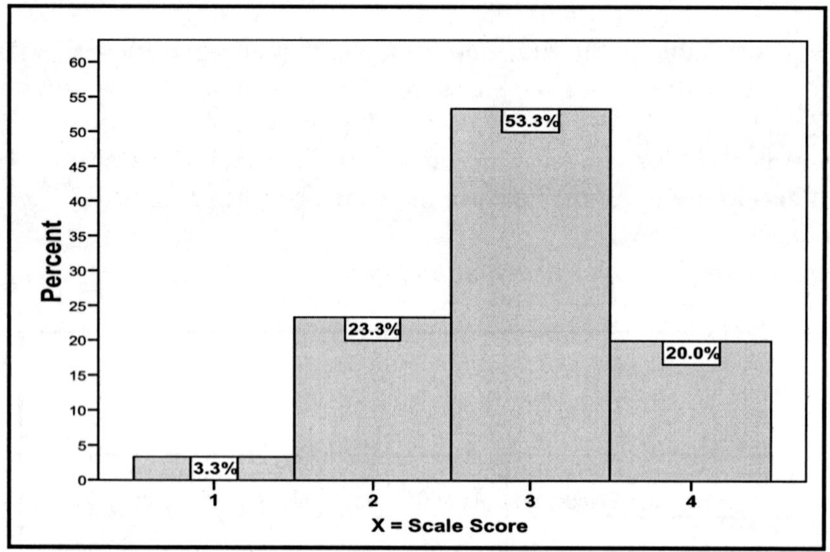

Figure 6.3 *Cumulative percent distribution for the data in Figure 6.1*

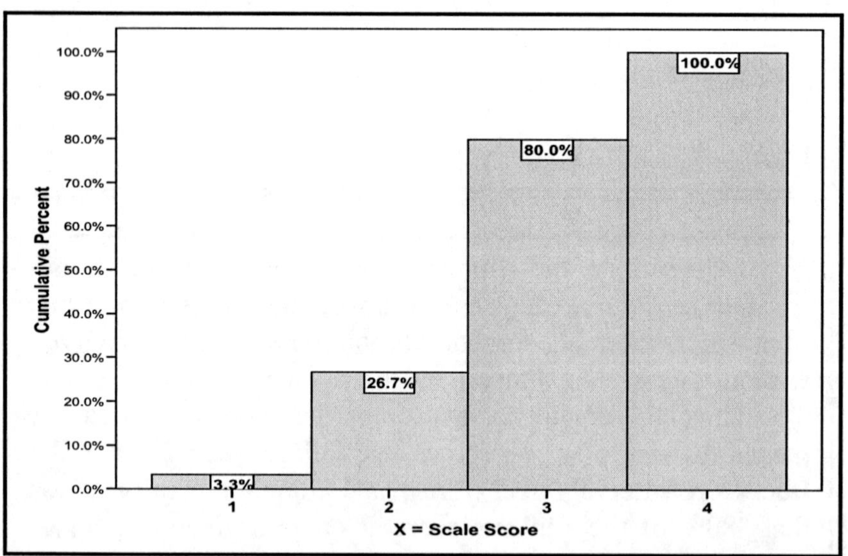

SPSS 15.0, as well as preceding and following versions of this statistical package, provides numerous data sets for users to practice with. The present example uses the SPSS data set **Employee data.sav,** with slight modifications. Namely, two variables, *Employee Code* (*ID*) and *Date of Birth*, were eliminated; *gender* was coded numerically (0 = male, 1 = female); and two variables (*salary* and *beginning salary*) were converted from their original "Dollar ($)" type to numeric type to permit calculations. The variables used here (and later in this book) are shown in Figure 6.4, with the first 22 (out of 474) observations from this data set. The meaning and coding of variables will be provided as necessary throughout the book.

Figure 6.4 *SPSS data file* **Employee data.sav**

*Employee data.sav [DataSet1] - SPSS Data Editor

File Edit View Data Transform Analyze Graphs Utilities Add-ons Window Help

0 :

	gender	educ	jobcat	salary	salbegin	jobtime	prevexp	minority
1	m	15	3	57000	27000	98	144	0
2	m	16	1	40200	18750	98	36	0
3	f	12	1	21450	12000	98	381	0
4	f	8	1	21900	13200	98	190	0
5	m	15	1	45000	21000	98	138	0
6	m	15	1	32100	13500	98	67	0
7	m	15	1	36000	18750	98	114	0
8	f	12	1	21900	9750	98	0	0
9	f	15	1	27900	12750	98	115	0
10	f	12	1	24000	13500	98	244	0
11	f	16	1	30300	16500	98	143	0
12	m	8	1	28350	12000	98	26	1
13	m	15	1	27750	14250	98	34	1
14	f	15	1	35100	16800	98	137	1
15	m	12	1	27300	13500	97	66	0
16	m	12	1	40800	15000	97	24	0
17	m	15	1	46000	14250	97	48	0
18	m	16	3	103750	27510	97	70	0
19	m	12	1	42300	14250	97	103	0
20	f	12	1	26250	11550	97	48	0
21	f	16	1	38850	15000	97	17	0
22	m	12	1	21750	12750	97	315	1

Figure 6.5 shows the SPSS printout for the histogram of the variable "previous experience" (in months) for the employees from the "Employee data" data set. To obtain this printout in SPSS, follow the steps:

1. Click **Graphs**, click **Legacy Dialogs**, click **Histogram**.

2. Click on the **Previous Experience (months)** and then click ▶ to move this variable into the **Variable** box.
3. Click **OK**.

The histogram in Figure 6.5 reveals that the frequency distribution of the employees' previous experience (in months) is ***positively skewed*** (the "skinny" tail is on the positive direction of the number line). Clearly, most employees in this institution start with relatively little (or no) previous experience. Yet, one can also expect data "outliers," particularly on the right side of the distribution; that is, unusually high levels of previous experience.

Figure 6.5 *Histogram for the variable "previous experience (months)" from the data set* "Employee data" *(Figure 6.4)*

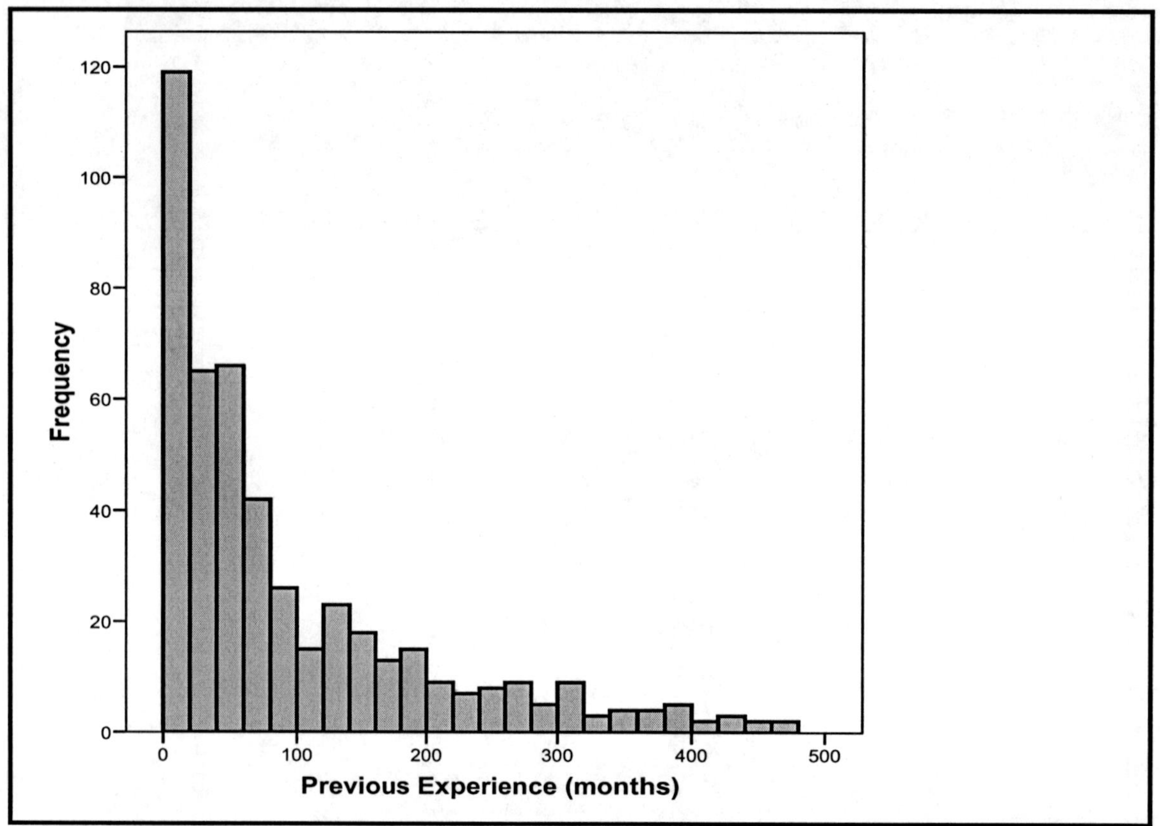

To obtain the **five-number summary** in SPSS (X_{min} = *lowest value*, Q_1 = *first quartile*, Q_2 = *second quartile*, Q_3 = *third quartile*, and X_{max} = *highest value*), follow the steps:

1. Click **Analyze**, click **Descriptive Statistics**, and click **Frequencies**.
2. Click on the **Previous Experience (months)** and then click ▶ to move this variable into the **Variable(s)** box.
3. Still in the dialog box **Frequencies**, and click on **Statistics**.
4. In the dialog box **Frequencies: Statistics**, check the boxes **Quartiles, Minimum,** and **Maximum**.
5. Click **Continue**.
6. Click **OK.**

The SPSS output is shown in Figure 6.6, where $X_{min} = 0$ and $X_{max} = 476$. The *first quartile* is the 25th *percentile*, $Q_1 = P_{25} = 19$ — the score at or below which 25% of all scores fall. The *second quartile* (*median*) is the 50th percentile, Q_2 = *Median* = P_{50} = 55 — the score at or below which 50% of all scores fall. The *third quartile* is the 75th percentile, $Q_3 = P_{75} = 140$ — the score at or below which 75% of all scores fall.

Figure 6.6 *Five-number summary*

Statistics

Previous Experience (months)

N	Valid	474
	Missing	0
Minimum		0
Maximum		476
Percentiles	25	19.00
	50	55.00
	75	140.00

The middle 50% of the scores fall between the 25th and the 75th percentiles. The difference between these two percentiles ($P_{75} - P_{25}$) is called **interquartile range (IQR)**. Thus, given that $P_{25} = Q_1$ and $P_{75} = Q_3$, the interquartile range is: IQR = $Q_3 - Q_1$. Using the results in Figure 6.6, the interquartile range for the scores on "previous experience" is: IQR = 140 – 19 = 121.

The five-number summary and the interquartile range are visually displayed in a graph referred to as a **box-plot**. For example, the five-number summary in Figure 6.6 is graphed with box-plot in Figure 6.7. The length of the box represents the interquartile range (IQR). The median is closer to the lower end of the box because the distribution of scores for the variable "previous experience" is positively skewed (see Figure 6.5). To obtain the **box-plot** in Figure 6.7 using SPSS, follow the steps:

1. Click **Graphs**, click **Legacy Dialogs**, click **Boxplot**.
2. Click **Simple**, click **Summaries of separate variables**, click **Define**.
3. Click on the **Previous Experience (months)** and then click ► to move this variable into **Boxes Represent**.
4. Click **OK**.

The box-plot information can be used to detect **outliers** (unusually high or low scores) in the distribution. Specifically, the **reasonable upper boundary** (RUB) and **reasonable lower boundary** (RLB) of the interval beyond which the outliers fall are determined as follows:

$$\text{RUB} = Q_3 + (1.5)(\text{IQR})$$
$$\text{RLB} = Q_1 - (1.5)(\text{IQR})$$

For the box plot in Figure 6.7, IQR = 140 – 19 = 121. Thus, the reasonable boundaries in this case are: RUB = 140 + (1.5)(121) = 321.5 and RLB = 19 – (1.5)(121) = -162.5. Also, given that $X_{min} = 0$, there are no scores that fall below the RLB (-162.5). Thus, there are no outliers in the lower tail of the distribution. Therefore, the "whisker" below the box ends at $X_{min} = 0$ and no observations are graphed below this whisker. On the other side, the highest score in this distribution, $X_{max} = 476$, exceeds the reasonable upper boundary (RUB = 321.5), thus indicating that there are outliers in upper tail of the distribution. Therefore, the "whisker" above the box ends at the RUB (321.5). In Figure 6.7, the *outliers* (scores above the upper whisker) are depicted with their identification numbers. For example, observation number 295 is the largest outlier (X_{max} = 476). If you sort the **Employee data** file in descending order, you will notice that there are 24 outliers — that is, 24 scores that exceed the RUB (321.5). To perform this in SPSS, follow the steps:

1 Click **Data** and click **Sort Cases ...**
2 Click **Previous experience (months),** then click ▶ to move this variable into the box **Sort by,** and select the radio-button **Descending** for the *Sort Order.*
3 Click **OK**.

Figure 6.7 *Box-plot for the variable "previous experience (months)" from the "Employee data"*

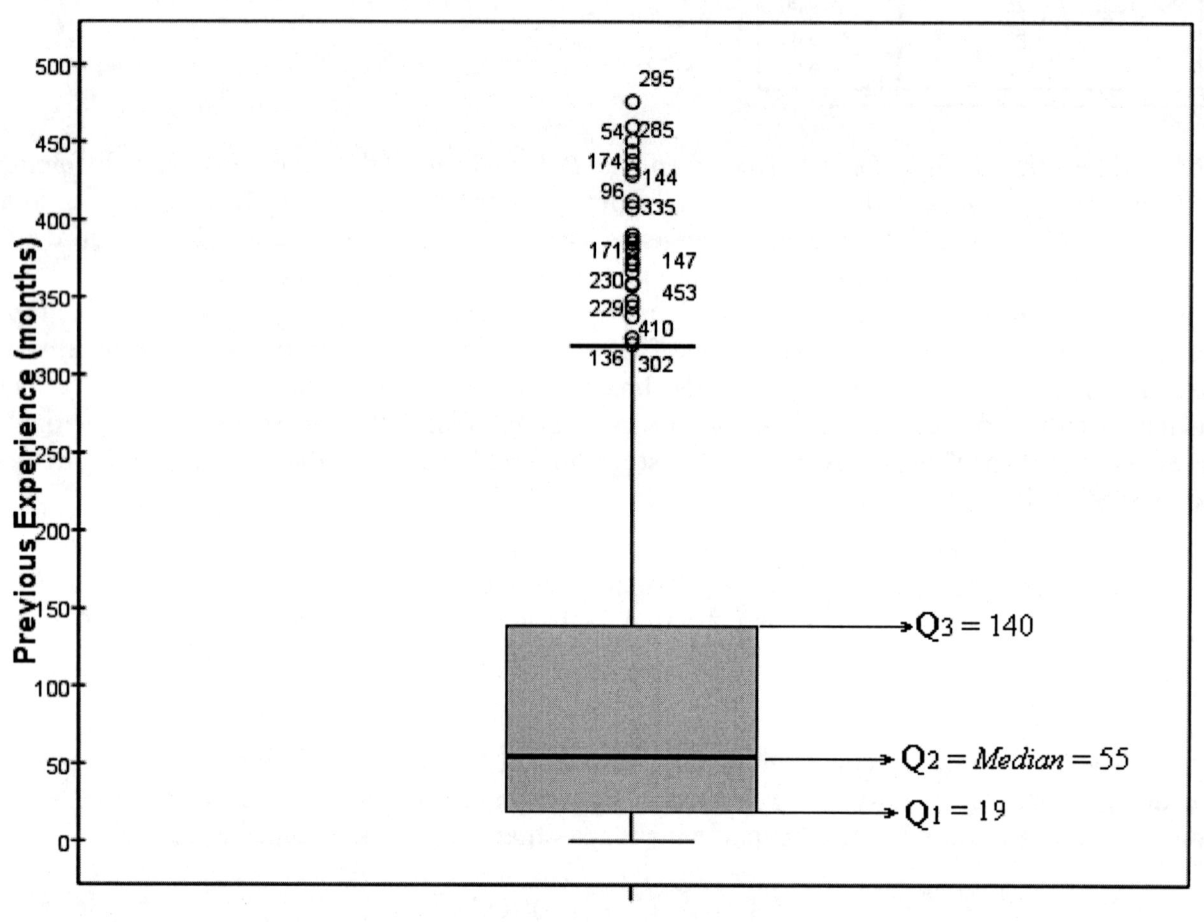

6.2 Describing Distributions

6.2.1 Percentiles

Given a distribution of scores (observations), a **percentile** is the score at or below which a certain percent of the scores fall. The notation of a percentile is the capital letter *P* with an index showing the percent of scores that fall at or below this percentile. For example, P_{25} stands for the 25th percentile — the score at or below which 25% of the scores fall. As shown in the previous section, the **quartiles** (Q_1, Q_2, and Q_3) of a distribution are the 25th, 50th, and 75th percentile, respectively. The second quartile (or 50th percentile) is referred to also as the **median** of the distribution. That is, $P_{25} = Q_1$, $P_{50} = Q_2 = median$, and $P_{75} = Q_3$.

Consider again the frequency table in Figure 6.1. The cumulative percent for the score of 3 is 80; that is, 80% of the scores fall at or below 3. The percentile translation is that the 80th percentile is 3 ($P_{80} = 3$). However, as pointed out in the note with Figure 6.1, it would be more accurate to say that "80% of the scores fall below 3.5" ($P_{80} = 3.5$) because a score of 3 on a continuous variable (trait) must be viewed as a score interval from 2.5 to 3.5. To obtain the quartiles (or any desired percentile) in SPSS, you can use the steps described for obtaining the five-number summary in Figure 6.6. However, in addition to selecting **Quartiles**, check **Percentile(s),** type the value of any other desired percentile and click **Add** to select this percentile. For example, the selection in Figure 6.8 will provide the quartiles (P_{25}, P_{50}, and P_{75}) and two additional percentiles, P_{27} and P_{73}.

Figure 6.8 *SPSS dialog box for frequency statistics*

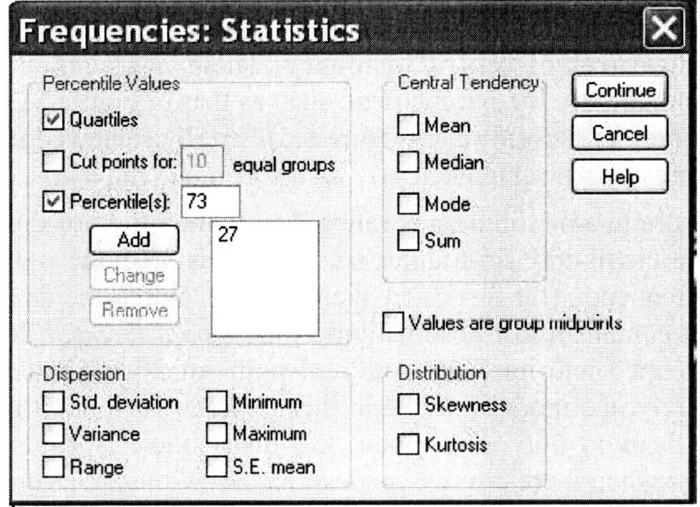

Note: When the distribution of scores is **normal**, P_{27} and P_{73} are often recommended to serve as the boundaries in defining *low*, *medium*, and *high* score categories (e.g., performance levels) for the distribution (Kelley, 1939).

Percentiles are widely used to report the performance of students at school, state, or national levels. In some cases scores are presented as percentiles within different reference groups. For example, the score of a student on a standardized math test can be reported to be at the 85th percentile (P_{85}) for the school population and at the 74th (P_{74}) percentile for the state population of students. In other words, this student did better than 85% of the students in his/her school and 74% of the students statewide on the math test.

It is also important to keep in mind that equal differences between percentiles do not indicate equal differences between the scores associated with these percentiles. That is, the percentiles do not form an *interval* scale — they merely form an *ordinal* scale (see, chapter 1.2). Therefore, arithmetic operations with percentiles are not permissible (e.g., it is not appropriate to add, subtract, or average percentiles). Additional comments on percentiles are provided with the discussion of normal distributions (see, 7.1.3).

Suppose now that the score of a student on a reading proficiency test is known, say 72, and the task is to determine what percent of the students who took the same test scored lower than this student. In general, the percent of scores that are less than or equal to a particular score, X, is referred to as the **percentile rank** of this score and denoted PR_X. Thus, the task is now to determine PR_{72} — the percentile rank of the reading proficiency score 72. If, for example, the frequency table for the reading proficiency scores shows that the cumulative percent for 72 is 65%, then $PR_{72} = 65$. In general, the percentile rank of a score is provided with the cumulative percent for this score. As another example, the frequency table in Figure 6.1 shows that the cumulative percent for the score of 3 is 80. Thus, the percentile rank of 3 is 80: $PR_{80} = 3$; [**Consider:** Given the note that accompanies Figure 6.1., would it be more accurate to say that $PR_{80} = 3.5$?]

NOTE [6.1] Quantiles is the general term for cutoff points that divide the ordered data into parts containing equal percent of observations (scores). For example, the *percentiles* are quantiles that divide the data into 100 parts each containing 1% of the data, whereas the *quartiles* are quantiles that divide the data into four parts each containing 25% of the data. The quantiles that divide the data into 10 parts each containing 10% of the data are called *deciles*, etc.

6.2.2 Measures of Central Tendency

Along with frequency tables and graphs, the description and comparison of distributions is facilitated by statistics referred to as **measures of central tendency**. These measures are located near the center when the distribution is (close to) symmetrical, such as that in Figure 6.2. This, however, is not true when the distribution is skewed (e.g., Figure 6.5). Briefly reviewed in this section are three frequently-used measures of central tendency — *mode*, *median*, and *mean*.

6.2.2.1 Mode. The most frequent score in a distribution is referred to as the **mode** of this distribution. For example, the mode for the distribution in Figures 6.1 and 6.2 is 3 (mode = 3) because this is the score with the highest frequency (for $X = 3$, frequency = 16). When the data are grouped into intervals, the interval that contains most observations is the *modal interval*. In Figure 6.5, for example, the scores are grouped into intervals with a "length" of 20 for better visual representation of the histogram. Clearly, the modal interval in this skewed distribution is the lowest score interval (0-20). When there is only one mode, the distribution is called *unimodal*. The distribution is called *bimodal* when there are two modes; that is, two nonadjacent scores (or score intervals) occur more frequently than their adjacent scores. In general, a distribution with two or more modes is referred to as *multimodal*.

6.2.2.2 Median. As noted earlier, the **median** is the score at or below which 50% of the distribution scores fall. Clearly, the median is also the 50th percentile, as well as the second quartile, of the distribution: $median = P_{50} = Q_2$. The median separates the distribution into two equal parts in the sense that 50% of the scores fall below the median and 50% fall above the median. This, however, does not mean that the median is the midpoint of the distribution interval (or the midpoint of the box in the box-plot graph of the distribution). For example, for the positively skewed distribution in Figure 6.5 (box-plot in Figure 6.7), the *median* (55) is much closer to the lower end of the distribution ($X_{min} = 0$) than to its upper end ($X_{max} = 476$). In fact, the median will be the midpoint of the distribution interval only when the distribution is perfectly symmetrical.

6.2.2.3 Mean. The arithmetic average of the scores in a distribution is referred to as the **mean** of this distribution. When the mean is calculated for a sample of scores, it is called *sample mean* and denoted $\overline{X}$ ("X bar"). In general, if the sample consists of n observations, $X_1, X_2, \ldots, X_n$, the formula for the sample mean is

$$\overline{X} = \frac{X_1 + X_2 + ... + X_n}{n} \text{ or, using the summation symbol, } \overline{X} = \frac{\sum_{i=1}^{n} X_i}{n}. \quad \textbf{(6.1)}$$

When the scores are tabulated in a frequency table, we can calculate the mean by using the frequencies of the distinct values. For example, out of the 30 observations tabulated in Figure 6.1, there only four distinct values: $X_1 = 1$, $X_2 = 2$, $X_3 = 3$, and $X_4 = 4$. The frequencies of these distinct values are: $f_1 = 1$, $f_2 = 7$, $f_3 = 16$, and $f_4 = 6$, respectively. Therefore, the mean of all 30 observations is

$$\overline{X} = \frac{\sum_{k=1}^{4} f_k X_k}{n} = \frac{f_1 X_1 + f_2 X_2 + f_3 X_3 + f_4 X_4}{30} = \frac{(1)(1) + (7)(2) + (16)(3) + (6)(4)}{30} = 2.90.$$

The difference between a score, X_i, and the mean is called **deviation score**: $\boldsymbol{x_i = X_i - \overline{X}}$; $(i = 1, 2, \ldots, n)$. The sum of the deviation scores always equals zero:

$$\sum x_i = \sum (X_i - \overline{X}) = 0. \quad \textbf{(6.2)}$$

6.2.2.4 Properties of the Mode, Median, and Mean. With a *nominal scale,* it is appropriate to report the mode, but not the median or the mean (Why?). With an *ordinal scale*, it is appropriate to report both the mode and the median, but not the mean (Why?). With an *interval scale* or a *ratio scale*, it is appropriate to report the mode, the median, and the mean (Why?). In this case, the relative location of these three measures depends on the shape of the distribution. Specifically, (a) when the distribution is *symmetrical* and *unimodal*, the mode, median, and mean coincide (mode = median = mean), (b) when the distribution is *positively skewed*, mode < median < mean, and (c) when the distribution is *negatively skewed*, mean < median < mode.

It is important to note that the median is more *robust* (less sensitive) to outliers in the distribution compared to the mean. To illustrate, take the sample of five observations: 2, 2, 6, 10, and 80. For this sample, the mean is 20 ($\overline{X} = 20$) and the median is 6. If we replace the "outlier" (80) in this sample with a number that is closer to the other four scores, say, 15, the resulting sample is: 2, 2, 6, 10, and 15. Now we have $\overline{X} = 7$ and median = 6. Thus, while the mean changed (from 20 to 7), the median did not. Therefore, it is useful to report both the mean and the median, particularly in the presence of outliers or skewed distributions. To obtain the mode, the median, and the mean in SPSS, you can follow the steps that provide the display in Figure 6.8 and then check the boxes for **Mean**, **Median**, and **Mode** (from the *Central Tendency* options in the right-hand panel of the dialog box).

6.2.3 Measures of Variation

Along with measures of central tendency, the distribution is described with *measures of score variation* that indicate the spread of scores in the distribution. Two key measures of score variation are the **variance** and the **standard deviation.**

6.2.3.1 Variance. For a sample of n scores, $X_1, X_2, \ldots, X_n$, with a mean $\overline{X}$, the *sum of squared deviations from the mean*, or briefly **sum of squared deviations** (SS), is

$$SS = \sum_{i=1}^{n} (X_i - \overline{X})^2 = (X_1 - \overline{X})^2 + (X_2 - \overline{X})^2 + \ldots + (X_n - \overline{X})^2. \quad \textbf{(6.3)}$$

The **sample variance,** denoted s^2, is defined as the ratio of SS to the number "sample size minus one" referred to as *degrees of freedom* ($df = n - 1$). That is,

$$s^2 = \frac{SS}{df} = \frac{\sum (X_i - \overline{X})^2}{n - 1}, \quad \textbf{(6.4)}$$

where the summation is for $i = 1, 2, \ldots, n$.

Let's calculate the variance for the sample of four scores: 2, 4, 4, 10. Given that the sample size is 4 and the mean is 5, we can use Formula 6.4 with $n = 4$ and $\overline{X} = 5$. The sample variance in this case is

$$s^2 = \frac{(2-5)^2 + (4-5)^2 + (4-5)^2 + (10-5)^2}{4-1} = \frac{9+1+1+25}{3} = \frac{36}{3} = 12.$$

When the score distribution is for the entire population, the *mean* is denoted by $\boldsymbol{\mu}$ (the lower case Greek letter "mu") and the *variance* is denoted by "sigma squared": $\boldsymbol{\sigma^2}$ (the lower case Greek letter "sigma"). The formula for the **population variance** is

$$\sigma^2 = \frac{\sum (X_i - \mu)^2}{N}, \quad \textbf{(6.5)}$$

where N is the population size and the summation is for $i = 1, 2, \ldots, N$.

NOTE [6.2] The sample variance s^2, calculated with Formula (6.4), is an **unbiased estimate** of the population variance $\boldsymbol{\sigma^2}$ obtained with Formula (6.5). This means that the mean of the sample variances, s^2, calculated for all possible random samples of sample size n equals the population variance, $\boldsymbol{\sigma^2}$. In statistical parlance, it is said that "the expected value of s^2 is $\boldsymbol{\sigma^2}$" and denoted as: $E(s^2) = \boldsymbol{\sigma^2}$. If, however, we divide SS by n, instead of $(n - 1)$, the resulting "sample variance" will no longer represent an unbiased estimate of the population variance, $\boldsymbol{\sigma^2}$. That is, the ratio SS/n is a *biased estimate* of $\boldsymbol{\sigma^2}$. This is why $SS/(n - 1)$ is preferred to SS/n for the calculation of sample variance.

6.2.3.2 Standard deviation. The square root of the variance is called the **standard deviation.** Specifically, $s = \sqrt{s^2}$ is the *sample standard deviation*, whereas $\sigma = \sqrt{\sigma^2}$ is the *population standard deviation*. Sometimes, the sample standard deviation is denoted SD. As shown in the previous section, the variance of the scores 2, 4, 4, and 10 is $s^2 = 12$. Thus, the standard deviation for this sample of four scores is $s = \sqrt{12} = 3.464$.

The standard deviation "compensates" for two major drawbacks of the variance. First, the variance "inflates" the actual deviations from the mean due to squaring these deviations — see Formula 6.4. Second, the unit of measurement for the variance is different from that for the scores and their mean (again due to squaring). By taking the square root of the variance, the standard deviation (a) reduces the inflated deviations from the mean and (b) remains on the same scale with the scores and their mean. For example, if 2, 4, 4, and 10 are measures of length in inches, the mean and the standard deviations are also measured in inches ($\overline{X} = 5$ inches and $s =$ 3.464 inches), but the variance is on a different scale ($s^2 = 12$ inches squared). For example, the summation $\overline{X} + s^2$ is meaningless (it puts together "apples and oranges"), but the summation $\overline{X} +$ s is permissible ($\overline{X} + s = 5 + 3.364 = 8.364$ inches). At the same time, however, the variance and the standard deviation are closely related and they both play a key role in the theory and practice of statistical data analysis.

6.2.3.3 Pooled variance. Suppose that two samples are randomly selected from a population. Let also n_1 and s_1^2 stand for the size and variance of the first sample, whereas n_2 and s_2^2 are their counterparts for the second sample. Since s_1^2 and s_2^2 represent two sample estimates of the same population variance, σ^2, their "weighed" for sample size average, referred to as **pooled variance**, s^2_{pooled}, represents a more accurate estimate of σ^2. The formula for s^2_{pooled} is

$$s^2_{\text{pooled}} = \frac{(n_1 - 1)s_1^2 + (n_2 - 1)s_2^2}{n_1 + n_2 - 2}, \qquad \textbf{(6.6)}$$

where the denominator, $n_1 + n_2 - 2$, is the sum of the degrees of freedom for the two sample variances: $n_1 + n_2 - 2 = (n_1 - 1) + (n_2 - 1)$.

If, for example, $n_1 = 36$, $s_1^2 = 12$, $n_2 = 21$, and $s_2^2 = 30$, the pooled variance is

$$s^2_{\text{pooled}} = \frac{(36-1)(12)+(21-1)(30)}{36+21-2} = \frac{1020}{55} = 18.54.$$

As you may notice, $s^2_{\text{pooled}} = 18.54$ is between the two sample variances (12 and 30), but closer to the one that comes from the larger sample ($s_1^2 = 12$). This is always the case. The pooled variance of more than two sample variances can be calculated by extending Formula 6.6.

6.2.3.4 Some basic rules. The following basic rules relate to changes that occur in the variance and standard deviation of scores as a result of adding or multiplying the same number (say, *constant c*) to each score.

Rule 1: The variance and the standard deviation of scores do not change when the same number (constant, c) is added to (or subtracted from) each score. Thus, under the transformation $Y = X + c$, we have:

$$s_Y^2 = s_{X+c}^2 = s_X^2.$$

(Clearly, the same holds for the standard deviation: $s_Y = s_{X+c} = s_X$.)

Rule 2: If the scores X are multiplied by a (positive or negative) constant, c, the variance of the transformed distribution, $Y = cX$, is the product of the variance of X and the squared value of the constant:

$$s_Y^2 = s_{cX}^2 = (c^2)(s_X^2).$$

. *Rule* 3: If the scores, *X*, are multiplied by a constant, *c*, the standard deviation of the transformed distribution, $Y = cX$, is the product of the standard deviation of *X* and the absolute value of the constant:

$$s_Y = s_{cX} = |c| s_X.$$

For example, if the standard deviation of *X* is $s_X = 15$ and the *X* values are multiplied by the negative number (-0.1) — that is, divided by (-10), the standard deviation of the transformed scores, $Y = (-0.1)X$, is:

$$s_Y = s_{-0.1X} = |-0.1| s_X = (0.1) s_X = (0.1)(15) = 1.5.$$

6.2.4 Standard Scores

Given the mean and the standard deviation for a sample (or population) of scores, each score, *X*, can be transformed into a standard score, z, which shows how many standard deviations is *X* below or above the mean. The formula for computing z scores is

Sample Data:	**Population Data:**	
$z = \dfrac{X - \bar{X}}{s}$	$z = \dfrac{X - \mu}{\sigma}$	**(6.7)**

Suppose that the mean and standard deviation for a sample are $\bar{X} = 50$ and $s = 10$, respectively. If $X = 60$ is a score from this sample, its *z* score is: $z = (X - \bar{X})/s = (60 - 50)/10 = 1$. The standard score $z = 1$ shows that 60 is one standard deviation above the sample mean. Likewise, the standard score for $X = 35$ is calculated as follows: $z = (35 - 50)/10 = -15/10 = -1.5$. Thus, 35 is one and a half standard deviations below the mean. [What is the *z* score for $X = 70$?]

The *z* scores present the deviations from the mean for *X* scores divided by the standard deviation of these scores. The sum of the *z* scores is zero because the sum of the deviations from the mean is zero (see Formula 6.2). The same holds for the mean of the z scores ($\bar{z} = 0$). Also, it can be easily seen that the standard deviation of the z scores always equals to one ($\sigma_z = 1$).

EXAMPLE 6.1 The z scores can be used to compare scores presented at different scales of measurement. Suppose that John has 45 points on a standardized math proficiency test, with the population mean and standard deviation for this test being $\mu = 30$ and $\sigma = 10$, respectively. At the same time, John has 92 points on a standardized reading proficiency test, with different mean and standard deviation for the population performance on this test (say, $\mu = 80$ and $\sigma = 12$). The question is on which test (math or reading) did John perform better? As John's scores in math proficiency (45) and reading proficiency (92) are presented on two different scales, it would be appropriate to compare the z-score equivalents of these two scores. Specifically, John's *z* score in math is $z = (45 - 30)/10 = 1.5$, whereas his z score in reading is $z = (92 - 80)/12 = 1$. As John scored one and a half standard deviations above the mean on the math test and one standard deviation above the mean on the reading test, he did better in math than in reading.

NOTE [6.3] The formula for converting *X* scores into *z* scores is a liner transformation of the *X* scores:

$$z = (1/\sigma)X - (\mu/\sigma)$$

6.2.5 Scale Transformation

Although the comparison of scores that come from different scales can be performed by comparing their z scores, sometimes it is necessary to present such scores on a common scale with desired mean and standard deviation. One reason for this is that negative (or zero) *z* scores may be misinterpreted in public reports of student performance. Suppose that the goal is to transform a distribution of scores, *X*, into a distribution of scores, *Y*, with desired mean and standard deviation (say, μ^* and σ^*, respectively). This can be performed in two steps:

1. Convert the *X* scores into *z* scores.
2. Calculate the new, *Y*, scores as follows: $Y = (z)\,\sigma^* + \mu^*$.

EXAMPLE 6.2 Using the information in Example 6.1, let's present John's scores in math ($X = 45$) and reading ($X = 92$) on a common scale with a desired mean of 50 and standard deviation of 10. This scale is known as the **T-scale** ($\mu = 50$, $\sigma = 10$). As shown in Example 6.1, John's *z* score in math is $z = 1.5$. Therefore, his math score on the T-scale is: $T_{math} = (1.5)(10) + 50 = 65$. Likewise, given that John's *z* score in reading is $z = 1$, his reading score on the T-scale is: $T_{reading} = (1)(10) + 50 = 60$. Higher *z* scores translate into higher T scores because of the positive linear relationship between *z* and T scores. Thus, the comparison of John's math and reading scores on either scale (*z* or T) shows that he did better in math than in reading.

EXAMPLE 6.3 This example shows how to transform a given distribution of scores into a distribution with a desired mean and standard deviation using SPSS. The survey scores, *X*, in Figure 6.1 are transformed into T-scores ($\mu = 50$, $\sigma = 10$), denoted in this example TX, using the following steps in SPSS:

1. Click **Analyze**, click **Descriptive Statistics,** and click **Descriptives ...**
2. Select **X**, then click ▶ to move this variable into the box **Variable(s)**, then check **Save standardized values as variables.**
3. Click **OK**.
4. Click **Transform**, click **Compute Variable ...**
5. Type **TX** in the box **Target Variable**, then type **10*ZX + 50** in the box **Numeric Expression** (see Figure 6.9, dialog box **Compute Variable**).

As shown in Figure 6.9 (left panel), two additional variables appear in the SPSS spreadsheet: ZX — representing the *z*-scores of *X*, and TX — representing the T-score equivalents of the original *X* scores.

NOTE [6.4] To transform a score distribution, *X*, into a new score distribution, *Y*, with a desired mean and standard deviation, multiply the z scores of *X* by the desired standard deviation and add the desired mean. The original scores *X* and their transformed values, *Y*, are linearly related and the *Y* distribution has exactly the same shape as the original *X* distribution. Thus, the z-scores, T-scores (or any other linear transformations of the original *X* scores) are normally distributed only if the original distribution of *X* scores is normal.

Figure 6.9 *SPSS transformation of X scores into z scores, ZX, and T scores, TX*

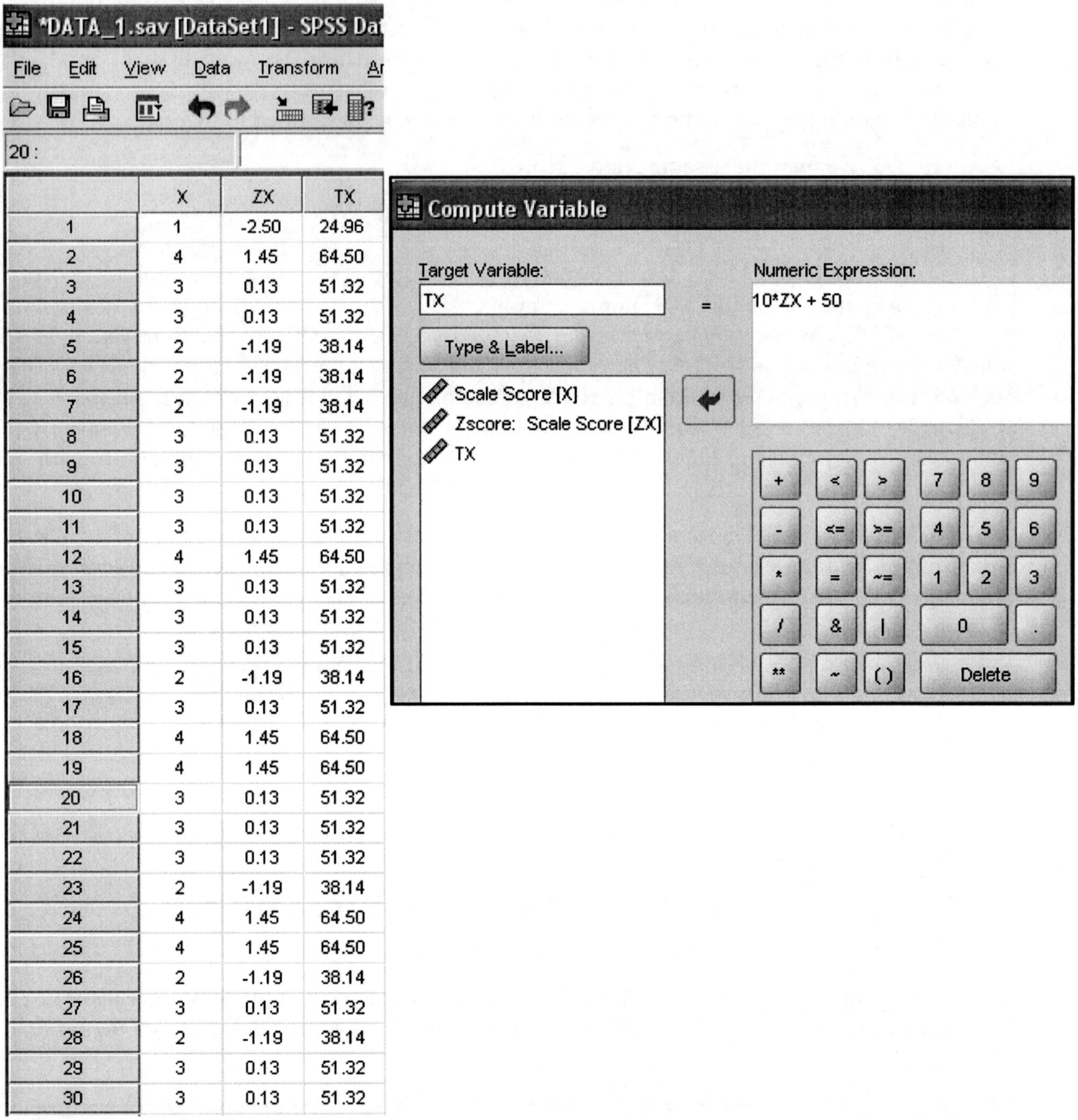

*DATA_1.sav [DataSet1] - SPSS Da

File Edit View Data Transform A

20 :

	X	ZX	TX
1	1	-2.50	24.96
2	4	1.45	64.50
3	3	0.13	51.32
4	3	0.13	51.32
5	2	-1.19	38.14
6	2	-1.19	38.14
7	2	-1.19	38.14
8	3	0.13	51.32
9	3	0.13	51.32
10	3	0.13	51.32
11	3	0.13	51.32
12	4	1.45	64.50
13	3	0.13	51.32
14	3	0.13	51.32
15	3	0.13	51.32
16	2	-1.19	38.14
17	3	0.13	51.32
18	4	1.45	64.50
19	4	1.45	64.50
20	3	0.13	51.32
21	3	0.13	51.32
22	3	0.13	51.32
23	2	-1.19	38.14
24	4	1.45	64.50
25	4	1.45	64.50
26	2	-1.19	38.14
27	3	0.13	51.32
28	2	-1.19	38.14
29	3	0.13	51.32
30	3	0.13	51.32

Compute Variable

Target Variable: TX = Numeric Expression: 10*ZX + 50

Type & Label...

Scale Score [X]
Zscore: Scale Score [ZX]
TX

\+ < > 7 8 9
\- <= >= 4 5 6
* = ~= 1 2 3
/ & | 0 .
** ~ ( ) Delete

Note: Verify that the z scores (ZX) have a mean of zero and a standard deviation of one, whereas the T scores (TX) have a mean of 50 and a standard deviation of 10. Use SPSS to compute the mean and standard deviation of ZX and TX: **Analyze → Descriptive Statistics → Descriptives.**

6.3 Summary

• The frequencies associated with a specific value of X in a frequency table are as follows: (a) **frequency** — the number of people with a score *X*, (b) **cumulative frequency** — the number of people with a score *X* or less, (c) **relative frequency** — the sample proportion of people with a score *X*, (d) **relative cumulative frequency** — the sample proportion of people with a score *X* or less [by multiplying the relative the cumulative frequency by 100, it is presented as a *cumulative percent.*]

• A **percentile** is the score at or below which a certain percent of the scores fall [e.g., the 25th percentile, P_{25}, is the score below which 25 percent of the scores fall.]

• The **five-number summary** of a frequency distribution is X_{min} = *lowest value*, Q_1 = *first quartile*, Q_2 = *second quartile*, Q_3 = *third quartile*, and X_{max} = *highest value*), where: $Q_1 = P_{25}$ (25th percentile — the score below which 25 percent of all scores fall), Q_2 = Median = P_{50} (50th percentile — the score below which 50 percent of all scores fall), and $Q_3 = P_{75}$ (75th percentile — the score below which 75 percent of all scores fall).

• The **measures of central tendency** in a distribution are (a) **mode** — the most frequent score in the distribution, (b) **median** — the score below which 50 percent of the scores fall, and (c) **mean** — the arithmetic average of the scores.

• With a *nominal scale,* it is appropriate to report the mode, but not the median or the mean. With an *ordinal scale*, it is appropriate to report both the mode and the median, but not the mean. With an *interval scale* or a *ratio scale*, it is appropriate to report the mode, the median, and the mean.

• The **measures of variation** are (a) **sum of squared deviations about the mean**, $SS = \Sigma(X - \bar{X})^2$, (b) **variance:** $s^2 = SS/(n - 1)$, and (c) **standard deviation**: $s = \sqrt{s^2}$.

• If s_1^2 and s_2^2 represent two sample estimates of the same population variance, σ^2, their "weighed" for sample size average is referred to as **pooled variance**.

• The variance and the standard deviation of scores do not change when the same number (constant, *c*) is added to (or subtracted from) each score.

• If the scores *X* are multiplied by a (positive or negative) constant, *c*, the variance of the transformed distribution, $Y = cX$, is the product of the variance of *X* and the squared value of the constant.

• If the scores *X* are multiplied by a constant, *c*, the standard deviation of the transformed distribution, $Y = cX$, is the product of the standard deviation of *X* and the absolute value of the constant.

• The **standard score**, z, for a score *X* shows how many standard deviations is *X* below or above the mean (Formula 6.7).

• The formula for converting *X* scores into *z* scores represents a liner transformation of the *X* scores. Therefore, the shape of the *z*-score distribution is the same as the shape of the original distribution of *X* scores.

• A score distribution, *X*, is transformed into a new score distribution, *Y*, with a desired mean and standard deviation, by multiplying the z scores of *X* by the desired standard deviation and adding the desired mean.

6.4 Study Questions

1. A unimodal distribution of scores from a relatively difficult test is

   A. negatively skewed, **B**. positively skewed, **C**. symmetrical.

2. What does it mean that the cumulative percent for a score of 10 is 74?
3. The five-number summary for a score distribution is: $X_{min} = 5$, $Q_1 = 10$, $Q_2 = 25$, $Q_3 = 50$, and $X_{max} = 135$. Given this, answer the questions: (a) what is median of the score distribution, (b) what is the interquartile range (IQR)?, (c) what are the reasonable upper boundary (RUB) and the reasonable lower boundary (RLB)?, and (d) are there any outliers?
4. Compute the mean, the variance, and the standard deviation for the distribution of four scores: 2, 2, 7, and 17.
5. Compute the pooled variance of the sample variances $s_1^2 = 10$ and $s_2^2 = 18$, given that they come from random samples with 36 and 27 observations, respectively.
6. Given that the variance of a score distribution, *X*, is $s_X^2 = 20$, what is the variance of the score distribution *Y* obtained from *X* through the use of the transformation (a) $Y = X + 5$, (b) $Y = 4X$, and (c) $Y = 4X + 5$ [*Hint*: use the basic rules in Section 6.2.3.4].
7. Given that John has 25 points on a standardized science test ($\mu = 22$, $\sigma = 9$) and 45 points on standardized reading test ($\mu = 40$, $\sigma = 20$), he did better on which of the two tests?
8. Using SPSS with the data file **Employee data.sav** (see Figure 6.4), provide the histogram and the five-number summary for the variable **salary** and transform the values of this variable into T-scores ($\mu = 50$, $\sigma = 10$).

CHAPTER 7

BASIC DISTRIBUTIONS

7.1 Normal Distribution

7.1.1 What is a Normal Distribution?

The numeric outcomes (observations) in many natural processes tend to conform to a bell-shaped distribution known as the **normal distribution**. Suppose that we toss a coin 100 times and X is the count of how many times the coin comes up "*heads*". If we repeat this "experiment" many times (say, 10,000), the frequency distribution of X values will have the shape of a normal distribution. Of course, it is much easier to conduct such an experiment using computer generations of random values (e.g., 1 or 0). Figure 7.1 shows the histogram for 5,000 scores on a math proficiency test. The continuous curve that approximates this histogram is a normal distribution curve. As another example, it is well known that IQ test scores conform to a normal distribution with a mean of 100 and a standard deviation of 15 ($\mu = 100$, $\sigma = 15$) — see Figure 7.4.

Figure 7.1 *Histogram of 5,000 math proficiency test scores, approximated by a normal curve*

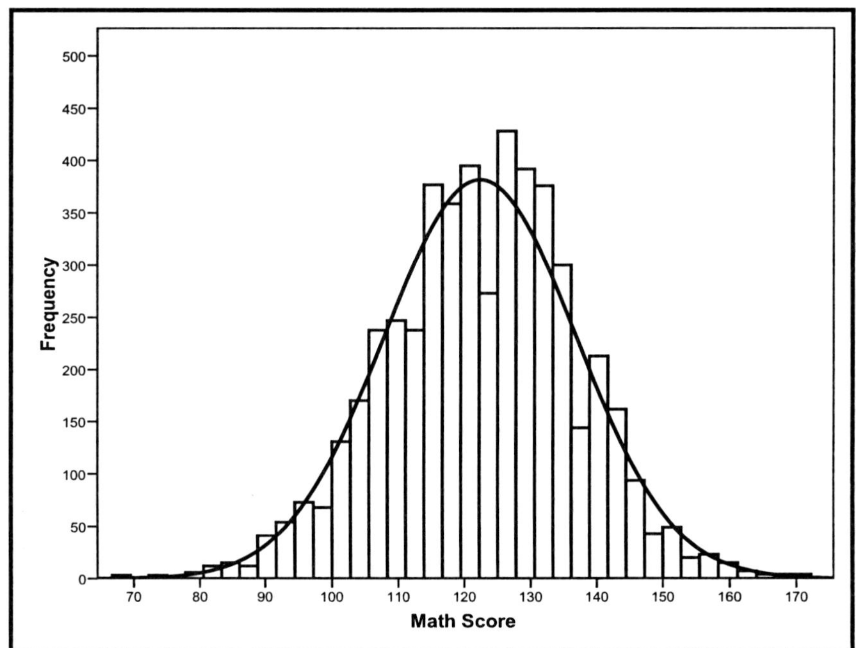

The exact location and shape of a normal distribution is determined as an analytic function of two parameters — *mean* and *standard deviation*. The notation $N(\mu, \sigma)$ is used to specify a normal distribution that has a mean, μ, and standard deviation, σ. For example, $N(\mu = 100, \sigma = 15)$ is the familiar IQ distribution. The normal distribution is also referred to as the **bell curve** distribution (because of its curved flaring shape), or the **Gaussian distribution,** because it was used by the German mathematician and scientist Karl F. Gauss (1977-1855) to analyze astronomical data. When the distribution of real scores on a given variable approximates a normal distribution we say that these scores follow the normal distribution (or, that the variable is normally-distributed).

In Figure 7.2, the upper panel shows two bell curves with equal standard deviations (σ = 0.5), but different means (μ = −0.5 and μ = 1), whereas the lower panel shows two bell curves with same mean (μ = 1), but different standard deviations (σ = 0.5 and σ = 1.3). Thus, the normal distributions in the upper panel, *N*(−0.5, 0.5) and *N*(1, 0.5), have the same shape but different locations, whereas those in the lower panel, *N*(1, 1.3) and *N*(1, 0.5), have the same location, but different shapes.

Figure 7.2 *Two normal curves with the same shape, but different location (upper panel), and two normal curves with the same location, but different shapes (lower panel)*

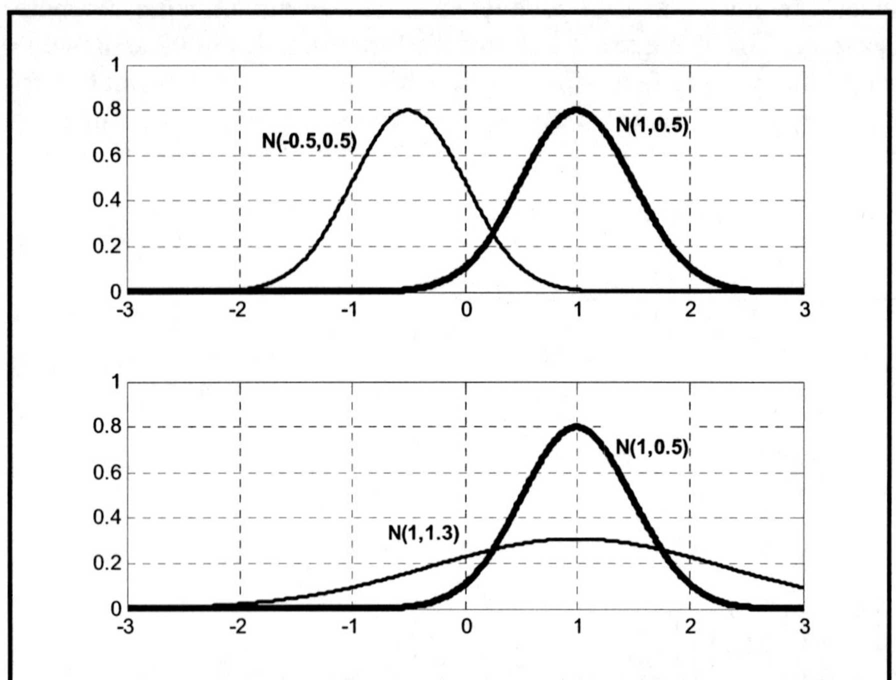

When the scores of a normal distribution are transformed into standard scores (*z*-scores), the resulting distribution is also normal, with a mean of zero (μ= 0) and a standard deviation of 1 (σ = 1). This distribution is called the **standard normal distribution** (or the **unit normal distribution**) and is denoted *N*(0,1). The bell curve for the standard normal distribution is shown in Figure 7.3. The exact shape of the standard normal distribution, *N*(0,1), is governed by the following analytic function of the standard scores, *z*:

$$f(z) = \frac{1}{\sqrt{2\pi}} e^{-0.5z^2}$$

where *e* is the exponential constant (*e* = 2.718, rounded to the third decimal digit) and π is the well known mathematical constant (π = 3.142, rounded to the third decimal digit).

Figure 7.3 *The standard normal distribution, N(0,1)*

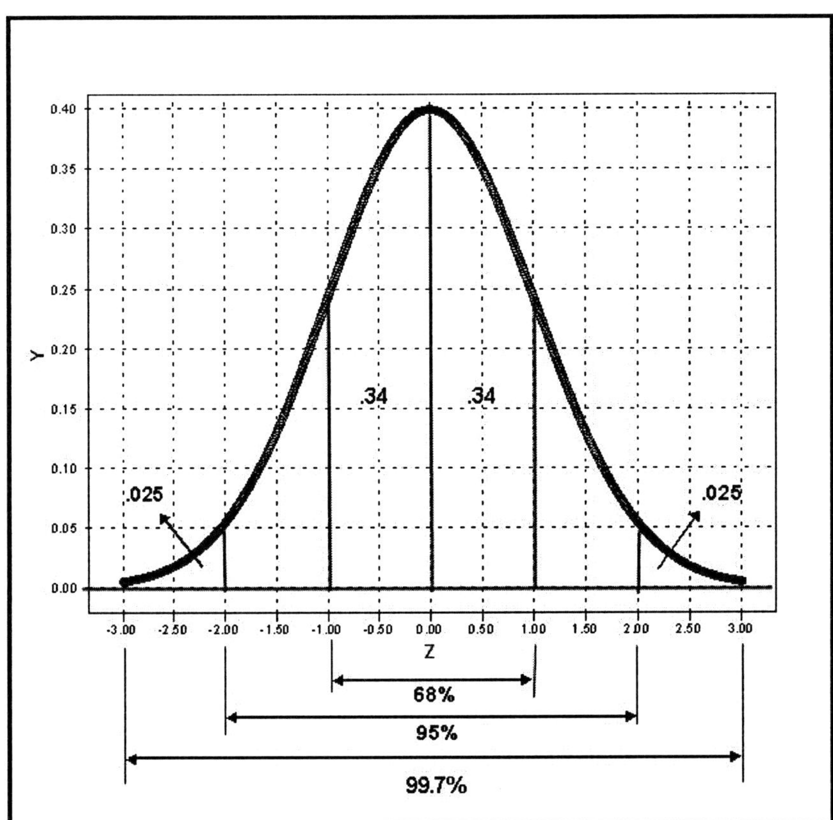

7.1.2 Basic Properties of the Normal Distribution

The bell curve of the normal distribution is (a) unimodal, (b) symmetric around the mean (which in this case coincides with the mode and the median), and (c) extended from $-\infty$ to $+\infty$; (∞ denotes "infinity"). As mentioned above, the location of the bell curve is determined by the mean, μ, and its shape is determined by the standard deviation, σ. The total area under the bell curve is 1 (i.e., 100%), and the area under the curve associated with a given interval on the scale is a proportion which is equivalent to the percent of scores that fall within that interval. The empirical rules in NOTE [7.1], referred to as "*sigma-rules*" provide quick estimates of the percent of scores that fall within certain intervals of a normal distribution with parameters μ and σ.

> **NOTE [7.1]** *Sigma-Rules*:
>
> - **1σ-rule**: about 68% of the scores fall within the interval $\mu \pm \sigma$.
> - **2σ-rule**: about 95% of the scores fall within the interval $\mu \pm 2\,\sigma$.
> - **3σ-rule**: almost all (99.7%) of the scores fall within the interval $\mu \pm 3\sigma$.

The estimates provided by these empirical rules are approximate. For example, the middle 95% of the scores actually fall within 1.96 standard deviations from the mean, but the 2σ-rule works for quick practical estimations. Figure 7.3 illustrates the sigma rules applied to the standard normal distribution with $\mu = 0$ and $\sigma = 1$, $N(0,1)$. The 3σ -rule shows that almost all of the *z* scores in the distribution (99.7%) fall between -3.0σ and $+3.0\sigma$, that is, between -3.0 and 3.0 because $\sigma = 1$. The 2σ-rule shows that about 95% of the *z* scores fall between -2.0 and $+2.0$; (more accurately, 95% of the *z* scores fall between -1.96 and $+1.96$). The 1σ-rule shows that about 68% of the z scores fall between -1.0 and $+1.0$.

The area under the $N(0,1)$ curve associated with the interval from -1.0 to $+1.0$ equals 0.68 — the proportion equivalent to 68% percent of the z scores that fall within this interval. Because the bell curve is symmetrical around the mean, the two areas under the $N(0,1)$ curve associated with the intervals $(-1, 0)$ and $(0, 1)$ are identical, and each of them is equal to 0.34 (one half of 0.68). Likewise, the sum of the two areas under the tails of the $N(0,1)$ that fall beyond the interval $(-2.0, 2.0)$ is 0.05, so each of them equals 0.025 or 2.5%.

7.1.3 Determining Percentiles and Percentile Ranks

7.1.3.1 Determining percentiles. Educators are often tasked determining percentiles and percentile ranks in a normal distribution of scores. For example, given the normal distribution of IQ scores, $N(\mu = 100, \sigma = 15)$, we may ask the question: "What is the IQ score that can serve as a *threshold* (cutoff point) to select students that fall in the top 20% of the IQ distribution?" This information may be necessary, say, to select participants for an advanced study program. Since in this example 80% of the scores in the IQ distribution fall below the IQ threshold of interest, we need to determine the 80th percentile, P_{80}—the score below which 80% of the scores fall—in the IQ distribution (see Figure 7.4). We can answer this question in two steps:

Step 1: The *area beyond* the *z* score corresponding to the 80th percentile is .20. In Table A-1, the area beyond (probability in upper tail) closest to .20 is .201, with a corresponding z score of 0.84. Thus, we take $z = 0.84$ as the z score corresponding to the 80th percentile (P_{80}) under the standard normal distribution, $N(0, 1)$.

Step 2: Formula 6.7 provides the z score for a score *X*. Conversely, given the z score, the original score, *X*, can be obtained by using the following equivalent equation:

$$X = (z)(\sigma) + \mu.$$

In this case, with *X* being the 80th percentile ($X = P_{80}$) in the IQ distribution, we have: $P_{80} = (0.84)(15) + 100 = 112.6$.

Thus, rounded to the nearest integer, IQ = 113 can serve as a cutting score to select students who perform in the top 20% percent on the IQ test.

7.1.3.2 Determining percentile ranks. Suppose we ask the question: "What percent of the IQ test takers score below 80?" The task is now to determine the percentile rank for the score of 80, PR_{80}—the percent of scores that fall below the score of 80. Given that $\mu = 100$ and $\sigma = 15$ for the IQ score distribution, we perform this task in three steps:

Step 1: We convert the score of 80 into a z score: $z = (80 - 100)/15 = -1.33$.

Step 2: Using Table A-1, we can see that the *area above* $z = 1.33$ is .092. Therefore, since $N(0,1)$ is symmetrical around zero, the *area below* $z = -1.33$ is also .092.

Step 3: Since the area below the IQ score of 80 is .092, $PR_{80} = 9.2$. That is, 9.2% of the scores fall below 80 (see Figure 7.4).

Figure 7.4 *IQ score distribution, N(μ = 100, σ = 15)*

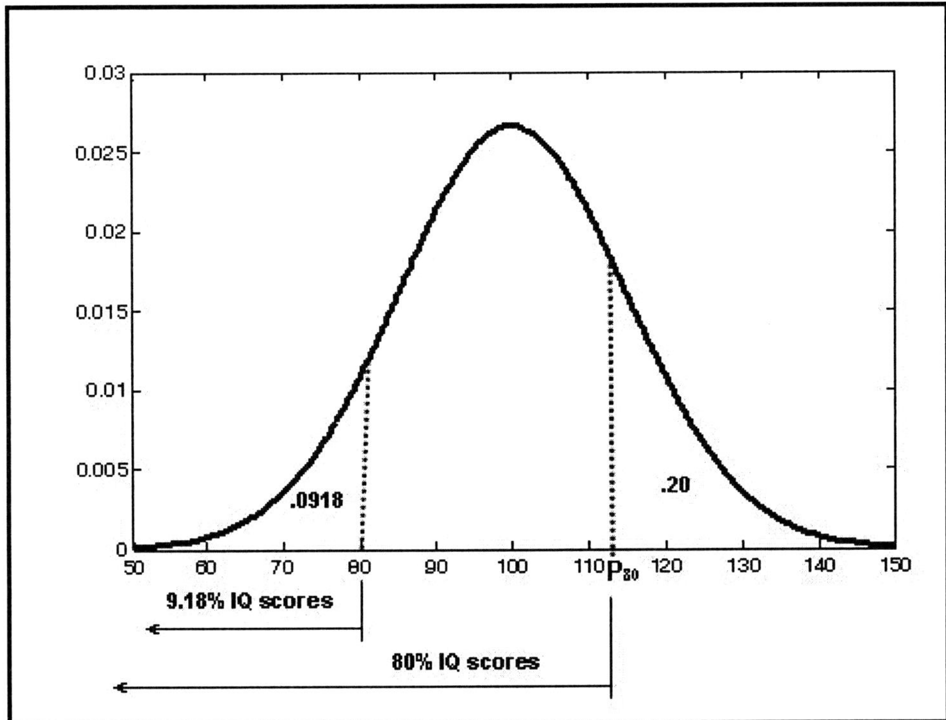

7.1.4 Sampling Distribution of the Mean

Suppose that we randomly select a sample of *n* observations from a (not necessarily normal) distribution and then calculate the sample mean, $\overline{X}$. If we keep repeating the random sampling of *n* people, allowing for replication (i.e., each sample may include observations from previous samples), the resulting distribution of sample means, $\overline{X}$, is referred to as the **sampling distribution of the mean**. The properties of the sampling distribution of the mean play a key role in constructing confidence intervals and testing hypotheses about population means.

NOTE [7.2] As known from the so-called **Central Limit Theorem**, the properties of the sampling distribution of the mean for samples with a sample size *n* are:

- The sampling distribution of the mean is **normal**, regardless of the shape of the population distribution.
- The mean of the sampling distribution of the mean equals the mean of the population distribution, that is:

$$\mu_{\overline{X}} = \mu \tag{7.1}$$

- The variance of the sampling distribution of the mean is *n* times smaller than the variance of the population distribution, that is:

$$\sigma^2_{\overline{X}} = \frac{\sigma^2}{n}, \tag{7.2}$$

- or, equivalently, the standard deviation of the sampling distribution is:

$$\sigma_{\overline{X}} = \frac{\sigma}{\sqrt{n}}. \text{ [referred to also as the \textbf{standard error of the mean}]} \tag{7.3}$$

EXAMPLE 7.1 Suppose that the students' scores on a state reading assessment are normally distributed and presented on a T-scale ($\mu = 50$ and $\sigma = 10$). We want to determine the interval that contains (a) the reading score of any randomly selected student and (b) the mean reading score of 25 randomly selected students. To answer question (a), we apply the 3σ-rule for the population distribution of individual scores, T($\mu = 50$, $\sigma = 10$). Specifically, almost all (99.7%) individual test scores, *X*, fall within the interval: $\mu \pm 3\sigma = 50 \pm (3)(10) = 50 \pm 30$. Thus, the reading score of any randomly-selected student will be between 20 and 80 (see Figure 7.5).

To answer question (b), we must use the sampling distribution of the mean for $n = 25$. Using Formula 7.3, the **standard error of the mean** is: $\sigma_{\overline{X}} = \sigma / \sqrt{n} = 10 / \sqrt{25} = 10/5 = 2$. Now, using the 3σ-rule for the sampling distribution of the mean ($\mu_{\overline{X}} = 50$, $\sigma_{\overline{X}} = 2$), we can say that, almost all (99.7%) samples with $n = 25$ will have their means, $\overline{X}$, within the following interval: $\mu_{\overline{X}} \pm 3\sigma_{\overline{X}} = 50 \pm (3)(2) = 50 \pm 6$. Thus, the mean score on the reading test for 25 randomly selected students is expected to be between 44 and 56 (see Figure 7.5).

Figure 7.5 *Distribution of reading test scores ($\mu = 50$, $\sigma = 10$) and sampling distribution of the mean ($\mu_{\overline{X}} = 50, \sigma_{\overline{X}} = 2$) for samples of 25 observations*

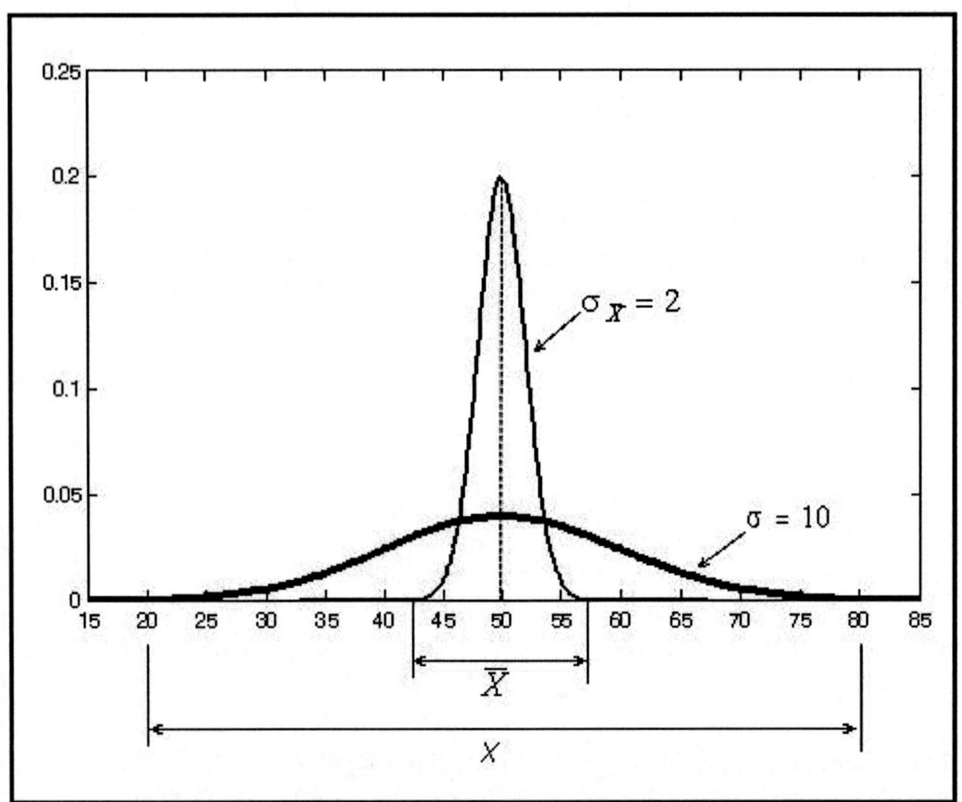

The 2σ-rule for the population distribution in Figure 7.5, T($\mu = 50$, $\sigma = 10$), shows that about 95% of reading test scores fall between 30 and 70. On the other hand, the 2σ-rule for the sampling distribution of the mean ($\mu_{\overline{X}} = 50, \sigma_{\overline{X}} = 2$) shows that about 95% of the sample means of all possible random samples of 25 observations ($n = 25$) fall between 46 and 54.

7.1.5 Normal Q-Q Plot

A simple test to whether the sample data come from a normal distribution is provided by a normal probability plot known as the **normal Q-Q plot** (normal quantile-quantile plot). Recall that *quantiles* are cutoff points (scores) that divide the ordered data into parts containing equal percent of observations. Examples of quantiles are percentiles, quartiles, and deciles (see NOTE [6.1]). The Q-Q plot is a plot of ordered data values against the associated quantiles of the normal distribution. If the data come from a normal distribution, the points of the plot should lie close to a straight line.

EXAMPLE 7.2 This example illustrates the use of SPSS for the normal Q-Q plot. The data represent the values of the variable named **prevexp** [previous experience (months)] in the SPSS data file **Employee data.sav** (see Figure 6.4). The SPSS steps for the Q-Q plot in this case are:

1. Click **Analyze**, click **Descriptive Statistics**, and click **Q-Q Plots**.
2. Click **Previous Experience (months)** and click ► to move it into th [illegible]
3. Keep the default option **Normal** in the list of options labeled **Test** [illegible]
4. Click OK.

The SPSS output is shown in Figure 7.6. As can be seen, the data for t[illegible] vious experience (months)" are not normally distributed because the dots of th[illegible] do not lie close to the straight line. This result can be expected given the positively sk[illegible] tribution of these data depicted in Figure 6.5.

Figure 7.6 *Normal Q-Q plot for the (positively skewed) distribution of the variable "previous experience (months)" in the SPSS file* **Employee data**

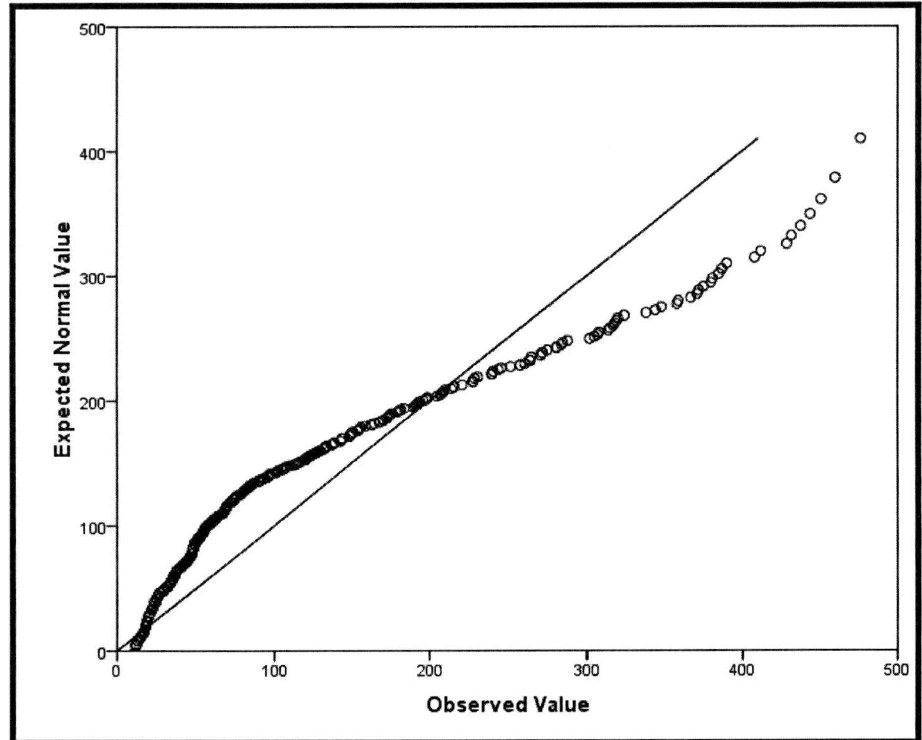

EXAMPLE 7.3 This example illustrates the normal Q-Q plot for 5,000 scores on a reading proficiency test. The histogram of the data is shown in Figure 7.7, whereas the normal Q-Q plot is provided in Figure 7.8. The normal distribution of the data suggested by the unimodal symmetrical histogram is supported by the normal Q-Q plot. Indeed, except for a slight deviation at the lower end, the dots of the Q-Q plot fall entirely on the straight line.

Figure 7.7 *Histogram of 5,000 scores on a reading proficiency test*

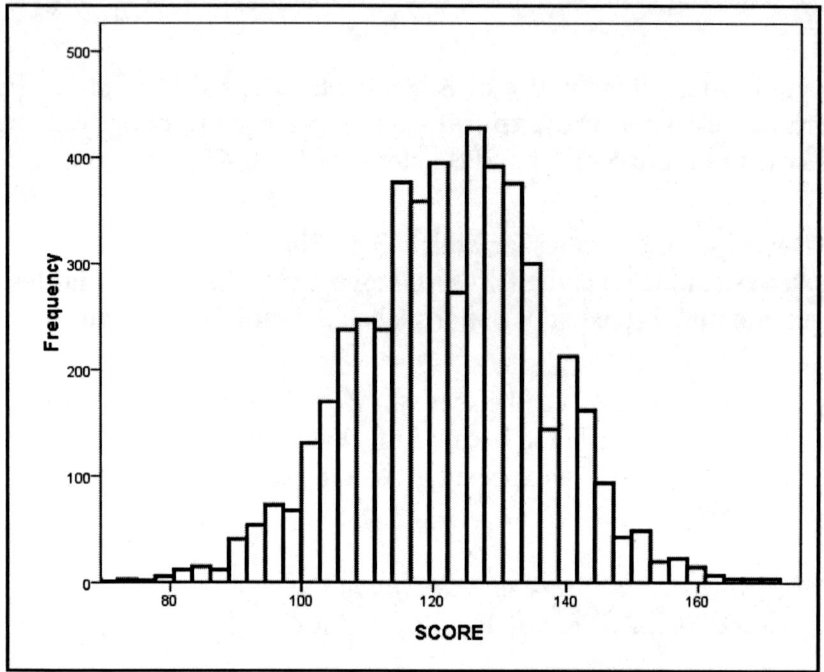

Figure 7.8 *Normal Q-Q plot for the reading proficiency test data*

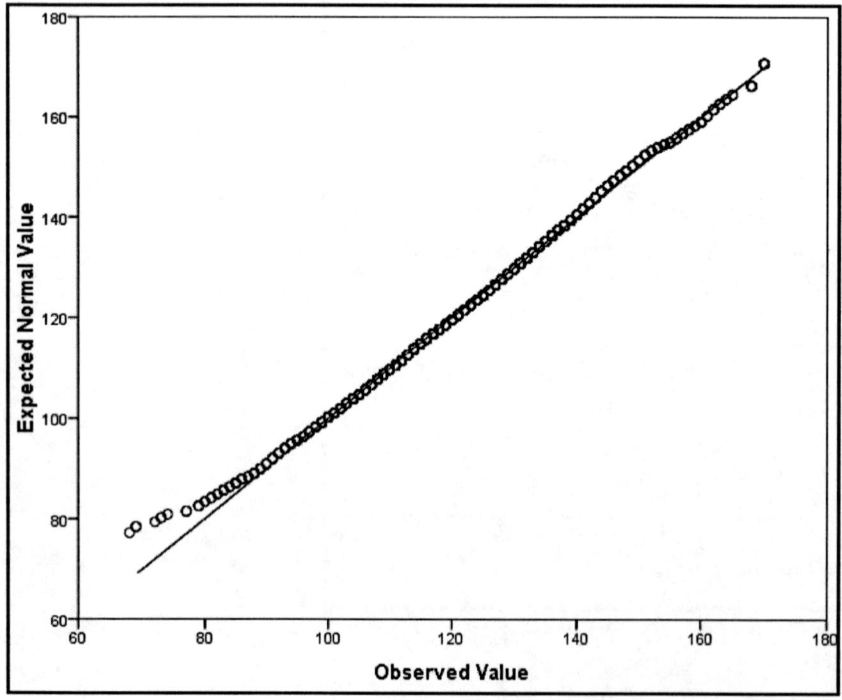

7.2 Student's *t*-Distribution

As noted earlier, $\sigma_{\overline{X}} = \sigma / \sqrt{n}$ is the standard deviation (or **standard error**) of $\overline{X}$ in the sampling distribution of the mean. Therefore, the z score of $\overline{X}$ in this distribution is

$$z = \frac{\overline{X} - \mu}{\frac{\sigma}{\sqrt{n}}}. \quad \textbf{(7.4)}$$

The z statistic from Equation 7.4 belongs to the standard normal distribution, $N(0, 1)$. When the population standard deviation, σ, is not known and is replaced by the sample standard deviation, s, the resulting statistic is referred to as a ***t*-statistic**:

$$t = \frac{\overline{X} - \mu}{\frac{s}{\sqrt{n}}}. \quad \textbf{(7.5)}$$

When the sample is large (e.g., $n > 100$), the *t*-statistic follows the standard normal distribution, $N(0, 1)$. When the sample is not large, the *t*-statistic follows the so-called **Student's *t*-distribution**. ["Student" was the publishing pseudonym of W. S. Gosset who derived the *t*-distribution while working as a statistician at the Guinness Brewery in Dublin (1908).] The *t*-distribution is similar in shape to the standard normal distribution, but it has thicker tails. The exact shape of the *t*-distribution is governed by its *degrees of freedom* (*df*). With one sample, $df = n - 1$. The larger the degrees of freedom, the closer the *t*-distribution is to the standard normal distribution (see Figure 7.6).

Figure 7.6 *The standard normal distribution, N(0,1), and t-distributions*

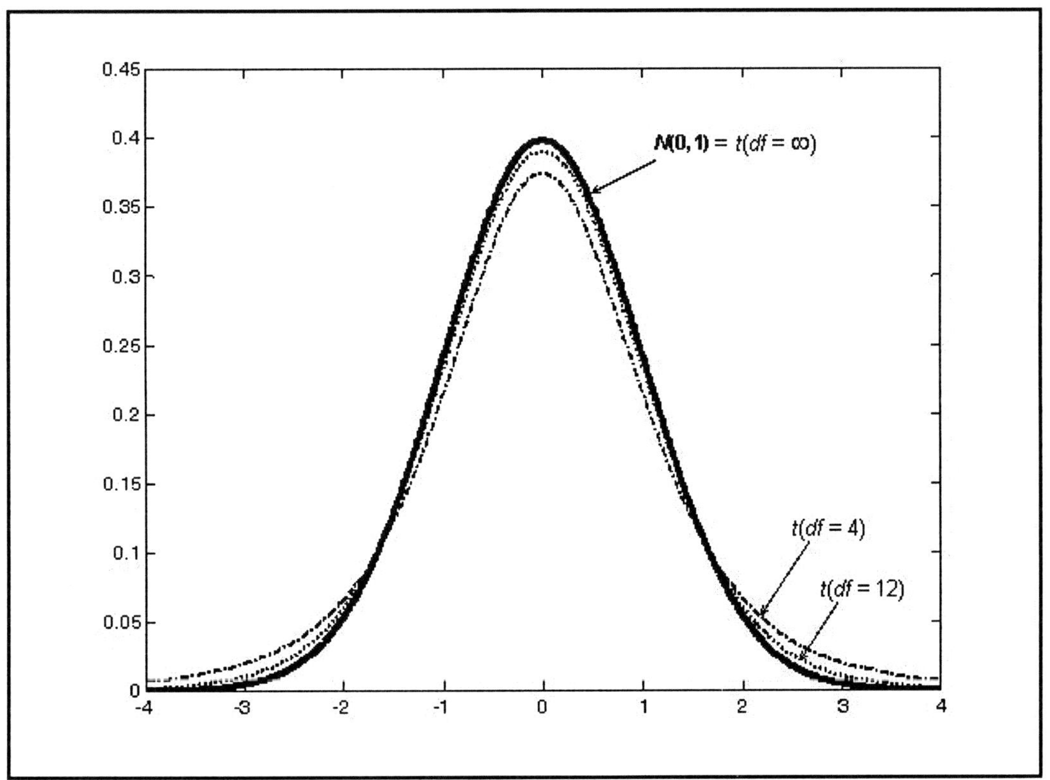

7.3 *F*-Distribution

Suppose we randomly select from a normal distribution a pair of samples with variance s_1^2 and s_2^2, respectively (the two samples may have different sample size — say, n_1 and n_2, respectively). The ratio of two sample variances from a normal distribution is called the ***F*-ratio**:

$$F = \frac{s_1^2}{s_2^2}. \tag{7.6}$$

If we keep repeating this random sampling allowing for replication (i.e., each selected sample may include observations from previous samples), the *F*-ratios are distributed according to a distribution called the ***F*-distribution**. The shape of the *F*-distribution is governed by the *degrees of freedom* (*df*) for the variance in the numerator ($df_1 = n_1 - 1$) and the variance in the denominator ($df_2 = n_2 - 1$) of the *F*-ratio. The *F*-distribution is named after the famous statistician R.A. Fisher (1890 - 1962).

As shown in Figure 7.7, the *F*-distribution is skewed to the right and can only have positive values because each *F*-value is a ratio of two positive numbers (s_1^2 and s_2^2). Also, when the degrees of freedom increase, the *F*-distribution gets closer to a normal distribution. As with any other probability distribution, the area below the curve of the *F*-distribution equals 1.0.

Figure 7.7 *F*-distributions for three pairs of degrees of freedom (df_1 and df_2).

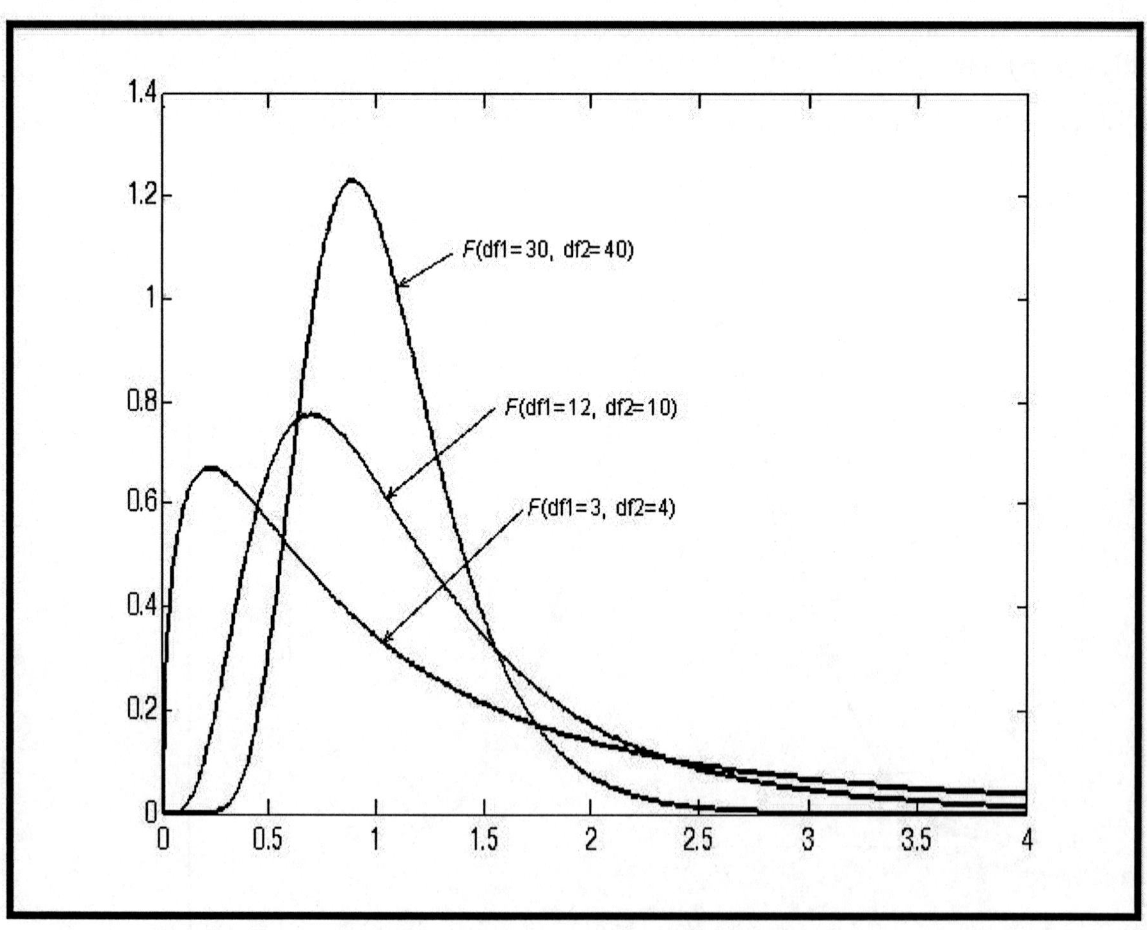

The *F*-distribution is used in numerous scenarios of hypothesis testing. The most common procedure is testing for equal population variances (i.e., $\sigma_1^2 = \sigma_2^2$). A key task in such testing is to determine the area under the *F*-curve that is to the right of (*beyond*) a given *F*-statistic (this area is referred to as the ***p*-value** associated with the *F*-statistic). The reverse task also occurs—given the area *beyond* (e.g., in the right tail of the F-distribution), determine its corresponding *F* value (referred to as a **critical value** — see Table A-4). More details on this topic are provided with the discussion of hypothesis testing later in this book.

7.4 Chi-square Distribution

Suppose that we randomly select *k* standard scores from the standard normal distribution, *N*(0,1) and calculate the sum of their squared values denoted as χ^2 ("chi-square").

$$\chi^2 = \sum_{i=1}^{k} z_i^2 = z_1^2 + z_2^2 + \ldots + z_k^2. \qquad \textbf{(7.7)}$$

If we keep repeating this sampling with replication (i.e., each sampling may include *z* scores that appear in previous samplings), the χ^2 sums are distributed according to the so-called **chi-square distribution.** The number of z scores in the sum χ^2 represents the *degrees of freedom* for the chi-square distribution (*df* = *k*), and the shape of the distribution is governed by its degrees of freedom. Figure 7.8 shows chi-square distributions with degrees of freedom 4 (χ_4^2) and 12 (χ_{12}^2).

Figure 7.8 *Chi-square distributions with degrees of freedom 4 and 12*

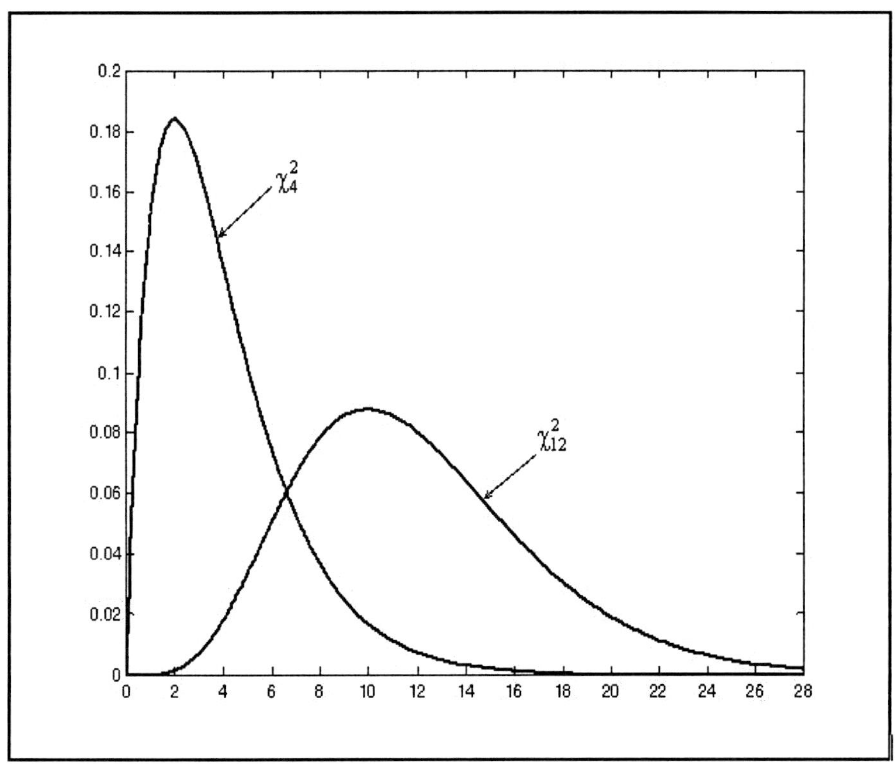

NOTE [7.3] The chi-square distribution with *k* degrees of freedom (χ_k^2) can be seen as a special case of the *F*-distribution with *k* degrees of freedom for the numerator ($df_1 = k$) and very large ("infinity") degrees of freedom for the denominator ($df_2 = \infty$), that is: $\chi_k^2 = F_{k,\infty}$. Thus, for the χ^2 distributions in Figure 7.8 we have: $\chi_4^2 = F_{4,\infty}$ and $\chi_{12}^2 = F_{12,\infty}$.

7.5 Summary

• The **normal distribution** is a unimodal bell curve distribution which exact shape is governed by its mean, μ, and standard deviation, σ. The mean (μ) determines the location and the standard deviation (σ) determines the shape of the normal distribution (e.g., see Figure 7.2).

• When the scores in a normal distribution are presented as standard (*z*-) scores, this distribution is transformed into a normal distribution with a mean of zero ($\mu = 0$) and a standard deviation of 1 ($\sigma = 1$) referred to as the **standard normal distribution** and denoted *N*(0, 1). The exact shape of the standard normal distribution is governed by the analytic function of the z-scores represented with Equation 7.1

• **Sigma-rules** for normal distribution: (a) **one-sigma rule** — about 68% of the scores fall within the interval $\mu \pm \sigma$, (b) **two-sigma rule** — about 95% of the scores fall within the interval $\mu \pm 2\sigma$, and (c) **three-sigma rule** — 99.7% of the scores fall within the interval $\mu \pm 3\sigma$.

•**The Central Limit Theorem** states that the sampling distribution of the mean (a) is normal, regardless of the shape of the original distribution, (b) its mean equals the mean of the original distribution, and (c) its variance is *n* times smaller than the variance of the original distribution, where *n* is the sample size — see NOTE [7.2].

• When the population standard deviation, σ, is not known and is replaced by the sample standard deviation, *s*, the ***t*-statistic**, $t = (\bar{X} - \mu)/(s/\sqrt{n})$, follows the **Student's t-distribution**.

• The *t*-distribution is similar in shape to the standard normal distribution, but it has thicker tails. The exact shape of the *t*-distribution is governed by its *degrees of freedom* (*df*). When the sample is large (e.g., $n > 100$), the *t*-statistic follows the standard normal distribution, *N*(0, 1).

• The ratio of two sample variances from a normal distribution is called the ***F*-ratio** ($F = s_1^2/s_2^2$). The *F*-ratios are distributed according to a distribution called the ***F*-distribution**. The shape of the *F*-distribution is governed by the *degrees of freedom* (*df*) for the variance in the numerator ($df_1 = n_1 - 1$) and the variance in the denominator ($df_2 = n_2 - 1$) of the *F*-ratio.

• The sum of *k* squared z-scores randomly selected from the standard normal distribution follows the so-called **chi-square (χ^2) distribution** with *k* degrees of freedom.

• The shape of the chi-square distribution is governed by its degrees of freedom. When the number for degrees of freedom is small, the shape of the chi-square distribution is positively skewed, but when this number increases, the chi-square distribution is getting close to a normal distribution (e.g., see Figure 7.8).

• The chi-square distribution with *k* degrees of freedom (χ_k^2) can be seen as a special case of the *F*-distribution with *k* degrees of freedom for the numerator ($df_1 = k$) and very large ("infinity") degrees of freedom for the denominator ($df_2 = \infty$).

7.6 Study Questions

1. Which parameters determine the location and the shape of the normal distribution?

2. For the IQ score normal distribution $N(\mu = 100, \sigma = 15)$, what percent of the population is expected to score (a) between 85 and 115, (b) higher than 115, and (c) lower than 70?

3. For a normal distribution with a mean of 50 and a standard deviation of 10 ($\mu = 50$, $\sigma = 10$), (a) what is the percentile rank for a score of 60? and (b) what is the 16th percentile?

4. If the distribution of *X* scores is positively skewed, the distribution of sample means for all possible random samples (with the same sample size) taken from the *X* distribution is

   A. positively skewed

   B. negatively skewed

   C. normal

   D. impossible to know

5. Given that the variance of a distribution of scores is 25 ($\sigma^2 = 25$), what is the standard error of the mean for a random sample of 36 observations?

6. Given that $s_1^2 = 12$ and $s_2^2 = 18$ are the variances of two random samples from the same normal distribution, with $n_1 = 51$ and $n_2 = 46$ for their respective sizes, compute the *F*-ratio and the degrees of freedom for its numerator and denominator.

7. With the "infinity" symbol (∞) representing large degrees of freedom, which of the following is true:

   A. $\chi_5^2 = F_{5,5}$

   B. $\chi_5^2 = F_{1,5}$

   C. $\chi_5^2 = F_{\infty,5}$

   D. $\chi_5^2 = F_{\infty,1}$

   E. $\chi_5^2 = F_{5,\infty}$

   F. None of the above

8. When the population standard deviation is not known and the sample standard deviation is used instead, the standardized deviation of a sample mean from the population mean is called

   A. z-statistic

   B. *t*-statistic

   C. *chi-square* statistic

   D. *F*-statistic

9. The F-distribution is named after the famous statistician

   A. W. S. Gosset

   B. K. Pearson

   C. R. A. Fisher

   D. None of the above

10. Using the SPSS data file **Employee data.sav**, test the variable **current salary** for normality by employing the normal Q-Q plot test. [*Hint*: see Example 7.2]

CHAPTER 8

HYPOTHESIS TESTING

8.1 What is Hypothesis Testing?

Hypothesis testing is a process of using statistical procedures and reasoning to make inferences about the population based on sample observations. Any hypothesis represents a statement about statistical relationships between population parameters (e.g., population means, proportions, variances, correlations, etc.). In research scenarios, each question is addressed by testing a **null hypothesis** (H_0) versus an **alternative hypothesis**, H_a. The null hypothesis states that the relationship targeted in the research question does not exist (e.g., H_0: *There is no difference between control and experimental groups on math proficiency scores* or H_0: *There is no correlation between test performance and anxiety*). In contrast, the alternative hypothesis states that the targeted relationship does exist.

Suppose that the research question concerns "*Whether high school students from school district A, who studied science using computer simulations, outperform the state norm of 50 points on a science proficiency test.*" The null hypothesis associated with this question states that, "On average, the students from school district A do not differ from the state norm (50 points) on the science proficiency test." In symbols, this null hypothesis is $\boldsymbol{H_0}$**:** $\boldsymbol{\mu = 50}$, where μ is the population mean of the students in school district A on the science proficiency test. The alternative hypothesis in this case is $\boldsymbol{H_a}$**:** $\boldsymbol{\mu > 50}$**;** (note that "$\mu > 50$" is a symbolic translation of the statement that "The students from school district A *outperform* the state norm of 50").

There are two types of error that may occur in hypothesis testing. **Type I error** occurs when we reject a true null hypothesis (that is, when we falsely reject H_0). *Prior* to testing a hypothesis, the researcher must decide what chances of making a Type I error are acceptable (e.g., based on the potential consequences of making a Type I error). The acceptable probability of making a Type I error is called the **level of significance** or **alpha (α) level**. Behavioral research most frequently uses $\alpha = .05$ and $\alpha = .01$. Selecting $\alpha = .05$, for example, means that we can "afford" up to 5% chances of making a Type I error.

Type II error occurs when we fail to reject a false null hypothesis. In other words, we make a Type II error when we falsely retain H_0. The probability of making a Type II error is denoted β ("beta"). While the acceptable probability of making a Type I error (level of significance), is selected by the researcher prior to testing a hypothesis, the probability of making a Type II error is not selected by the researcher. Instead, with all other conditions being equal, the probability of making a Type II error, β, is inversely related to the selected level of significance, α. For example, with all other factors the same, selecting $\alpha = .01$ will lead to higher probability of making Type II error than selecting $\alpha = .05$.

EXAMPLE 8.1 Suppose we want to know the consequences of making Type I error and Type II error in a jury verdict. Under the judicial assumption that "the defendant is innocent until proven guilty," the null hypothesis is H_0: "*The defendant is innocent.*" Type I will occur if the jury falsely rejects this null hypothesis. Therefore, the outcome of making a Type I error is "giving a guilty verdict to an innocent person." Conversely, a Type II error will occur if the jury falsely retains H_0. Thus, the outcome of making a Type II error is "acquitting a guilty person."

The probability of rejecting a false null hypothesis is called the **power** of the test. In other words, the *power* indicates the chances of being correct when rejecting the null hypothesis. Higher power in testing for differences means greater chances to detect such differences when they exist. As most of the time the researcher's goal is to reject the null hypothesis, it is important to determine and report the power in testing H_0 versus H_a.

NOTE [8.1] The definitional statement of *Type II error* ("failure to reject a false null hypothesis") is a logical negation of the *power* statement "reject a false null hypothesis." Therefore, if one of these two statements is true, the other is false. This, in turn, proves that *power* and *probability of making Type II error*, β, are related as follows:

$$\textbf{Power} = 1 - \beta \tag{8.1}$$

Thus, if β = .20, then power = .80. In other words, if there are 20% chances of making a Type II error, there are 80% chances of rejecting the null hypothesis when it is indeed false (e.g., of detecting differences when they exist).

8.2 When To Reject (or Not) the Null Hypothesis?

The statistical procedures involved in testing hypotheses depend on the specific *testing scenario* — the type of hypothesis being tested, the information that is available about the target population, sample(s), etc. One scenario, for example, is when we test a null hypothesis that two populations have equal means (H_0: $\mu_1 = \mu_2$) versus an alternative hypothesis that they do not have equal means (H_a: $\mu_1 \neq \mu_2$) and we know the population variances (σ_1^2 and σ_2^2). A variation of this scenario is when the population variances are not known, so we use their sample estimates (s_1^2 and s_2^2) instead. Other scenarios may involve testing about other population parameters such as proportions, correlations, etc.

In any testing scenario, a decision must be made about the null hypothesis (*reject* or *fail to reject* H_0). The correctness of this decision is based on proper understanding of the process of hypothesis testing. Generally, the **testing of a null hypothesis** *versus* **an alternative hypothesis** (H_0 versus H_a) is a five-step process:

1. A level of significance, α, is selected *prior* to testing H_0 versus H_a.
2. Depending on the testing scenario, a statistic, referred to as **test statistic,** is calculated from the sample.
3. It is theoretically given that "If H_0 is true, the test statistic must belong to a specific distribution, referred to as the **hypothesized distribution.**" [Depending on the testing scenario, this can be the *standard normal distribution*, *t*-distribution, *F*-distribution, or *chi-square* distribution.]
4. Given the hypothesized distribution and the test statistic, the probability that the test statistic belongs to the hypothesized distribution (*p*-value) is estimated.

5. **H_0 is rejected if $p < \alpha$** (i.e., the chances that the test statistic belongs to the hypothesized distribution are smaller than those specified by the level of significance, α). **Otherwise, we fail to reject H_0.**

Figure 8.1 illustrates a general scenario of making a decision about H_0 (*reject* or *fail to reject*). The hypothesized distribution is presented as positively skewed (like the *F*-distribution or the *chi-square* distribution), but it can also be symmetrical — say, like the standard normal distribution or the *t*-distribution. The test statistic is denoted *TS*, but in a specific scenario this will be a statistic calculated from the sample(s) (e.g., *z*-statistic, *t*-statistic, *F*-statistic, or χ^2-statistic). The shaded area (α) shows the *level of significance* selected by the researcher prior to testing H_0. The darker part of this area (*p*) — the *area beyond TS*, represents the probability that *TS* belongs to the hypothesized distribution. For illustration, it is assumed here that $\alpha = .05$ and $p = .032$. Because $p < \alpha$, the probability that *TS* belongs to the hypothesized distribution is smaller than the probability specified by the level of significance. In other words, selecting $\alpha = .05$ means that we can "afford" up to 5% chances of error in rejecting H_0. At the same time, $p = .032$ indicates that the actual chances of making an error by rejecting H_0 are 3.2% (smaller than the 5% error rate that we can "afford"). Therefore, we reject the null hypothesis, H_0, at the .05 level of significance.

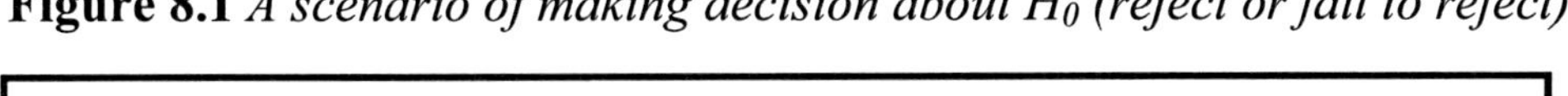

Figure 8.1 *A scenario of making decision about H_0 (reject or fail to reject)*

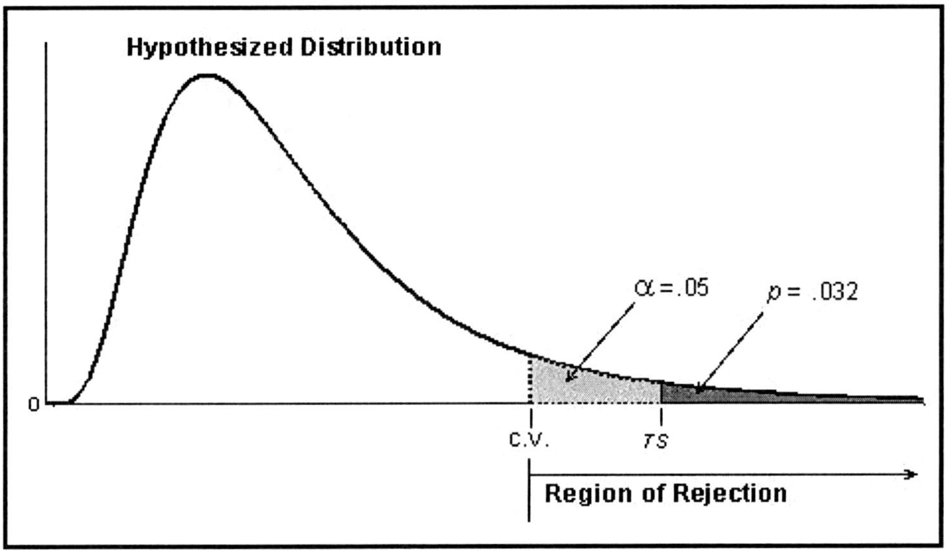

In Figure 8.1, the notation **C.V.** stands for **critical value** — the score associated with the shaded area that represents the level of significance, α. As α is selected prior to testing H_0 versus H_a, the C.V. does not depend on the test statistic, *TS*. In fact, *the C.V. always belongs to the hypothesized distribution, whereas the TS does so only when H_0 is true*. This is because the *TS* is based on a sample that comes from the hypothesized distribution *only when H_0 is true*. When H_0 is false, the *TS* can be entirely outside of the hypothesized distribution, thus producing a negligible *p*-value (e.g., $p < .001$). The critical value, C.V., can be determined by using a statistical table or some electronic tool (e.g., online calculators) of critical values for the *standard normal distribution, t-, F-,* or *chi-square* distributions — see Appendix, Tables A-1, A-2, A-3, and A-4.

NOTE [8.2] As shown in Figure 8.1, **we reject H_0 at the level of significance, α** (e.g., α = .05), when the sample-based test statistic, *TS*, falls in the interval beyond the critical value, C.V. (hence the name of this interval: **region of rejection**). Thus, there are two equivalent criteria for rejecting H_0: $p < \alpha$ or **TS > C.V.** (in absolute value). Scenarios in which the *region of rejection* is on the left tail (or split in the two tails) of the hypothesized distribution are discussed in the next sections.

8.3 Testing Hypotheses about the Mean

8.3.1 One-sample Case for the Mean

One-Sided Test. Suppose that the scores on a math proficiency test for the high school students in a given state are normally distributed and presented on a T-scale (μ = 50, σ = 10). Suppose also that the superintendent of a school district in this state claims that the high school students in this school district outperform the state norm of 50 points on the math proficiency test. This claim is based on the fact that the mean score of 25 randomly-selected high school students from this school district on the math proficiency test is 55 points (i.e., $n = 25$ and $\overline{X} = 55$).

If μ denotes the mean of the math proficiency test scores for the population of high school students in the superintendent's school district, then the claim that this school district's students "outperform" the state norm of 50 points on the math proficiency test can be translated as follows: μ > 50. Therefore, to check this claim, we define the following null and alternative hypotheses:

$$H_0: \mu = 50 \qquad \textbf{(8.2)}$$

$$H_a: \mu > 50.$$

In this case, H_a: μ > 50 is a **right-sided alternative hypothesis** [In other cases, H_a can be **left-sided** (e.g., μ < 50) or **non-directional** (e.g., μ ≠ 50).]

Clearly, if the null hypothesis (H_0: μ = 50) is true, the school district sample comes from the normal distribution of the state population, N(μ = 50, σ = 10). Therefore, the school district sample mean, $\overline{X} = 55$, must belong to the sampling distribution of the mean for the state population. According to the central limit theorem, this sampling distribution is normal, with a mean $\mu_{\overline{X}} = \mu = 50$ and a standard deviation $\sigma_{\overline{X}} = \sigma / \sqrt{n} = 10 / \sqrt{25} = 10/5 = 2$ (see Figure 7.5). Thus, if H_0 is true, $\overline{X} = 55$ must belong to the distribution N(μ = 50, $\sigma_{\overline{X}} = 2$). To make a decision about H_0 (*reject* or *fail to reject*), let's follow the five-step process described in section (8.2):

1. We select α = .05 as the level of significance.

2. To estimate the chances that $\overline{X} = 55$ belongs to the hypothesized normal distribution, N(μ = 50, $\sigma_{\overline{X}} = 2$), we determine the z-score for $\overline{X}$:

$$z = \frac{\overline{X} - \mu}{\sigma_{\overline{X}}} = \frac{55 - 50}{2} = 2.5.$$

3. Thus, if H_0 is true, the test statistic $z = 2.5$ must belong to the standard normal distribution, $N(0, 1)$.

4. As the alternative hypothesis is right-sided (H_a: $\mu > 50$), we place $\alpha = .05$ in the right tail of the distribution $N(0, 1)$ — see Figure 8.2. Looking at Table A-1 we see that the z-critical value is $z_\alpha = 1.65$. The area beyond the test statistic ($z = 2.5$) is .0062 [rounded to .006 in Table A-1]. Thus, the actual probability of making a Type I error (to falsely reject H_0) in this case is $p = .0062$.

5. **We reject H_0**, thus retaining the alternative hypothesis (H_a: $\mu > 50$), because the actual probability of falsely rejecting H_0 is smaller than the selected level of significance ($p < \alpha$). Equivalently, the test statistic ($z = 2.5$) exceeds the critical value ($z_\alpha = 1.65$), thus leading to the same decision to reject H_0.

Figure 8.2 *Right-sided test for the mean*

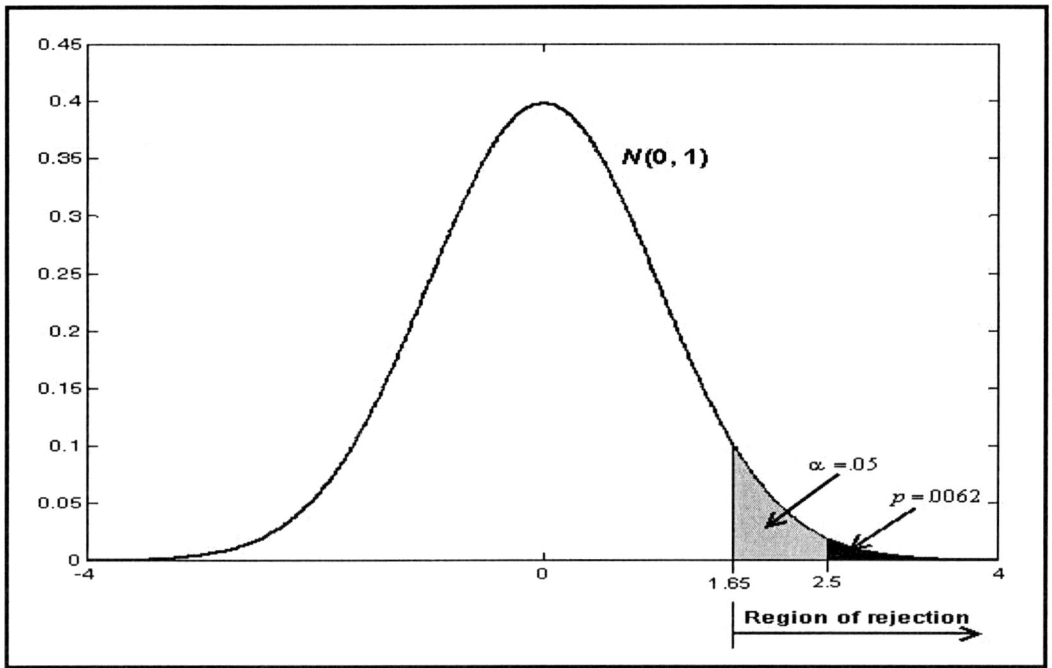

Two-sided test. Suppose now a second scenario in which, with everything else the same, the superintendent just wants to know whether the high school students from the given school district *differ* from the state norm of 50 points on the math proficiency test. In this case, the null hypothesis, H_0: $\mu = 50$, is tested against a **non-directional alternative hypothesis**, H_a: $\mu \neq 50$. This case is referred to also as **two-sided** (or **two-tailed**) **test**. [The non-directional test is performed here for illustration as we already know that $\mu > 50$ and, thus, $\mu \neq 50$.]

To perform the two-sided test, we repeat the first three steps in the right-sided test procedure described above. In Step 4, however, we split $\alpha = .05$ in the two tails of the standard normal distribution because this is a non-directional (two-sided) test. Thus, we place $\alpha/2 = .025$ in each tail of the distribution $N(0, 1)$ — see Figure 8.3. From Table A-1 we determine the critical value $z_{\alpha/2} = 1.96$ that corresponds to $\alpha/2 = .025$ in the right tail of $N(0, 1)$. Because the standard normal distribution, $N(0, 1)$, is symmetrical around zero, the critical value for $\alpha/2 = .025$ in the left tail of the distribution is -1.96. Thus, we have two critical values in this case: $\pm$ 1.96. As already shown in Step 2 with the one-sided test scenario above, the test statistic is $z = 2.5$. Since this test statistic exceeds 1.96 (the absolute value of the critical values ± 1.96), we still reject the null hypothesis H_0: μ = 50 and retain its non-directional alternative, H_a: μ ≠ 50, at the .05 level of significance.

Figure 8.3 *Non-directional (two-sided) test for the mean*

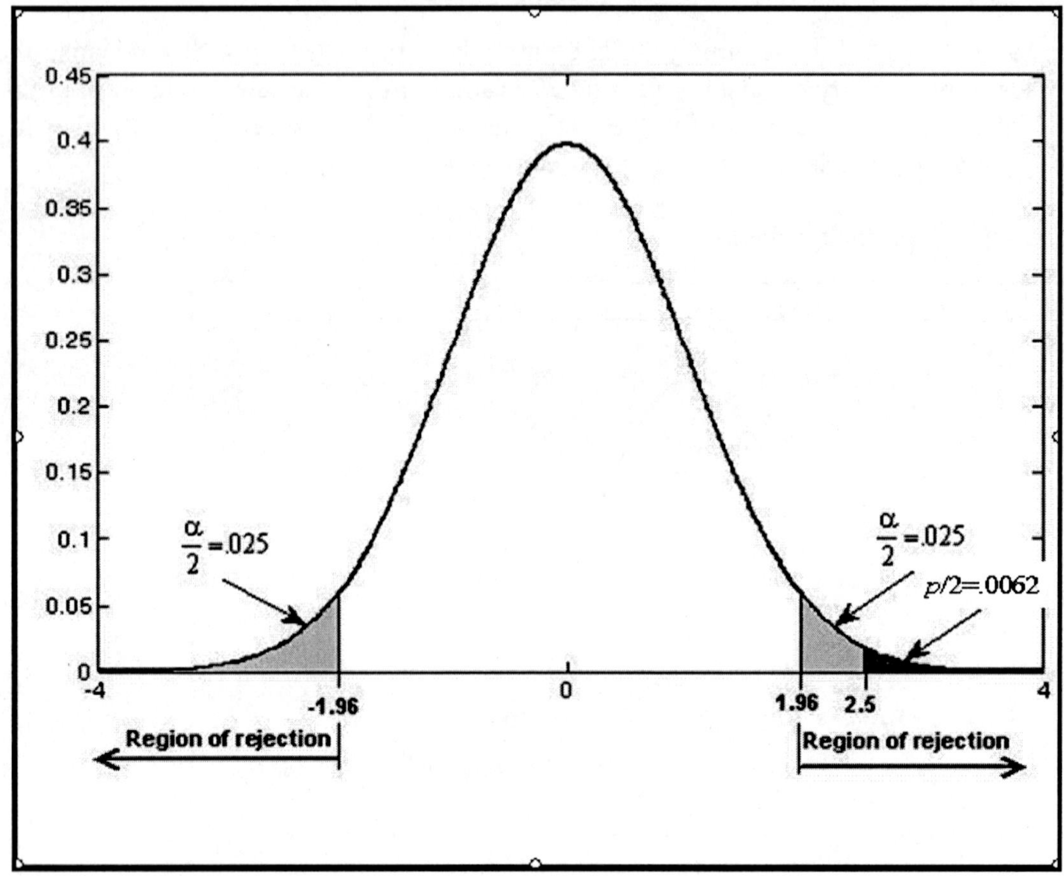

NOTE [8.3]. As you may notice, **the *power* of the one-sided test** (Figure 8.2) **is higher than that with the two-sided test** (Figure 8.3). That is, the one-sided test increases the chances for the researcher to reject H_0 when it is indeed false. This is because, with the test statistic being the same in both cases, the one-sided test produces a smaller *p*-value than the two-sided test. In this example, with $z = 2.5$ in both cases, the *p*-value for the one-sided test is $p = .0062$ (see Figure 8.2), whereas the *p*-value for the two-sided test is $p = .0062 + .0062 = .0124$ (see Figure 8.3).

Confidence interval for μ. By rejecting H_0: μ = 50 and retaining the alternative hypothesis H_a: μ > 50, we came to the conclusion that the school district's population outperforms the state norm of 50 points on the math proficiency test. However, we still don't know *how large* of a difference there is between the school district's population mean, μ, and the state norm, 50. Such information can be obtained by determining an interval within which the unknown mean, μ, falls. This interval is referred to as a **confidence interval (CI) for μ**.

Given the sample information ($n = 25$ and $\overline{X} = 55$) and the population standard deviation ($\sigma = 10$), the task is to construct a confidence interval for the population mean, μ. It is assumed that the standard deviation for the school district population is the same as that for the state population, σ = 10. As we already know, the standard error of the sample mean, $\overline{X}$, in this example is: $\sigma_{\overline{X}} = \sigma/\sqrt{n} = 10/\sqrt{25} = 10/5 = 2$. We also know that 95% of the sample means fall within an interval of ±1.96 standard errors around μ (see Figure 7.5). Thus, we can expect with 95% confidence that μ will fall within an interval of ±1.96 standard errors around $\overline{X}$. That is:

$$95\%\text{CI (for } \mu) = \overline{X} \pm (1.96)\sigma_{\overline{X}}. \quad \textbf{(8.3)}$$

With $\overline{X} = 55$ and $\sigma_{\overline{X}} = 2$, the 95% CI for the school district's population mean, μ, is then: 95%CI = 55 ± (1.96)(2) = 55 ± 3.92. So, the 95%CI for μ is from 51.08 to 58.92 (see Figure 8.4).

Figure 8.4 *95% confidence interval for μ*

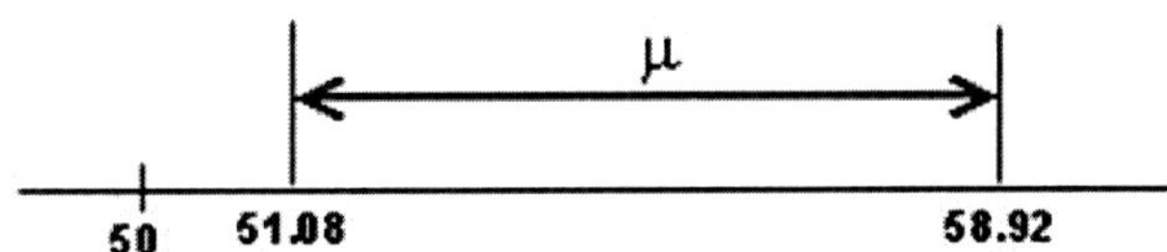

The 95%CI for μ in Figure 8.4 clearly shows that we can reject H_0: μ = 50 and retain the alternative H_a: μ > 50. The 95%CI also shows that μ exceeds 50 by at least 1.08, but not more than 8.92 points on the math proficiency test. This information can be used to evaluate the **practical importance** of the difference between the school district's mean, μ, and the state norm, 50. Suppose that a difference of *at least 10 points over the state norm* is considered to be practically important for the school district's performance on the math proficiency test (say, to qualify for additional funding for the math education program in this school district). If this is the case, in this example the difference between the school district's students' performance and the state norm of 50 points on the math proficiency test is statistically significant, but not practically important, because its smallest possible magnitude is 1.08 (not 10) points.

NOTE [8.4] The confidence interval for μ is non-directional (two-sided). In Formula 8.3, 95% "confidence" means 5% error (that is, α = .05) which entails the use of a critical value based on splitting α, that is: $z_{\alpha/2} = 1.96$ (see Figure 8.3). With 90%CI, for example, α = .10, so the critical value is $z_{\alpha/2} = 1.65$. In general, if the population standard deviation, σ, is known, the standard error of $\overline{X}$ is $\sigma_{\overline{X}} = \sigma/\sqrt{n}$ and the critical value is $z_{\alpha/2}$, so the formula for the confidence interval (CI) for μ is:

$$CI = \overline{X} \pm (z_{\alpha/2})\left(\frac{\sigma}{\sqrt{n}}\right). \quad \textbf{(8.4)}$$

When the population standard deviation, σ, is not known and its sample estimate, s, is used instead, the standard error of $\overline{X}$ is $s_{\overline{X}} = s/\sqrt{n}$. In this case, a critical value from the t-distribution ($t_{\alpha/2}$) is used to develop a confidence interval for μ:

$$CI = \overline{X} \pm (t_{\alpha/2})\left(\frac{s}{\sqrt{n}}\right). \quad \textbf{(8.5)}$$

EXAMPLE 8.2 Suppose that a sample of 64 observations is randomly selected from a normal distribution with (unknown) mean μ. Given that the mean and the standard deviation for this sample are 25 and 4, respectively, let us determine the 95%CI for μ. As the population standard deviation, σ, is not known, we will use Formula 8.5 with $n = 64$, $\overline{X} = 25$, and $s = 4$. We set $\alpha = .05$, and there are 63 degrees of freedom for this sample ($df = n - 1 = 64 - 1 = 63$). To construct the 95%CI, we use Table A-2 to find that the critical value ($t_{\alpha/2}$) with 63 degrees of freedom is $t_{\alpha/2} = 2.00$. Given this, we apply Formula 8.5 and we have:

$95\%CI = 25 \pm (2.00)\left(\frac{4}{\sqrt{64}}\right) = 25 \pm (2.00)\left(\frac{4}{8}\right) = 25 \pm 1$. Thus, the 95%CI for μ is from 24 to 26.

EXAMPLE 8.3 Using the confidence interval for μ constructed in Example 8.2, let us test the null hypothesis in two scenarios: (a) H_0: μ = 25.7 versus H_a: μ ≠ 25.7 and (b) H_0: μ = 30 versus H_a: μ < 30, at the .05 level of significance. The 95%CI for μ, as well as the values against which μ is compared (25.7 and 30), are depicted in Figure 8.5.

Figure 8.5 *95%CI for μ compared to two hypothesized values, 25.7 and 30*

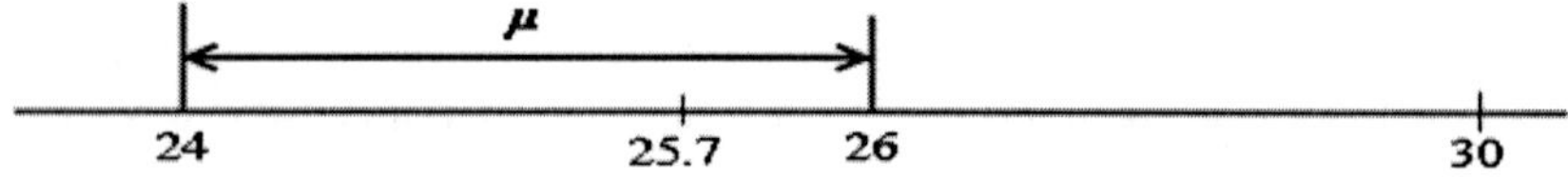

In scenario (a), H_0: μ = 25.7 versus the non-directional alternative H_a: μ ≠ 25.7, we fail to reject H_0 because the hypothesized value, 25.7, falls within the 95%CI for μ, so it is possible that μ = 25.7 [of course, this does not mean that H_0 is necessarily true but we have no evidence that it is not]. In scenario (b), H_0: μ = 30 versus the left-sided alternative H_a: μ < 30, we reject H_0 because the entire 95%CI for μ is below the hypothesized value, 30. In this case, we can also say that μ < 30 by at least 4, but not more than 6 points. In this same fashion, using the 95%CI for μ we can test μ against any hypothesized value, at the .05 level of significance.

NOTE [8.5] **The main advantages of using a confidence interval (CI) for μ in hypothesis testing,** compared to the five-step procedure described earlier in this section, are that we can (a) test μ against numerous hypothesized values simultaneously and (b) determine the smallest and the largest possible difference between μ and the hypothesized value when H_0 is rejected. **Keep in mind, however, that the CI testing is non-directional and, therefore, less powerful in retaining a one-sided alternative hypotheses.** In any case, it is strongly recommended (and most professional journals in education and related fields require) that confidence intervals are reported.

In Formulas 8.4 and 8.5, the amount that we add and subtract from $\overline{X}$ to obtain the CI for μ is referred to as the **margin of error** (*ME*); that is: CI = $\overline{X} \pm ME$. In the case of Formula 8.4, for example, the margin of error is

$$ME = (z_{\alpha/2})\left(\frac{\sigma}{\sqrt{n}}\right). \tag{8.6}$$

We can reduce the margin error by (a) increasing the sample size, *n*, and/or (b) increasing the probability for Type I error, α, thus obtaining a smaller critical value, $z_{\alpha/2}$. For example, with $\alpha = .05$ (95%CI), the critical value is $z_{\alpha/2} = 1.96$, whereas with $\alpha = .10$ (90%CI), the critical value is smaller: $z_{\alpha/2} = 1.65$. Smaller *ME* narrows the confidence interval (CI) for μ, thus providing a more accurate estimation of μ and increasing the power in hypothesis testing by making it more likely to reject H_0.

NOTE [8.6]. A 95%CI for μ means that if we construct all possible 95%CIs using the sample means of all possible samples of size *n*, 95% of these confidence intervals would contain μ and 5% would not. Therefore, a specific 95%CI either contains μ or it does not. The same holds for 90%CI, 99%CI, etc.

Using SPSS to test H_0: μ = *a*. Testing hypotheses about the population mean, μ, compared to a hypothesized value, *a*, can be easily performed using SPSS. Let's illustrate this using the familiar SPSS data file **Employee data** (see Figure 6.4). We are interested in the variable "**educ**" — years of education for the employees in the data set. The SPSS label for this variable is **Educational Level (years)**. Suppose that we want to know whether the educational level for the population of employees exceeds 10 years. To answer this question, we test the null hypothesis H_0: μ = 10 versus H_a: μ > 10, say, at the .05 level of significance. In SPSS, this can be done by following the steps below:

1. Click **Analyze**, click **Compare Means**, and click **One-Sample T Test.**
2. Click on **Educational Level (years)** and then click ► to move this variable into the box **Test Variable(s)** — see Figure 8.6.
3. In the box **Test Value**, enter the hypothesized value (10) specified in the null hypothesis, H_0 (see Figure 8.6).
4. Click **OK**.

Figure 8.6 *One-sample t-test using SPSS with the Employee data file*

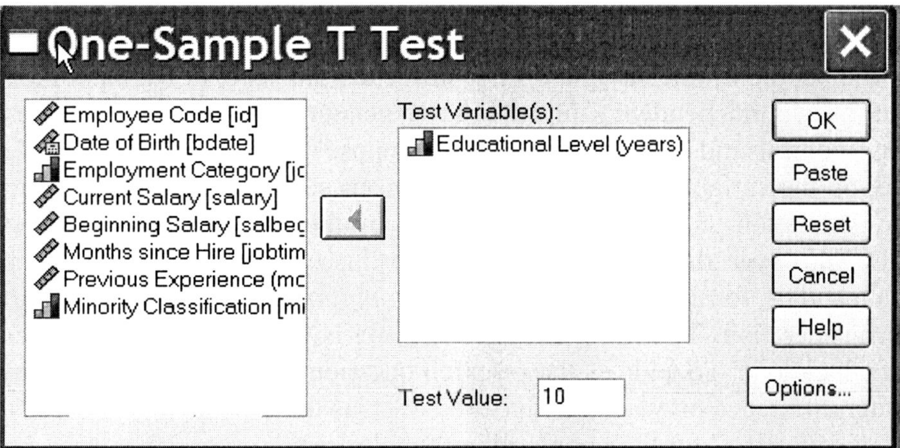

The SPSS output is provided in Figure 8.7. As the p-value associated with the t-statistic (p = .000) is smaller than the level of significance (α = .05), we reject the null hypothesis, H_0: μ = 10. Further, we see that the 95%CI for the difference (μ - 10) is from 3.23 to 3.75, so $\mu > 10$ by at least 3.23, but not more than 3.77. Thus, the educational level of the employees exceeds 10 years by a magnitude between 3.23 and 3.77 years.

Figure 8.7 *SPSS output for the one-sample t-test (H_0: μ = 10)*

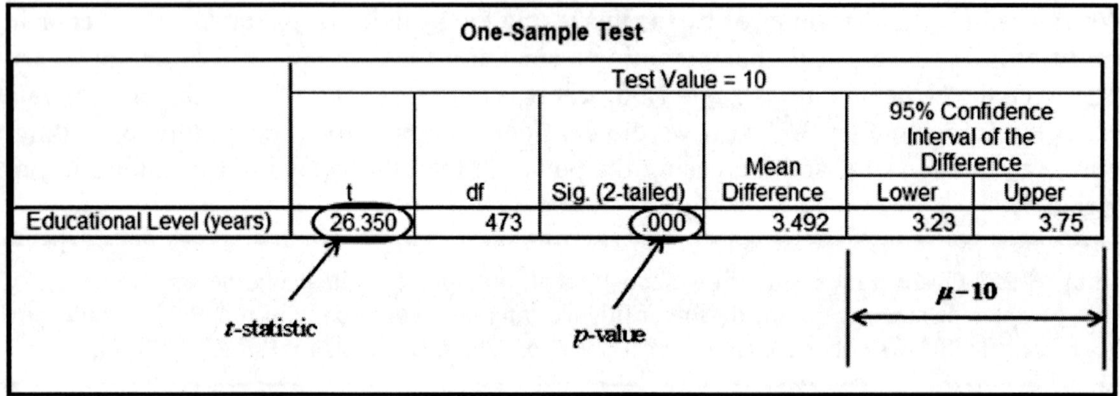

One-Sample Test

	Test Value = 10					
					95% Confidence Interval of the Difference	
	t	df	Sig. (2-tailed)	Mean Difference	Lower	Upper
Educational Level (years)	26.350	473	.000	3.492	3.23	3.75

It is also important that we start practicing the presentation of results in a format and style requested for educational research documents such as papers, course projects, dissertations, etc. Hereafter, our efforts in this regard will be reflected in summary notes that present results according to requirements documented in the Manual of the American Psychological Association (APA, 2001) — **APA style**. For example, an APA style presentation of the results in Figure 8.7 is provided in NOTE [8.7].

NOTE [8.7] Reporting in APA style: The results from the one-sample t-test in Figure 8.7 show that there is a statistically significant difference between the mean educational level (in years) for the population of employees and the hypothesized value of 10 years, $t(473) = 26.35, p < .001$. The 95 percent confidence interval for this difference shows that, on average, the educational level of the employees exceeds the hypothesized value of 10 years by a magnitude of 3.23 to 3.75 years.

8.3.2 Two-sample Case for the Mean: Independent Samples

There are many situations in educational research that lead to testing hypotheses about two population means. In this section we discuss testing hypotheses for two **independent samples** — i.e., the scores of the people in one sample do not influence the scores of the people in the other sample. Examples of two independent samples are two gender groups (males, females), two treatment groups (e.g., control and experimental), etc. Suppose that we are interested in possible gender differences on the variable discussed in the previous section: years of education (educational level) for the population of employees represented by the sample of 474 observations in the SPSS data file **Employee data** (see Figure 6.4). In this case, μ_1 will stand for the mean of the *male population* and μ_2, for the mean of the *female population*, on years of education for the employees under consideration. The **independent variable** is "gender" and the **dependent variable** is "years of education." To address the research question, we will test the null hypothesis, "There is no gender difference on years of education" versus the alternative, "There is a gender difference in years of education" for the population of employees:

$$H_0: \mu_1 = \mu_2$$
$$H_a: \mu_1 \neq \mu_2. \quad \textbf{(8.7)}$$

The hypotheses in (8.7) represent a general case referred to as a **two-sample case for the mean.** The null and alternative hypotheses in (8.7) can also be represented as follows:

$$H_0: \mu_1 - \mu_2 = 0$$
$$H_a: \mu_1 - \mu_2 \neq 0. \quad \textbf{(8.8)}$$

Of course, depending on the research question, the alternative hypothesis can be also right-sided (H_a: $\mu_1 - \mu_2 > 0$) or left-sided (H_a: $\mu_1 - \mu_2 < 0$). The logic of testing in the two-sample case for the mean (H_0: $\mu_1 - \mu_2 = 0$) is analogous to that in one-sample case for the mean (H_0: $\mu - a = 0$, where a is a specified number). In both cases, we (a) calculate an appropriate test statistic from the sample(s) and determine the p-value associated with this statistic, or (b) construct an appropriate confidence interval. In the two-sample case for the mean, the confidence interval for the mean difference $\mu_1 - \mu_2$ is constructed around the *difference* of the two sample means, $\overline{X}_1 - \overline{X}_2$, using the standard error of this difference, $s_{\overline{X}_1 - \overline{X}_2}$. The formula for $s_{\overline{X}_1 - \overline{X}_2}$ takes on two different forms depending on the two population variances, so it is necessary to determine whether the variances of the two populations are equal $(\sigma_1^2 = \sigma_2^2)$ or not equal $(\sigma_1^2 \neq \sigma_2^2)$. The test for equal population variances is referred to as the **homogeneity of variance** test (see NOTE [8.8]).

NOTE [8.8] Testing for homogeneity of variance. Suppose that two samples are randomly selected from two populations with unknown means (μ_1 and μ_2) and variances (σ_1^2 and σ_2^2). The sample size, mean, and variance for each sample are known: n_1, $\overline{X}_1$, s_1^2, for the first sample, and n_2, $\overline{X}_2$, s_2^2, for the second sample (for convenience, we assume here that s_1^2 is the larger variance). The test of the null hypothesis "equal population variances" $(H_0^*: \sigma_1^2 = \sigma_2^2)$ against the alternative "not equal population variances" $(H_a^*: \sigma_1^2 \neq \sigma_2^2)$ is performed as follows:

1. Calculate the F-ratio of the two sample variances, referred to as the F-statistic:

$$F = \frac{s_1^2}{s_2^2}, \quad \textbf{(8.9)}$$

where s_1^2 is the larger sample variance. As we already know, the *degrees of freedom* for this F-statistic are $df_1 = n_1 - 1$, for the variance in the numerator, and $df_2 = n_2 - 1$, for the variance in the denominator (see Chapter 7.3).

2. Find the F-critical value, using Table A-4 for $df_1 = n_1 - 1$, $df_2 = n_2 - 1$, and the selected level of significance (say, $\alpha = .05$).

3. Reject the null hypothesis of "equal population variances" $(H_0^*: \sigma_1^2 = \sigma_2^2)$ if the F-statistic exceeds the F-critical value. Equivalently, if the p-value associated with the F-statistic is obtained (e.g., by using SPSS), reject $H_0^*: \sigma_1^2 = \sigma_2^2$ when $p < \alpha$ (see Figure 8.1).

EXAMPLE 8.4 Suppose that the sample size and the variance for two samples are n_1 = 25, $s_1^2 = 18$ and n_2= 41, $s_2^2 = 12$, respectively. The first sample is randomly selected from a population with a variance σ_1^2, while the second sample is randomly selected from a population with a variance σ_2^2. To test for homogeneity of variance in this case, we follow the three-step approach described in NOTE [8.8]. First, the *F*-ratio in this example is $F = 18/12 = 1.5$. Second, given the level of significance (say, $\alpha = .05$) and the degrees of freedom ($df_1 = n_1 - 1 = 24$ and $df_2 = n_2 - 1 = 40$), we use Table A-4 to find the *F*-critical value: $F_{c.v} = 1.79$. Third, we fail to reject the null hypothesis of "equal population variances" because the *F*-statistic (1.5) does not exceed the *F*-critical value (1.79). Thus, we assume equal population variances: $\sigma_1^2 = \sigma_2^2$. The formulas for $s_{\overline{X}_1 - \overline{X}_2}$ and degrees of freedom (*df*) are provided in Table 8.1.

Table 8.1 *Formulas for the standard error* $s_{\overline{X}_1 - \overline{X}_2}$ *and the degrees of freedom (df) with the t-test for* H_0: $\mu_1 - \mu_2 = 0$ (*two-sample case for the mean*).

Equal variances: $\sigma_1^2 = \sigma_2^2$	**Not equal variances:** $\sigma_1^2 \neq \sigma_2^2$
$s_{\overline{X}_1 - \overline{X}_2} = \sqrt{s^2\left(\frac{1}{n_1} + \frac{1}{n_2}\right)}$, where $s^2 = \frac{(n_1 - 1)s_1^2 + (n_2 - 1)s_2^2}{n_1 + n_2 - 2}$ is the **pooled estimate of the population variance** (see Formula 6.6).	$s_{\overline{X}_1 - \overline{X}_2} = \sqrt{\frac{s_1^2}{n_1} + \frac{s_2^2}{n_2}}$
$df = n_1 + n_2 - 2$	$df = \frac{(A + B)^2}{A^2/(n_1 - 1) + B^2/(n_2 - 1)}$, where $A = \frac{s_1^2}{n_1}$ and $B = \frac{s_2^2}{n_2}$.

After determining whether the population variances are equal (or not equal), we can proceed with testing the null hypothesis of equal population means (H_0: $\mu_1 - \mu_2 = 0$).

- **Conducting a *t*-test for H_0: μ_1 - μ_2 = 0.** The test statistic used with this approach is the following *t*-statistic:

$$t = \frac{\overline{X}_1 - \overline{X}_2}{s_{\overline{X}_1 - \overline{X}_2}}. \qquad \textbf{(8.10)}$$

The decision about the null hypothesis (H_0: $\mu_1 - \mu_2 = 0$) is based on the *p*-value associated with this statistic under a *t*-distribution with certain degrees of freedom, *df*. Specifically, we reject H_0 when the *p*-value is smaller than the level of significance, α ($p < \alpha$).

• **Constructing a confidence interval (CI) to test H_0: $\mu_1 - \mu_2 = 0$.** The confidence interval for the difference $\mu_1 - \mu_2$ can be constructed as follows:

$$\text{CI} = \overline{X} \pm (t_{\alpha/2})(s_{\overline{X}_1 - \overline{X}_2}), \tag{8.11}$$

where $t_{\alpha/2}$ is the *t*-critical value associated with the pre-established level of significance, α. The notation $t_{\alpha/2}$ indicates that α is "split in half" in the two tails of the *t*-distribution because the confidence interval (CI) is non-directional. We reject the null hypothesis (H_0: $\mu_1 - \mu_2 = 0$) when "zero" does not belong to the confidence interval for the difference ($\mu_1 - \mu_2$) — that is, when the hypothesized $\mu_1 - \mu_2 = 0$ cannot occur at the selected level of confidence. Otherwise, we fail to reject H_0.

Figure 8.8 *Three cases of confidence intervals for μ_1 - μ_2 and their interpretation*

Scenario A: Testing H_0: $\mu_1 - \mu_2 = 0$ against H_0: $\mu_1 - \mu_2 \neq 0$.

$\mu_1 - \mu_2$

-2.5 4.5

Interpretation: Fail to reject H_0: $\mu_1 - \mu_2 = 0$ because "zero" belongs to the confidence interval thus making it possible that $\mu_1 - \mu_2 = 0$; [*Hint*: Always fail to reject H_0 when the lower end of the confidence interval (CI) for μ_1 - μ_2 is a negative number and the upper end is a positive number because this implies that "zero" belongs to the confidence interval.]

Scenario B: Testing H_0: $\mu_1 - \mu_2 = 0$ against H_0: $\mu_1 - \mu_2 > 0$.

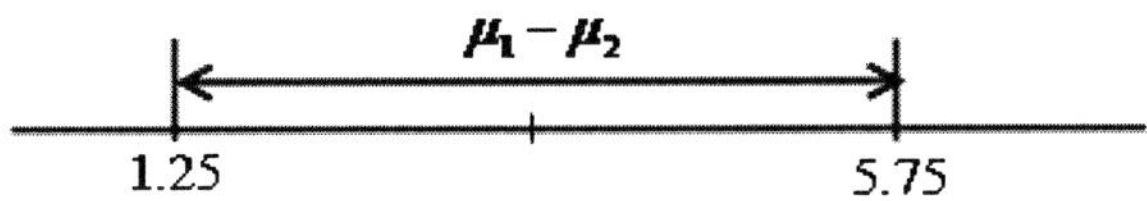

Interpretation: Reject H_0 and retain the alternative H_0: $\mu_1 - \mu_2 > 0$ because the difference $\mu_1 - \mu_2$ can take only positive values. Specifically, $\mu_1 > \mu_2$ by at least 1.25, but not more than 5.75.

Scenario C: Testing H_0: $\mu_1 - \mu_2 = 0$ against H_0: $\mu_1 - \mu_2 < 0$.

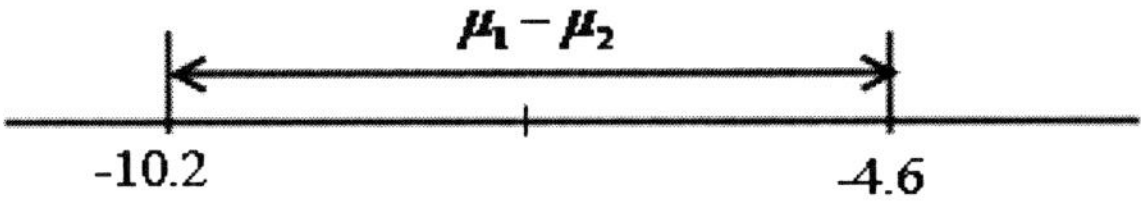

Interpretation: Reject H_0 and retain the alternative H_0: $\mu_1 - \mu_2 < 0$ because the difference $\mu_1 - \mu_2$ can take only negative values. Specifically, $\mu_1 < \mu_2$ by at least 4.6, but not more than 10.2.

- **Using SPSS to test H_0: $\mu_1 - \mu_2 = 0$.** The SPSS file **Employee data** (see Figure 6.4) is used here to test H_0: $\mu_1 - \mu_2 = 0$, where μ_1 and μ_2 are the population means on **Educational Level** (years of education) for males and females, coded **m** and **f**, respectively. The SPSS steps are:

  1. Click **Analyze**, click **Compare Means**, and click **Independent-Samples T Test**.
  2. Click **Educational Level** and then click ► to move this variable into the box **Test Variable(s)** (as shown in Figure 8.9).
  3. Click **gender** and then click ► to move this variable into the box **Grouping Variable**.
  4. Click **Define Groups**, type **m** in the box **Group 1** and type **f** in the box **Group 2**.
  5. Click **OK**.

The resulting SPSS table **Independent Samples Test** is shown in Figure 8.9.

Figure 8.9 *SPSS t-test for two independent samples*

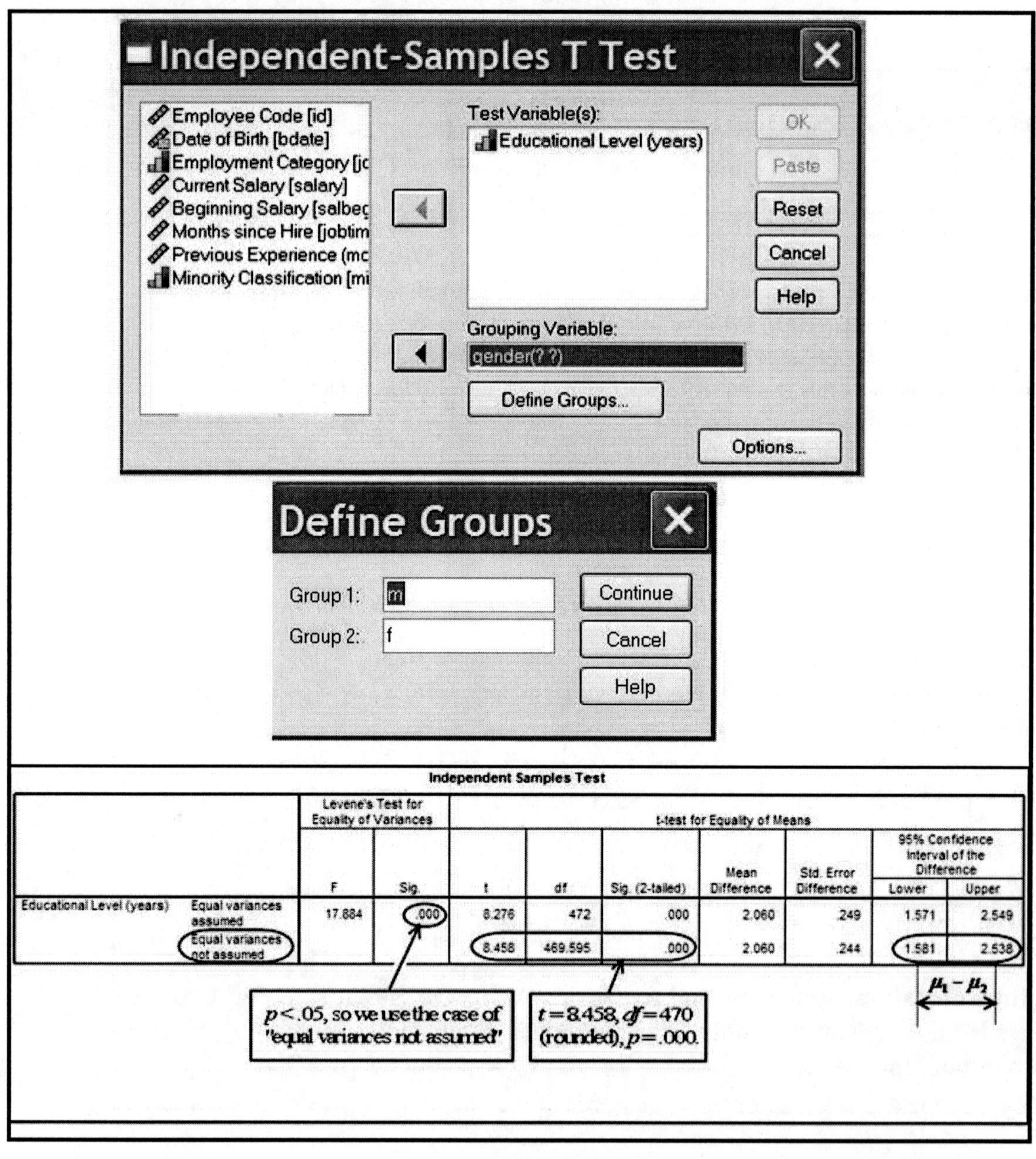

Independent Samples Test

		Levene's Test for Equality of Variances		t-test for Equality of Means						
									95% Confidence Interval of the Difference	
		F	Sig.	t	df	Sig. (2-tailed)	Mean Difference	Std. Error Difference	Lower	Upper
Educational Level (years)	Equal variances assumed	17.884	.000	8.276	472	.000	2.060	.249	1.571	2.549
	Equal variances not assumed			8.458	469.595	.000	2.060	.244	1.581	2.538

As the p-value in the Levene's test for equality of variances is sufficiently small (p = .000), we reject the null hypothesis of equal variances and interpret the results related to the case "equal variances not assumed" in the SPSS table **Independent Samples Test.** The t-test for equality of means test shows that there is a statistically significant difference between males and females on years of education, $t(470) = 8.46, p < .001$. Rounded to the nearest hundredth, the 95%CI for the difference $\mu_1 - \mu_2$ is (1.58, 2.54), so $\mu_1 > \mu_2$ by at least 1.58, but no more than 2.54. Thus, there is gender disparity in years of education in favor of males for the population of employees.

8.3.3 Two-sample Case for the Mean: Dependent Samples

Many research situations in educational research involve testing hypotheses about two samples for which the scores in one sample are related to those in the other sample. These are called **dependent samples**. For example, studies that use pretest and posttest data deal with dependent samples because the pretest and posttest scores are correlated — typically, high pretest scores relate to high posttest scores and low pretest scores relate to low posttest scores. Another example of two dependent samples are the survey responses of husbands and their wives on household-related questions (e.g., on a Likert-type scale).

- **Testing H_0: $\mu_1 = \mu_2$ for two dependent samples**. The two-sample case for the mean with dependent samples is discussed here in the context of pretest-posttest data. Specifically, the data in Table 8.2 represent the pretest scores (X_1) and posttest scores (X_2) on an anxiety test of ten students (n = 10) before and after participating in two therapy sessions that were intended to reduce anxiety.

Table 8.2 *Pretest-posttest anxiety measures*

Student ID	Pretest X_1	Posttest X_2	Difference D
1	32	28	**4**
2	38	38	**0**
3	26	22	**4**
4	35	30	**5**
5	19	18	**1**
6	20	20	**0**
7	30	28	**2**
8	36	33	**3**
9	44	40	**4**
10	30	29	**1**

In this example, the alternative hypothesis is H_a: $\mu_1 > \mu_2$, because it is expected that the anxiety measures prior to the therapy sessions would be higher than those after such sessions. Written in the "difference" format discussed in the previous section, the null and alternative hypotheses are:

$$H_0: \mu_1 - \mu_2 = 0$$
$$H_a: \mu_1 - \mu_2 > 0$$

In Table 8.2, $D = X_1 - X_2$, which is the difference between the two dependent samples (pretest and posttest) on the anxiety scale. If s_D is the standard deviation of this difference, the standard error of the mean difference, $\overline{D} = \overline{X}_1 - \overline{X}_2$, is:

$$s_{\overline{D}} = \frac{s_D}{\sqrt{n}}. \quad \textbf{(8.12)}$$

Given the *standard error of the difference*, $s_{\overline{D}}$, the test statistic for H_0: $\mu_1 - \mu_2 = 0$ is:

$$t = \frac{\overline{D}}{s_{\overline{D}}} = \frac{\overline{D}}{\frac{s_D}{\sqrt{n}}}. \quad \textbf{(8.13)}$$

• **Confidence interval for $\mu_1 - \mu_2$ with two dependent samples.** Given the mean difference, $\overline{D}$, and its standard error, $s_{\overline{D}}$, the confidence interval for $\mu_1 - \mu_2$ is

$$\text{CI} = \overline{D} \pm (t_{\alpha/2})\left(\frac{s_D}{\sqrt{n}}\right), \quad \textbf{(8.14)}$$

where $t_{\alpha/2}$ is the critical value for the respective level of significance under a *t*-distribution with degrees of freedom $df = n - 1$; [$t_{\alpha/2}$ is based on splitting α because the confidence interval in non-directional.]

For the data in Table 8.2, we will test H_0: $\mu_1 - \mu_2 = 0$ at the $\alpha = .05$ level. The mean and the standard deviation of the difference, *D*, are $\overline{D} = 2.40$ and $s_D = 1.838$, respectively. Using Formula 8.12, we calculate $s_{\overline{D}} = 1.838/\sqrt{10} = 0.581$. Then, using Formula 8.13, we obtain the *t*-statistic: $t = \overline{D}/s_{\overline{D}} = 2.40/0.581 = 4.13$. Given that the alternative hypothesis H_a: $\mu_1 - \mu_2 > 0$ is right-sided, we place $\alpha = .05$ in the right tail of the *t*-distribution ($df = n - 1 = 10 - 1 = 9$) thus obtaining the right-sided critical value $t_\alpha = 1.833$ (see Table A-2). As the test statistic (4.13) exceeds the critical value (1.833), we reject H_0 at the .05 level. To estimate the magnitude of the pretest-posttest decrease in student anxiety, we construct the 95% confidence interval for the difference $\mu_1 - \mu_2$ using Formula 8.14: 95%CI = 2.40 ± (2.262)(0.581) = 2.40 ± 1.31; [The critical value is now $t_{\alpha/2} = 2.262$ (see Table A-2) because the CI is non-directional.] Thus, the 95%CI for $\mu_1 - \mu_2$ is: 95%CI = (1.09, 3.71). This indicates that $\mu_1 > \mu_2$ by at least 1.09, but no more than 3.71. We can say now that the students' anxiety decreased over the period of therapy sessions by a magnitude from 1.09 to 3.71 points on the anxiety scale.

• **Using SPSS to test H_0: $\mu_1 = \mu_2$ for two dependent samples.** The SPSS entry for the data in Table 8.2 is shown in Figure 8.10 (left panel). To test the null hypothesis (H_0: $\mu_1 = \mu_2$) in the context of these data using SPSS, follow the steps:

1. Click **Analyze**, click **Compare Means**, and click **Paired-Samples T Test**.
2. While holding the **Ctrl** key, click **X1**, click **X2**, and then click ▶ to move these two variables into the box **Paired Variables** — see Figure 8.10 (right panel).
3. Click **OK**.

The key table in the resulting SPSS output (**Paired Samples Test** table) is provided at the bottom in Figure 8.10. As can be seen, the results in this table match those obtained in the previous section: $\overline{D} = 2.40$, $s_D = 1.838$, $s_{\overline{D}} = 0.581$, $t = 4.13$, and 95%CI = (1.09, 3.71).

Figure 8.10 *SPSS t-test for two dependent (paired) samples*

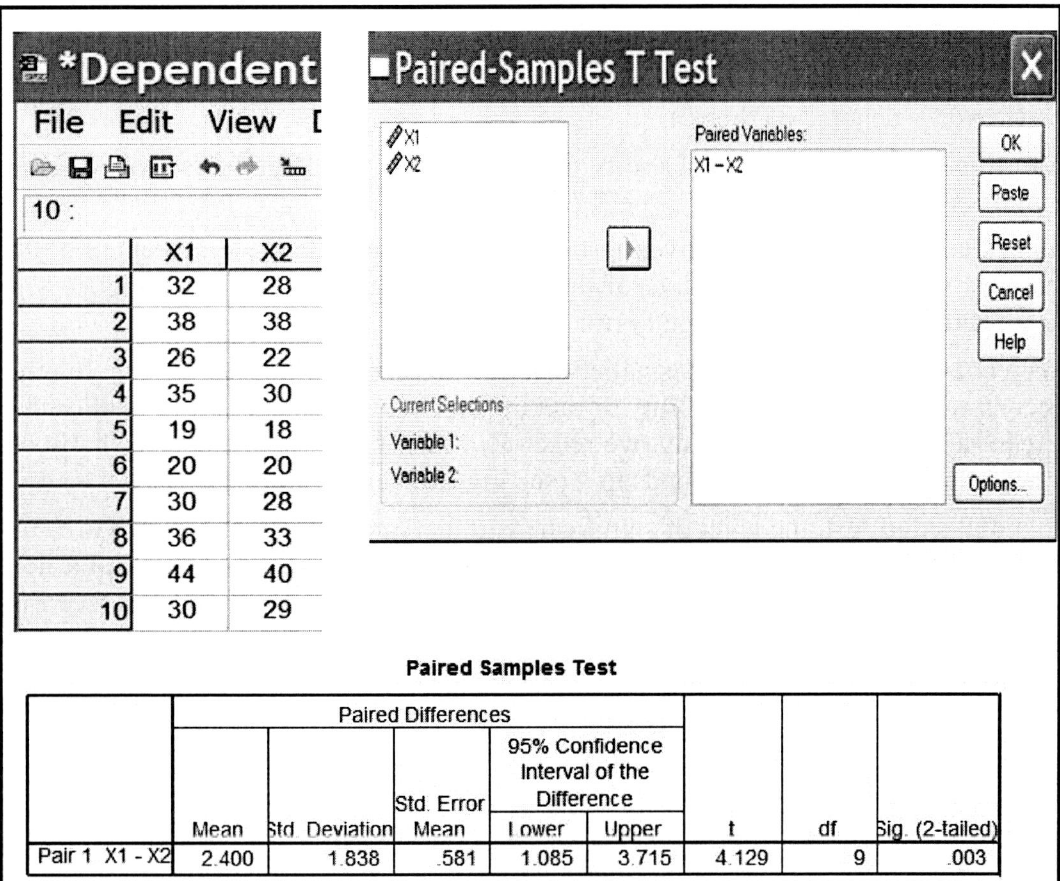

	X1	X2
1	32	28
2	38	38
3	26	22
4	35	30
5	19	18
6	20	20
7	30	28
8	36	33
9	44	40
10	30	29

Paired Samples Test

	Paired Differences					t	df	Sig. (2-tailed)
				95% Confidence Interval of the Difference				
	Mean	Std. Deviation	Std. Error Mean	Lower	Upper			
Pair 1 X1 - X2	2.400	1.838	.581	1.085	3.715	4.129	9	.003

8.4 Summary

This chapter describes the general logic of hypothesis testing. The topic of testing hypotheses about population mean(s) is addressed in the context of a one-sample case for the mean (H_0: $\mu = a$) and a two-sample case for the mean (H_0: $\mu_1 = \mu_2$) in the cases of independent samples and dependent samples. The testing procedures and related analytic tools (formulas) are illustrated with examples and SPSS applications. A brief bulleted summary of this chapter follows.

- **Hypothesis testing** is a process of using statistical procedures and reasoning to make inferences about the population based on sample observations. Any hypothesis represents a statement about statistical relationships between population parameters (e.g., population means, proportions, variances, correlations, etc.).
- A research question is addressed by testing a **null hypothesis** (H_0) versus an **alternative hypothesis**, H_a. The null hypothesis states that the relationship targeted with the question does not exist, whereas its alternative states that the relationship does exist.
- **Type I error** occurs when we reject a true null hypothesis (that is, when we falsely reject H_0). *Prior* to testing a hypothesis, the researcher must decide what chances of making a Type I error are acceptable.

• The acceptable probability of making a Type I error is referred to as the **level of significance** [or **alpha (α) level**]. For example, $\alpha = .05$ (traditionally used in behavioral research) indicates that up to 5% chances of error are acceptable when H_0 is rejected.

• **Type II error** occurs when we fail to reject a false null hypothesis. The probability of making a Type II error is denoted β ("beta").

• The **power** of the test is the probability of rejecting the null hypothesis when it is indeed false. With β being the probability of Type II error, **Power = 1 – β.**

• The ***p*-value** associated with a given test statistic is the probability represented by the area beyond the test statistic under the curve of the hypothesized distribution (see Figure 8.1). The *p*-value is the actual probability of Type I error.

• We **reject H_0** when the *p*-value is smaller than the level of significance ($p < \alpha$). In other words, we reject H_0 when the actual probability of making an error in doing so (p) is smaller than that which we can "afford" (α). Equivalently, we reject H_0 when the test statistic exceeds (in absolute value) the critical value that corresponds to α (see Figure 8.1).

• With a **one-sided test**, the level of significance, α, is represented by a one-tail area under the curve of the hypothesized distribution (see Figure 8.2 for a right-tail test). With a non-directional (two-sided) test, α is "split" in the two-tails of the hypothesized distribution (see Figure 8.3; note that in this case the area beyond the test statistic is only "half" of the *p*-value, $p/2$).

• The testing of H_0**: μ = *a*** (one-sample case for the mean) is performed by using a *z*-test, when the population standard deviation, σ, is known, or a *t*-test when a sample standard deviation, *s*, is used instead. Likewise, the confidence interval for **μ** is computed by Formula 8.4, when σ is known, or Formula 8.5 when its sample estimate, *s*, is used instead.

• To test H_0**: $\mu_1 - \mu_2 = 0$** (independent samples) the researcher must first know whether the population variances are equal or not equal. This is called the **homogeneity of variance assumption** $(H_0^*: \sigma_1^2 = \sigma_2^2)$, and it is tested by the *F*-test described in NOTE [8.8]. The formulas for the standard error of the sample mean difference, $s_{\bar{X}_1 - \bar{X}_2}$, are provided in Table 8.1. The *t*-test statistic is computed by Formula 8.10 and the confidence interval for the difference $\mu_1 - \mu_2$ is computed by Formula 8.11.

• The testing of H_0**: $\mu_1 - \mu_2 = 0$** (dependent samples) is based on a *t*-test statistic — the ratio of the mean difference between the paired observation in the two dependent samples, $\bar{D} = \bar{X}_1 - \bar{X}_2$, and its standard error, $s_{\bar{D}}$ (Formula 8.13). The confidence interval for $\mu_1 - \mu_2$ is computed by Formula 8.14.

8.5 Study Questions

1. When a false null hypothesis is retained, this is a matter of

   A. Type I error, **B.** Type II error, **C.** Power, **D.** None of the above.

2. The probability of rejecting a false null hypothesis is called

   A. Type I error, **B.** Type II error, **C.** Power, **D.** None of the above.

3. If there are 20% chances of retaining a false null hypothesis, the chances of rejecting this hypothesis are

   A. 20% **B.** 50%, **C.** 80%, **D.** None of the above.

4. Given is the SPSS data set **Pretest-Posttest** for the pretest and posttest scores on a math test of 30 students of which 11 are males ($n_1 = 11$) and 19 are females ($n_2 = 19$). Answer the following questions and perform the related tasks as requested:

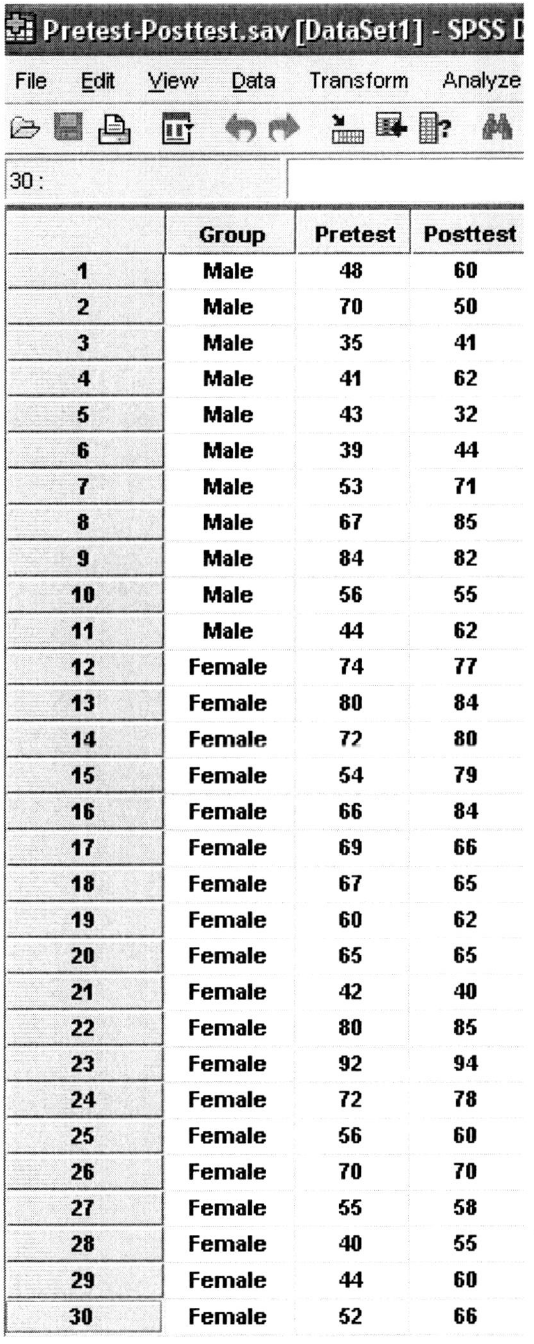

	Group	Pretest	Posttest
1	Male	48	60
2	Male	70	50
3	Male	35	41
4	Male	41	62
5	Male	43	32
6	Male	39	44
7	Male	53	71
8	Male	67	85
9	Male	84	82
10	Male	56	55
11	Male	44	62
12	Female	74	77
13	Female	80	84
14	Female	72	80
15	Female	54	79
16	Female	66	84
17	Female	69	66
18	Female	67	65
19	Female	60	62
20	Female	65	65
21	Female	42	40
22	Female	80	85
23	Female	92	94
24	Female	72	78
25	Female	56	60
26	Female	70	70
27	Female	55	58
28	Female	40	55
29	Female	44	60
30	Female	52	66

4.1 Test the claim that females outperform males on the posttest given that for Group 1 (males) the mean and the standard deviation on the posttest are 58.55 and 16.56, whereas for Group 2 (females) they are 69.89 and 13.13, respectively. Perform this manually by first testing for homogeneity of variance [see Example 8.4] and then computing the *t*-test statistic as well as the 95% CI [see Formulas 8.10 and 8.11]. Use the .05 level of significance.

4.2 Test the claim in 4.1 using SPSS [enter the data in SPSS as shown in the left panel. Use gender coding, say 1 = male, 2 = female].

4.3 Test the claim that the students (males and females together) have improved their math test performance over the time period from the pretest to the posttest. Perform the testing at the .05 level of significance using SPSS [see Figure 8.10]

4.4 Test whether males and females differ in the change (gain) from pretest to posttest. [*Hint*: First compute a new variable, say **gain**, which equals the change from pretest to posttest: gain = Posttest – Pretest. Then use the *t*-test for independent samples to compare males and females on gain as the dependent variable.]

5. For the SPSS data file **Employee data.sav** (see Figure 6.4), use SPSS to test the claim that there is a statistically significant increase in dollar amount from **beginning salary** to **current salary** for the population of employees.

6. For the SPSS data file **Employee data.sav**, use SPSS to test the claim that the average current salary for the population of employees exceeds $30,000.

7. Still for the SPSS data file **Employee data.sav**, test the claim that males and females do not differ in salary increase from **beginning salary** to **current salary.**

CHAPTER 9

HYPOTHESIS TESTING FOR PROPORTIONS

Many questions the field of education and the social sciences lead to testing hypotheses about proportions (or their percentage equivalents). For example, a school principal may want to know whether more than 30 percent of the students are getting parental help on homework assignments. As another example, a state governor may decide to sign a bill on additional funding for free school lunch programs if more than 60 percent of the state population of students are eligible for free lunch. A third example is when a researcher wants to know whether the percent of supporters of a sensitive issue might change after a video session on that issue. Or, a polling agency may want to determine whether Republicans and Democrats nationwide support at equal rates a recently-proposed bill on tax relief. Although such questions are usually asked in "percentages," the related statistical hypotheses always relate to population proportions. This is due to theoretical considerations which are beyond the scope of this book. Of course, this is not a problem for the interpretation of the results of such hypothesis tests, given that the translation from percentages to proportions and vice-versa is straightforward.

9.1 One-Sample Case for Proportion

• **Testing H_0: $P = a$.** This section deals with testing whether the proportion of individuals who fall into one of two possible categories (e.g., "Yes" = support a tax bill, "No" = do not support a tax bill), P, equals a hypothesized value, a. It is clear that if P is the proportion of individuals in the category of interest (e.g., "Yes"), then $1 - P$ is the proportion of individuals in the other category (e.g., "No"). When necessary, the category of interest will be referred to in this section as the **reference category** and the other category, as the **complementary category**.

Consider the example in which a school principal wants to know whether more than 30 percent of the students are getting help from their parents on homework assignments. If P stands for the population proportion of students in this school who are getting such help, the null hypothesis in this case is H_0: $P = .30$. As the question is whether *more* than 30 percent of students are getting parental help on their homework assignments, H_0 is tested against the (right-sided) alternative hypothesis H_a: $P > .30$. Thus, the two hypotheses are:

$$H_0: P = .30$$

$$H_a: P > .30.$$

Suppose now that out of 70 students who were randomly selected to complete a school survey, 28 responded that they were getting help from their parents on homework assignments. Thus, 28/70 = .40 is the sample proportion of students getting parental help on homework assignments ($p = .40$). Just like the standard error of the sample mean, $s_{\bar{X}}$, is used to test hypotheses about the mean (see Chapter 8), the standard error of the sample proportion, s_p, is used to test hypotheses about proportions.

For large samples, the sampling distribution of p approximates a normal distribution, with the mean of this distribution being the population proportion $\boldsymbol{P}$ in the null hypothesis (in this case, H_0: $\boldsymbol{P} = .30$). The standard deviation of the sampling distribution of p, called the **standard error of the sample proportion**, is

$$s_p = \sqrt{\frac{P(1-P)}{n}}, \qquad (9.1)$$

where n is the sample size.

Thus, given $n = 70$, the standard error of the sample proportion for H_0: $\boldsymbol{P} = .30$ is:

$$s_p = \sqrt{\frac{(.30)(1-.30)}{70}} = \sqrt{\frac{(.30)(.70)}{70}} = 0.0548.$$

Given the hypothesized values of the population proportion, $\boldsymbol{P}$, the sample proportion, $\boldsymbol{p}$, and its standard error, s_p, the **test statistic** for the null hypothesis is

$$z = \frac{p-P}{s_p}. \qquad (9.2)$$

As in our example we have $\boldsymbol{P} = .30$, $p = .40$, and $s_p = 0.0548$, the test statistic for H_0: $\boldsymbol{P} = .30$ is

$$z = \frac{.40 - .30}{0.0548} = \frac{.10}{0.0548} = 1.825.$$

Given that the alternative hypothesis is right-sided (H_a: $\boldsymbol{P} > .30$), we place $\alpha = .05$ [the level of significance selected in this case] in the right-tail of the standard normal distribution, thus obtaining the critical value: $z_\alpha = 1.645$. As the test statistic ($z = 1.825$) exceeds the critical value ($z_\alpha = 1.645$), **we reject the null hypothesis** (H_0: $\boldsymbol{P} = .30$). Thus, more than 30 percent of the students are getting parental help on their homework assignments.

NOTE [9.1] The z-test for proportions (Equation 9.2) assumes that the sampling distribution of the proportion, p, is approximately normal. This assumption holds relatively well when the hypothesized proportion is close to .50 (i.e., H_0: $\boldsymbol{P} = .50$). If this is not the case, the assumption still holds when the sample size, n, is sufficiently large — according to a widely used rule, n must be equal to or larger than the ratio $5/P_{\text{min}}$, that is

$$n \geq \frac{5}{P_{\text{min}}}, \qquad (9.3)$$

where P_{min} is the smaller number of the hypothesized proportion, P, and the difference $1 - P$. For example, if H_0: $\boldsymbol{P} = .85$, then $1 - .85 = .15$, so in this case $P_{\text{min}} = .15$ (the smaller number of .85 and .15). Thus, we have $5/P_{\text{min}} = 5/.15 = 33.33$. Therefore, to be safe regarding the assumption of normality for the sampling distribution of p, the sample size must be at least 34 ($n \geq 34$).

• **Constructing a confidence interval for *P*.** Before going over an example of how to construct a confidence interval for ***P***, we will provide the following important clarification:

> **NOTE [9.2] When constructing a *confidence interval* (CI) for the population proportion, *P*,** the standard error of the sample proportion, s_p, is estimated by replacing the hypothesized ***P*** in Formula 9.1 with the sample proportion *p*, that is:
>
> $$s_p = \sqrt{\frac{p(1-p)}{n}}. \qquad \textbf{(9.4)}$$
>
> Then the confidence interval (CI) for the population proportion, ***P***, is computed as follows:
>
> $$\text{CI} = p \pm (z_{\alpha/2})(s_p), \qquad \textbf{(9.5)}$$
>
> where $z_{\alpha/2}$ is the critical value for "half alpha" (α/2) in the right tail of the standard normal distribution. For example, with 95%CI, $z_{\alpha/2}$ = 1.96 (see Table A-1).

Taking into account NOTE [9.2], we will construct the 95% confidence interval for the population proportion, ***P***, of the students who are getting parental help in homework assignments. Specifically, with $p = .40$ and $n = 70$ in Equation 9.4, we obtain:

$$s_p = \sqrt{\frac{(.40)(1-.40)}{70}} = \sqrt{\frac{(.40)(.60)}{70}} = 0.0586.$$

Then, using Equation 9.5 with $p = .40$, $s_p = 0.0586$, and $z_{\alpha/2} = 1.96$, we compute the 95% confidence interval for ***P*** as follows: 95%CI = .40 ± (1.96)(0.0586) = .40 ± 0.1149 = (.285, .515). Thus, we fail to reject the null hypothesis (H_0: ***P*** = .30) because the hypothesized value for ***P*** (.30) belongs to the 95%CI (from .285 to .515). The decision to retain H_0 is different from that reached with the one-sided test (where we rejected H_0). This is because the 95%CI is non-directional and "splitting" α decreases the chances to reject H_0 (i.e., lowers the test power) when the alternative hypothesis is one-sided (e.g., compare Figures 8.2 and 8.3).

• **Using SPSS to test H_0: *P* = *a*.** The SPSS data file **tv-survey** (available with the SPSS package) is used to illustrate testing of H_0: ***P*** = *a* using SPSS**.** The data consist of the responses of 906 individuals on seven survey questions about reasons why they are watching a given TV show. The first 12 cases are provided in Figure 9.1. The variable names are abbreviations of the labels that describe the reason for watching the TV show: **any** = "any reason," **bored** = "there are no other popular shows on at that time," **critics** = "the critics still give the show good reviews," **peers** = "other people still watch the show," etc. The scores on each of the variable are 1 ("Yes"), for a positive response, or 0 ("No"), for a negative response on the respective survey question.

Figure 9.1 *SPSS data file **tv-survey.sav** (n = 906)*

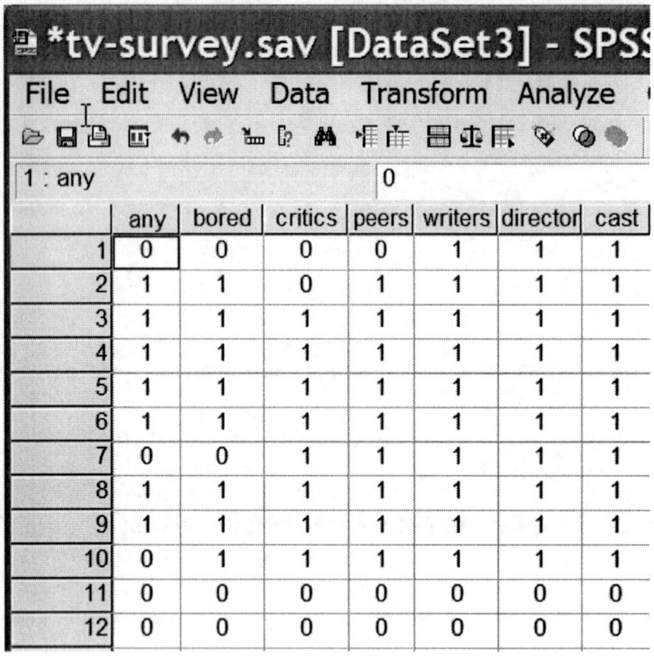

*tv-survey.sav [DataSet3] - SPSS

File Edit View Data Transform Analyze

1 : any 0

	any	bored	critics	peers	writers	director	cast
1	0	0	0	0	1	1	1
2	1	1	0	1	1	1	1
3	1	1	1	1	1	1	1
4	1	1	1	1	1	1	1
5	1	1	1	1	1	1	1
6	1	1	1	1	1	1	1
7	0	0	1	1	1	1	1
8	1	1	1	1	1	1	1
9	1	1	1	1	1	1	1
10	0	1	1	1	1	1	1
11	0	0	0	0	0	0	0
12	0	0	0	0	0	0	0

EXAMPLE 9.1 Suppose we want to know whether half of the people who watch the TV show do so because "other people still watch the show" (variable **peers).** In SPSS, the hypothesized proportion is named *test proportion.* In this case the test proportion is .50, so we test the null hypothesis H_0: $\boldsymbol{P}$ = .50 against the nondirectional alternative H_a: $\boldsymbol{P} \neq .50$. Because the test proportion is .50, the sampling distribution of the proportion, *p*, is approximately normal, so we can use the *z*-test (see NOTE [9.1]). To perform this in SPSS, follow the steps below:

1. Click **Analyze**, click **Nonparametric Tests**, then click **Binomial.**
2. Click **Other people still watch the show [peers]** and then click ▶ to move this variable into the box **Test Variable List** (see Figure 9.1); [In SPSS, .50 is the default option for test proportion, so there is no need to type .50 in the box **Test Proportion**.]
3. Click **OK.**

The SPSS table **Binomial Test** is shown in Figure 9.2. The *p*-value with the *z*-test (*p* = .09) indicates that H_0: $\boldsymbol{P}$ = .50 is not rejected at the .05 level. Thus, the observed proportion of people who responded "Yes" (i.e., they watch the TV show because "other people still watch the show"), .53, is not significantly different from the hypothesized proportion, .50. In fact, the same holds for the other category ("No") because the test proportion in this example is .50.

NOTE [9.3] When the test proportion is .50, SPSS provides a two-sided *p*-value (e.g., this is the case with *p* = .09 in the SPSS output in Figure 9.2). **If the test proportion is different from .50, SPSS provides a one-sided *p*-value**. Thus, if we have a two-sided alternative hypothesis about a test proportion different from .50, we must *double* the one-sided *p*-value reported with SPSS. For example, if we test H_0: $\boldsymbol{P}$ = .20 against H_a: $\boldsymbol{P} \neq .20$, and SPSS reports *p* = .032, we must make a decision about H_0 based on *p* = .064 (i.e, "two times .032"). In either case, the sample size should be sufficiently large to use the *z*-test (see NOTE [9.1]).

Figure 9.2 *SPSS test for H_0: P = .50*

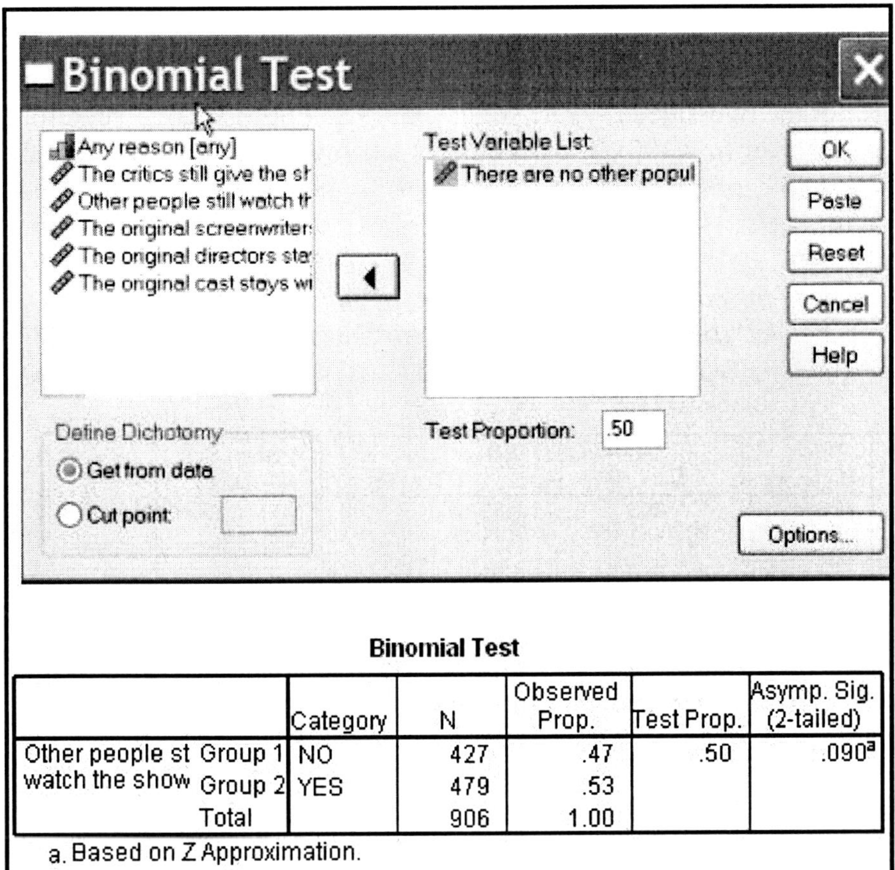

Binomial Test

		Category	N	Observed Prop.	Test Prop.	Asymp. Sig. (2-tailed)
Other people st watch the show	Group 1	NO	427	.47	.50	.090[a]
	Group 2	YES	479	.53		
	Total		906	1.00		

a. Based on Z Approximation.

EXAMPLE 9.2 Using the **tv-survey** data in Example 9.1, suppose that a previous survey has shown that, in general, 14% of the people watch a given TV show regardless of whether the original cast stays with the show. To check if this holds true for the **tv-survey** data, we test the null hypothesis H_0: $\boldsymbol{P}$ = .14 against H_a: $\boldsymbol{P} \neq .14$ for the proportion of people who responded "No" (score 0) on the variable **"the original cast stays with the show"; (**this variable is named **"cast"** in the SPSS data file — see Figure 9.1).

Thus, the category of interest in this case is "No" for the variable "**cast.**" Before we use the SPSS steps described in Example 9.1, an important clarification is necessary. Namely, SPSS is testing the proportion for the category which appears with the first case for the respective variable in the SPSS data set. As shown in Figure 9.1, the first case for the variable named "**cast**" is a score of 1 (category "Yes"). Thus, instead of testing H_0: $\boldsymbol{P}$ = .14 for the reference "No" category, SPSS will perform the equivalent test (H_0: $\boldsymbol{P}$ = .86) for its complementary category ("Yes"). Taking this into account, the SPSS steps are as follows:

1. Click **Analyze**, click **Nonparametric Tests**, then click **Binomial.**
2. Click **The original cast stays with the show [cast]** and then click ▶ to move this variable into the box **Test Variable List.**
3. In the box **Test Proportion**, change the default SPSS test proportion (.50) to **.86.**
4. Click **OK.**

The SPSS output is given in Figure 9.3. In this case, the test proportion (.86) is different from .50. Therefore, considering NOTE [9.3], we must double the one-sided (1-tailed) p-value reported in Figure 9.3 ($p = .006$) to obtain the two-sided p-value in testing H_0: $\boldsymbol{P} = .86$ against H_a: $\boldsymbol{P} \neq .86$ for the category "Yes" (or, equivalently, H_0: $\boldsymbol{P} = .14$ against H_a: $\boldsymbol{P} \neq .14$, for the category of interest, "No"). Thus, for the two-sided p-value we have: $p = (2)(.006) = .012$. Therefore, we reject H_0: $\boldsymbol{P} = .14$ at the .05 level ($p < .05$). Clearly, the **tv-survey** data do not support the finding in a previous survey that 14% of the people watch a given TV show regardless of whether the original cast stays with the show.

Figure 9.3 *SPSS test of H_0: $\boldsymbol{P} = .84$ for category "Yes" (or, equivalently, H_0: $\boldsymbol{P} = .14$ for category "No") with the variable "**the original cast stays with the show [cast]**"*

Binomial Test

		Category	N	Observed Prop.	Test Prop.	Asymp. Sig. (1-tailed)
The original cast stays with the show	Group 1	YES	805	.89	.86	.006[a]
	Group 2	NO	101	.11		
	Total		906	1.00		

a. Based on Z Approximation.

9.2 Testing H_0: $P_1 = P_2$ for Independent Samples

This section deals with testing hypotheses about two population proportions, $\boldsymbol{P_1}$ and $\boldsymbol{P_2}$, given their respective sample estimates, p_1 and p_2, in two *independent* random samples. This scenario will occur, for example, if a polling agency wants to determine whether Republicans and Democrats nationwide support at equal rates a recently proposed bill on tax relief. In this case, the null hypothesis H_0: $\boldsymbol{P_1} = \boldsymbol{P_2}$ is tested against the alternative hypothesis H_a: $\boldsymbol{P_1} \neq \boldsymbol{P_2}$, where $\boldsymbol{P_1}$ and $\boldsymbol{P_2}$ are the population proportions of Republicans and Democrats, respectively, who support the tax relief bill. Another example would be when a State Board of Education wants to know if the rate of male science teachers who prefer to teach physics to boys is higher than the rate of female science teachers who prefer to teach physics to boys. This time H_0: $\boldsymbol{P_1} = \boldsymbol{P_2}$ must be tested against the one-sided alternative hypothesis H_a: $\boldsymbol{P_1} > \boldsymbol{P_2}$, where $\boldsymbol{P_1}$ and $\boldsymbol{P_2}$ are the population proportions of male and female science teachers, respectively, who prefer to teach physics to boys. In general, $\boldsymbol{P_1}$ and $\boldsymbol{P_2}$ are the proportions of people in the two populations under comparison that fall in the category of interest — e.g., giving a "Yes" response to a "Yes/No" question.

• **z-test for H_0: $P_1 = P_2$.** The equivalent form of H_0: $\boldsymbol{P_1} = \boldsymbol{P_2}$ is H_0: $\boldsymbol{P_1} - \boldsymbol{P_2} = 0$. The sample estimate of the population difference $\boldsymbol{P_1} - \boldsymbol{P_2}$ is the difference p_1 - p_2, where p_1 is the sample estimate of $\boldsymbol{P_1}$ (say, from a random sample with size n_1) and p_2 is the sample estimate of $\boldsymbol{P_2}$ (say, from a random sample with size n_2). The sampling distribution of the difference between independent sample proportions ($p_1 - p_2$) is approximately normal when the sample sizes n_1 and n_2 are relatively large and each of the following four products is greater than 5: n_1p_1, $n_1(1 - p_1)$, n_2p_2, and $n_2(1 - p_2)$. Under this condition, the **standard error of $p_1 - p_2$** is estimated as follows:

$$s_{p_1-p_2} = \sqrt{p(1-p)\left(\frac{1}{n_1}+\frac{1}{n_2}\right)}, \qquad (9.6)$$

where p is the sample proportion calculated for the two samples together: $p = \frac{X_1 + X_2}{n_1 + n_2}$, and X_1 and X_2 are the frequency (counts) of people in the reference category in the first and second sample, respectively (i.e., $p_1 = X_1/n_1$ and $p_2 = X_2/n_2$). Then the sample statistic for testing the null hypothesis, H_0: $\boldsymbol{P_1} - \boldsymbol{P_2} = 0$, is the following z-statistic:

$$z = \frac{p_1 - p_2}{s_{p_1-p_2}}. \qquad (9.7)$$

EXAMPLE 9.3 Let's go back to the example in which a State Board of Education wants to know if the rate of male science teachers who prefer to teach physics to boys is higher than the rate of female science teachers who prefer to teach physics to boys. As stated at the beginning of this section, H_0: $\boldsymbol{P_1} = \boldsymbol{P_2}$ is tested in this case against the one-sided alternative H_a: $\boldsymbol{P_1} > \boldsymbol{P_2}$, where $\boldsymbol{P_1}$ and $\boldsymbol{P_2}$ are the population proportions of male and female science teachers, respectively, who prefer to teach physics to boys. Suppose now that the question "Do you prefer to teach physics to boys?" has been asked to 50 male science teachers and 40 female science teachers and the responses were "Yes" for 38 male teachers and 22 female teachers. This sample information translates into relevant notations as follows: $n_1 = 50$, $n_2 = 40$, $X_1 = 38$, and $X_2 = 22$. The two sample proportions are then: $p_1 = 38/50 = .76$ and $p_2 = 22/40 = .55$. The necessary condition for using the z-test statistic (Equation 9.7) is met in this case because the two samples sizes are relatively large and each of the four (*sample size* x *proportion*) products exceeds 5: $n_1p_1 = (50)(.76) = 38$, $n_1(1 - p_1) = (50)(.24) = 12$, $n_2p_2 = (40)(.55) = 22$, and $n_2(1 - p_2) = (40)(.45) = 18$. Thus, we can use Formula 9.6 to estimate $s_{p_1-p_2}$ — the standard error of the difference between the two sample proportions (p_1 - p_2), and to calculate the z-statistic (see Formula 9.7) for H_0: $\boldsymbol{P_1} - \boldsymbol{P_2} = 0$.

With $p = (X_1 + X_2)/(n_1 + n_2) = (38 + 22)/(50 + 40) = 60/90 = .6667$, $n_1 = 50$, and $n_2 = 40$, we use Formula 9.6 to calculate the standard error of the difference $p_1 - p_2$:

$$s_{p_1-p_2} = \sqrt{(.6667)(1-.6667)\left(\frac{1}{50}+\frac{1}{40}\right)} = 0.10.$$

Then, given that $p_1 - p_2 = .76 - .55 = .21$ and $s_{p_1-p_2} = .10$, we use Formula 9.7 to obtain the test statistic: $z = (p_1 - p_2)/s_{p_1-p_2} = .21/.10 = 2.10$. As the alternative hypothesis in this case is right-sided, H_a: $\boldsymbol{P_1}$ - $\boldsymbol{P_2} > 0$, the critical value z_α (for $\alpha = .05$ in the right tail of the standard normal distribution) is $z_\alpha = 1.645$. Thus, we reject H_0: $\boldsymbol{P_1}$ - $\boldsymbol{P_2} = 0$ at the .05 level of significance because the test statistic ($z = 2.10$) exceeds the critical value ($z_\alpha = 1.645$). In other words, the data in this hypothetical example support the expectation that the percentage of male science teachers who prefer to teach physics to boys is higher than that of female science teachers who prefer to teach physics to boys.

• **Constructing a confidence interval for $P_1 - P_2$.** Assuming that there is an approximately normal sampling distribution for the difference between the two independent sample proportions ($p_1 - p_2$), we can use the standard error of this difference (see Formula 9.6) to compute a confidence interval for the difference between the two population proportions, $P_1 - P_2$:

$$\text{CI} = (p_1 - p_2) \pm (z_{\alpha/2})(s_{p_1-p_2}), \tag{9.8}$$

where $z_{\alpha/2}$ is the two-sided *z*-critical value for the selected level of significance, α; (e.g., for a 95%CI: $z_{\alpha/2} = 1.96$, for a 90%CI: $z_{\alpha/2} = 1.645$, and for a 99%CI: $z_{\alpha/2} = 2.576$).

EXAMPLE 9.4 Let's compute the 95%CI for $P_1 - P_2$ for the case in Example 9.3. Given that $p_1 - p_2 = .21$, $z_{\alpha/2} = 1.96$, and $s_{p_1-p_2} = .10$, the confidence interval of interest is computed as follows: 95%CI = .21 ± (1.96)(.10) = .21 ± .196 = (.014, .406). Thus, the difference $P_1 - P_2$ is between .014 and .406, which indicates that $P_1 > P_2$ by at least .014, but no more than .406. In other words, the percentage of male teachers who prefer to teach physics to boys is higher than that of female teachers who prefer to teach physics to boys by a magnitude from 1.4% to 40.6%.

The large range (between 1.4% and 40.6%) of possible difference between the population rates of male and female science teachers who prefer to teach physics to boys is of little value when it comes to making accurate decisions about the practical importance of this difference. Larger sample sizes will lower the relatively large standard error in this case ($s_{p_1-p_2} = .10$). This will reduce the margin of error of the confidence interval, $ME = (z_{\alpha/2})(s_{p_1-p_2})$, thus improving the accuracy of the estimate about the magnitude of $P_1 - P_2$. In general, obtaining a small margin of error improves the accuracy of decisions about both the statistical significance and the practical importance of the differences between two population proportions or other population parameters (means, variances, etc.).

• **Conducting a *chi-square* test for H_0: $P_1 = P_2$.** The *z*-test for H_0: $P_1 = P_2$ with independent samples (illustrated in Example 9.3) can be equivalently replaced by a *chi-square* (χ^2) test for a 2 x 2 contingency table. For example, to test H_0: $P_1 = P_2$ for the case described in Example 9.3 using the χ^2 test, we arrange the sample frequency information for this example in a 2 x 2 contingency table (see Table 9.1). Here, $n_{11} = 38$ and $n_{21} = 22$ represent the frequency of male and female science teachers, respectively, who fall in the reference category "Yes" — i.e., teachers who prefer to teach physics to boys (see, $X_1 = 38$ and $X_2 = 22$ in Example 9.3). The first row total ($R_1 = 50$) is the sample size for male science teachers and the second row total ($R_2 = 40$) is the sample size for female science teachers ($n_1 = 50$ and $n_2 = 40$ in Example 9.3). The total sample size for male and female science teachers together is $N = 90$.

Table 9.1 *Contingency table for χ^2-test of H_0: $P_1 = P_2$*

	Yes	No	**Row totals**
Males	$n_{11} = 38$	$n_{10} = 12$	$R_1 = 50$
Females	$n_{21} = 22$	$n_{20} = 18$	$R_2 = 40$
Column totals	$C_1 = 60$	$C_2 = 30$	$N = 90$

As in Example 9.3, $\boldsymbol{P_1}$ and $\boldsymbol{P_2}$ are the population proportions of male and female science teachers, respectively, in the "Yes" category (i.e., who prefer to teach physics to boys). With the notations in Table 9.1, the *chi-square* (χ^2) statistic for H_0: $\boldsymbol{P_1 = P_2}$ is:

$$\chi^2 = \frac{N(n_{11}n_{20} - n_{10}n_{21})^2}{R_1 R_2 C_1 C_2}. \qquad \textbf{(9.9)}$$

Using Formula 9.9 with the data in Table 9.1, we calculate

$$\chi^2 = \frac{(90)[(38)(18) - (12)(22)]^2}{(50)(40)(60)(30)} = 4.41.$$

The degrees of freedom with the chi-square test for a contingency table with R rows and C columns are: $df = (R - 1)(C - 1)$. Thus, for a 2 x 2 contingency table, $df = (2 - 1)(2 - 1) = 1$. Using Table A-3, with $\alpha = .05$ for the level of significance and $df = 1$, we find the chi-square critical value: $\chi^2_\alpha = 3.84$. Thus, we reject H_0: $\boldsymbol{P_1 = P_2}$ because the test statistic ($\chi^2 = 4.41$) exceeds the critical value ($\chi^2_\alpha = 3.84$) at the .05 level of significance.

NOTE [9.4]. In testing $\boldsymbol{H_0}$: $\boldsymbol{P_1 = P_2}$ for two independent samples, the *chi-square* test is equivalent to the *z*-test. The sample statistics of these two tests are related as follows: $z^2 = \chi^2$ (see Formula 9.7 for z and Formula 9.9 for χ^2). For example, $\chi^2 = 4.41$, obtained with the data in Table 9.1, equals the squared value of the *z*-statistic ($z = 2.1$) obtained with the same data in Example 9.3. An advantage of the *chi-square* test is that it provides accurate probability statements about H_0 *even with small sample sizes*. The *z*-test requires larger samples, but when its assumptions are met, it is conducted with the more familiar standard normal distribution, $N(0, 1)$. In addition, the confidence interval associated with the z-test approach (Formula 9.8) provides useful information about the direction and magnitude of the difference $\boldsymbol{P_1 - P_2}$ (e.g., in decisions about the practical importance of this difference).

• **Using SPSS to test $\boldsymbol{H_0}$: $\boldsymbol{P_1 = P_2}$.** We can test H_0: $\boldsymbol{P_1 = P_2}$ for independent samples using the chi-square test in SPSS. To illustrate this for the example with physics teachers, the data in Table 9.1 are entered in SPSS as shown in Figure 9.3, with variables: **Gender** (1 = Male, 2 = Female), **Response** (1 = "Yes," 0 = "No"), and **Count** — the frequency of science teachers for each of the four combinations of Gender and Response categories.

Figure 9.3 *Science teachers data*

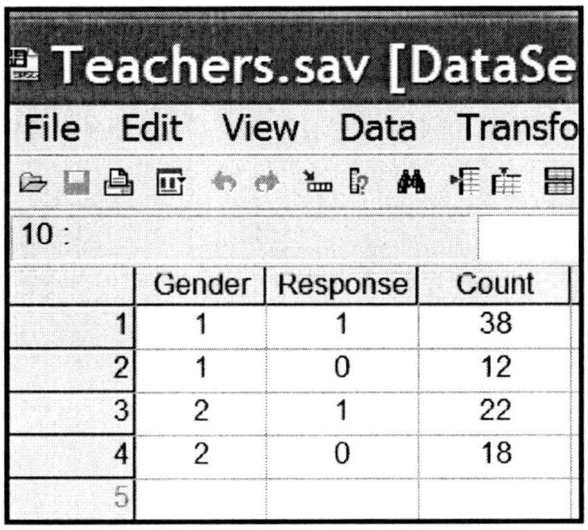

Teachers.sav [DataSe

File Edit View Data Transfo

10 :

	Gender	Response	Count
1	1	1	38
2	1	0	12
3	2	1	22
4	2	0	18
5			

As before, P_1 and P_2 are the population proportions of male and female science teachers, respectively, in the response category "Yes" (i.e., who prefer to teach physics to boys). To perform the chi-square test for H_0: $P_1 = P_2$ in SPSS, follow the steps:

1. Click **Data** and click **Weight Cases**.
2. Click **Weight Cases by** in the **Weight Cases** dialog box.
3. Click Count and click ▶ to move this variable into the **Frequency Variable** box.
4. Click **OK**.
5. Click **Analyze**, click **Descriptive Statistics**, and click **Crosstabs**.
6. Click **Gender** and then click ▶ to move it into the box **Row(s)**.
7. Click **Response** and then click ▶ to move it into the box **Column(s)**.
8. Click **Statistics** and check the **Chi-square** box.
9. Click **OK**.

The resulting SPSS output is given in Figure 9.4. The most frequently reported Pearson chi-square test statistic is the same that we obtained using Formula 9.9 in the previous section: $\chi^2 = 4.41$ (with $df = 1$). Given that the corresponding p-value ($p = .036$) is smaller than the level of significance in this case ($\alpha = .05$), we reject H_0: $P_1 = P_2$. The APA-style report of the Pearson chi-square test result is: $\chi^2(1, N = 90) = 4.41, p = .036$.

Figure 9.4 *SPSS output for the chi-square test of H_0: $P_1 = P_2$ for independent samples*

Gender * Response Crosstabulation

Count

		Response		
		No	Yes	Total
Gender	Male	12	38	50
	Female	18	22	40
Total		30	60	90

Chi-Square Tests

	Value	df	Asymp. Sig. (2-sided)	Exact Sig. (2-sided)	Exact Sig. (1-sided)
Pearson Chi-Square	4.410[b]	1	.036		
Continuity Correction[a]	3.516	1	.061		
Likelihood Ratio	4.413	1	.036		
Fisher's Exact Test				.044	.030
Linear-by-Linear Association	4.361	1	.037		
N of Valid Cases	90				

$\chi^2(df = 1) = 4.41, p = .036$

9.3 Testing H_0: $P_1 = P_2$ for Dependent Samples

In this section, H_0: $\boldsymbol{P_1 = P_2}$ is tested against H_a: $\boldsymbol{P_1 \neq P_2}$ for two *dependent* samples. In general, dependent samples occur when (a) the same individuals are measured twice on the same variable, say, before and after an *event*, (b) the same individuals are measured on two different variables, or (c) two (naturally or experimentally) matched groups of individuals are compared on the same variable. For example, the first scenario occurs when a researcher wants to know whether the percent of supporters of a sensitive issue would change after a video session on that issue. The second scenario will be illustrated here using the **tv-survey** data (see Figure 9.1) to determine whether an equal percent of people watch a TV show because "there are no other popular shows on at that time" or because "other people are still watching the show." The third scenario of two dependent samples occurs, for example, when husbands and wives are compared on the percent of positive responses on a survey of satisfaction with their kids' school performance

When H_0: $\boldsymbol{P_1 = P_2}$ is tested for two dependent samples, the data is organized in a (2 x 2) contingency table. This is illustrated in Table 9.2 for the scenario in which the same group of individuals answer ("Yes" or "No") a given question *before* and *after* an "event" (e.g., therapy session, movie, presidential debate, etc.). The **research question** is whether there is a change in the proportion of positive responses ("Yes") from before to after the event. The numeric values assigned to the frequencies **A**, **B**, **C**, and **D** are provided in Table 9.2 for illustrative purposes.

Table 9.2 Contingency table for testing H_0: $\boldsymbol{P_1 = P_2}$ with dependent samples

		AFTER [event]		
		No	**Yes**	Totals
BEFORE [event]	**Yes**	**A = 10**	**B = 20**	30
	No	**C = 24**	**D = 26**	50
Totals		34	46	$n = 80$

Note. **A** and **D** indicate the "before-after" response *change*.

• **Conducting a *chi-square* test for H_0: $P_1 = P_2$ (dependent samples).** The χ^2- test for the null hypothesis H_0: $\boldsymbol{P_1 = P_2}$ with dependent samples is called the **McNemar test** for change (McNemar, 1960, pp. 260-262). Using the notations in Table 9.2, the McNemar's test statistic is computed as follows:

$$\chi^2 = \frac{(A-D)^2}{A+D}. \qquad \textbf{(9.10)}$$

To make a decision about H_0: $\boldsymbol{P_1 = P_2}$, this χ^2-statistic is compared against a χ^2 critical value with degrees of freedom of 1 (df = 1) at the selected level of significance, α: χ^2_α (see Table A-3). We reject H_0: $\boldsymbol{P_1 = P_2}$ when the χ^2-statistic exceeds the critical value (i.e, $\chi^2 > \chi^2_\alpha$). For example, at the .05 level, $\chi^2_\alpha = 3.84$ (see Table A-3, α = .05 and df = 1). Let's use McNemar's test with the data in Table 9.2 at the .05 level of significance. Given the "change" frequencies (**A** = 10 and **D** = 26), the χ^2-test statistic is: $\chi^2 = (10 - 26)^2/(10 + 26) = (-16)^2/36 = 256/36 = 7.111$. In this case, then, we reject the null hypothesis because the χ^2-statistic (7.111) exceeds the chi-square critical value at the .05 level with $df = 1$ (3.84).

• **Conducting a z-test for H_0: $P_1 = P_2$ (dependent samples).** Again using the notations in Table 9.2, the sample proportions for the "Yes" category *before* and *after* the event are: $p_1 = (\mathbf{A} + \mathbf{B})/n$ and $p_2 = (\mathbf{B} + \mathbf{D})/n$, respectively. The sampling distribution of the difference $p_1 - p_2$ is approximately normal when A + D > 10 or B + C > 10. If this is the case, the z-statistic for H_0: $P_1 = P_2$ can be computed by taking the square root of the χ^2-statistic provided with Formula 9.10. Indeed, given the familiar relationship $z^2 = \chi^2$ (when $df = 1$), we have:

$$z = \sqrt{\chi^2}. \tag{9.11}$$

Given the data in Table 9.2, we found $\chi^2 = 7.111$. Thus, the z-statistic for the null hypothesis, H_0: $P_1 = P_2$, in this case is: $z = \sqrt{7.111} = 2.67$. The z-critical value for the non-directional alternative, H_a: $P_1 \neq P_2$, at the .05 level is: $z_{\alpha/2} = 1.96$ (see Table A-1). We reject H_0: $P_1 = P_2$ because the z-statistic (2.67) exceeds the z-critical value (1.96). As expected, the two equivalent (χ^2- and z-) tests led to the same decision about H_0: $P_1 = P_2$.

NOTE [9.5] Taking into account Formula 9.10, we can represent Formula 9.11 as follows:

$$z = (A - D)/\sqrt{A + D}. \tag{9.12}$$

• **Constructing a confidence interval for P_1 - P_2 with dependent samples.** As noted earlier, the sampling distribution of the difference $p_1 - p_2$ for dependent samples is approximately normal when A + D > 10 or B + C > 10. Under this assumption, the standard error of the difference $p_1 - p_2$ can be estimated as follows:

$$s_{p_1 - p_2} = \frac{\sqrt{A+D}}{n} \tag{9.13}$$

The confidence interval of the difference P_1 - P_2 with dependent samples is then

$$\mathrm{CI} = (p_1 - p_2) \pm (z_{\alpha/2})(s_{p_1 - p_2}), \tag{9.14}$$

For example, let's compute the 95%CI for $P_1 - P_2$ using the data in Table 9.2. The two sample proportions in this case are: $p_1 = (\mathbf{A} + \mathbf{B})/n = (10 + 20)/(80) = 30/80 = .375$ and $p_2 = (\mathbf{B} + \mathbf{D})/n = (20 + 26)/(80) = 46/80 = .575$. Thus, their difference is: $p_1 - p_2 = .375 - .575 = -.20$. Using Formula 9.13, the standard error of this difference is:

$$s_{p_1 - p_2} = \sqrt{A + D}/n = \sqrt{10 + 26}/80 = 6/80 = 0.075.$$

Using Formula 9.14 with $p_1 - p_2 = -.20$, $z_{\alpha/2} = 1.96$, and $s_{p_1 - p_2} = 0.075$, we compute the 95% confidence interval for the population difference, $P_1 - P_2$, as follows:

$$95\%\mathrm{CI} = (-.20) \pm (1.96)(0.075) = (-.20) \pm 0.147 = (-.347, -.053).$$

As $P_1 - P_2$ is a negative number (between −.347 and −.053), we can be 95% confident that $P_1 < P_2$ by at least .053, but no more than .347. **Conclusion**: There is a statistically significant "before-after" increase in positive ("Yes") responses in the range from 5.3% to 34.7%.

• **Using SPSS to test H_0: $P_1 = P_2$ (dependent samples).** We once again use the familiar SPSS data file **tv-survey** (see Figure 9.1) to test whether an equal percent of people watch a TV show because "there are no other popular shows on at that time" or because "other people are still watching the show." The two dependent samples in this case are the scores (1 = "Yes", 0 = "No") of the same people on two variables in the **tv-survey** data file: **bored** ["there are no other popular shows on at that time"] and **peer** [other people are still watching the show].

To perform the McNemar's χ^2-test in SPSS, follow the steps:

1. Click **Analyze**, click **Descriptive Statistics**, and click **Crosstabs**.
2. Click **There are no other popular shows on at that time [bored]** and then click ► to move this variable into the box **Row(s)**.
3. Click **Other people are still watching the show [peer]** and then click ► to move this variable into the box **Column(s)**.
4. Click **Cells** and then check (√) the **Total** box in the panel *Percentages* [this provides the percent values of A, B, C, and D relative to the total sample size, *n*.]
5. Click **Continue.**
6. Back in the **Crosstabs** dialog box, click **Statistics** and then check (√) the **McNemar** box (as shown in Figure 9.5).
7. Click **Continue.**
8. Click **OK.**

Figure 9.5 *Selecting the McNemar test in SPSS*

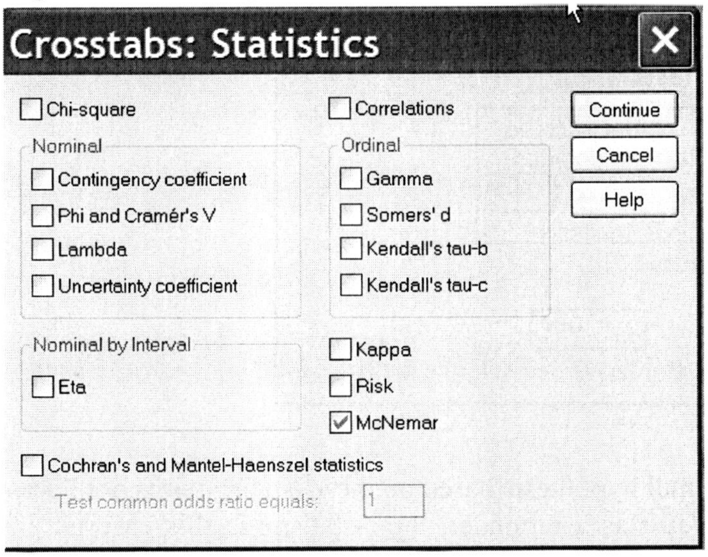

The resulting SPSS output is shown in Figure 9.6. The top panel is the 2 x 2 contingency table with "Yes"-"No" responses on the two variables used in this example: **bored** ["There are no other popular shows on at that time"] and **peer** ["Other people are still watching the show"]. This table provides the key information necessary for the computation of the χ^2-statistic (Formula 9.10) and the confidence interval for $P_1 - P_2$ (Formula 9.14): **A** = 32, **D** = 56, n = 906, p_1 =.502, and p_2 = .529. Thus, using Formula 9.10, $\chi^2 = (\mathbf{A} - \mathbf{D})^2/(\mathbf{A} + \mathbf{D}) = (32 - 56)^2/(32 + 56) =$

$(-24)^2/88 = 576/88 = 6.54$. The p-value for this test statistic ($p = .014$) is reported in the lower panel in Figure 9.6. As the p-value is smaller than the .05 level of significance used in this example ($p < \alpha$), we reject the null hypothesis, H_0: $\boldsymbol{P_1} = \boldsymbol{P_2}$; [we can reach the same conclusion using that the χ^2- statistic (6.54) exceed the χ^2-critical value for $\alpha = .05$ and $df = 1$: $\chi^2_\alpha = 3.84$].

Figure 9.6 *SPSS crosstabulation for the two categories ("Yes"/"No") of the variables named* ***bored*** *and* ***peer*** *in the* ***tv-survey*** *data file.*

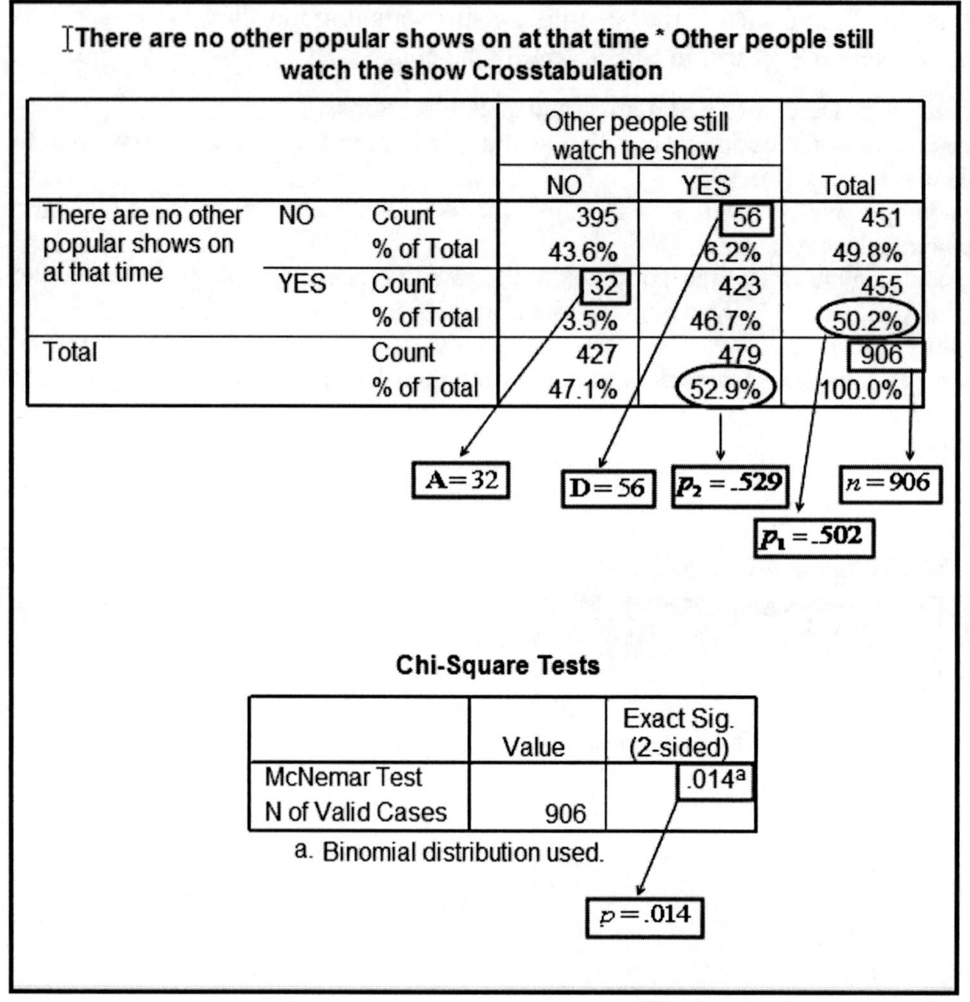

There are no other popular shows on at that time * Other people still watch the show Crosstabulation

			Other people still watch the show		Total
			NO	YES	
There are no other popular shows on at that time	NO	Count	395	56	451
		% of Total	43.6%	6.2%	49.8%
	YES	Count	32	423	455
		% of Total	3.5%	46.7%	50.2%
Total		Count	427	479	906
		% of Total	47.1%	52.9%	100.0%

Chi-Square Tests

	Value	Exact Sig. (2-sided)
McNemar Test		.014[a]
N of Valid Cases	906	

a. Binomial distribution used.

After making a decision about the null hypothesis based on the χ^2-statistic, it is not necessary to do so with the equivalent z-test [Just as a reminder, the z-statistic in this case is: $z = \sqrt{\chi^2} = \sqrt{6.54} = 2.56$, which exceeds the two-sided z-critical value, $z_{\alpha/2} = 1.96$.]. However, given that the null hypothesis is rejected, it would be useful to compute the 95% confidence interval for the difference $\boldsymbol{P_1} - \boldsymbol{P_2}$. First, using Formula 9.13, we estimate the standard error of the difference $p_1 - p_2$: $s_{p_1-p_2} = \sqrt{A + D} / n = \sqrt{32 + 56} / 906 = 0.0104$. Then, given $p_1 - p_2 = .502 - .529 = -.027$ and the two-sided z-critical value $z_{\alpha/2} = 1.96$, we use Formula 9.14 to compute the 95 percent confidence interval for $\boldsymbol{P_1} - \boldsymbol{P_2}$: 95%CI = $(-.027) \pm (1.96)(0.0104) = (-.027) \pm .0204 = (-.047, -.007)$. This indicates that the population difference $\boldsymbol{P_1} - \boldsymbol{P_2}$ is a negative number between −.047 and −.007. Therefore, $P_1 < P_2$ by at least .007, but no more than .047. **Conclusion:** The percentage of people who watch a TV show because "there is no other popular shows on at that time" is smaller than that of people who do so because "other people are still watching the show" by a magnitude from 0.7% to 4.7%.

NOTE [9.6] The McNemar's test and the *t*-test for paired samples with the dichotomous dependent variable (e.g., 1 = "Yes" and 0 = "No") are equivalent in testing H_0: $P_1 = P_2$ (with a negligible difference in the *p*-values yielded by these two tests). The same holds true for the confidence intervals for the difference $P_1 - P_2$ obtained with the *t*-test and Formula 9.14 in this section. For example, the 95%CI = (−.047, −.007) obtained here with the **tv-survey** data (variables **bored** and **peer**) is identical to the 95%CI provided by the SPSS *t*-test for paired samples using the same data [Check this on your own.]

9.4 Summary

This chapter deals with testing hypotheses about proportions in the one-sample case for proportion (H_0: $P = a$) and two-sample case for proportion (H_0: $P_1 = P_2$), with the latter case addressed for both independent and dependent samples. The testing procedures involve the use of a *z*-test, confidence interval, or *chi-square* (χ^2) test. Along with a brief theoretical discussion of these procedures and related analytic tools (formulas), their practical use is illustrated with examples and SPSS applications. A bulleted summary of the content of this chapter follows.

• **In testing hypotheses about proportions**, there are two possible categories into which the individuals from a study population may fall. Such categories can be, for example, (a) the dichotomous responses to a specific question ("Yes" or "No"), and (b) the *presence* or *lack* of a specific characteristic (e.g., *pass* or *fail* a proficiency test), etc. If P denotes the proportion of individuals who fall in the category of interest (i.e., reference category), then $1 - P$ is the proportion of those who fall in the other category.

• **The testing of H_0: $P = a$** (one-sample case for proportion) is performed by the use of a z-test statistic (Formula 9.2) and/or a confidence interval (Formula 9.5). Either approach requires that the sampling distribution of the proportion p be approximately normal — an assumption that holds under the condition $n \geq 5/P_{min}$ (see NOTE [9.1]).

• **The testing of H_0: $P_1 = P_2$ for independent samples** is performed by the use of a z-test statistic (Formula 9.7) and/or a confidence interval (Formula 9.8). Either approach requires that the sampling distribution of the difference $p_1 - p_2$ be approximately normal — an assumption which is satisfied when the samples are relatively large and each of the following four products is greater than 5: n_1p_1, $n_1(1 - p_1)$, n_2p_2, and $n_2(1 - p_2)$. A *chi-square* test can also be used to test H_0: $P_1 = P_2$, with the data arranged in a 2 x 2 contingency table (see Table 9.1). When the z-test assumption of normality is met, the z-test and the χ^2-test are equivalent. Also, the squared value of the *z*-statistic (Formula 9.7) equals the χ^2-statistic (Formula 9.9), that is: $z^2 = \chi^2$. An advantage of the χ^2-test is that it provides accurate probability statements about H_0: $P_1 = P_2$ even with small sample sizes (see NOTE [9.4]).

• **The testing of H_0: $P_1 = P_2$ for dependent samples** is performed by a χ^2-test called the **McNemar test** for change. The 2 x 2 contingency table for this test is shown in Table 9.2. The

research question is whether there is a change in the proportion of positive responses ("Yes") from before to after the event (e.g., therapy sessions, movie, presidential debate, etc.). The χ^2-statistic is computed by Formula 9.10. Equivalently, the null hypothesis, H_0: $P_1 = P_2$, can be tested by using a z-test if the sampling distribution of the difference $p_1 - p_2$ is approximately normal — an assumption which is met when the following is true for the frequencies in the contingency table: A + D > 10 or B + C > 10 (see Table 9.2). Under this assumption, the z-statistic is computed by Formula 9.11 (or, equivalently, by Formula 9.12). The confidence interval for the difference $P_1 - P_2$ is computed by using Formulas 9.13 and 9.14 (in this order).

• The McNemar's test and the t-test for paired samples with the dichotomous dependent variable (e.g., 1 = "Yes" and 0 = "No") are equivalent in testing H_0: $P_1 = P_2$ (see NOTE [9.6]).

9.5 Study Questions

1. In testing hypotheses about proportions, what is the "reference category"?

2. In testing H_0: $P = a$, what do P and a represent?

3. In testing H_0: $P_1 = P_2$ for independent samples, what do P_1 and P_2 represent?

4. In testing H_0: $P_1 = P_2$ for dependent samples, what do P_1 and P_2 represent?

5. Which null hypothesis relates to the research question: "Does the proportion of minority students in a school district correspond to the expected percent of such students for the residential boundaries of this school district?"

A. H_0: $P = a$,

B. H_0: $P_1 = P_2$ for independent samples,

C. H_0: $P_1 = P_2$ for dependent samples.

6. Which null and alternative hypotheses relate to the research question: "Do boys and girls in a large school district have equal rates of positive attitudes toward math?"

A. H_0: $P = a$ against H_a: $P \neq a$,

B. H_0: $P_1 = P_2$ against H_a: $P_1 > P_2$ for independent samples,

C. H_0: $P_1 = P_2$ against H_a: $P_1 \neq P_2$ for dependent samples,

D. None of the above.

7. Which null and alternative hypotheses relate to the research question: "Is there a decrease in the percent of students who think that they 'don't like math' after seeing the movie *Beautiful Mind*?"

A. H_0: $P = a$ against H_a: $P < a$,

B. H_0: $P_1 = P_2$ against H_a: $P_1 \neq P_2$ for independent samples,

C. H_0: $P_1 = P_2$ against H_a: $P_1 < P_2$ for dependent samples,

D. None of the above.

8. When the research question is whether there is a change in the proportion of positive responses ("Yes") from before to after the event, the appropriate test is

    A. the chi-square test for independent samples
    B. the z-test for one-sample case for proportion
    C. the McNemar's test for dependent samples

9. Using the SPSS data file **tv-survey** (Figure 9.1), test the appropriate hypothesis to answer the question whether half of the people watch a TV show just for "any reason" [*Hint*: Replicate the procedure in Example 9.1 for the variable named **any** – the first column in Figure 9.1.]

10. Suppose that you want to answer the following research question: "Do girls who are taught science by a male teacher *pass* a proficiency test in science at a higher rate compared to girls who are taught science by a female teacher?" Suppose also that, using a random sampling of students academic records, you have found that out of 50 girls taught science by a male teacher, 38 have passed the test, whereas out of 72 girls taught science by a female teacher, 56 have passed the test. Answer the research question by completing the following tasks:

    10.1 Formulate the appropriate null and alternative hypotheses (H_0 and H_a).

    10.2 Test H_0 against H_a using the z-test at $\alpha = .05$ [*Hint*: see Example 9.3].

    10.3 Compute the 95%CI for $\boldsymbol{P_1 = P_2}$ [*Hint*: see Example 9.4].

    10.4 Develop the 2 x 2 contingency table and conduct the χ^2-test. [*Hint*: see Table 9.1 and χ^2-test with these data.]

    10.5 Test H_0 against H_a using SPSS [*Hint*: see Figure 9.3 and SPSS steps].

11. The 2 x 2 table provided here below shows the frequencies of (**correct/incorrect**) responses of 100 randomly selected examinees on two key items from a certification test. The test developers claim that Item 2 is easier than Item 1 (i.e., higher proportion of examinees will respond correctly to Item 2). Test the claim at the .10 level of significance using (a) the χ^2-test, (b) z-test, and (c) 90% CI.

		Item 2		
		Incorrect	**Correct**	Totals
Item 1	**Incorrect**	**14**	**46**	60
	Correct	**30**	**10**	40
		44	56	$n = 100$

12. Provided in Figure 9.7 are the frequencies of responses on attitude toward mathematics (1 = positive, 0 = negative) for students under two experimental conditions in a six-week treatment targeting changes in students' attitude toward math (1 = treatment, 2 = control). Using SPSS, test the claim (at the .05 level of significance) that the treatment group students reported positive attitude toward math at higher rate compared to the control group students. [*Hint*: see the testing related to the data in Figure 9.3]

Figure 9.7 *Frequency of responses on attitude toward math for two treatment groups of students*

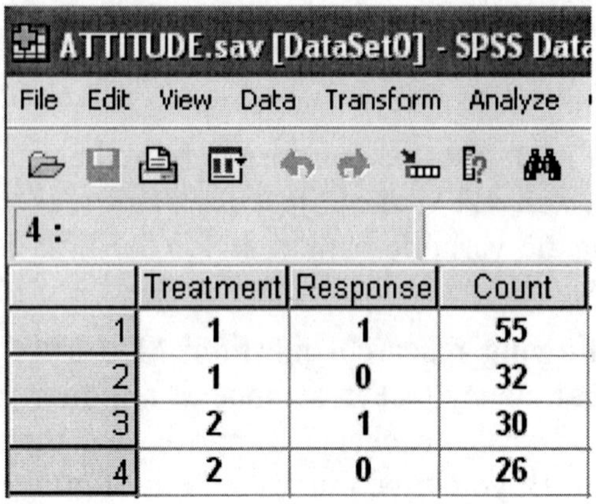

ATTITUDE.sav [DataSet0] - SPSS Data

File Edit View Data Transform Analyze

4 :

	Treatment	Response	Count
1	1	1	55
2	1	0	32
3	2	1	30
4	2	0	26

CHAPTER 10

CORRELATION AND SIMPLE REGRESSION

Many research questions in education, psychology, and other behavioral fields deal with whether two variables are related and, if they are, determining the type of relationship and its strength. For example, is verbal ability related to academic achievement? Is anxiety related to test performance? Is motivation related to task involvement? Is depression related to social functioning? To answer such questions, measures of relationship (or *correlation*) between two variables are needed.

Most people have an intuitive understanding of the existence of a correlation between two variables. For example, when asked about the correlation between IQ and academic performance (GPA), people usually say that "the higher a student's IQ, the higher his/her GPA," thus showing an understanding that there is a positive linear relationship between IQ and GPA. Specifically, the correlation has to do with the degree to which the students maintain the same relative position (or ranks) on IQ score and GPA. Or, when asked about the correlation between anxiety and test performance, most people realize that "the higher the test anxiety an examinee feels, the lower his/her test performance will be," thereby indicating that there is a negative correlation between anxiety and test performance. When a relationship between two variables exists, the question is to what degree one variable explains (or predicts) the other variable. This question can be addressed by a statistical method known as *simple linear regression.*

10.1 Correlation between Two Variables

10.1.1 What is Linear Relationship (Correlation) between Two Variables?

Figure 10.1 provides an excerpt from the SPSS data file **World95 survey** (available with SPSS). The data come from the World95 survey for 107 countries. These data are used here to illustrate the relationship between two variables — **Percent of females who read** and **Average female life expectancy**. The scatterplot in Figure 10.1 reveals that there is a linear relationship between these two variables, whereby a high *percentage of females who read* tends to be associated (paired) with high *average female life expectancy* and, conversely, a low *percentage of females who read* tends to be paired with low *average female life expectancy*. The dots group along a straight line with a *positive slope* (i.e., the direction of the dots is from the lower left to the upper right). In statistical parlance, there is a positive linear relationship (positive correlation) between the two variables.

In general, a **positive linear relationship** (**positive correlation**) between two variables, X and Y, occurs when high values on X tend to be associated with high values on Y and, conversely, low values on X tend to be associated with low values on Y. In previous research, positive correlations have been found, for example, between (a) motivation and academic success, (b) social functioning and mental health, (c) verbal ability and proficiency test performance, (d) teacher quality and student success, etc.

Figure 10.1 *Excerpt from the SPSS data file* ***World95.sav*** *(available with SPSS)*

*World95.sav [DataSet1] - SPSS Data Editor

File Edit View Data Transform Analyze Graphs Utilities Add-ons Window Help

16 : country Bulgaria

	country	populatn	density	urban	religion	lifeexpf	lifeexpm	literacy
1	Afghanistan	20500	25	18	Muslim	44	45	29
2	Argentina	33900	12	86	Catholic	75	68	95
3	Armenia	3700	126	68	Orthodox	75	68	98
4	Australia	17800	2	85	Protstnt	80	74	100
5	Austria	8000	94	58	Catholic	79	73	99
6	Azerbaijan	7400	86	54	Muslim	75	67	98
7	Bahrain	600	828	83	Muslim	74	71	77
8	Bangladesh	125000	800	16	Muslim	53	53	35
9	Barbados	256	605	45	Protstnt	78	73	99
10	Belarus	10300	50	65	Orthodox	76	66	99
11	Belgium	10100	329	96	Catholic	79	73	99
12	Bolivia	7900	7	51	Catholic	64	59	78
13	Bosnia	4600	87	36	Muslim	78	72	86
14	Botswana	1359	2	25	Tribal	66	60	72
15	Brazil	156600	18	75	Catholic	67	57	81
16	Bulgaria	8900	79	68	Orthodox	75	69	93

Figure 10.1 *Positive linear relationship (positive correlation) between "percent of females who read" and "average female life expectancy"*

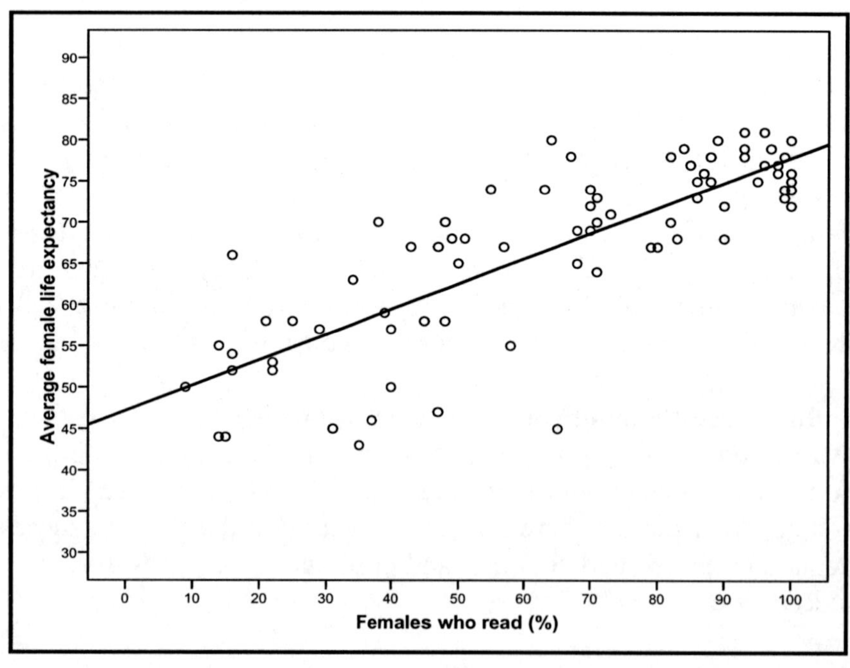

Also for the World95 survey data, the scatterplot in Figure 10.2 reveals a linear relationship between measures of **Birth rate per 1000 people** and **Average female life expectancy,** but this time a high *birth rate* tends to associate with low *average female life expectancy* and, conversely, a low *birth rate* tends to associate with high *average female life expectancy*. The dots group along a straight line with a *negative slope* (i.e., the direction of the dots is from the upper left to the lower right).

In general, **negative linear relationship (negative correlation)** between two variables, X and Y, occurs when high values on X tend to be associated with low values on Y and, conversely, low values on X tend to be associated with high values on Y. In previous research, negative correlations have been found, for example, between (a) anxiety and test performance, (b) college stress and academic success, (c) depression and motivation, (d) social support and isolation, etc.

Figure 10.2 *Negative linear relationship (negative correlation) between "birth rate" and "average female life expectancy"*

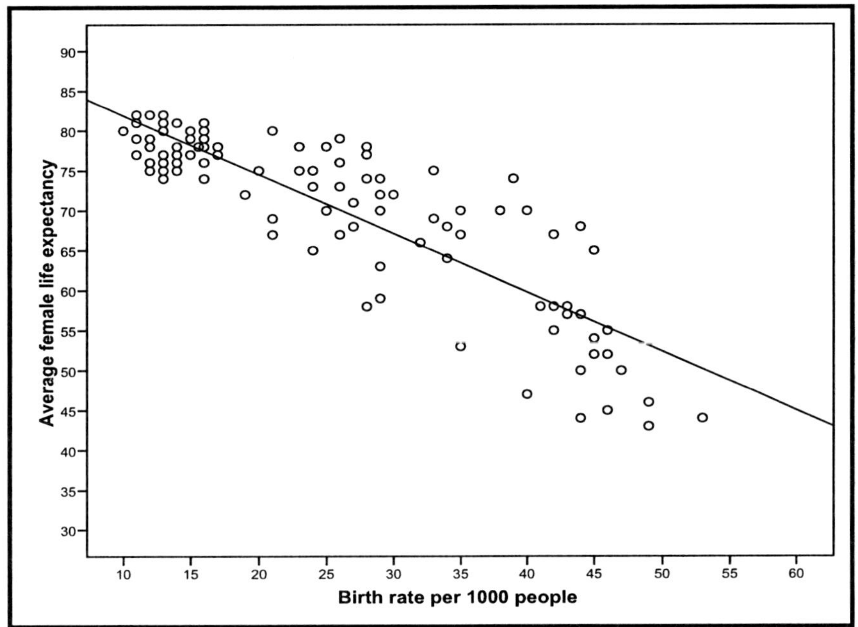

Still using the World95 survey data, the scatterplot in Figure 10.3 reveals that there is neither a positive, nor a negative linear relationship between the variables **population density** ("number of people per square kilometer") and **average female life expectancy.** In this case, we say that that there is **no correlation** between the two variables. In this chapter, *correlation* is short for "linear correlation" or *linear relationship* between two variables. Thus, "no correlation between X and Y" means that there is no linear relationship between X and Y, but it does not mean that there is no relationship between X and Y at all — e.g., there might be some nonlinear relationship between X and Y (e.g., see Figure 10.5a).

Figure 10.3 *Lack of linear relationship (no correlation) between "population density" and "average female life expectancy"*

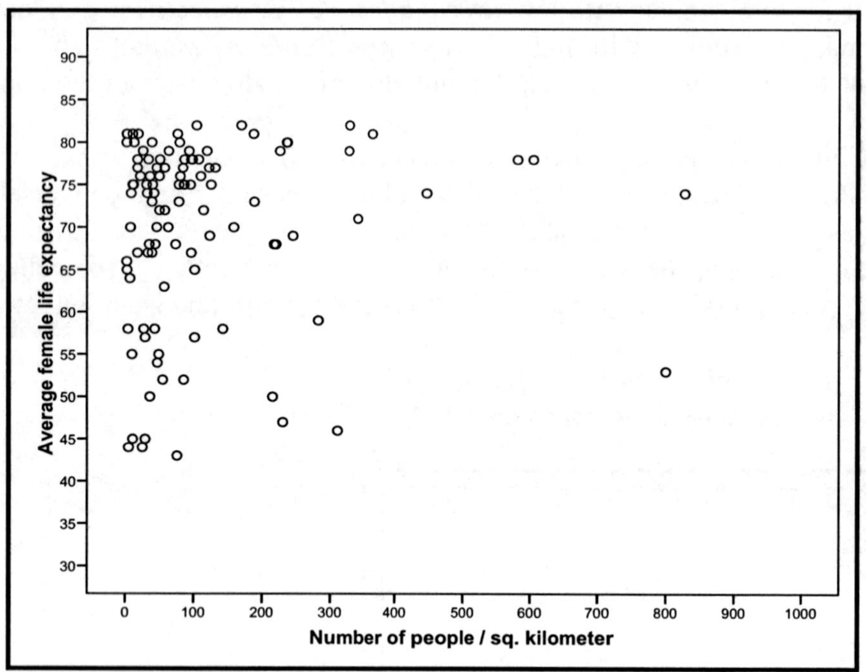

Figures 10.1, 10.2, and 10.3 show that *average female life expectancy* is positively correlated with *female literacy*, negatively correlated with *birth rate*, and is not correlated with *population density*.

10.1.2 The Pearson Product-Moment Correlation Coefficient

Pearson *r*. Although the scatterplot of the relationship between two variables, *X* and *Y*, is useful, more accuracy is needed to determine the presence (or absence) of a linear relationship between *X* and *Y*, its direction (positive, negative), and its strength. Such information is provided by the *Pearson product-moment correlation coefficient (Pearson r)* developed by the English statistician Karl Pearson (1857-1936). The Pearson r can take on values from -1.0 and $+1.0$, with a positive r indicating a positive linear relationship, and a negative r, a negative linear relationship between *X* and *Y*. The closer the absolute value of r to 1.0, the stronger the correlation (graphically, the closer the dots are to a straight line in the scatterplot for *X* and *Y*). When $r = 0$, there is no linear relationship between *X* and *Y*. The extreme positive value, $r = 1.0$, indicates that there is a *perfect positive correlation* between *X* and *Y* (all dots in the scatterplot fall on a straight line with a positive slope). The extreme negative value, $r = -1.0$, indicates that there is a *perfect negative correlation* between *X* and *Y* (all dots in the scatterplot fall on a straight line with a negative slope).

NOTE [10.1] A rule of thumb for interpreting the size of the Pearson r is based on its absolute value as follows: (a) .90 to 1.00 = **very high correlation**, (b) .70 to .90 = **high correlation**, (c) .50 to .70 = **moderate correlation**, (d) .30 to .50 = **low correlation**, and (e) .00 to .30 = **very low (if any) correlation**.

With the data in Figure 10.1 $r = .819$, thus indicating the presence of a strong positive linear relationship (high positive correlation) between the variables *average female life expectancy* and *female literacy* (percent of females who read). With the data in Figure 10.2, $r = -.862$, which indicates that there is a strong negative linear relationship (high negative correlation) between *average female life expectancy* and *birth rate*. Note that the negative relationship between X and Y in Figure 10.2 is stronger than the positive relationship between X and Y in Figure 10.1. With the data in Figure 10.3, the Pearson r is close to zero ($r = .128$) which indicates that there is a very weak (if any) linear relationship between *average female life expectancy* and *population density*.

Calculation of the Pearson *r*. The calculation of the Pearson r is described here by first introducing the concept of *covariance* between two variables, X and Y. Given the X and Y scores for a sample of size n, the covariance of X and Y (denoted s_{XY}) is the mean cross-product of the deviation scores, that is

$$s_{XY} = \frac{\sum(X - \bar{X})(Y - \bar{Y})}{n - 1}. \quad \textbf{(10.1)}$$

As can be seen, the covariance of a variable, X, with itself equals the variance of this variable, that is: $s_{XX} = s_X^2$.

If there is a positive linear relationship between X and Y, s_{XY} is a positive number. This is because people with X scores above the mean $\bar{X}$ tend to have Y scores above the mean $\bar{Y}$, and those with X scores below $\bar{X}$ tend to have Y scores below $\bar{Y}$, which results in positive cross-products $(X - \bar{X})(Y - \bar{Y})$. Indeed, (a) when X is above $\bar{X}$ and Y is above $\bar{Y}$, both deviation scores, $(X - \bar{X})$ and $(Y - \bar{Y})$, are positive, so their product is positive, and (b) when X is below $\bar{X}$ and Y is below $\bar{Y}$, both $(X - \bar{X})$ and $(Y - \bar{Y})$ are negative, but their product is positive.

If there is a negative linear relationship between X and Y, s_{XY} is negative because people with X scores above $\bar{X}$ tend to have Y scores below $\bar{Y}$, and vice versa, which results in negative cross-products $(X - \bar{X})(Y - \bar{Y})$. That is, positive deviation scores $(X - \bar{X})$ tend to associate with negative deviation scores $(Y - \bar{Y})$, and vice versa, so their cross-products are negative numbers.

Unlike in the case of Pearson r, the value of s_{XY} does not vary between -1.0 and 1.0 because it depends on the units of measurement for X and Y. In fact, the Pearson r is obtained by dividing the covariance by the product of the standard deviations of X and Y:

$$r_{XY} = \frac{s_{XY}}{s_X s_Y} \quad \textbf{(10.2)}$$

After replacing s_{XY} in Formula (10.2) with its expression in Formula (10.1), we have:

$$r_{XY} = \frac{\Sigma(X - \bar{X})(Y - \bar{Y})}{(n-1)s_X s_Y}. \quad \textbf{(10.3)}$$

Further, given that $z_X = (X - \bar{X})/s_X$ and $z_Y = (Y - \bar{Y})/s_Y$, Formula (10.3) can be presented as

$$r_{XY} = \frac{1}{n-1}\sum z_X z_Y. \quad \textbf{(10.4)}$$

Formula 10.4 shows that the Pearson *r* equals the sum of cross-products of the standard scores for *X* and *Y* (z_X and z_Y) divided by the degrees of freedom ($n - 1$). There are other equivalent formulas for the Pearson *r*, but they are not provided here as the computations in this chapter are facilitated through the use of SPSS rather than using manual computations.

Testing the Pearson *r* for statistical significance. While the Pearson r_{XY} provides information about the direction and strength of a linear relationship between *X* and *Y* for a sample of measures on *X* and *Y*, it is very important to determine whether there is a linear relationship between *X* and *Y* in the entire population to which the sample belongs. With ρ_{XY} denoting the correlation between *X* and *Y* in the population, the task is then to test the null hypothesis H_0: $\rho_{XY} = 0$ versus the alternative H_a: $\rho_{XY} \neq 0$. When $\rho_{XY} = 0$ (and only then), the sampling distribution of the correlation coefficient *r*, calculated for a sample of size *n*, is symmetrical and follows the *t* distribution with $n - 2$ degrees of freedom. The test statistic for testing H_0: $\rho_{XY} = 0$ is

$$t = r\sqrt{\frac{n-2}{1-r^2}}. \quad \textbf{(10.5)}$$

For example, if $r = .25$ is obtained for 36 persons ($n = 36$), the *t*-statistic obtained with Formula 10.5, is $t = 1.50$. With 34 degrees of freedom ($df = n - 2 = 36 - 2 = 34$), the *t-critical value* at the .05 level of significance is 2.032 (see Table A-2). As the absolute value of the test statistic (1.50) does not exceed the critical value (2.032), there is not sufficient evidence to reject H_0: $\rho_{XY} = 0$. Since the correlation coefficient, $r = .25$, is not statistically significant (at $\alpha = .05$), there is no evidence of a linear relationship between *X* and *Y* in the population; [check whether this holds if $r = .25$ is obtained with $n = 160$.]

EXAMPLE 10.1 Figure 10.4 (left panel) shows the data for 24 individuals on three survey questions (q1, q2, and q3). The correlation coefficients for each pair of questions are given in a correlation matrix obtained through the use of SPSS (Figure 10.4, right panel). Each cell contains a correlation coefficient, *r*, its *p*-value, and the number of observations used for the calculation of *r* [in this case $n = 24$ in all cells, as there are no missing observations in the SPSS data file]. For example, the cell for the pair of questions q1 and q2, contains $r_{12} = .525$, $p = .008$, and $n = 24$. Given that the *p*-value associated with the Pearson correlation coefficient for questions q1 and q2, r_{12}, is sufficiently small ($p = .008$), we can say that there is a statistically significant correlation between these two questions at the .01 level of significance based on 24 observations, $r(24) = .525$, $p < .01$. That is, there is a linear relationship between questions q1 and q2 for the population from which the sample of 24 observations has been randomly selected. However, there is not a statistically significant correlation between q1 and q3, $r(24) = .093$, $p = .667$, or between q2 and q3, $r(24) = .008$, $p = .969$. This means that neither q1 and q3, nor q2 and q3 are linearly related in the study population.

Figure 10.4 *SPSS output for Pearson correlations among three survey questions*

*SURVEY ITEMS.sav [DataSet0]

File Edit View Data Transform

28 :

	q1	q2	q3
1	4	4	4
2	4	4	4
3	3	4	5
4	5	3	5
5	5	5	3
6	3	3	4
7	4	4	4
8	3	3	5
9	4	4	3
10	4	4	5
11	4	4	5
12	4	5	5
13	4	4	5
14	4	5	5
15	4	4	5
16	3	3	4
17	5	5	5
18	4	4	5
19	4	4	4
20	4	4	5
21	3	4	4
22	5	5	5
23	4	5	4
24	3	4	4

Correlations

		q1	q2	q3
q1	Pearson Correlation	1	.525**	.093
	Sig. (2-tailed)		.008	.667
	N	24	24	24
q2	Pearson Correlation	.525**	1	.008
	Sig. (2-tailed)	.008		.969
	N	24	24	24
q3	Pearson Correlation	.093	.008	1
	Sig. (2-tailed)	.667	.969	
	N	24	24	24

**. Correlation is significant at the 0.01 level (2-tailed).

The Pearson correlation coefficient between questions q1 and q2 is statistically significant, $r(24) = .525, p = .008$. That is, there is a linear relationship between these two questions for the population from which the sample of 24 observations was randomly selected.

Factors affecting the Pearson *r*. To better understand which factors affect the Pearson *r* (and why?), it is important to keep in mind that the Pearson *r* is an index of the linear relationship between two variables. Thus, $r = 0.0$ indicates that there is no linear relationship between the two variables, but there might be some nonlinear relationship between them. In Figure 10.5a, for example, $r = 0.0$, but there is a curvilinear relationship between two variables (say, age and physical strength). Figure 10.5b illustrates a scenario in which $r = 0.0$ when calculated over a restricted range of variable values, although there is a linear relationship between the two variables over a larger range of their measures. In another scenario, there may not be a linear relationship between two variables for a sample of persons ($r = 0.0$), but there might be a linear relationship between the variables for some subgroups of persons from the total sample. This is illustrated in Figure 10.5c, where there is a positive linear relationship between *X* and *Y* for one subgroup (females) and, conversely, a negative linear relationship between *X* and *Y* for another subgroup (males), despite the fact that there is no linear relationship ($r = 0.0$) for the total sample. In this case, calculating and interpreting correlation coefficients for separate subgroups is more useful than interpreting the lack of linear relationship ($r = 0.0$) for the entire sample.

Figure 10.5. *Scatterplots illustrating (a) curvilinear relationship, (b) restricted range, and (c) correlations by subgroups (e.g., females and males).*

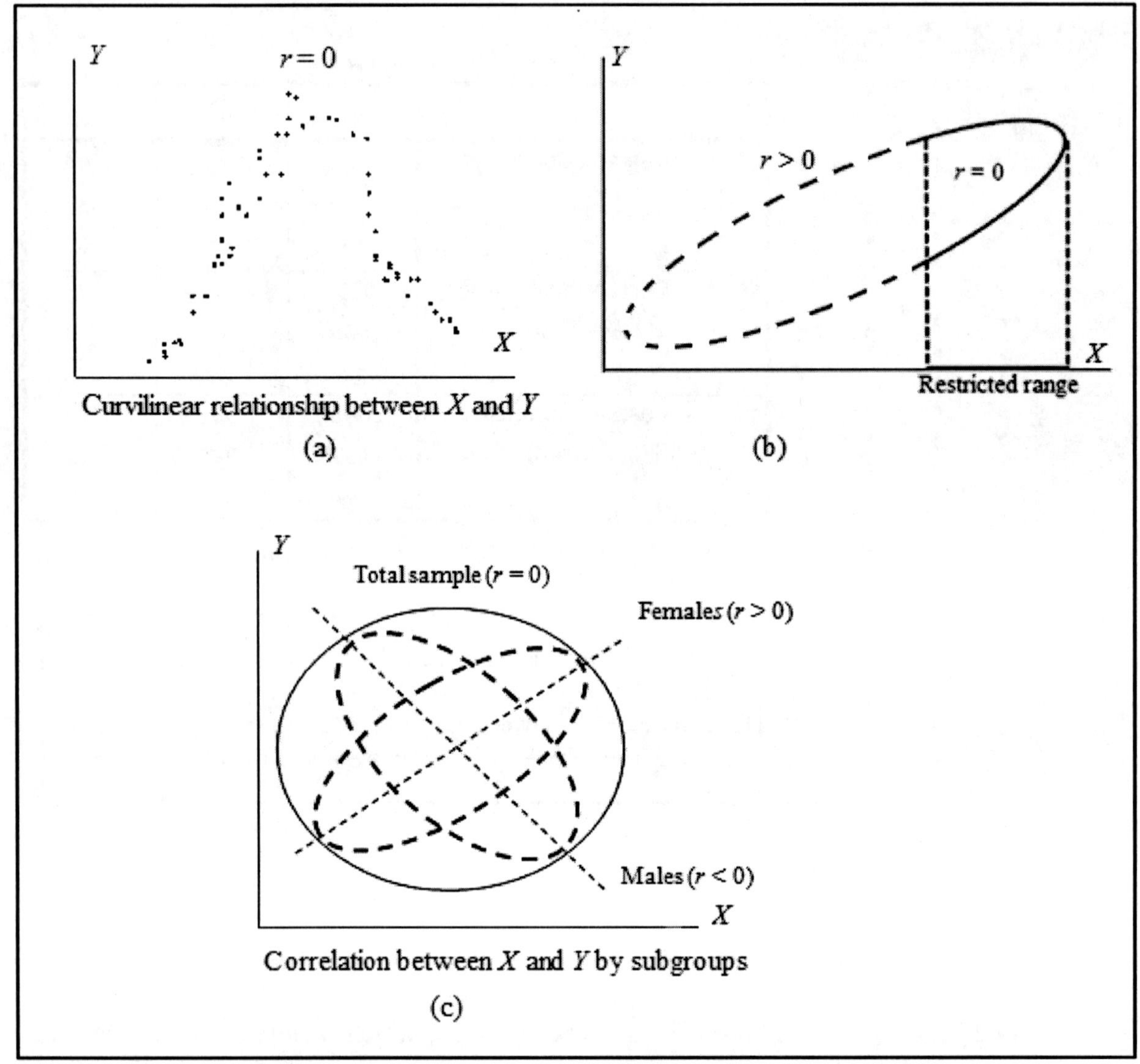

Linear transformations and the Pearson *r*. Linear transformations on *X* and/or *Y* do not affect the size of the Pearson *r*. Suppose that $X^* = bX + a$ and $Y^* = cX + d$ are linear transformations on *X* and *Y*, respectively. Such transformations are often used to represent *X* and *Y* on a common scale (e.g., to convert the *X* and *Y* scores into standard scores z_X and z_Y, respectively). If the slopes in these two linear transformations (*b* and *c*) have the same sign (both positive or both negative), the transformation does not affect the correlation coefficient, i.e., $r_{X^*Y^*} = r_{XY}$. If, however, *b* and *c* have opposite signs, the size of the correlation remains the same, but its sign changes ($r_{X^*Y^*} = -r_{XY}$). For example, if $r_{XY} = -.82$ and the transformations are $X^* = 5X + 10$ and $Y^* = 1.5Y - 4$, the correlation coefficient does not change ($r_{X^*Y^*} = -.82$) because the slopes (5 and 1.5) are both positive. An important implication is that the correlation coefficient does not change when the values of *X* and *Y* are transformed into standard (z-) scores ($\mu = 0$; $\sigma = 1$) or into scores on other scales such as the T-scale ($\mu = 50$; $\sigma = 10$) or the *norm curve equivalent* (*NCE*) scale ($\mu = 50$; $\sigma = 21$).

Coefficient of determination, r^2. The Pearson r is a measure of the linear relationship between two variables, but it is also used to determine the degree to which the individual differences in one variable can be associated with the individual differences in another variable. Specifically, the square of the correlation coefficient, referred to as the *coefficient of determination*, r^2, indicates what proportion of the variance in one of the correlated variables is associated with the variance in the other variable. For example, if $r = .30$ is the correlation between "motivation" and "task performance", then $r^2 = .09$. This shows that nine percent of an individual's differences in motivation is associated with their differences in task performance (or vice versa).

The Venn diagrams in Figure 10.6 provide a graphical illustration of the coefficient of determination, r^2, where each circle represents the variance of one variable. When the focus in interpreting r^2 is on the degree to which the variance in Y is associated with the variance in X, the variable Y is called the **dependent variable** and X, the **independent variable**. The larger the overlap between the two circles, the higher the proportion of the variance in Y associated with the variance in X. The lack of overlap in Figure 10.6a shows that there is no correlation between X and Y or, equivalently, that none of the variance in Y is explained by the variance in X. The overlap in Figure 10.6b, however, illustrates that 16 percent of the variance in Y is explained by the variance in X.

Figure 10.6. *Venn diagram of shared (common) variance in variables X and Y*

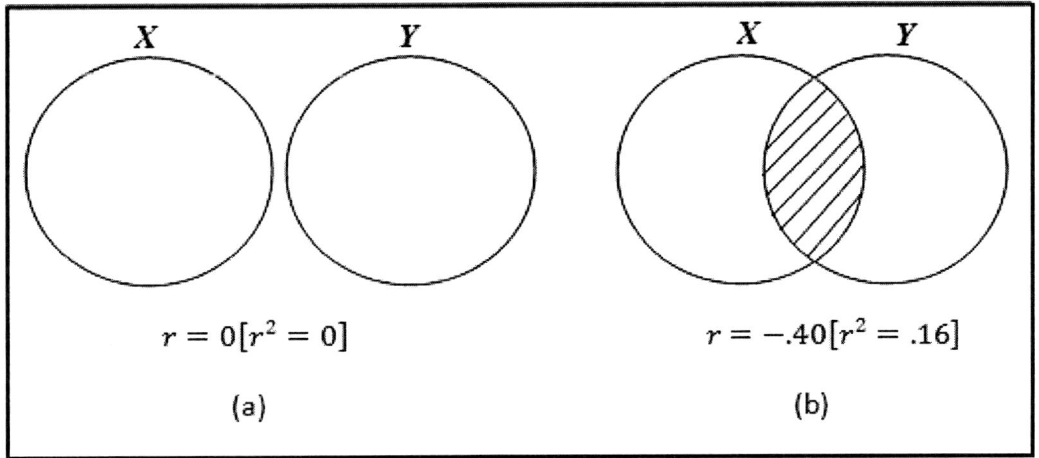

Correlation and causation. As noted earlier, the coefficient of determination, r^2, shows what proportion of the variance in Y is associated with the variance in X, but this does not necessarily mean that individual differences in Y are caused by individual differences in X. That is, **correlation does not necessarily mean causation**. For example, using the SPSS World95 survey data (see Figure 10.2), the correlation between "percent of females who read" and "average female life expectancy" was $r = .819$. Then, $r^2 = (.819)^2 = .671$ indicates that 67.1 percent of the differences in average female life expectancy worldwide is associated with differences in the percent of females who read. There is no logical basis, however, to believe that differences in literacy across countries *cause* differences in average life expectancy among these countries. Most likely, literacy and average life expectancy are correlated because they are both causally affected by a third variable (say, "standard of living") or even by several other variables.

NOTE [10.2] Hereafter, the terms "associated with," "accounted for by," and "explained by" are used synonymously in interpreting r^2 as a proportion of the variance in Y associated with (accounted for by, explained by) the variance in X. However, they *do not imply causality*.

10.2 Simple Linear Regression

10.2.1 Correlation, Prediction, and Causation

The linear relationship between two variables can be used to predict values on one of the variables from values on the other variable. If the goal is to predict scores on Y from scores on X, then Y is called the *dependent variable* and X, the *independent variable*. The dependent variable, Y, is also referred to as the *criterion variable* and X, the *predictor* variable. Which of two variables is considered Y (criterion) and which one is considered X (predictor) depends on the research question. For example, given that there is a positive correlation between IQ test scores and grade-point average (GPA), we may want to predict GPA from IQ scores. In this case, the dependent variable is Y = GPA and the independent variable is X = IQ.

It is important to reiterate that correlation does not necessarily mean causation. A high (positive or negative) correlation between X and Y indicates that scores on Y can be accurately predicted from scores on X, but this does not imply that changes in X *cause* changes in Y. For example, using data from the World95 survey (see, Figure 10.1), we can predict *average female life expectancy* from *female literacy* although there is no causal relationship between these two variables. In a more extreme example, it is possible to predict mental ability from shoe size for children of age, say 5 to 16, although the existence of a correlation between these two variables does not make sense. In fact, the correlation between these two variables "vanishes" after partialling out the common cause (age). In general, when two variables are affected by a common cause, the correlation between them is referred to as a *spurious correlation* — a concept that will be discussed later in this book.

It is important to keep in mind that the emphasis in predictive research is on practical applications, not on causal explanations. Of course, results in predictive research can be very useful in generating cause-and-effect hypotheses. Conversely, the chances of accurate prediction increase when the selection of predictor variables is based on their theoretical relationship with the criterion variable.

10.2.2. The Regression Line

Suppose that a sample of scores on X and Y is available and the goal is to predict Y scores from X scores with future samples in which only X scores are available. This is illustrated for the SPSS data provided in the Study Question section in Chapter 8 (Question 4). The task is to predict students' posttest math scores from their pretest scores. In Figure 10.7, the scatterplot reveals a positive linear relationship between the pretest (X) and posttest (Y) scores (r = .786). The straight line fitting the scatterplot can be used to predict scores on Y from scores on X. Specifically, for any value of X, the predicted Y value (denoted $\hat{Y}$) is located on the straight line.

The difference between an actual Y score and its predicted value, $\hat{Y}$, is referred to as prediction **error**: $e = Y - \hat{Y}$ [see its graphical illustration for the leftmost dot in Figure 10.7]. The Y scores for data points (●) above the prediction line are associated with positive errors ($e > 0$), whereas those below the prediction line are associated with negative errors ($e < 0$). The **total er-**

ror with the straight line prediction is the **sum of squared errors**: $SSE = \sum e^2 = \sum(Y - \hat{Y})^2$. Among all possible prediction lines, the one that produces the smallest total error (sum of squared errors) is the line of "best fit," or the **regression line**. With this approach, known as the **least squares method**, the line of the best fit produces the smallest sum of squared distances from the actual data points (•) to the prediction line. The prediction with a regression line is referred to as **simple linear regression** because only one predictor is used to predict *Y* from *X* (or, "regress *Y* on *X*").

Figure 10.7 *Regression line for the prediction of posttest scores from pretest scores*

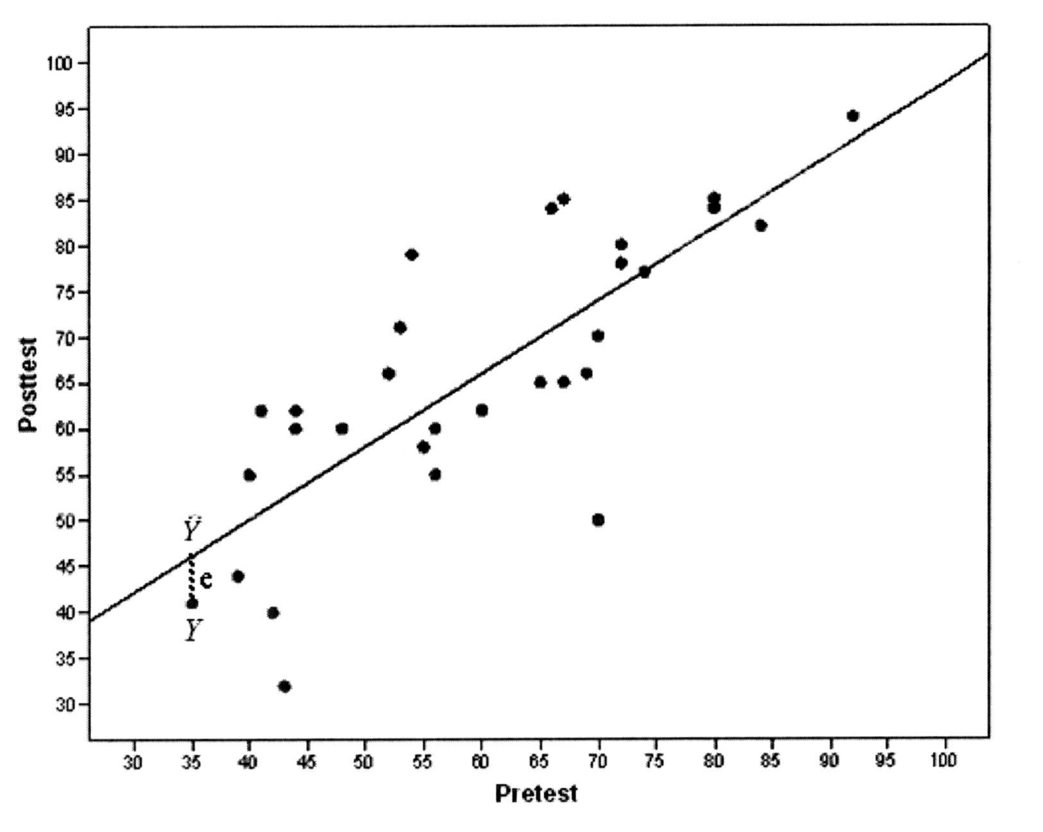

The general analytic form of the regression line is provided with the equation

$$\hat{Y} = bX + a \qquad \textbf{(10.6)}$$

where *b* is the **slope** and *a* is the **intercept** of the regression line. The slope, *b*, governs the steepness of the regression line. The intercept, *a*, shows the intersection point of this line on the vertical axis (*Y*). Indeed, by replacing $X = 0$ in Equation 10.6, we obtain $\hat{Y} = a$. That is, (0, *a*) is the intersection point of the prediction line and the vertical axis (*Y*). With the least squares method, the slope and the intercept for the line of best fit are calculated as follows:

$$b = r_{XY}\left(\frac{S_Y}{S_X}\right) \qquad \textbf{(10.7)}$$

$$a = \bar{Y} - b\bar{X} \qquad \textbf{(10.8)}$$

where:

r_{XY} = correlation between X and Y,
s_X = standard deviation of the X scores,
s_Y = standard deviation of the Y scores,
$\overline{X}$ = mean of the X scores, and
$\overline{Y}$ = mean of the Y scores.

In Formula 10.7, the standard deviations are always positive ($s_X > 0$, $s_Y > 0$). Therefore, the slope, b, and the correlation coefficient, r_{XY}, have the same sign. Given this, a positive slope (b) indicates a positive direction, and a negative slope, a negative direction of the regression line.

> **NOTE [10.3] The data point with coordinates $(\overline{X}, \overline{Y})$ always belongs to the regression line.** This can be seen by replacing X with $\overline{X}$ in Equation 10.6, $\hat{Y} = b\overline{X} + a$, and then comparing this expression for $\hat{Y}$ with that for $\overline{Y}$, obtained from Equation 10.8: $\overline{Y} = b\overline{X} + a$. Thus, $\hat{Y} = \overline{Y}$, which shows that $\overline{Y}$ is the predicted Y score for $X = \overline{X}$.

EXAMPLE 10.2 For the pretest-posttest data in Chapter 8 (Study Question 4), r_{XY} = .786, $\overline{X}$ = 59.67, $\overline{Y}$ = 65.73, s_X = 15.112, and s_Y = 15.245. Using Formulas 10.7 and 10.8, we obtain b = (.786)(15.245)/15.112 = 0.793 and a = 65.73 – (0.793)(59.67) = 18.412 for the slope and intercept, respectively. Thus, the equation of the regression line is $\hat{Y}$ = 0.793X + 18.412. By replacing X with a specific value in this equation, say X = 60, we obtain $\hat{Y}$ = (0.793)(60) + 18.412 = 65.99. In other words, a student who earns a score of 60 on the pretest will have a predicted posttest score of 66 (rounded to the nearest integer).

To use SPSS with the data in this example, follow the steps:

1. Click **Analyze,** click **Regression**, and click **Linear**.
2. Click **Posttest** and click ► to enter this variable in the box **Dependent Variable**.
3. Click Pre**test** and click ► to enter this variable in the box **Independent Variable.**
4. Click **OK**.

The resulting SPSS output is provided in Figure 10.8. The first step in the interpretation of the results in the SPSS output is to determine whether the correlation between the dependent variable (posttest, Y) and the independent variable (pretest, X) is statistically significant. In the **Model Summary** table, R = .786 is the Pearson correlation coefficient between X and Y. The F-test for statistical significance of this correlation coefficient is reported with the **ANOVA** table in the SPSS output. Clearly, the correlation coefficient (R = .786) is statistically significant at the .001 level, $F(1, 28) = 45.127, p < .001$. This means that there is a positive linear relationship between the dependent variable (posttest, Y) and the independent variable (pretest, X) for population in this example. The next step is to interpret the *coefficient of determination*. In this case, R^2 = .617 (see **Model Summary** table), thus indicating that 61.7 percent of the variance in the posttest scores, Y, is accounted for by the variance in the pretest scores, X. The **Coefficients** table provides the slope and the intercept for the regression line: b = 0.792 and a = 18.449 [the difference between the SPSS values for b and a and those obtained with manual computations earlier in this example (b = 0.793 and a = 18.412) is due to rounding errors]. Thus, the simple linear regression equation for the prediction of posttest scores, Y, from pretest scores, X, is:

$$\hat{Y} = (0.792)X + 18.449.$$

Figure 10.8 *SPSS output for the simple linear regression of posttest to pretest scores.*

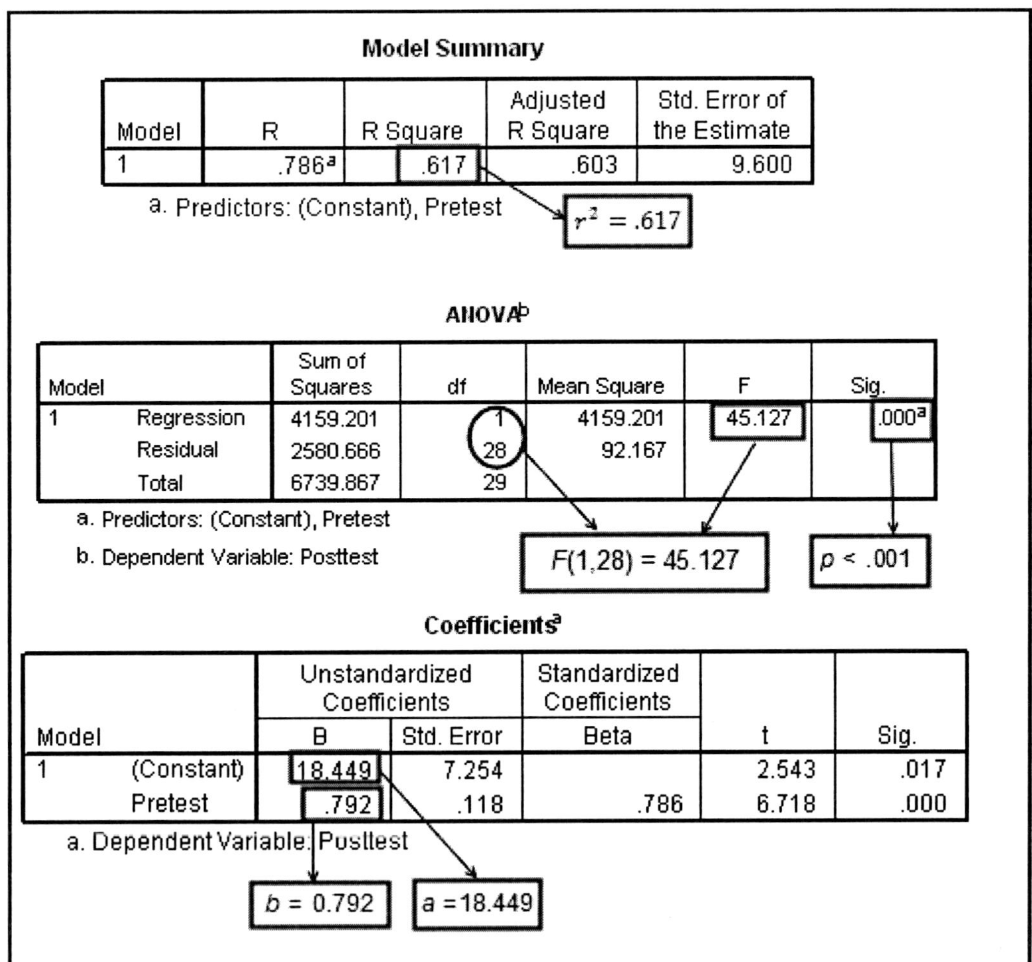

Model Summary

Model	R	R Square	Adjusted R Square	Std. Error of the Estimate
1	.786[a]	.617	.603	9.600

a. Predictors: (Constant), Pretest

ANOVA[b]

Model		Sum of Squares	df	Mean Square	F	Sig.
1	Regression	4159.201	1	4159.201	45.127	.000[a]
	Residual	2580.666	28	92.167		
	Total	6739.867	29			

a. Predictors: (Constant), Pretest

b. Dependent Variable: Posttest

Coefficients[a]

Model		Unstandardized Coefficients		Standardized Coefficients	t	Sig.
		B	Std. Error	Beta		
1	(Constant)	18.449	7.254		2.543	.017
	Pretest	.792	.118	.786	6.718	.000

a. Dependent Variable: Posttest

NOTE [10.4] In Figure 10.8, the F-test for statistical significance of the correlation between Y and X (**ANOVA** table) can be equivalently replaced by the t-test for statistical significance of the slope (b = 0.792) in the **Coefficients** table. In this case, the t-statistic (t = 6.718 is also statistically significant at the .001 level. However, when two or more independent variables are used to predict the independent variable, Y, the F-test in the **ANOVA** table is for the statistical significance of the prediction by all predictors together, whereas the t-tests in the **Coefficients** table are for statistical significance of the unique contribution of each predictor to the prediction of Y; [this will be discussed in Chapter 13].

10.2.3 Interpretation of the Slope

In general, the slope, b, in a simple linear regression equation equals the ratio "change in $\hat{Y}$ to change in X" for any X value and any magnitude of change in X:

$$b = \frac{\Delta \hat{Y}}{\Delta X}, \tag{10.9}$$

where ΔX denotes the change in X and $\Delta \hat{Y}$ denotes the associate change in the predicted score, $\hat{Y}$.

With $\Delta X = 1$, $b = \Delta\hat{Y}/1 = \Delta\hat{Y}$. Thus, **the slope in the simple regression equation indicates the change in the predicted Y score associated with a unit change in the predictor variable, X.**

Figure 10.9 depicts the regression equation $\hat{Y} = 0.5X + 4$. The positive slope ($b = 0.5$) indicates that when the X scores increase, the predicted scores ($\hat{Y}$) also increase. For example, when X increases from 2 to 3 ($\Delta X = 1$), the predicted score increases by 0.5 ($\Delta\hat{Y} = 0.5$). Likewise, if X increases from 5 to 9 ($\Delta X = 4$), the predicted score increases by two units ($\Delta\hat{Y} = 2$). When the slope is negative, an increase in X ($\Delta X > 0$) yields a decrease in $\hat{Y}$ ($\Delta\hat{Y} < 0$).

NOTE [10.5] To find the predicted score, $\hat{Y}$, given X, we replace X with its given value in the regression equation. However, to find the change in the predicted score, given the change in X, we use the equation $\Delta\hat{Y} = (b)(\Delta X)$, which follows directly from Formula 10.9.

EXAMPLE 10.3 Suppose that the regression equation for the prediction of students' Grade Point Average (GPA) from their verbal ability (VA) scores on a T-scale ($\mu = 50$, $\sigma = 10$) is as follows: $\widehat{GPA} = 0.05(VA) - 0.1$. Suppose also that we want to know (a) the predicted GPA for students with a verbal ability score of 50 and (b) how do the predicted GPAs of John and Mary compare, if Mary scored higher than John on verbal ability test by 20 points.

To address the first question, we replace $VA = 50$ in the regression equation thus obtaining: $\widehat{GPA} = 0.05(50) - 0.1 = 2.40$. To answer the second question, we use the formula for change in the predicted score, given the slope and the change in X: $\Delta\hat{Y} = (b)(\Delta X)$. In this case, $b = 0.05$ and $\Delta X = 20$ (the difference between verbal ability scores of John and Mary), so we have: $\Delta\hat{Y} = (0.05)(20) = 1$. Further, the slope is positive ($b = 0.05$) which indicates a positive direction of the regression line. Thus, students with higher verbal ability scores have higher predicted GPAs and, therefore, Mary's predicted GPA is 1 point higher than the GPA of John.

Figure 10.9 The regression slope ($b = 0.5$) as a change-rate ($\Delta\hat{Y}/\Delta X$).

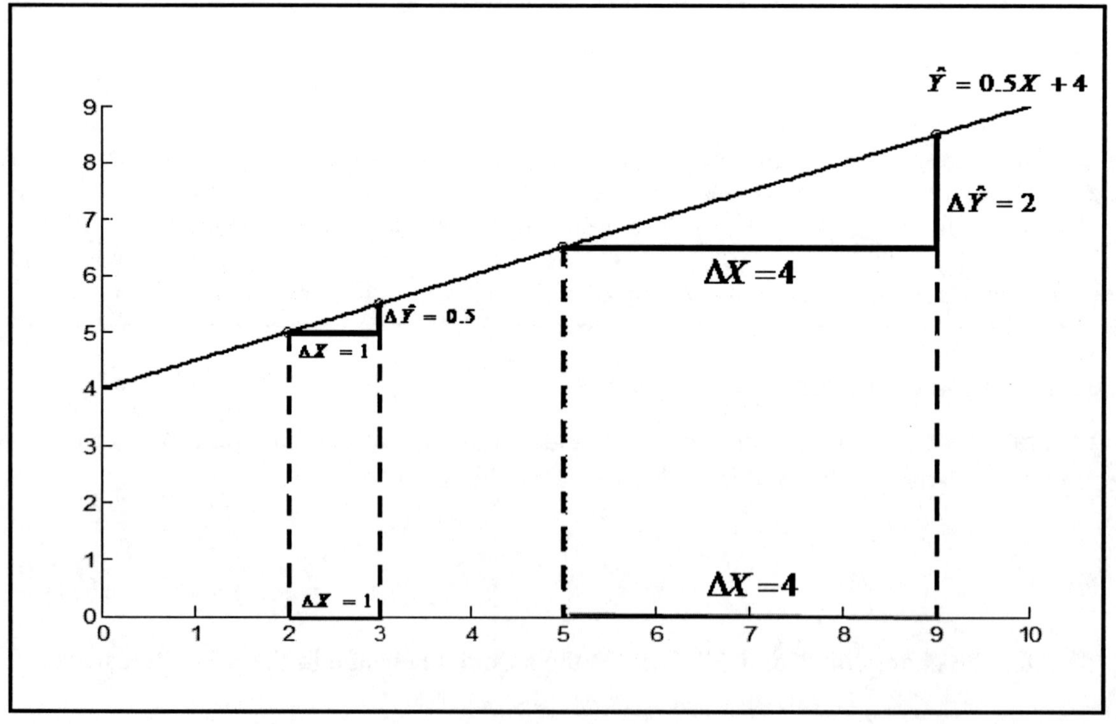

10.2.4 Conditional Distributions of *Y* Scores

Suppose $\hat{Y} = 0.75X + 5$ is the regression equation for predicting *aggressiveness* from *anger*; (Y = aggressiveness, X = anger). All individuals with a given score X have the same predicted score, $\hat{Y}$. However, the actual Y scores of people with the same X score are spread around their predicted score and form a distribution called **conditional distribution of *Y* scores given *X***. The *mean* of the conditional distribution for a given X is the predicted Y value, $\hat{Y}$. For example, Figure 10.10 illustrates the conditional distributions of Y scores (aggressiveness) for three different values of the independent variable (anger): $X = 10$, $X = 20$, and $X = 30$.

The simple linear regression assumes (a) **normality** — the conditional distributions of Y values across X values are normal and (b) **homoscedasticity** — the conditional distributions have equal variances. Given also that the simple linear regression assumes a linear relationship between X and Y, as well as independence of the Y scores, there are four assumptions with the simple linear regression: (a) linearity, (b) independence, (c) normality, and (d) homoscedasticity.

Under the assumption of homoscedasticity, all conditional distributions of actual Y values have the same variance, denoted $\sigma^2_{Y.X}$. The standard deviation of the conditional distributions of actual Y values, $\sigma_{Y.X}$, is called the **standard error of estimate**. The sample estimate of $\sigma_{Y.X}$ is denoted $s_{Y.X}$ (read "standard deviation of Y given X") and computed as

$$s_{Y.X} = s_Y\sqrt{1 - r^2}, \qquad \textbf{(10.10)}$$

where s_Y is the standard deviation of Y for the sample and r is the correlation between X and Y.

For example, with the sample data used to develop the equation $\hat{Y} = 0.75X + 5$ for the prediction of *aggressiveness* from *anger*, $s_Y = 5$ and $r = .866$. Using Formula 10.10, the standard error of estimate is $s_{Y.X} = (5)\sqrt{1 - (.866)^2} = 2.5$. Thus, $s_{Y.X} = 2.5$.

Figure 10.10 *Three conditional distributions of Y values with the simple linear regression for the prediction of aggressiveness from anger: $\hat{Y} = 0.75X + 5$.*

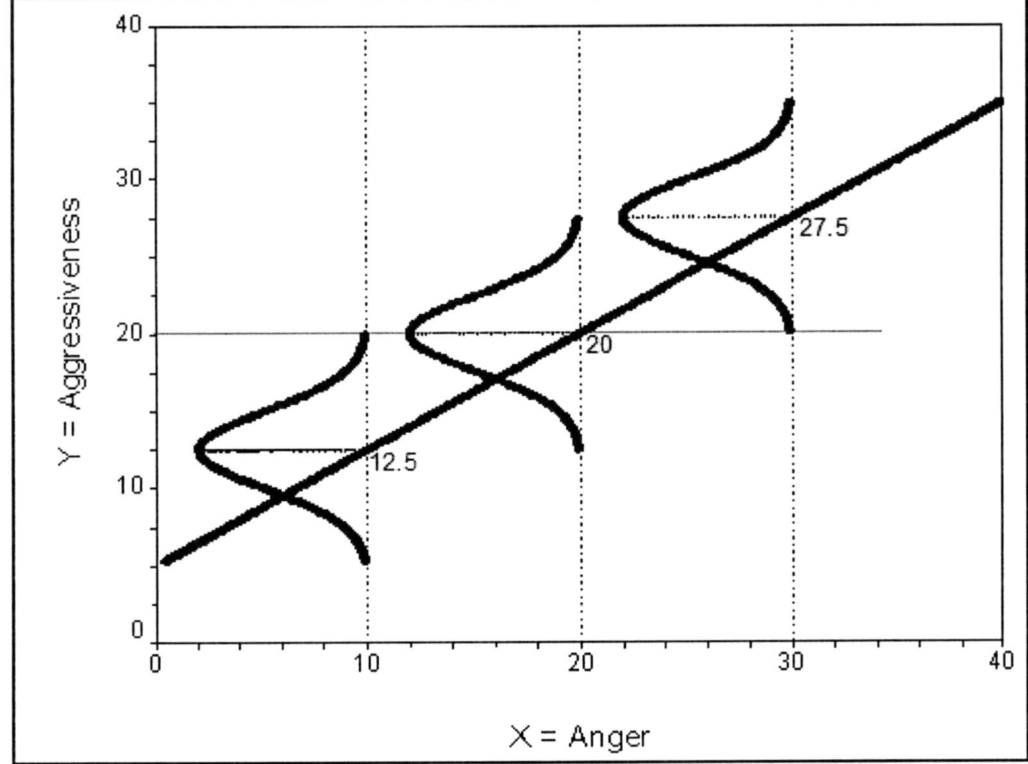

Given the standard error of estimate, $s_{Y.X}$, we can use the "3-sigma rule" for normal distributions to determine the interval of (almost) all actual Y values given X (see NOTE [7.1]). For example, we computed $s_{Y.X}$ = 255 for the conditional distributions of Y values in Figure 10.10. Thus, using that the predicted Y scores for $X = 10$ is $\hat{Y} = 12.5$, we can say that almost all (99.7%) of the Y scores for $X = 10$ fall within the interval: $\hat{Y} \pm 3s_{Y.X} = 12.5 \pm (3)(2.5) = 12.5 \pm 7.5$, that is between 5 and 20. Likewise, we can see that almost all Y values for $X = 20$ fall between 12.5 to 27.5 and that almost all Y values for $X = 30$ fall between 20 and 35.

Suppose now that people are considered "at risk" for aggressiveness if their Y score (on the aggressiveness scale) exceeds 20 points. None of the persons with 10 points on the *anger* scale ($X = 10$) is "at risk" for aggressiveness because almost all Y scores in the conditional distribution for $X = 10$ are between 5 and 20 (below the cutting score of 20 points for aggressiveness). At the same time, 50% of the people with a score of 20 on the anger scale ($X = 20$) are "at risk" for aggressiveness and almost all (100%) of those with 30 points on the anger scale ($X = 30$) are "at risk" for aggressiveness [Why?]

NOTE [10.6] With small samples (e.g., $n < 30$), Formula 10.10 underestimates the standard error of estimate, $s_{Y.X}$. This bias can be corrected by multiplying $s_{Y.X}$ by $\sqrt{(n-1)/(n-2)}$.

EXAMPLE 10.4 Provided below are the SPSS data and regression output for the prediction of **motivation** (Y) from **task involvement** (X), which is labeled "Task" in the SPSS file.

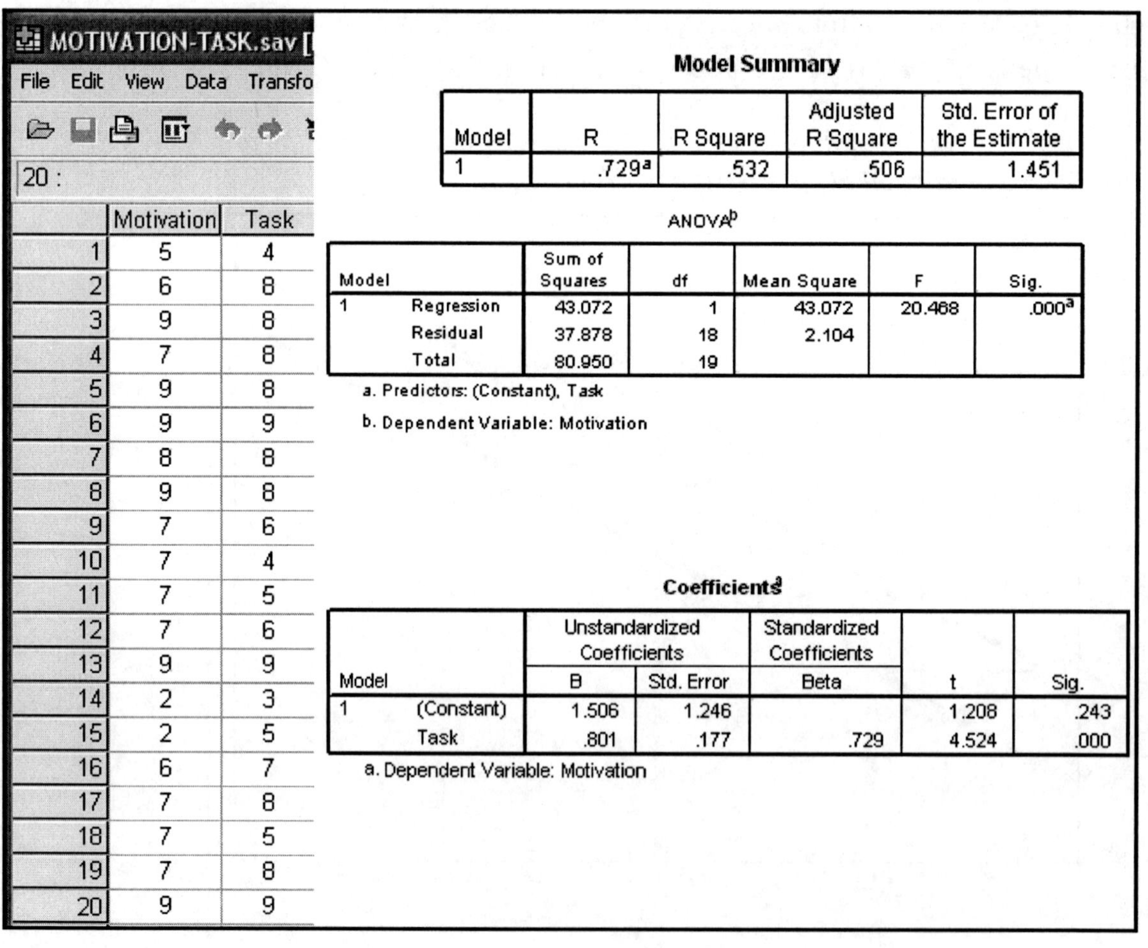

MOTIVATION-TASK.sav

	Motivation	Task
1	5	4
2	6	8
3	9	8
4	7	8
5	9	8
6	9	9
7	8	8
8	9	8
9	7	6
10	7	4
11	7	5
12	7	6
13	9	9
14	2	3
15	2	5
16	6	7
17	7	8
18	7	5
19	7	8
20	9	9

Model Summary

Model	R	R Square	Adjusted R Square	Std. Error of the Estimate
1	.729[a]	.532	.506	1.451

ANOVA[b]

Model		Sum of Squares	df	Mean Square	F	Sig.
1	Regression	43.072	1	43.072	20.468	.000[a]
	Residual	37.878	18	2.104		
	Total	80.950	19			

a. Predictors: (Constant), Task

b. Dependent Variable: Motivation

Coefficients[a]

Model		Unstandardized Coefficients		Standardized Coefficients	t	Sig.
		B	Std. Error	Beta		
1	(Constant)	1.506	1.246		1.208	.243
	Task	.801	.177	.729	4.524	.000

a. Dependent Variable: Motivation

Suppose that, for people with a task involvement score of 5, we want to determine (a) the predicted score on motivation, (b) the interval that contains their actual scores on motivation, and (c) their probability to "pass" a cutting score of 7 points on motivation. Given the results in the **ANOVA** table, we can say that the prediction of motivation from task involvement is statistically significant at the .001 level, $F(1, 18) = 20.468$, $p < .001$. From the **Coefficients** table, we use the slope ($b = 0.801$) and the intercept ($a = 1.506$) to obtain the regression equation for the prediction of motivation (Y) from task involvement (X):

$$\hat{Y} = (0.801)X + 1.506.$$

Now we can answer questions (a), (b), and (c) as follows:

(a) By replacing $X = 5$ in the above regression equation we obtain the predicted motivation score for people with a task involvement score of 5:

$$\hat{Y} = (0.801)(5) + 1.506 = 5.511.$$

(b) To determine the interval that contains the actual scores on motivation (Y) for people with 5 points on task involvement ($X = 5$), we use the assumption that these scores are distributed according to a normal distribution with a mean that equals the predicted Y score for $X = 5$ (5.511) and a standard deviation equal to the standard error of estimate, $s_{Y.X}$. In this case, $s_{Y.X} =$ 1.451 (reported in the **Model Summary** table). Thus, the interval of interest can be obtained by using the "3-sigma rule":

$$\hat{Y} \pm 3s_{Y.X} = 5.11 \pm (3)(1.451) = 5.511 \pm 4.353 = (1.158, 9.864).$$

Rounding the ends of this interval to the nearest integer, we see that the motivation scores for people with 5 points on task involvement fall between 1 and 10 points.

(c) For people with 5 points on task involvement ($X = 5$), the actual motivation scores are on a normal distribution with mean $Y = 5.511$ and standard deviation $s_{Y.X} = 1.451$. The question about their probability to "pass" a cutting score of 7 points on motivation becomes: "What is the area above a score of 7 under the normal curve with a mean of 5.511 and a standard deviation of 1.451?" This normal curve is the conditional normal distribution of motivation (Y) scores for people with 5 points on task involvement ($X = 5$) — like the normal curves in Figure 10.10, but for convenience it can be depicted horizontally as shown here below.

The z-score for $X = 7$ is $z = (7 - 5.511)/1.451 = 1.026$. The area "beyond" this score under the standard normal curve equals .1524 [in Table A-1, z = 1.026 is between z = 1.02 and z = 1.03]. Thus, people with 5 points on task involvement have a probability of .1524 (15.24% chances) to "pass" the cutting score of 7 points on the motivation scale.

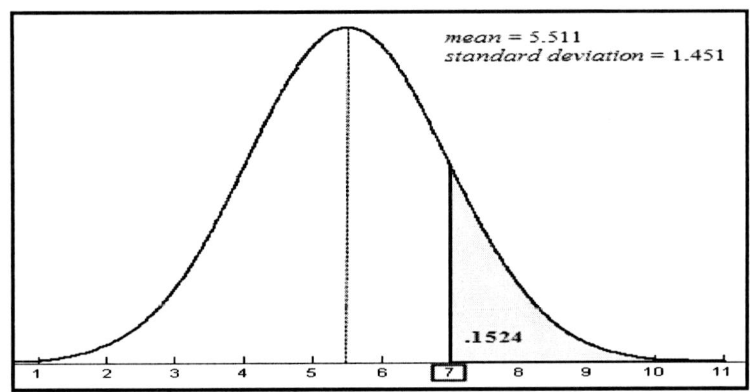

10.2.5 Assumptions with Simple Linear Regression

As mentioned earlier, there are four principal assumptions which justify the use of a simple linear regression for the purposes of predicting a dependent variable, Y, from an independent variable, X: **linearity**, **independence**, **normality**, and **homoscedasticity**. Violations of these assumptions threaten the accuracy of the prediction.

Linearity. The assumption of linearity is met when the relationship between X and Y is linear. Although the scatterplot of Y versus X can be used as a visual check for linearity, the Pearson correlation coefficient, r_{XY}, must be statistically significant to claim that the relationship between X and Y is linear. We can use the *t*-test in Formula 10.5 or, equivalently, the *F*-test reported with the SPSS output for simple linear regression.

Independence. The assumption of independence is met when the scores on the dependent variable, Y, are independent. This assumption would be violated, for example, when the Y scores are obtained for students who work in groups. With high certainty, the assumption of independence is met when the observations come from random samples.

Normality. The assumption of normality in simple linear regression means that the conditional distributions of Y scores across fixed values of X are normal distributions (see Figure 10.10). This assumption implies that the *residuals* (differences between the observed and predicted Y values) are normally distributed.

Let's illustrate the assessment of the normality assumption using SPSS with the data in Example 10.4, but this time using **Task** as the dependent variable and Motivation as the independent variable [this case is addressed with study question 21 at the end of the chapter].

1. Click **Analyze**, click **Regression**, and click **Linear**.
2. Click **Task** and click ▶ to move it into the box **Dependent.**
3. Click **Motivation** and click ▶ to move it into the box **Independent(s)**.
4. At the bottom of the dialog box **Linear Regression**, click **Plots**.
5. In the bottom panel *Standardized Residual Plots*, check **Normal probability plot**.
6. Check **Continue.**
7. Check **OK**.

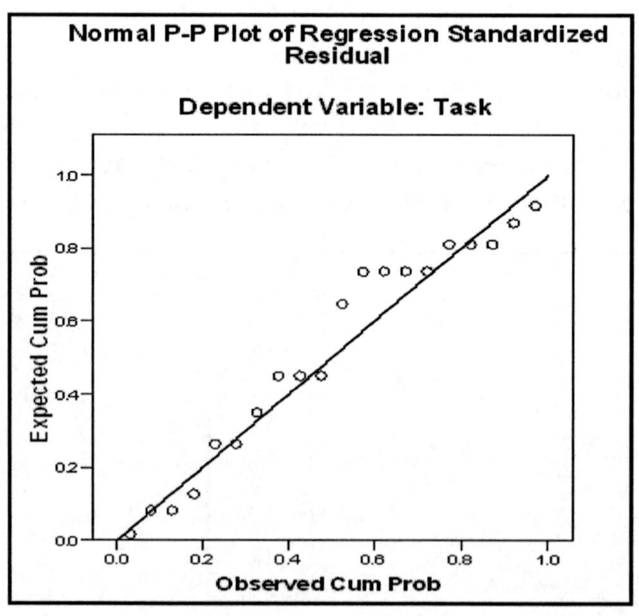

The assumption of normality is met if the scatterplot of the observed and expected cumulative probabilities for standardized residuals stretches along a straight line in the normal P-P plot. As can be seen, this criterion is met for the P-P plot with the SPSS data in this example.

. • **Homoscedasticity.** The assumption of homoscedasticity, referred to also as the assumption of **constant variance**, requires that the conditional distributions of Y values across fixed X values have the same variance (see Figure 10.10).

The homoscedasticity can be assessed by plotting the residuals ($e = Y - \hat{Y}$) against the predicted values. We illustrate this here using SPSS again with the data in Example 10.4, but using **Task** as the dependent variable (i.e., Y = Task, X = Motivation). All steps in using SPSS are the same as those just described with the testing for normality using the same data. The only exception is that **Step 5** in the previous list of seven steps is now replaced as follows:

> Step 5: In the dialog box **Linear Regression Plots**, click ***ZRESID** and click ► to move it into the box **Y:** Then click ***ZPRED** and click ► to move it into the box **X:** [see Figure 10.11, left panel.]

Figure 10.11 *SPSS dialog box and output for graphical assessment of homoscedasticity*

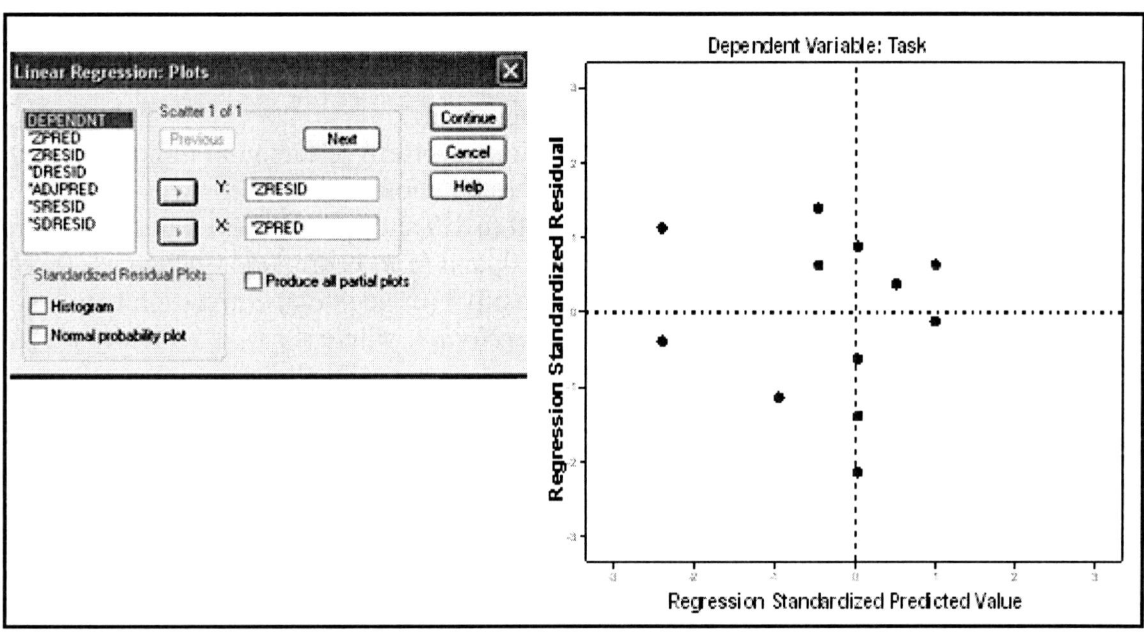

The assumption of homoscedasticity (constant variance) is supported when the dots in the scatterplot are randomly spread around zero — that is, there is no pattern of increase or decrease in the residuals when the predicted values increase. The examination of the scatterplot in Figure 10.11 (right panel) shows that the assumption of homoscedasticity is not violated with the regression of *task involvement* on *motivation*.

Let us also note that "task involvement" is a directly observable variable, whereas "motivation" is a typical latent trait (unobservable variable). Depending on the research question, motivation can be predicted from task involvement (see Example 10.4) or, conversely, task involvement can be predicted from motivation (see study question 21 at the end of the chapter). Any of these two cases may be embedded in a more complex model of relationships investigated with advanced statistical methods (e.g., structural equation modeling — see Chapter 24).

10.3 SUMMARY

This chapter introduces the concepts of linear relationship (correlation) between two variables and simple linear regression. Some major points are summarized here in the form of responses to questions addressed in this chapter.

What is correlation between two variables?

In general, the correlation between two variables reveals the nature and the strength of their relationship (e.g., linear or curvilinear), if such relationship exists. The discussion of correlation in this chapter is restricted to linear relationship between two variables. A *positive correlation* (i.e., positive linear relationship) between two variables, X and Y, exists when high X values relate to high Y values and low X values relate to low Y values. Conversely, a *negative correlation* between X and Y exists when high X values relate to low Y values and low X values relate to high Y values. Graphically, the scatterplot for X and Y reveals (a) a positive correlation when the dots group along a straight line with a positive slope (i.e., the direction of the dots is from the lower left to the upper right), and (b) a negative correlation when dots group along a straight line with a negative slope (i.e., the direction of the dots is from the upper left to the lower right). In either case, the closer the dots to the straight line, the stronger the (positive or negative) correlation. When neither a positive, nor a negative correlation between two variables exists, there is no correlation (linear relationship) between them.

What is the Pearson product-moment correlation coefficient?

The Pearson product-moment correlation coefficient (briefly, Pearson r) indicates the direction (positive or negative) and the strength of a linear relationship between two variables, X and Y. Specifically, Pearson r takes on values from -1.0 to 1.0 and indicates (a) a positive correlation, when $r > 0$, (b) a negative correlation, when $r < 0$, and (c) no correlation, when $r = 0$. The closer the Pearson r to 1.0 (or -1.0), the stronger the positive (or negative) correlation between X and Y. Theoretically, $r = 1$indicates *perfect positive correlation*, whereas $r = -1$ indicates *perfect negative correlation* between X and Y. In both cases ($r = 1$ or $r = -1$), all data points in the scatterplot for X and Y fall on a straight line with a positive or negative slope, respectively. A rule of thumb for interpreting the size of Pearson r is based on its absolute value (sign ignored) as follows: (a) .90 to 1.00 = very high correlation, (b) .70 to .90 = high correlation, (c) .50 to .70 = moderate correlation, (d) .30 to .50 = low correlation, and (e) .00 to .30 = very low (if any) correlation.

What is a statistically significant Pearson *r*?

As the Pearson r is sample dependent, it is important to determine whether a linear relationship between two variables, X and Y, exists in the population from which the sample has been randomly selected. With ρ_{XY} denoting the correlation between X and Y in the population, the null hypothesis H_0: $\rho_{XY} = 0$ is tested versus the alternative H_a: $\rho_{XY} \neq 0$. When H_0 is rejected at a given level of significance (say, $\alpha = .05$), the sample-based Pearson r is referred to as statistically significant correlation coefficient thus indicating that there is a linear relationship between X and Y for the study population.

Which factors affect the Pearson *r*?

The size of the Pearson r is affected by factors such as sample size, range of X and Y values in the sample, and nature of the relationship between X and Y. It is important to keep in mind that when the Pearson r is equal (or close) to zero, thus indicating the lack of linear relationship between X and Y for the sample at hand, this might be due to (a) the presence of a curvilinear relationship between X and Y, (b) restricted range of X and Y values, or (c) the presence of, say, two groups in the sample for one of which the Pearson r is positive, and for the other, negative (see, Figure 10.5). Linear transformations on the values of one (or both) of the variables X and Y do not affect the size of the Pearson r.

What is coefficient of determination?

The square of the correlation coefficient (r^2), referred to as the *coefficient of determination*, indicates what proportion of the variance in one of the variables is associated with the variance in the other variable. For example, if $r = -.30$ is the Pearson correlation between anxiety and test performance for a sample of students, $r^2 = .09$ indicates that nine percent of the student variation in test performance is accounted for by their variation on the anxiety scale. This, however, does not mean that nine percent of the student differences in test performance are "caused" by their anxiety differences. It is very important to keep in mind that *correlation does not necessarily indicate causation.*

What is simple linear regression?

A simple linear regression uses the linear relationship between two variables X and Y to predict values of one variable (Y = criterion) from the other variable (X = predictor). For any value of X, the predicted Y value, $\hat{Y}$, is located on a straight line. The difference between the actual Y score and its predicted value, $\hat{Y}$, is referred to as prediction *error*: $e = Y - \hat{Y}$. The straight line that produces the smallest total error (sum of all squared errors) is called the line of *best fit*, or *regression line*. The prediction with a regression line is referred to as *simple linear regression* because only one predictor is used to predict Y from X (or, to "regress Y on X").

In the equation of the regression line, $\hat{Y} = bX + a$, the slope, b, indicates the direction (steepness of the regression line), whereas the intercept, a, indicates its location (where the regression line intersects the vertical axis, Y). For interpretation purposes, it is important to note that the slope, b, shows the change in the predicted score, $\hat{Y}$, associated with a one-unit change in the predictor variable, X. Also, the sign of the slope (positive or negative) is always the same as the sign of the Pearson correlation between X and Y.

What are the assumptions with simple linear regression?

The simple linear regression method is based on the assumptions of (a) *linearity* — there is a linear relationship between X and Y, (b) *independence* — the scores on the dependent variable, Y, are independent, (c) *normality* – the conditional distribution of Y scores for persons with the same X score is normal, and (d) *homoscedasticity* – all conditional distributions have equal variances.

10.4 Study Questions

1. If high scores on X correspond to high scores on Y, there is a positive linear relationship (positive correlation) between X and Y. This statement

(A) is true.

(B) is false.

(C) might be true, but additional information is needed.

(D) might be false, but additional information is needed.

2. The closer the scatterplot data points to a straight line, the stronger the correlation between the two variables. This statement is

(A) true for a positive correlation only.
(B) true for a negative correlation only.
(C) false for any (positive or negative) correlation.
(D) true for any (positive or negative) correlation.

3. If *X* and *Y* are given in standard (*z*-score) form, their correlation and covariance are equal ($r_{XY} = s_{XY}$). This statement

(A) is false.
(B) is true.
(C) might be true, but additional information is needed.
(D) might be false, but additional information is needed.

4. The correlation between *X* and *Y* is $r_{XY} = .50$. After increasing the values of *X* by 0.1 and those of *Y* by 0.3, the correlation between the resulting *X* and *Y* values is

(A) 0.00
(B) .90
(C) −1.00
(D) .50
(E) 1.00

5. The correlation between the raw scores and the *z*-scores of any variable is

(A) −1.00
(B) .50
(C) 1.00
(D) −.50
(E) 0.00

6. The correlation between IQ scores (*X*) and academic achievement (*Y*) for gifted students is mostly likely to be close to

(A) 1.00
(B) . 50
(C) -1.00
(D) 0.00
(E) -.50

7. Given that the correlation between *X* and *Y* in a given school is $r = -.85$ for boys and $r = .79$ for girls, the correlation between *X* and *Y* for all students (regardless of gender) in this school is most likely to be close to

(A) 0.00
(B) 1.00
(C) .50
(D) −.50
(E) −1.00

8. Is the relationship between age and physical strength curvilinear over any year-time interval (Yes/No)?

9. Does the sign of the Pearson r indicate the strength of the linear relationship between the two variables (Yes/No)?

10. Is the Pearson r based on the raw scores different from the Pearson r based on the z-scores for the same group of people (Yes/No)?

11. After squaring the Pearson r, is r^2 greater than the absolute value of r (Yes/No)?

12. Does the high positive correlation between rates of smoking and rates of lung cancer prove that smoking causes lung cancer (Yes/No)?

13. Is the correlation $r = .80$ stronger than the correlation $r = -.85$ (Yes/No)?

14. If $r = -.40$ is the correlation between depression and self-esteem, what percent of the variance in self-esteem are accounted for by the variance in depression?

(A) 40%
(B) 50%
(C) 80%
(D) 16%
(F) None of the above

15. The difference between an actual Y score and its predicted value is called a (an)

(A) intercept.
(B) best fit.
(C) slope.
(D) standard error of estimate.
(E) None of the above.

16. Given that $r_{XY} = .60$, $s_X = 20$, and $s_Y = 10$, the regression coefficient, b, for the prediction of Y from X is

(A) 1.20
(B) 1.00
(C) .30
(D) .90
(E) None of the above.

17. Given is the regression equation $\hat{Y} = -0.50X + 10$. If X increases by a score of 4, the predicted Y score will

(A) increase by 0.50
(B) decrease by 0.50
(C) increase by 4.00
(D) decrease by 2.00
(E) None of the above.

18. Given that, for the sample used to develop the regression equation, the mean on X is 10 and the mean on Y is 22.75, the predicted Y score for persons with $X = 10$ is

(A) 0.00
(B) 10.00
(C) 22.75
(D) 1.00
(E) None of the above.

19. For a large sample (say, $n = 200$) used in the prediction of Y from $X, r_{XY} = -.60$ and the variance in Y is $s_Y^2 = 100$. What is the standard error of estimate, $s_{Y.X}$?

(A) 4.00
(B) 80.00
(C) 6.32
(D) 8.00
(E) None of the above.

20. Given is the regression equation $\hat{Y} = 1.5X + 10$ for the prediction of vitality (Y) from hours of daily exercise (X) in a rehabilitation program. The standard error of estimate is $s_{Y.X} = 1$. For persons who exercise two hours per day, the predicted score on vitality is ________, but their actual vitality scores may vary from ________ to ________. [*Hint*: see Example 10.4]

21. Answer the questions (a), (b), and (c) asked in Example 10.4, but changing the role of the variables "motivation" and "task involvement" — namely, use "task involvement" as the dependent variable (Y) and "motivation" as the independent variable (X). Thus, for people with a motivation score of 5, determine (a) the predicted task involvement score, (b) the interval that contains their actual scores on task involvement, and (c) their probability to "pass" a cutting score of 7 points on task involvement.

CHAPTER 11

PARTIAL AND PART CORRELATION

This chapter examines the correlation (linear relationship) between two variables after removing the effect of a third variable, which is influencing this correlation, from both variables or just from one of them. The related concepts of *partial correlation* and *part correlation*, respectively, are critical to understanding the relationship between two variables or among multiple variables in the context of subsequent topics such as multiple regression and structural equation modeling.

11.1 Partial Correlation

When two variables, *X* and *Y*, are correlated with a third variable, *Z*, the correlation between *X* and *Y* after removing variance that they share with Z from each of them is referred to as a **partial correlation between *X* and *Y* controlling for *Z*.** The partial correlation, denoted $r_{XY.Z}$, can help us to better understand the nature of the Pearson correlation between *X* and *Y*. One explanation, the **common cause hypothesis**, hold that *X* and *Y* are correlated because they are both affected by a third variable (*common cause*), Z. This hypothesis is depicted in Figure 11.1.a. For example, it is known in behavioral research that there is a high positive correlation between *shoe size* and *reading skills* of children from, say, 5 to 16 years old. However, it is also known that this correlation "vanishes" when controlling for *age* which represents a common cause of *shoe size* and *reading skills*. Thus, with *X* = *shoe size*, *Y* = *reading skills*, and Z = *age*, the partial correlation between *X* and *Y*, controlling for Z, equals zero ($r_{XY.Z} = 0$).

Figure 11.1 *Partialling out a common cause or mediator, Z, from X and Y*

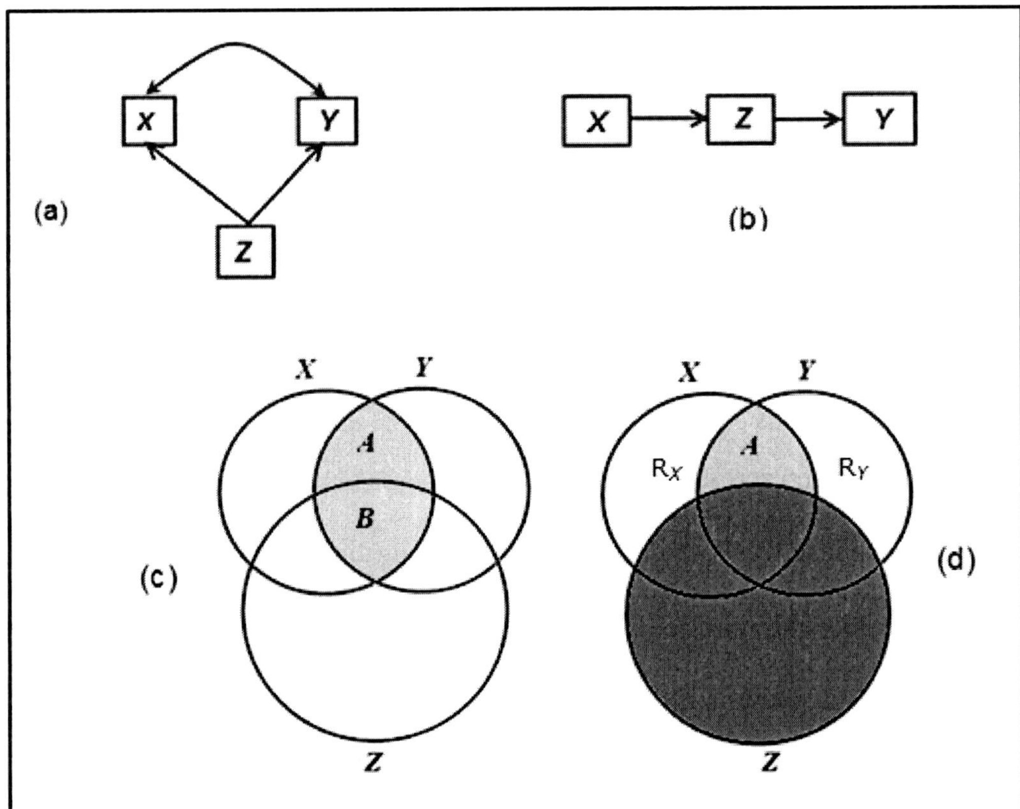

When the correlation between *X* and *Y* exists solely because of the influence of a common cause, *Z,* it is referred to as a **spurious** correlation between *X* and *Y.* Thus, the correlation between *shoe size* and *reading skills* is a spurious because it equals zero when controlling for the common cause of these two variables, *age*. It must be noted that, while in this example the partial correlation is zero, in other cases it might be greater or smaller than the Pearson correlation between *X* and *Y*, r_{XY}. Some authors consider "illusory correlation" to be a better term than "spurious correlation" with the argument it is not the correlation itself that is spurious, but rather the inference that the existence of a significant correlation coefficient signifies the existence of a significant or causal relationship.

Another frequently sought explanation of the Pearson correlation between *X* and *Y*, called the **mediation hypothesis**, is that *X* and *Y* are correlated through the mediation of a third variable (*mediator*), Z. This hypothesis is depicted in Figure 11.1.b, where the correlation between *X* and *Y* is **mediated** by Z. For example, it is often hypothesized in educational studies that the correlation between *Socioeconomic Status* (*X*) and *Academic Achievement* (*Y*) is mediated by *Motivation* (*Z*). The topic of mediation is addressed in more details later in this book.

The partial correlation $r_{XY.Z}$ is called a **first-order partial correlation** to indicate that the effect of only one variable, *Z*, is removed from *X* and *Y.* By the same logic, the Pearson correlation between *X* and *Y*, r_{XY}, is called a **zero-order correlation** between *X* and *Y*; [Examples of higher order partial correlations, which control for two or more variables, are provided in Chapter 13.] In Figure 11.1.c, the Pearson correlation between *X* and *Y* is depicted by the area (*A* + *B*) — the overlap between the two circles depicting the variances of *X* and *Y.* In Figure 11.1.d, the parts that remain in *X* and *Y*, after "removing" Z from both of them, are called ***residualized X*** and ***residualized Y***, denoted R_X and R_Y, respectively. Thus, the partial correlation between *X* and *Y*, controlling for Z, is depicted by part A — the overlap between R_X and R_Y.

NOTE [11.1] The Pearson correlation between R_X and R_Y equals the partial correlation between *X* and *Y* controlling for *Z*. The values of the residuals R_X and R_Y can be obtained as follows:

- Using a simple linear regression to predict *X* from *Z*, the difference between the observed and predicted *X* values represents the residualized *X*, that is: $R_X = X - \hat{X}$.
- Using a simple linear regression to predict *Y* from *Z*, the difference between the observed and predicted Y values represents the residualized *Y*, that is: $R_Y = Y - \hat{Y}$.

[In SPSS, the regression residuals are provided directly by using the option **Save** in the dialog box **Linear Regression.]**

Analytically, the partial correlation between *X* and *Y* controlling for *Z* is provided by the following formula

$$r_{XY.Z} = \frac{r_{XY} - (r_{XZ})(r_{YZ})}{\sqrt{(1 - r_{XZ}^2)(1 - r_{YZ}^2)}}, \qquad \mathbf{(11.1)}$$

where r_{XY}, r_{XZ}, and r_{YZ} are Pearson zero-order correlations.

EXAMPLE 11.1 Suppose the Pearson correlations among three variables, *X* = *reading comprehension*, *Y* = *ability to solve math word problems*, and *Z* = *general reasoning skills*, are as follows: $r_{XY} = .42$, $r_{XZ} = .33$, and $r_{YZ} = .78$. Suppose also that we hypothesize that *reading comprehension* and *ability to solve math word problems* are both affected by the *general reasoning skills* of the students. This hypothesis is depicted in Figure 11.1.a, with *X* = *reading compre-*

hension, Y = *ability to solve math word problems*, and Z = *general reasoning skills*. The task is to estimate the correlation between reading comprehension and ability to solve math word problems controlling for general reasoning skills. Using Formula 11.1 with the Pearson correlation coefficients given in this case, we obtain the partial correlation of interest:

$$r_{XY.Z} = \frac{.42 - (.33)(.78)}{\sqrt{(1 - .33^2)(1 - .78^2)}} = \frac{0.1626}{0.5907} = 0.28.$$

Thus, after controlling for general reasoning skills, the Pearson correlation between reading comprehension and ability to solve math word problems dropped from .42 to .28. That is, for a group of students with the same general reasoning skills, the Pearson correlation between reading comprehension and ability to solve math word problems is .28.

NOTE [11.2] The partial correlation between X and Y controlling for Z equals the Pearson correlation between X and Y for people with the same score on Z.

In Example 11.1, and in most cases, the partial correlation between two variables is smaller than the original Pearson correlation between these two variables. However, there are situations in which the partial correlation turns out to be larger than the original Pearson correlation. When this occurs, the control variable, Z, is called **suppressor** variable because it "suppresses" a part (if not all) of the variance shared by X and Y which is due to measurement artifacts. Here is an example of a *suppression* in the correlation between two variables.

EXAMPLE 11.2 Suppose X is the time (in hours) that students have spent preparing for a high-stakes test, Y is their score on this test, and Z is their level of fear of failing the test. Suppose also that $r_{XY} = .18$, $r_{XZ} = .85$, and $r_{YZ} = -.20$. As the correlation between the students' test preparation time and their test performance is surprisingly small (.18), let us examine this correlation controlling for fear of failing the test. Using Formula 11.1., the partial correlation between X and Y controlling for Z is

$$r_{XY.Z} = \frac{.18 - (.85)(-.20)}{\sqrt{[1 - .85^2][1 - (-.20)^2]}} = \frac{.35}{.5161} = .68.$$

Thus, the partial correlation between X and Y controlling for Z ($r_{XY.Z} = .68$) is much higher than the original Pearson correlation between X and Y ($r_{XY} = .18$). Removing the *fear of taking the test* led to removing ("suppressing") invalid components in the variance shared by test *preparation time* and *test performance* thus causing an increase in the Pearson correlation between these two variables. Therefore, for people equally afraid of taking the high-stake test, the correlation between test preparation time and test performance is .68.

EXAMPLE 11.3 This example illustrates the computation of partial correlations using SPSS. The SPSS data file shown here contains three variables: *PI* = *Principal Isolation*, *TPD* = *Teacher Professional Development*, and *SAP* = *Student Academic Performance*. The scores on these variables are based on a random sample of 20 schools in a large urban area. The *PI* scores come from a survey on principal's feelings of isolation, with higher scores indicating that the principal perceives a higher level of professional isolation. The *TPD* scores come from a teacher survey, with higher scores indicating higher level of school support for the professional development of teachers in a given school. The *SAP* scores represent an overall evaluation score of the academic performance of the students in the school.

MEDIATION.sav [DataSet1] - SP
File Edit View Data Transform An
20 :

	PI	TPD	SAP
1	12	15	32
2	16	12	40
3	20	8	28
4	22	10	22
5	10	45	38
6	25	12	26
7	28	9	20
8	18	11	24
9	30	5	12
10	32	10	22
11	33	4	49
12	36	8	18
13	38	3	8
14	27	7	15
15	38	4	22
16	40	3	18
17	41	4	15
18	44	5	12
19	46	4	10
20	22	9	20

In general, the professional *isolation* of a school principal is defined as a lack of (or insufficient) communication with teachers about their professional development and other related issues. The negative impact of the principal isolation on teacher and school performance is well documented in the empirical and popular literature on this topic. In fact, the data in this example also tend to support this finding. Using SPSS (as shown in Example 10.1), we find that the Pearson correlations among the variables, *principal isolation* (*PI*), *teacher professional development* (*TPD*), and *student academic performance* (*SAP*) are:

$$r_{PI,TPD} = -.68, (p = .001);$$
$$r_{PI,SAP} = -.609, (p = .004), \text{ and}$$
$$r_{TPD,SAP} = .465, (p = .039).$$

As indicated by the *p*-values (in parentheses), all correlation coefficients are statistically significant. The negative correlation between *PI* and *TPD* (−.68), as well as that between *PI* and *SAP* (−.609), signal that the principal isolation may have a significant negative impact on teacher professional development and student academic performance. The task is now to determine whether the correlation between *PI* and *SAP* (.456) is mediated by *TPD*. With the notations $X = PI$, $Y = SAP$, and $Z = TPD$, this is case is depicted in Figure 11.1.b.

Thus, the task is reduced to computing the partial correlation between principal isolation and student academic performance controlling for teacher professional development, $r_{XY.Z}$. To perform this task in SPSS, enter the data of the 20 observations listed above and follow the steps:

1. Click **Analyze**, click **Correlate**, and click **Partial**.
2. While holding the **Ctrl** key, click **Principal Isolation [PI]** and **Student Academic Performance [SAP]** and then click ▶ to move them into the box **Variables**.
3. Still in the *Partial Correlations* dialog box, click **Teacher Professional Development** [TPD] and click ▶ to move it into the box **Controlling for** [see Figure 10.13, upper panel.]
4. Click **OK**.

The resulting SPSS output is shown in Figure 11.2 (lower panel). As can be seen, the partial correlation between principal isolation and student academic performance controlling for teacher professional development (−.451) is not statistically significant at the .05 level ($p = .053$). This is determined in SPSS by a *t*-test with degrees of freedom $df = n - 3$ (in this case, $df = 20 - 3 = 17$); [Recall that the degrees of freedom with the *t*-test for statistical significance of the Pearson zero-order correlation are $df = n - 2$, see Formula 10.5.] Thus, after removing the effect of teacher professional development, the original statistically significant negative correlation between principal isolation and student academic performance (−.609, $p = .001$) dropped to a statistically nonsignificant correlation (−.451, $p = .053$). With a larger sample, this partial correlation will probably turn out to be statistically significant, yet still lower in absolute value than the original

Pearson correlation between principal isolation and student academic performance. We can conclude then that the relationship between principal isolation and student academic performance is probably mediated by teacher professional development.

Figure 11.2 *SPSS computation of the partial correlation between Principal Isolation and Student Academic Performance controlling for Teacher Professional Development*

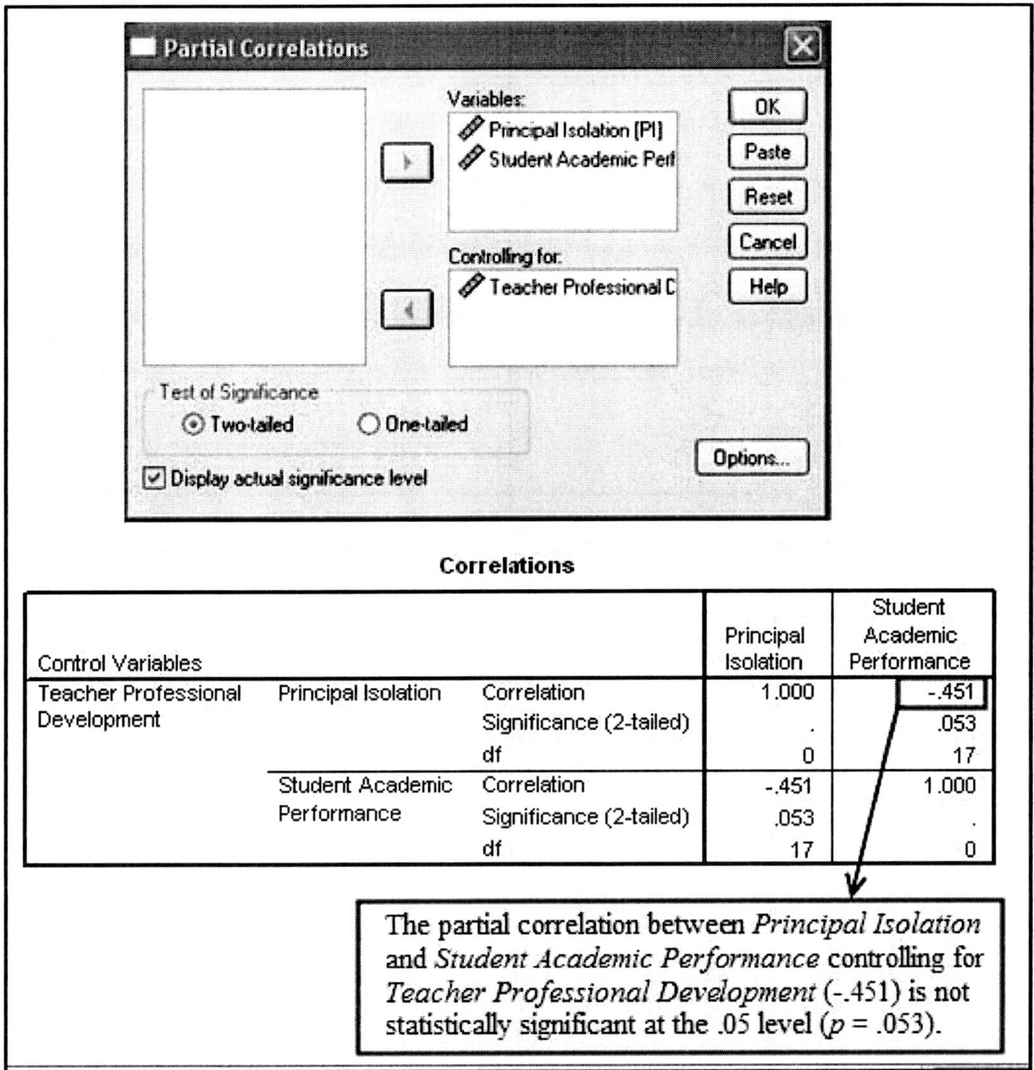

Correlations

Control Variables			Principal Isolation	Student Academic Performance
Teacher Professional Development	Principal Isolation	Correlation	1.000	-.451
		Significance (2-tailed)	.	.053
		df	0	17
	Student Academic Performance	Correlation	-.451	1.000
		Significance (2-tailed)	.053	.
		df	17	0

11.2 Part Correlation

There are situations in which a researcher wants to know the correlation between two variables, X and Y, after removing the effect of a third variable, Z, from only *one* of the two variables. In this case, when X is used to explain Y, the variable Z is removed *only from* X thus preserving Y "intact" (see Figure 11.3). The correlation between the (intact) dependent variable, Y, and the residualized independent variable, X, after removing Z only from X, is called a **part correlation** between X and Y controlling for Z. The part correlation, referred to also as a *semi-partial* correlation, is denoted $r_{Y(X.Z)}$. In Figure 11.3, the part correlation between X and Y partialling out Z from X is presented by the shaded area (A) — the overlap between the intact Y and the residualized X (denoted R_X). The squared partial correlation, $r^2_{Y(X.Z)}$, indicates what proportion is part *A* from the intact *Y* — i.e., what proportion of the variance in *Y* is accounted for by the variance in *X* controlling for *Z*. For example, if the part correlation is $r_{Y(X.Z)} = .21$, its squared value is $(.21)^2 = .0441$ which indicates that 4.41% of the variance in *Y* is explained by *X* controlling for *Z*. We can also say that "4.41% of the variance in *Y* is uniquely explained by the variance in *X* controlling for *Y*."

Figure 11.3 *Part correlation between Y and X partialling out Z from X.*

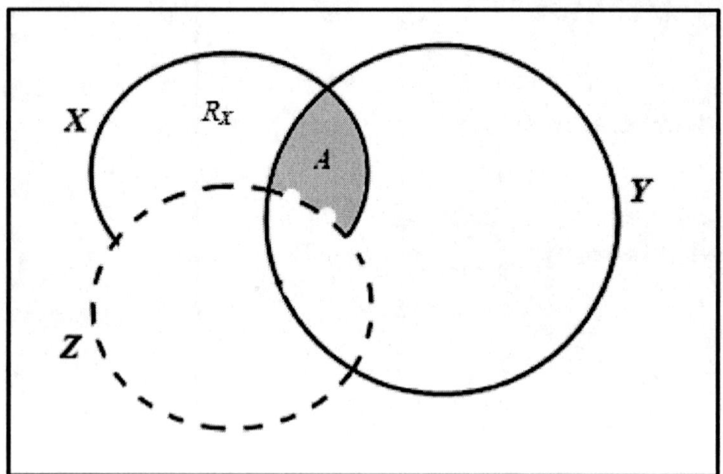

If we use a simple linear regression to predict *X* from *Z*, the differences between the observed and predicted *X* values are, in fact, the residual values in *X* after removing *Z* from *X* (that is, $R_X = X - \hat{X}$). Thus, the Pearson correlation between the *Y* scores and the residual scores, R_X, equals the part correlation $r_{Y(X.Z)}$. Analytically, the part correlation can be estimated as follows:

$$r_{Y(X.Z)} = \frac{r_{XY} - (r_{XZ})(r_{YZ})}{\sqrt{1 - r_{XZ}^2}}. \quad \textbf{(11.2)}$$

EXAMPLE 11.4 Suppose a six-month program intervention took place with the purpose of increasing the students' math proficiency. Among other things, **the researcher wants to determine the correlation between the level of *parental support* that the students have received during the six-month program intervention and their *math proficiency upon finishing the program*, removing the effect of pre-intervention differences in math proficiency**. The students participating in the program took a standardized math proficiency test prior to and after the program and responded to survey questions about parental support during the six-month time period of program intervention. With the notations *X* = *pretest*, *Y* = *posttest*, and *Z* = *parental support*, the Pearson correlations among these variables are: $r_{XY} = .82$, $r_{XZ} = .35$, and $r_{YZ} = .46$. Note that the researcher's question translates into the task of computing the part correlation between *Z* and *Y*, partialling out *X* from *Y*. Taking this into account, we use Formula 11.2 as follows:

$$r_{Z(Y.X)} = \frac{r_{YZ} - (r_{XY})(r_{XZ})}{\sqrt{1 - r_{XY}^2}} = \frac{.46 - (.82)(.35)}{\sqrt{1 - (.82)^2}} = \frac{.1730}{.5724} = .302.$$

Thus, the part correlation of interest in this example is $r_{Z(Y.X)} = .302$. In other words, the correlation between parental support and post-intervention math proficiency, controlling for pre-intervention differences in math proficiency of the students, is .302; [Note that $r_{ZY} = .46$ is higher than $r_{Z(Y.X)} = .302$.]

> **NOTE [11.3]** With the notations X_1, X_2, and X_3 for three variables, the **partial correlation** between X_1 and X_2 controlling for X_3 is denoted $\boldsymbol{r_{12.3}}$. The **part correlation** between X_1 and X_2, partialling out X_3 only from X_2, is denoted $\boldsymbol{r_{1(2.3)}}$. With the notations X_1, X_2, and Y, the **partial correlation** between Y and X_1 controlling for X_2 is denoted $r_{Y1.2}$. The **part correlation** between Y and X_1 partialling out X_2 only from X_1 is denoted $r_{Y(1.2)}$.

11.3 Summary

This chapter introduces the concepts of *partial correlation* and *part correlation* between two variables controlling for a third variable. Later in this book, partial and part correlations are discussed for cases which control for two or more variables (e.g., Chapter 13). A brief summary of this chapter follows in order of its content presentation.

11.3.1 Partial correlation

- **Partial correlation** between two variables, X and Y, controlling for a third variable, Z, is **the correlation between** X and Y after removing from their variances the variance that they share with Z. This partial correlation is denoted $\boldsymbol{r_{XY.Z}}$. The variable Z, removed from both X and Y, is called the *control variable*.

- The partial correlation, $r_{XY.Z}$, is used primarily when it is hypothesized that (a) Z is a common cause of X and Y or (b) Z is a mediator for the correlation between X and Y (e.g., see Figure 11.1).

- When the correlation between X and Y exists solely because it is affected by a common cause, Z, it is called **spurious** correlation between X and Y (e.g., X = *shoe size*, Y = *reading skills*, Z = *age*).

- The partial correlation between X and Y controlling for Z is called **first-order partial correlation** to indicate that only one variable is removed from X and Y, whereas the original Pearson correlation between X and Y is called **zero-order correlation** to indicate that no variable is removed from X and Y.

- The partial correlation $r_{XY.Z}$ equals the Pearson correlation between the residual scores R_X and R_Y which represent the residuals in simple linear regressions used to predict X from Z and Y from Z, respectively (i.e., $R_X = X - \hat{X}$ and $R_Y = Y - \hat{Y}$). Alternatively, this partial correlation can be estimated by using Formula 11.1.

- The partial correlation between X and Y controlling for Z can be lower, higher, or equal to the original Pearson correlation between X and Y.

- The partial correlation between X and Y controlling for Z equals the Pearson correlation between X and Y for people with the same score on Z.

- When the partial correlation $r_{XY.Z}$ is higher than the original Pearson correlation, r_{XY}, the control variable, Z, is called **suppressor** variable because it "suppresses" a part (if not all) of the variance shared by X and Y which is due to measurement artifacts.

- $r_{Y1.2}$ denotes the partial correlation between Y and X_1 controlling for X_2.

11.3.2 Part correlation

- **Part correlation** between X and Y partialling out Z only from X is the Pearson correlation between the (intact) Y and the residualized part of X obtained after removing Z from X (see Figure 11.2). This part correlation is denoted $r_{Y(X.Z)}$. The part correlation is referred to also as *semipartial* correlation.
- **The squared partial correlation** $r^2_{Y(X.Z)}$ indicates what proportion of the variance in Y is uniquely explained (accounted for) by the variance in X controlling for Z.
- $r_{Y(1.2)}$ denotes the part correlation between Y and X_1 partialling out X_2 only from X_1.

11.4 Study Questions

1. It has been found that there is a strong positive correlation between *hospital admissions for heart stroke* and *ice cream sales* [?!] Circle two of the following words which have to do with this weird correlation:

   mediation, residual, spurious, temperature, money, insurance, medication

2. Another "weird" correlation is the negative correlation between *income* and *longevity*. Circle two of the following words which have to do with such correlation:

   mediation, money, health, temperature, residual, ethnicity, suppression

3. It is hypothesized that *parental support* affects the *grade point average* (GPA) of the students through their *motivation*. Given the Pearson correlations $r_{XY} = .28$, $r_{XZ} = .45$, and $r_{YZ} = .52$, where X = parental support, Y = GPA, and Z = motivation, the correlation between parental support and GPA, removing the effect of motivation from both of them, is

   (A) .0539, **(B)** .0201, **(C)** .0603, **(D)** .0558.

4. Taking into account NOTE [11.3] for three variables, X_1, X_2, and X_3, which of the following notations represents the correlation between X_2 and X_1 partialling out X_3 only from X_1:

   (A) $r_{21.3}$, **(B)** $r_{12.3}$, **(C)** $r_{1(2.3)}$, **(D)** $r_{2(1.3)}$.

5. The Pearson correlations among X_1, X_2, and X_3 are $r_{12} = -.35$, $r_{13} = -.27$, and $r_{23} = .62$. Given this, the correlation between X_2 and X_3 partialling out X_1 only from X_2 is

   (A) .5610, **(B)** .5826, **(C)** .6200, **(D)** .4832.

6. The data table below contains 20 observations on three variables: X_1 = *self-reliance*, X_2 = *motivation*, and Y = *task involvement*.

X_1	5	6	9	7	9	9	8	9	7	7	7	7	9	2	2	6	7	7	7	9
X_2	6	8	9	8	8	6	8	8	6	5	6	6	8	4	7	3	7	5	7	4
Y	4	8	8	8	8	9	8	8	6	4	5	6	9	3	5	7	8	5	8	9

   Compute the part correlation between task involvement and self-reliance, partialling out motivation from self-reliance, by using SPSS with two approaches: (a) compute the Pearson correlations r_{Y1}, r_{Y2}, and r_{12}, and then use Formula 11.2 to compute the requested part correlation, and (b) regress X_1 on X_2 and then correlate the residual from this simple linear regression ($R_{X_1} = X_1 - \widehat{X_1}$) with Y.

CHAPTER 12

NONPARAMETRIC TESTS

There are situations in testing hypotheses when the underlying assumptions are either not met or are difficult to test, particularly with small samples. For example, the *t*-test for independent or dependent samples (see Chapter 9) assumes that the data belong to an interval scale and that the dependent variable is normally distributed. Thus, the *t*-test is not appropriate with ordinal data (e.g., individuals ranked according to a given trait) or skewed distributions of data. As another example, the Pearson correlation coefficient is not appropriate for measuring the relationship between two categorical variables — e.g., an association between *ethnicity* and *type of sport* practiced by college students. Statistical tests to examine differences between groups on ordinal data or skewed distributions of data, as well as tests for relationships between categorical variables, are called **nonparametric tests**. A logical question a researcher might ask is, "Why not use nonparametric tests all of the time, since they are *distribution free* and do not require testing for assumptions?" One major argument against doing so is that, when their assumptions are met, parametric tests (e.g., *z*-tests, *t*-tests, or *F*-tests) are more powerful than their nonparametric counterparts. That is, the parametric tests yield higher chances of detecting hypothesized differences when those differences actually exist. There are multiple excellent sources on nonparametric tests (e.g., books, articles, software, and online materials), including discussions of their advantages and disadvantages compared to parametric tests (e.g., Conover, 1998; Hollander & Wolfe, 1973; Lehmann, 1975; Nikitin, 1995). This chapter presents only several of the widely-used nonparametric tests available in SPSS.

12.1 The Man-Whitney U Test

The **Man-Whitney *U* test** is a nonparametric test for assessing whether two independent samples of ordinal data come from the same population. When the null hypothesis is not rejected, the conclusion is that the two samples do not differ on the dependent variable. Thus, the Man-Whitney *U* test can be viewed as the nonparametric analog of the *t*-test for independent samples. Unlike the *t*-test, the Man-Whitney *U* test can be used with small samples and does not require a normal distribution of the data. The trade-off is that, with normally distributed data, the *t*-test is more powerful than the Man-Whitney *U* test (i.e., it makes it easier to detect differences between two independent samples when such differences exist).

With the Man-Whitney *U* test, the scores are converted to *ranks* (ordinal scores) in the combined sample of the two independent samples and then the test evaluates whether the mean ranks for the two groups differ significantly from each other based on a test *U*-value computed from the ranks in the two samples. The calculation of this *U* value is described in Example 12.1.

EXAMPLE 12.1 The calculation of the Mann-Whitney *U* value is described here using the portfolio scores assigned by instructors to students in two independent samples as follows

Sample 1: 20, 42, 60, 64, 70, 78, 80 ($n_1 = 7$);

Sample 2: 30, 42, 42, 55, 64, 72, 85, 88, 92 ($n_2 = 9$).

To calculate the U value, follow the steps:

1. Combine the two samples, order the scores from highest to lowest, and assign a rank to each score corresponding to the position (denoted ID) of this score in the combined sample. For equal scores, the "tied" rank equals the mean of the IDs for the equal scores (see Table 12.1).
2. In Samples 1 and 2, assign to each score its rank from the combined sample.
3. Calculate R_1 = sum of ranks for the observations in Sample 1 (here: $R_1 = 55.5$).
4. Calculate R_2 = sum of ranks for the observations in Sample 2 (here: $R_2 = 80.5$).
5. Calculate U_1 and U_2 using the formulas:

$$U_1 = n_1 n_2 + \frac{n_1(n_1+1)}{2} - R_1 \quad \textbf{(12.1)}$$

$$U_2 = n_1 n_2 + \frac{n_2(n_2+1)}{2} - R_2 \quad \textbf{(12.2)}$$

In this example,

$$U_1 = (7)(9) + \frac{(7)(7+1)}{2} - 55.5 = 35.5$$

$$U_2 = (7)(9) + \frac{(9)(9+1)}{2} - 80.5 = 27.5$$

6. U equals the smaller number of U_1 and U_2. Thus, in this case $\boldsymbol{U} = \mathbf{27.5}$.

Table 12.1 *Calculation of R_1 and R_2 for the U value*

Combined Sample			Sample 1		Sample 2	
ID	Score	Rank	Score	Rank	Score	Rank
1	20	**1**	20	1	30	2
2	30	**2**	42	4	42	4
3	42	**4**	60	7	42	4
4	42	**4**	64	8.5	55	6
5	42	**4**	70	10	64	8.5
6	55	**6**	78	12	72	11
7	60	**7**	80	13	85	14
8	64	**8.5**	**$R_1 = 55.5$**		88	15
9	64	**8.5**			92	16
10	70	**10**			**$R_2 = 80.5$**	
11	72	**11**				
12	78	**12**				
13	80	**13**				
14	85	**14**				
15	88	**15**				
16	92	**16**				

Note. "Tied" ranks are highlighted — e.g., the rank for the score of 64 in the combined sample is 8.5 = the mean of the IDs for this score (8 and 9).

For samples with 20 or less observations, the critical values for U are usually provided in statistical tables for the U distribution. In this case, given $n_1 = 7$ and $n_2 = 9$, the U-critical value for a two-tailed test at the .05 level ($\alpha/2 = .025$) is $U_{\alpha/2} = 13$ [see Table A-5 for $n_1 = 7$, $n_2 = 9$, and $\alpha = .025$]. Unlike the testing rule that we use with the z-test or t-test, in the Mann-Whitney test the null hypothesis is rejected if the test U-value is *smaller* than the critical U-value. In this example, the test U-value ($U = 27.5$) is greater than the critical U-value ($U_{\alpha/2} = 13$). Therefore, we fail to reject the null hypothesis. Thus, there is no statistically significant difference between the portfolio scores in the two samples of students.

NOTE [12.1] With the Mann-Whitney U test, we reject the null hypothesis when the computed test value for U is *smaller* than the critical value for U at the respective level of significance, α.

For samples with more than 20 observations ($n_1 > 20$ and $n_2 > 20$), the U distribution is approximately normal, with the *mean* and *standard deviation* calculated as follows:

$$\mu_U = \frac{n_1 n_2}{2} \quad \text{and} \quad \sigma_U = \sqrt{\frac{n_1 n_2 (n_1 + n_2 + 1)}{12}}, \qquad \textbf{(12.3)}$$

where n_1 and n_2 are the sample sizes of Samples 1 and 2, respectively.

With the U-value calculated as shown in Example 12.1, the z- statistic that corresponds to U under the normal distribution is:

$$z = \frac{U - \mu_U}{\sigma_U}. \qquad \textbf{(12.4)}$$

As this is the familiar z-test, we reject the null hypothesis when the z-statistic obtained by Formula 12.4 *exceeds* the z-critical value in absolute units (sign ignored). For example, in the case of a non-directional test with a level of significance of .05 ($\alpha = .05$), the critical value is $z_{\alpha/2} = 1.96$, so the null hypothesis will be rejected if the absolute value of the z-statistic exceeds 1.96.

EXAMPLE 12.2 This example illustrates how to conduct the Mann-Whitney U test with the data from Example 12.1 using SPSS. The SPSS data layout is shown in Figure 12.1 (left panel). The variable **Score** contains the portfolio scores for the combined Samples 1 and 2, whereas the variable **Sample** provides the coding for the samples (1 = Sample 1, 2 = Sample 2). To perform the Mann-Whitney U test with these data, follow the steps:

1. Click **Analyze**, click **Nonparametric Tests**, and then click **Independent Samples**.
2. Click Score and click ▶ to move it into the box **Test Variable List**.
3. Click **Sample** and click ▶ to move it into the box **Grouping Variable**.
4. Click **Define Groups** and then type **1** in the box **Group 1** and type **2** in the box **Group 2**.
5. The box **Mann-Whitney U** is checked by default, so just click **Continue**.
6. Click **OK**.

The resulting SPSS output is also shown in Figure 12.1 (right panel).

Figure 12.1 *SPSS data and output with the Mann-Whitney U test for independent samples*

Mann-Whitney Data.s

File Edit View Data Tran

16 :

	Score	Sample
1	20	1
2	30	2
3	42	2
4	42	1
5	42	2
6	55	2
7	60	1
8	64	1
9	64	2
10	70	1
11	72	2
12	78	1
13	80	1
14	85	2
15	88	2
16	92	2

Ranks

	Sample	N	Mean Rank	Sum of Ranks
Score	1	7	7.93	55.50
	2	9	8.94	80.50
	Total	16		

$R_1 = 55.5$ $R_2 = 80.5$

Test Statistics[b]

	Score
Mann-Whitney U	27.500
Wilcoxon W	55.500
Z	-.425
Asymp. Sig. (2-tailed)	.671
Exact Sig. [2*(1-tailed Sig.)]	.681[a]

a. Not corrected for ties.

b. Grouping Variable: Sample

$U = 27.5$

$z = -0.425$

$p = .671$

The SPSS output provides the U value which we computed in Example 11.1 ($U = 27.5$), as well as two intermediate sums in this computation ($R_1 = 55.5$ and $R_2 = 80.5$). It also provides the value of the z-statistic (see Formula 12.4) and two p-values associated with this statistic — an exact two-tailed p-value ($p = .681$), which is not corrected for tied ranks, and a two-tailed p-value ($p = .671$) which is corrected for tied ranks and is based on an approximated z-statistic. In most cases these two p-values are very close or almost equal. Although the p-value(s) are very large, thus clearly indicating that we cannot reject the null hypothesis, it is more appropriate to test the null hypothesis by comparing the U value (27.7) to the respective U critical value (as we did in Example 12.1). This is because the sample sizes are smaller than 20 ($n_1 = 7$ and $n_2 = 9$) and, therefore, there is no evidence that the z-test in this case is valid.

12.2 The Wilcoxon Signed-Rank Test for Dependent Samples

In Chapter 8 (Section 8.3.3) we discussed the t-test for two dependent samples. This test, however, is not appropriate when the dependent scores in the two samples are ordinal, when the samples are small, and/or when the data distributions are skewed. In such cases we can use a nonparametric test referred to as the **Wilcoxon matched-pairs signed-rank test** (or briefly, the **Wilcoxon signed-rank test**).

The null hypothesis tested with the Wilcoxon signed-rank test states that "there is no difference in the paired (dependent) populations of scores on the dependent variable." Just like with the *t*-test for dependent samples, the Wilcoxon signed-rank test involves the computation of the difference between the dependent scores (e.g., pretest and posttests data) for each person. The absolute values of the difference scores are ranked and then each rank is assigned the sign (positive or negative) of the respective difference. The sum of the ranks with the less frequent sign is called the *T*-value. **The null hypothesis is rejected when the computed *T*-value is *smaller* than the critical *T*-value at a specified level of significance.**

For samples with more than 25 observations ($n > 25$), the sampling distribution of the computed *T*-value is approximately normal, with a *mean* and *standard deviation* computed as follows:

$$\mu_T = \frac{n(n+1)}{4} \quad \text{and} \quad \sigma_T = \sqrt{\frac{n(n+1)(2n+1)}{24}}. \qquad \textbf{(12.5)}$$

In this case, the null hypothesis is tested with the following *z*-statistic:

$$z = \frac{T - \mu_T}{\sigma_T}. \qquad \textbf{(12.6)}$$

As with other *z*-tests, we reject the null hypothesis when the *z*-statistic obtained by Formula 12.6 *exceeds* the *z*-critical value in absolute units (sign ignored).

EXAMPLE 12.3 This example illustrates the use of SPSS for the Wilcoxon signed-rank test using the pretest-posttest data in Figure 12.2 (left panel). These data represent subjective, interview-based, scores on attitude toward smoking cigarettes before and after a movie of health hazards from smoking cigarettes was shown to high school students. Lower scores indicate lower tolerance toward smoking cigarettes. Thus, the expectation is that the "treatment" (movie) will be associated with a decrease in pretest to posttest scores on attitude toward smoking. Given the ordinal nature of the data and their pretest-posttest dependency, the Wilcoxon signed-rank test is appropriate. We will test the null hypothesis that there is no decrease in pretest to posttest scores versus the one-sided alternative (that there is such a decrease). In this example, we set the level of significance at $\alpha = .01$ [jut for illustration]. To use SPSS for this test, follow the steps:

1. Click **Analyze**, click **Nonparametric Tests**, and click **2 Related Samples**.
2. Click **Pretest**, click **Posttest**, and then click ▶ to move them into the box **Test Pair(s) List**.
3. The box **Wilcoxon** is checked by default in SPSS (as shown here), so just click **OK**.

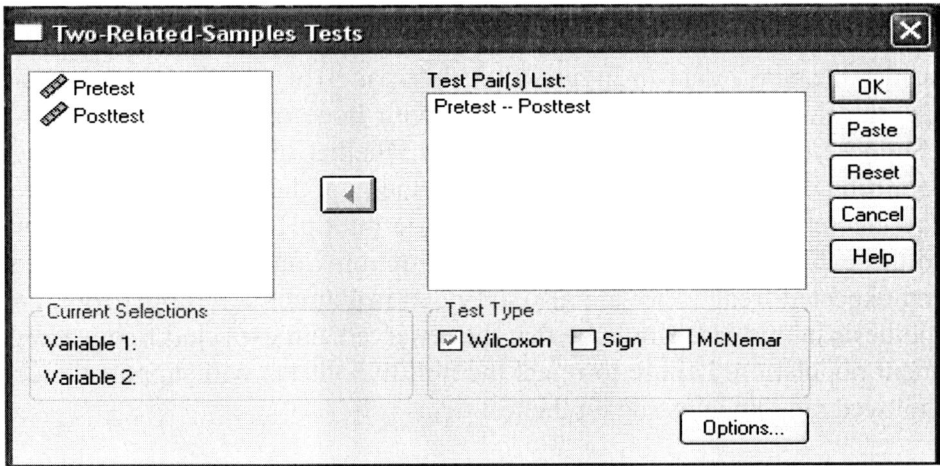

Figure 12.2 *SPSS data and output for the Wilcoxon signed-rank test for dependent samples*

*Smoking Data.sav [DataS

File Edit View Data Transform

10 :

	Pretest	Posttest
1	18	12
2	20	18
3	9	9
4	12	8
5	4	7
6	12	8
7	15	15
8	7	6
9	10	10
10	6	4

Ranks

		N	Mean Rank	Sum of Ranks
Posttest - Pretes	Negative Ranks	6[a]	4.00	24.00
	Positive Ranks	1[b]	4.00	4.00
	Ties	3[c]		
	Total	10		

a. Posttest < Pretest

b. Posttest > Pretest

c. Posttest = Pretest

$T = 4$

Test Statistics[b]

	Posttest - Pretest
Z	-1.696[a]
Asymp. Sig. (2-tailed)	.090

a. Based on positive ranks.

b. Wilcoxon Signed Ranks Test

$z = -1.696$

$p = .09$

In the SPSS output, the results in the table **Ranks,** column **N**, show that there are six 6 negative ranks and one positive rank for the difference (Posttest – Pretest) scores. As indicated earlier, the T value with the Wilcoxon signed-rank test equals the sum of the ranks with the less frequent sign. Thus, in this case $T = 4$ because the positive ranks are less frequent and their sum equals 4. The critical T-value, for a one-sided test at the .01 level ($\alpha = .01$) is $T_\alpha = 5$ [see Table A-6]. Thus, we reject the null hypothesis because the computed T value ($T = 4$) is less than the critical T-value ($T_\alpha = 5$).

As shown in Figure 12.2, SPSS also reports the z-statistic (computed by Formula 12.6) and the p-value associated with this statistic, but in this case we do not take them into account since the sample size ($n = 10$) is smaller than 25, which invalidates the use of the z-test. Thus, by rejecting the null hypothesis, we can say that the "treatment" (a movie on health hazards from smoking) yields a statistically significant decrease in pretest to posttest scores on tolerance toward smoking cigarettes for the study population of high school students.

12.3 Chi-Square Goodness-of-fit Test

Consider the SPSS data in Figure 12.3 (left panel) where the entries stand for the responses of 27 students on a multiple-choice item with three options (1, 2, and 3) in a teacher-made test. Suppose that the teacher wants to know whether the students' responses on this test item can be attributed to random guessing. Under the hypothesis that responses reflect random guessing, the theoretical expectation is that the three multiple-choice options would be equally attractive to these 27 students and, therefore, each option would be selected by 9 students. The observed and expected frequencies are also provided in Figure 12.3 (upper right panel). Clearly, the null hypothesis in this case would be that the observed and expected frequencies do not differ for this student population. Failure to reject the null hypothesis will support the conclusion that students employed random guessing on the test item.

The general case for this example relates to testing for population differences between **observed frequencies** that come from direct empirical observations, and **expected frequencies** developed on the basis of a hypothesis. Such testing is usually performed by using a *chi-square* (χ^2) test called the **chi-square goodness-of-fit test**. The chi-square (χ^2) test statistic for comparing observed and expected frequencies is computed as follows:

$$\chi^2 = \sum \frac{(O-E)^2}{E} \tag{12.7}$$

where O = observed frequency, E = expected frequency, and the summation is across all nominal categories (say, K categories). The null hypothesis that there are no population differences between the observed and expected frequencies is rejected when the χ^2 test statistic exceeds the χ^2 critical value (with *degrees of freedom* = $K - 1$) at a specified level of significance, α.

EXAMPLE 12.4 Let's use the chi-square goodness-of-fit test with the frequency data in Figure 12.3 (left panel) to test the hypothesis of random guessing on the multiple-choice item at the .05 level. Using Formula 12.7 with the frequencies in Figure 12.3 (upper right panel), we obtain $\chi^2 = 2.0$. The χ^2 critical value, with 2 degrees of freedom ($df = K - 1 = 3 - 1 = 2$) and $\alpha = .05$, is $\chi^2_\alpha = 5.99$ (see Table A-3). Thus, we fail to reject the null hypothesis because the χ^2 test statistic (2.0) does not exceed the χ^2 critical value (5.99). This provides statistical evidence that student responses on the test item can be attributed to random guessing. To conduct the same test using the SPSS, follow the steps:

1. Click **Analyze**, click **Nonparametric Tests**, and click **Chi-Square**.
2. Click **Option** and click ► to move it into the box **Test Variable List**.
3. Keep the SPSS defaults **Get from data** (for *Expected Range*) and **All categories equal** (for *Expected Values*), as shown in the dialog box *Chi-Square Test* provided here below.
4. Click **OK**.

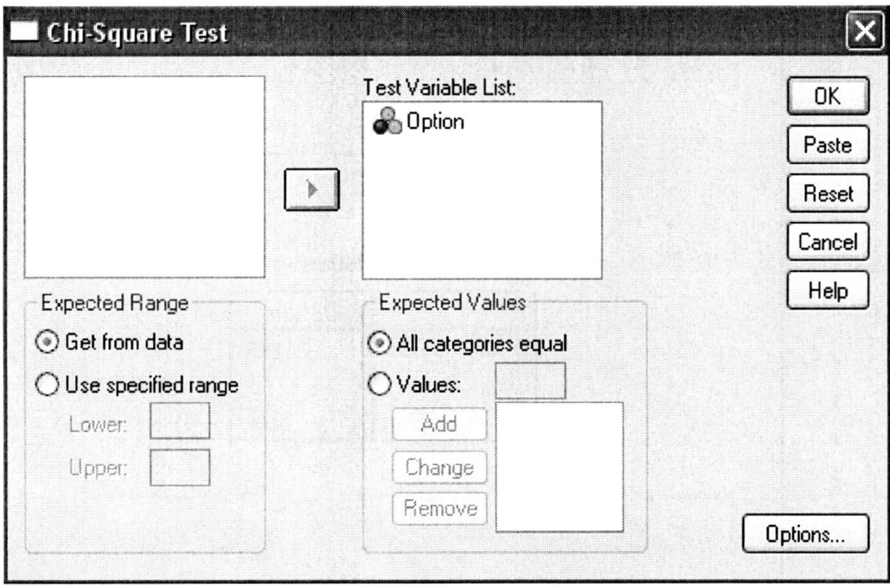

The resulting SPSS output is also provided in Figure 12.3 (lower right panel — tables **Option** and **Tests Statistics**). Note that the χ^2 test value is the same as the one obtained by manual computations ($\chi^2 = 2.0$). As the *p*-value associated with this statistic ($p = .368$) exceeds the level of significance adopted in this example ($\alpha = .05$), we fail to reject the null hypothesis, $\chi^2(2) = 2.0$, $p = .368$. Thus, with both manual computations and a chi-square goodness-of-fit test run in SPSS, the null hypothesis is *not* rejected. This means that there is no difference between the population distributions of observed and expected frequencies across the three multiple-choice options of this particular test item. Taking into account that the expected frequencies are developed under the hypothesis that students employed random guessing, we can conclude that the observed student responses on the test item can be attributed to random guessing.

Figure 12.3 *Goodness-of-fit test for observed and expected frequencies across three categories*

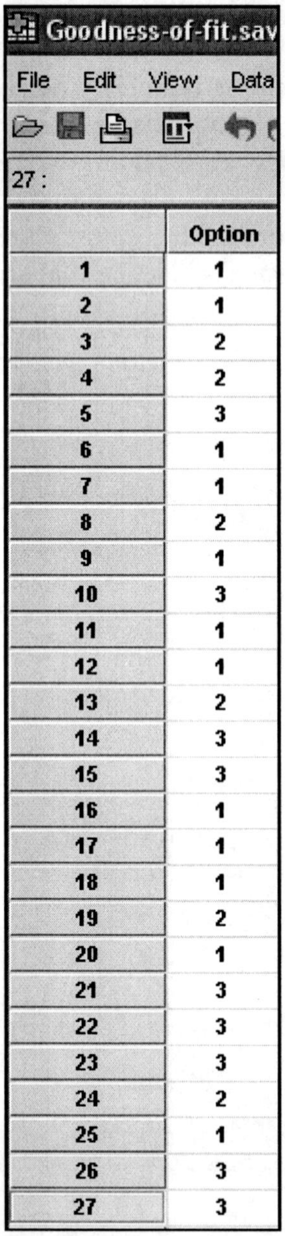

Goodness-of-fit.sav

File Edit View Data

27 :

	Option
1	1
2	1
3	2
4	2
5	3
6	1
7	1
8	2
9	1
10	3
11	1
12	1
13	2
14	3
15	3
16	1
17	1
18	1
19	2
20	1
21	3
22	3
23	3
24	2
25	1
26	3
27	3

	Multiple-Choice Options		
Frequencies	Option 1	Option 2	Option 3
Observed (O)	12	6	9
Expected (E)	9	9	9

$$\chi^2 = \frac{(12-9)^2}{9} + \frac{(6-9)^2}{9} + \frac{(9-9)^2}{9} = \frac{9}{9} + \frac{9}{9} + \frac{0}{9} = \frac{18}{9} = 2.0.$$

Option

	Observed N	Expected N	Residual
1	12	9.0	3.0
2	6	9.0	-3.0
3	9	9.0	.0
Total	27		

Test Statistics

	Option	
Chi-Square[a]	2.000	→ $\chi^2 = 2.0$
df	2	→ $df = 2$
Asymp. Sig.	.368	→ $p = .368$

As already noted, the expected frequencies with the chi-square goodness-of-fit test are developed under the assumption that a specific hypothesis (or claim, expectation, etc.) is correct. In Example 12.4, the assumption of random guessing led to equal expected frequencies across the three multiple-choice options with the test item. There are situations in which the expected frequencies are not "evenly" distributed across all nominal categories, but this does not change the chi-square test procedure. The next two examples illustrate this trough manual computations and then using SPSS to conduct the goodness-of-fit test with the same data.

EXAMPLE 12.5 Suppose that the ethnic distribution for the population in a given demographic area is: 50% Caucasian, 20% African-American, 15% Hispanic, 5% Asian, and 10% Other. The superintendent of a school district in this demographic area claims that the ethnic makeup of students in this school district matches the proportions for the five ethnic groups in the demographic area. Out of 80 students randomly selected from the superintendent's school district, there were 32 Caucasian, 18 African-American, 20 Hispanic, 7 Asian, and 3 Other students. Let's test the superintendent's claim at the .05 level of significance. In Table 12.2, we tabulate the observed frequencies, the expected frequencies, and the different components involved in the computation of the χ^2 test statistic in Formula 12.7. Note that the expected frequencies are not "evenly" distributed across the five nominal categories (ethnic groups). Indeed, the expected frequencies are 40 for Caucasians (50% of 80), 16 for African-Americans (20% of 80), 12 for Hispanic (15% of 80), 4 for Asians (5% of 80), and 8 for Other (10% of 80).

Table 12.2 *Computation of the chi-square test statistic for ethnic group frequencies*

ETHNICITY	Observed frequency (*O*)	Expected frequency (*E*)	$O - E$	$(O - E)^2$	$(O - E)^2/E$
Caucasian	32	40	−8	64	**1.600**
Afr-American	18	16	2	4	**0.250**
Hispanic	20	12	8	64	**5.333**
Asian	7	4	3	9	**2.250**
Other	3	8	−5	25	**3.125**
***Chi-square* test statistic** = $\sum [O - E)^2/E]$ = **12.558**					

Thus, the chi-square test statistic is $\chi^2 = 12.558$. With five nominal categories in this case ($K = 5$), there are 4 degrees of freedom ($df = K - 1 = 5 - 1 = 4$). The χ^2 critical value, with $df = 4$ and $\alpha = .05$, is $\chi^2_\alpha = 9.49$ (see Table A-3). **As the chi-square test statistic (12.558) exceeds the critical value (9.49), we reject the null hypothesis at the .05 level of significance**. Therefore, there is no evidence to support the superintendent's claim that the ethnic makeup of students in the school district is the same as that for the entire population in this demographic area.

EXAMPLE 12.6 This example illustrates the use of SPSS for the chi-square goodness-of-fit test performed manually in Example 12.5 (or other similar cases). Again, given are the observed frequencies of 80 students across five ethnic groups: 32, 18, 20, 7, 3. The expected frequencies (40, 16, 12, 4, 8) for these students are developed based on the superintendent's claim presented above. To use SPSS for the chi-square goodness-of-fit test with these data, follow the steps:

1. Enter the five ethnic categories and their observed frequencies in SPSS (as shown here), but make sure to use numeric codes for these categories and then label the codes in SPSS — say, **1** = **Caucasian**, **2** = **African-American**, **3** = **Hispanic**, **4** = **Asian**, and **5** = **Other**.

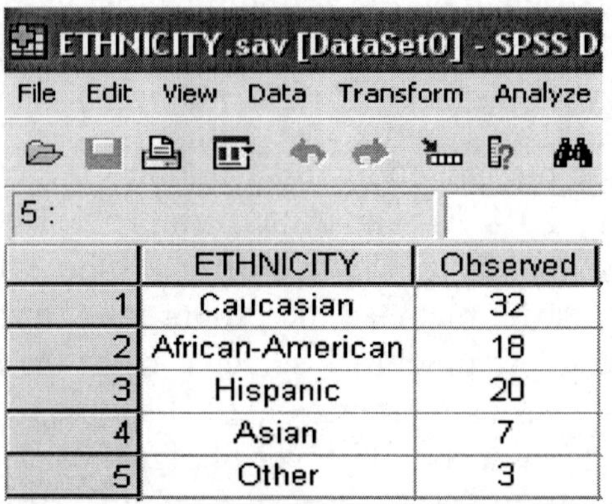

2. Click **Data**, and click **Weight Cases**.
3. Select the radio-button **Weight cases by**, then click **Observed**, and click ► to move it into the box **Frequency Variable**.
4. Click **OK**.
5. Click **Analyze**, click **Nonparametric Tests**, and click **Chi-Square**.
6. Click **ETHNICITY**, select the radio-button **Values**, type **40** in the white pane to the right, and then click **Add**. The type 16, click Add, type 12, click Add, etc., until you enter all expected frequencies the box, as shown here below.

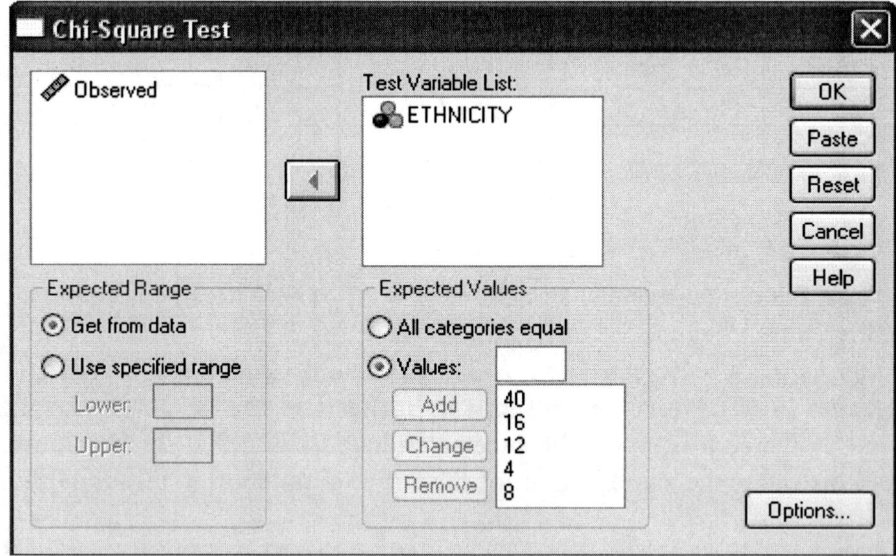

7. Click **OK**.

The resulting SPSS output is shown in Figure 12.5. Note that the chi-square test value is the same as the one we obtained through manual calculation in Table 12.2 ($\chi^2 = 12.558$). The *p*-

value reported in SPSS for this test statistic (p = .014) is less than the level of significance in this case (α = .05). Therefore, we reject the null hypothesis at the .05 level, $\chi^2(4) = 12.558$, p = .014.

Figure 12.5 *SPSS output for the chi-square goodness-of-fit test with the data in Table 12.2*

ETHNICITY

	Observed N	Expected N	Residual
Caucasian	32	40.0	-8.0
African-America	18	16.0	2.0
Hispanic	20	12.0	8.0
Asian	7	4.0	3.0
Other	3	8.0	-5.0
Total	80		

Test Statistics

	ETHNICITY
Chi-Square[a]	12.558
df	4
Asymp. Sig.	.014

→ p = .014

NOTE [12.2] With the SPSS file **ETHNICITY.sav**, given in Step 1 of the directions for using SPSS in Example 12.6, you can obtain the output in Figure 12.5 by using SPSS syntax as follows:

1. Click **File**, click **New**, and click **Syntax**.
2. In the SPSS Syntax Editor, type the following three syntax lines:

```
WEIGHT BY Observed.
    NPAR TESTS CHISQUARE = ETHNICITY(1, 3)
    / EXPECTED = 40 16 12 4 8.
```

3. Still in the SPSS Syntax Editor, click **Run**, and click **All**.

When the null hypothesis is rejected with the chi-square goodness-of-fit test, it is important to determine which categories are major contributors to the overall statistical discrepancy between observed and expected frequencies. This can be done by computing the **standardized residual (*SR*)** between observed and expected frequencies for each category:

$$SR = \frac{O - E}{\sqrt{E}} \quad \textbf{(12.8)}$$

When the *SR* for a given category exceeds 2.0 in absolute value, this indicates that the difference between the observed and expected frequencies in that category is a major contributor to the statistical significance of the χ^2 value. For example, using the SPSS output in Figure 12.5, we can apply Formula 12.8 by dividing the residuals to the square root of the expected frequencies reported in the table ETHNICITY (Figure 12.5, left panel) thus obtaining the following standardized residuals for the respective five ethnic categories: −1.26, 0.50, 2.31, 1.50, and −1.77. Thus, the only category with *SR* greater than 2.0 in absolute value, and therefore the only major contributor to the significance of the χ^2 value, is the ethnic group *Hispanic* (*SR* = 2.31).

12.4 Chi-Square Test for Association

When a research question seeks to determine a possible association between two categorical variables, another chi-square test, the **chi-square test for association**, can be used. [The chi-square test for association is also referred to as the *chi-square test of homogeneity* (or the *chi-square test for independence*), but the preference here is on the term "association."] For example, educators and parents in a large school district may want to know whether the gender of the students relates to their success (pass or fail) on a mathematics proficiency test. Thus, the question relates to a possible association between the two categorical variables *gender* and *success* (pass/fail) on the math proficiency test. In general, each of the two variables may have two or more categories. For example, in a question about an association between *ethnicity* and *employment category* in a large corporation, there can be six ethnic groups and eight employment categories. **The null hypothesis states that there is no association between the two categorical variables.**

When each variable has two categories, the frequencies of people across all categories are tabulated in a 2 x 2 contingency table. This case was addressed with testing hypothesis about proportions (Chapter 9, Sections 9.2 and 9.3). Therefore, this section deals with the more general case of *R* x *C* contingency tables, where the number of rows, *R*, is the number of categories in one variable, and the number of columns, *C*, is the number of categories in the other variable.

The chi-square test for association between categorical variables is discussed here using data from the SPSS data file **Employee data.sav.**, which was also used in Chapter 6 (Figure 6.4). Specifically, we will test for an association between two categorical variables in this data file: *minority classification* (0 = no minority, 1 = minority) and *employment category* (1 = Clerical, 2 = Custodial, 3 = Manager). Table 12.3 illustrates the corresponding 2 x 3 contingency table. The frequencies in this table were obtained using **Crosstabs** in SPSS for *minority classification* and *employment category* [**Analyze →Descriptive Statistics → Crosstabs.**]

Table 12.3 *Contingency table for minority classification and employment category*

		Employment category			
		Clerical	Custodial	Manager	Totals
Minority Classification	No minority	$O_{11} = 276$	$O_{12} = 14$	$O_{13} = 80$	$R_1 = 370$
	Minority	$O_{21} = 87$	$O_{22} = 13$	$O_{23} = 4$	$R_2 = 104$
	Totals	$C_1 = 363$	$C_2 = 27$	$C_3 = 84$	$n = 474$

In Table 12.3, *O* = observed frequency, *R* = row marginal (total), and *C* = column marginal (total). For example, $O_{23} = 4$ indicates that the observed frequency in the cell located in the second horizontal row and the third column equals 4 (i.e., there are 4 minority persons in the employment category "manager"). In general, O_{ij} = observed frequency in the cell located at row *i* and column *j* (here, *i* = 1, 2 and *j* = 1, 2, 3).

The null hypothesis states that there is no association between the two categorical variables. Each observed frequency, O_{ij}, is associated with an expected frequency, E_{ij}, which is theoretically defined as follows:

$$E_{ij} = \frac{R_i C_j}{n}, \qquad \textbf{(12.9)}$$

where R_i = total in row i, C_j = total in column j, and n = sample size. For example, the expected frequency associated with the observed frequency O_{23} ($i = 2, j = 3$) is:

$$E_{23} = (R_2)(C_3)/n = (104)(84)/474 = 18.43.$$

The values of all observed and expected frequencies, as well as the computation of the χ^2 test statistic, are provided in Table 12.4. The computed χ^2 value (26.171) is compared to a χ^2 critical value for degrees of freedom computed as follows: $df = (R - 1)(C - 1) = (2 - 1)(3 - 1) = 2$. With $df = 2$ and a $\alpha = .05$ level of significance, the critical value is $\chi^2_\alpha = 5.99$ (see Table A-3). Thus, we reject the null hypothesis because the χ^2-test statistic ($\chi^2 = 26.171$) exceeds the critical value ($\chi^2_\alpha = 5.99$).

Table 12.4 *Chi-square test for association between the variables "minority classification" and "employment category" in the SPSS data file* ***Employee data.sav****.*

Group	Observed frequency (***O***)	Expected frequency (***E***)	***O – E***	***(O – E)²***	***(O – E)²/E***	***SR*** = $(O - E)/\sqrt{E}$
No minority Clerical	$O_{11} = 276$	$E_{11} = 283.354$	−7.354	54.081	**0.191**	−0.44
No minority Custodial	$O_{12} = 14$	$E_{12} = 21.076$	−7.076	50.070	**2.376**	−1.54
No minority Manager	$O_{13} = 80$	$E_{13} = 65.570$	14.430	208.225	**3.176**	1.78
Minority Clerical	$O_{21} = 87$	$E_{21} = 79.646$	7.354	54.081	**0.679**	0.82
Minority Custodial	$O_{22} = 13$	$E_{22} = 5.924$	7.076	50.070	**8.452**	2.91*
Minority Manager	$O_{23} = 4$	$E_{23} = 18.430$	−14.430	208.225	**11.298**	−3.36*
Chi-square **test statistic** = $\sum [O - E)^2/E]$ = **26.171**						

Note. The *SR* values with an asterisk (*) are statistically significant as they exceed 2.0 in absolute value.

The last column in Table 12.4 provides the values of the **standardized residual (*SR*)** — the standard difference between the observed and expected frequency (see Formula 12.8). As noted earlier, when the standardized residual (*SR*) for a given category exceeds 2.0 in absolute value, this indicates that the difference between the observed and expected frequencies in that category is a major contributor to the statistical significance of the χ^2 value. The *SR* values in Table 12.4 show that there are two categories (cells) that can be viewed as major contributors to the statistically significant χ^2 value in this case (26.171). Namely, the "minority-custodial" (*SR* = 2.91) and "minority-manager" (*SR* = -3.36) categories. Further, given the positive sign of the SR in the former and its negative sign in the latter case, we can conclude that the overall association between *minority classification* and *employment category* is due primarily to the fact that people classified as minority are overrepresented in the custodial position, but underrepresented in the manager position.

When the number of variable categories is relatively large, manual computations of the chi-square test for association, as illustrated in Table 12.4, can be tedious and time consuming. Fortunately, as shown with the next example, the chi-square test for association between two categorical variables is available with SPSS.

EXAMPLE 12.7 This example illustrates how to conduct the chi-square test for association between *minority classification* and *employment category* using SPSS. Upon opening the SPSS file *Employee data.sav* (**File → Open → Data → Employee data**), follow the steps:

1. Click **Analyze**, click **Descriptive Statistics,** and click **Crosstabs.**
2. Click **Minority Classification** and click ▶ to move it into the box **Row(s).**
3. Click **Employment Category** and click ▶ to move it into the box **Column(s).**
4. Click **Statistics** (at the bottom of the dialog box *Crosstabs*).
5. Check **Chi-square** (upper left corner in the dialog box *Crosstabs: Statistics*).
6. Click **Continue.**
7. Click **Cells** (at the bottom of the dialog box *Crosstabs*).
8. The box **Observed** is checked by default in SPSS, so just check **Expected,** and check **Standardized** (in the panel *Residual*), as shown in the dialog box *Crosstabs: Cell Display*.

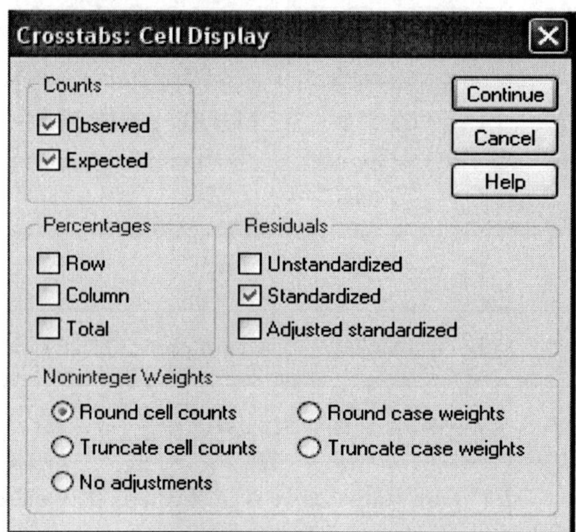

9. Click **Continue.**
10. Click **OK.**

The SPSS output is shown in Figure 12.6. As can be seen, the values for the expected frequencies and standard residuals in Table 12.4 are identical to those provided in the figure (upper panel).The notations $O = 4$, $E = 18.4$, and $SR = -3.4$ for the numbers in the cell located at the second row and third column of the table help to illustrate the meaning of the numbers presented in the 2 x 3 contingency table.

As can be seen, the Pearson chi-square value (26.172) reported in SPSS [lower panel in Figure 12.6] equals the χ^2 value computed manually in Table 12.4 (26.171), with a negligible difference due to computational rounding. In addition, SPSS reports the *p*-value associated with the χ^2 value. Given that this *p*-value is very small (p = .000), we reject the null hypothesis, $\chi^2(2) = 26.17$, $p < .001$. Thus, we conclude that there is a strong statistical evidence of an association between *minority classification* and *employment category* for the study population of employees. Also, the standardized residuals show that minority group in this population is overrepresented in the custodial position, but underrepresented in the manager position.

Figure 12.6 *SPSS output with the chi-square test for association between minority classification and employment category*

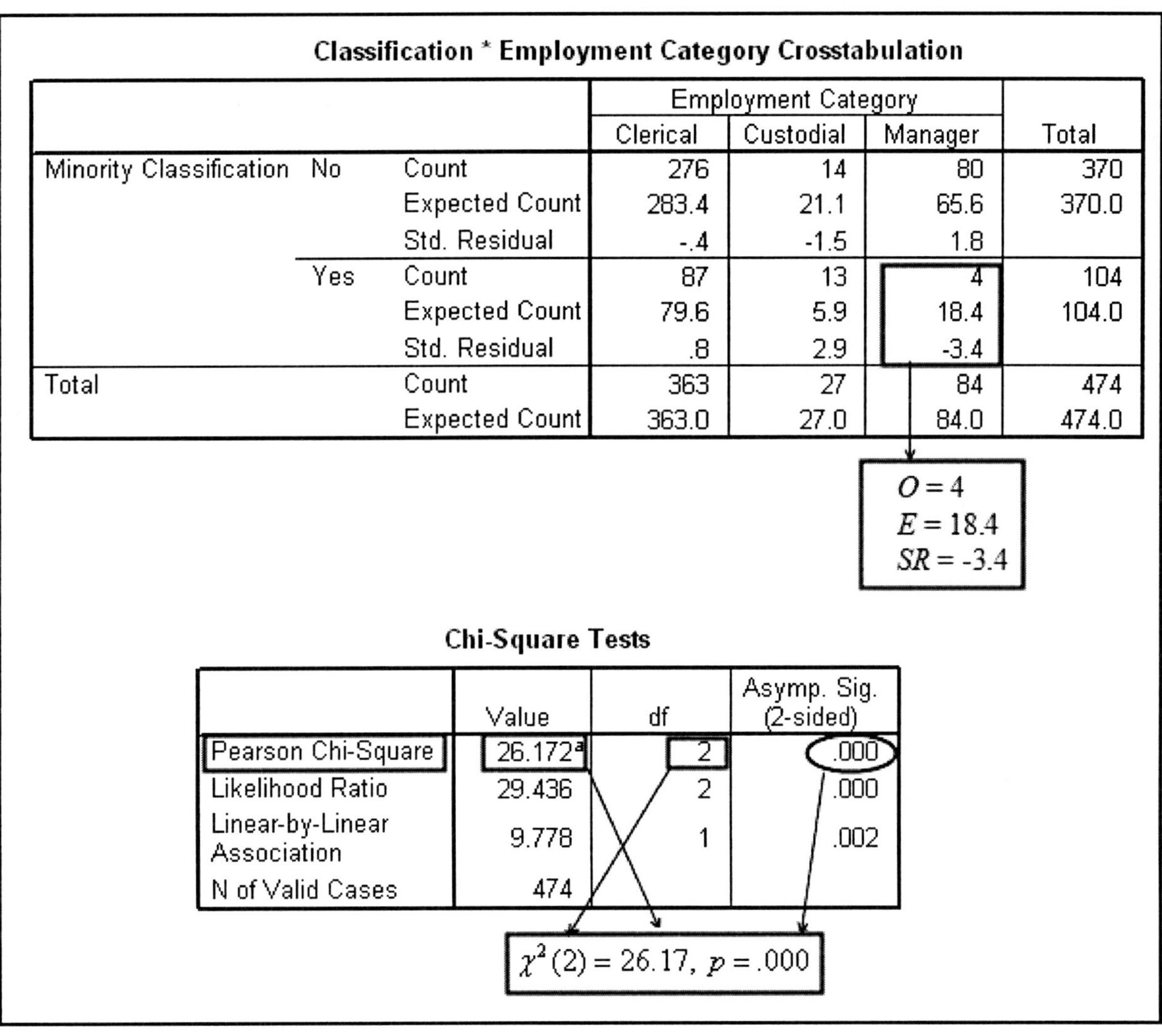

Classification * Employment Category Crosstabulation

			Employment Category			Total
			Clerical	Custodial	Manager	
Minority Classification	No	Count	276	14	80	370
		Expected Count	283.4	21.1	65.6	370.0
		Std. Residual	-.4	-1.5	1.8	
	Yes	Count	87	13	4	104
		Expected Count	79.6	5.9	18.4	104.0
		Std. Residual	.8	2.9	-3.4	
Total		Count	363	27	84	474
		Expected Count	363.0	27.0	84.0	474.0

$O = 4$
$E = 18.4$
$SR = -3.4$

Chi-Square Tests

	Value	df	Asymp. Sig. (2-sided)
Pearson Chi-Square	26.172[a]	2	.000
Likelihood Ratio	29.436	2	.000
Linear-by-Linear Association	9.778	1	.002
N of Valid Cases	474		

$\chi^2(2) = 26.17,\ p = .000$

12.5 Summary

This chapter presents *nonparametric* tests that are commonly used with ordinal data, small samples, or when the assumptions of normality or equal variances of the population distributions are not met. Nonparametric tests for hypotheses about frequency distributions of categorical variable(s) are also discussed. Here is a brief summary of the content in this chapter.

The Man-Whitney *U* test

- The Man-Whitney *U* test is a nonparametric test used for assessing whether two independent samples of ordinal data come from the same population. This test is a nonparametric analog of the *t*-test for independent samples.

- Unlike the *t*-test, the Mann-Whitney *U* test can be used with ordinal data and does not assume that the data is normally distributed, but it is less powerful than a *t*-test.

- With the Man-Whitney *U* test, the scores are converted into *ranks* (ordinal scores) in the combined sample of the two independent samples and then the test evaluates whether the mean ranks for the two groups differ significantly from each other based on a test *U*-value computed from the ranks in the two samples.

- With the Mann-Whitney *U* test, the null hypothesis is rejected when the computed test value for *U* is *smaller* than the critical value for *U* at the respective level of significance. [Note that this is the opposite of the way hypotheses are rejected using *z*-tests or *t*-tests.]

- For samples with more than 20 observations ($n_1 > 20$ and $n_2 > 20$), the *U* distribution is approximately normal, the *mean* and *standard deviation* are estimated by Formula 12.3 and the z-test value, by Formula 12.4.

The Wilcoxon signed-rank test for dependent samples

- The Wilcoxon signed-rank test is the nonparametric analog of the *t*-test for dependent samples. The Wilcoxon signed-rank test can be used with ordinal data and does not assume that the data are normally distributed, but it is also less powerful than the *t*-test.

- The Wilcoxon signed-rank test involves the computation of the difference between the dependent scores (e.g., pretest and posttests data) for each person. The absolute values of the difference scores are ranked and then each rank is assigned the sign (positive or negative) of the respective difference. The sum of the ranks with the less frequent sign is called *T*-value.

- With the Wilcoxon signed-rank test, the null hypothesis is rejected when the computed *T*-value is *smaller* than the critical *T*-value at the respective level of significance. [Note that, like with the Man-Whitney *U* test, this is the opposite of the way hypotheses are rejected using *z*-tests or *t*-tests.]

- For samples with more than 25 observations ($n > 25$), the sampling distribution of the computed *T*-value is approximately normal, the *mean* and *standard deviation* are estimated by Formula 12.5, and the z-test value, by Formula 12.6.

Chi-square goodness-of-fit test

- The **chi-square goodness-of-fit test** is used to test for population differences between *observed frequencies* that come from direct empirical observations, and *expected frequencies* developed on the basis of some hypothesis. The (observed and expected) frequencies are related to the categories of a single categorical variable (e.g., ethnicity, professional occupation, etc.).

• The *chi-square* (χ^2) *test statistic* is calculated as the sum of the ratios $(O - E)^2/E$ across all categories, where O and E stand for observed and expected frequencies, respectively. If the summation is over K categories, the degrees of freedom for the χ^2 test are: $df = K - 1$.

• With the chi-square goodness-of-fit test, the null hypothesis is rejected when the χ^2 test statistic exceeds the critical χ^2 value at a specified level of significance, α. Or, equivalently, the null hypothesis is rejected when the p-value associated with the χ^2 test statistic is smaller than the level of significance ($p < \alpha$).

• When the *standardized residual* (*SR*) for a given category exceeds 2.0 in absolute value, the difference (residual) between the observed and expected frequencies in that category is considered a major contributor to a statistically significant χ^2 test value (see Formula 12.8).

Chi-square test for association

• The chi-square test for association is used to test for a possible association between two categorical variables. Each variable may have two or more categories (e.g., 5 ethnic groups and 7 professional occupations).

• The *chi-square* (χ^2) *test statistic* is calculated as the "sum of the ratios $(O - E)^2/E$," where O and E stand for observed and expected frequencies, respectively, across all categories. With the frequencies arranged in a contingency table with R rows and C columns, the degrees of freedom for the χ^2 test are: $df = (R - 1)(C - 1)$.

• Under the null hypothesis that there is no association between the two categorical variables, the *expected frequencies* are computed by Formula 12.9.

• With the chi-square test for association, the null hypothesis is rejected when the χ^2 test statistic exceeds the critical χ^2-value at a specified level of significance, α. Or, equivalently, the null hypothesis is rejected when the p-value associated with the χ^2 test statistic is smaller than the level of significance ($p < \alpha$).

• When the standardized residual (*SR*) for a given category exceeds 2.0 in absolute value, this indicates that the difference between the observed and expected frequencies in that category is a major contributor to the statistically significant of the χ^2 value (see Formula 12.8).

12.6 Study Questions

[The multiple-choice question may allow for more than one correct answer]

1. Nonparametric tests are used in testing for score differences in two samples because they are

   A. more powerful than their parametric counterparts
   B. suitable for skewed distribution(s)
   C. suitable for small samples
   D. suitable for ordinal data
   E. All of the above.

2. With which test(s) the null hypothesis is rejected when the computed test statistic is smaller than the critical value as a specified level of significance?

A. z-test
B. t-test
C. Mann-Whitney U test
D. Wilcoxon signed-rank test
E. Chi-square goodness-of-fit test
F. Chi-square test for association.

3. Suppose that the research question is whether male and female teachers in a given school differ in their evaluations of the school principal on overall job performance. Given are the following evaluation scores provided by 10 female teachers and 8 male teachers on a 10-point scale, with higher scores reflecting more positive evaluations

Female teachers: 3, 3, 4, 5, 5, 6, 8, 8, 9, 10

Male teachers: 4, 7, 7, 8, 9, 10, 10, 10.

Answer the question by using the Mann-Whitney U test (at the .05 level of significance) via (a) manual computations [as in Example 12.1], and (b) SPSS [as in Example 12.2].

4. The school counselor in a large urban school conducted a session on personal and social consequences from aggressive behavior. The session consisted of a movie and a follow-up discussion with 26 participants randomly selected from existing school records on students' behavior. After the session, the school counselor collected observations on the participants' behavior within a two-month period of time. The pre-session and post-session evaluations, with higher scores indicating higher level of aggressive behavior, are as follows:

Pre-session: 22, 28, 16, 20, 9, 10, 20, 26, 30, 22, 12, 16, 19, 20, 20, 24, 28, 30, 22, 9, 10, 18, 22, 24, 13, 19;
Post-session: 18, 18, 17, 13, 8, 7, 14, 29, 28, 23, 8, 18, 19, 17, 20, 16, 15, 30, 20, 10, 8, 16, 20, 16, 10, 15.

Test whether there is a decrease in students' aggressive behavior for the pre-session to post-session period of time using SPSS at the .05 level of significance. [*Hint*: see Example 12.3]

5. Suppose that the responses of 42 randomly selected students on a multiple-choice test with three options, A, B, and C, are as follows: 12 students choose A, 22 students choose B, and 8 students choose C. Test whether the students responses on this test item can be attributed to random guessing. Conduct the testing at the .05 level (a) without using SPSS and (b) using SPSS. [*Hint*: see Examples 12.4]

6. Test whether the students in a graduate school of education have preference regarding four optional courses (say, C1, C2, C3, and C4), given that a random data collection on this matter showed that 20 students have registered for C1, 15 for C2, 22 for C3, and 15 for C4. Conduct the testing at the .10 level (a) without using SPSS and (b) using SPSS.

7. Test whether there are music preferences (*Jazz*, *Country*, *Classical*, and *Pop*) among adults and teenagers given the preferences of randomly selected 50 adults and 50 teenagers. Conduct the testing at the .05 level of significance using SPSS. [*Hint*: see Example 12.7]

	Jazz	*Country*	*Classical*	*Pop*
Adults	10	18	13	9
Teenagers	8	12	5	25

CHAPTER 13

MULTIPLE REGRESSION

In Chapter 10 we used *simple linear regression* to explain or predict one dependent variable from a single independent variable. Here the concept of simple linear regression is extended to that of **multiple linear regression** in which one dependent variable is explained or predicted from two or more independent variables. Although the terms *explanation* and *prediction* are sometimes used interchangeably in this chapter, it is important to emphasize that they correspond to two differing general goals in research. Namely, the purpose of **explanation** focuses on an attempt to understand how people's differences on a variable of interest (dependent variable) are *explained* (*accounted for*) by their differences on two or more independent variables. The purpose of **prediction**, instead, is to provide accurate predictions of values of the dependent variable from values of the independent variables. It must be emphasized, however, that **neither explanation nor prediction imply causality** in the framework of correlations and regressions.

13.1 The Concept of Multiple Regression

While a simple linear regression is useful in explaining (or predicting) a dependent variable of interest, Y, from a single independent variable, X, more comprehensive explanations (or more accurate predictions) are obtained by using two or more appropriate independent variables. For example, students' differences on a vocabulary test can be useful in explaining their differences on a *reading comprehension* test, but adding independent variables such as *IQ scores*, *grade in reading assigned by a teacher*, *test anxiety*, and *motivation* will further improve our understanding of factors that relate to reading comprehension. This can be achieved by using a **multiple regression** — an extension of simple linear regression that involves two or more independent variables to explain (or predict) one dependent variable.

The SPSS data shown in Figure 13.1 (left panel) represent the scores of 30 students on three tests: Y = *Reading comprehension*, X_1 = *Vocabulary*, and X_2 = *Test anxiety*. The Pearson correlation coefficients among the variables are: $r_{Y1} = .396$ ($p = .031$), $r_{Y2} = -.475$ ($p = .008$), and $r_{12} = -.131$ ($p = .489$). The correlation between Y and X_1 is statistically significant and its squared value is $R^2 = (.396)^2 = .1568$. Thus, 15.68% of the variance in reading comprehension is explained by the variance in vocabulary. Likewise, the correlation between Y and X_2 is statistically significant and its squared value is $R^2 = (-.457)^2 = .2088$. Thus, 20.88% of the variance in reading proficiency is explained by the variance in anxiety. It is logical to expect that X_1 and X_2 together explain more of the variance in Y than each of them separately. Graphically, this is depicted in Figure 13.1 (right panel), where the circle for the variance in Y represents the sum of squared deviations for Y, referred to as the **sum of squares total**:

$$SS_{Total} = \sum(Y - \bar{Y})^2 \qquad \textbf{(13.1)}$$

Given the description of the parts of the Y variance in Figure 13.1 (bottom of right panel), $SS_{Total} = A + B + C + SSE$. As the part $A + C$ represents the correlation between Y and X_1, this part accounts for 15.68% of the Y variance (SS_{Total}). Likewise, $B + C$ represents the correlation between Y and X_2, thus accounting for 20.88% of the variance in Y. However, we still do not know what percent of the variance in Y is explained jointly by X_1 and X_2, which is represented by the part $A + B + C$. We can determine this by using a multiple regression with Y as the dependent variable and X_1 and X_2 as independent variables (predictors).

Figure 13.1 *SPSS data and Venn diagram for the variances of reading comprehension (Y), vocabulary (X_1), and anxiety (X_2).*

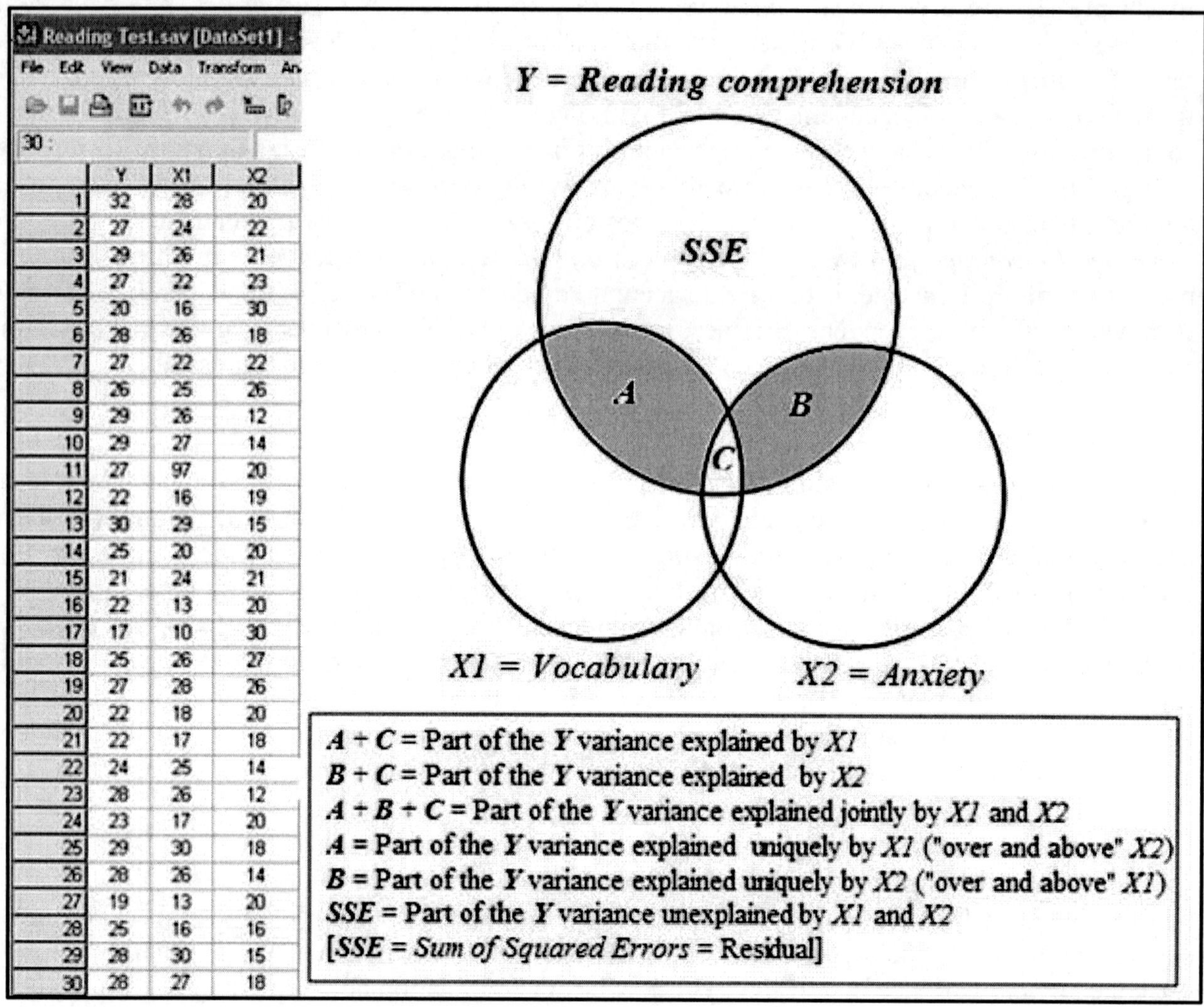

	Y	X1	X2
1	32	28	20
2	27	24	22
3	29	26	21
4	27	22	23
5	20	16	30
6	28	26	18
7	27	22	22
8	26	25	26
9	29	26	12
10	29	27	14
11	27	97	20
12	22	16	19
13	30	29	15
14	25	20	20
15	21	24	21
16	22	13	20
17	17	10	30
18	25	26	27
19	27	28	26
20	22	18	20
21	22	17	18
22	24	25	14
23	28	26	12
24	23	17	20
25	29	30	18
26	28	26	14
27	19	13	20
28	25	16	16
29	28	30	15
30	28	27	18

The general form of a multiple regression equation with two predictors, X_1 and X_2, is

$$\hat{Y} = b_1X_1 + b_2X_2 + a, \quad (13.2)$$

where b_1 and b_2 are the regression coefficients for X_1 and X_2, respectively, and a is the intercept (i.e., a equals the predicted Y value when all predictors equal zero: $a = \hat{Y}$ for $X_1 = X_2 = 0$). The prediction of Y is affected not only by the correlations between Y and each of the predictors, X_1 and X_2, but also by the correlation between X_1 and X_2. It is assumed that the relationship between Y and X_1 is the same for any fixed value of X_2 and, conversely, the relationship between Y and X_2 is the same for any fixed values of X_1. The Pearson correlation between the actual and predicted

Y scores ($r_{Y\hat{Y}}$), is called the **coefficient of multiple correlation** between Y and the predictors. The multiple correlation is denoted $\boldsymbol{R}$, with a subscript when necessary to specify the predictors being used to obtain the predicted scores, $\hat{Y}$. For example, $\boldsymbol{R}_{Y.12}$(read "Y dot one two") is used when Y is predicted from X_1 and X_2, whereas $\boldsymbol{R}_{Y.123}$ is used when Y is predicted from X_1, X_2, and X_3. The squared multiple correlation, $\boldsymbol{R}^2$, referred to as the **coefficient of multiple determination**, indicates the proportion of the variance in Y explained by the variance in all predictors together. With the notations in Figure 13.1 (right panel), $\boldsymbol{R}^2$ indicates what proportion is the shared variance (A + B + C) of the total variance in Y and the variance in X_1 and X_2, i.e.,

$$\boldsymbol{R}^2 = \frac{A+B+C}{Y} = \frac{SS_{Total}-SSE}{SS_{Total}} = \frac{Sum\ of\ squares\ due\ to\ regression}{Total\ sum\ of\ squares}, \quad \textbf{(13.3)}$$

where SSE is the **sum of squared errors** with the regression. Specifically, as with the simple linear regression, the prediction error in multiple regression is defined by the difference between actual and predicted Y values ($e = Y - \hat{Y}$). Thus, the *sum of squared errors*, referred to also as the *regression residual*, is

$$SSE = \Sigma(Y - \hat{Y})^2. \quad \textbf{(13.4)}$$

Graphically, the predicted Y values, $\hat{Y}$, from a multiple regression equation with two predictors fall on a "regression plane" that cuts through a three-dimensional space which is determined by the perpendicular axis of X_1, X_2, and Y (see Figure 13.2). As with simple linear regression, the "best fit" is the plane that yields the *smallest sum of squared errors* (*SSE*). This plane of the "best fit" is referred to as the **regression plane**.

Figure 13.2 *Regression plane for predicting Y from X_1 and X_2*

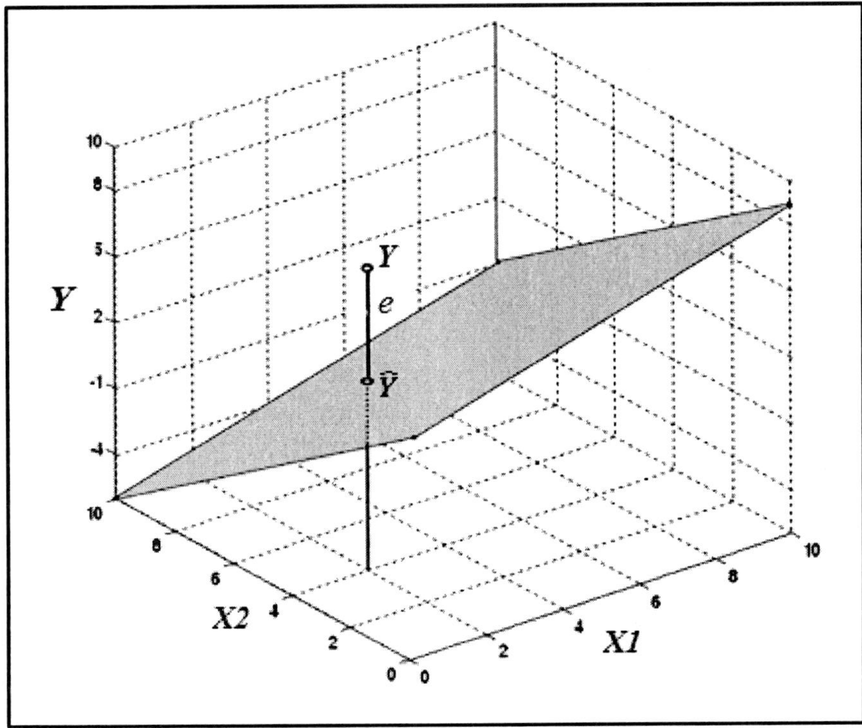

The SPSS steps for multiple regression with the data in Figure 13.1, where Y = **Reading comprehension**, X1 = **Vocabulary**, and X2 = **Anxiety**, are as follows:

1. Click **Analyze**, click **Regression**, and click **Linear**.
2. Click **Reading comprehension** and then click ▶ to move it into the box **Dependent**.
3. While holding the **Ctrl** key, click **Vocabulary**, click **Anxiety**, and then click ▶ to move them into the box **Independent(s)**.
4. Click **Statistics** (bottom of the dialog box *Linear Regression*).
5. Check **Part and partial correlations** (in the box *Linear Regression: Statistics*).
6. Click **Continue,** and click **OK.**

The resulting SPSS output is shown in Figure 13.3. The first step in the interpretation of the results is to determine whether the two predictors together account for a statistically significant proportion of the variance in *Y* (*Reading comprehension*). This will be the case if we reject the null hypothesis which states that "the coefficient of determination for the population, R^2_{pop}, is zero":

$$H_0\text{: } R^2_{pop} = 0 \qquad \textbf{(13.5)}$$

Keeping in mind the diagram in Figure 13.1., to reject this null hypothesis means that A + B + C ≠ 0 for the population. In Figure 13.3, the results from the *F*-test for H_0 are reported in the **ANOVA** table. As can be seen, the *F*-statistic is statistically significant, $F(2, 27) = 6.899$, $p = .004$, thus providing evidence that the variance in *Y* accounted for by the two predictors does not equal zero for the population. Specifically, the coefficient of determination in the **Model Summary** table, $R^2 = .338$, indicates that 33.8% of the students' differences in reading comprehension are accounted for by their differences in vocabulary and test anxiety. Given the unstandardized regression coefficients (**Coefficients** table), the multiple regression equation for predicting the dependent variable, *Y* (*Reading comprehension*) from X_1 (*Vocabulary*) and X_2 (*Anxiety*) is:

$$\hat{Y} = 0.083\,X_1 - 0.326\,X_2 + 29.877. \qquad \textbf{(13.6)}$$

The interpretation of the regression coefficient for an independent variable (predictor) is similar to the interpretation of the slope in simple linear regression but under the assumption that the values of the other predictor(s) are fixed. For example, the positive regression coefficient for X_1 in Equation 13.6 ($b_1 = 0.083$) indicates that the predicted score, $\hat{Y}$, increases by 0.083 when X_1 increases by one unit assuming that the value of X_2 does not change. The negative regression coefficient for X_2 ($b_2 = -0.326$) indicates that the predicted score, $\hat{Y}$, decreases by 0.326 when X_2 increases by one unit assuming that the value of X_1 does not change. Further, using Equation 13.6, the predicted *Y* (Reading comprehension) score for a student with, say, 20 points on the Vocabulary test ($X_1 = 20$) and 30 points on the Anxiety test ($X_2 = 30$) is:

$$\hat{Y} = (0.083)(20) - (0.326)(30) + 29.877 = 21.76.$$

NOTE [13.1] With Equation 13.6, the predicted *Y* value equals the sample mean of *Y* ($\hat{Y} = \bar{Y}$) when the values of the predictors are replaced by the sample means ($\bar{X}_1$ and $\bar{X}_2$). Graphically, the dot with coordinates ($\bar{X}_1$, $\bar{X}_2$, $\bar{Y}$) always falls on the regression plane.

Figure 13.3 *SPSS output from multiple linear regression of Reading comprehension on Vocabulary and Anxiety*

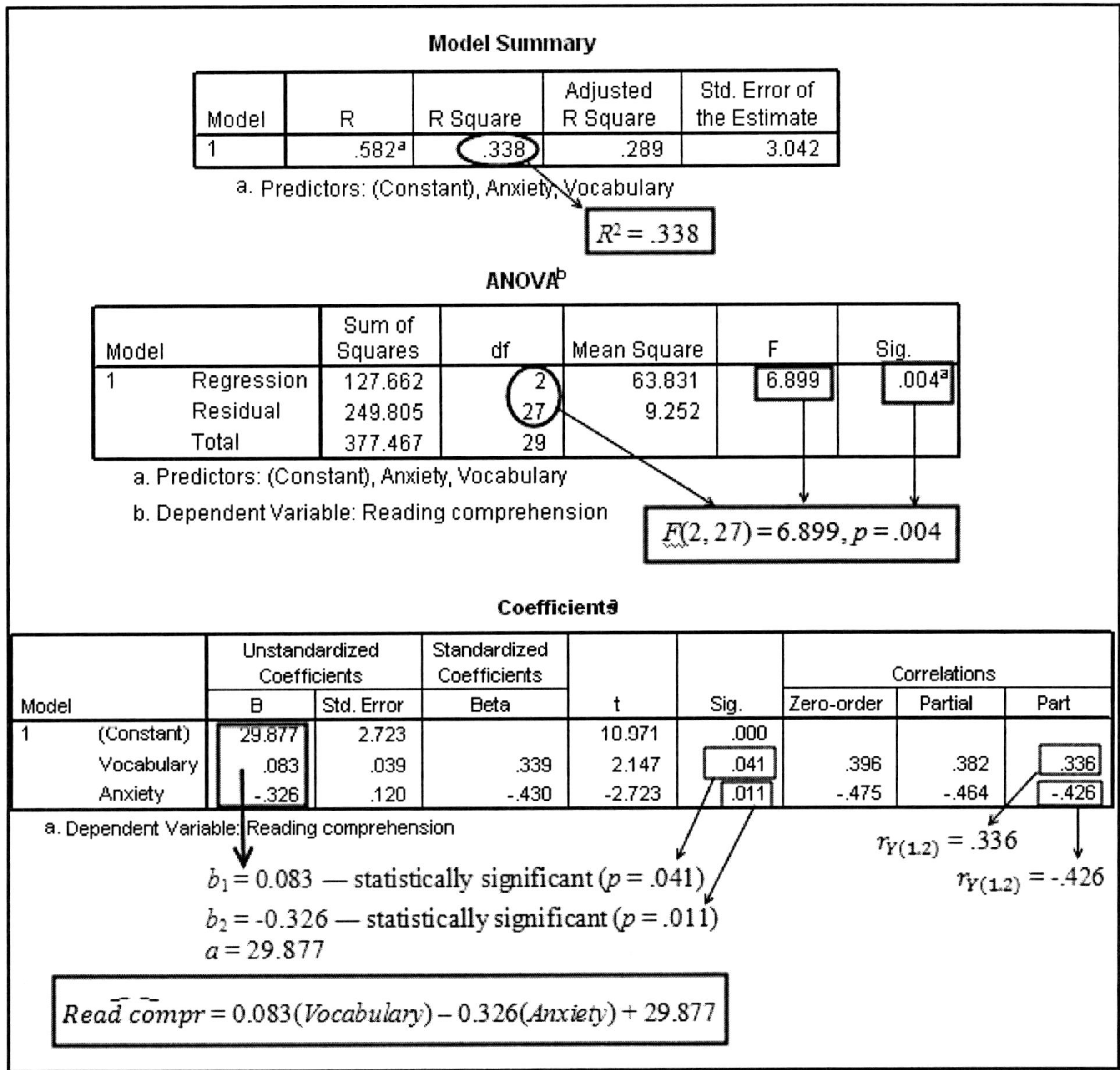

Model Summary

Model	R	R Square	Adjusted R Square	Std. Error of the Estimate
1	.582[a]	.338	.289	3.042

a. Predictors: (Constant), Anxiety, Vocabulary

ANOVA[b]

Model		Sum of Squares	df	Mean Square	F	Sig.
1	Regression	127.662	2	63.831	6.899	.004[a]
	Residual	249.805	27	9.252		
	Total	377.467	29			

a. Predictors: (Constant), Anxiety, Vocabulary

b. Dependent Variable: Reading comprehension

Coefficients[a]

Model		Unstandardized Coefficients		Standardized Coefficients	t	Sig.	Correlations		
		B	Std. Error	Beta			Zero-order	Partial	Part
1	(Constant)	29.877	2.723		10.971	.000			
	Vocabulary	.083	.039	.339	2.147	.041	.396	.382	.336
	Anxiety	-.326	.120	-.430	-2.723	.011	-.475	-.464	-.426

a. Dependent Variable: Reading comprehension

After establishing the overall statistical significance of R^2 and the multiple regression equation, we move to examining the statistical significance of the regression coefficients for the two predictors, *vocabulary* ($b_1 = 0.083$) and *Anxiety* ($b_2 = -0.326$). In this case, each of them is statistically significant at the .05 level ($p = .041$ and $p = .011$, respectively). This indicates that each predictor has its own *unique* contribution to R^2 (that is, to the explanation of the variance in the dependent variable, Y = *reading comprehension*). Again using the diagram notations in Figure 13.1 as a reference, this means that $A \neq 0$ and $B \neq 0$ for the population. The magnitude of the unique explanatory contribution of a given predictor is indicated by the squared value of its part correlation with the dependent variable (see *part correlations* in Chapter 11).

In Figure 13.3, the part correlation between Y and X_1, partialling out X_2 from X_1, is: $r_{Y(1.2)} = .336$. Thus, $(.336)^2 = .1129$ shows that 11.29% of the variance in *reading comprehension* is uniquely accounted for by the variance in *Vocabulary* ("over and above" the explanatory contribution of *Anxiety*). Likewise, the part correlation between *Y* and X_2, partialling out X_1 from X_2, is: $r_{Y(2.1)} = -.426$. Thus, $(-.426)^2 = .1815$ shows that 18.15% of the variance in *Reading comprehension* is uniquely accounted for by the variance in *anxiety* ("over and above" the explanatory contribution of *Vocabulary*). Back to the diagram in Figure 13.1, these results indicate that part *A* represents 11.29% and part *B* represents 18.15% of the total variance in *Y*. Clearly, for the data in Figure 13.1, *Anxiety* is relatively more important than *Vocabulary* for the explanation (or prediction) of *Reading comprehension*.

NOTE [13.2] The *t*-statistic for statistical significance of the regression coefficient, *b*, for a given predictor equals the ratio of *b* to its standard error: ***t* = *b*/SE(*b*).** For example, the *t*-statistic for the *b* coefficient of *Anxiety* in Figure 13.3 (*Coefficients* table) is $t = -.326/.120 = -2.72$. The *p*-value for the *t*-statistic is the area beyond this statistic under the *t*-distribution with degrees of freedom: $df = n - k - 1$, where *n* is the sample size and *k* is the number of predictors. A statistically significant *b* ($p < .05$) indicates that the unique contribution of the predictor, over and above that of all other predictors, in accounting for variance in *Y* is statistically significant (i.e., does not equal zero for the population).

Standardized regression equation. When the values of *Y*, X_1, and X_2 are transformed into *z*-scores (z_Y, z_1, and z_2, respectively) and then the *z*-scores of *Y* are predicted from the *z*-scores of X_1, and X_2, the regression equation is called a **standardized regression equation** and its general form is:

$$\hat{z}_Y = \beta_1 z_1 + \beta_2 z_2 \qquad \textbf{(13.7)}$$

The standardized regression coefficient (e.g., β_1 or β_2) for a given predictor is a close "relative" of the *part correlation* between *Y* and this predictor, while controlling for the other predictor(s). In Equation 13.7, the intercept is omitted as it is equal to zero. This is because the mean of the z-scores equals zero and, taking into account NOTE [13.1], the dot with coordinates (0, 0, 0) always falls on the regression plane (that is, $\bar{z}_1 = \bar{z}_2 = 0$ yields $\hat{z} = \bar{z} = 0$).

While the raw score regression coefficients in Equation 13.2 (b_1 and b_2) are useful for interpretations using the original metric for the predictors, the standardized coefficients in Equation 13.7 (β_1 or β_2) indicate the relative explanatory importance of the predictors regardless of their original units of measurement. Specifically, the higher the absolute value of the standardized regression coefficient for a predictor, the larger the explanatory contribution of this predictor. In Figure 13.3, the standardized regression coefficient for *Anxiety* ($\beta_2 = -.430$) exceeds in absolute value the standardized regression coefficient for *Vocabulary* ($\beta_1 = .339$) thus indicating that the unique explanatory contribution of *Anxiety* is larger than that of *Vocabulary*; [Equivalently, the relative explanatory importance of the predictors can be determined by comparing the squared values of their part correlations with the dependent variable.]

In general, a multiple regression model is tested for statistical significance (H_0: $R^2_{pop} = 0$) using the following *F*-statistic:

$$F = \frac{R^2/k}{(1-R^2)/(n-k-1)}, \qquad \textbf{(13.8)}$$

where R^2 is the coefficient of determination computed for the sample and k is the number of predictors (independent variables) in the multiple regression model. If H_0 is true, this F-statistic belongs to the F-distribution with k degrees of freedom in the numerator and $n - k - 1$ degrees of freedom in the denominator.

For example, the F-statistic in Figure 13.3 (ANOVA table), $F = 6.899$, is computed by Formula 13.8, with $R^2 = .338$, $k = 2$ (number of predictors), and $n = 30$ (sample size):

$$F = \frac{.338/2}{(1-.338)/(30-2-1)} = 6.893.$$

As this computation uses a rounded value of R^2 (.338), the resulting F-value (6.893) is slightly different from that in Table 13.3 ($F = 6.899$). The p-value for this F-statistic, under the F-distribution with two degrees of freedom in the numerator ($k = 2$) and 27 degrees of freedom in the denominator ($n - k - 1 = 30 - 2 - 1 = 27$), is given in Figure 13.3 (ANOVA table: $p = .004$).

13.2 Comparison of Full and Restricted Regression Models

The logic of multiple regression with two predictors carries over into multiple regression with more than two predictors. However, adding more predictors does not necessarily improve the multiple regression model. For example, if two predictors, X_1 and X_2, account for the same amount of variance in the dependent variable, Y, as four predictors, X_1, X_2, X_3, and X_4, the two-predictor multiple regression model is more practical and cost efficient (e.g., reducing expenses in collecting data on X_3 and X_4). Consider the four-predictor multiple regression model

$$\hat{Y} = b_1X_1 + b_2X_2 + b_3X_3 + b_4X_4 + a. \quad \textbf{(13.9)}$$

After removing some predictors, say X_3 and X_4, the resulting multiple regression model is

$$\hat{Y} = b_1X_1 + b_2X_2 + a \quad \textbf{(13.10)}$$

The multiple regression model in Equation 13.9 is called a **full regression model**, whereas the model in Equation 13.10 is called a **restricted regression model**. If R^2_{full} is the coefficient of determination with the full model and R^2_{restr} is that with the restricted model, the question is whether the difference $R^2_{change} = R^2_{full} - R^2_{restr}$ is statistically significant. This question calls for testing the null hypothesis:

$$H_0\colon R^2_{change} = 0 \quad \textbf{(13.11)}$$

A failure to reject H_0 would indicate that the full and restricted regression models account for the same proportion of variance in the dependent variable, Y, at the population level. In such case, the explanatory contribution of X_3, and X_4, over and above that provided by X_1 and X_2, is not statistically significant. Thus, given that the full and restricted regression models are equally effective in explaining the variance in Y, it would be better to use the more parsimonious restricted model.

In general, if the full model has k predictors and the restricted model has r predictors (selected from the predictors in the full model), the test statistic for H_0 is

$$F = \frac{R^2_{change}/(k-r)}{\left(1-R^2_{full}\right)/(n-k-1)}, \tag{13.12}$$

where n is the sample size. If H_0 is true, this F-statistic belongs to the F distribution with $(k - r)$ degrees of freedom in the numerator and $(n - k - 1)$ degrees of freedom in the denominator.

For example, suppose that for a sample of 85 observations ($n = 85$), we have $R^2_{full} = .435$, for a full regression model with four predictors ($k = 4$), and $R^2_{restr} = .412$, for a restricted model that contains only two of the predictors in the full model ($r = 2$). Thus, $R^2_{change} = .435 - .412 = .023$ and, using Formula 13.12, the F-statistic for H_0 is

$$F = \frac{(.023)/(4-2)}{(1-.435)/(85-4-1)} = \frac{.023/2}{.565/80} = 1.63.$$

To test H_0 at the .05 level of significance, the F-statistic (1.63) is compared to the critical value $F_{cv} = 3.11$ for 2 degrees of freedom in the numerator ($k - r = 4 - 2 = 2$), 80 degrees in the denominator ($n - k - 1 = 85 - 4 - 1 = 80$), and $\alpha = .05$ (see Table A-4). As the computed F-statistic (1.63) does not exceed the F-critical value (3.11), the null hypothesis (H_0: $R^2_{change} = 0$) is not rejected. Thus, the full model with four predictors and the restricted model with only two of those predictors are equally effective in explaining the variance in Y. Therefore, it would be better to use the more parsimonious restricted regression model.

EXAMPLE 13.1 In this example we illustrate the use of SPSS for the comparison of full and restricted regression models. In SPSS, the model used first is the restricted model (Model 1). Then the full model (Model 2) is conducted. The SPSS output reports the change in R^2 from Model 1 to Model 2 (R^2_{change}) and information about its statistical significance (F-statistic computed by Formula 13.12 and its p-value). The data come from a study on predicting *mental health* ($Y = MH$) from *vitality* (*VT*), *social functioning* (*SF*), *physical functioning* (*PF*), *health perception* (*HP*), and *body pain* (*BP*). The data file, titled **MENTAL_HEALTH**, is available (in SPSS format) at the website accompanying this textbook [http://cehd.gmu.edu/book/dimitrov].

In this example, the **full model** includes all five predictors (*VT, SF, PF, HP, BP*). Using SPSS for this model (as shown in section 13.1), we can see that its coefficient of determination ($R^2_{full} = .663$) is statistically significant, $F(5, 75) = 29.566$, $p = .000$. However, the SPSS results also show that the regression coefficients for two predictors, *HP* and *BP*, are not statistically significant at the .05 level (see the results for Model 2 in Figure 13.4). Therefore, we define the restricted model in this example by removing *HP* and *BP* from the full model thus obtaining a **restricted model** (Model 1 in SPSS) with three predictors: *VT, SF*, and *PF*.

To compare Model 1 (restricted) versus Model 2 (full) in SPSS, follow the steps:

1. Click **Analyze**, click **Regression**, and click **Linear**.
2. Click **Reset** to clear the dialog box (if there is some information from previous analyses).
3. Click **MH** and click ▶ to move it to the **Dependent** box.
4. Hold down the **Ctrl** key, click **VT**, **SF**, and **PF**, and click ▶ to move them to the **Independent** box. [Thus, the predictors with the restricted model (Model 1) are entered first.]
5. Click **Next**.

6. Hold down the **Ctrl** key, click **HP** and **BP**, and then click ▶ to move them to the **Independent** box [this adds HP and BP to the restricted model to form the full model.]
7. Click **Statistics**. The options **Estimates** and **Model fit** should already be selected by default in SPSS, so click **R Squared Change**, **Descriptives**, and **Part and partial correlations**.
8. Click **Continue**
9. Click **OK**.

The SPSS output is provided in Figure 13 (without descriptive statistics and correlations).

The results in the **Model Summary** table show that the three predictors in the restricted model (Model 1: *VT*, *SF*, and *PF*) account for a statistically significant amount of the variance in *mental health*, $R^2 = .645$, $F(3, 77) = 46.64$, $p = .000$. However, the change in R^2 from Model 1 to Model 2 is not statistically significant, $R^2_{change} = .018$, $F(2, 75) = 2.046$, $p = .136$. This indicates that *health perception* and *body pain* do not account for a statistically significant proportion of the variance in *mental health* over and above the proportion accounted for by the independent variables in the restricted model (*vitality*, *social functioning*, and *physical functioning*). As the three-predictor restricted model (Model 1) and the five-predictor full model (Model 2) do not differ in how much variance in *mental health* they account for, it would be better to use the restricted model. Given the unstandardized coefficients for Model 1 in Figure 13.4, the regression equation for the restricted model is

$$\widehat{MH} = (0.248)VT + (0.614)SF + (0.269)PH - 24.198.$$

Following the description and interpretation of the results provided in the previous section for the SPSS output in Figure 13.3, we can interpret the results in Figure 13.4 separately for Model 1 and Model 2. To illustrate, notice that the part correlation between the dependent variable (*mental health*) and the independent variable *social functioning* is .425 in Model 1 and .292 in Model 2. This is because when Model 1 is used, two predictors (*vitality* and *physical functioning*) are removed from social functioning, thus obtaining .425, whereas when Model 2 is used, four predictors (*vitality*, *physical functioning*, *health perception*, and *body pain*) are removed from *social functioning* thus lowering its part correlation with *mental health* to .292. The notations for part and partial correlations with more than two predictors are illustrated in NOTE [13.3].

NOTE [13.3] With the notations Y = *mental health*, X_1 = *vitality*, X_2 = *social functioning*, X_3 = *physical functioning*, X_4 = *health perception*, and X_5 = *body pain*, the **part correlation** between *mental health* (Y) and *social functioning* (X_2) in Model 1 is the correlation between Y and X_2 partialling out X_1 and X_3 from X_2. This part correlation is denoted $r_{Y(2.13)}$. The **part correlation** between mental health (Y) and social functioning (X_2) in Model 2, however, is the correlation between Y and X_2 partialling out X_1, X_3, X_4, and X_5 from X_2. This part correlation is denoted $r_{Y(2.1345)}$. Thus, as reported in Figure 13.4, $r_{Y(2.13)} = .425$ and $r_{Y(2.1345)} = .292$. The part correlation between the dependent variable, Y, and any other predictor in Model 1 (or Model 2) is denoted and interpreted in a similar fashion.

Likewise, the **partial correlation** between *mental health* and *social functioning* (Y and X_2) in Model 1 is $r_{Y2.13} = .581$, whereas the **partial correlation** between the same two variables in Model 2 is: $r_{Y2.1345} = .449$. The partial correlation between the dependent variable, Y, and any other predictor in Model 1 (or Model 2) is denoted and interpreted in a similar fashion.

Figure 13.4 *SPSS multiple regression results for Model 1 (restricted) versus Model 2 (full).*

Model Summary

Model	R	R Square	Adjusted R Square	Std. Error of the Estimate	Change Statistics				
					R Square Change	F Change	df1	df2	Sig. F Change
1	.803[a]	.645	.631	12.349	.645	46.642	3	77	.000
2	.814[b]	.663	.641	12.185	.018	2.046	2	75	.136

a. Predictors: (Constant), Physical functioning, Vitality, Social functioning

b. Predictors: (Constant), Physical functioning, Vitality, Social functioning, Body pain, Health perception

$R^2_{change} = .018, F(2, 75) = 2.046, p = .136$

ANOVA[c]

Model		Sum of Squares	df	Mean Square	F	Sig.
1	Regression	21338.521	3	7112.840	46.642	.000[a]
	Residual	11742.368	77	152.498		
	Total	33080.889	80			
2	Regression	21946.028	5	4389.206	29.564	.000[b]
	Residual	11134.861	75	148.465		
	Total	33080.889	80			

a. Predictors: (Constant), Physical functioning, Vitality, Social functioning

b. Predictors: (Constant), Physical functioning, Vitality, Social functioning, Body pain, Health perception

c. Dependent Variable: Mental health

Coefficients[a]

Model		Unstandardized Coefficients		Standardized Coefficients	t	Sig.	Correlations		
		B	Std. Error	Beta			Zero-order	Partial	Part
1	(Constant)	-24.198	8.926		-2.711	.008			
	Vitality	.248	.088	.239	2.815	.006	.604	.305	.191
	Social functioning	.614	.098	.545	6.257	.000	.752	.581	.425
	Physical functioning	.269	.088	.217	3.056	.003	.420	.329	.208
2	(Constant)	-31.759	10.693		-2.970	.004			
	Vitality	.290	.091	.279	3.201	.002	.604	.347	.214
	Social functioning	.517	.119	.459	4.357	.000	.752	.449	.292
	Physical functioning	.249	.087	.201	2.853	.006	.420	.313	.191
	Health perception	.191	.098	.172	1.949	.055	.555	.220	.131
	Body pain	.075	.082	.075	.920	.360	-.394	.106	.062

a. Dependent Variable: Mental health

13.3 Multicollinearity

Multicollinearity occurs when there are moderate to high correlations among the predictors in a multiple regression. In general, three major problems stem from multicollinearity in multiple regression.

1. When the correlation among some predictors increases, the proportion of the variance in the dependent variable, Y, that is uniquely explained by these predictors decreases. The

explanatory effects of correlated predictors are confounded due to the considerable amount of variance that such predictors share. In Figure 13.1, for example, the presence of multicollinearity for the two predictors depends on the magnitude of part *C*. In this particular example there is no danger of multicollinearity as the correlation between the two predictors, X_1 (*vocabulary*) and X_2 (*anxiety*) is not statistically significant, $r_{12} = -.131$, $p = .489$. Thus, the proportion of the variance in *Y* depicted by part *C* is negligible. Imagine, however, that as circles X_1 and X_2 increasingly overlap, part *C* gets larger while parts *A* and *B* get smaller. In this hypothetical situation the coefficient of determination, R^2 — depicted by the overlap between *Y* and the two predictors ($A + B + C$), may remain the same while the unique parts *A* and *B* decrease.

2. In multiple regression, the regression coefficient for a predictor is interpreted as "the change in the predicted value associated with a one-unit change in the predictor while holding the other predictors constant." However, this interpretation is not quite valid when there is multicollinearity because, when the predictors are correlated, changes (increases or decreases) in one predictor are associated with changes in the other predictors and, therefore, it is unrealistic to "hold the other predictors constant."

3. As can be inferred from Formula 13.13, discussed below, the standard error of the regression coefficients increases when the correlation among the predictors increases. Thus, the higher the multicollinearity, the lower the accuracy of the multiple regression prediction.

Given the problems associated with multicollinearity, it is important to know the degree to which multicollinearity exists. The degree to which a given predictor, X_j, correlates with the other predictors, thus causing multicollinearity, can be determined by regressing this predictor on the other predictors — that is, using a multiple regression to predict X_j from the other predictors. By doing this, the resulting coefficient of determination (denoted R_j^2) will show how much X_j correlates with the other predictors. Clearly then, the difference $1 - R_j^2$, called **tolerance** of X_j, will indicate the degree of nonredundancy between X_j and the remaining predictors.

The tolerance may take on values from 0.00 to 1.00. The closer the tolerance to 1.00, the lower the multicollinearity caused by the predictor X_j. Ideally, tolerance of 1.00 will occur when $R_j^2 = 0$ (that is, X_j does not correlate with any of the other predictors). In this case, X_j is said to be **orthogonal** to the other predictors. Conversely, the closer the tolerance to zero, the higher the contribution of X_j to multicollinearity.

The reciprocal of the tolerance, $1/(1 - R_j^2)$, is called the **variance inflation factor (*VIF*)** for the predictor X_j. Clearly, when $R_j^2 = 0$, the lowest (and best) possible value of the variance inflation factor is 1.00 (*VIF* = 1). Conversely, the closer R_j^2 is to 1.00, the larger the *VIF* and thus the larger the contribution of X_j to multicollinearity. A good rule of thumb is that if a predictor has a *VIF* greater than 10 its contribution to multicollinearity should be a concern. The "inflation" comes from the presence of the *VIF* in the formula for the variance of the regression coefficient for X_j, Var(b_j):

$$\text{Var}(b_j) = \frac{s_e^2}{(n-1)s_j^2} \times \frac{1}{1-R_j^2}, \tag{13.13}$$

where *n* is the sample size, s_j^2 is the variance of the predictor X_j, and s_e^2 is the *error variance* —

i.e, the squared standard error of estimate [in SPSS, the **standard error of estimate** is reported in the **Model Summary** table — in Figure 13.3, s_e = 3.042.]. The smallest variance of the regression coefficient b_j will occur when $R_j^2 = 0$ (or, equivalently, when $VIF = 1$). Conversely, the larger the VIF, the larger (more "inflated") is the variance of b_j. However, larger Var(b_j) yields less accurate multiple regression predictions in future samples.

EXAMPLE 13.2 This example illustrates how to interpret the SPSS output for *tolerance* and *variance inflation factor* (*VIF*) using Model 2 (the full regression model) in Example 13.1. Using the SPSS data file MENTAL_HEALTH, follow the steps:

1. Click **Analyze**, click **Regression**, and click **Linear**.
2. Click **Reset** to clear the dialog box.
3. Click **MH**, and click ▶ to move it to the **Dependent** box.
4. Hold down the **Ctrl** key, click **VT, SF, PH, HP**, and **BP**, and then click ▶ to move them to the **Independent** box.
5. Click **Statistics.** The options **Estimates** and **Model fit** should already be selected by default in SPSS, so click **Part and partial correlations**, and click **Collinearity diagnostics**.
6. Click **Continue.**
7. Click **OK.**

Figure 13.5 presents only the *Coefficients* table from the resulting SPSS output. The other two tables, *Model Summary* and *ANOVA*, are provided with Model 2 in Figure 13.4.

Figure 13.5 *Selected SPSS output with the multiple regression for prediction of mental health vitality, social functioning, physical functioning, health perception, and body pain.*

Coefficients[a]

Model		Unstandardized Coefficients		Standardized Coefficients			Correlations			Collinearity Statistics	
		B	Std. Error	Beta	t	Sig.	Zero-order	Partial	Part	Tolerance	VIF
1	(Constant)	-31.759	10.693		-2.970	.004					
	Vitality	.290	.091	.279	3.201	.002	.604	.347	.214	.591	1.692
	Social functioning	.517	.119	.459	4.357	.000	.752	.449	.292	.405	2.470
	Physical functioning	.249	.087	.201	2.853	.006	.420	.313	.191	.902	1.108
	Health perception	.191	.098	.172	1.949	.055	.555	.220	.131	.577	1.733
	Body pain	.075	.082	.075	.920	.360	-.394	.106	.062	.669	1.495

a. Dependent Variable: Mental health

The examination of the *Collinearity Statistics* column in Figure 13.5 shows that, following the rule of thumb for the lack of multicollinearity ($VIF < 10$), there should not be a serious concern about multicollinearity in this case because even the largest *VIF* (2.470) is much smaller than 10. *Physical functioning* is the predictor that correlates the least with the other predictors as its *tolerance* value (.902) is very close to 1.00 (total lack of correlation with the other predictors). Thus, *physical functioning* is almost orthogonal to the remaining predictors. It is also interesting to note that the predictor that contributes the most to multicollinearity, *social functioning* (Tolerance = .405, VIF = 2.470), is at the same time the most important predictor in terms of its unique contribution to explaining the variance of *mental health* (with the largest standardized coefficient, *Beta* = .459). The unique explanatory contribution of *social functioning* is estimated by squaring its part correlation with *mental health*: $(.292)^2 = .0853$. Thus, 8.53% of the variance in *mental health* is uniquely accounted for by *social functioning*. Clearly, it would be a mistake to exclude *social functioning* from the regression model based solely on its relative contribution to multicollinearity.

13.4 Cross-validation

When a multiple regression model is developed for predictions with future samples, the accuracy of the prediction is critical to making valid interpretations and decisions based on predicted scores. The sample initially used to develop a multiple regression equation is called the **screening sample**. The regression coefficients obtained with the screening sample are aimed at maximizing the coefficient of multiple determination, R^2. Therefore, the coefficient of multiple determination with the screening sample, R^2_{scr}, is always greater than its counterpart produced by the original regression equation applied to any other sample (called the **calibration sample**), R^2_{cal}. The difference between these two coefficients of determination ($\varepsilon = R^2_{scr} - R^2_{cal}$) is called **shrinkage** in R^2.

The estimation of R^2 shrinkage is called **cross-validation**. When the shrinkage is small, it would be useful to combine the screening and calibration samples and use the resulting regression equation in future predictions. The regression coefficients produced by the combined sample are more stable because the size of the combined sample is greater than that for either the screening or calibration sample. If it is difficult to obtain a calibration sample and the original sample is sufficiently large, one can randomly split the original sample into two (screening and calibration) samples to estimate the R^2 shrinkage. The smaller the R^2 shrinkage, the better the regression equation will cross-validate in applications with future samples.

The amount of R^2 shrinkage depends, among other things, on the ratio of "sample size to number of predictors" (n/k). With all other conditions being equal, the larger this ratio, the smaller the R^2 shrinkage. According to a recommended rule (Stevens, 2002), about 15 observations per predictor are needed for a multiple regression equation to make accurate predictions with future samples. For example, it has been demonstrated that with 15/1 ratio, the R^2 shrinkage is small (less than .05), with a probability of .90, if the coefficient of determination for the population is $R^2_{pop} = .50$.

13.5 Statistical power, Effect size, and Sample size

As noted earlier in this chapter, a first step in the analysis of multiple regression results is to test the null hypothesis H_0: $R^2_{pop} = 0$ (see Equation 13.5). The **power** of this test (***P*** = probability to reject H_0 when it is indeed false) depends on the following four factors: *level of significance* (α), *sample size* (*n*), *number of predictors* (*k*), and *effect size* (*ES*), defined as

$$ES = R^2_{pop}/(1 - R^2_{pop}) \qquad \textbf{(13.14)}$$

Cohen and Cohen (1983) provided the following sample size formula for prespecified values of **P**, α, and ES:

$$n = \frac{L}{ES} + k + 1, \qquad \textbf{(13.15)}$$

where L is a parameter, reported in Cohen's statistical power tables (Cohen & Cohen, 1983), that depends on ***P***, α, and *k*. Table 13.1 provides *L* values for α = .05 and selected values of ***P*** and *k*.

EXAMPLE 13.3 Suppose that a R^2_{pop} as small as .25 is of interest for a multiple regression equation with four predictors. What sample size is necessary to reach a power of .90 to detect the pre-specified R^2_{pop} = .25 at the .05 level of significance? For $\boldsymbol{P}$ = .90 (power), k = 4 (number of predictors), and α = .05 (level of significance), Table 13.1 provides the L value = 15.41. On the other hand, using Formula 13.14 with R^2_{pop} = .25, we obtain the effect size: ES = .25/(1 – .25) = 0.3333. Now, using Equation 13.15, we obtain the necessary sample size: n = 15.41/0.3333 + 4 + 1 = 51.23 (or, rounded to the nearest integer, n = 51). Thus, a sample of 51 observations is needed if we want to reject the null hypothesis (H_0: R^2_{pop}= 0) at the .05 level of significance, with a power of .90, given that the actual R^2_{pop} is as small as .25.

Table 13.1 *Cohen's L values for sample size in multiple regression (α = .05)*

	Power								
k	.50	.60	.70	.75	.80	.85	.90	.95	.99
1	3.84	4.90	6.17	6.94	7.85	8.98	10.51	13.00	18.37
2	4.96	6.21	7.70	8.59	9.64	10.92	12.65	15.44	21.40
3	5.76	7.15	8.79	9.77	10.90	12.30	14.17	17.17	23.52
4	6.42	7.92	9.68	10.72	11.94	13.42	15.41	18.57	25.24
5	6.99	8.59	10.45	11.55	12.83	14.39	16.47	19.78	26.73
6	7.50	9.19	11.14	12.29	13.62	15.26	17.42	20.86	28.05
7	7.97	9.73	11.77	12.96	14.35	16.04	18.28	21.84	29.25
8	8.41	10.24	12.35	13.59	15.02	16.77	19.08	22.74	30.36
9	8.81	10.71	12.89	14.17	15.65	17.45	19.83	23.59	31.39
10	9.19	11.15	13.40	14.72	16.24	18.09	20.53	24.39	32.37
11	9.56	11.58	13.89	15.24	16.80	18.70	21.20	25.14	33.29
12	9.90	11.98	14.35	15.74	17.34	19.28	21.83	25.86	34.16
13	10.24	12.36	14.80	16.21	17.85	19.83	22.44	26.55	35.00
14	10.55	12.73	15.22	16.67	18.34	20.36	23.02	27.20	35.81
15	10.86	13.09	15.63	17.11	18.81	20.87	23.58	27.84	36.58
16	11.16	13.43	16.03	17.53	19.27	21.37	24.13	28.45	37.33
18	11.73	14.09	16.78	18.34	20.14	22.31	25.16	29.62	38.76
20	12.26	14.71	17.50	19.11	20.96	23.20	26.13	30.72	40.10
22	12.77	15.30	18.17	19.83	21.74	24.04	27.06	31.77	41.37
24	13.02	15.87	18.82	20.53	22.49	24.85	27.94	32.76	42.59
28	14.17	16.93	20.04	21.83	23.89	26.36	29.60	34.64	44.87
32	15.02	17.91	21.17	23.04	25.19	27.77	31.14	36.37	46.98
36	15.82	18.84	22.23	24.18	16.41	29.09	32.58	38.00	48.96
40	16.58	19.71	23.23	25.25	27.56	30.33	33.94	39.54	50.83
50	18.31	21.72	25.53	27.71	30.20	33.19	37.07	43.07	55.12

Note: k = number of predictors; k = 1 is the case of simple linear regression.

13.6 Outliers and Influential Data Points

When the sample that is used to develop a regression equation contains **outliers** (extreme observations), the estimates of the regression coefficients and other regression parameters (e.g., R^2) can be very inaccurate. A similar negative effect is attributed to the so-called **influential data points** — observations that are not necessarily outliers, but that negatively "influence" the stability of the regression coefficients by increasing their standard error, thereby damaging the accuracy of prediction with future samples. It is, therefore, very important to always examine the data for outliers and influential data points. Outliers may occur due to data errors (e.g., data recording or data entry). Outliers not related to data errors occur when there are observations whose magnitudes on variables involved in the regression model are unusually small or large compared to the majority of observations in the sample. Suppose that a researcher predicts students' *academic achievement* (Y = GPA) from their *motivation* (X_1) and *family income* (X_2) using a random sample which happen to include a couple of students from very wealthy families. Thus, there will be a couple of observations on the predictor X_2 that are unusually high for this sample. In this case we say that there are outliers on X (i.e., on predictors). If the sample includes a couple of students with unusually (high or low) GPA, on the other hand, we can say that there are outliers on Y. It may happen that some observations produced outliers on Y as well as some of the predictors (X).

In general, outliers and influential data points require a special examination to build a better model and to better understand the phenomenon under study. The decision whether to delete an outlier (or influential data point) from a data set should be based on criteria established in advance. Presenting results obtained with and without outliers and/or influential data points may enhance a researcher's final conclusions.

Fortunately, SPSS (and other major statistical packages) provide indices for detecting outliers and influential data points. Among the indices available with the SPSS multiple regression analysis, the most recommended are:

- **Studentized deleted residual** — This index is used to detect outliers on Y. For any observation, the studentized deleted residual (*sdr*) is calculated for the sample, with this observation excluded ("deleted"). As the *sdr* index follows a Student t distribution, there should be a "red flag" for an outlier on Y when the studentized deleted residual for an observation is greater than 3.00 in absolute value, that is $|sdr| > 3.00$.
- **Leverage value** – This index is used to detect outliers on X, that is, observations with extremely high or low values on some predictors. A leverage value, denoted h_{ij} (for observation i on predictor j), is considered large when it exceeds $3(k + 1)/n$, where k is the number of predictors and n is the sample size. For example, with n = 100 and $k = 4$, a leverage greater than $3(4 + 1)/100 = 0.15$ is large.
- **Cook's distance** – This index is used to detect influential data points. It should be noted that an observation may not be an outlier and, yet, may still negatively influence the estimates of the regression coefficients and thereby cause problems with the accuracy of prediction with future samples. The *Cook's distance* (*CD*) index, proposed by Cook (1977), considers the effect of deleting an observation on the residual of all observations. It measures the impact of a specific observation on the estimates of regression parameters; (the calculation of the *CD* involves the sum of squared dif-

ferences between the predicted *Y* scores obtained with, and then without, the specific observation). All *CD* values are positive, but a *CD* value greater than 1.00 is considered large (i.e., *CD* > 1.00 indicates an influential data point).

EXAMPLE 13.4 This example illustrates how to use SPSS to detect outliers and influential data points. The data set MENTAL_HEALTH is used again, so the SPSS steps 1-7, described in Example 13.2, can be repeated here for the prediction of *mental health* from five predictors (*vitality, social functioning, physical functioning, health perception*, and *body pain*). To add information about outliers and influential data points, it suffices to insert the following two steps right after step 6 in Example 13.2:

- Click **Save.** In the dialog box ***Linear Regression: Save***, select **Cook's** and **Leverage values** (left panel), and select **Standardized deleted** (right panel).
- Click **Continue.**

Now, three additional variables appear in the SPSS Data Editor: **sdr_1** (studentized deleted residual), **coo_1** (Cook's distance), and **leve_1** (leverage value). The **Residuals Statistics** table reported in the SPSS output provides descriptive information (*min, max, mean, SD*, and *n*) for all residual statistics available in the **Linear Regression: Save** box (see Figure 13.6).

Figure 13.6 *Residual statistics for detecting outliers and influential data points in the prediction of mental health from vitality, social functioning, physical functioning, health perception, and body pain*

Residuals Statistics[a]

	Minimum	Maximum	Mean	Std. Deviation	N
Predicted Value	24.03	92.38	67.70	16.563	81
Std. Predicted Value	-2.637	1.490	.000	1.000	81
Standard Error of Predicted Value	1.642	8.386	3.097	1.192	81
Adjusted Predicted Value	16.73	91.70	67.98	17.093	81
Residual	-31.794	35.969	.000	11.797	81
Std. Residual	-2.609	2.952	.000	.968	81
Stud. Residual	-3.494	3.238	-.009	1.049	81
Deleted Residual	-58.681	43.274	-.274	14.118	81
Stud. Deleted Residual	-3.793	3.468	-.014	1.082	81
Mahal. Distance	.466	36.905	4.938	5.581	81
Cook's Distance	.000	1.831	.040	.207	81
Centered Leverage Value	.006	.461	.062	.070	81

a. Dependent Variable: Mental health

In the **Residuals Statistics** table, both the minimum and maximum values for *Stud. Deleted Residual* (*sdr*) are greater than 3.00 in absolute value (–3.793 and 3.468, respectively) thus indicating the presence of at least two outliers on *Y*. These outliers can be identified by selecting cases that satisfy the condition |**sdr_1**| > 3.00 for the values in the column named **sdr_1** in the SPSS Data Editor. Further, the maximum value for the *Cook's Distance* index (1.577) is greater than 1.00 thus indicating that there is at least one influential data point. Likewise, the influential data points can be identified by selected cases that satisfy the condition **coo_1 > 1.00** (i.e., $CD > 1.00$) for the values in the column named **coo_1** in the SPSS Data Editor. To decide whether the maximum value of the *Centered Leverage Value* is a "red flag" for the presence of (at least one) outlier on X, we compare this value (0.461) to $3(k + 1)/n = 3(5 + 1)/81 = 0.222$; [in this example, $n = 81$, $k = 4$]. As the maximum leverage value (0.461) exceeds the "cutoff" value (0.222), there is at least one outlier among the predictors, X. Thus, there are at least two outliers on the dependent variable (Y = mental health), at least one outlier on the predictors, X, and at least one influential data point in the MENTAL_HEALTH data [http://cehd.gmu.edu/book/dimitrov].

13.7 Categorical Predictors in Multiple Regression

Suppose that the performance of high school students on a standardized math test (e.g., as a part of a state assessment program) is predicted from these students' gender and their teacher-assigned grade in math. With the notations *SMT* = *standardized math test score*, *TGM* = *teacher grade in math,* and *Gender* (0 = male, 1 = female), the regression equation for this prediction is:

$$\widehat{SMT} = 0.5(TGM) + 1.5(Gender) + 50$$

The interpretation of the regression coefficient for the categorical predictor (*Gender*) is possible solely because of the dichotomous coding (0 = male, 1 = female) of this predictor. What this dichotomous coding tells us is that, given that the regression coefficient for gender (1.5) is a positive number, the gender group with a higher coding value (here, 1 = female) will have a higher predicted score $(\widehat{SMT})$. Thus, among students who get the same teacher-assigned grade in math (*TGM*), females will have a predicted score 1.5 points higher than males.

It is impossible to interpret a categorical predictor when there are more than two categories. For example, it is not appropriate to use *ethnicity* as a predictor with four categories (e.g., 1 = Caucasian, 2 = African-American, 3 = Hispanic, 4 = Asian) because "a one-unit change" in this predictor cannot be defined. A way out of this situation is to use dummy coding that generates new predictors with two categories. As an illustration, we can create a dichotomous "ethnic" variable, say *CAUC* (Caucasian – Not Caucasian), by using the following dummy coding: *EC* = 1, if the person is Caucasian, and *EC* = 2, if this person is not Caucasian. Another dichotomous "ethnic" variable can be *HISP* (Hispanic – Not Hispanic), using the dummy coding: *HISP* = 1, if the person is Hispanic, and *HISP* = 2, if not. Including the categorical variables *CAUC* and *HISP* as predictors in a multiple regression equation would be appropriate because they are both dichotomous, therefore the interpretation of their regression coefficients is meaningful. How many (and what) new variables to create via dummy coding is up to the researcher.

EXAMPLE 13.5 This example illustrates the use of a multiple regression for the prediction of test scores of students from their gender and ethnicity using SPSS. The data are provided in Figure 13.8, where *SCORE* is the SPSS name for the dependent variable (test score). *Gender* is a dichotomous categorical variable (1 = male, 2 = female), so it can be used directly as a predictor. *Ethnicity* cannot be used directly as a predictor because in this case it has three categories (1 = Caucasian, 2 = African-American, and 3 = Hispanic). For the purpose of illustration, a new "ethnic" variable, named *CAUC,* is created with two categories (1 = Caucasian, 0 = Other). The category "Other" combines the African-American and Hispanic ethnic groups. This is done in SPSS by recoding *Ethnicity* into a new variable *CAUC* following the steps described in Figure 13.8 (right panel).

Figure 13.7 *SPSS recoding of Ethnicity into CAUC in a multiple regression for the prediction of SCORE (test score) from Gender (1 = male, 2 = female) and CAUC (1 = Caucasian, 0 = Other).*

EXAMPLE 13_6.sav [DataSet1] - SPSS Da

File Edit View Data Transform Analyze Graph

21 :

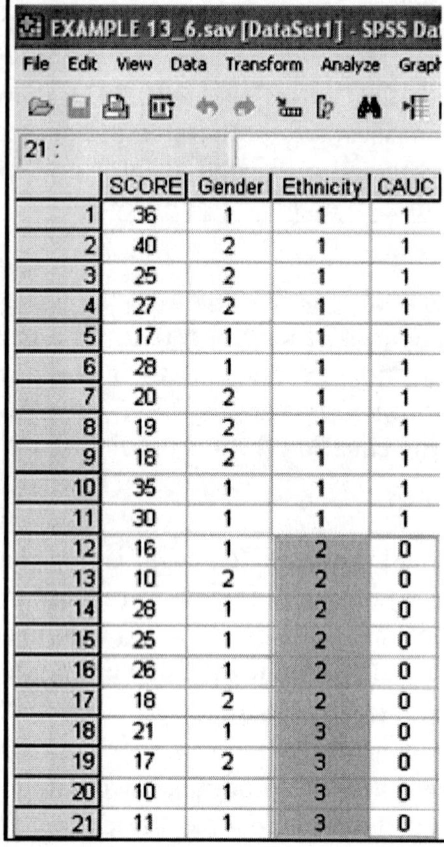

	SCORE	Gender	Ethnicity	CAUC
1	36	1	1	1
2	40	2	1	1
3	25	2	1	1
4	27	2	1	1
5	17	1	1	1
6	28	1	1	1
7	20	2	1	1
8	19	2	1	1
9	18	2	1	1
10	35	1	1	1
11	30	1	1	1
12	16	1	2	0
13	10	2	2	0
14	28	1	2	0
15	25	1	2	0
16	26	1	2	0
17	18	2	2	0
18	21	1	3	0
19	17	2	3	0
20	10	1	3	0
21	11	1	3	0

Using SPSS to recode *Ethnicity* into *CAUC*

Enter the data (21 observations) for *SCORE*, *Gender*, and *Ethnicity* in a SPSS data sheet and follow the steps:

1. Click **Transform**, and click **Recode into Different Variables.**
2. Click **Ethnicity**, and then click ▶ to move into the box **Numeric Variable → Output Variable.**
3. In the box **Name** (panel *Output Variable*), type **CAUC** and click **Change** [in this way **CAUC** also moves into the box **Numeric Variable → Output Variable.**]
4. Click **Old and New Values.**
5. Type **1** in the **Old Value** box, type **1** in the **New Value** box, and click **Add.**
6. Type **2** in the **Old Value** box, type **0** in the **New Value** box, and click **Add.**
7. Type **3** in the **Old Value** box, type **0** in the **New Value** box, and click **Add.**
8. Click **Continue.**
9. Click **OK.**

Note. After completing steps 1-9, click on *Variable View* (at the bottom of the SPSS data sheet) and assign the following values to the CAUC categories: 1 = "Caucasian", 0 = "Other."

The SPSS results in Figure 13.8 (ANOVA table) show that the two predictors (*Gender* and *CAUC*) account for a statistically significant proportion of the variance in the dependent variable, *SCORE* (*test score*), $F(2, 18) = 7.063$, $p = .005$. Specifically $R^2 = .440$ indicates that 44% of the test score differences are accounted for by differences in gender and *CAUC* (Caucasian versus Other). Further, the regression coefficients are statistically significant, at the .05 level, for both gender ($p = .034$) and *CAUC* ($p = .017$). Thus, each predictor has its own unique contribution to the (44%) overall explanation of the test score variance. Taking into account the coding for gender (1 = male, 2 = female), its negative regression coefficient (–6.793) indicates that, for examinees from the same *CAUC* group (Caucasian or Other), the predicted test score for females is 6.793 lower than that for males. On the other hand, taking into account the ethnic coding in *CAUC* (1 = Caucasian, 0 = Other), its positive regression coefficient (7.692) indicates that, for same gender examinees, the predicted test score for Caucasians is 7.692 higher than the predicted score of the other ethnic groups (African-American or Hispanic).

In Example 13.5 both predictors are categorical, but more often in applied research we see multiple regression models that include both continuous and categorical predictors. For example, instead of (or in addition to) gender, the regression model for predicting the students' test scores may include continuous variables such as motivation, anxiety, family income, etc.

Figure 13.8 SPSS output with a multiple regression for predicting *SCORE (test score) from Gender (1 = male, 2 = female) and CAUC (1 = Caucasian, 0 = Other)*

Model Summary

Model	R	R Square	Adjusted R Square	Std. Error of the Estimate
1	.663[a]	.440	.377	6.635

a. Predictors: (Constant), CAUC, Gender

ANOVA[b]

Model		Sum of Squares	df	Mean Square	F	Sig.
1	Regression	621.857	2	310.928	7.063	.005[a]
	Residual	792.429	18	44.024		
	Total	1414.286	20			

a. Predictors: (Constant), CAUC, Gender

b. Dependent Variable: SCORE

Coefficients[a]

Model		Unstandardized Coefficients		Standardized Coefficients	t	Sig.
		B	Std. Error	Beta		
1	(Constant)	28.389	4.903		5.791	.000
	Gender	-6.793	2.954	-.410	-2.300	.034
	CAUC	7.692	2.927	.468	2.628	.017

a. Dependent Variable: SCORE

13.8 Interaction Between Predictors in Multiple Regression

13.8.1 What is Interaction between Predictors?

As noted earlier in this chapter, the interpretation of the regression coefficient for one predictor is based on the assumption that the relationship between the dependent variable, *Y*, and this predictor is the same when the values of the other predictors are fixed. Consider, for example, the multiple regression equation with two predictors, X_1 and X_2:

$$\hat{Y} = b_1X_1 + b_2X_2 + a \quad \textbf{(13.16)}$$

If we replace X_2 with a specific value, the last two terms in Equation 13.16 ($b_2X_2 + a$) represent a numeric constant. For example, if $X_2 = 5$, this constant is $5b_2 + a$. Thus, for any fixed value of X_2, Equation 13.16 turns into a simple linear regression equation for predicting *Y* from X_1:

$$\hat{Y} = b_1X_1 + (b_2X_2 + a) \quad \textbf{(13.17)}$$

When X_2 takes on different fixed values in Equation 13.17, the intercept in this equation ($b_2X_2 + a$) changes, but the slope (b_1) remains the same. Graphically, this means that when X_2

takes on different fixed values, the resulting regression lines are parallel as they have the same slope (b_1). In Figure 13.9 (left panel), the two parallel regression lines are produced from Equation 13.17 for $X_2 = 0$ and $X_2 = 1$ [details are provided in Example 13.7.] Given that the relationship between Y and X_1 is measured by the slope (b_1), it is clear that this relationship does not change across fixed values of X_2 in Equation 13.16. In the literature on multiple regression, the stability of the relationship between Y and X_1 across fixed values of X_2 is defined as a *lack of interaction* between the two predictors, X_1 and X_2, in accounting for variance in Y (e.g., Aiken & West, 1991; Cohen & Cohen, 1983; Pedhazur, 1997).

There are, however, situations in which theoretical and/or empirical findings suggest that the relationship between Y and X_1 changes across fixed values of X_2. For example, it is likely that the performance of students on a high-stake proficiency test relates to their preparation efforts for the test (e.g., as measured by a total survey score on study time for the test, homework completion, class participation, and teacher grade). This relationship, however, may depend on the teaching strategy (e.g., curriculum oriented versus test oriented) adopted by the students' teachers. In this case, Y = *test performance*, X_1 = *preparation efforts*, and X_2 = *teaching strategy* (e.g., 0 = curriculum oriented, 1 = test oriented).

Following Cohen and Cohen (1983), we can say that **two predictors, X_1 and X_2, interact when they have a joint (shared) contribution, *over and above* the sum of their separate contributions, to accounting for variance in Y.** The occurrence of interaction between two predictors, X_1 and X_2, results in the presence of their product, X_1X_2, as an additional predictor in the regression equation. Thus, if the two predictors in Equation 13.16 interact, this regression equation is extended as follows:

$$\hat{Y} = b_1X_1 + b_2X_2 + b_3(X_1X_2) + a \qquad \textbf{(13.18)}$$

To show that in this case the relationship between Y and X_1 is not the same across fixed values of X_2, we assume that X_2 is fixed and then rearrange the terms in the right-hand side of Equation 13.18 as follows: $\hat{Y} = b_1X_1 + b_2X_2 + b_3(X_1X_2) + a = (b_1 + b_3X_2)X_1 + (b_2X_2 + \text{a})$. When X_2 is fixed to a specific value, the term $(b_1 + b_3X_2)$ is a constant which represents the slope of the relationship between Y and X_1. This slope is called a **simple slope**. The term $(b_2X_2 + a)$ is also a constant, but it equals the intercept of the simple linear regression for predicting Y from X_1:

$$Y = (b_1 + b_3X_2)X_1 + (b_2X_2 + \text{a}). \qquad \textbf{(13.19)}$$

Clearly, when X_1 and X_2 interact in accounting for variance in Y, the relationship between Y and X_1 depends on the values of X_2 because the slope that measures this relationship $(b_1 + b_3X_2)$ involves X_2. For example, if X_2 takes on values 0, 1, 2, 3, etc., the simple slope $(b_1 + b_3X_2)$ takes on values b_1, $b_1 + b_3$, $b_1 + 2b_3$, $b_1 + 3b_3$, etc. Thus, the value of b_3 indicates the amount of change in the slope of the regression of Y on X_1 $(b_1 + b_3X_2)$ that results from a one-unit change in X_2.

EXAMPLE 13.6 This example provides a graphical illustration of (a) lack of interaction between X_1 and X_2, implied by Equation 13.16, and (b) presence of interaction between X_1 and X_2, implied by Equation 13.18. The predictor X_2 is the categorical variable *gender* (say, 0 = male, 1 = female). For generality, the dependent variable and the predictor X_1 are not specified here. As noted earlier, when X_2 takes on a specific value, Equation 13.16 turns into a simple linear regression for predicting Y from X_1 (see Equation 13.17). Likewise, Equation 13.18 turns into Equation 13.19. Therefore, the two possible values of X_2 in this example (0 and 1) are replaced in Equations 13.17 and 13.19 for the two cases, (a) and (b), respectively.

(a) With $X_2 = 0$ in Equation 13.17, we obtain the simple linear regression for predicting Y from X_1 for males: $\hat{Y} = b_1X_1 + a$. With $X_2 = 1$ in this equation, we obtain the simple linear regression for predicting Y from X_1 for females: $\hat{Y} = b_1X_1 + (b_2 + a)$. With the slope being the same (b_1) in both equations, their regression lines are parallel (Figure13.9, left panel).

(b) With $X_2 = 0$ in Equation 13.19, the simple linear regression for predicting Y from X_1 for males is: $\hat{Y} = b_1X_1 + a$. With $X_2 = 1$ in this equation, the simple linear regression for predicting Y from X_1 for females is: $\hat{Y} = (b_1 + b_3)X_1 + (b_2 + a)$. This time the slope in the regression equations for males (b_1) is not the same as that in the regression equation for females ($b_1 + b_3$) and, therefore, the two regression lines are not parallel — see Figure 13.9 (right panel).

Figure 13.9 *Relationship between Y and X_1 for fixed values of X_2 (gender: 0 = male, 1 = female) in the case of (a) no interaction between X_1 and X_2* — Equation 13.17 (left panel), *and (b) interaction between X_1 and X_2 — Equation 13.19 (right panel)*

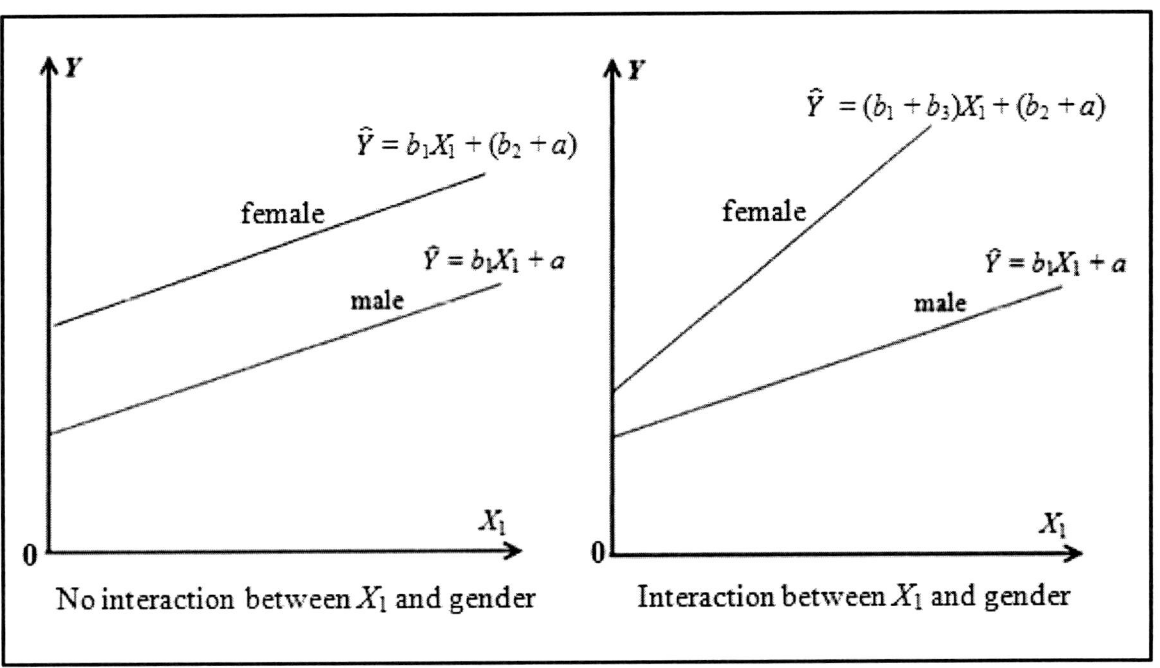

In this example X_2 is a categorical variable (gender), but it can also be a continuous variable. An example of interaction between two continuous predictors is when the relationship between *academic success* (Y = GPA) and *attitude toward school* (X_1) depends on *family income* (X_2). Of course, "interaction between X_1 and X_2" also means "interaction between X_2 and X_1," that is, the relationship between Y and X_2 is not the same across fixed values of X_1.

NOTE [13.4] When X_1 and X_2 interact in accounting for variance in Y, it is also said that X_2 is a **moderator** in the relationship between Y and X_1. [Or, X_1 is a moderator in the relationship between Y and X_2.] For example, Figure 13.9 (right panel) illustrates the case in which gender is *moderating* the relationship between Y and X_1 (whatever their specific meaning might be).

13.8.2 Testing for Interaction between Predictors

The validity of an approach to testing for interaction between predictors in multiple regression is based on the definition that **two predictors, X_1 and X_2, interact when they have a joint contribution, *over and above* the sum of their separate contributions, to accounting for variance in Y** (Cohen & Cohen, 1983). A proper translation of this definition shows that testing for interaction between X_1 and X_2 means testing for statistical significance of their "pure" joint contribution, after partialling out their separate contributions, to accounting for variance in Y. In the context of Equation 13.18, such a "pure" joint contribution of X_1 and X_2 is evidenced when the regression coefficient for the X_1X_2 product (b_3) is statistically significant. This is because, as we already know (see NOTE [13.2]), the statistical significance of the regression coefficient for a predictor indicates that the unique contribution of this predictor to accounting for variance in Y is statistically significant (i.e., not equal to zero for the population).

EXAMPLE 13.7 This example illustrates how to use SPSS to test for interaction between *vocabulary* (X_1) and *anxiety* (X_2) in the prediction of reading comprehension (Y), with the data provided in Figure 13.1. To obtain the product X_1X_2 in SPSS follow the steps:

1. In the SPSS *Data Editor* box, click **Transform,** and click **Compute.**
2. In the *Compute Variable* dialog box, **type the** name of the **product** variable, **X1X2,** in the **Target Variable** box, and type **X1*X2** in the **Numeric Expression** box.
3. Click ***OK.***

In step 2, **X1X2** is the name of the product variable, whereas **X1*X2** is an algebraic expression for the values of this variable, obtained by multiplying the values of **X1** and **X2.** In this example, the product variable, **X1X2,** was labeled **Vocabulary x Anxiety.** Figure 13.10 presents only the **Coefficients** table from the resulting SPSS output. As the regression coefficient for the predictor **X1X2** (the product of **X1** and **X2**) is not statistically significant (p = .301), there is no statistically significant interaction between *vocabulary* **(X1)** and *anxiety* **(X2)** in accounting for variance in *reading comprehension* **(*Y*)**.

Figure 13.10 *Testing for interaction between two predictors (vocabulary and anxiety) used to predict reading comprehension*

Coefficients[a]

Model		Unstandardized Coefficients		Standardized Coefficients		
		B	Std. Error	Beta	t	Sig.
1	(Constant)	39.103	9.147		4.275	.000
	Vocabulary	-.327	.390	-1.332	-.838	.410
	Anxiety	-.771	.438	-1.017	-1.761	.090
	Vocabulary x Anxiety	.020	.019	1.705	1.056	.301

a. Dependent Variable: Reading comprehension

There is no statistically significant interaction between *vocabulary* and *anxiety* in accounting for variance in *reading comrehension* (p = .301).

In the presence of interaction, it might be better to divide the sample into groups by score levels on one predictor (e.g., low, medium, high) and to determine the predictive effect of the other predictor for each group separately. The presence of interaction between predictors, however, does not depend on the level of correlation (multicollinearity) between them.

NOTE [13.4] Testing for interaction between X_1 and X_2 in accounting for variance in Y can also be performed by comparing the full versus the restricted model (see section 13.2) defined as follows:

Restricted model: $\hat{Y} = b_1X_1 + b_2X_2 + a$ (see Equation 13.16)
Full model: $\hat{Y} = b_1X_1 + b_2X_2 + b_3(X_1X_2) + a$ (see Equation 13.18).

Evidence of interaction between X_1 and X_2 is obtained when the R^2_{change} is statistically significant (see Formula 13.12). The use of SPSS for this purpose is illustrated in Example 13.1. This test is equivalent to the test for statistical significance of the regression coefficient b_3 (see Example 13.7). Both tests target the statistical significance of the contribution of the product X_1X_2, *over and above* the contribution of X_1 and X_2, to accounting for variance in Y.

13.8.3 Centering Predictors

As the purpose in Example 13.7 was to test for interaction between *vocabulary* and *anxiety* in accounting for variance in *reading comprehension*, we were only interested in whether the regression coefficient for the product of the two predictors was statistically significant. It is worth noting, however, that the regression coefficients for *vocabulary* and *anxiety* in Figure 13.10 arc not statistically significant (p = .410 and p = .090, respectively, but that they are both statistically significant in Figure 13.3 (p = .041 and p = .011, respectively). This is because, in general, the predictors X_1 and X_2 are both highly correlated with their product, X_1X_2, which increases their multicollinearity and, therefore, decreases their unique explanatory contribution to accounting for variance in Y. As a result, there are always fewer chances to find statistical significance of the regression coefficients for each predictor when their product is included in the regression equation (e.g., Figure 13.10), compared to the case when the product is not included (e.g., Figure 10.3).

The multicollinearity in regression equations that contain the product of two predictors can be substantially reduced by **centering** the predictors (e.g., Aiken & West, 1991). This means to replace the scores on each predictor with their deviations from the sample mean — that is, to replace the scores on X_1 with the deviation scores $(X_1 - \bar{X}_1)$ and the scores on X_2 with the deviation scores $(X_2 - \bar{X}_2)$. With centered predictors, Equation 13.18 takes the form

$$\hat{Y} = b_1(X_1 - \bar{X}_1) + b_2(X_2 - \bar{X}_2) + b_3(X_1 - \bar{X}_1)(X_2 - \bar{X}_2) + a \qquad \textbf{(13.20)}$$

If the purpose is only to test interaction between X_1 and X_2 (as with Example 13.7), there is no benefit from centering the predictors because both Equations 13.18 and 13.20 provide the same values for the regression coefficient b_3, its standard error, and the t-test for its statistical significance. Beyond this, there are two main advantages of using Equation 13.20 instead of Equation 13.18. First, the multicollinearity produced by the *centered* predictors and their product in Equation 13.20 is much smaller than that produced by the *non-centered* predictors and their product in Equation 13.18. This yields smaller standard errors of the regression coefficients b_1

and b_2 for the centered predictors (Equation 13.20) compared to those for their non-centered counterparts (Equation 13.18). Thus, centered predictors render more meaningful interpretation of the regression coefficients than non-centered predictors.

The second major advantage of using centered predictors is that with the non-centering method, the regression coefficient of X_1 in Equation 13.18 estimates the relationship between X_1 and Y when $X_2 = 0$ [Indeed, with $X_2 = 0$ in Equation 13.18, we obtained the relationship between Y and X_1: $\hat{Y} = b_1X_1 + a$.]. However, a value of zero for predictors is unrealistic (or impossible) for most measurement scales in education and related fields. Aiken and West (1983) commented on this problem by using an example in which the *strength* of athletes (Y) is predicted from their *height* (X_1) and *weight* (X_2). When the predictors are not centered, the relationship between strength and height is measured by the regression coefficient for height assuming "zero weight." This clearly is impossible (at least while the law of gravity holds) thus making the interpretation meaningless. This problem does not occur with centered predictors because then the regression coefficient b_1, which measures the relationship between Y and X_1, is estimated when X_2 equals the sample *mean* ($\bar{X}_2$), not *zero*. Thus, the regression coefficient for the relationship between strength (Y) and height (X_1) is estimated for athletes with average weight (X_2 = *mean* weight), which makes practical sense and renders meaningful interpretations.

As another example, an empirical study by Suldo, Shaunessy, and Hardesty (2008) includes testing for interaction between *stress* (X_1) and *coping style* (X_2) in predicting *mental health* (Y). The predictors were centered and evidence of interaction between them was sought by testing R^2_{change} for statistical significance (see NOTE [13.4]). The testing was conducted multiple times for different copying styles (e.g., X_2 = *positive appraisal coping*, X_2 = *anger coping*, etc.). It was found, for example, that the relationship between *mental health* (Y) and *stress* (X_1) depends on the level (low, high) of *coping* styles such as *positive appraisal coping* and *positive appraisal coping.* In other words, each of these *coping* styles is moderating (buffering) the relationship between mental health and stress (Suldo, Shaunessy, & Hardesty, 2008).

Predictors do not necessarily have to be centered around their mean score. Instead, the "center" can be, say, an appropriate cutting score on each predictor. For example, if the academic performance of college freshmen (*FGPA*) is predicted from their *SAT* scores and high school academic performance (*HGPA*), both predictors can be centered using some cutting scores of interest — say, $SAT_{\text{cut}} = 1100$ and $HGPA_{\text{cut}} = 3.00$. Then the regression equation, with a product term for interaction between the two predictors, has the following form:

$$\widehat{FGPA} = b_1(SAT - 1100) + b_2(HGPA - 3) + b_3(SAT - 1100)\,(HGPA - 3) + a.$$

If the regression coefficient for the product term (b_3) is statistically significant, this would indicate an interaction between the two predictors (*SAT* and *HGPA*). Alternately, one can use the testing procedure described in NOTE [13.4]. Even in the presence of interaction, the interpretation of the regression coefficients (b_1 and b_2) would be meaningful because the two predictors are centered properly. For example, the regression coefficient for the relationship between college success (*FGPA*) and *SAT* is estimated for students with a high school GPA of 3.00 (*HGPA* = 3), which might be the cutting score for acceptance into college.

There is typically no reason to center the dependent variable Y when centering the predictors because subtracting (or adding) a constant from the values of Y has no effect on the regression coefficients in equations that contain interactions. A comprehensive discussion of interaction between predictors can be found in Aiken and West (1991).

13.9 Selection of Predictors in Multiple Regression

Given a set of potential predictors, determining how many and which predictors to select depends on various considerations (e.g., practical, theoretical, statistical, and circumstantial). It is methodologically sound that researchers specify criteria for "best" set of predictors before conducting regression analysis. Particular attention should be paid to errors which occur when relevant predictors are omitted or irrelevant predictors are included into the regression equation. Such errors are referred to as **specification errors**. Caution is required when predictors are deleted from the equation (e.g., with the purpose of reducing multicollinearity) because the removal of relevant predictors is a serious specification error. Described in this section are five approaches to statistical selection of predictors in multiple regression - forward, backward, stepwise, blockwise, and hierarchical selection.

- **Forward selection** — the first step in this approach consists of selecting the predictor that has the highest zero-order (Pearson *r*) correlation with the criterion variable, *Y*. At any subsequent step, the predictor producing the greatest increase in R^2 (i.e., the highest squared part correlation with *Y*) enters the equation if it meets the criterion of inclusion (e.g., statistical significance at the .05 level) – if not, the procedure terminates. A major drawback of the forward selection is that, once a predictor enters the equation, it stays in the equation although it might have lost its initial importance when new predictors are added to the equation.
- **Backward** selection (elimination) — this method begins with all predictors in the equation and removes them one at a time until the final equation is obtained. At each step, the predictor that produces the smallest increase in R^2 (i.e., the smallest squared part correlation with *Y*) is selected and tested for removal (e.g., it is removed if its squared part correlation with *Y* is not statistically significant at the .05 level).
- **Stepwise selection** — this approach combines the methods of forward selection and backward elimination. It works as a forward selection, but at each step the predictors which remain in the equation are reexamined for possible backward elimination. In this way, predictors that were suitable to enter the equation at previous steps but that lost much of their predictive power when additional predictors were added, may be removed from the regression equation. This is an important advantage of the stepwise selection over the forward selection.
- **Blockwise selection** — with this approach, predictors are grouped into "blocks" (e.g., Block 1 – demographic variables, Block 2 – academic performance, and Block 3 – behavioral variables). The assignment of variables to blocks and the order of the blocks is should be based on some theoretical and/or empirical considerations. First, a stepwise selection is conducted for the predictors in the first block. With the other blocks, one at a time, a stepwise selection is conducted for the predictors in each block and the predictors that have survived the immediately preceding stepwise selection remain in the equation.
- **Hierarchical regression** — with this method, intact blocks (meaningful units) of predictors are forced into the regression equation, one at a time, to determine their unique contribution (R^2 change) to the prediction of the criterion variable, *Y*. Also, forcing some blocks (e.g., treatment variables) into the equation and conducting blockwise selection on others is a very useful combination in many research applications of multiple regression.

Enright (1996) used a hierarchical regression analysis to predict career indecision from self-doubting career beliefs, disability status, age, and gender. The decision to use these four predictors stemmed from past research and a preliminary analysis of predictive relationships between the criterion (career indecision) and potential predictors. The hierarchical regression included two steps. First, a multiple regression model was conducted with three predictors: age, gender, and self-doubting career belief. Second, a multiple regression analysis was conducted with these three predictors and the fourth predictor (disability status). The R^2 change from step 1 to step 2 was used to determine the significance of the prediction effect of disability status, over and above the combined prediction effect of age, gender, and self-doubting career belief. Additional regressions were performed to test the significance of interaction effects. The results from these tests strengthened the conclusions about the prediction of career indecision.

13.10 APA Style Table for Multiple Regression Results

APA style summary for multiple regression results is illustrated here for the results provided in Figure 13.4, where a restricted regression model with three predictors (Model 1) is compared to a full regression model with five predictors (Model 2) in the prediction of mental health. This represents a hierarchical regression analysis, where the restricted model is used first (Step 1) and then two more predictors are added to form the full model (Step 2). The APA-style summary of the results is provided in Table 13.2.

Table 13.2

Summary of Hierarchical Regression Analysis for Variables Predicting Mental Health (N = 81)

	Variable	*B*	SE B	B	R^2
Step 1					0.64***
	Vitality	0.25	0.09	.24**	
	Social functioning	0.61	0.10	.54***	
	Physical functioning	0.27	0.09	.22**	
Step 2					.66***
	Vitality	0.29	0.09	.28**	
	Social functioning	0.52	0.12	.46***	
	Physical functioning	0.25	0.09	.20**	
	Health perception	0.19	0.10	0.17	
	Body pain	0.08	0.08	0.08	

Note. R^2_{change} = .02 for Step 2 ($p > .05$).

** $p < .01$. *** $p < .001$.

13.11 Summary

The general form of a multiple regression model with two predictors is given with Equation 13.2. For an initial (screening) sample of observations, the estimates of the regression parameters (b_1, b_2, and a) minimizes the sum of squared errors, $\sum e^2 = \sum(Y - \hat{Y})^2$. Geometrically, the equation of the "best" fit for a regression model with two predictors is the "regression plane" that cuts through a three-dimensional space which is determined by the perpendicular axis of X_1, X_2, and Y (see Figure 13.2). The general form of a multiple regression model for the prediction of a variable Y from k predictors ($k \geq 2$) is

$$\hat{Y} = b_1X_1 + b_2X_2 + \ldots + b_kX_k + a$$

Geometrically, the equation of the "best fit" in this general case represents a surface (not flat, for $k > 2$) cutting through (k + 1) dimensional space. In this chapter, multiple regression is discussed in light of explanatory or predictive, not causal applications.

- **Multiple correlation**
  Multiple correlation, denoted $R_{Y.12...k}$, is the Pearson correlation between the actual values of the dependent variable, Y, and its predicted values, $\hat{Y}$, produced by a multiple regression equation with k predictors. The squared value of the multiple correlation, $R^2_{Y.12...k}$(or, just R^2), called *coefficient of multiple determination*, indicates the proportion of the variance in Y accounted for by all predictors.

- **Interpretation of regression coefficients**
  The regression coefficient for a given predictor indicates the change in the predicted Y value produced by a one-unit change in this predictor, while controlling for all other predictors. This interpretation assumes that there is no interaction between the predictor and other predictors (i.e., the Pearson correlation between Y and the predictor is the same for any combination of fixed values of the other predictors).

- **Standardized regression equation**
  Regression equation based on the standard z-scores of the criterion and predictor variables is called standardized regression equation: $\hat{z}_Y = \beta_1 z_1 + \beta_2 z_2 + \ldots + \beta_k z_k$. Note that the intercept is zero. This is because when the predictors take their mean values ($\overline{X}_1, \overline{X}_2, \ldots, \overline{X}_k$), the predicted Y score equals the *mean* ($\hat{Y} = \overline{Y}$) — thus, when the z-scores take their mean values, $\overline{z}_1 = \overline{z}_2 = \ldots = \overline{z}_k = 0$, the predicted score is $\hat{z}_Y = \overline{z}_Y = 0$. The "beta weights" (standardized regression coefficients) provide information about the relative importance (unique predictive effect) of the predictors – the higher the absolute value of the "beta" weight, the more important the predictor. The regression coefficient with the original (raw-score) multiple regression equation do not provide such information, as they are measured on different scales, but they are more useful for interpretation purposes. The raw-score regression equation and its standardized counterpart produce the same coefficient of multiple determination, R^2.

- **Significance of the multiple regression model**
  The F statistic in Equation 13.8 (reported with the SPSS output for multiple regression) is used to test the null hypothesis that the coefficient of determination is zero for the study popula-

tion, $H_0{:}R^2_{pop} = 0$. This null hypothesis is equivalent also to the null hypothesis stating that all regression coefficient are zero for the study population, H_0: $B_1 = B_2 = \ldots = B_k = 0$. If there is a sufficient evidence to reject H_0 (the Type I error rate is smaller than the adopted level of statistical significance, $p < \alpha$), the multiple regression model is statistically significant.

- **Significance of multiple regression coefficients**

A multiple regression coefficient, b_j, is statistically significant if its population value, B_j, is not zero. The null hypothesis H_0: $B_j = 0$ is tested by using the t statistic calculated by dividing the regression coefficient by its standard error: $t = b_j/SE(b_j)$. The standard error of the regression coefficient, $SE(b_j)$, equals the square root of its variance, $\text{Var}(b_j)$.

- **Comparison of full and restricted regression models**

Two regression models are referred to as *full* model and *restricted* model if the latter includes only some of the predictors in the former. The null hypothesis, tested with the F statistic in Formula 13.12, is that the population coefficients of determination for the full model and its counterpart for the restricted models are equal, H_0: $R^2_{full} = R^2_{restr}$. Failure to reject H_0 indicates that the full and restricted models have the same predictive effect. In such case it is better to use the more parsimonious (restricted) regression model.

- **Multicollinearity**

When multicollinearity (moderate to high correlations among predictors) occurs, the unique predictive effect of each predictor decreases (even if the joint predictive effect, R^2, is significant and large enough). The higher the multicollinearity, the larger the standard error for the regression coefficients and, thus, the lower the accuracy of prediction with future samples. Also, with highly correlated predictors, it is somewhat artificial to assume changes in one predictor, holding the other predictors fixed, when interpreting regression coefficients. After regressing one predictor, X_j, on the other predictors, the coefficient of determination, R^2_j, indicates the degree of redundancy (overlap) between X_j and the other predictors. Therefore, the difference $1 - R^2_j$, referred to as *tolerance*, indicates the degree of nonredundancy between X_j and the other predictors. The tolerance can take on values from 0 to 1, with 0 being the worse case (X_j totally "overlaps" with the other predictors) and 1 being the ideal case (X_j is orthogonal to all other predictors). The ratio $1/(1 - R^2_j)$, called *variance inflation factor* (*VIF*), also indicates the degree of multicollinearity caused by the predictor X_j. Specifically, *VIF* indicates the degree of "inflation" in the variance of the regression coefficient b_j due to correlation between X_j and the other predictors (see, Formula 13.13). When researchers eliminate predictors with the purpose of reducing multicollinearity, they have to be aware of potential specification errors that may result from omitting relevant predictors.

- **Cross-Validation**

The coefficient of determination for the original (screening) sample, R^2_{scr} is always greater than its counterpart produced by the original regression equation when applied to any other (calibration) sample, R^2_{cal}. The estimation of R^2 *shrinkage* ($R^2_{scr} - R^2_{cal}$) is called *cross-validation*. The smaller the shrinkage, the more accurate the regression prediction. It is very useful, for example, to combine the screening and calibration samples and use the regression equation obtained for the combined sample for prediction with future samples. Or, if the screening sample is large enough, split it into two (screening and calibration) samples to conduct cross-validation. The amount of R^2 *shrinkage* depends, among other things, on the ratio "sample size to number of predictors" (n/k). With the recommended 15/1 ratio (15 subjects per predictor), the R^2 *shrinkage* is small (less than .05), with a probability of .90, if the coefficient of determination for the population is R^2_{pop} = .50.

- **Statistical power method for sample size**

Statistical power methods for determining sample size involve the effect size for multiple regression: $ES = R^2_{pop}/(1 - R^2_{pop})$, where R^2_{pop} is the coefficient of determination for the study population. The effect size enables researchers to address issues of both statistical and practical significance. Formula 13.15 (Cohen & Cohen, 1983) is used to determine the sample size with prespecified values for statistical power, level of statistical significance, and effect size.

- **Outliers and influential data points**

In multiple regression, the sum of squared errors (*SSE*) is very sensitive to "outliers" (extreme data points). The data may also include "influential data points" (not necessarily outliers) which have undue effect on the estimates of the regression parameters. Among the indices for detecting outliers and influential data points, provided with the SPSS output for multiple regression, three were highlighted in this chapter – *studentized deleted residual (sdr), leverage*, and *Cook's distance* (*CD*). Specifically, (a) outliers on the criterion variable, *Y*, are "signaled" when *sdr* exceeds 3.00 in absolute value, (b) outliers on predictors, *X*, are detected when the leverage exceeds the "cutoff" value $3(k + 1)/n$, where k is the number of predictors and n is the sample size, and (c) influential data points are detected when the $CD > 1.00$.

- **Interaction in multiple regression**

There is an interaction between two predictors, X_1 and X_2, in accounting for variance in the dependent variable, Y, the relationship between *Y* and one predictor is not the same across fixed values of the other predictor. In the presence of interaction between predictors, the interpretation of their regression coefficients is meaningless. To account for possible interaction between X_1 and X_2, their product is included in the regression model (see Equation 13.18). If the regression coefficient for this product (b_3 in Equation 13.18) is statistically significant, there is an interaction between X_1 and X_2. Alternately, one can use the R^2_{change} test for interaction between X_1 and X_2 (see NOTE [13.4]). If a given predictor is involved in interaction with $_{\text{other}}$ predictors, it might be better to conduct the multiple regression analysis with the other predictors, separately for different subsamples of people assigned to different levels (e.g., low, medium, and high) or fixed values of this predictor. Centering the predictors (around their *mean* or a *cutting score* of interest) enhance the interpretability of the regression coefficients for X_1 and X_2 (b_1 and b_2, respectively, in Equation 13.18).

- **Selection of predictors in multiple regression**

This chapter describes five approaches to statistical selection of predictors in multiple regression - forward, backward, stepwise, blockwise, and hierarchical selection. In the forward selection, the predictor with the highest zero-order correlation with the criterion variable, *Y*, is selected first and then, at each subsequent step, the predictor with the greatest increment in R^2, if the criterion for inclusion is met (e.g., $p < .05$). The backward selection elimination begins with all predictors in the equation and removes them one at a time. At each step, the predictor that produces the smallest increment in R^2 is selected and tested for removal. The stepwise selection works as a forward selection, but at each step the predictors which are in the equation are reexamined for possible backward elimination. With the blockwise selection, the predictors are initially grouped in "blocks" based on substantive theory or empirical models. A stepwise selection is conducted with the predictors in the first block and then with the other blocks, one at a time, using the predictors in each block and the predictors that have survived the immediately preceding stepwise selection. In hierarchical regression analysis, intact blocks of predictors are forced into the equation, one a time, to determine how they influence the prediction of the criterion variable (by examining R^2 *change*). It is important that researchers specify criteria for "best" set of predictors before conducting regression analysis. Particular attention should be paid to potential *specification errors* which occur when relevant predictors are omitted or irrelevant predictors are included into the regression equation.

13.12 Study Questions

1. Predictions with multiple regression emphasize

   (A) causal explanation
   (B) group comparison
   (C) predictive applications
   (D) substantive theory
   (E) None of the above.

2. Suppose the regression equation $\widehat{TP}$ = 0.25 (VA) -0.20(ANX) + 10 is used to predict test performance (*TP*) from verbal ability (*VA*) and anxiety (*ANX*). If John and Mary have the same verbal ability score, but John's anxiety score is higher that of Mary by 6 units, then the predicted *TP* score of John, compared to the predicted *TP* score of Mary, is

   (A) higher by 1.00
   (B) lower by 0.20
   (C) lower by 1.00
   (D) lower by 0.20
   (E) None of the above.

3. If the multiple correlation is $\boldsymbol{R}$ = .90, what percent of the variance in the dependent variable, *Y*, is accounted for by the predictors?

   (A) 60% **(B)** 0% **(C)** 30% **(D)** 81% **(E)** None of the above.

4. In a multiple regression, the "total sum of squares" for *Y* is SS_{Total} = 100 and the "sum of squared errors" is *SSE* = 30. What percent of the variance in *Y* is accounted for by the predictors?

   (A) 70% **(B)** 49% **(C)** 30% **(D)** 100% **(E)** None of the above

5. The relative importance of the predictors in multiple regression is indicated by

   (A) unstandardized regression coefficients
   (B) partial correlations
   (C) zero-order correlations
   (D) standardized regression coefficients
   (E) None of the above.

6. In a multiple regression with predictors X_1, X_2, and X_3, the proportion of variance in *Y* uniquely associated with X_2 (over and above X_1 and X_3) is provided by the value of

   (A) $r_{Y2.13}$, **(B)** $r^2_{Y2.13}$, **(C)** $r_{Y(2.13)}$, **(D)** $r^2_{Y(2.13)}$, **(E)** None of the above.

7. For a sample of 60 subjects, a multiple regression equation with seven predictors produced $R^2 = .75$. After excluding two predictors, the resulting multiple regression equation produced $R^2 = .68$. Test whether the two regression equations differ in accounting for variance in the dependent variable [*Hint*: use Formula 13.12.]

8. Among the problems associated with multicollinearity in multiple regression are
   (A) unrealistic interpretation of regression coefficients
   (B) low (if any) unique contribution of individual predictors
   (C) low accuracy of prediction with future samples
   (D) All of the above.

9. If the *tolerance* of a predictor is .85, its *variance inflation factor* (*VIF*) is

   (A) 1.00 **(B)** 0.7225 **(C)** 1.1765 **(D)** 0.0225 **(E)** None of the above.

10. About how many subjects are necessary in a multiple regression with four predictors to attain a power of .85 to detect $R^2_{pop} = .25$ at the .05 level of significance? [*Hint*: see Example 13.3]

    (A) 45 **(B)** 85 **(C)** 25 **(D)** 110 **(E)** None of the above.

11. Does a *leverage* of 0.25 indicate an "outlier" in a multiple regression with three predictors for a sample of 60 subjects (Why?).

12. Given the SPSS output with a multiple regression for predicting *mental health* ($Y = MH$) from *vitality* (*VT*) and *health perception* (*HP*) using the **MENTAL_HEALTH** data describe and interpret these results [*Hint*: see Figure 13.3 and related discussion.] Also, obtain this SPSS output on your own using the **MENTAL_HEALTH** data; [http://cehd.gmu.edu/book/dimitrov].

Model Summary

Model	R	R Square	Adjusted R Square	Std. Error of the Estimate
1	.724[a]	.524	.512	14.206

a. Predictors: (Constant), Health perception, Vitality

ANOVA[b]

Model		Sum of Squares	df	Mean Square	F	Sig.
1	Regression	17340.179	2	8670.090	42.963	.000[a]
	Residual	15740.710	78	201.804		
	Total	33080.889	80			

a. Predictors: (Constant), Health perception, Vitality

b. Dependent Variable: Mental health

Coefficients[a]

Model		Unstandardized Coefficients		Standardized Coefficients	t	Sig.	Correlations		
		B	Std. Error	Beta			Zero-order	Partial	Part
1	(Constant)	2.895	7.266		.398	.691			
	Vitality	.504	.085	.485	5.949	.000	.604	.559	.465
	Health perception	.463	.091	.417	5.114	.000	.555	.501	.399

a. Dependent Variable: Mental health

13. To test for interaction between the two predictors in the previous question (14), vitality and *health perception*, their product (named VT_HP) was added in the regression model with these two predictors. Given the **Coefficients** table from the resulting SPSS output,

   a. make a conclusion about the presence of interaction between *vitality* and *health perception* in accounting for variance in *mental health* and
   b. explain the differences in the values of the *t*-statistics (and *p*-values) for the regression coefficients provided here and those in the table **Coefficients** given in Question 14. In addition, obtain the **Coefficients** table provided here using the **MENTAL_HEALTH** data [http://cehd.gmu.edu/book/dimitrov].

Coefficients[a]

Model		Unstandardized Coefficients		Standardized Coefficients		
		B	Std. Error	Beta	t	Sig.
1	(Constant)	52.027	24.983		2.082	.041
	Vitality	-.311	.406	-.299	-.766	.446
	Health perception	-.202	.336	-.182	-.602	.549
	VT_HP	.011	.005	1.125	2.052	.044

a. Dependent Variable: Mental health

14. Using the **MENTAL_HEALTH** data, replicate the testing for interaction between *vitality* and *health perception* in the previous question (15) using the R^2_{change} test [see NOTE [13.4].

CHAPTER 14

ONE-FACTOR ANALYSIS OF VARIANCE

In Chapter 8 we learned how to test the null hypothesis of no difference between two population means using a t-test for two independent samples. Suppose, however, that a researcher wants to know about possible differences among three or more population means. Examples of such questions are, (a) Are there differences among four ethnic groups of students (Caucasian, African-American, Hispanic, and Asian) in mathematics proficiency?, (b) Does the academic achievement (GPA) of students depend on their parents' educational level (lower than high school, high school, bachelor degree, graduate degree)?, or (c) Are there differences among students with ADHD, students with ADD, and students without disabilities in self-regulation? [ADHD = Attention Deficit Hyperactivity Disorder, ADD = Attention Deficit Disorder.]

One way to address such questions is to use multiple t-tests for all possible pairs of groups. With three groups (G1, G2, and G3), three t-tests must be conducted, as there are three possible pairs of groups: (G1, G2), (G1, G3), and (G2, G3). With four groups, six t-tests are required, as there are six pairs of groups: (G1, G2), (G1, G3), (G1, G4), (G2, G3), (G2, G4), and (G3, G4). In general, with k groups, there are $k(k-1)/2$ possible pairs of groups. For example, testing for mean differences among six groups ($k = 6$) would involve 15 t-tests: $(6)(6-1)/2 = (6)(5)/2 = 30/2 = 15$. This approach, referred to as conducting **pairwise t-tests**, has several limitations. First, if we set the level of significance for each t-test at α (say, $\alpha = .05$), the level of significance for the overall question ("Are there mean differences among all groups?") will actually be higher than α. Specifically, if α is used for each t-test, the "overall" α (denoted α^*) is

$$\alpha^* = 1 - (1 - \alpha)^c, \tag{14.1}$$

where c is the number of all pairwise comparisons. For example, as shown above, when six groups are compared ($k = 6$), there are 15 comparisons ($c = 15$). If $\alpha = .05$ is used with each of the 15 t-tests in this case, then the "overall" level of statistical significance is

$$\alpha^* = 1 - (1 - .05)^{15} = 1 - (.95)^{15} = .54.$$

Thus, if the overall (*omnibus*) null hypothesis were true (i.e., if there were no mean differences among the six groups) and all 15 t-tests were conducted at the .05 level of significance, then the probability that at least one of the 15 tests would result in Type I error (false rejection) is .54.

The overall level of significance, α^*, is called also **family-wise α** because it relates to the overall question about differences among the "family" of groups. To keep the family-wise α^* at a prespecified level, Bonferroni suggested the following adjustment of α for each separate t-test:

$$\alpha = \alpha^*/c, \tag{14.2}$$

where c is the number of pairwise comparisons. For example, to keep $\alpha^* = .05$ in the above case of 15 pairwise t-tests, each of these tests must be conducted at a much lower level of significance, namely: $\alpha = .05/15 = .0033$. The **Bonferroni adjustment** is most useful with a relatively small number of groups (e.g., 3 or 4) because with many groups the number of comparisons, c, is very large, thereby making the adjusted α for separate t-tests extremely small.

Another limitation of using pairwise *t*-tests to compare groups is that they do not address the omnibus null hypothesis of no differences among the means for the "family" of groups. An omnibus test of the null hypothesis, which keeps the family-wise level of significance, α^*, at a desired level, is provided by a method known as the **analysis of variance** (ANOVA).

14.1 The Concept of One-Factor Analysis of Variance

When the groups being compared represent different categories (levels) of a single categorical variable, the analysis of variance is referred to as a **one-factor ANOVA** (or **one-way ANOVA**). The categorical (grouping) variable is the **independent variable** (or **factor**), whereas the variable on which the groups are compared is the **dependent variable**. For example, when four ethnic groups (e.g., Caucasian, African-American, Hispanic, and Asian) are compared on test scores, there is one independent variable (factor) with four levels: *ethnicity*. The dependent variable in this case is *test score*. Similarly, when three teaching methods are compared on their effect on students' GPA, there is one factor with three levels — *teaching method*, and the dependent variable is GPA. Or, when three types of drugs (e.g., Drug A, Drug B, and Placebo) are compared on their effect on depression, the 3-level independent variable (factor) is *type of drug*, and the dependent variable is *depression*.

In ANOVA, the **null hypothesis** states that the populations represented by the groups have equal means on the dependent variable. For example, if three methods of teaching are compared on their effects on GPA for a population of students, the null hypothesis is

$$H_0\colon \mu_1 = \mu_2 = \mu_3 \qquad \textbf{(14.3)}$$

where μ_1, μ_2, and μ_3 represent the *mean* of the GPAs for the population of students taught under Method 1, Method 2, or Method 3, respectively. The **alternative hypothesis** is that not all population means are equal (i.e., at least two population means are different):

$$H_0\colon (\mu_1 \neq \mu_2) \text{ OR } (\mu_1 \neq \mu_3) \text{ OR } (\mu_2 \neq \mu_3). \qquad \textbf{(14.4)}$$

To further clarify the meaning of the population means (μ_1, μ_2, and μ_3), we can say that μ_1 is the theoretical mean of the distribution of scores (GPAs) for the population of students if they were all taught under Method 1. Likewise, μ_2 is the theoretical mean of the distribution of scores for the same population of students if they were all taught under Method 2. Clearly, μ_3 is the theoretical mean of the distribution of scores for the population of students if they were all taught under Method 3. Thus, one population of individuals "generates" three theoretical distributions of scores, called **population distributions**, assuming that all individuals were submitted independently to each of the three conditions (methods of teaching), one at a time — Method 1, Method 2, or Method 3, respectively. As it is not possible to repetitively and independently submit the entire student population to three different teaching methods, an appropriate research design is used under which three groups (samples) of students are randomly selected and each group is randomly assigned to one method of teaching. A test statistic, computed from the sample scores, is then used to make a decision about the null hypothesis (reject or fail to reject) at a selected (family-wise) level of significance.

The logic of ANOVA for three groups carries over into cases of more than three groups. The ANOVA null and alternative hypotheses in the general case of, say, K groups are

$$H_0\colon \mu_1 = \mu_2 = \ldots = \mu_K \quad \textbf{versus} \quad H_0\colon (\mu_i \neq \mu_j) \text{ for some } i \text{ and } j \text{ groups; } (i, j = 1, 2, \ldots, K). \qquad \textbf{(14.5)}$$

14.2 Assumptions in ANOVA

As described in the previous section, when conducting a one-factor ANOVA with K groups (levels), each group is interpreted as a random sample from a theoretical distribution of scores. Thus, there are K distributions of scores (or K populations). There are three primary assumptions in ANOVA: *independence*, *normality*, and *homogeneity of variance*. The assumption of **independence** means that the sample observations (scores) are independent of each other. A violation of this assumption would occur, for example, if the study participants work in groups, thereby influencing each other's responses on test questions. The assumption of **normality** means that each theoretical distribution of scores is normal. The **homogeneity of variance** assumption means that the variances of all (normal) theoretical distributions of scores are equal. In other words, all population variances are equal. Figure 14.1 illustrates the normality and homogeneity of variance assumptions for one-factor ANOVA with three groups.

Figure 14.1 *Illustration of the normality and homogeneity of variance assumptions (H_0 is false)*

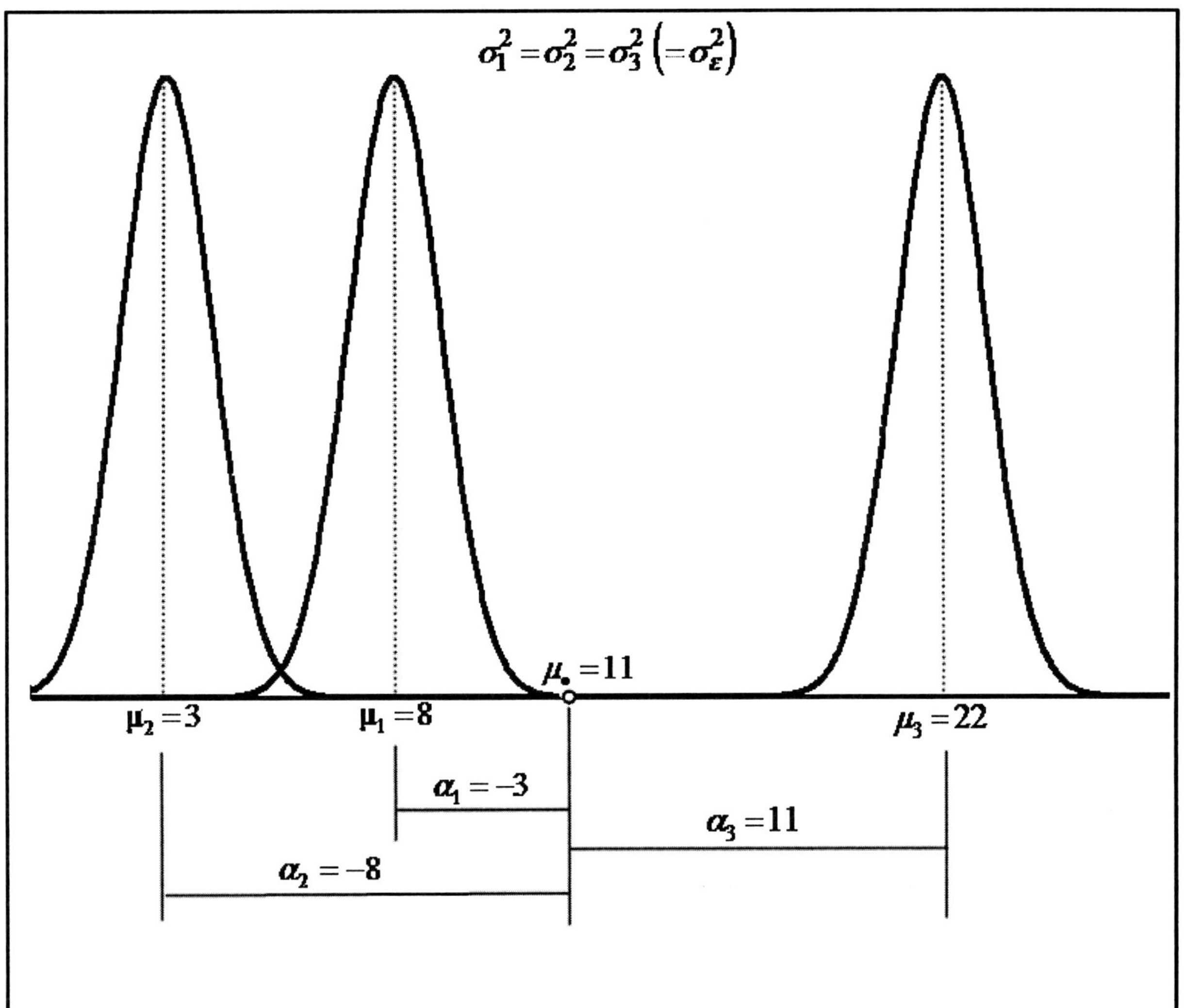

Suppose the normal distributions in Figure 14.1 represent the theoretical distributions of scores for three ethnic populations of students in a large urban area on a questionnaire about motivation to learn. In this hypothetical case, the population means are not equal ($\mu_1 = 8$, $\mu_2 = 3$, and $\mu_3 = 22$), thus indicating that the null hypothesis is false. To satisfy the homogeneity of variance assumption, the population variances are considered equal ($\sigma_1^2 = \sigma_2^2 = \sigma_3^2$) and a single variance notation (σ_ϵ^2) is used for each of them. The **population variance,** σ_ϵ^2, is also called **error variance** or **random variance**. Here σ_ϵ^2 represents the score variation among students from the same ethnic population. Generally, σ_ϵ^2 measures the variation (differences) among individuals submitted to the same ANOVA condition(s) — e.g., same teaching method, same preventive treatment, same gender, etc.

14.3 Effects in ANOVA

The discussion in this section is based on the illustration in Figure 14.1 for one-factor ANOVA with three groups, but it holds for the general case of, say, K groups. The *mean* of all population means being compared in ANOVA is called the **grand mean** ($\mu.$). In Figure 14.1, the grand mean is: $\mu. = (\mu_1 + \mu_2 + \mu_3)/3 = (8 + 3 + 22)/3 = 33/3 = 11$. The deviation of a given population mean from the grand mean is called the **effect** for this population. For the case depicted in Figure 14.1, the population effects are:

$$\alpha_1 = \mu_1 - \mu. = 3 - 11 = -8,$$
$$\alpha_2 = \mu_2 - \mu. = 8 - 11 = -3, \text{ and} \qquad \textbf{(14.6)}$$
$$\alpha_3 = \mu_3 - \mu. = 22 - 11 = 11.$$

Clearly, *negative effects* occur when the population mean is below the grand mean and, conversely, *positive effects* are produced when the population mean is above the grand mean. Also, as the effects represent deviations about the mean, their sum equals zero. For the effects in (14.6), for example, we have: $\alpha_1 + \alpha_2 + \alpha_3 = (-8) + (-3) + 11 = -11 + 11 = 0$.

It can be seen that the null hypothesis (H_0: $\mu_1 = \mu_2 = \mu_3$) can be equivalently presented as follows: H_0: $\alpha_1^2 + \alpha_2^2 + \alpha_3^2 = 0$. Indeed, when all population means are equal, then all effects equal zero and, thus, the sum of their squared values is zero: $\alpha_1^2 + \alpha_2^2 + \alpha_3^2 = 0^2 + 0^2 + 0^2 = 0$. Working backward, $\alpha_1^2 + \alpha_2^2 + \alpha_3^2 = 0$ is possible *only if* $\alpha_1^2 = \alpha_2^2 = \alpha_3^2 = 0$. That is, if all effects are zero: $\alpha_1 = \alpha_2 = \alpha_3 = 0$ (i.e., $\mu_1 = \mu_2 = \mu_3$). In the general case involving K groups, the null and alternative hypotheses in Equation (14.5) can be represented as follows:

$$H_0\text{: } \alpha_1^2 + \alpha_2^2 + \ldots + \alpha_k^2 = 0; \text{ [shortly, } \textstyle\sum \alpha^2 = 0] \qquad \textbf{(14.7)}$$

$$H_a\text{: } \alpha_1^2 + \alpha_2^2 + \ldots + \alpha_k^2 \neq 0; \text{ [shortly, } \textstyle\sum \alpha^2 \neq 0]$$

In reality, the population means on the dependent variable Y (μ_1, μ_2, and μ_3) are not known and are, therefore, replaced with their sample estimates ($\bar{Y}_1$, $\bar{Y}_2$, and $\bar{Y}_3$, respectively). Consequently, if the three samples have the same sample size, n, the *sample grand mean* is $\bar{Y}_\bullet = (\bar{Y}_1 + \bar{Y}_2 + \bar{Y}_3)/3$. [If the sample sizes are not equal, then $\bar{Y}_\bullet$ is computed as a "weighted" mean of $\bar{Y}_1$, $\bar{Y}_2$, and $\bar{Y}_3$ — see section 6.2.2.3] The sample estimates of the α-effects are then computed as

$$\hat{\alpha}_1 = \bar{Y}_1 - \bar{Y}_\bullet,\ \hat{\alpha}_2 = \bar{Y}_2 - \bar{Y}_\bullet, \text{ and } \hat{\alpha}_3 = \bar{Y}_3 - \bar{Y}_\bullet \qquad \textbf{(14.8)}$$

As noted earlier, the concept of ANOVA effects and their properties are illustrated here for the case of three groups, but they hold for the general case involving more than three groups.

14.4 Within-group and Between-group Variance

In one-factor ANOVA with K groups, presuming that the assumptions of normality and homogeneity of variance hold, there are K normal distributions of scores which will all have the same variance, σ_ϵ^2. As stated in section 14.1, this variance represents the variation **within** each population; that is, the variation among subjects submitted to the same ANOVA condition(s) (e.g., ethnicity, teaching method, etc.). As such, the sample variance within each group is a sample estimate of σ_ϵ^2.

The "pooled" variance of the sample variances of all groups represents a more accurate estimate of σ_ϵ^2 than each sample variance separately. This "pooled" variance is called **within-groups variance** or **mean squares within ($\mathrm{MS_W}$).** Formula 6.6, which gives the pooled variance of two sample variances, can be directly extended here to obtain $\mathrm{MS_W}$ for K groups:

$$\mathrm{MS_W} = \frac{(n_1 - 1)s_1^2 + (n_2 - 1)s_2^2 + \ldots + (n_K - 1)s_K^2}{n_1 + n_2 + \ldots + n_K - K}, \qquad \textbf{(14.9)}$$

where $n_1, n_2, \ldots, n_K$ and $s_1^2, s_2^2, \ldots, s_K^2$ are the sample sizes and variances for the K groups. The denominator in Formula 14.9 indicates the degrees of freedom for $\mathrm{MS_W}$:

$$df_W = n_1 + n_2 + \cdots + n_K - K \qquad \textbf{(14.10)}$$

On the other hand, the variance of the sample means of the K groups is called **between-groups variance** or **mean squares between ($\mathrm{MS_B}$)**:

$$\mathrm{MS_B} = \frac{n_1(\bar{Y}_1 - \bar{Y}_\bullet)^2 + n_2(\bar{Y}_2 - \bar{Y}_\bullet)^2 + \ldots + n_K(\bar{Y}_K - \bar{Y}_\bullet)^2}{K - 1}, \qquad \textbf{(14.11)}$$

where $\bar{Y}_1, \bar{Y}_2, \ldots, \bar{Y}_K$ are the sample means for the K groups and $\bar{Y}_\bullet$, called the **grand mean**, is the mean of all observations in the K groups. The squared deviation of each sample mean from the grand mean, $(\bar{Y}_k - \bar{Y}_\bullet)^2$, is multiplied by the sample size, n, to take into account the number of observations producing the sample mean; ($k = 1, \ldots, K$). The degrees of freedom for $\mathrm{MS_B}$ is

$$df_B = K - 1. \qquad \textbf{(14.12)}$$

NOTE [14.1] In a **balanced ANOVA design** all K groups contain the same number of observations, $n_1 = n_2 = \ldots = n_K$ ($= n$), so Formulas 14.9, 14.10, and 14.11 become respectively:

$$\mathrm{MS_W} = \frac{s_1^2 + s_2^2 + \ldots + s_K^2}{K} \qquad \textbf{(14.13)}$$

$$df_W = K(n - 1) \qquad \textbf{(14.14)}$$

$$\mathrm{MS_B} = \frac{n[(\bar{Y}_1 - \bar{Y}_\bullet)^2 + (\bar{Y}_2 - \bar{Y}_\bullet)^2 + \ldots + (\bar{Y}_K - \bar{Y}_\bullet)^2]}{K - 1} \qquad \textbf{(14.15)}$$

EXAMPLE 14.1 This example illustrates the computation of the MS_W and MS_B for a balanced ANOVA design. The data are provided in Figure 14.2 (left panel). The data entry in SPSS (which will be used in a next example) is provided in the right panel of this figure. There are three ethnic groups ($K = 3$) with four observations per group ($n = 4$). The scores indicate the improvement made by middle school students on a math test as a result of an experimental school program that incorporates bilingual (English-Spanish) interpretation of mathematics concepts and principles. Not all students in each ethnic group (1 = Caucasian, 2 = African-American, and 3 = Hispanic) participated in this school program, but for the purposes of this example, this information is irrelevant [it will be used in an example of a two-factor ANOVA design in the next chapter.] Given the sample variances of the three ethnic groups, the within-groups variance (MS_W) in this balanced design is computed using Formula 14.13 with $K = 3$; in this case $MS_W = 37.33$. The between-groups variance (MS_B) is computed using Formula 14.15, with $K = 3$, $n = 4$, sample means $\bar{Y}_1 = 8$, $\bar{Y}_2 = 10$, and $\bar{Y}_3 = 18$, and a grand mean $\bar{Y}_{\bullet} = 12$. As shown with the computations in Figure 14.2 (left panel), $MS_B = 112$.

Figure 14.2 *Computation of the* ***mean squares within*** *(MS_W) and* ***mean squares between*** *(MS_B) using data for three ethnic groups in a one-factor balanced ANOVA design with four observations per group (n = 4).*

ETHNICITY			
Caucasian	**Afr-Amer**	**Hispanic**	
11	12	24	
7	8	28	
10	11	6	
4	9	14	
$\bar{Y}_1 = 8$	$\bar{Y}_2 = 10$	$\bar{Y}_3 = 18$	$\bar{Y}_{\bullet} = 12$
$s_1^2 = 10.00$	$s_2^2 = 3.33$	$s_3^2 = 98.67$	

$$MS_W = \frac{10.00 + 3.33 + 98.67}{3} = 37.33$$

$$MS_B = \frac{4[(8-12)^2 + (10-12)^2 + (18-12)^2]}{3-1} = \frac{(4)(56)}{2} = 112$$

ETHNIC-BILINGUAL.sav [D

File Edit View Data Transform

12 :

	SCORE	Ethnicity
1	11	1
2	7	1
3	10	1
4	4	1
5	12	2
6	8	2
7	11	2
8	9	2
9	24	3
10	28	3
11	6	3
12	14	3

The *mean squares within* ($MS_W = 37.33$) is entirely random in nature, as it represents a sample-based estimate of the error variance, σ_ϵ^2. The *mean squares between* ($MS_B = 112$), on the other hand, consists of two parts: a random part and a part due to differences among the groups (if such differences do exist).

14.5 Linear Model for One-factor ANOVA

Let Y_{ik} denote the score of person i from population k in a one-factor ANOVA with K groups (k = 1, 2, ..., K). The deviation of Y_{ik} from its population mean, μ_k, is the *random error* (*residual*) of this score: $\varepsilon_{ik} = Y_{ik} - \mu_k$. As we already know, the deviation of μ_k from the grand mean for all K populations, $\mu_\bullet$, is the *effect* associated with μ_k: $\propto_k = \mu_k - \mu_\bullet$ (see Equations 14.6). In a one-factor ANOVA, it is assumed that any score, Y_{ik}, can be represented as a sum of the grand mean, $\mu_\bullet$, the effect $\propto_k$, and the residual of the score, ε_{ik}. That is,

$$Y_{ik} = \mu_\bullet + \propto_k + \varepsilon_{ik} \qquad \textbf{(14.16)}$$

Equation (14.16) is referred to as a **linear model** for the data in a one-factor ANOVA. The same holds when the unknown population parameters in the right-hand side of Equation 14.16 are replaced with their sample estimates: $\hat{\mu}_\bullet = \bar{Y}_\bullet$, $\widehat{\propto}_k = \bar{Y}_k - \bar{Y}_\bullet$, and $\hat{\varepsilon}_{ik} = Y_{ik} - \bar{Y}_k$ (denoted e_{ik}). Thus,

$$Y_{ik} = \bar{Y}_\bullet + \widehat{\propto}_k + e_{ik} \qquad \textbf{(14.17)}$$

OR:

$$Y_{ik} = \bar{Y}_\bullet + (\bar{Y}_k - \bar{Y}_\bullet) + (Y_{ik} - \bar{Y}_k). \qquad \textbf{(14.18)}$$

For the data in Figure 14.2, the group means are $\bar{Y}_1 = 8$, $\bar{Y}_2 = 10$, and $\bar{Y}_3 = 18$, and the grand mean is $\bar{Y}_\bullet = 12$. Using equation 14.8, we compute the estimates of the group effects: $\hat{\alpha}_1 = 8 - 12 = -4$, $\hat{\alpha}_2 = 10 - 12 = -2$, and $\hat{\alpha}_3 = 18 - 12 = 6$ [as already known, the sum of all effects is zero: $(-4) + (-2) + 6 = 0$]. With Y_{ik} denoting the score of person i in group k (i = 1, 2, 3, 4; k = 1, 2, 3), we have: $Y_{11} = 11$, $Y_{21} = 7$, $Y_{31} = 10$, and $Y_{41} = 4$ for the scores of in the first column (Group 1 = Caucasian), $Y_{12} = 12$, $Y_{22} = 8$, $Y_{32} = 11$, and $Y_{42} = 9$ for the scores in the second column (Group 2 = African-American), and $Y_{13} = 24$, $Y_{23} = 28$, $Y_{33} = 6$, and $Y_{43} = 14$ for the scores in the third column (Group 3 = Hispanic). To illustrate the linear model for the score $Y_{21} = 7$, we use Equation 14.17 with $\bar{Y}_\bullet = 12$, $\hat{\alpha}_1 = -4$, and $e_{ik} = Y_{21} - \bar{Y}_1 = 7 - 8 = -1$. Thus,

$$Y_{21} = \bar{Y}_\bullet + \hat{\alpha}_1 + e_{ik} = 12 + (-4) + (-1) = 12 - 4 - 1 = 12 - 5 = 7.$$

Understanding the linear nature of the ANOVA data is important for understanding ANOVA and its relation to multiple regression in the framework of a general liner model.

14.6 Testing the ANOVA Null Hypothesis

The logic of the ANOVA test for statistical significance is based on the nature of the mean squares within (MS_W) and mean squares between (MS_B) under the assumption that the ANOVA null hypothesis, H_0, is true — see H_0 in (14.5). Specifically, as mentioned previously, MS_W is entirely random in nature while MS_B consists of a random part and a part due to differences among the population means (if such differences exist). When H_0 is true, there are no differences among the population means and, therefore, MS_B is then also entirely random in nature. Clearly, when H_0 is true, the MS_W and MS_B are both random (but not necessarily equal), and each represents an estimate of the random variance for the population, σ_ϵ^2. On the other hand, it is known that the ratio of two sample estimates of the same population variance is distributed according to the F-distribution (see Equation 7.6).

Thus, **if thc ANOVA null hypothesis (H_0: $\mu_1 = \mu_2 = \ldots = \mu_K$) is true, the ratio of the *mean squares between* (MS_B) to *mean squares within* (MS_W) follows the F-distribution:**

$$F = \frac{MS_B}{MS_W}. \tag{14.19}$$

In Formula 14.19, MS_B is used as a numerator out of convenience, since it is typically larger than the denominator (MS_W). The **degrees of freedom** for the numerator are given in Formula (14.12), while Formula 14.10 [or Formula 14.14 for a balanced design] provides the degrees of freedom for the denominator.

To test H_0: $\mu_1 = \mu_2 = \mu_3$ for the ANOVA design presented in Example 14.1 at the .05 level of significance, we compute the F-statistic for $MS_B = 112$ and $MS_W = 37.33$: $F = 112/37.33 = 3.00$. The degrees of freedom are: $df_B = K - 1 = 3 - 1 = 2$ and $df_W = K(n - 1) = (3)(4 - 1) = 9$. For $\alpha = .05$, the critical value under the F-distribution with two degrees of freedom for the numerator ($df_B = 2$) and nine degrees of freedom for the denominator ($df_W = 9$) is $F_{cv} = 4.26$. We fail to reject H_0 as the test statistic ($F = 3.00$) does not exceed the critical value ($F_{cv} = 4.26$). Thus, there are no statistically significant differences in math improvement among the ethnic groups.

EXAMPLE 14.2 This example illustrates how to use SPSS to test the null hypothesis in a one-factor (one-way) ANOVA. We test H_0: $\mu_1 = \mu_2 = \mu_3$ for the ANOVA design presented in Example 14.1 at the .05 level of significance. To perform this in SPSS, follow the steps:

1. Enter the data in SPSS as shown in Figure 14.1 (right panel).
2. Click **Analyze**, click **General Linear Model**, and click **Univariate.**
3. Click **SCORE** and click ▶ to move it into the box **Dependent Variable.**
4. Click **Ethnicity** and click ▶ to move it into the box **Fixed Factor(s).**
5. Click **OK.**

The SPSS output is given in Figure 14.3. The omnibus F-test in the ANOVA shows that there are no statistically significant differences among the ethnic groups (Caucasian, African-American, and Hispanic) in math improvement scores at the .05 level of significance, $F(2, 9) = 3.00$, $p = .10$. Note also that the values of MS_B (112), MS_W (37.33), and F (3.00) are equal to those obtained with the manual computations in Figure 14.2.

Figure 14.3 *SPSS output for ANOVA with the data in Figure 14.1 (right panel)*

Tests of Between-Subjects Effects

Dependent Variable: SCORE

Source	Type III Sum of Squares	df	Mean Square	F	Sig.
Corrected Model	224.000[a]	2	112.000	3.000	.100
Intercept	1728.000	1	1728.000	46.286	.000
Ethnicity	224.000	2	112.000	3.000	.100
Error	336.000	9	37.333		
Total	2288.000	12			
Corrected Total	560.000	11			

$MS_B = 112$

$MS_W = 37.333$

$F(2, 9) = 3.00, p = .10$

14.7 Multiple Comparisons

When the omnibus F-test in ANOVA indicates that the null hypothesis (H_0: $\mu_1 = \mu_2 = \ldots = \mu_K$) is false (that is, not all K population means are equal) and there are more than two groups ($K > 2$), there is a need to determine exactly *which* differences are statistically significant. This is achieved by using statistical procedures referred to as **multiple comparison (MC)** techniques. In Example 14.2, for instance, there was no need to conduct multiple comparisons because the omnibus F-test did not lead to rejection of the null hypothesis (H_0: $\mu_1 = \mu_2 = \mu_3$). When this is necessary, there are numerous methods of conducting multiple comparisons, each with their advantages and limitations, that are discussed in the literature and included in major statistical packages. This section provides a brief description and SPSS illustrations of only a few (out of more than a dozen) MC methods available in SPSS.

MC methods that involve the comparison of all possible pairs of means after rejecting the omnibus H_0, are called **post hoc comparisons**. In contrast, MC methods that test hypotheses specified *prior* to testing the omnibus null hypothesis are called **planned comparisons**.

14.7.1 Post Hoc Comparisons

This section briefly describes two frequently-used post hoc tests for multiple comparisons: the Tukey method and the Bonferroni method (both are available in SPSS).

14.7.1.1 The Tukey method of multiple comparisons. With the Tukey MC method, all K sample means are ranked in *decreasing* order of their algebraic values from the largest ($\bar{Y}_1$) to the smallest ($\bar{Y}_K$) as follows: $\bar{Y}_1, \bar{Y}_2, \ldots, \bar{Y}_j, \ldots, \bar{Y}_K$. First, the largest difference is tested for statistical significance (H$_0$: $\bar{Y}_1 - \bar{Y}_K = 0$) using the so-called **studentized range statistic**:

$$q_1 = \frac{\bar{Y}_1 - \bar{Y}_K}{s_{\bar{Y}}}, \quad \textbf{(14.20)}$$

where $s_{\bar{Y}}$, the *standard error of the mean* for the dependent variable, Y, is computed as follows:

$$s_{\bar{Y}} = \sqrt{\frac{\text{MS}_\text{W}}{n}} \qquad [\text{MS}_\text{W} = \textit{mean squares within}] \quad \textbf{(14.21)}$$

If the studentized range statistic q_1 is not statistically significant, the null hypothesis H$_0$: $\bar{Y}_1 - \bar{Y}_K = 0$ is retained and the MC process stops, since there is no reason to expect that some of the smallest differences between $\bar{Y}_1$ and the other sample means (excluding $\bar{Y}_K$) would be statistically significant. If, however, H$_0$: $\bar{Y}_1 - \bar{Y}_K = 0$ is rejected, then the second largest difference is tested for statistical significance (H$_0$: $\bar{Y}_1 - \bar{Y}_{K-1} = 0$), and so on. After the testing of differences that involve $\bar{Y}_1$ is completed, the cycle is repeated for differences that involve the next largest mean, $\bar{Y}_2$; that is: $\bar{Y}_2 - \bar{Y}_K$ and, if necessary, $\bar{Y}_2 - \bar{Y}_{K-1}$, and so on. This process continues until the smallest difference ($\bar{Y}_{K-1} - \bar{Y}_K$) is tested for statistical significance (assuming, of course, that all preceding tests were statistically significant).

For concreteness, suppose that the omnibus null hypothesis with three population means (H_0: $\mu_1 = \mu_2 = \mu_3$) is rejected. The Tukey MC ranking of sample means (from largest to smallest) is: $\bar{Y}_1$, $\bar{Y}_2$, and $\bar{Y}_3$. One possible scenario of MC testing in this case is:

Step 1: Testing $\bar{Y}_1 - \bar{Y}_3$ (say, statistically significant).
Step 2: Testing $\bar{Y}_1 - \bar{Y}_2$ (say, not statistically significant).
Step 3: Testing $\bar{Y}_2 - \bar{Y}_3$ (say, statistically significant).

Under this hypothetical scenario, the conclusion would be (a) reject H_0: $\mu_1 = \mu_3$, (b) retain (fail to reject) H_0: $\mu_1 = \mu_2$, and (c) reject H_0: $\mu_2 = \mu_3$.

NOTE [14.2] With a balanced ANOVA design (in which all samples are of the same size, *n*), the Tukey MC method is simplified by finding the minimum difference between two sample means that is necessary to reject the null hypothesis which compares the means of the populations from which the samples were selected. This minimum difference is called the ***honest significance difference*** (*HSD*).

14.7.1.2 Bonferroni method of multiple comparisons. The Bonferroni MC method uses the Student's *t*-test for pairwise comparisons of population means. This method controls for the overall (family-wise) Type I error rate by using the *Bonferroni adjustment* described earlier in this chapter (see Equation 14.2). When the omnibus null hypothesis in ANOVA involves a small number (e.g., 3 or 4) population means, the Bonferroni MC test is more powerful than the Tukey MC test, but with a larger number of groups, the Tukey MC test is more powerful.

EXAMPLE 14.3 This example illustrates how to use SPSS for the Tukey MC method. The omnibus null hypothesis for the ANOVA design in Example 14.2 was H_0: $\mu_1 = \mu_2 = \mu_3$. As H_0 was not rejected, the Tukey post hoc test is conducted here only for the sake of illustration. To perform this test, you can use the SPSS steps described in Example 14.2, inserting the following steps between steps 4 and 5: Click **Post Hoc**, then check the **Tukey** box, and click **Continue**.

The SPSS output for multiple comparisons in this case is shown in Figure 14.4; arrows were added to illustrate the pairwise comparisons between ethnic groups (1 = Caucasian, 2 = African-American, and 3 = Hispanic) on their improvement in math test performance during an experimental school program for integrative bilingual education. The pairs of groups not related by arrows can be ignored, as they are the same as those connected with arrows but in reverse order. As expected, none of the pairwise comparisons is statistically significant, as indicated by the *p*-values for the differences $\bar{Y}_1 - \bar{Y}_2$ ($p = .890$), $\bar{Y}_1 - \bar{Y}_3$ ($p = .105$), and $\bar{Y}_2 - \bar{Y}_3$ ($p = .208$).

Figure 14.4 *SPSS output for the Tukey method of post hoc comparisons of three groups*

Multiple Comparisons

Dependent Variable: SCORE
Tukey HSD

(I) Ethnicity	(J) Ethnicity	Mean Difference (I-J)	Std. Error	Sig.	95% Confidence Interval Lower Bound	Upper Bound
1	→ 2	-2.00	4.320	.890	-14.06	10.06
	→ 3	-10.00	4.320	.105	-22.06	2.06
2	1	2.00	4.320	.890	-10.06	14.06
	→ 3	-8.00	4.320	.208	-20.06	4.06
3	1	10.00	4.320	.105	-2.06	22.06
	2	8.00	4.320	.208	-4.06	20.06

Based on observed means.

14.7.2 Planned Comparisons

14.7.2.1 Contrasts for planned multiple comparisons. Suppose the omnibus null hypothesis is H_0: $\mu_1 = \mu_2 = \mu_3$, where μ_1 and μ_2 are the population means of two experimental groups and μ_3 is the population mean of the control group. Instead of running a post hoc test for all pairs of means, suppose we have decided a priori to compare each experimental group to the control group. That is, we are interested in testing two specific hypotheses: H_{01}: $\mu_1 = \mu_3$ and H_{02}: $\mu_2 = \mu_3$. We can test these two hypotheses using a post hoc MC method (e.g., Tukey or Bonferroni) but, with all other conditions being equal, the planned tests are more powerful than their post hoc counterparts.

As with the *t*-test for two population means, the null hypotheses H_{01} and H_{02} can be represented as H_{01}: $\mu_1 - \mu_3 = 0$ and H_{02}: $\mu_2 - \mu_3 = 0$, respectively. The difference $\mu_1 - \mu_3$ is called a *contrast* for H_{01}, denoted Ψ_1. Likewise, the difference $\mu_2 - \mu_3$ is called a *contrast* for H_{02}, denoted Ψ_2. Thus, the representation of H_{01} and H_{02} with contrasts is H_{01}: $\Psi_1 = 0$ and H_{02}: $\Psi_2 = 0$. As the standard form of a contrast includes all means involved in the omnibus null hypothesis, in this case we have:

$$\Psi_1 = (1)\mu_1 + (0)\mu_2 + (-1)\mu_3 \qquad \textbf{(14.22)}$$

$$\Psi_2 = (0)\mu_1 + (1)\mu_2 + (-1)\mu_3. \qquad \textbf{(14.23)}$$

Clearly, each contrast (Ψ_1 and Ψ_2) represents a linear combination of the population means. Note also that the sum of the coefficients in each contrast equals zero [for Ψ_1: 1 + 0 – 1 = 0 and for Ψ_2: 0 + 1 – 1 = 0.] The sample estimates of Ψ_1 (= $\mu_1 - \mu_3$) and Ψ_2 (= $\mu_2 - \mu_3$) are the differences $\widehat{\Psi}_1 = \bar{Y}_1 - \bar{Y}_3$ and $\widehat{\Psi}_2 = \bar{Y}_2 - \bar{Y}_3$, respectively. Thus, the testing of H_{01} and H_{02} is equivalent to testing $\widehat{\Psi}_1$ and $\widehat{\Psi}_2$, respectively, for statistical significance.

If we decide to test whether the average effect of the two experimental groups equals the effect of the control group, we need to plan a third null hypothesis,

$$H_{03}: \frac{\mu_1+\mu_2}{2} = \mu_3. \qquad \textbf{(14.24)}$$

The contrast representation of this hypothesis is H_{03}: $\mu_1 + \mu_2 - 2\mu_3 = 0$. Thus, the contrast for H_{03} is the following linear combination of the population means;

$$\Psi_3 = (1)\mu_1 + (1)\mu_2 + (-2)\mu_3. \qquad \textbf{(14.25)}$$

Note again that the sum of all coefficients for Ψ_3 (1, 1, −2) equals zero.

In general, a **contrast** Ψ among *K* population means is a linear combination of the means

$$\Psi = c_1\mu_1 + c_2\mu_2 + \cdots + c_K\mu_K, \qquad \textbf{(14.26)}$$

where the sum of all coefficients is zero: $c_1 + c_2 + \cdots + c_K = 0$. The sample estimate of Ψ is:

$$\widehat{\Psi} = c_1\bar{Y}_1 + c_2\bar{Y}_2 + \ldots + c_K\bar{Y}_K. \qquad \textbf{(14.27)}$$

Contrasts that involve only two means are called **simple contrasts** (e.g., Ψ_1 and Ψ_2) and contrasts that involve more than two means are called **complex contrasts** (e.g., Ψ_3). Each contrast is designed to test a specific planned hypothesis using the following *t*-test statistic:

$$t = \widehat{\Psi} / s_{\widehat{\Psi}}, \qquad \textbf{(14.28)}$$

where $\widehat{\Psi}$ is computed using Equation 14.27, and its *standard error*, $s_{\widehat{\Psi}}$, is computed as

$$s_{\widehat{\Psi}} = \sqrt{MS_W\left(\frac{c_1^2}{n_1} + \frac{c_2^2}{n_2} + \cdots + \frac{c_K^2}{n_K}\right)} \quad \textbf{(14.29)}$$

In Formula 14.29, MS_W is the *mean squares within* (see Formula 14.9), $n_1, n_2, \ldots, n_K$ are the sample sizes of the K groups, and $c_1, c_2, \ldots, c_K$ are the coefficients of the contrast $\widehat{\Psi}$ (Equation 14.27). For example, for the contrast $\widehat{\Psi}_3$ presented in Equation 14.25: $c_1 = 1$, $c_2 = 1$, and $c_3 = -2$.

14.7.2.2 Dunnett method of multiple comparisons. The Dunnett MC method is designed to compare each of the population means to one prespecified mean. The group that represents the population with the prespecified mean is called a **reference group** [in SPSS the reference group is called the **control group**]. Suppose that in the case of three groups the decision, made *a priori*, is to compare the population means for the first two groups (μ_1 and μ_2) to the population mean for the third group (μ_3). With the third group being the reference (control) group, we can use the Dunnett MC method to test H_{01}: $\mu_1 = \mu_3$ and H_{02}: $\mu_2 = \mu_3$. In contrast form, H_{01}: $\Psi_1 = 0$ and H_{02}: $\Psi_2 = 0$, where the two contrasts are: $\Psi_1 = \mu_1 - \mu_3$ [coefficients 1 0 −1] and $\Psi_2 = \mu_2 - \mu_3$ [coefficients 0 1 −1.] The testing of H_{01} and H_{02} is performed using the *t*-statistic in Formula 14.28, with $\widehat{\Psi}_1 = \bar{Y}_1 - \bar{Y}_3$ and $\widehat{\Psi}_2 = \bar{Y}_2 - \bar{Y}_3$, respectively. The standard errors of $\widehat{\Psi}_1$ and $\widehat{\Psi}_2$ are estimated via Formula 14.29, given the sample sizes of the three groups (n_1, n_2, n_3) and the contrast coefficients of the contrasts, $\widehat{\Psi}_1$ ($c_1 = 1$, $c_2 = 0$, $c_3 = -1$) and $\widehat{\Psi}_2$ ($c_1 = 0$, $c_2 = 1$, $c_3 = -1$). The *t* critical values can be found in a statistical table for the Dunnett MC test (e.g., see Glass & Hopkins, 1996). This table is not provided here because manual calculations with Formulas 14.28 and 14.29 are tedious and not targeted in this book. An illustration of the Dunnett MC test using SPSS is provided in Example 14.4.

EXAMPLE 14.4 This example demonstrates how to use SPSS to conduct the Dunnett MC test. The data in Figure 14.2 are used again, but this time to conduct planned comparisons of each of the first two groups (Caucasian and African-American) to the third group (Hispanic), used as a control group. The planned comparisons are then H_{01}: $\mu_1 - \mu_3 = 0$ and H_{02}: $\mu_2 - \mu_3 = 0$. A left-sided directional test is used because, given the nature of the bilingual program (English-Spanish), it is expected that the third ethnic group (Hispanic) will benefit more than the other two groups from this program. To use SPSS, repeat the first four steps described in Example 14.2 and add the selections shown in Figure 14.5 as follows:

- Click **Post Hoc**, and then select the **Dunnett** box, select the left radio button < **Control** (to indicate left-sided test), and select **Last** in the *Control Category* (to indicate that the reference category in this case is the last group, 3 = Hispanic).

The SPSS output table is shown in Figure 14.6. The results indicate that there is a statistically significant difference in math improvement scores between the first group (Caucasian) and the third group (Hispanic) at the .05 level of significance ($p = .040$). Specifically, given that this is a left-sided test, the upper bound of the 95 percent confidence interval for this difference (−0.58) indicates that the first group (Caucasian) has no more than 0.58 test points lower improvement on the math test than the third (Hispanic) group.

Figure 14.5 *SPSS dialog box for multiple comparisons, with the selection of the left-sided Dunnett test for the comparison of the first two groups (1 = Caucasian, 2 = African-American) to the last group (3 = Hispanic) as a control group.*

Univariate: Post Hoc Multiple Comparisons for Observed Means

Factor(s): Ethnicity

Post Hoc Tests for: Ethnicity

Continue | Cancel | Help

Equal Variances Assumed

☐ LSD ☐ S-N-K ☐ Waller-Duncan
☐ Bonferroni ☑ Tukey Type I/Type II Error Ratio: 100
☐ Sidak ☐ Tukey's-b ☑ Dunnett
☐ Scheffe ☐ Duncan Control Category: Last
☐ R-E-G-W F ☐ Hochberg's GT2 Test
☐ R-E-G-W Q ☐ Gabriel ○ 2-sided ◉ < Control ○ > Control

Equal Variances Not Assumed

☐ Tamhane's T2 ☐ Dunnett's T3 ☐ Games-Howell ☐ Dunnett's C

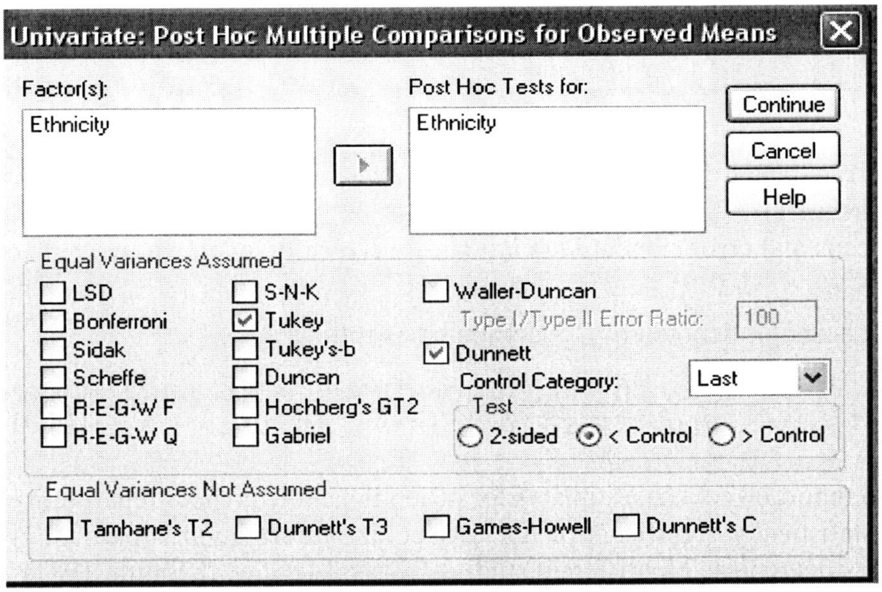

Note that the planned comparisons (in combination with a one-sided test) increased the power of the test, which enabled us to detect the difference between the Caucasian and Hispanic groups, whereas the post hoc Tukey comparisons showed no statistical significance for this difference (p = .105) (see Example 14.3). The difference between the second group (African-American) and the third group (Hispanic) is not statistically significant, but its p-value (.083) is much smaller than that reported with the Tukey post hoc test for this difference (p = .208) (see Example 14.3).

Figure 14.6 *SPSS output table for the one-sided Dunnett sided test comparing two ethnic groups (1 = Caucasian, 2 = African-American) to a third ethnic group (3 = Hispanic) as a control group*

Multiple Comparisons

Dependent Variable: SCORE
Dunnett t (<control)[a]

(I) Ethnicity	(J) Ethnicity	Mean Difference (I-J)	Std. Error	Sig.	95% Confidence Interval Upper Bound
1	3	-10.00*	4.320	.040	-.58
2	3	-8.00	4.320	.083	1.42

Based on observed means.

*. The mean difference is significant at the .05 level.

a. Dunnett t-tests treat one group as a control, and compare all other groups against it.

Effect Size

n Differences

r the difference between two population means in ANOVA, say μ_i and standardized absolute value of this difference

$$\delta_{i,j} = \frac{|\mu_i - \mu_j|}{\sigma_\varepsilon}, \tag{14.30}$$

e σ_ε is the population error standard deviation. That is, $\sigma_\varepsilon = \sqrt{\sigma_\varepsilon^2}$, where σ_ε^2 is the population rror variance (e.g., see Figure 14.1).

As the population means and error standard deviations are typically unknown, we replace them with their sample estimates: $\hat{\mu}_i = \bar{Y}_i$, $\hat{\mu}_j = \bar{Y}_j$, and $\hat{\sigma}_\varepsilon = \sqrt{\text{MS}_\text{W}}$ (see Formula 14.9). Thus, the sample estimate of the effect size $\delta_{i,j}$, denoted $d_{i,j}$, is computed as follows:

$$d_{i,j} = \frac{|\bar{Y}_i - \bar{Y}_j|}{\sqrt{MS_W}}. \tag{14.31}$$

It is recommended to report effect size estimates for group mean differences regardless of whether the difference are statistically significant or not. Effect size information is particularly useful for meta-analysis of results reported in different studies (Glass, McGaw, & Smith, 1981).

When the ANOVA assumption of equal variances is not met, it would be better to replace the denominator in Formula 14.31, $\sqrt{\text{MS}_\text{W}}$, with the standard deviation of one of the groups being compared — typically, the control group (Glass, 1976). For example, if the Dunnett MC test is used when the population variances are not equal, the effect size of the difference between the means of a given group, *i*, and the control group, *c*, can be estimated as follows:

$$d_{i,c} = \frac{\bar{Y}_i - \bar{Y}_c}{s_c}, \tag{14.32}$$

where s_c is the sample standard deviation of the control group, *c*.

> **NOTE [14.3]** Cohen (1988) suggested the following guidelines for interpreting the magnitude of the effect size of the difference between two means, *d*:
>
> (a) **small:** $d = .2$, (b) **medium**: $d = .5$, and (c) **large**: $d = .8$

14.8.2 Omnibus Effect Size

Along with measuring the effect size of mean differences (Formulas 14.31 and 14.32), it is also important to estimate an **omnibus effect size** — the proportion of the total variance in the dependent variable, *Y*, accounted for by the differences among the groups being compared. In one-factor ANOVA, an omnibus effect size is estimated by the ratio of the *between-groups variation* (SS_B – sum of squares between) to the *total variation* (SS_T – sum of squares total), referred to as the η^2 (**eta squared**) effect size:

$$\eta^2 = \frac{SS_B}{SS_T}. \tag{14.33}$$

Recall that in one-factor ANOVA with K groups SS_B is the numerator in F(that is: $SS_B = n_1(\bar{Y}_1 - \bar{Y}_\bullet)^2 + n_2(\bar{Y}_2 - \bar{Y}_\bullet)^2 + \cdots + n_K(\bar{Y}_K - \bar{Y}_\bullet)^2$. Also, ! squared deviations from the grand mean, $\bar{Y}_\bullet$, for the observations in all / $\sum\sum(Y_{ij} - \bar{Y}_\bullet)^2$, where Y_{ij} is the score of subject i in group j ; (j = 1, 2, ...

As η^2 shows the amount of variation in Y accounted for by the particular sample, an adjustment of η^2 for the population, denoted ω been proposed (Hays, 1963):

$$\omega^2 = \frac{\mathrm{SS_B} - (K-1)\mathrm{MS_W}}{\mathrm{SS_T} + \mathrm{MS_W}}, \qquad \textbf{(14.34)}$$

where K is the number of groups and $\mathrm{MS_W}$ is the *mean squares within* (see Formulas 14.9).

NOTE [14.4] Cohen (1988) suggested the following guidelines for interpreting the magnitude of the effect size η^2 (or ω^2):

(a) **small:** η^2 = .01, (b) **medium:** η^2= .06, and (c) **large**: η^2 = .14.

EXAMPLE 14.5 This example illustrates how to estimate η^2 using SPSS. The omnibus effects size adjusted for the population (ω^2) and the effect sizes for mean differences in multiple comparisons (d) are not reported in SPSS, but their computation is also illustrated here using information provided in the SPSS output. The null hypothesis tested with the one-factor ANOVA in this example is H_0: $\mu_1 = \mu_2 = \mu_3$, for the means of three ethnic groups of high school students (1 = Caucasian, 2 = African-American, 3 = Hispanic) on motivation for academic achievement. The data in Figure 14.7 (left panel) is taken from Example 13.5.

The SPSS steps for ANOVA in this example are described in Figure 14.7 (right panel). The SPSS output is provided in Figure 14.8. For space considerations, the descriptive statistics are not shown in Figure 14.8: $\bar{Y}_1$= 26.82 (s_1= 7.88), $\bar{Y}_2$ = 20.50 (s_2=6.98), $\bar{Y}_3$=14.75 (s_3= 5.19). The results from the Levene's test for equal variances show that the null hypothesis of "equal variances in the dependent variable across groups" cannot be rejected, $F(2, 18) = 0.54$, $p = .592$. Thus, the ANOVA assumption of equal variances is met. The F-test results in the *Tests of Between-Subjects Effects* table indicate that we *can* reject the ANOVA null hypothesis (H_0: $\mu_1 = \mu_2 = \mu_3$) at the .05 level, $F(2, 18) = 4.46$, $p = .027$. The effect size reported in this table is $\eta^2 = .331$. According to Cohen's classification, this is a *large* effect size (see NOTE [14.4]). In other words, 33.1% of the variance in the dependent variable (motivation for academic achievement) is accounted for by the differences in this variable among the three ethnic groups. Note that SPSS reports "partial eta squared," which in the case of one-factor ANOVA equals η^2 [*partial* η^2 is discussed for ANOVAs with more than one factor, see Chapter 15.]

The effect size adjusted for the population, ω^2, is obtained using Formula 14.34 for three groups (K = 3) and the values for the components in this formula that are reported in Figure 14.8: $\mathrm{SS_B}$ = 468.399, $\mathrm{SS_T}$ = 1414.286, and $\mathrm{MS_W}$ = 52.549.

$$\omega^2 = \frac{\mathrm{SS_B} - (K-1)\mathrm{MS_W}}{\mathrm{SS_T} + \mathrm{MS_W}} = \frac{468.399 - (3-1)(52.549)}{1414.286 + 52.549} = 0.25.$$

results from the Tukey post hoc test for pairwise comparisons among the ethnic ndicated that only the mean difference between the Caucasian and Hispanic groups is ically significant (p = .027). The 95% confidence interval for this difference shows that the ucasian group scored higher that the Hispanic group by an amount that varies largely (from 1.27 to 22.87) on the motivation scale. This large variation is due to a large standard error of this difference (4.233) which, in turn, is due to the very small sample size in this illustrative example. To estimate the effect size of the population mean difference between the two groups ($\mu_1 - \mu_3$), we use Formula 14.31 because, as indicated by the Levene's test, the assumption of equal variances is met. Given that $\bar{Y}_1 - \bar{Y}_3$= 12.07 and MS_W = 52.549 (see Figure 14.8), we obtain:

$$d_{1,3} = \frac{|\bar{Y}_1 - \bar{Y}_3|}{\sqrt{MS_W}} = \frac{|12.07|}{\sqrt{52.549}} = \frac{12.07}{7.2491} = 1.66.$$

Although the other two pairwise group differences are not statistically significant, it is still useful to report their effect sizes. Using Formula 14.31 with the values reported in Figure 14.8, $\bar{Y}_1 - \bar{Y}_2$ = 6.32, $\bar{Y}_2 - \bar{Y}_3$ = 5.75, and MS_W = 52.549, we obtain $d_{1,2}$= 0.87, for the difference between the Caucasian and African-American groups, and $d_{2,3}$ = 0.79 for the difference between the African-American and Hispanic groups. Keep in mind that the sample size in this example is very small which makes it difficult to reach statistical significance in all pairwise comparisons.

Figure 14.7 *SPSS steps for one-factor ANOVA comparing three ethnic groups on motivation for academic achievement*

Example 14_5.sav [DataSet1]

File Edit View Data Transform An

21 :

	MOTIVATION	Ethnicity
1	36	1
2	40	1
3	25	1
4	27	1
5	17	1
6	28	1
7	20	1
8	19	1
9	18	1
10	35	1
11	30	1
12	16	2
13	10	2
14	28	2
15	25	2
16	26	2
17	18	2
18	21	3
19	17	3
20	10	3
21	11	3

To perform the SPSS analysis, enter the 21 observations, as shown in the left panel, assign the coding values for Ethnicity (1 = Caucasian, 2 = African-American, 3 = Hispanic), and follow the steps:

1. Click **Analyze**, click **General Linear Model**, and click **Univariate**.
2. Click **MOTIVATION**, and click ▶ to move it into the box **Dependent Variable**. Then click **Ethnicity**, and click ▶ to move it into the box **Fixed Factor(s)**.
3. Click **Options**, check the boxes **Descriptive Statistics**, **Estimates of Effect size**, and **Homogeneity tests**, and then click **Continue**.
4. Click **Post Hoc**, then click **Ethnicity**, click ▶ to move it into the box **Post Hoc Tests for**, check the **Tukey** box, and click **Continue**.
5. Click **OK**.

Figure 14.8 *SPSS ANOVA output for the comparison of three ethnic groups (1 = Caucasian, 2 = African-American, 3 = Hispanic) on motivation for academic achievement*

Levene's Test of Equality of Error Variances [a]

Dependent Variable: Motivation for academic achievement

F	df1	df2	Sig.
.540	2	18	.592

Tests the null hypothesis that the error variance of the dependent variable is equal across groups.

The ANOVA assumption of equal variances is met ($p > .05$)

Tests of Between-Subjects Effects

Dependent Variable: Motivation for academic achievement

Source	Type III Sum of Squares	df	Mean Square	F	Sig.	Partial Eta Squared
Corrected Model	468.399[a]	2	234.200	4.457	.027	.331
Intercept	7589.920	1	7589.920	144.434	.000	.889
Ethnicity	468.399	2	234.200	4.457	.027	.331
Error	945.886	18	52.549			
Total	12249.000	21				
Corrected Total	1414.286	20				

a. R Squared = .331 (Adjusted R Squared = .257)

SS_B SS_T SS_W MS_W $\eta^2 = SS_B / SS_T = .331$

Multiple Comparisons

Dependent Variable: Motivation for academic achievement
Tukey HSD

(I) Ethnicity	(J) Ethnicity	Mean Difference (I-J)	Std. Error	Sig.	95% Confidence Interval Lower Bound	95% Confidence Interval Upper Bound
Caucasian	African-American	6.32	3.679	.226	-3.07	15.71
	Hispanic	12.07*	4.233	.027	1.27	22.87
African-American	Caucasian	-6.32	3.679	.226	-15.71	3.07
	Hispanic	5.75	4.679	.452	-6.19	17.69
Hispanic	Caucasian	-12.07*	4.233	.027	-22.87	-1.27
	African-American	-5.75	4.679	.452	-17.69	6.19

Based on observed means.

*. The mean difference is significant at the .05 level.

$\bar{Y}_1 - \bar{Y}_3$ $p < .05$

Note. It is important to emphasize that the very small sample size in this example is convenient for data entry and illustration, but would be unacceptable for using ANOVA in a real study.

14.9 Determining the Sample Size

In Chapter 13 (Section 13.5) we discussed an approach to determining sample size for multiple regression based on a prespecified level of significance, power, effect size, and number of predictors (Cohen & Cohen, 1983). The ANOVA analog of this approach to determining sample size is also based on preliminary information about the **level of significance** (α), **power** (*P*), **effect size** (*d*), **population error variance** (σ_ε^2), and **number of groups or treatment levels**(*K*) (Hinkle & Oliver, 1983). The task is to determine the sample size that is needed in a one-factor ANOVA to reject the null hypothesis at a specified level of significance, α, with a desired test power, *P*, and practically-important effect size, *d*. Typically, the practical importance of the effect size *d* is determined by the researcher based on previous research findings and/or considerations related to policy or accountability demands. In one-factor ANOVA with *K* groups, the effect size of interest, *d*, is the largest effect size across all pairs of groups.

Suppose we decide that the largest effect size among all pairs of four groups ($K = 4$) in a one-factor ANOVA must be at least 0.50 to be practically important. The related sample-size question is, for example, "How large must the sample be in order to detect a difference of a half standard deviation ($d = .50$), for the largest separation between two ANOVA groups, at the .05 level of significance and with a power of .85?" Using Table 14.1 for $K = 4$, $\alpha = .05$, $d = .50$, and power of .85 ($P = .85$), we can see that the sample size must be $n = 98$ (i.e., 98 observations are needed in this case).

Table 14.1 *Sample size (n) for one-factor ANOVA with K groups and effect size (d) to be detected with power = .85 at the α = .05 level of significance*

α = .05 **power = .85**	Effect size				
Number of groups (*K*)	*d* = 0.5	*d* = 0.75	*d* = 1.0	*d* = 1.25	*d* = 1.5
2	72	32	19	13	9
3	87	39	22	15	11
4	98	44	25	17	12
5	108	48	28	18	13
6	116	52	30	19	14
7	123	55	31	20	14
8	129	57	32	21	15

Note. The complete sample-size tables for two α -levels (α = .05 and α = .01) and six power values (.75, .80, .85, .90, .95, and .99) are provided by Hinkle and Oliver (1983).

14.10 Consequences of Violating the ANOVA Assumptions

As described in Section 14.2, there are three primary assumptions in ANOVA— *independence, normality*, and *homogeneity of variance*. **Independence** means that the sample observations are independent of each other, **normality** means that the theoretical distribution of scores are normal, and **homogeneity of variance** means that the variances of all theoretical distributions of scores are equal. There is also an assumption of **linearity** according to which an individual score, Y_{ik}, can be represented as a sum of the grand mean, $\mu_{\bullet}$, the effect $\propto_k$, and the residual of the score, ε_{ik} (see Equation 14.16). A statistical method is considered "robust" based on the degree to which the results obtained through this method remain accurate. A comprehensive review of studies on the robustness of ANOVA (Glass, Peckham, & Sanders, 1972) reached the following conclusions:

- Violations of the **normality** assumption have negligible consequences on the chances for Type-I and Type-II error in testing the null hypothesis unless (a) the population distributions are highly skewed, (b) the *n*'s (sample sizes of the groups) are very small, and/or (c) one-sided tests are used [which applies only in the special case of ANOVA with two groups ($K = 2$)].
- Violations of the **homogeneity of variance** assumption ($\sigma_1^2 = \sigma_2^2 = \ldots = \sigma_K^2$) have negligible consequences on the chances for Type-I and Type-II error when the ANOVA design is *balanced* (i.e., all *n*'s are equal). When the design is not balanced, violations of this assumption affect the degrees of freedom of the *F*-distribution for the ANOVA test which, in turn, yields either "conservative" or "liberal" results. Specifically, when larger variances (σ_k^2's) come from larger samples (n_k's), the results are **conservative** — make it more difficult to reject the null hypothesis (H_0) than it should actually be (i.e., the *F*-critical value inferred from the results is larger than it actually is). Conversely, when larger n_k's relate to smaller σ_k^2's, the ANOVA results are **liberal** — make it easier to reject H_0 than it should actually be (i.e., the *F*-critical value inferred from the results is smaller than it actually is).
- Violations of the **independence** assumption have serious consequences on the accuracy of the ANOVA results. Specifically, when the observations are not independent (i.e., the scores within groups influence each other), ANOVA yields liberal results, thus allowing the researcher to reach conclusions about the presence of treatment effects when they may not exist at all. As suggested in the literature (e.g., Glass & Hopkins, 1996), when individual observations within experimental groups (e.g., classrooms) are not independent, it would be better to compute the group means and conduct an ANOVA test using the groups as observational units.
- Violations of the **linearity** assumption occur when the differences among groups in a one-factor ANOVA model are not the same across distinct subgroups of people. For example, if the ANOVA groups represent different types of treatment, it may happen that the differences between some (or all) pairs of treatments are not the same for males and females. This is referred to as an "interaction" between treatment and gender. In such case a two-factor (*Treatment* x *Gender*) ANOVA should be employed [see Chapter 15.]

NOTE [14.5] In SPSS, the *homogeneity of variance* assumption in ANOVA is tested by the **Levene's test of equality of error variances**. The lack of statistical significance with this test ($p > .05$) indicates that the population variances are equal. If, however, the Levene's test indicates that the homogeneity of variance assumption is not met ($p < .05$), there are two "lucky" scenarios for reaching safe conclusions about the null hypothesis:

- If *conservative* results (larger σ_k^2's and n_k's are paired) suggest rejection of H_0, we can safely conclude that H_0 is false at the specified level of significance, α.
- If *liberal* results (larger n_k's and smaller σ_k^2 are paired) suggest retention of H_0, we can safely retain (fail to reject) H_0 at the specified level of significance, α.

14.11 Interpretation of SPSS Output for One-factor ANOVA

The interpretation of SPSS output for one-factor ANOVA is illustrated here for the results in Figure 14.9. Three ethnic groups of fifth grade students in a large urban school district (1 = Caucasian, 2 = African-American, 3 = Hispanic) are compared on a standardized reading test. The data consist of 2230 observations randomly selected from real records for this student population. The SPSS data file, **RMS-5.sav**, is available at http://cehd.gmu.edu/book/dimitov. This file also contains data on the students' gender and scores on math and science tests, but it is not used in this example. The ANOVA was performed with **Reading** as the dependent variable and **Ethnicity** as the independent variable (factor) using the five-step process described in Figure 14.7. The results are described and interpreted in APA style, adding some minor clarifications and illustrative computations.

The means and standard deviations of reading scores for the three ethnic groups are given in Table 14.2 [APA style]. In Figure 14.9, the results from the Levene's test indicate that the homogeneity of variance assumption is met, $F(2, 2227) = 1.54$, $p = .214$. The normal Q-Q plot for the reading scores (not shown here) indicated that the score distribution is close to normal. The ANOVA F-test results show that there are statistically significant differences in reading among the three ethnic groups, $F(2, 2227) = 33.35$, $p < .001$. The omnibus effect size for the sample data is $\eta^2 = .029$, thus indicating that 2.9 percent of the variance in reading scores is accounted for by score differences among the three ethnic groups. By the Cohen's guidelines for interpreting η^2 (Cohen, 1988), the effect size of .029 is small. Further, the results from the Tukey post hoc multiple comparisons indicate that there is a statistically significant difference between the Caucasian group and the other two ethnic groups ($p < .001$), but not between the African-American and the Hispanic groups ($p = .918$). The 95 percent confidence intervals for the differences show that the Caucasian group outperformed the African-American group, by a score between 2.03 and 3.91 and the Hispanic group by a score between 1.91 and 4.46.

The effect sizes of group differences are not provided in SPSS, but they are calculated here to provide pairwise effect size information. As the Levene's test showed that the population variances are equal, we use Formula 14.31, with the values for the components in this formula taken from the SPSS output in Figure 14.9: $MS_W = 75.982$, $\bar{Y}_1 - \bar{Y}_2 = 2.97$, $\bar{Y}_1 - \bar{Y}_3 = 3.19$, and $\bar{Y}_2 - \bar{Y}_3 = 0.22$. With this, the pairwise effect sizes for the three ethnic groups (1 = Caucasian, 2 = African-American, 3 = Hispanic) are: $d_{1,2} = |2.97|/\sqrt{75.982} = 0.34$, $d_{1,3} = |3.19|/\sqrt{75.982} = 0.37$, and $d_{2,3} = |0.22|/\sqrt{75.982} = 0.02$. Thus, the Caucasian group outperformed the African-American and Hispanic groups by an effect size of a small to medium magnitude (0.34 and 0.37, respectively), whereas the effect size for the difference between the African-American and Hispanic groups was negligible (0.02).

Table 14.2 *Means and Standard Deviations for Three Ethnic Groups on Reading*

Ethnicity	*N*	*M*	*SD*
Caucasian	993	29.52	8.70
African- American	889	26.56	8.56
Hispanic	348	26.34	9.15

Figure 14.9 *SPSS output for one-factor ANOVA comparing three ethnic groups on reading*

Descriptive Statistics

Dependent Variable:Reading

Ethnicity	Mean	Std. Deviation	N
1	29.52	8.696	993
2	26.56	8.564	889
3	26.34	9.150	348
Total	27.84	8.842	2230

Levene's Test of Equality of Error Variances

Dependent Variable:Reading

F	df1	df2	Sig.
1.545	2	2227	.214

Tests of Between-Subjects Effects

Dependent Variable:Reading

Source	Type III Sum of Squares	df	Mean Square	F	Sig.	Partial Eta Squared
Corrected Model	5068.565[a]	2	2534.283	33.354	.000	.029
Intercept	1357107.404	1	1357107.404	17860.990	.000	.889
Ethnicity	5068.565	2	2534.283	33.354	.000	.029
Error	169211.128	2227	75.982			
Total	1903166.000	2230				
Corrected Total	174279.693	2229				

Multiple Comparisons

Reading
Tukey HSD

(I) Ethnicity	(J) Ethnicity	Mean Difference (I-J)	Std. Error	Sig.	95% Confidence Interval Lower Bound	95% Confidence Interval Upper Bound
1	2	2.97*	.402	.000	2.03	3.91
	3	3.19*	.543	.000	1.91	4.46
2	1	-2.97*	.402	.000	-3.91	-2.03
	3	.22	.551	.918	-1.08	1.51
3	1	-3.19*	.543	.000	-4.46	-1.91
	2	-.22	.551	.918	-1.51	1.08

14.12 Summary

Analysis of variance (ANOVA) is used as an omnibus test of differences among K groups (H_0: $\mu_1 = \mu_2 = \ldots = \mu_K$). In the case of two groups ($K = 2$), ANOVA and the t-test for independent samples provide equal results about the probability for Type-I error in rejecting H_0: $\mu_1 = \mu_2$. In the case of more than two groups ($K > 2$), however, ANOVA maintains the overall probability of Type-I error (family-wise α^*) at a pre-specified level, whereas this probability is inflated when the method of pairwise t-tests is used instead.

- **Assumptions in ANOVA**
  There are three primary assumptions in ANOVA— *independence*, *normality*, and *homogeneity of variance*. **Independence** means that the sample observations are independent of each other, **normality** means that the theoretical distribution of scores are normal, and **homogeneity of variance** means that the variances of all theoretical distributions of scores are equal. There is also an assumption of **linearity** according to which an individual score, Y_{ik}, can be represented as a sum of the grand mean, $\mu_\bullet$, the effect α_k, and the residual of the score, ε_{ik}.

- **Effects in ANOVA**
  The deviation of a population mean from the grand mean ($\alpha_k = \mu_k - \mu_\cdot$) is called **effect** for this population; ($k = 1, 2, \ldots, K$). The sum all effects equals zero: $\sum \alpha_k = 0$. The sum of all squared effects equals zero only when H_0 is true, that is H_0: $\sum \alpha_k^2 = 0$.

- **Within-group and between-group variance**
  The "pooled" variance of the sample variances of all groups represents an estimate of the population error variance, σ_ϵ^2, called the *within-groups variance* or **mean squares within** (MS_W). The variance of the sample means of the K groups is called *between-groups variance* or **mean squares between** (MS_B). While MS_W is entirely random, MS_B consists of two parts — a random part and a part due to differences among the population means (if such differences exist).

- **Testing the null hypothesis in ANOVA**
  When H_0 is true, there are no differences among the population means. In this case, the MS_B and MS_W are both random thus each representing an estimate of the population error variance, σ_ϵ^2. Therefore, when H_0 is true, the ratio of MS_B and MS_W is distributed according to the F-distribution, $F = MS_B/MS_W$. With this F-ratio, the degrees of freedom are $K - 1$, for the numerator, and $(n_1 + n_2 + \cdots + n_K - K)$ for the denominator. The null hypothesis is rejected when the computed test statistic ($F = MS_B/MS_W$) exceeds the F-critical value at the specified level of significance, α [or, equivalently, when the p-value of the F-statistic is smaller than the specified level of significance: $p < \alpha$.]

- **Multiple comparisons**
  When the omnibus null hypothesis (H_0: $\mu_1 = \mu_2 = \ldots = \mu_K$) is rejected, **multiple comparisons** (MC) techniques are used to determine exactly which differences are statistically significant. MC methods that involve the comparison of all possible pairs of means after rejecting the omnibus H_0 are called **post hoc comparisons** (e.g., the Tukey and Bonferroni MC methods). In contrast, MC methods are called **planned comparisons** when they test hypotheses specified *prior* to testing the omnibus null hypothesis (e.g., the Dunnett MC method). Each planned null hypothesis is tested by testing a specific **contrast** Ψ — a linear combination of the group means, where the sum of all coefficients is zero, by using a t-statistic for this contrast (Formula 14.28).

- **Effect size**

The **effect size** of the difference between two population means in ANOVA is defined by the standardized absolute value of this difference (see Formula 14.30). When the assumption of equal variances is met, Formula 14.31 is recommended for the estimation of the effect size. If this assumption is not met, Formula 14.32 can be used instead. The proportion of the total variance in the dependent variable, *Y*, accounted for by the differences among the groups is referred to as an **omnibus effect size,** η^2 (Formula 14.33). As η^2 (eta squared) shows the amount of variation in *Y* accounted for by the group differences for a particular sample, an adjustment of η^2 for the population, denoted ω^2 **(omega squared)**, is also used (Formula 14.34).

- **Determining the sample size**

The approach to determining sample size for ANOVA is based on prespecified values for the **level of significance** (α), **power** (*P*), **effect size** (*d*), **and number of groups**, *K*. In general terms, the sample-size question is: "How large must the sample be in order to detect a difference with an effect size *d*, for the largest separation between two ANOVA groups, at the specified level of significance, α, and power *P*?" Sample-size tables for the .05 and .01 levels of significance and different power values are available in the literature (Hinkle & Oliver, 1983).

- **Consequences of violating the ANOVA assumptions**

Violations of the **normality** assumption have negligible consequences on the chances for Type-I and Type-II error in testing the null hypothesis unless (a) the population distributions are highly skewed, (b) the *n*'s (sample sizes of the groups) are very small, and/or (c) one-sided tests are used [which applies only for the special case of ANOVA with two groups ($K = 2$)].

Violations of the **homogeneity of variance** assumption have negligible consequences on the chances for Type-I and Type-II error when the ANOVA design is *balanced* (equal *n*'s). When the design is not balanced, ANOVA yields either "conservative" or "liberal" results.

Violations of the **independence** assumption have serious consequences on the accuracy of the ANOVA results. When the individual observations within experimental groups are not independent, it would be better to compute the group means and conduct ANOVA by using the groups as observational units.

Violations of the **linearity** assumption occur when the differences among groups in a one-factor ANOVA model are not the same across distinct subgroups of people (e.g., males, females). In this case, it is recommended that researchers use ANOVA with two (or more) factors defined by such subgroups (e.g., gender).

14.13 Study Questions

1. To keep the family-wise α* at the .05 level when using pairwise *t*-tests for the null hypothesis in ANOVA with 3 groups, what level of significance, α, is required for each separate *t*-test? [*Hint*: use Formula 14.2.]
2. What are the three primary assumptions in ANOVA?
3. In one-factor ANOVA for the comparison of four ethnic groups on communication skills, the population error variance, σ_ϵ^2, represents difference in communication skills among

   (a) people from different ethnic groups,

   (b) people from the same ethnic group,

   (c) None of the above.

4. For the data in Figure 14.2, compute the effect estimates for the three ethnic groups, $\hat{\alpha}_1$, $\hat{\alpha}_2$, and $\hat{\alpha}_3$ [*Hint*: use Formula 14.8.]

5. Two dosages of a drug (D_1 and D_2) and a placebo are used in a treatment for reducing anxiety. Using a one-factor ANOVA design, the researcher plans to test (a) whether the two drug dosages produce different effects and (b) whether the joint average effect of the two drugs is different from the placebo effect in reducing anxiety. The null hypotheses for these two questions are H_{01}: $\mu_1 = \mu_2$ and H_{02}: $(\mu_1 + \mu_2)/2 = \mu_3$, where μ_1, μ_2, and μ_3 are the population means of the treatment groups taking dosage D_1, dosage D_2, and placebo, respectively. Among the triplets of contrast coefficients (c_1 c_2 c_3) given below, which one is appropriate to test for H_{01} and which one for H_{02}? [*Hint*: see Section 14.7.2.1]

   A. (1 0 −1), **B.** (1 −1 0), **C.** (2 0 −1), **D.** (1 1 −2), **E.** (1 −1 2).

6. Figure 14.4 provides the SPSS output for the Tukey pairwise post hoc comparisons between three ethnic groups (1 = Caucasian, 2 = African-American, and 3 = Hispanic) on their improved performance on a math test as a result of a new school program for integrative bilingual education. The estimate of the within-groups variance is provided in both Figures 14.2 and 14.3 ($MS_W = 37.333$). Given these results, use Formula 14.31 to compute the effect size of the mean difference for each pair of the three ethnic groups [disregard the fact that none of the pairwise differences is statistically significant].

7. Given the results from the SPSS output in Figure 14.3, compute the omnibus effect size η^2 (*eta squared*) and its adjusted for the population version, ω^2 (*omega squared*), using Formulas 14.33 and 14.34, respectively; [ignore the fact that the main effect of Ethnicity is not statistically significant, $F(2, 9) = 3.00, p = .10$].

8. Suppose you have decided that the largest effect size among all pairs of six treatment groups must be at least one standard deviation large to be practically important. How many observations must you use in a one-factor ANOVA design to detect the desired effect size at the .05 level of significance with a test power of .85? [*Hint*: use Table 14.1.]

9. Suppose that the ANOVA *F*-test provides evidence to reject the null hypothesis at the .05 level ($p < .05$). At the same time, however, the Levene's test indicates that the ANOVA assumption of equal variances is not met. If the examination of the results shows that larger variances are paired with larger samples, what would be your decision about H_0 at the .05 level (reject or fail to reject)? (*Hint*: see NOTE [14.5]).

10. Using the SPSS data file **RMS-5.sav** [http://cehd.gmu.edu/book/dimitov], perform a one-factor AVOVA to test for differences in math test scores (variable **math**) among three ethnic groups (variable **Ethnicity**) coded in this data file as follows: 1 = Caucasian, 2 = African-American, and 3 = Hispanic. Follow the analysis described in Section 14.11 for the comparison of the same three groups on *reading* and the interpretations provided there for the results in Figure 14.9. [To test the distribution of math scores for normality, use the normal Q-Q plot approach described in Chapter 7, Section 7.1.5.]

CHAPTER 15

TWO- AND THREE-FACTOR ANOVA

The analysis of variance (ANOVA) is not limited to a single factor. The variety and complexity of phenomena and relationships investigated in educational research often dictate the use of two, three, or more factors such as ethnicity, gender, teaching method, demographic area, etc. For example, using one-factor ANOVA to compare ethnic groups on math proficiency does not allow the researcher to test whether the ethnic differences in math proficiency remain the same for males and females. If some (or all) ethnic differences depend on gender, there is an interaction between ethnicity and gender. The presence of such an interaction may mask existing ethnic differences that remain undetected with one-factor ANOVA. In general, an **interaction** between two factors means that the difference in the dependent variable between any two levels of one factor varies across levels of the other factor. Using ANOVA with two or more factors allows the researcher to (a) investigate the role of different sources of error in accounting for the variance in the dependent variable, (b) detect and interpret interactions between factors, and (c) increase the power of tests for differences among factor levels and interactions among factors.

15.1 Two-factor ANOVA

15.1.1 Null Hypotheses in Two-factor ANOVA

Consider again Example 14.1 (Chapter 14, Section 14.4) but this time, in addition to ethnicity, we will also take gender into account to explain differences in math scores. The data layout in Figure 14.2 is now extended to that shown in Figure 15.1 to include two factors: gender and ethnicity. The scores indicate the improvement made by middle schools students on a math test as a result of an experimental school program that incorporates bilingual (English-Spanish) interpretation of mathematics concepts and principles.

In Figure 15.1 (left panel), the column means ($\bar{Y}_{\bullet 1}$, $\bar{Y}_{\bullet 2}$, $\bar{Y}_{\bullet 3}$) are sample estimates of the population means ($\mu_{\bullet 1}$, $\mu_{\bullet 2}$, $\mu_{\bullet 3}$) for the three ethnic groups, whereas the row means ($\bar{Y}_{1\bullet}$, $\bar{Y}_{2\bullet}$) are sample estimates of the population means ($\mu_{1\bullet}$, $\mu_{2\bullet}$) for females and males, respectively. The sample grand mean ($\bar{Y}_{\bullet\bullet}$) is an estimate of the population grand mean ($\mu_{\bullet\bullet}$). The SPSS entry (right panel) shows the scores and the coding values for Ethnicity (1 = Caucasian, 2 = African-American, 3 = Hispanic) and Gender (0 = female, 1 = male). Under this **two-factor ANOVA** (or **two-way ANOVA**) model, the following three null hypotheses are testable:

H_{01}: $\mu_{1\bullet} = \mu_{2\bullet}$; [**No gender differences** (ethnicity ignored)]
H_{02}: $\mu_{\bullet 1} = \mu_{\bullet 2} = \mu_{\bullet 3}$; [**No ethnic differences** (gender ignored)]
H_{03}: **There is NO interaction between *Gender* and *Ethnicity*.**

In the general case of two factors, with J levels in Factor A and K levels in Factor B, the null hypotheses with the (A x B) two-factor ANOVA are:

H_{01}: $\mu_{1\bullet} = \mu_{2\bullet} = \ldots = \mu_{J\bullet}$ **(15.1)**
H_{02}: $\mu_{\bullet 1} = \mu_{\bullet 2} = \ldots = \mu_{\bullet K}$ **(15.2)**
H_{03}: There is NO interaction between factors A and B. **(15.3)**

When H_{01} is rejected, we say that there is a statistically significant **main effect** of factor A. Likewise, when H_{02} is rejected, there is a statistically significant **main effect** of factor B. When H_{03} is rejected, there is a statistically significant **interaction** between the factors A and B. The notation (J x K) ANOVA indicates that this is a two-factor ANOVA with J levels in the first factor and K levels in the second factor. For example, Figure 15.1 depicts a 2 x 3 ANOVA ($J = 2$, $K = 3$), which can be referred to also as *Gender* x *Ethnicity* ANOVA. The order of the factors is irrelevant, but typically A x B means that A is the "row" factor and B is the "column" factor.

Figure 15.1 *Data layout for two-factor (gender x ethnicity) ANOVA*

	ETHNICITY			
GENDER	Caucasian	Afr-Amer	Hispanic	
Female	11, 7	12, 8	24, 28	$\bar{Y}_{1\bullet} = 15$
Male	10, 4	11, 9	6, 14	$\bar{Y}_{2\bullet} = 9$
	$\bar{Y}_{\bullet 1} = 8$	$\bar{Y}_{\bullet 2} = 10$	$\bar{Y}_{\bullet 3} = 18$	$\bar{Y}_{\bullet\bullet} = 12$

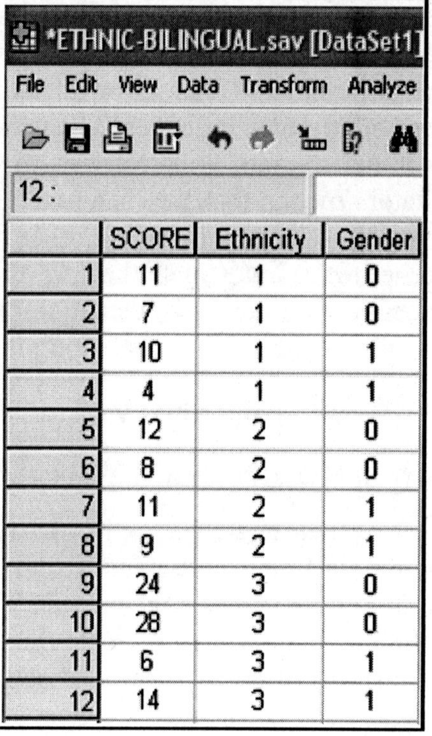

*ETHNIC-BILINGUAL.sav [DataSet1]

File Edit View Data Transform Analyze

12 :

	SCORE	Ethnicity	Gender
1	11	1	0
2	7	1	0
3	10	1	1
4	4	1	1
5	12	2	0
6	8	2	0
7	11	2	1
8	9	2	1
9	24	3	0
10	28	3	0
11	6	3	1
12	14	3	1

15.1.2 Assumptions in Two-factor ANOVA

The assumptions of *normality*, *homogeneity of variance*, and *independence* in one-factor ANOVA remain in two-factor ANOVA. The difference is that the population distribution and its error variance, σ_ε^2, are not the same in one- and two-factor ANOVA models. For the ANOVA model in Figure 15.1, for example, there are six population distributions of scores for students with the same gender and ethnicity. That is, the two scores in each cell represent a random sample of two observations ($n = 2$) from the population distribution of scores for students with the same gender and ethnicity. For example, the cell mean for Caucasian females (first row, first column), $\bar{Y}_{11} = 9$, is a sample estimate of the population mean for all Caucasian females, μ_{11}. Likewise, the other five cell means, $\bar{Y}_{12} = 10$, $\bar{Y}_{13} = 26$, $\bar{Y}_{21} = 7$, $\bar{Y}_{22} = 10$, and $\bar{Y}_{23} = 10$ are estimates of the population cell means, μ_{12}, μ_{13}, μ_{21}, μ_{22}, and μ_{23}, respectively. Under the ANOVA assumptions of normality and homogeneity of variance, all six population distributions are normal and have equal variances, $\sigma_{11}^2 = \sigma_{12}^2 = \sigma_{13}^2 = \sigma_{21}^2 = \sigma_{22}^2 = \sigma_{23}^2$, denoted σ_ε^2 (*population error variance*) — see Figure 15.2 [compare to Figure 14.1].

Figure 15.2 *Population distributions for 2 x 3 ANOVA*

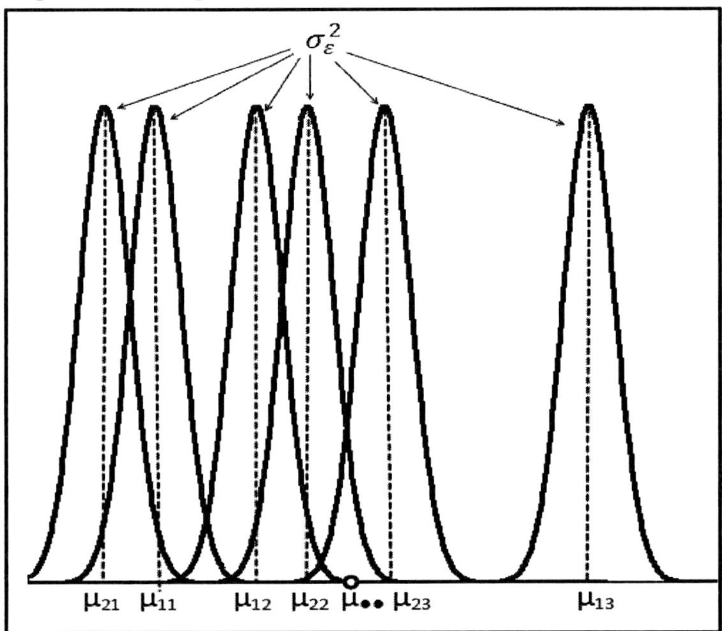

15.1.3 Effects in Two-factor ANOVA

The concept of effects in one-factor ANOVA, introduced in Chapter 14 (Section 14.3), is extended here to that of effects in two-factor ANOVA. Consider a two-factor (A x B) ANOVA with *J* levels for factor A and *K* levels for factor B. If depicted in a two-way (*J* x *K*) ANOVA table, there are *J* horizontal rows (factor A), *K* columns (factor B), and *JK* cells. There are three types of effects with the two-factor ANOVA:

- **Row effects** (for the levels of factor A):

$$\alpha_j = \mu_{j\bullet} - \mu_{\bullet\bullet}\ ;\ (j = 1, 2, \ldots, J) \quad \textbf{(15.4)}$$

- **Column effects** (for the levels of factor B)

$$\beta_k = \mu_{\bullet k} - \mu_{\bullet\bullet}\ ;\ (k = 1, 2, \ldots, K) \quad \textbf{(15.5)}$$

- **Cell effects** (interaction terms):

$$\alpha\beta_{jk} = \mu_{jk} - (\mu_{\bullet\bullet} + \alpha_j + \beta_k) \quad \textbf{(15.6)}$$

After replacing the values of $\alpha_{j\bullet}$ and $\beta_{\bullet k}$ from (15.4) and (15.5) into (15.6) and using some simple algebra, the interaction term can be represented as follows:

$$\alpha\beta_{jk} = \mu_{jk} - \mu_{j\bullet} - \mu_{\bullet k} + \mu_{\bullet\bullet} \quad \textbf{(15.7)}$$

As Equation 15.6 shows, the interaction term $\alpha\beta_{jk}$ is obtained by subtracting from the cell mean (μ_{jk}) the total effect ($\mu_{\bullet\bullet}$), the row effect (α_j), and the column effect (β_k). Thus, the interaction term is obtained from the cell mean after "partialling" out all other effects (total effect, row effect, and column effect) that affect the cell mean. While Equation 15.6 clarifies the meaning of interaction terms, $\alpha\beta_{jk}$, Equation 15.7 is more convenient for computations of their sample estimate (see Figure 15.3).

Figure 15.3 *Estimation of effects in two-factor ANOVA*

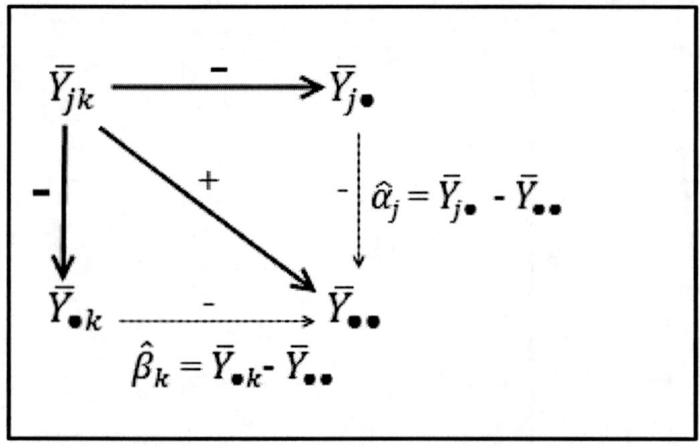

Thus, α_j is the effect produced by the row mean $\mu_{j\bullet}$, β_k is the effect produced by the column mean $\mu_{\bullet k}$, and $\alpha\beta_{jk}$ is the effect produced by the cell mean μ_{jk}. If Y_{ijk} is the score of person *i* in the cell located at row *j* and column *k*, the deviation of this score from the cell mean is the *error term* for the score, $\varepsilon_{ijk} = Y_{ijk} - \mu_{jk}$, referred to also as the **random effect** of score Y_{ijk}.

In the general case of *J* levels in Factor A and *K* levels in Factor B, each "effect" represents a deviation from the mean and, therefore, the sum of all row effects equals zero ($\sum \alpha_j = 0$), the sum of all column effects equals zero ($\sum \beta_k = 0$), and the sum of all interaction terms equals zero ($\sum\sum \alpha\beta_{jk} = 0$); ($j$ = 1, 2, …, J; k = 1, 2, …, K). However, the sum of squared effects for the levels of a factor (or interaction between factors) equals zero *only if* the null hypothesis for this factor (or interaction between factors) is true. Thus, the null hypotheses with the (A x B) two-factor ANOVA (see Equations 15.1-15.3) can be represented by using row effects, column effects, and interaction terms, respectively:

Main effect of factor A, H_{01}: $\sum \alpha_j^2 = 0$, **(15.8)**

Main effect of factor B, H_{02}: $\sum \beta_k^2 = 0$, **(15.9)**

Interaction between factors A and B, H_{03}: $\sum\sum (\alpha\beta_{jk})^2 = 0$, **(15.10)**

where the summations are for j = 1, 2, …, J and k = 1, 2, …, K.

EXAMPLE 15.1 This example illustrates how to calculate sample estimates of row effects, column effects, and interaction terms in two-factor ANOVA using the data in Figure 15.1. The estimation of error terms is also illustrated. Using the computation formulas provided in Figure 15.3, we obtain sample estimates of the effects of gender levels (row effects), ethnic levels (column effects), and interaction terms as follows:

Effects of gender levels (row effects): $\hat{\alpha}_1 = \bar{Y}_{1\bullet} - \bar{Y}_{\bullet\bullet} = 15 - 12 = 3$,

$\hat{\alpha}_2 = \bar{Y}_{2\bullet} - \bar{Y}_{\bullet\bullet} = 9 - 12 = -3$.

Effects of ethnic levels (column effects): $\hat{\beta}_1 = \bar{Y}_{\bullet 1} - \bar{Y}_{\bullet\bullet} = 8 - 12 = -4$,

$\hat{\beta}_2 = \bar{Y}_{\bullet 2} - \bar{Y}_{\bullet\bullet} = 10 - 12 = -2$,

$\hat{\beta}_3 = \bar{Y}_{\bullet 3} - \bar{Y}_{\bullet\bullet} = 18 - 12 = 6$.

Interaction terms: $\widehat{\alpha\beta}_{11} = \bar{Y}_{11} - \bar{Y}_{1\bullet} - \bar{Y}_{\bullet 1} + \bar{Y}_{\bullet\bullet} = 9 - 15 - 8 + 12 = 21 - 23 = -2$,
$\widehat{\alpha\beta}_{12} = \bar{Y}_{12} - \bar{Y}_{1\bullet} - \bar{Y}_{\bullet 2} + \bar{Y}_{\bullet\bullet} = 10 - 15 - 10 + 12 = 22 - 25 = -3$,
$\widehat{\alpha\beta}_{13} = \bar{Y}_{13} - \bar{Y}_{1\bullet} - \bar{Y}_{\bullet 3} + \bar{Y}_{\bullet\bullet} = 26 - 15 - 18 + 12 = 38 - 33 = 5$,
$\widehat{\alpha\beta}_{21} = \bar{Y}_{21} - \bar{Y}_{2\bullet} - \bar{Y}_{\bullet 1} + \bar{Y}_{\bullet\bullet} = 7 - 9 - 8 + 12 = 19 - 17 = 2$,
$\widehat{\alpha\beta}_{22} = \bar{Y}_{22} - \bar{Y}_{2\bullet} - \bar{Y}_{\bullet 2} + \bar{Y}_{\bullet\bullet} = 10 - 9 - 10 + 12 = 22 - 19 = 3$,
$\widehat{\alpha\beta}_{23} = \bar{Y}_{23} - \bar{Y}_{2\bullet} - \bar{Y}_{\bullet 3} + \bar{Y}_{\bullet\bullet} = 10 - 9 - 18 + 12 = 22 - 27 = -5$.

The estimation of error terms for an individual observation, $\varepsilon_{ijk} = Y_{ijk} - \mu_{jk}$, is performed by replacing the population cell mean, μ_{jk}, with its sample estimate, $\bar{Y}_{jk}$. Thus, $\hat{\varepsilon}_{ijk} = Y_{ijk} - \bar{Y}_{jk}$. For example, the error terms for the two observations in the first cell (i = 1, k = 1) in Figure 15.1 are: $\hat{\varepsilon}_{111} = Y_{111} - \bar{Y}_{11} = 11 - 9 = 2$ and $\hat{\varepsilon}_{211} = Y_{211} - \bar{Y}_{11} = 7 - 9 = -2$. Likewise, the error terms of the observations for the "Male-Hispanic" cell (i = 2, k = 3) are: $\hat{\varepsilon}_{123} = Y_{123} - \bar{Y}_{23} = 6 - 10 = -4$ and $\hat{\varepsilon}_{223} = Y_{223} - \bar{Y}_{23} = 14 - 10 = 4$, etc. Note that the sum of error terms within a cell equals zero, and that the sum of all row effects equals zero ($\sum \hat{\alpha}_j = 3 - 3 = 0$), the sum of all column effects equals zero ($\sum \hat{\beta}_k = -4 - 2 + 6 = 0$), and the sum of all interaction terms equals zero ($\sum \sum \widehat{\alpha\beta}_{jk} = -2 - 3 + 5 + 2 + 3 - 5 = 0$).

15.1.4 Linear Model for the Data in Two-factor ANOVA

The **linear model** for the data in two-factor ANOVA is an extension of its counterpart for one-factor ANOVA (see Chapter 14, Section 14.5) to accommodate for the presence of two factors and a possible interaction between them:

$$Y_{ijk} - \mu_{\bullet\bullet} + \alpha_j + \beta_k + \alpha\beta_{jk} + \varepsilon_{ijk}, \tag{15.11}$$

where Y_{ijk} is the score of person i in the cell located at row j and column k, and ε_{ijk} is the error term of Y_{ijk} ($\varepsilon_{ijk} = Y_{ijk} - \mu_{jk}$). The variance of error terms, ε_{ijk}, across all observations for the population within a cell is the *population error variance*, σ_ε^2 (see Figure 15.2). According to the ANOVA linear model in Equation 15.11, each individual score can be represented as a sum of five effects: total effect ($\mu_{\bullet\bullet}$), row effect ($\alpha_{j\bullet}$), column effect ($\beta_{k\bullet}$), interaction effect ($\alpha\beta_{jk}$), and random effect (ε_{ijk}). By moving the grand mean ($\mu_{\bullet\bullet}$) from the right-hand side in Equation 15.11 into its left-hand side (with an opposite sign), we obtain the linear model for the deviation of individual scores from the grand mean:

$$Y_{ijk} - \mu_{\bullet\bullet} = \alpha_j + \beta_k + \alpha\beta_{jk} + \varepsilon_{ijk}. \tag{15.12}$$

The deviation ($Y_{ijk} - \mu_{\bullet\bullet}$) is the building unit of the total variability in the dependent variable, Y. By squaring both sides of Equation 15.12 and using some summation algebra, we can see that the total variation in Y equals the sum of the squared effects of rows, columns, interaction terms, and error terms:

$$\sum\sum\sum(Y_{ijk} - \mu_{\bullet\bullet})^2 = \sum \alpha_j^2 + \sum \beta_k^2 + \sum\sum(\alpha\beta_{jk})^2 + \sum\sum\sum \varepsilon_{ijk}^2 \tag{15.13}$$

where the triple summation is across subjects (i), rows (j), and columns (k). Note that the first three terms in the right-hand side in Equation 15.13 are used to represent the three null hypotheses in two-factor ANOVA (Equations 15.8, 15.9, and 15.10, respectively).

15.1.5 Sum of Squares in Two-factor ANOVA

Let's assume that the two-factor (A x B) ANOVA design is *balanced*, with n observations in each cell (j, k), where $j = 1, 2, \ldots, J$ and k = 1, 2, …, K. This simplifies the analytic presentation without any loss of generality for the case when the ANOVA design is unbalanced. The sample estimate of the sum in the left-hand side in Equation 15.13 is the **total sum of squares** (SS_T). That is,

$$SS_T = \sum\sum\sum(Y_{ijk} - \bar{Y}_{\bullet\bullet})^2, \qquad \textbf{(15.14)}$$

where the triple summation is across $i = 1, 2, \ldots, n$; $j = 1, 2, \ldots, J$, and $k = 1, 2, \ldots, K$. The four components of the SS_T (estimates of the four terms in the right-hand side in Equation 15.13) are:

- **Sum of squares for factor A:**

$$SS_A = (nK)\sum \hat{\alpha}_j^2 = (nK)\sum(\bar{Y}_{j\bullet} - \bar{Y}_{\bullet\bullet})^2, \qquad \textbf{(15.15)}$$

where (nK) is the number of observations used in the computation of the row mean, $\bar{Y}_{j\bullet}$.

- **Sum of squares for factor B:**

$$SS_B = (nJ)\sum \hat{\beta}_k^2 = (nJ)\sum(\bar{Y}_{\bullet k} - \bar{Y}_{\bullet\bullet})^2, \qquad \textbf{(15.16)}$$

where (nJ) is the number of observations used in the computation of the column mean, $\bar{Y}_{\bullet k}$.

- **Sum of squares for the A x B interaction:**

$$SS_{AB} = n\sum\sum(\widehat{\alpha\beta}_{jk})^2 = n\sum\sum(\bar{Y}_{jk} - \bar{Y}_{j\bullet} - \bar{Y}_{\bullet k} + \bar{Y}_{\bullet\bullet})^2, \qquad \textbf{(15.17)}$$

where n is the number of observations used in the computation of the cell mean, $\bar{Y}_{jk}$.

- **Sum of squares within cells:**

$$SS_W = \sum\sum\sum \hat{\varepsilon}_{ijk}^2 = \sum\sum\sum(Y_{ijk} - \bar{Y}_{jk})^2 \qquad \textbf{(15.18)}$$

Thus, the sample-based equivalent of Equation 15.13 for partitioning the total variability into four components is

$$\mathbf{SS_T = SS_A + SS_B + SS_{AB} + SS_W.} \qquad \textbf{(15.19)}$$

EXAMPLE 15.2 This example illustrates how to calculate the sum of squares for the two-factor ANOVA data in Figure 15.1, where factor A = *Gender* and Factor B = *Ethnicity*. Using Equations 15.15, 15.6, and 15.7, with some intermediate results from Example 15.1, two observations per cell ($n = 2$), two levels of factor A ($J = 2$), and three levels of factor B ($K = 3$), we obtain

$$SS_A = (nK)\sum \hat{\alpha}_j^2 = (2)(3)(\hat{\alpha}_1^2 + \hat{\alpha}_2^2) = (6)[3^2 + (-3)^2] = (6)(9 + 9) = (6)(18) = 108,$$

$$SS_B = (nJ)\sum \beta_k^2 = (2)(2)(\beta_1^2 + \beta_2^2 + \beta_3^2) = (4)[(-4)^2 + (-2)^2 + 6^2] = (4)(16 + 4 + 36) = 224,$$

$$SS_{AB} = n\sum\sum(\widehat{\alpha\beta}_{jk})^2 = (2)[(\widehat{\alpha\beta}_{11})^2 + (\widehat{\alpha\beta}_{12})^2 + (\widehat{\alpha\beta}_{13})^2 + (\widehat{\alpha\beta}_{21})^2 + (\widehat{\alpha\beta}_{22})^2 + (\widehat{\alpha\beta}_{23})^2]$$
$$= (2)[(-2)^2 + (-3)^2 + 5^2 + 2^2 + 3^2 + (-5)^2] = (2)(4 + 9 + 25 + 4 + 9 + 25) = (2)(76) = 152.$$

To calculate $SS_W = \sum\sum\sum \hat{\varepsilon}^2_{ijk}$, we use the values provided in Example 15.1 of four error terms in two cells [$\hat{\varepsilon}_{111} = 2$, $\hat{\varepsilon}_{211} = -2$, $\hat{\varepsilon}_{123} = -4$, $\hat{\varepsilon}_{223} = 4$] and the values of the eight error terms in the remaining four cells [the computation of which is not shown here for space consideration] thus obtaining the sum of squares within cells:

$$SS_W = \hat{\varepsilon}^2_{111} + \hat{\varepsilon}^2_{211} + \ldots + \hat{\varepsilon}^2_{123} + \hat{\varepsilon}^2_{223}$$
$$= 2^2 + (-2)^2 + 2^2 + (-2)^2 + (-2)^2 + 2^2 + 3^2 + (-3)^2 + 1^2 + (-1)^2 + (-4)^2 + 4^2 = 76.$$

As all terms in the right-hand side of Equation15.19 are now known, we can compute the *sum of squares total*:

$SS_T = SS_A + SS_B + SS_{AB} + SS_W = 108 + 224 + 152 + 76 = 560.$
Thus, we have: $SS_A = 108$, $SS_B = 224$, $SS_{AB} = 152$, $SS_W = 76$, and $SS_T = 560$.

15.1.6 Mean Squares in Two-factor ANOVA

By taking the ratio of each sum of squares (SS) to its degrees of freedom (*df*), we can obtain the **mean squares (MS)** — estimates of the population variances of the effects for factor A, factor B, their interaction (A x B), and the population variance, σ^2_ε. The degrees of freedom for the sum of squares (SS_A, SS_B, SS_{AB}, and SS_W) are obtained as follows:

$$df_A = J - 1,\ df_B = K - 1,\ df_{AB} = (J - 1)(K - 1), \text{ and } df_W = JK(n - 1) \qquad \textbf{(15.20)}$$

Thus, the corresponding mean squares are:

$$MS_A = \frac{SS_A}{J - 1},\ MS_B = \frac{SS_B}{K - 1},\ MS_{AB} = \frac{SS_{AB}}{(J - 1)(K - 1)}, \text{ and } MS_W = \frac{SS_W}{JK(n - 1)}. \qquad \textbf{(15.21)}$$

EXAMPLE 15.3 This example illustrates how to calculate the mean squares for the two-factor ANOVA data in Figure 15.1. Using the formulas for mean squares in (15.21), with $n = 2$, $J = 2$, $K = 3$, and the sum of squares obtained in Example 15.2 ($SS_A = 108$, $SS_B = 224$, $SS_{AB} = 152$, and $SS_W = 76$), we have:

$$MS_A = \frac{SS_A}{J - 1} = \frac{108}{2 - 1} = 108,$$

$$MS_B = \frac{SS_B}{K - 1} = \frac{224}{3 - 1} = 112,$$

$$MS_{AB} = \frac{SS_{AB}}{(J - 1)(K - 1)} = \frac{152}{(2 - 1)(3 - 1)} = 76, \text{ and}$$

$$MS_W = \frac{SS_W}{JK(n - 1)} = \frac{76}{(2)(3)(2 - 1)} = 12.667.$$

The within-cells variance for the sample, MS_W, is entirely random, thus representing an estimate of the population error variance, σ^2_ε. In general, MS_A consists of two parts (variance components): a random part and a part that is due to differences (if any) among the levels of factors A. Likewise, MS_B consists of two parts: a random part and a part due to differences (if any) among the levels of factors B. Finally, MS_{AB} also consists of a random part and a part due to interaction (if any) between the two factors, A and B.

15.1.7 Testing the Null Hypotheses in Two-factor ANOVA

As discussed earlier, three null hypotheses are testable in two-factor ANOVA — two main effects and an interaction effect (see, 15.8, 15.9, and 15.10):

Main effect of factor A, H_{01}: $\sum \alpha_j^2 = 0$,
Main effect of factor B, H_{02}: $\sum \beta_k^2 = 0$,
Interaction between factors A and B, H_{03}: $\sum\sum(\alpha\beta_{jk})^2 = 0$.

The logic behind the *F*-test for the null hypothesis in one-factor ANOVA (Chapter 14, Section 14.6) carries over into testing the three null hypotheses in two-factor ANOVA. For example, if H_{01} is true, MS_A does not contain a variance component due to differences among the levels in factor A and, therefore, consists only of a random variance component. In other words, when H_{01} is true, MS_A represents a sample estimate of the population error variance, σ_ε^2. Thus, when H_{01} is true, MS_A and MS_W represent two sample estimates of the same population variance, σ_ε^2, and, therefore, their ratio must follow the *F*-distribution. This yields the following *F*-statistic for H_{01} (main effect of factor A):

$$F_A = \frac{MS_A}{MS_W} \tag{15.22}$$

Likewise, the following *F*-statistics are used to test H_{02} (the main effect of factor A) and H_{03} (the interaction between factors A and B), respectively:

$$F_B = \frac{MS_B}{MS_W} \text{ and } F_{AB} = \frac{MS_{AB}}{MS_W} \tag{15.23}$$

> **NOTE [15.1] The *F*-test for a specific main effect in two-factor ANOVA is generally more powerful than the *F*-test for that effect in one-factor ANOVA.** This is because the MS_W with the former (*within-cell variance*) is smaller than the MS_W with the latter (*within-column variance*).

EXAMPLE 15.4 This example illustrates how to calculate the *F*-ratios and how to use them in testing the null hypotheses for the two-factor ANOVA data in Figure 15.1 (factor A = *Gender* and Factor B = *Ethnicity*) at the .05 level of significance. The values of the dependent variable in this case are scores that indicate the improvement made by middle school students on a math test as a result of an experimental school program that incorporates bilingual (English-Spanish) interpretation of mathematics concepts and principles (see Chapter 14, Example 14.1). We will briefly refer to these scores here as "math gain scores."

As the mean squares for these data are already known from Example 15.3 ($MS_A = 108$, $MS_B = 112$, $MS_{AB} = 76$, and $MS_W = 12.667$), we use directly Formulas 15.22 and 15 as follows:

$$F_A = \frac{MS_A}{MS_W} = \frac{108}{12.667} = 8.526;\ F_B = \frac{MS_B}{MS_W} = \frac{112}{12.667} = 8.842;\text{ and } F_{AB} = \frac{MS_{AB}}{MS_W} = \frac{76}{12.667} = 6.00$$

Using Formulas 15.20, we compute the degrees of freedom (*df*) for each *F*-ratio. Note that the two-factor ANOVA design in Figure 15.1 is balanced, with two observations per cell ($n = 2$), two levels of factor A ($J = 2$), and three levels of factor B ($K = 3$). First, all *F*-ratios have the same denominator (MS_W) with 6 degrees of freedom ($df_W = 6$). That is, $df_W = JK(n - 1) = (2)(3)(2 - 1) = 6$. The degrees of freedom for the numerators of *F*-ratios are: $df_A = J - 1 = 2 - 1 = 1$, $df_B = K - 1 = 3 - 1 = 2$, and $df_{AB} = (J - 1)(K - 1) = (2 - 1)(3 - 1) = 2$.

The ANOVA null hypotheses (H_{01}, H_{02}, and H_{03}) in this example are:

Main effect of gender, H_{01}: $\mu_{1\bullet} = \mu_{2\bullet}$ [or, H_{01}: $\sum \alpha_j^2 = 0$; ($j = 1, 2$)]
Main effect of ethnicity, H_{02}: $\mu_{\bullet 1} = \mu_{\bullet 2} = \mu_{\bullet 3}$ [or, H_{02}: $\sum \beta_k^2 = 0$; ($k = 1, 2, 3$)]
Interaction (*gender* x *ethnicity*), H_{03}: $\sum\sum(\alpha\beta_{jk})^2 = 0$; ($j = 1, 2$; $k = 1, 2, 3$).

The first null hypothesis, H_{01}, is tested by comparing the F_A test value (8.526) against the critical *F*-value for $\alpha = .05$, $df_A = 1$, and $df_W = 6$ [see Table A-4]. Because the computed F_A value (8.526) exceeds the critical *F*-value (5.99), we reject H_{01}. Thus, there is a statistically significant main effect of gender at the .05 level. In other words, males and females differ on their mean scores on the dependent variable (math gain score).

The second null hypothesis, H_{02}, is also rejected since the computed *F*-value ($F_B = 8.842$) exceeds the critical *F*-value (5.14) for $\alpha = .05$, $df_B = 2$, and $df_W = 6$. Thus, there is a statistically significant difference between the means of at least two of the three ethnic groups. Which particular groups are different can be determined using multiple comparisons (e.g., the Tukey post hoc test). This is illustrated in Example 15.5.

Finally, H_{03} is also rejected since the computed *F*-value ($F_{AB} = 6.00$) is greater than the critical *F*-value (5.14) for $\alpha = .05$, $df_{AB} = 2$, and $df_W = 6$. This indicates that there is a statistically significant interaction between gender and ethnicity.

Note that the two-factor ANOVA test in this example provides evidence of differences among the three ethnic groups, whereas this was not the case with the one-factor ANOVA for the same data in Example 14.2 (Chapter 14). This occurred because the computed *F*-value here is $F_B = MS_B/MS_W = 108/12.667 = 8.842$, whereas the *F*-value with the one-factor ANOVA is smaller: $F_B = MS_B/MS_W = 108/37.333 = 3.00$. The larger *F*-ratio with the two-factor ANOVA (8.842) is due to its smaller denominator ($MS_W = 12.667$) compared to that with the one-factor ANOVA reported in Figure 14.3 ($MS_W = 37.333$) — see NOTE [15.1].

15.1.8 Omnibus Effect Size in Two-factor ANOVA

The measure of omnibus effect size, η^2 (eta squared) presented in Chapter 14 (Section 14.8.2) is applicable for the main and interaction effects in a two-factor (A x B) ANOVA.

$$\eta^2 = \frac{SS_{effect}}{SS_T}, \quad \textbf{(15.24)}$$

where SS_T is the *sum of squares total* (see Equation 15.14) and SS_{effect} is the sum of squares of the "effect" A, B, or A x B. That is, (a) for factor A: $SS_{effect} = SS_A$ (Equation 15.15), (b) for factor B: $SS_{effect} = SS_B$ (Equation 15.16), and (c) for the (A x B) interaction: $SS_{effect} = SS_{AB}$ (Equation 15.17). For example, for the two factor (*Gender* x *Ethnicity*) ANOVA in Examples

15.2, 15.3, and 15.4, we have $SS_A = 108$, $SS_B = 224$, $SS_{AB} = 152$, and $SS_W = 76$. Using Equation 15.19, we obtain: $SS_T = SS_A + SS_B + SS_{AB} + SS_W = 108 + 224 + 152 + 76 = 560$. Given this, we use Equation 15.24 to obtain the effect size for factor A (η_A^2), factor B (η_B^2), and the interaction between them (η_{AB}^2) as follows:

$$\eta_A^2 = \frac{SS_A}{SS_T} = \frac{108}{560} = .193,\ \eta_B^2 = \frac{SS_B}{SS_T} = \frac{224}{560} = .400, \text{ and } \eta_{AB}^2 = \frac{SS_{AB}}{SS_T} = \frac{152}{560} = .271.$$

Thus, following the Cohen's guidelines described in NOTE [14.4], we find that all three effect sizes are large.

In ANOVA with two or more factors, an effect size measure called **partial eta squared** ($p\eta^2$) is also used to indicate the proportion of the variability in the dependent variable, *Y*, accounted for by a given effect (A, B, or A x B) after "partialling out" (controlling for) the contribution of all other effects. The formula for partial eta squared is

$$p\eta^2 = \frac{SS_{effect}}{SS_{effect} + SS_W}, \quad \textbf{(15.25)}$$

where SS_{effect} is the same as with η^2 (i.e., SS_A, SS_B, or SS_{AB}) and SS_W is the *sum of squares within cells* (or *sum of squares error*) — see Equation 15.18.

Using the sum of squares values with the above calculations of the effects η_A^2, η_B^2, and η_{AB}^2, we use Formula 15.25 to compute their partial counterparts as follows:

$$p\eta_A^2 = \frac{SS_A}{SS_A + SS_W} = \frac{108}{108+76} = .587,$$

$$p\eta_B^2 = \frac{SS_B}{SS_B + SS_W} = \frac{224}{224+76} = .747, \text{ and}$$

$$p\eta_{AB}^2 = \frac{SS_{AB}}{SS_{AB} + SS_W} = \frac{152}{152+76} = .667.$$

NOTE [15.2] Eta squared for an effect is always smaller than its partial eta squared ($\eta^2 < p\eta^2$). This is because the denominator for η^2 (SS_T) in Formula 15.24 is larger than the denominator for $p\eta^2$ ($SS_{effect} + SS_W$) in Formula 15.25, as the latter is a part of the former (see Equation 15.19). Also, **the Cohen's guidelines for (small, medium, and large) effect size do not apply for the partial eta squared** because its denominator changes across effects (e.g., A, B, and A x B, as shown here above).

In the context of two-factor ANOVA, the "translation" of Formula 14.34 (in Chapter 14) for **omega squared** (ω^2) — the effect size adjusted for the population — is straightforward:

$$\omega^2 = \frac{SS_{effect} - (df_{effect})MS_W}{SS_T + MS_W}, \quad \textbf{(15.26)}$$

where df_{effect} is the degrees of freedom for the effect (see Formulas 15.20).

For example, given that $SS_A = 108$, $SS_B = 224$, and $SS_{AB} = 152$ [which we already used in the computations of η^2 and $p\eta^2$], we can now use Formula 15.26 to compute omega squared for factor A ($\omega_{\hat{A}}^2$), factor B ($\omega_{\hat{A}}^2$), and their interaction ($\omega_{\hat{AB}}^2$) as follows:

$$\omega_{\hat{A}}^2 = \frac{SS_A - (df_A)MS_W}{SS_T + MS_W} = \frac{108 - (1)(76)}{560 + 76} = .050,$$

$$\omega_{\hat{B}}^2 = \frac{SS_B - (df_B)MS_W}{SS_T + MS_W} = \frac{224 - (2)(76)}{560 + 76} = .113, \text{ and}$$

$$\omega_{\hat{AB}}^2 = \frac{SS_{AB} - (df_{AB})MS_W}{SS_T + MS_W} = \frac{152 - (2)(76)}{560 + 76} = .00.$$

15.1.9 Types of Interaction in Two-factor ANOVA

There are two types of interaction that may occur in two-factor ANOVA — ordinal or disordinal interaction. **Ordinal interaction** is when the order of the mean scores for the levels in one factor is the same across the levels of other factor. **Disordinal interaction** is when the order of mean scores for the levels in one factor is not the same across the levels of other factor. The three plots in Figure 15.4 illustrate the hypothetical cases of (a) no interaction, (b) an ordinal interaction, and (c) a disordinal interaction between two factors — *gender* (male, female) and type of school (public, private), where the dependent variable, *Y*, is attitude toward school. The cell means, $\bar{Y}_{jk}$, are presented on the vertical axis. Keep in mind, however, that in a real study there must be evidence that the *F*-test for interaction is statistically significance in order to proceed with the interpretation of the interaction plot (see F_{AB} in Equation 15.23).

Figure 15.4 *Three hypothetical cases of (a) no interaction, (b) ordinal interaction, and (c) disordinal interaction) in a two-factor ANOVA with factors gender (male, female) and type of school (public, private)*

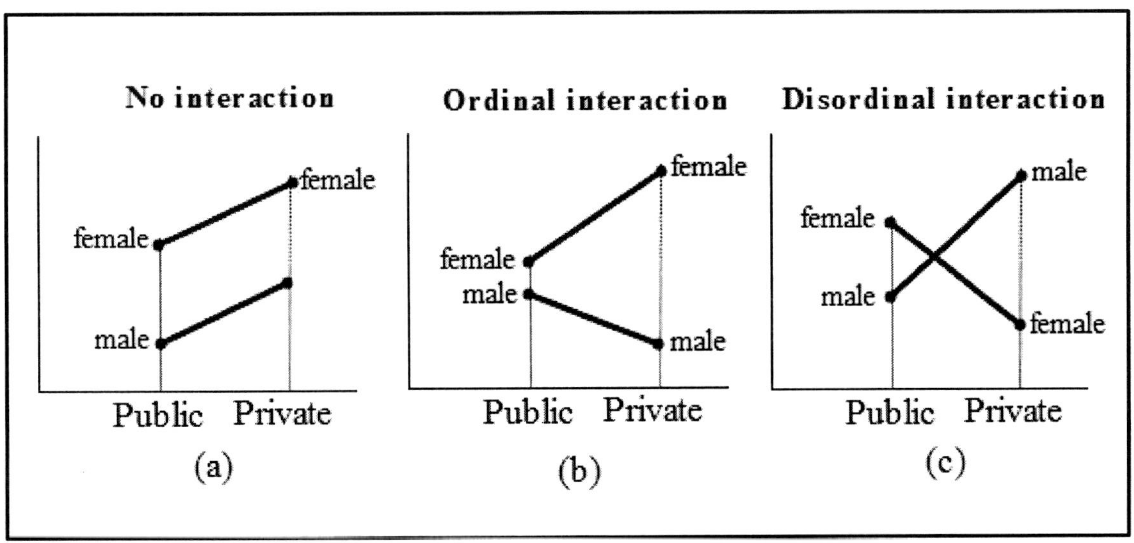

15.1.10 Testing for Simple Main Effects

When the interaction in a two-factor ANOVA is statistically significant, the interpretation of main effects is of little interest regardless of their statistical significance. For example, with the interactions depicted in Figure 15.4 (b and c) there would likely be no statistically significant main effect of gender. Clearly, interpreting the (lack of) main effect for gender in each of these two scenarios would mask existing gender differences across public and private schools. It would be important, therefore, to test for gender differences separately for public and private schools. This is referred to as testing for *simple main effects* of gender across public and private schools.

In general, if the (A x B) interaction in a two-factor ANOVA is statistically significant, **testing for simple main effects** of factor A is performed by testing the difference between any two levels of factor A across the levels of factor B. Likewise, one can perform testing for simple main effects of factor B across the levels of factor A. Which simple main effects to test (A or B, but not both) depends on which one is of interest to the researcher. For a *balanced* (A x B) ANOVA design, with *n* observation in each (A x B) cell, we can compare any two levels of factor A (say, A_j and A_m) at a given level of factor B (say, B_k) by using the following *t*-statistic:

$$t = \frac{\bar{Y}_{jk} - \bar{Y}_{mk}}{\sqrt{\frac{2MS_W}{n}}}, \qquad \textbf{(15.27)}$$

where $\bar{Y}_{jk}$ is the mean for the cell (A_j, B_k), located at the "intersection" of levels A_j and B_k, $\bar{Y}_{mk}$ is the mean for the cell (A_m, B_k), located at the "intersection" of levels A_m and B_k, and MS_W is the *mean squares within* (see Formulas 15.21).

15.1.11 Using SPSS for Two-factor ANOVA

This section addresses the use of SPSS for two-factor ANOVA and presentation of the results in APA format, along with some technical comments.

EXAMPLE 15.5 This example illustrates how to use SPSS for the two-factor ANOVA in Example 15.4, with Tukey post hoc comparisons among the three ethnic groups and graphical representation of the interaction between gender and ethnicity. APA-style summaries and discussion of results are also provided. The SPSS data layout is presented in Figure 15.1 (right panel), with the values of the dependent variable (SCORE = math gain score) and the coding values for the two factors: *Gender* (0 = Female, 1 = Male) and *Ethnicity* (1 = Caucasian, 2 = African-American, 3 = Hispanic). The SPSS steps used for this illustration are:

1. Click **Analyze**, click **General Linear Model**, and click **Univariate**.
2. Click **SCORE**, and click ► to move it into the box
3. Click **Gender**, click **Ethnicity**, and click ► to move them into the box **Fixed Factor(s).**
4. Click **Options**, check the boxes **Descriptive statistics**, **Estimates of effect size**, and **Homogeneity tests**, and then click **Continue**.
5. Click **Post Hoc**, click **Ethnicity**, and click ► to move it into the box **Post Hoc Tests for**
6. Check the **Tukey** box and click **Continue**.
7. Click **Plots**, click **Ethnicity**, and click ►to move it into the box **Horizontal Axis**.
8. Then click **Gender**, and click ►to move it into the box **Separate Lines,** and click **Add** [make sure that the interaction term ***Ethnicity*Gender*** appears in the box **Plots**.
9. Click **OK**.

The resulting SPSS output is provided in Figure 15.5. The **Leve Variances** table is not shown because it did not provide a test value [sample size per cell, $n = 2$]. The descriptive statistics (means and interaction plot are not shown in the SPSS output either, but the format) in Table 15.1 and Figure 15.6, respectively.

Just for comparison, we can see first that the "boxed" values in t **Subjects Effects** table are exactly the same as those obtained through manu Example 15.2 (for SS_A, SS_B, SS_{AB}, SS_W, SS_T), Example 15.3 (for MS_A, MS_B, MS_A ample 15.4 (for F_A, F_B, F_{AB}, and their degrees of freedom), and in this section (for $p\eta_A$, $p\eta^2_{AB}$) [factor A = *Gender*, factor B = *Ethnicity*].

The values of the omnibus effect size, η^2, for the main effect of factor A (η^2_A), main fect of factor B (η^2_B), and the interaction A x B (η^2_{AB}), are not provided with the SPSS output, but they can be easily computed using Formula 15.24 for the SS values provided with the SPSS output. As shown in the previous section for these data, we have: $\eta^2_A = .193$, $\eta^2_B = .400$, and $\eta^2_{AB} = .271$. Recall that Cohen's guidelines for the magnitude of an effect size (small, medium, large) apply for *eta squared* (η^2), but not for *partial eta squared* ($p\eta^2$) estimates. Likewise, *omega squared* (ω^2), the effect size adjusted for the population, can be computed with Formula 15.26 using the values for the components in this formula provided with the SPSS output. Specifically, as shown in the previous section, we have $\omega^2_A = .050$, $\omega^2_B = .113$, and $\omega^2_{AB} = .00$.

The results in the SPSS output, including those not shown in Figure 15.5, are summarized (in APA style) in Tables 15.1, 15.2, 15.3, and Figure 15.6. Specifically, Table 15.1 provides the means and standard deviations of the groups (by gender and ethnicity) on the dependent variable (math gain score). Table 15.2 summarizes the results in the **Tests of Between-Subjects Tests** table, whereas Table 15.3 summarizes the results in the **Multiple Comparisons** table included in Figure 15.5. The interaction between gender and ethnicity is depicted in Figure 15.6.

In this example we asked whether there were gender differences in the dependent variable (math gain score) and whether such differences may vary across the three ethnic groups. The results in Table 15.2 indicate that there is a statistically significant main effect for gender, $F(1, 6) = 8.53$, $p = .03$, $p\eta^2 = .59$, a statistically significant main effect for ethnicity, $F(2, 6) = 8.84$, $p = .02$, $p\eta^2 = .75$, and a statistically significant interaction between gender and ethnicity, $F(2, 6) = 6.00$, $p = .04$, $p\eta^2 = .67$, at the .05 level of significance. As mentioned previously, when there is a statistically significant interaction, the main effects are of little interest regardless of their statistical significance. They are interpreted here only for the sake of illustration.

The *partial eta squared* ($p\eta^2$) measure of effect size for gender (.59) indicates that 59 percent of the students' differences in math gain scores is accounted for by gender differences, controlling for the effects of ethnicity and the interaction between gender and ethnicity. Likewise, the value of $p\eta^2$ for ethnicity (.75) shows that 75 percent of the differences in math gain scores are accounted for by differences among the ethnic groups, controlling for the effects of gender and the interaction between gender and ethnicity. Also, $p\eta^2 = .67$ for the interaction effect size shows that the interaction between gender and ethnicity accounts for 67 percent of the differences in math gain scores controlling for the effects of gender and ethnicity.

15.5 *Selected SPSS output for the two-factor (Gender x Ethnicity) ANOVA*

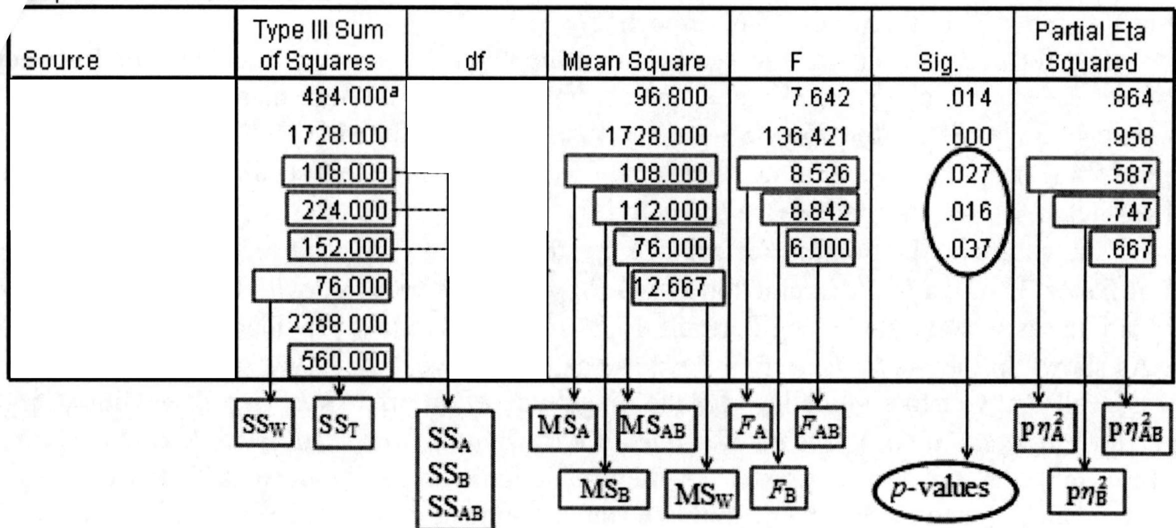

Tests of Between-Subjects Effects

Dependent Variable: SCORE

Source	Type III Sum of Squares	df	Mean Square	F	Sig.	Partial Eta Squared
	484.000[a]		96.800	7.642	.014	.864
	1728.000		1728.000	136.421	.000	.958
	108.000		108.000	8.526	.027	.587
	224.000		112.000	8.842	.016	.747
	152.000		76.000	6.000	.037	.667
	76.000		12.667			
	2288.000					
	560.000					

Multiple Comparisons

Dependent Variable: SCORE
Tukey HSD

(I) Ethnicity	(J) Ethnicity	Mean Difference (I-J)	Std. Error	Sig.	95% Confidence Interval Lower Bound	95% Confidence Interval Upper Bound
Caucasian	African-American	-2.00	2.517	.720	-9.72	5.72
	Hispanic	-10.00*	2.517	.017	-17.72	-2.28
African-American	Caucasian	2.00	2.517	.720	-5.72	9.72
	Hispanic	-8.00*	2.517	.044	-15.72	-.28
Hispanic	Caucasian	10.00*	2.517	.017	2.28	17.72
	African-American	8.00*	2.517	.044	.28	15.72

Based on observed means.

*. The mean difference is significant at the .05 level.

Table 15.1

Means and Standard Deviations for Math Gain Score by Gender and Ethnicity

	Female			Male			Total		
Ethnicity	*n*	*M*	*SD*	*N*	*M*	*SD*	*N*	*M*	*SD*
Caucasian	2	9.00	2.83	2	7.00	4.24	4	8.00	3.16
African-American	2	10.00	2.83	2	10.00	1.41	4	10.00	1.83
Hispanic	2	26.00	2.83	2	10.00	5.66	4	18.00	9.93

Table 15.2

Analysis of Variance for Math Performance

Source	*df*	*F*	$p\eta^2$	*p*
Gender (G)	1	8.53	0.59	0.03
Ethnicity (E)	2	8.84	0.75	0.02
G X E	2	6.00	0.67	0.04
S within group error	6	(12.67)		

Note. The value enclosed in parentheses is the *mean square error* (MS_W). S = subjects.

Table 15.3

Multiple Comparisons for Math Gain Score Among Ethnic Groups

Ethnic Groups	ΔM	SEΔM	95% CI for ΔM	
Caucasian — African-American	2.00	2.52	−9.72	5.72
Caucasian — Hispanic	10.00*	2.52	−17.72	−2.28
African-American — Hispanic	−8.00*	2.52	−15.72	−0.28

Note. ΔM = Mean difference. SEΔM = Standard error of ΔM.

$*p < .05$.

Figure 15.6 *Interaction between gender and ethnicity on math gain score*

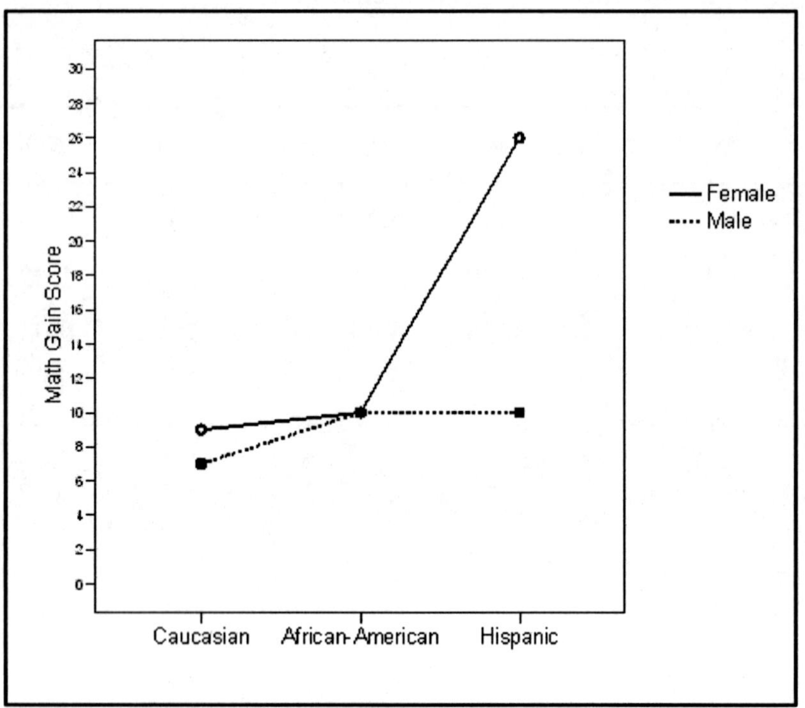

While $p\eta^2$provides useful effect-size information, it cannot be used to compare effect sizes across different effects because the denominator in the formula for $p\eta^2$ varies across the effects (see Formula 15.25). For the same reason, Cohen's guidelines for interpreting the magnitude of effect sizes (.01 = small, .06 = *medium*, and .14 = *large*) do not apply for $p\eta^2$ (Cohen, 1988). Comparison of effect sizes across different effects can be achieved by reporting the omnibus *eta squared* (η^2) statistic. For the data in this example, the computations in Section 15.1.8 show that there are large effect sizes for gender (η^2 = .193), ethnicity (η^2 = .400), and the interaction between gender and ethnicity (η^2 = .271). Clearly, the largest effect size is associated with the effect of ethnicity (.400), which indicates that 40 percent of the differences in math gain scores are accounted for by gain score differences among the three ethnic groups (Caucasian, African-American, and Hispanic).

Given the statistically significant main effect for ethnicity, the Tukey post hoc method of multiple comparisons was used to determine which ethnic groups differ in math gain scores. The results in Table 15.3 indicate that, at the .05 level, there is no statistically significant difference between the Caucasian and African-American groups ($p > .05$), but there is a statistically significant difference between the Caucasian and Hispanic groups ($p < .05$), as well as between the African-American and Hispanic groups ($p < .05$). Specifically, the results provided by the 95 percent confidence interval for the difference between the means of two groups indicate that the Hispanic group outperformed both the Caucasian group (by a difference between 2.28 and 17.72) and the African-American group (by a difference between 0.28 and 15.72) in math gain scores. Evidently, the Hispanic group in the study population of middle school students benefited most from the experimental school program that incorporates bilingual (English-Spanish) interpretation of mathematics concepts and principles.

As noted earlier, the results on main effects are provided here only to illustrate their APA style presentation. When there is a statistically significant interaction, the main effects are of little interest and can even be misleading. The examination of Figure 15.6 provides more refined information about our major interest in this example — whether there are gender differences in math gain scores across ethnic groups. Specifically, while there are no gender differences for the Caucasian and African-American groups, there is a substantial difference between females (M = 26, SD = 2.83, n = 2) and males (M = 10, SD = 5.66, n = 2) for the Hispanic group in favor of the female students. To test the simple main effect of gender for the Hispanic group, we use Formula 15.27 with $n = 2$, $\bar{Y}_{13} = 26$, $\bar{Y}_{23} = 10$, and $MS_W = 12.67$ (see Table 15.2) to compute the t-statistic:

$$t = \frac{\bar{Y}_{13} - \bar{Y}_{23}}{\sqrt{\frac{2MS_W}{n}}} = \frac{26 - 10}{\sqrt{\frac{(2)(12.67)}{2}}} = 4.50.$$

As the t-statistic (4.50) exceeds the critical t-value (2.447), at the .05 level and with $df = 6$ (see Table A-2), we can conclude that there is a statistically significant simple effect of gender in math gain score (in favor of females) for the Hispanic group of students. This, however, is not the case for the other two ethnic groups. Specifically, the t-statistics for the Caucasian and African-America groups are $t = 0.56$ and $t = 0.00$, respectively, which do not exceed the critical t-value (2.447). The results indicate that the Hispanic female students benefit most from a school program that incorporates bilingual (English-Spanish) interpretation of mathematics concepts and principles. The differences in math gain scores among all other groups—Hispanic (males), Caucasian (males and females), and African-American (males and females)—are negligible.

15.2 Three-factor ANOVA

The logic of two-factor ANOVA carries over directly into ANOVA with three or more factors. Suppose a researcher wants to study whether the motivation for academic achievement of high school students varies according to their gender, ethnicity, and socio-economic status. This question can be addressed by using ANOVA with three factors (gender, ethnicity, and socio-economic status) and the dependent variable "motivation for academic achievement." For concreteness, suppose the three factors are: A = *gender* (male, female), B = *ethnicity* (Caucasian, African-American, Hispanic, Asian), and C = *socio-economic status,* as measured by family income (low, medium, and high). The notation 2 x 4 x 3 ANOVA indicates that this is a three-factor ANOVA, where factor A has 2 levels, factor B has 4 levels, and factor C has 3 levels.

The notations with the two-factor (A x B) AVOVA, used in the previous section, are extended with the three-factor (A x B x C) ANOVA to take into account the presence of a third factor, C. Specifically,

μ_{jkl} = mean of the cell (j, k, l) [the "intersection" of level j of factor A, level k of factor B, and level l of factor C]

$\mu_{j\bullet\bullet}$ = population mean for level j of factor A across all levels of factors B and C; ($j = 1, 2, \ldots, J$),

$\mu_{\bullet k\bullet}$ = population mean for level k of factor B across all levels of factors A and C; ($k = 1, 2, \ldots, K$),

$\mu_{\bullet\bullet l}$ = population mean for level l of factor C across all levels of factors A and B; ($l = 1, 2, \ldots, L$),

$\mu_{\bullet\bullet\bullet}$ = grand mean (of all observations across all levels of factors A, B, and C);

$\alpha_j = \mu_{j\bullet\bullet} - \mu_{\bullet\bullet\bullet}$ [effect of level *j* in factor A],

$\beta_k = \mu_{\bullet k\bullet} - \mu_{\bullet\bullet\bullet}$ [effect of level *k* in factor B],

$\gamma_l = \mu_{\bullet\bullet l} - \mu_{\bullet\bullet\bullet}$ [effect of level *l* in factor C],

$\alpha\beta_{jk} = \mu_{jk} - (\mu_{\bullet\bullet\bullet} + \alpha_j + \beta_k)$ [interaction term of cell (*j*, *k*)],

$\alpha\gamma_{jl} = \mu_{jl} - (\mu_{\bullet\bullet\bullet} + \alpha_j + \gamma_l)$ [interaction term of cell (*j*, *l*)],

$\beta\gamma_{kl} = \mu_{kl} - (\mu_{\bullet\bullet\bullet} + \beta_k + \gamma_l)$ [interaction term of cell (*k*, *l*)],

$\alpha\beta\gamma_{jkl} = \mu_{jkl} - (\mu_{\bullet\bullet\bullet} + \alpha_j + \beta_k + \gamma_l + \alpha\beta_{jk} + \alpha\gamma_{jl} + \beta\gamma_{kl})$ [interaction term of cell (*j*, *k*, *l*)]

$\varepsilon_{ijkl} = Y_{ijkl} - \mu_{jkl}$ [error term for the score of subject *i* within cell (*j*, *k*, *l*)]

σ_ε^2 = *population error variance* [the within-cell variance of the error terms, ε_{ijkl}].

The **assumptions of normality, homogeneity of variance, and independence of observations** hold for ANOVA with three (or more) factors. With the 2 x 3 x 4 ANOVA, for example, there are 24 cells (i.e., 24 population distributions of scores). Under the assumptions of normality and homogeneity of variance, all 24 population (within-cells) distributions are normal and have equal variances, σ_ε^2 [compare to the 2 x 3 ANOVA case depicted in Figure 15.2.]

Under the **linear model** for the data with three-factor ANOVA, the score of any subject *i* in cell (*j*, *k*, *l*) is a linear sum of the effects, interaction terms, and error term as follows:

$$Y_{ijkl} = \mu_{\bullet\bullet\bullet} + \alpha_j + \beta_k + \gamma_l + \alpha\beta_{jk} + \alpha\gamma_{jl} + \beta\gamma_{kl} + \alpha\beta\gamma_{jkl} + \varepsilon_{ijkl}. \quad \textbf{(15.28)}$$

There are seven null hypotheses testable with the tree-factor ANOVA:

Main effect of factor A, H_{01}: $\mu_{1\bullet\bullet} = \mu_{2\bullet\bullet} = \ldots = \mu_{J\bullet\bullet}$ [or, H_{01}: $\sum \alpha_j^2 = 0$]

Main effect of factor B, H_{02}: $\mu_{\bullet 1\bullet} = \mu_{\bullet 2\bullet} = \ldots = \mu_{\bullet K\bullet}$ [or, H_{02}: $\sum \beta_k^2 = 0$]

Main effect of factor C, H_{03}: $\mu_{\bullet\bullet 1} = \mu_{\bullet\bullet 2} = \ldots = \mu_{\bullet\bullet L}$ [or, H_{03}: $\sum \gamma_l^2 = 0$]

A x B interaction, H_{04}: There is no A x B interaction [or, H_{04}: $\sum\sum(\alpha\beta_{jk})^2 = 0$]

A x C interaction, H_{05}: There is no A x C interaction [or, H_{05}: $\sum\sum(\alpha\gamma_{jl})^2 = 0$]

A x C interaction, H_{06}: There is no B x C interaction [or, H_{06}: $\sum\sum(\beta\gamma_{kl})^2 = 0$]

A x B x C interaction, H_{07}: There is no A x B x C interaction [or, $\sum\sum\sum(\alpha\beta\gamma_{jkl})^2 = 0$]

The *F*-test for the three null hypotheses in two-factor ANOVA applies to testing the null hypotheses with three-factor ANOVA. The *F*-statistics in this case are:

Main effects: $F_A = \dfrac{MS_A}{MS_W}$ (for H_{01}), $F_B = \dfrac{MS_B}{MS_W}$ (for H_{02}), and $F_C = \dfrac{MS_C}{MS_W}$ (for H_{03}),

Dual interactions: $F_{AB} = \dfrac{MS_{AB}}{MS_W}$ (for H_{04}), $F_{AC} = \dfrac{MS_{AC}}{MS_W}$ (for H_{05}), and $F_{BC} = \dfrac{MS_{BC}}{MS_W}$ (for H_{06}),

Triple interaction: $F_{ABC} = \dfrac{MS_{ABC}}{MS_W}$ (for H_{07}).

Evidently, the testing for main effects and dual interactions (between two factors) is the same as with two-factor ANOVA. However, the power of the *F*-tests with three-factor ANOVA is higher than that with the two-factor ANOVA because the MS_W with the former is generally smaller than the MS_W with later [Why?]

The new element in the transition from a two-factor ANOVA to a three-factor ANOVA is the "triple" (three-factor) interaction A x B x C. Generally, a **three-factor interaction** occurs when there is an interaction between two factors at some level(s) of the third factor, but this interaction changes (or disappears) at some other level(s) of the third factor. A three-factor interaction in a 2 x 2 x 2 ANOVA is depicted in Figure 15.7. The factors are *gender* (boys, girls), *test performance* (fail, pass), and *test form* — a sample of middle school students was randomly split and each group randomly assigned to take a Physics test in either multiple-choice items (MCI) or open-ended items (OEI) format. The total scores on the test represent the dependent variable, *Y*. The mean score in *Y* for boys and girls who failed or passed the test, $\bar{Y}_{jk}$, is presented on the vertical axis, separately for the MCI and OEI test forms. The plots in Figure 15.7 are based on a real data analysis which showed that the three-factor interaction is statistically significant, thus opening the door for interpretation of the interaction plots. As can be seen, girls consistently outperform boys on the MCI test form, but the difference remains the same (in direction and magnitude) for students who failed and for those who passed the test. This trend cannot be generalized across test forms, as the picture for the OEI test form is quite different — for students who failed the test, girls did slightly better than boys, whereas for students who passed the test, boys did much better than girls.

Figure 15.7 *Three-factor interaction among* ***gender, test performance,*** *and* ***test form*** *for the test scores of middle school students*

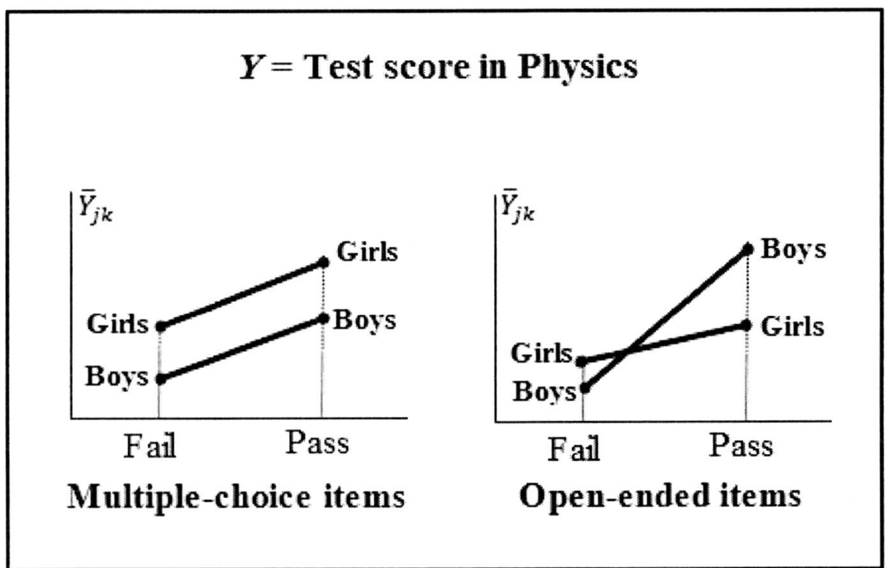

NOTE [15.3] To proceed with the interpretation of interaction plots, there must be statistical evidence for the presence of interaction. For a three-factor interaction, such evidence is provided (or not) by the respective *F*-test (see F_{ABC} for H_{07}).

EXAMPLE 15.6 This example illustrates how to use SPSS to conduct a three-factor ANOVA and how to interpret the results. The SPSS data file **EX_15_6.sav** is available on the website of this book [http://cehd.gmu.edu/book/dimitrov]. The data consist of 597 observations on the following five variables: **Treatment** (0 = Control, 1 = Experimental), **Race** (1 = White, 2 = Black, 3 = Other), **ESL** = English as a Second Language (0 = No, 1 = Yes), **Content** = Scores on a *content knowledge* test (on a T-scale, *Mean* = 50, *SD* = 10), and **Procedural** = Scores on a *procedural knowledge* test (also on a T-scale). The first 10 (out of 597) observations are shown in Figure 15.8. The three factors are Treatment, Race, and ESL, so a 2 x 3 x 2 ANOVA is employed with *content knowledge* as the dependent variable. [The use of *procedural knowledge* as the dependent variable to conduct a three-way ANOVA is requested with study question 7 at the end of this chapter.]

The research question is whether an experimental program in teaching science makes a difference in the students' content knowledge, taking into account the students' race and whether English is their second language (ESL). Gender is not considered here because preliminary analyses showed that gender was not involved in any statistically significant main or interaction effects. The null hypotheses with the 2 x 3 x 2 ANOVA in this case relate to main effect of Treatment (T), main effect of Race (R), main effect of ESL, three pairwise interactions between factors (T x R, T x ESL, R x ESL), and a three-factor interaction, T x R x ESL.

Figure 15.8 *SPSS data file* **EX_15_6.sav** *— the first 10 (out of 597) observations*

*EX_15_6.sav [DataSet1] - SPSS Data Editor

File Edit View Data Transform Analyze Graphs Utilities Add-

597 :

	Treatment	Race	ESL	Content	Procedural
1	1	1	0	63.07	49.24
2	0	1	0	53.94	59.43
3	1	1	0	70.75	41.09
4	1	1	0	55.52	42.73
5	1	1	0	34.38	42.77
6	0	1	0	55.42	51.53
7	1	1	0	56.33	64.18
8	1	1	0	40.36	40.38
9	0	1	0	43.88	40.06
10	0	1	1	41.03	48.69

Following the SPSS steps described in Example 15.5 for a two-factor ANOVA, but this time using three fixed factors (**Treatment, Race**, **ESL**) and **Content** as a dependent variable, we obtain the SPSS output provided in Figure 15.9. For space consideration, the results are not summarized in APA style, but this can be done following the illustration in Tables 15.1, 15.2, and 15.3 for two-factor ANOVA. The three-factor interaction plots provided with the SPSS output, edited for APA format, are shown in Figure 15.10.

Figure 15.9 *Selected SPSS output for the three-factor (Treatment x Race x ESL) ANOVA*

Levene's Test of Equality of Error Variances[a]

Dependent Variable: Content knowledge

F	df1	df2	Sig.
.690	11	585	.749

Tests the null hypothesis that the error variance of the dependent variable is equal across groups.

a. Design: Intercept+Treatment+Race+ESL+Treatment * Race+Treatment * ESL+Race * ESL+Treatment * Race * ESL

Tests of Between-Subjects Effects

Dependent Variable: Content knowledge

Source	Type III Sum of Squares	df	Mean Square	F	Sig.	Partial Eta Squared
Corrected Model	3318.698[a]	11	301.700	3.136	.000	.056
Intercept	631669.899	1	631669.899	6565.713	.000	.918
Treatment	659.372	1	659.372	6.854	.009	.012
Race	1562.842	2	781.421	8.122	.000	.027
ESL	925.942	1	925.942	9.624	.002	.016
Treatment * Race	187.207	2	93.603	.973	.379	.003
Treatment * ESL	262.617	1	262.617	2.730	.099	.005
Race * ESL	1012.715	2	506.357	5.263	.005	.018
Treatment * Race * ESL	622.999	2	311.500	3.238	.040	.011
Error	56281.302	585	96.207			
Total	1552100.000	597				
Corrected Total	59600.000	596				

a. R Squared = .056 (Adjusted R Squared = .038)

Multiple Comparisons

Dependent Variable: Content knowledge
Tukey HSD

(I) Race	(J) Race	Mean Difference (I-J)	Std. Error	Sig.	95% Confidence Interval Lower Bound	Upper Bound
WHITE	BLACK	2.2959*	.86199	.022	.2704	4.3213
	OTHER	.0979	1.32339	.997	-3.0117	3.2074
BLACK	WHITE	-2.2959*	.86199	.022	-4.3213	-.2704
	OTHER	-2.1980	1.36511	.242	-5.4056	1.0096
OTHER	WHITE	-.0979	1.32339	.997	-3.2074	3.0117
	BLACK	2.1980	1.36511	.242	-1.0096	5.4056

Based on observed means.

*. The mean difference is significant at the .05 level.

Figure 15.10
Three-factor (Treatment × Race × ESL) Interaction for Test Scores on Content Knowledge

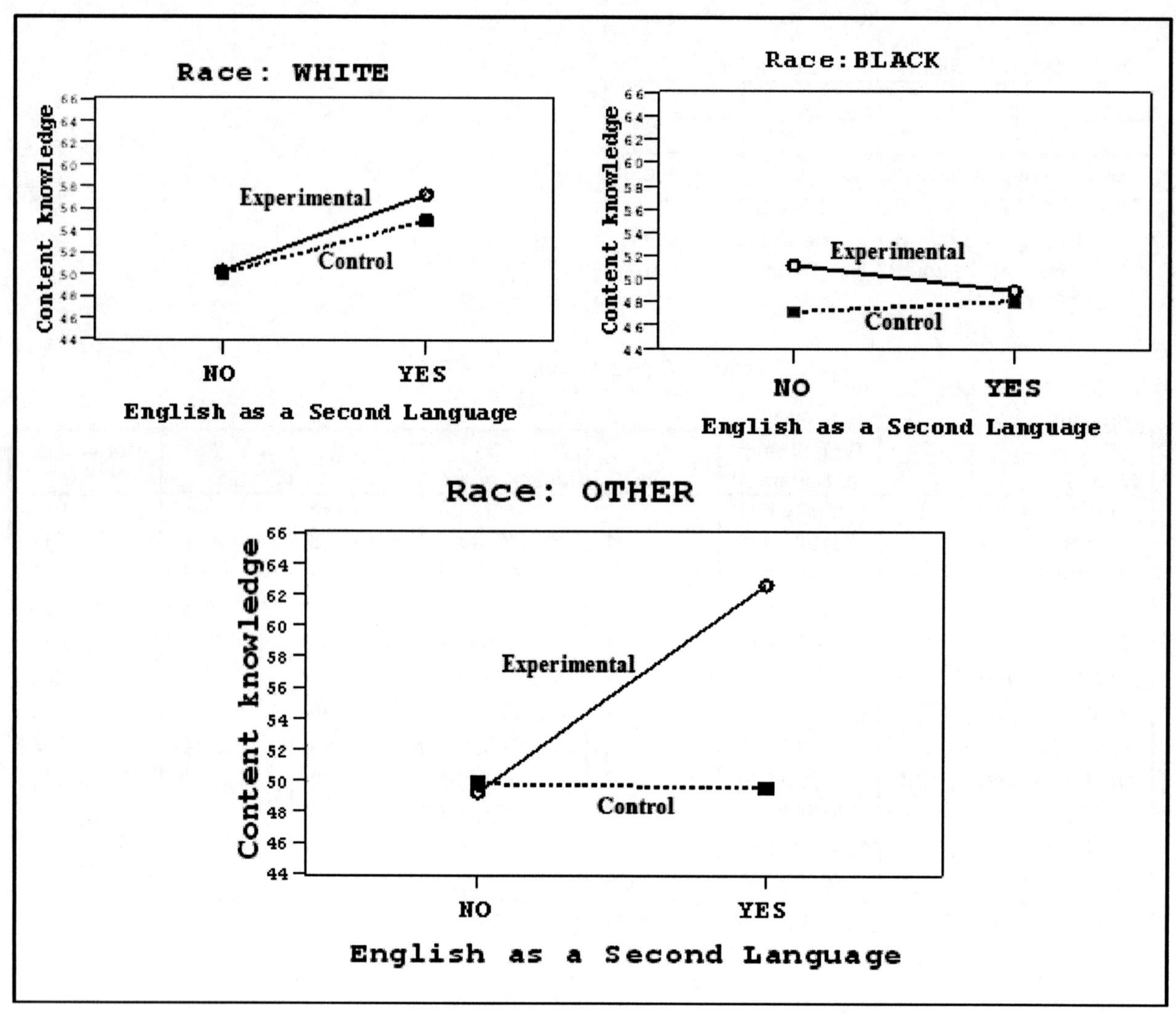

The results from the Levene's test show that the homogeneity of variance assumption is met for the data in this example, $F(11, 585) = 0.69$, $p = .75$. For space consideration, the means and standard deviations are not shown in Figure 15.9, but they are reported here. The results from the tests of between-subjects effects indicate that there is a statistically significant main effect of Treatment, $F(1, 585) = 6.85$, $p < .01$, $p\eta^2 = .01$, with higher scores for the experimental group ($M = 53.25$, $SD = 1.00$, $n = 198$) compared to the control group ($M = 49.92$, $SD = 0.79$, $n = 399$). There was also a statistically significant main effect of ESL, $F(2, 585) = 9.62$, $p < .01$, $p\eta^2 = .02$, with higher scores for the students with English as a second language ($M = 53.56$, $SD = 1.12$, $n = 159$) than those with native English speakers ($M = 49.61$, $SD = 0.61$, $n = 438$). The main effect for Race was also statistically significant, $F(2, 585) = 8.12$, $p < .001$, $p\eta^2 = .03$. The results from the Tukey post hoc test for Race, reported in Figure 15.9, show that the White group outperformed the Black group ($p < .05$) by a difference that varies between 0.27 and 4.32 units on the test scale, but there were no other differences among the three racial groups.

Although the three main effects are statistically significant, they are of little interest, as there is a statistically significant interaction between Race and ESL, $F(2, 585) = 5.26, p < .01$), $p\eta^2 = .02$, as well as a statistically significant three-factor interaction, Treatment x Race x ESL, $F(2, 585) = 3.24, p < .05, p\eta^2 = .01$. Recall that the main research question in this example is whether an experimental program in teaching science makes a difference in the students' content knowledge, taking into account the students' race and whether English is their second language. In the presence of an interaction, the statistically significant main effect of Treatment cannot be generalized across the levels of Race and ESL. Therefore, the difference between the experimental and control groups must be examined in the context of the three-factor interaction depicted in Figure 15.10.

The three-factor interaction plots in Figure 15.10 were obtained by running a two-factor (Treatment x ESL) ANOVA separately for each level of the factor Race. This is achieved by first "splitting" the SPSS file by Race [click **Data**, click **Split File**, select **Organize output by groups**, select **Race**, and click ▶ to move it into the box **Groups Based on].** Then run the two-factor (Treatment x ESL) ANOVA as shown with the SPSS steps in Example 15.5.

The results showed that the interaction between Treatment and ESL was not statistically significant for the White and Black racial groups, but it was statistically significant for the "Other" group ($p < .05$). Clearly, the largest difference between the experimental and control groups is for students in the "Other" group for whom English is a second language (ESL = 1). This result, however, must be interpreted with caution, given the relatively small number of observations in the "Other" group ($n = 67$) compared to the number of observations in White ($n = 305$) and Black ($n = 225$) groups. Moreover, the number of observations by Race becomes even smaller when distributed by cells across the levels of the other two factors, Treatment and ESL.

In addition, as the data in this example **(EX_15_6.sav)** do not produce a balanced three-factor ANOVA design, we cannot test for simple main effects using the *t*-test calculated by Formula 15.27. Thus, assuming valid data prerequisites for the results in this example, we can conditionally summarize that the experimental group outperforms the control group, but while the treatment effect is negligible for students from the White and Black racial groups, regardless of their ESL status, it is well pronounced in favor of the students from the "Other" racial group for whom English is a second language.

NOTE [15.4] When the ANOVA design is not balanced, we cannot use Formula 15.27 (or other formulas that assume balanced ANOVA) to test for simple main effects. Procedures for simple main effects with unbalanced ANOVA are beyond the scope of this chapter, but more on this topic can be found on the website for this book, http://cehd.gmu.edu/book/dimitrov.

15.3 Summary

Using ANOVA with two or more factors allows for (a) investigating the role of different sources in accounting for the variance in the dependent variable, (b) detecting and interpreting interactions between factors, and (c) increasing the power of tests for differences among factor levels and interactions among factors.

- **Assumptions in ANOVA**

  The three primary assumptions in one-factor ANOVA, *independence, normality*, and *homogeneity of variance*, remain in place for ANOVA with two or more factors. The difference is that, with adding a new factor in ANOVA, the population distributions (subjects submitted to the same ANOVA conditions) become more homogeneous and, as a result, the population error variance, σ_ε^2, becomes smaller (e.g., compare Figures 14.1 and 15.2).

- **Effects in two-factor ANOVA**

  There are three types of effects in two-factor (A x B) ANOVA, α_j — *row effects* (for the levels of factor A), β_k — *column effects* (for the levels of factor B), and $\alpha\beta_{jk}$— *cell effects* (interaction terms), defined with Equations 15.4, 15.5, and 15.6, respectively.

- **Null hypotheses in two-factor ANOVA**

  There are three testable null hypotheses with two-factor ANOVA, with *J* levels in Factor A and *K* levels in Factor B,:

  main effect of A, H_{01}: $\mu_{1\bullet} = \mu_{2\bullet} = \ldots = \mu_{J\bullet}$ [or, H_{01}: $\sum \alpha_j^2 = 0$],
  main effect of B, H_{02}: $\mu_{\bullet 1} = \mu_{\bullet 2} = \ldots = \mu_{\bullet K}$ [or, H_{02}: $\sum \beta_k^2 = 0$], and
  interaction A x B, H_{03}: There is NO interaction between factors A and B
  [or, H_{03}: $\sum\sum(\alpha\beta_{jk})^2 = 0$.]

- **Linear model for the data in two-factor ANOVA**

  Under the linear model assumption in two-factor ANOVA, any observed score can be represented as a sum of the total effect ($\mu_{\bullet\bullet}$), row effect (α_j), column effect (β_k), cell effect ($\alpha\beta_{jk}$), and error "effect" (ε_{ijk}) for this observation:

  $$Y_{ijk} = \mu_{\bullet\bullet} + \alpha_j + \beta_k + \alpha\beta_{jk} + \varepsilon_{ijk}.$$

- **Testing the null hypotheses in two-factor ANOVA**

  The null hypotheses in two-factor ANOVA (H_{01}, H_{02}, and H_{03}) are tested by using the *F*-statistics: $F_A = MS_A/MS_W$, $F_B = MS_B/MS_W$, and $F_{AB} = MS_{AB}/MS_W$, respectively.

- **Measures of effect size in two-factor ANOVA**

  Eta squared (η^2) measures an omnibus effect size of an "effect" (A, B, or A x B) by indicating what proportion of the total variability in the dependent variable (SS_T) is accounted for by this effect (see Formula 15.24). *Partial eta squared* ($p\eta^2$) indicates the proportion of the variability in the dependent variable, *Y*, accounted for by a given effect after "partialling out" (controlling for) the contribution of all other effects (see Formula 15.25). Omega squared (ω^2) is an adjustment of η^2 for the population (see Formula 15.26). The Cohen's guidelines for interpreting the magnitude of the effect size η^2 (*small*: η^2 = .01, *medium*: η^2= .06, and *large*: η^2 = .14) do not apply for partial eta squared, $p\eta^2$ (Cohen, 1988).

- **Types of interaction in two-factor ANOVA**

There are two types of interaction that may occur in two-factor ANOVA — ordinal or disordinal interaction. *Ordinal interaction* is when the order of the mean scores for the levels in one factor is the same across the levels of other factor. *Disordinal interaction* is when the order of mean scores for the levels in one factor is not the same across the levels of other factor (see Figure 15.4).

- **Testing for simple main effects in two-factor ANOVA**

If the (A x B) interaction in a two-factor ANOVA is statistically significant, *testing for simple main effects* of factor A is performed by testing the difference between any two levels of factor A across the levels of factor B. With a balanced ANOVA design, the testing for simple main effects can be performed by using the t-test statistic in Formula 15.27.

- **Three-factor ANOVA**

The logic of two-factor ANOVA carries over directly into ANOVA with three or more factors. The main difference is that, with a three factor (A x B x C) ANOVA, there are seven testable null hypotheses — main effects of A, B, and C, interactions between two factors (A x B, A x C, and B x C), and a three-factor interaction, A x B x C. A statistically significant A x B x C interaction means that the interaction pattern between any two factors is not the same across the levels of the third factor (e.g., see Figure 15.10).

15.4 Study Questions

1. Table 15.4.1 provides the data layout for a two-factor ANOVA with factors Gender (1 = Female, 2 = Male) and Treatment (1 = Control, 2 = Experimental) with two observations within each cell ($n = 2$). Using these data, (a) compute the row means, the column means, and the grand mean, and (b) compute the row effects, column effects, and interaction terms. [*Hint*: see Formula 15.4-15.7.]

Table 15.4.1

	Control	Experimental
Female	1, 3	40, 16
Male	2, 6	30, 14

2. For the two-factor ANOVA data in Table 15.4.1, compute (a) the sum of squares (SS_A, SS_B, and SS_{AB}) and (b) the mean squares (MS_A, MS_B, MS_{AB}, and MS_W), where factor A = *Gender* and factor B = *Treatment*. [*Hint*: see Sections 15.1.5 and 15.1.6]

3. Given the data layout in Table 15.4.1, (a) formulate the null hypotheses for the two-factor ANOVA and (b) test the null hypotheses by computing the F-statistics (F_A, F_B, and F_{AB}), where factor A = *Gender* and factor B = *Treatment*. [*Hint*: see Section 15.1.7]

4. For the two-factor ANOVA data in Table 15.4.1, compute the effect sizes (a) eta squared (η^2), (b) partial eta squared ($p\eta^2$), and (c) omega squared (ω^2) for A, B, and AB, where factor A = *Gender* and factor B = *Treatment*. [Hint: see Section 15.1.8]

5. For the two-factor ANOVA data in Table 15.4.1, use SPSS to analyze the data and then present and interpret the results (in APA format). [*Hint*: see Example 15.5]

6. Table 15.4.2 provides the data layout for a two-factor ANOVA. The dependent variable GAIN indicates the "gain" score of students in reading under two treatment conditions labeled Treatment (1 = Control, 2 = Experimental), which represent two different approaches to teach reading. The variable Ability has three levels (1 = Low, 2 = Middle, and 3 = High) indicating the student's reading ability prior to "treatment." The research question is whether the treatment conditions make a difference in the students' gain score on reading and does the difference depend on the prior ability level of the students in reading. Use SPSS to perform the two-factor (Treatment x Ability) ANOVA and then present and interpret the results in APA format. Make sure to test for simple main effects in case there is a statistically significant interaction between Treatment and Ability [*Hint*: see Section 15.1.10].

Table 15.4.2

QUESTION 15_6.sav [DataSet1] - SPSS Da

File Edit View Data Transform Analyze Graph

1 : GAIN 30

	GAIN	Treatment	Ability
1	30	1	1
2	50	1	1
3	12	1	2
4	8	1	2
5	15	1	3
6	5	1	3
7	4	2	1
8	8	2	1
9	10	2	2
10	14	2	2
11	5	2	3
12	7	2	3

7. Using the SPSS data file **EX_15_6.sav** [http://cehd.gmu.edu/book/dimitrov], perform the three-factor (Treatment x Race x ESL) ANOVA and interpret the results, as shown in Example 15.6, but this time use the variable **Procedural** (the students' scores on procedural knowledge) as the dependent variable. Present the results in APA style following the format in Tables 15.1, 15.2, and 15.3 adapted for the three-factor ANOVA in this case.

CHAPTER 16

ANALYSIS OF COVARIANCE

In Chapters 4 and 5 we discussed two key characteristics (*randomization* and *control*) of true experimental research. In addition to *experimental control*, which is achieved primarily by manipulating treatment conditions, researchers should consider the possibility of using *statistical control* to determine treatment effects and other sources that account for the variation in the dependent variable. In the framework of analysis of variance (ANOVA), statistical control can be achieved by controlling the variation in the dependent variable which is due to one (or more) variables in addition to the independent variable (e.g., type of treatment, gender, etc.). The procedure for statistical control of such "extraneous" variables (covariates) in the analysis of variance is called **analysis of covariance** (ANCOVA).

16.1 The Logic behind ANCOVA

16.1.1 Basic Concepts in ANCOVA

Suppose that, as often occurs in educational research, intact groups (e.g., classrooms) were randomly selected and assigned to three approaches to teaching math to fifth grade students (computer aided instruction, problem-solving oriented instruction, and traditional math instruction) in a pretest-posttest experimental design. As this is a nonrandomized pretest-posttest control group design, possible *selection bias* is a serious threat to internal validity (see Chapter 5, Section 5.3.1). In other words, the differences among the treatment groups on the posttest can be partly (or entirely) due to pre-treatment group differences on the math test. Due to an expected positive correlation between the pretest and posttest scores, the groups with higher pretest scores are expected to have higher posttest scores. In other words, the mean scores of the groups on the posttest "covary" with their scores on the pretest. Therefore, the group differences on the "covariate" (pretest scores) must be taken into account when comparing the groups on posttest scores. In ANCOVA this is achieved by "adjusting" the posttest mean scores of the groups to take into account the group differences on the pretest. Then the groups are compared on the adjusted posttest scores by using ANOVA. Thus, ANCOVA is actually ANOVA with *adjusted group means* obtained under the assumption that the groups have equal "start" on the covariate.

In general, a **covariate** is an extraneous variable, X, that is controlled for when testing for group differences on a dependent variable, Y. When selecting a covariate, researchers must take into account several things. First, there must be a linear relationship between the covariate and the dependent variable (i.e., the correlation r_{XY} must be statistically significant). Second, the covariate must be meaningfully related to the dependent variable. Third, the identification of the groups being compared must not be (explicitly or implicitly) based on their scores on the covariate. For example, it is not appropriate to use the IQ test scores of students as a covariate when comparing, say, high GPA versus low GPA students on an analytic reasoning test because the identification of GPA-based groups is (implicitly) dependent on their IQ scores. It must also be noted that using ANCOVA with intact groups does not compensate for the lack of complete randomization and, therefore, awareness of the ANCOVA assumptions and limitations is critical.

16.1.2 Adjusted Group Means in ANCOVA

The ANCOVA adjustment of group means on the dependent variable, *Y*, in order to control for group differences on a covariate, *X*, is depicted in Figure 16.1, where the *Y* values are posttest scores and the *X* values are pretest scores for two compared groups: *Experimental* and *Control.* The logic remains the same when there are more than two groups. Using a simple linear regression, the dependent variable, *Y*, is regressed on the covariate, *X*, for each group separately. It is assumed that the resulting regression lines are parallel — this assumption is called **homogeneity of regression slopes.** That is, the slopes of the regression equations for the prediction of posttest scores from pretest scores are assumed to be equal for the two groups. Due to a positive correlation between the pretest and posttest scores, the experimental group (E) has a higher mean on the posttest ($\bar{Y}_E$) since it has higher mean on the pretest ($\bar{X}_E$). That is, $\bar{X}_E > \bar{X}_C$ so $\bar{Y}_E > \bar{Y}_C$.

Figure 16.1 *ANCOVA adjustment of posttest group means for pretest differences*

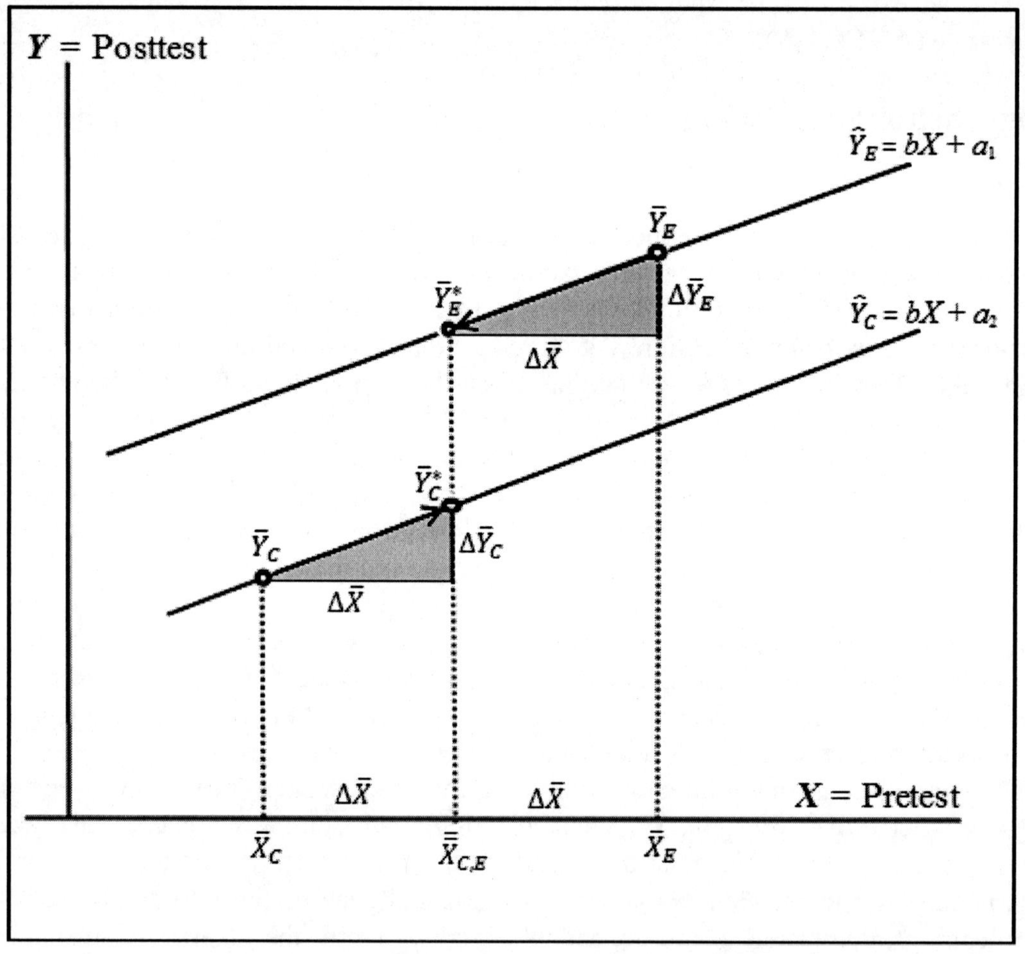

Suppose that the two groups have an equal "start" on the pretest, $\bar{\bar{X}}_{C,E}$, which will be the midpoint between their actual pretest means, $\bar{X}_C$ and $\bar{X}_E$. By replacing $\bar{\bar{X}}_{C,E}$ in the regression equation for the control group, the predicted *Y* score will equal the "adjusted" posttest mean for this group ($\bar{Y}_C^*$). Likewise, by replacing $\bar{\bar{X}}_{C,E}$ in the regression equation for the experimental group, the predicted *Y* score will equal the "adjusted" posttest mean for this group ($\bar{Y}_E^*$). Recall that when the sample mean of the predictor, $\bar{X}$, replaces X in a simple linear regression equation, the predicted Y score equals the sample mean on Y; that is, $\hat{Y} = \bar{Y}$ (see Chapter 10, NOTE [10.3]). In Figure 16.1, $\Delta\bar{Y}_C$ represents the magnitude of "upward" adjustment for the mean of the control group, whereas $\Delta\bar{Y}_E$ is the magnitude of the "downward" adjustment for the mean of the experimental group. As can be seen, the two shaded triangles are identical and, therefore, their sides $\Delta\bar{Y}_C$ and $\Delta\bar{Y}_E$ are equal. Thus, $\Delta\bar{Y}_C = \Delta\bar{Y}_E$ shows that the amount of the ANCOVA (downward and upward) adjustment is the same for each group. Specifically, taking into account Equation 10.9 for the slope in a simple linear regression equation ($b = \Delta\hat{Y}/\Delta X$), it is clear that the magnitude by which the group means are adjusted is $\Delta\bar{Y}_C = \Delta\bar{Y}_E = b\Delta\bar{X}$, where $\Delta\bar{X}$ is half the distance between $\bar{X}_C$ and $\bar{X}_E$: $\Delta\bar{X} = (\bar{X}_E - \bar{X}_C)/2$. Thus,

$$\Delta\bar{Y}_C = \Delta\bar{Y}_E = \left(\frac{b}{2}\right)(\bar{X}_E - \bar{X}_C). \qquad \textbf{(16.1)}$$

The adjusted means in Figure 16.1 are then computed as follows:

$$\bar{Y}_C^* = \bar{Y}_C + \left(\frac{b}{2}\right)(\bar{X}_E - \bar{X}_C) \text{ and } \bar{Y}_E^* = \bar{Y}_E - \left(\frac{b}{2}\right)(\bar{X}_E - \bar{X}_C) \qquad \textbf{(16.2)}$$

Note that the assumption of parallel regression lines (equal slopes, b) is critical in the derivation of Equations 16.1 and 16.2. Clearly, the amount of the posttest "penalty" assigned to the experimental group, for being higher on the pretest, is the same as the amount of the posttest "bonus" given to the control group, for being lower on the pretest. After obtaining the adjusted means, their comparison is achieved by the ANOVA procedure—hence the statement "ANCOVA is an ANOVA with adjusted means." The null hypothesis in one-factor ANCOVA with K groups is

$$H_0^*: \mu_1^* = \mu_2^* = \ldots = \mu_K^* \qquad \textbf{(16.3)}$$

versus the alternative hypothesis $H_a^*: \mu_j^* \neq \mu_k^*$ for at least one (j, k) pair; ($j, k = 1, 2, \ldots, K$), where $\mu_1^*, \mu_2^*, \ldots, \mu_K^*$ are the adjusted population means.

The testing of H_0^* versus H_a^* is performed by the ANOVA F-test, but for adjusted means:

$$F = \frac{\text{MS}_\text{B}^*}{\text{MS}_\text{W}^*}, \qquad \textbf{(16.4)}$$

where MS_B^* is the ANCOVA *mean square between groups* (for the adjusted means) and MS_W^* is the ANCOVA *mean square within groups* (the variance of the reduced error terms, $\hat{\varepsilon}_{ij}^*$'s, obtained after regressing Y on the covariate, X — see Figure 16.2). If the null hypothesis, H_0^*, is true, the F-ratio in Formula 16.4 will belong to an F-distribution with $(K - 1)$ degrees of freedom for the numerator and $(N - K - 1)$ degrees of freedom for the denominator, where K is the number of groups and N is the number of observations in all K groups.

16.1.3 Increased Test Power with ANCOVA

Along with "equating" groups on the covariate (e.g., reducing *selection bias* in a pretest-posttest design), ANCOVA increases the power in testing for group differences on the dependent variable, Y. Specifically, ANCOVA reduces the estimate of the population error variance, MS_W, thus increasing the power of the F-test [recall that MS_W is the denominator in the F-statistic in the ANOVA test for group differences — see Chapter 14, Equation 14.19). This is depicted in Figure 16.2, where $\hat{\varepsilon}_{ij}$ is the error estimate for an individual score on the dependent variable, say Y_{ij} for subject i from group j, in a one-factor ANOVA ($\hat{\varepsilon}_{ij} = Y_{ij} - \bar{Y}_j$). The variance of the error estimates, $\hat{\varepsilon}_{ij}$'s, is the mean square within, MS_W, in ANOVA. The subject's score on the covariate (e.g., pretest) X is denoted X_{ij} and its deviation from the mean of group j on X is denoted ΔX_{ij} (i.e., $\Delta X_{ij} = X_{ij} - \bar{X}_j$). With the ANCOVA regression of Y on the covariate X for group j, part of the ANOVA error term, $\hat{\varepsilon}_{ij}$, becomes known. Specifically, $\hat{\varepsilon}_{ij} = \Delta Y_{ij} + \hat{\varepsilon}^*_{ij}$, where the ΔY_{ij} is "explained" by the regression and $\hat{\varepsilon}^*_{ij}$ ($= Y_{ij} - \hat{Y}_{ij}$) is the remaining unexplained part of $\hat{\varepsilon}_{ij}$. As can be seen from the shaded triangle in Figure 16.2, the part by which $\hat{\varepsilon}_{ij}$ is reduced as a result of the ANCOVA regression of Y on X is: $\Delta Y_{ij} = b(\Delta X_{ij}) = b(X_{ij} - \bar{X}_j)$, where b is the slope. Thus,

$$\hat{\varepsilon}_{ij} = b(X_{ij} - \bar{X}_j) + \hat{\varepsilon}^*_{ij} \tag{16.5}$$

Figure 16.2 *Individual error terms with ANOVA (ε_{ij}) and ANCOVA (ε^*_{ij})*

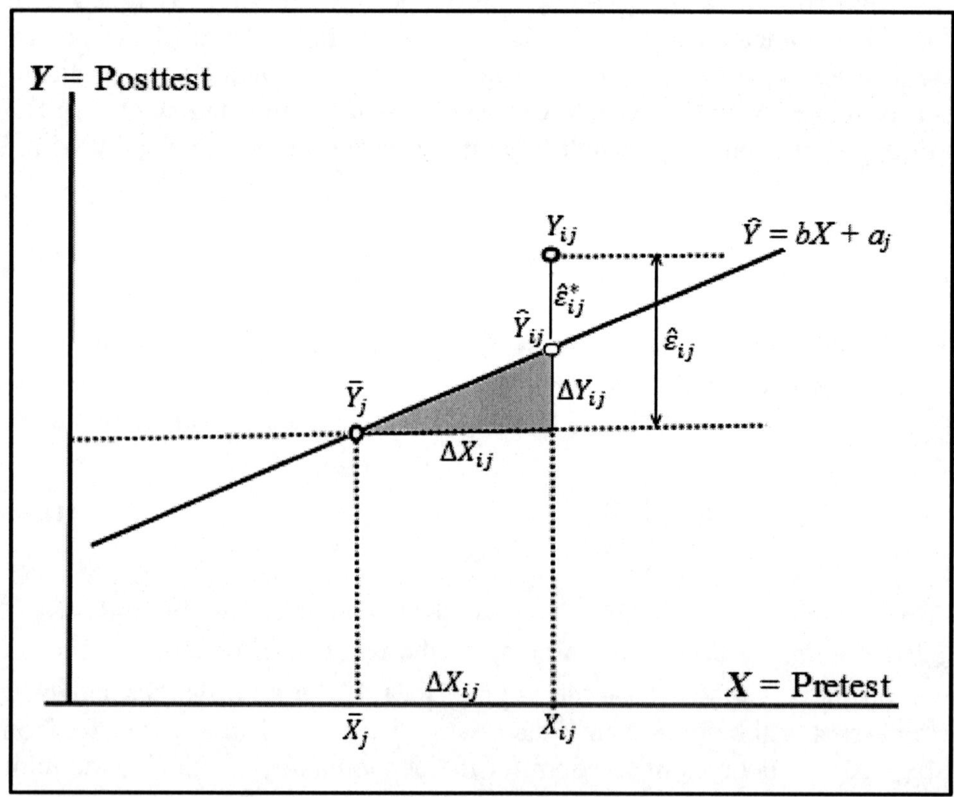

Clearly, the error term for an individual score in ANCOVA ($\hat{\varepsilon}^*_{ij} = Y_{ij} - \hat{Y}_{ij}$) is smaller than its error term in ANOVA ($\hat{\varepsilon}_{ij} = Y_{ij} - \bar{Y}_j$) in absolute value. Thus, if MS^*_W is the denominator of the F-ratio in testing for differences among the adjusted group means with ANCOVA (see

Formula 16.4) and MS_W is the denominator of the F-ratio in testing for differences among unadjusted group means (ANOVA), we have $MS_W^* < MS_W$. This is because MS_W^* is the variance of the smaller error terms, $\hat{\varepsilon}_{ij}^*$, whereas MS_W is the variance of larger error terms, $\hat{\varepsilon}_{ij}$'s. It is expected, then, that the F-test in ANCOVA is more powerful than the F-test in ANOVA. This is generally true, although one degree of freedom is lost from the within-group error variance in ANCOVA due to the presence of one covariate. That is, $df_W^* = df_W - 1$, where df_W^* are the degrees of freedom for MS_W^* — the denominator of the F-ratio in ANCOVA, and df_W are the degrees of freedom for MS_W — the denominator of the F-ratio in ANOVA [with two covariates, two degrees of freedom are lost, etc.] For one-factor ANOVA with K groups and N observations in all K groups, $df_W = N - K$, so $df_W^* = N - K - 1$.

16.1.4 Assumptions in ANCOVA

As ANCOVA is, in fact, an ANOVA with adjusted means, the ANOVA assumptions of normality, homogeneity of variance, and independent observations are required by ANCOVA as well. In addition, it is assumed in ANCOVA that (a) the dependent variable, Y, and the covariate, X, are linearly related, and (b) regressing Y on X produces parallel regression lines (that is, equal regression slopes) across the compared groups. This assumption of equal regression slopes is also referred to as the **homogeneity of regression slopes** assumption in ANCOVA. Although ANCOVA is considered relatively robust with respect to violations of the homogeneity of regression slopes assumption (Glass, Peckham, & Sanders, 1972), testing for this assumption is an important initial step when conducting ANCOVA. Researchers should also be aware that unreliable covariate scores pose a serious threat to the validity of the ANCOVA results.

16.2 Performing ANCOVA and Interpreting the Results

Prior to technically performing an ANCOVA (e.g., using SPSS), the researcher must select a covariate, X, which is meaningfully related to the dependent variable, Y. As noted earlier, it is inappropriate to use as a covariate a variable which explicitly or implicitly relates to the grouping variable. For example, it is not appropriate to use the IQ score as a covariate when comparing groups that represent levels of academic ability (e.g., low, medium, and high). As the adjustment of group means in ANCOVA is based on the presumption that the groups have equal starting points on the covariate, it is important to decide first whether such a presumption is truly realistic for the context of the study.

For comparison purposes, Example 16.1 provides the results from a one-factor ANOVA on posttest scores and then the same data are used in Example 16.2 using ANCOVA with the pretest as a covariate. The data represent fictitious pretest and posttest scores on a science test of three groups of students (two experimental and one control) assigned to three types of gender-oriented approaches to teaching science (EXP_1: only male students, EXP_2: only female students, and CONTROL: both male and female students). In the SPSS layout of the data (see Figure 16.3), the variables are: **Pretest**, **Posttest**, and **Treatment** — the ANOVA factor with three levels (1 = EXP_1, 2 = EXP_2, and 3 = CONTROL).

EXAMPLE 16.1 This example examines the ANOVA results for differences among the three treatment groups on the posttest, without controlling for pretest group differences. Using the SPSS steps for a one-factor ANOVA (see Example 14.2), with **Posttest** as the dependent variable and **Treatment** as a grouping variable (fixed factor), we obtain the output shown in Figure 16.3 (right panel). The data consist of 18 observations shown in Figure 16.3 (left panel). The results from the Levene's test of equality of error variances show that the ANOVA assumption of homogeneity of variance is met, $F(2, 15) = 1.00$, $p > .05$. However, as indicated by the results from the omnibus ANOVA F-test, there are no statistically significant differences among the treatment groups on the posttest, at the .05 level, $F(2, 15) = 1.94$, $p > .05$.

Figure 16.3 *SPSS data and output from one-factor ANOVA for posttest scores*

*EX_16_1.sav [DataSet1] - SPSS Dat

File Edit View Data Transform Analyze

18 :

	Pretest	Posttest	Treatment
1	12	26	1
2	10	22	1
3	7	20	1
4	14	34	1
5	12	28	1
6	11	26	1
7	11	32	2
8	12	31	2
9	6	20	2
10	18	41	2
11	10	29	2
12	11	31	2
13	6	23	3
14	13	35	3
15	15	44	3
16	15	41	3
17	7	28	3
18	9	30	3

Levene's Test of Equality of Error Variances[a]

Dependent Variable: Posttest

F	df1	df2	Sig.
.999	2	15	.391

Tests the null hypothesis that the error variance of the dependent variable is equal across groups.

a. Design: Intercept+Treatment

The homogeneity of variance assumption is met ($p > .05$)

Tests of Between-Subjects Effects

Dependent Variable: Posttest

Source	Type III Sum of Squares	df	Mean Square	F	Sig.
Corrected Model	172.111[a]	2	86.056	1.936	.179
Intercept	16260.056	1	16260.056	365.760	.000
Treatment	172.111	2	86.056	1.936	.179
Error	666.833	15	44.456		
Total	17099.000	18			
Corrected Total	838.944	17			

a. R Squared = .205 (Adjusted R Squared = .099)

There are no statistically significant differences among the treatment groups on posttest, $F(2, 15) = 1.94$, $p = .179$.

EXAMPLE 16.2 In this example we test for differences among the three treatment groups (1 = EXP_1, 2 = EXP_2, and 3 = CONTROL) on the posttest using an ANCOVA to control for group differences on the pretest. The choice of the pretest as a covariate is very appropriate given the substantive relationship between the pretest and posttest scores and the strong Pearson correlation between them, $r(18) = .85$, $p < .001$.

As noted earlier, an important first step when using ANCOVA is to test the homogeneity of regression slopes assumption. Using SPSS with the data in Figure 16.3 (left panel), the test of this assumption is performed as follows:

1. Click **Analyze**, click **General Linear Model**, and click **Univariate**.
2. Click **Posttest**, and click ▶ to move it into the box **Dependent Variable**.
3. Click **Treatment**, and click ▶ to move it into the box **Fixed Factor(s)**.
4. Click **Pretest**, and click ▶ to move it into the box **Covariate(s)**.
5. Click **Model** and then select the radio button for **Custom** under **Specify Model**.

6. Move **Treatment** and **Pretest** from the **Factor & Covariates** box to the **Model** box.
7. While holding down the "Shift" key, highlight both **Treatment** and **Pretest** and then click ► to move them in the **Model** box [they appear as an interaction term **Treatment*Pretest**.]
8. Click **Continue** and then click **OK.**

In the SPSS output (Figure 16.4), the source "Treatment*Pretest" is not statistically significant, $F(2, 12) = 0.35$, $p > .05$. This indicates that the factor (Treatment) and the covariate (Pretest) do not interact and, thus, the assumption of homogeneity of regression slopes is met.

Figure 16.4 *ANCOVA testing for the homogeneity of regression slopes assumption*

Tests of Between-Subjects Effects

Dependent Variable: Posttest

Source	Type III Sum of Squares	df	Mean Square	F	Sig.
Corrected Model	795.606[a]	5	159.121	44.059	.000
Intercept	103.757	1	103.757	28.730	.000
Treatment	10.128	2	5.064	1.402	.284
Pretest	503.690	1	503.690	139.468	.000
Treatment * Pretest	2.554	2	1.277	.354	.709
Error	43.338	12	3.612		
Total	17099.000	18			
Corrected Total	838.944	17			

a. R Squared = .948 (Adjusted R Squared = .927)

The homogeneity of regression slopes assumption is met, $F(2, 12) = 0.35, p > .05$.

After testing the homogeneity of regression slopes assumption, we proceed with the ANCOVA to test for differences among the treatment groups in the posttest controlling for their pretest differences. Using again the data in Figure 16.3 (left panel), the SPSS steps are:

1. Click **Analyze**, click **General Linear Model**, and click **Univariate**.
2. Click **Reset**.
3. Click **Posttest**, and click ► to move it into the box **Dependent Variable**.
4. Click **Treatment**, and click ► to move it into the box **Fixed Factor(s).**
5. Click **Pretest**, and click ► to move it into the box **Covariate(s)**.
6. Click **Options**, check the boxes for **Estimates of effect size** and **Homogeneity tests**, then click Treatment under **Estimated Marginal Means** and click ► to move it into the box **Display Means for** [this is to display the adjusted group means with ANCOVA.]
7. Click **Continue** and then click **OK**.

The resulting SPSS output is provided in Figure 16.5.

Figure 16.5 *SPSS output with ANCOVA for pretest scores controlling for pretest scores*

Levene's Test of Equality of Error Variances[a]

Dependent Variable: Posttest

F	df1	df2	Sig.
.096	2	15	.909

Tests the null hypothesis that the error variance o the dependent variable is equal across groups.

a. Design: Intercept+Pretest+Treatment

Tests of Between-Subjects Effects

Dependent Variable: Posttest

Source	Type III Sum of Squares	df	Mean Square	F	Sig.	Partial Eta Squared
Corrected Model	793.052[a]	3	264.351	80.644	.000	.945
Intercept	132.319	1	132.319	40.366	.000	.742
Pretest	620.941	1	620.941	189.427	.000	.931
Treatment	182.822	2	91.411	27.886	.000	.799
Error	45.892	14	3.278			
Total	17099.000	18				
Corrected Total	838.944	17				

a. R Squared = .945 (Adjusted R Squared = .934)

$F(2, 14) = 27.89, p < .001, p\eta^2 = .80.$

Treatment

Dependent Variable: Posttest

Treatment	Mean	Std. Error	95% Confidence Interval	
			Lower Bound	Upper Bound
EXP_1	26.102[a]	.739	24.517	27.687
EXP_2	30.157[a]	.740	28.569	31.744
CONTROL	33.908[a]	.740	32.321	35.495

a. Covariates appearing in the model are evaluated at the following values: Pretest = 11.06.

The results from the Levene's test show that the assumption of homogeneity of variance is also met, $F(2, 15) = 0.10, p > .05$; [recall that this assumption is required in both ANOVA and ANCOVA]. The *F*-test for effect of Treatment shows that there *are* statistically significant differences among the treatment groups (EXP_1, EXP_2, and CONTROL) on the posttest scores when controlling for pretest group differences, $F(2, 14) = 27.89, p < .001, p\eta^2 = .80$. Note that when we used ANOVA with the same data without controlling for pretest group differences, no statistically significant differences in the posttest were found among the treatment groups (see Example 16.1). As indicated in Section 16.1.3, this is due to the reduction of the *within-groups error variance* produced by regressing *Y* on *X* in ANCOVA, which, in turn, increases the power of the *F*-test in ANCOVA compared to the *F*-test in ANOVA. Indeed, the ANCOVA within-groups error variance (or *mean square within*) in Figure 16.5 is $MS^*_W = 3.278$, which is much smaller than its ANOVA counterpart in Figure 16.3, $MS_W = 44.456$.

As the omnibus ANCOVA test indicates statistically significant differences among the adjusted means of the three treatment groups, a post-hoc multiple comparisons test is needed. However, the post-hoc tests discussed in Chapter 14 (Section 14.7.1) are not appropriate with ANCOVA, as they do not take into account the adjusted means. Instead, an SPSS syntax with appropriate contrast coding can be used. This is illustrated in Figure 16.6, using the adjusted group means obtained with ANCOVA in this example [sample estimates of the adjusted means are provided with the table **Treatment** in Figure 16.5.]. In Figure 16.6, the syntax lines with contrasts for testing null hypotheses are based on the rules of contrast coding described in Chapter 14 (Section 14.7.2.1). Thus, **Treatment 1 -1 0** is the contrast comparing the first two treatment groups (EXP_1 versus EXP_2). Likewise, the syntax line **Treatment 1 0 -1** is the contrast comparing the first and third groups (EXP_1 versus CONTROL), and **Treatment 0 1 -1** is the contrast comparing the second and third groups (EXP_2 versus CONTROL). The variables Pretest, Posttest, and Treatment must appear in the SPSS syntax with the names that they have in the SPSS data file. The last syntax line ends with a period (.).

Figure 16.6 SPSS syntax for ANCOVA post-hoc tests

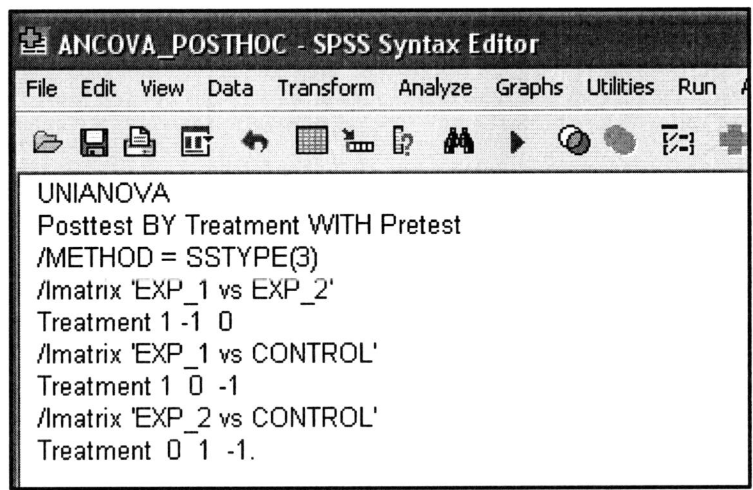

Once you have the syntax lines in the SPSS Syntax Editor, as shown in Figure 16.6, click on **Run** and then click on **All**. The SPSS output provides three "custom hypothesis tests" for the ANCOVA post-hoc group comparisons: 'EXP_1 versus EXP_2,' EXP_1 versus CONTROL,' and 'EXP_2 versus CONTROL.' For space considerations, only the first custom hypothesis test (EXP_1 versus EXP_2) is shown in Figure 16.7, but an APA-style summary of the results from all three tests is provided with Table 16.1.

NOTE [16.1] The SPSS syntax in Figure 16.6 is provided to illustrate the use of "contrasts" with adjusted means as such contrasts can also be used for planned comparisons in ANCOVA [e.g., the syntax lines **Treatment 1 1 −2** and **/lmatrix 'EXP_1 and EXP_2 vs CONTROL'** will produce a planned comparison for the joint effect of the first two experimental groups versus the control group.] However, if the goal is only to obtain post-hoc pairwise comparisons of adjusted means (as shown in Table 16.1), instead of using the syntax in Figure 16.6, we can just add the following selection in **Step 6** of the list of SPSS steps for ANCOVA described below Figure 16.4: Check the box **Compare main effects.**

Figure 16.7 *Selected SPSS output for post-hoc ANCOVA comparisons*

Custom Hypothesis Tests #1

Contrast Results (K Matrix)[a]

Contrast			Dependent Variable Posttest
L1	Contrast Estimate		-4.055
	Hypothesized Value		0
	Difference (Estimate - Hypothesized)		-4.055
	Std. Error		1.046
	Sig.		.002
	95% Confidence Interval for Difference	Lower Bound	-6.299
		Upper Bound	-1.811

a. Based on the user-specified contrast coefficients (L') matrix: EXP_1 vs EXP_2

Test Results

Dependent Variable: Posttest

Source	Sum of Squares	df	Mean Square	F	Sig.
Contrast	49.230	1	49.230	15.018	.002
Error	45.892	14	3.278		

Table 16.1

Multiple Comparisons for Adjusted Posttest Group Means Using the Pretest as a Covariate

Contrast comparison	ΔM	SEΔM	df_{contrast}	df_{error}	F	95% CI for ΔM	
EXP_1 — EXP_2	−4.06	1.05	1	14	15.02**	−6.30	−1.81
EXP_1 — CONTROL	−7.81	1.05	1	14	55.74***	−10.05	−5.56
EXP_2 — CONTROL	−3.75	1.05	1	14	12.83**	−6.00	−1.51

Note. ΔM = Difference of adjusted means. SEΔM = Standard error of ΔM.

*$p < .05$. ** $p < .01$. *** $p < .001$.

The results in Table 16.1 show that all pairwise comparisons of adjusted group means on the posttest, using the pretest as a covariate, are statistically significant at the .01 (or lower) level. Specifically, the difference between the adjusted posttest means of the EXP_1 and EXP_2 groups is statistically significant, $F(1, 14) = 15.02, p < .01$, and its 95 percent confidence interval shows that the EXP_1 group performed lower than the EXP_2 group by a difference that may vary from 1.81 to 6.30 units on the posttest scale of the science test. Likewise, the EXP_1 group performed lower than the CONTROL group, $F(1, 14) = 55.74, p < .001$, by a difference that may vary from 5.56 to 10.05 posttest units. Finally, the EXP_2 group also performed lower than the CONTROL group, $F(1, 14) = 12.83, p < .01$, by a difference that may vary from 1.51 to 6.00 posttest units.

Thus, given that the EXP_1 group consists only of male students, the EXP_2 group consists only of female students, and the CONTROL group consists of both female and male students, the ANCOVA results suggest that the best posttest results on the science test, controlling for the pretest scores, were obtained by the mixed gender group (CONTROL), followed by the group of female students, and then by the group of male students. Recall, however, that the data in this illustrative example are fictitious, so all "findings" are hypothetical.

16.3 ANCOVA versus ANOVA on Gain Score

As pretest-posttest measures are frequently available in education studies, ANCOVA is usually the method of choice. However, using only ANCOVA prevents researchers from examining the treatment effect in terms of "change" from pretest to posttest. In fact, sometimes (if not more often) the question about "change effects" is the right question to ask in education and related fields. In the framework of analysis of variance, testing for group differences in change from pretest to posttest (gain) can be achieved by using ANOVA with the gain score as a dependent variable. The **gain score** is the difference between the posttest scores, Y, and the pretest scores, X (i.e., Gain = $Y - X$).

The use of gain scores in measurement of change has been criticized due to a (generally false) assertion that the difference between the scores is less reliable than the scores themselves (e.g., Cronbach & Furby, 1970; Linn & Slindle, 1977). This assertion is true *only if* the pretest scores and the posttest scores have equal (or proportional) variances and equal reliability. When this is not the case, as happens in many situations, the reliability of the gain score is high (e.g., Overall & Woodward, 1975; D. Rogosa, Brandt, & Zimowski, 1982). The unreliability of the gain score does not preclude valid testing of the null hypothesis about mean gain score in a population of examinees. If the gain score is unreliable, however, it is not appropriate to correlate the gain score with other variables in a population of examinees (Mellenbergh, 1999). Thus, without ignoring the caution urged by some authors, researchers should be aware that there are situations when gain scores are useful.

EXAMPLE 16.3 This example illustrates how to conduct an ANOVA on gain score using the data from the ANCOVA in Example 16.2. This is achieved by computing a new variable, GAIN, by subtracting Pretest from Posttest scores in the SPSS data set shown in Figure 16.3 and then using one-factor ANOVA with **GAIN** as the dependent variable and **Treatment** as a three-level fixed factor (1 = EXP_1, 2 = EXP_2, and 3 = CONTROL) [The SPSS steps for one-factor ANOVA are described in Chapter 14, Example 14.2]. The SPSS output from ANOVA on GAIN is provided in Figure 16.8.

Figure 16.8 *ANOVA on gain score for pretest and posttest data*

Levene's Test of Equality of Error Variances

Dependent Variable: GAIN

F	df1	df2	Sig.
.696	2	15	.514

Tests of Between-Subjects Effects

Dependent Variable: GAIN

Source	Type III Sum of Squares	df	Mean Square	F	Sig.	Partial Eta Squared
Corrected Model	177.333[a]	2	88.667	7.615	.005	.504
Intercept	6498.000	1	6498.000	558.034	.000	.974
Treatment	177.333	2	88.667	7.615	.005	.504
Error	174.667	15	11.644			
Total	6850.000	18				
Corrected Total	352.000	17				

a. R Squared = .504 (Adjusted R Squared = .438)

Multiple Comparisons

Dependent Variable: GAIN
Tukey HSD

(I) Treatment	(J) Treatment	Mean Difference (I-J)	Std. Error	Sig.	95% Confidence Interval	
					Lower Bound	Upper Bound
EXP_1	EXP_2	-4.33	1.970	.104	-9.45	.78
	CONTROL	-7.67*	1.970	.004	-12.78	-2.55
EXP_2	EXP_1	4.33	1.970	.104	-.78	9.45
	CONTROL	-3.33	1.970	.240	-8.45	1.78
CONTROL	EXP_1	7.67*	1.970	.004	2.55	12.78
	EXP_2	3.33	1.970	.240	-1.78	8.45

Based on observed means.

*. The mean difference is significant at the .05 level.

The Levene's test indicates that the homogeneity of the variance assumption is met, $F(2, 15) = 0.70$, $p > .05$. The results in the table **Tests of Between-Subjects Effects** show that there are statistically significant differences among some treatment groups on gain score, $F(2, 15) = 7.62$, $p < .01$, $p\eta^2 = .50$. Moreover, the multiple comparisons results obtained with the Tukey post-hoc test indicate that the only statistically significant difference is between the EXP_1 and CONTROL groups ($p = .004$). The 95 percent confidence interval for this difference shows that the gain of the EXP_1 (only males) group is lower than the gain of the CONTROL (males and females) group for the pretest-posttest change on the science test. Note that this was not the case when we conducted an ANCOVA with these data, where all pairwise group differences were statistically significant on the posttest, controlling for group differences on the pretest (see Table 16.1). This, of course, should not be a surprise given that ANOVA on gain score and ANCOVA address different questions about group differences on pretest-posttest data.

16.4 Summary

• Analysis of covariance (ANCOVA) is a statistical method that combines the analysis of variance (ANOVA) with regression analysis with the purpose to (a) increase the test power and (b) equate the compared groups on an "extraneous" variable (covariate) that is linearly related to the dependent variable.

• The statistical control provided by ANCOVA in a quasi-experimental design (e.g., using randomly selected classrooms as intact units) does not "transform" this design into a truly randomized experimental design. Therefore, caution is needed in this regard when interpreting ANCOVA results.

• With quasi-experimental pretest-posttest designs, the main purpose of ANCOVA is to adjust the posttest means for differences among the groups on the pretest because such differences are likely to occur with intact groups.

• With randomized pretest-posttest designs, the main purpose of ANCOVA is to reduce error variance because the random assignment of subjects to groups guards against systematic bias.

• The criteria for selecting a covariate, *X*, in ANCOVA with a dependent variable *Y* are that (a) *X* must be meaningfully related to *Y*, (b) there must be a linear relationship between *X* and *Y*, and (c) the identification of groups compared with ANCOVA must not (explicitly or implicitly) be based on their scores on the covariate, *X* — e.g., it is not appropriate to use the IQ score as a covariate in ANCOVA comparison of groups with low, medium, and high academic achievement.

• In ANCOVA, the group means on the dependent variable, *Y*, are adjusted for group differences on the covariate, *X*, by regressing *Y* on *X* for each group separately.

• ANCOVA is ANOVA with adjusted means.

• In addition to the ANOVA assumptions (normality, homogeneity of variance, and independence of observations), ANCOVA assumes that (a) there is a linear relationship between the covariate, *X*, and the dependent variable, *Y*, and (b) when regressing *Y* on *X* for each group, all regression coefficients are equal for the population [*homogeneity of regression slopes*]. Also, the validity of the ANCOVA results is in doubt when the covariate scores are unreliable.

• The ANCOVA adjustment of group means is of the same amount ($\Delta\bar{Y}$) for each group [see Equation 16.1 for the value of $\Delta\bar{Y}$ with two groups.] The error of score Y_{ij}, for subject *i* from group *j* in a one-factor ANOVA ($\hat{\varepsilon}_{ij} = Y_{ij} - \bar{Y}_j$), is larger than the error of this score in ANCOVA ($\hat{\varepsilon}^*_{ij} = Y_{ij} - \hat{Y}_{ij}$) because the latter is a part of the former (see Figure 16.2 and Equation 16.5). That is, $\hat{\varepsilon}^*_{ij} < \hat{\varepsilon}_{ij}$.

• The error variance with ANCOVA (MS^*_W = variance of the $\hat{\varepsilon}^*_{ij}$'s) is smaller than the error variance with ANOVA (MS_W = variance of the $\hat{\varepsilon}_{ij}$'s) because $\hat{\varepsilon}^*_{ij} < \hat{\varepsilon}_{ij}$. Therefore, the *F*-test with ANCOVA is more powerful than that with ANOVA [see Equation 14.19 and 16.4].

• If the ANCOVA null hypothesis of equal adjusted group means is true, the *F*-ratio (see Formula 16.4) belongs to a *F*-distribution with ($K - 1$) the degrees of freedom for the numerator and ($N - K - 1$) degrees of freedom for the denominator, where *K* is the number of groups and *N* is the number of observations in all *K* groups.

• ANCOVA and ANOVA on gain score with pretest-posttest data provide different information about the treatment effect. While ANCOVA compares groups on the posttest under the hypothetical assumption that they have equal "start" on the pretest, ANOVA on gain score compares the groups on their "change" from pretest to posttest.

• The assumptions of randomization, linear relationship between the pretest and posttest scores, and homogeneity of regression slopes underlie the use of both ANCOVA and ANOVA on gain score.

16.5 Study Questions

1. What are the main purposes of ANCOVA?

2. What are the criteria for selecting a covariate in ANCOVA?

3. What are the ANCOVA assumptions?

4. Does the reliability of the covariate matter? (Why?)

5. Is it appropriate to use the height of participants in a sport event when groups of short versus tall participants are compared on their average performance on 100 meter dash?

6. What is the main purpose of ANCOVA with randomized pretest-posttest designs?

7. If there is a positive linear relationship between the covariate, *X*, and dependent variable, *Y*, for which of two groups compared in ANCOVA the adjustment of the mean is downward:

A. The group with lower sample mean on *X*,
B. The group with higher sample mean on *X*,
C. For both groups,
D. The group with larger sample size,
E. The group with smaller sample size.

8. What are the implications of the fact that the error term for any individual score with ANCOVA ($\hat{\varepsilon}^*_{ij} = Y_{ij} - \hat{Y}_{ij}$) is smaller than the error term for this score with ANOVA ($\hat{\varepsilon}_{ij} = Y_{ij} - \bar{Y}_j$) in absolute value?

9. In ANCOVA with pretest-posttest data, the magnitude of adjustment of posttest means for groups with higher pretest means is larger than that for groups with lower pretest means — True or False?

10. For one-factor ANCOVA comparing four groups with 100 observations in all four groups, the degrees of freedom for the numerator and denominator of the ANCOVA *F*-ratio are

A. 4 and 100, **B.** 3 and 99, **C.** 3 and 95, or **D.** 3 and 96, respectively.

CHAPTER 17

MULTIPLE REGRESSION AND ANOVA

In Chapter 14 (Section 14.7.2) we introduced the concept of contrasts for multiple comparisons in one-factor ANOVA. Now we will capitalize on this concept in using multiple regression with contrast-coded predictors for ANOVA purposes. The focus is on planned ANOVA comparisons.

17.1 One-Factor ANOVA via Multiple Regression

17.1.1 Contrast Coding for ANOVA with Two Groups

Consider first conducting an ANOVA with two groups (say, males and females). The null hypothesis is H_0: $\mu_1 = \mu_2$, where μ_1 and μ_2 are the population means for males and females, respectively, on the dependent variable, Y. As H_0: $\mu_1 - \mu_2 = 0$, we can use the contrast notations in Section 14.7.2 to represent H_0: $\Psi = 0$, where Ψ is the contrast $(1)\mu_1 + (-1)\mu_2$. Recall that the sum of all contrast coefficients is zero [here, $1 + (-1) = 0$].

The contrast coefficients (1 −1) can be used as **contrast coding** for gender (1 = male, and −1 = female). Then H_0 can be tested by regressing the dependent variable, Y, on the categorical predictor X (Gender), $Y = bX + a$. If the regression coefficient, b, is statistically significant, we reject H_0 at the specified level of significance (say, $\alpha = .05$). This "rule" of testing H_0 is based on the relationship between the regression coefficient, b, and the difference between the sample means $\bar{Y}_1$ and $\bar{Y}_2$ (for males and females, respectively). This is depicted in Figure 17.1, where 1 and −1 are the sample "means" of males and females, respectively, on the categorical predictor X (1 = male, −1 = female). Thus, the predicted Y score is $\hat{Y}_1 = \bar{Y}_1$, for males, and $\hat{Y}_2 = \bar{Y}_2$, for females (see NOTE [10.3]). Using the property of the slope, $b = \Delta\hat{Y}/\Delta X$ (see Equation 10.9), with $\Delta\hat{Y} = \Delta\bar{Y} = \bar{Y}_1 - \bar{Y}_2$ and $\Delta X = 2$ (the distance between −1 and 1), we obtain

$$b = \frac{1}{2}(\bar{Y}_1 - \bar{Y}_2) \qquad \textbf{(17.1)}$$

Figure 17.1 *Regressing Y on the contrast-coded predictor X (Gender)*

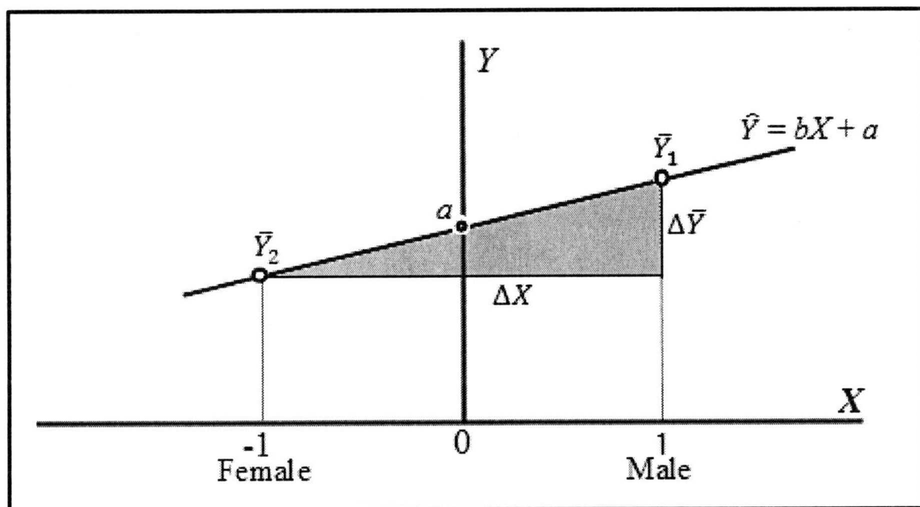

Equation 17.1 shows that testing the group mean difference $(\bar{Y}_1 - \bar{Y}_2)$ for statistical significance is equivalent to testing the regression coefficient (b) for statistical significance. Thus, when the regression coefficient, b, is statistically significant, we reject H_0.

17.1.2 Contrast Coding for One-factor ANOVA with Three Groups

The use of a multiple regression with contrast-coded predictors for an ANOVA with three or more groups is particularly useful in testing for planned hypotheses.. Suppose that in a one-factor ANOVA with three groups the first two groups are participants in two variations of an experimental treatment (E_1 and E_2) and the third group are participants in the control condition (C) of the experiment. If the researcher wants to compare the two experimental groups and then their combined effect versus the effect of the control group, the regular ANOVA with post-hoc comparisons would not work. Instead, the following two planned null hypotheses must be tested:

$$H_{01}: \mu_1 = \mu_2 \text{ and } H_{02}: \frac{\mu_1 + \mu_2}{2} = \mu_3 , \qquad \textbf{(17.2)}$$

where μ_1 and μ_2 are the population means for the two experimental groups and μ_3 is the population mean for the control group. As described in Chapter 14 (Section 14.7.2), H_{01} can be written as H_{01}: $\mu_1 - \mu_2 = 0$ [or H_{01}: $(1)\mu_1 + (-1)\mu_2 + (0)\mu_3 = 0$]. Thus, the contrast representation of this null hypothesis is H_{01}: $\Psi_1 = 0$, where Ψ_1 is the contrast $(1)\mu_1 + (-1)\mu_2 + (0)\mu_3$. Likewise, H_{02} can be represented as H_{02}: $\mu_1 + \mu_2 - 2\mu_3 = 0$, so its contrast form is H_{02}: $\Psi_2 = 0$, where Ψ_2 is the contrast $\mu_1 + \mu_2 - 2\mu_3$. The sample estimates of the contrasts Ψ_1 and Ψ_2 are:

$$\hat{\Psi}_1 = \bar{Y}_1 - \bar{Y}_2 \text{ and } \hat{\Psi}_2 = \bar{Y}_1 + \bar{Y}_2 - 2\bar{Y}_3 \qquad \textbf{(17.3)}$$

We can test H_{01} and H_{02} by regressing the dependent variable, Y, on two contrast-coded predictors, X_1 and X_2, as follows:

$$\text{Contrast code for } X_1\text{:}\ \mathbf{1 \ \ {-1} \ \ 0} \qquad \textbf{(17.4)}$$

$$\text{Contrast code for } X_2\text{:}\ \mathbf{1 \ \ 1 \ \ {-2}}. \qquad \textbf{(17.5)}$$

The general form of the regression equation in this case is $\hat{Y} = b_1X_1 + b_2X_2 + a$. As with the case of two groups presented earlier in this section, it can be shown that testing the coefficients b_1 and b_2 for statistical significance is equivalent to testing the contrasts $\hat{\Psi}_1$ and $\hat{\Psi}_2$ for statistical significance. Specifically, it can be shown that **each regression coefficient (b) equals the ratio of the corresponding contrast to the sum of squared coding values of the contrast**. Thus,

$$b_1 = \frac{\hat{\Psi}_1}{1^2 + (-1)^2 + 0^2} = \frac{\hat{\Psi}_1}{2} = \frac{\bar{Y}_1 - \bar{Y}_2}{2}, \qquad \textbf{(17.6)}$$

$$b_2 = \frac{\hat{\Psi}_2}{1^2 + 1^2 + (-2)^2} = \frac{\hat{\Psi}_2}{4} = \frac{\bar{Y}_1 + \bar{Y}_2 - 2\bar{Y}_3}{4}. \qquad \textbf{(17.7)}$$

Thus, if b_1 is statistically significant, we reject H_{01}. Likewise, if b_2 is statistically significant, we reject H_{02}. The testing of H_{01} and H_{02}, at the .05 level, is illustrated next by using a multiple linear regression with the contrast coded predictors X_1 and X_2 in (17.4) and (17.5), respectively.

EXAMPLE 17.1 In this example, H_{01}: $\mu_1 = \mu_2$ and H_{02}: $\frac{\mu_1 + \mu_2}{2} = \mu_3$ are tested using the data from Chapter 16 (see Examples 16.1, 16.2, and 16.3). The data are pretest and posttest scores on a science test of three groups of students assigned to three types of gender-oriented approaches to teaching science (EXP_1: only male students, EXP_2: only female students, and CONTROL: both male and female students). In Example 16.3, an ANOVA on gain score was used to compare the groups on change from pretest to posttest. Here, using GAIN as a dependent variable, the ANOVA comparison is between the first two groups (H_{01}) and then between their average effect versus the effect of the third group (H_{02}). Figure 17.2 (left panel) shows the data and the contrast-coded predictors X_1 and X_2 as shown in (17.4) and (17.5). The coding values in X_1 equal 1 for the subjects in the first treatment group, -1 for the subjects in the second group, and 0 for the subjects in the third group, thus reflecting the contrast coding for H_{01} **(1 −1 0)**. The coding values in X_2 equal 1 for the first group, 1 for the second group, and -2 for the third group, thus reflecting the contrast coding for H_{02} **(1 1 −2)**.

Figure 17.2 *Multiple regression with contrast-coded predictors X_1 and X_2 for ANOVA testing*

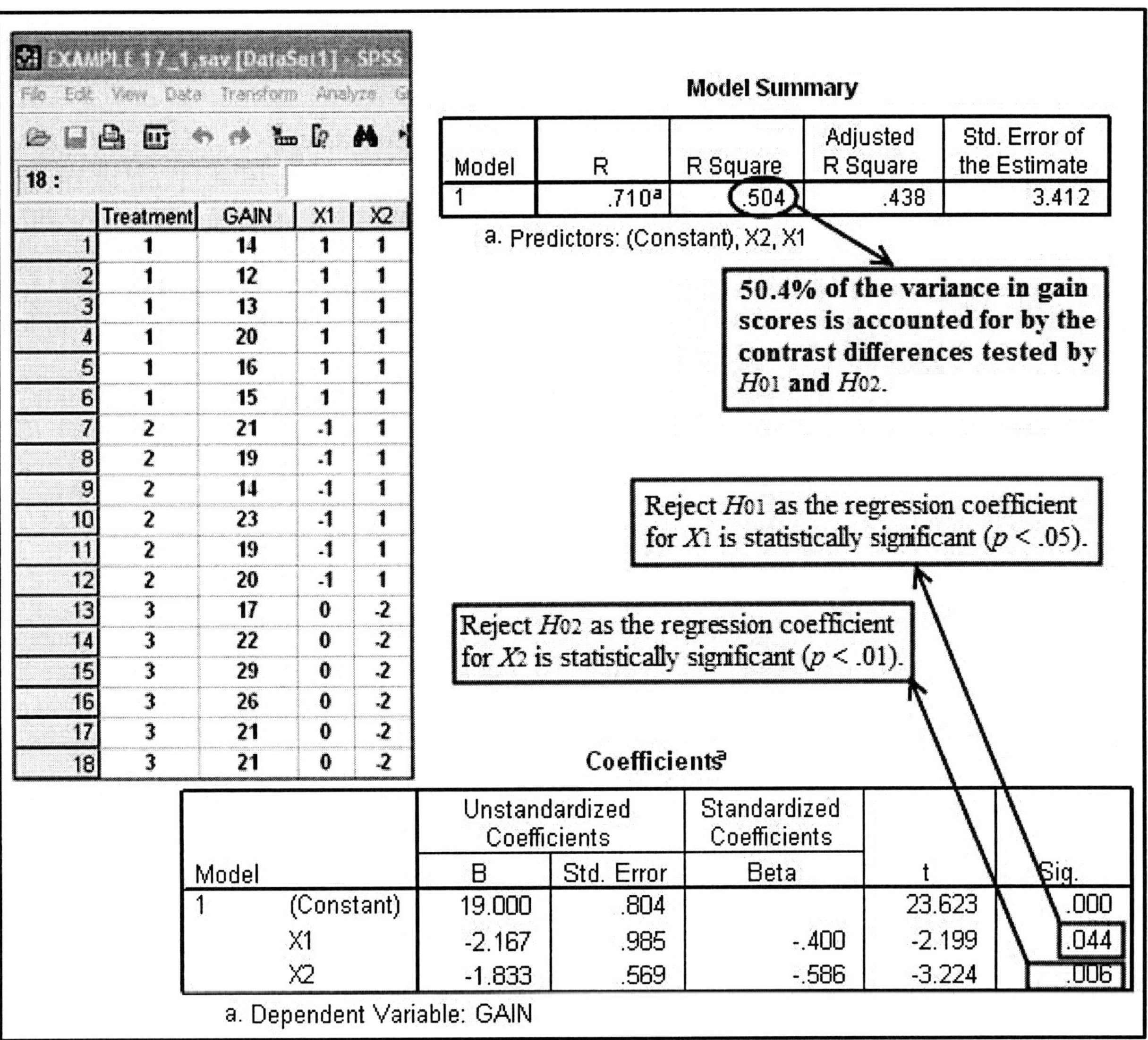

	Treatment	GAIN	X1	X2
1	1	14	1	1
2	1	12	1	1
3	1	13	1	1
4	1	20	1	1
5	1	16	1	1
6	1	15	1	1
7	2	21	-1	1
8	2	19	-1	1
9	2	14	-1	1
10	2	23	-1	1
11	2	19	-1	1
12	2	20	-1	1
13	3	17	0	-2
14	3	22	0	-2
15	3	29	0	-2
16	3	26	0	-2
17	3	21	0	-2
18	3	21	0	-2

Model Summary

Model	R	R Square	Adjusted R Square	Std. Error of the Estimate
1	.710[a]	.504	.438	3.412

a. Predictors: (Constant), X2, X1

Coefficients[a]

Model		Unstandardized Coefficients		Standardized Coefficients		
		B	Std. Error	Beta	t	Sig.
1	(Constant)	19.000	.804		23.623	.000
	X1	-2.167	.985	-.400	-2.199	.044
	X2	-1.833	.569	-.586	-3.224	.006

a. Dependent Variable: GAIN

Selected SPSS output from regressing GAIN on the contrast-coded predictors X_1 and X_2 is shown in Figure 17.2. The results in the **Coefficients** table show that we reject H_{01} as the regression coefficient for the predictor X_1, with the contrast coding for H_{01} (1 −1 0), is statistically significant (p = .044). Taking into account Equation 17.6, the negative sign of the regression coefficient for X_1 (−2.167) indicates that the mean of the first group (EXP_1 = only males) is *lower* than the mean of the second group (EXP_2 = only females). Note that this difference was not detected by the regular ANOVA on gain score reported in Chapter 16 (Figure 16.8), where the post-hoc test for the difference between the first two groups (EXP_1 and EXP_2) was not statistically significant (p = .104). This illustrates the higher power of testing planned comparisons with contrast coding compared to regular ANOVA tests with the same data. We also reject H_{02}, as the regression coefficient for the predictor X_2, with the contrast coding for H_{02} (1 1 −2), is statistically significant (p = .006). Taking into account Equation 17.7, the negative sign of this regression coefficient (−1.833) indicates that the average gain score of the first two groups (only males and only females), $(\mu_1 + \mu_2)/2$, is *smaller* than the gain score of the third group, μ_3, which consists of both males and females. This difference cannot be tested with the regular one-factor ANOVA (see Example 16.3). Furthermore, the R-square value reported with the SPSS output in Figure 17.2 (R^2 = .504) indicates that 50.4 percent of the variance in the dependent variable (gain score in science) is accounted for by the contrast differences tested by H_{01} and H_{02}.

17.1.3 Orthogonal Contrasts

As noted in Chapter 14 (Section 14.7.2), a **contrast,** Ψ, among K population means is a linear combination of the means ($\Psi = c_1\mu_1 + c_2\mu_2 + \cdots + c_K\mu_K$), where the sum of coefficients equals zero ($c_1 + c_2 + \cdots + c_K = 0$). To use a multiple regression to conduct an ANOVA with K groups, it is necessary to employ K – 1 contrast codes. Thus, one contrast-coded predictor (X) is needed for an ANOVA with two groups, two contrast-coded predictors (X_1 and X_2) for an ANOVA with three groups, three contrast-coded predictors (X_1, X_2, and X_3) for an ANOVA with four groups, etc.

Two contrasts are considered **orthogonal** to each other when the sum of the paired products of their coefficients equals zero. For example, the contrast codes (1 −1 0) and (1 1 −2), which we used for H_{01} and H_{02} in the previous section— see (17.4) and (17.5), are orthogonal since the sum of the paired products of their coefficients equals zero: (1)(1) + (−1)(1) + (0)(2) = 1 – 1 + 0 = 0. Table 17.1 presents three pairs of null hypotheses for three-group ANOVAs that yield orthogonal contrast codes: (H_{01}, H_{02}), (H_{03}, H_{04}), and (H_{05}, H_{06}). The two null hypotheses in each pair can be tested by using a multiple regression with the respective contrast-coded predictors, X_1 and X_2. The regression coefficients b_1 and b_2 are also presented in Table 17.1 — each as a ratio of the corresponding contrast to the sum of squared coding values of the contrast (see Equations 17.7 and 17.7). We can use three multiple regressions to test all three pairs of null hypotheses, but this is hardly necessary in a real study. It is important to note that the choice of which contrast codes should be used must be guided by theoretical knowledge or empirical expectations about group differences on the dependent variable.

Note also that if we "couple" null hypotheses from different pairs in Table 17.1, the two contrast codes are not orthogonal to each other. For example, if we test H_{02} and H_{03} using multiple regression, the contrast codes for H_{02} (1 1 −2) and H_{03} (1 0 −1) are not orthogonal as the sum of their paired products does not equal zero: (1)(1) + (1)(0) + (−2)(−1) = 1 + 0 + 2 = 3. This **nonorthogonality** implies some degree of redundancy between the two contrast-coded predictors. Questions addressed with null hypotheses that produce nonorthogonal contrast codes are not fully independent. That is, knowing the answer to one question provides some "clues" about the answer to the other question.

NOTE [17.1] Contrast-coded predictors in a multiple regression with unbalanced ANOVA designs (when there is an unequal number of observations across factor levels or cells) are not independent even when the contrast codes are defined as orthogonal [i.e., the sum of their code values equal zero and the sum of their paired products equal zero.] The case of dependent (correlated) contrasts is addressed in the discussion of multivariate analysis of variance later in this book (Chapter 21, Section 21.7).

Table 17.1 *Three pairs of orthogonal contrast-coded predictors, X_1 and X_2, for testing pairs of ANOVA null hypotheses (H_{01}, H_{02}), (H_{03}, H_{04}), and (H_{05}, H_{06}) using multiple regression.*

Null hypothesis	Contrast code	Check for orthogonality	Regression coefficient
H_{01}: $\mu_1 = \mu_2$ H_{02}: $\dfrac{\mu_1+\mu_2}{2} = \mu_3$	X_1: **1 −1 0** X_2: **1 1 −2**	$(1)(1) + (-1)(1) + (0)(-2)$ $= 1 - 1 + 0 = 0$	$b_1 = \dfrac{\bar{Y}_1 - \bar{Y}_2}{2}$ $b_2 = \dfrac{\bar{Y}_1 + \bar{Y}_2 - 2\bar{Y}_3}{4}$
H_{03}: $\mu_1 = \mu_3$ H_{04}: $\dfrac{\mu_1+\mu_3}{2} = \mu_2$	X_1: **1 0 −1** X_2: **1 −2 1**	$(1)(1) + (0)(-2) + (-1)(1)$ $= 1 + 0 - 1 = 0$	$b_1 = \dfrac{\bar{Y}_1 - \bar{Y}_3}{2}$ $b_2 = \dfrac{\bar{Y}_1 + \bar{Y}_3 - 2\bar{Y}_2}{4}$
H_{05}: $\mu_2 = \mu_3$ H_{06}: $\dfrac{\mu_2+\mu_3}{2} = \mu_1$	X_1: **0 1 −1** X_2: **−2 1 1**	$(0)(-2) + (1)(1) + (-1)(1)$ $= 0 + 1 - 1 = 0$	$b_1 = \dfrac{\bar{Y}_2 - \bar{Y}_3}{2}$ $b_2 = \dfrac{\bar{Y}_2 + \bar{Y}_3 - 2\bar{Y}_1}{4}$

In the case of an ANOVA with four groups, a set of three null hypotheses must be tested via a single multiple regression analysis. An example of orthogonal contrast-coded predictors in this case is provided with the following set of null hypotheses [using the star notation to differentiate these hypotheses from those presented in Table 17.1]:

H_{01}^*: $\mu_1 = \dfrac{\mu_2 + \mu_3 + \mu_4}{3}$, with a contrast-coded predictor X_1: **3 −1 −1 −1,**

H_{02}^*: $\mu_2 = \dfrac{\mu_3 + \mu_4}{2}$, with a contrast-coded predictor X_2: **0 2 −1 −1**, and

H_{03}^*: $\mu_3 = \mu_4$, with a contrast-coded predictor X_3: **0 0 1 −1**.

The product of the contrast-coded predictors X_1 and X_2 equals zero, thus indicating that they are orthogonal to each other: $X_1X_2 = (3)(0) + (-1)(2) + (-1)(-1) + (-1)(-1) = 0 - 2 + 1 + 1 = 0$. Likewise, it can be seen that $X_1X_3 = 0$ and $X_2X_3 = 0$. Thus, X_1, X_2, and X_3 represent an **orthogonal set of contrast-coded predictors.** A similar coding scheme can be used to obtain orthogonal contrast-coded predictors in a multiple regression for one-factor ANOVA with more than four groups. With five groups, for example, an orthogonal set of four contrast-coded predictors is:

X_1: **4 −1 −1 −1 −1**,
X_2: **0 3 −1 −1 −1**,
X_3: **0 0 2 −1 −1**, and
X_4: **0 0 0 1 −1**.

In any case, the null hypothesis associated with a specific contrast-coded predictor is rejected if the regression coefficient of this predictor is statistically significant. As noted earlier, this is because each regression coefficient equals the ratio of the corresponding contrast to the sum of the squared coding values of the contrast. In the general case of a **contrast** Ψ for K population means, the sample estimate of this contrast is $\widehat{\Psi} = c_1\bar{Y}_1 + c_2\bar{Y}_2 + \ldots + c_K\bar{Y}_K$, so the regression coefficient, b, for the predictor with the contrast coding $c_1, c_2, \ldots, c_K$ is

$$b = \frac{\widehat{\Psi}}{\sum c^2} = \frac{c_1\bar{Y}_1 + c_2\bar{Y}_2 + \ldots + c_K\bar{Y}_K}{c_1^2 + c_2^2 + \ldots + c_K^2}. \quad \textbf{(17.8)}$$

Clearly, testing $\widehat{\Psi}$ for statistical significance is equivalent to testing b for statistical significance.

17.2 Two-Factor ANOVA via Multiple Regression

The approach to using multiple regression with contrast-coded predictors for one-factor ANOVA is applicable to the case of two-factor ANOVA as well. It is just a matter of appropriate coding. Consider, for example, a two-factor (A x B) ANOVA, where factor A has three levels (A_1, A_2, A_3) and factor B has two levels (B_1, B_2). With a (3 x 2) ANOVA we have 6 cells (i.e., 6 groups), so we need to conduct a multiple regression with 5 contrast-coded predictors. The coding scheme with five contrast-coded predictors (X_1, X_2, X_3, X_4, and X_5) depends on the hypotheses of interest.

Given that factor A has three levels, we can have two (3 – 1 = 2) hypotheses about the effects of factor A. Thus, the first two contrast-coded predictors (X_1 and X_2) will be used to test for two effects of factor A. Factor B has two levels, so there is only one hypothesis (2 – 1 = 1) about this factor — the main effect of B, which will be tested by the third contrast-coded predictor (X_3). The remaining two contrast-coded predictors (X_4 and X_5) will be used to test interaction hypotheses defined by the "products" $X_4 = X_1X_3$ and $X_5 = X_2X_3$. Specifically, the null hypothesis tested by X_4 states that "there is no interaction between the differences tested by X_1 and X_3." Likewise, the null hypothesis tested by X_5 states that "there is no interaction between the differences tested by X_2 and X_3." A set of five null hypotheses that yield orthogonal contrast-coded predictors under this coding scheme are provided in Table 17.2. Note that the contrast coding for $X_4 = X_1X_3$ is obtained by "multiplying" the contrast codes for X_1 and X_3, just like removing parentheses in algebraic multiplications without adding the resulting terms:

(1 −1 0)(1 −1) = (1)(1) (1)(−1) (−1)(1) (−1)(−1) (0)(1) (0)(−1) = **1 −1 −1 1 0 0.**

Similarly, the contrast coding for $X_5 = X_2X_3$ is obtained by "multiplying" the codes for X_2 and X_3:

(1 1 −2)(1 −1) = (1)(1) (1)(−1) (1)(1) (1)(−1) (−2)(1) (−2)(−1) = **1 −1 1 −1 −2 2.**

Table 17.2 *Five null hypotheses with (3 x 2) ANOVA that produce orthogonal contrast-coded predictors (X_1, ..., X_5) for testing these hypotheses via multiple regression*

Null hypothesis	**Contrast-coded predictor**
H_{01}: $\mu_{1A} = \mu_{2A}$	X_1: **1 −1 0**
H_{02}: $\frac{\mu_{1A} + \mu_{2A}}{2} = \mu_{3A}$	X_2: **1 1 −2**
H_{03}: $\mu_{1B} = \mu_{2B}$	X_3: **1 −1**
H_{04}: There is no interaction between the differences defined by H_{01} $(\mu_{1A} - \mu_{2A})$ and H_{03} $(\mu_{1B} - \mu_{2B} = 0)$	$X_4 = X_1X_3$: **(1 −1 0)(1 −1)** = **1 −1 −1 1 0 0**
H_{05}: There is no interaction between the differences defined by H_{02} $\left(\frac{\mu_{1A} + \mu_{2A}}{2} - \mu_{3A} = 0\right)$ and H_{03} $(\mu_{1B} - \mu_{2B} = 0)$	$X_5 = X_2X_3$: **(1 1 −2)(1 −1)** = **1 −1 1 −1 −2 2**

Table 17.3 presents the contrast coding in Table 17.2 by (A x B) cells. Note, for example, that the contrast codes for factor A, X_1 (1 −1 0) and X_2 (1 1 −2), are repeated across the levels of factor B (B_1 and B_2) thus obtaining the contrast coding for factor A in all six cells. Also, the coding in column X_4 is obtained by multiplying columns X_1 and X_3. Likewise, the coding in column X_5 is obtained by multiplying columns X_2 and X_3. In SPSS applications, the coding value for a given (A x B) cell must be assigned to each observation in this cell. Further, X_1, X_2, X_3, X_4, and X_5 represent an orthogonal set of contrast-coded predictors. Indeed, the ANOVA design is balanced and (a) the sum of all coefficients for any predictor equals zero and (b) the sum of the paired products of the coefficients for any two predictors also equals zero — e.g., for X_2 and X_3 we have: $(1)(1) + (1)(1) + (-2)(1) + (1)(-1) + (1)(-1) + (-2)(-1) = 1 + 1 - 2 - 1 - 1 + 2 = 0$.

The coding scheme in Table 17.3 is illustrated in Example 17.2, where the interpretation of the two interaction products, $X_4 = X_1X_3$ and $X_5 = X_2X_3$, is clarified in the context of the specific factors used in this example (A = Socio-economic status, B = Gender).

Table 17.3 *Contrast-coded predictors for A x B ANOVA*

Factor A	Factor B	X_1	X_2	X_3	X_4	X_5
A_1	B_1	1	1	1	1	1
A_2	B_1	−1	1	1	−1	1
A_3	B_1	0	−2	1	0	−2
A_1	B_2	1	1	−1	−1	−1
A_2	B_2	−1	1	−1	1	−1
A_3	B_2	0	−2	−1	0	2

EXAMPLE 17.2 This example illustrates how to conduct a multiple regression with contrast-coded predictors to test the ANOVA null hypotheses defined in Table 17.2. The data represent reading scores of 30 middle school students grouped by two factors — *socio-economic status* (SES) with three levels (high, medium, low) and *gender* (female, male). The coding scheme shown in Table 17.3 is provided for these data in Figure 17.3.

Figure 17.3 *Multiple regression with five contrast-coded predictors for a two-factor (SES x Gender) ANOVA of reading scores*

EXAMPLE 17_2.sav [DataSet2] - SPSS Data Editor

File Edit View Data Transform Analyze Graphs Utilities Add-ons Window Help

30 :

	Reading	SES	Gender	X1	X2	X3	X4	X5
1	232	High	Female	1	1	1	1	1
2	288	High	Female	1	1	1	1	1
3	261	High	Female	1	1	1	1	1
4	280	High	Female	1	1	1	1	1
5	295	High	Female	1	1	1	1	1
6	240	Middle	Female	-1	1	1	-1	1
7	235	Middle	Female	-1	1	1	-1	1
8	212	Middle	Female	-1	1	1	-1	1
9	256	Middle	Female	-1	1	1	-1	1
10	253	Middle	Female	-1	1	1	-1	1
11	180	Low	Female	0	-2	1	0	-2
12	192	Low	Female	0	-2	1	0	-2
13	126	Low	Female	0	-2	1	0	-2
14	118	Low	Female	0	-2	1	0	-2
15	168	Low	Female	0	-2	1	0	-2
16	112	High	Male	1	1	-1	-1	-1
17	116	High	Male	1	1	-1	-1	-1
18	119	High	Male	1	1	-1	-1	-1
19	288	High	Male	1	1	-1	-1	-1
20	294	High	Male	1	1	-1	-1	-1
21	123	Middle	Male	-1	1	-1	1	-1
22	212	Middle	Male	-1	1	-1	1	-1
23	126	Middle	Male	-1	1	-1	1	-1
24	140	Middle	Male	-1	1	-1	1	-1
25	203	Middle	Male	-1	1	-1	1	-1
26	123	Low	Male	0	-2	-1	0	2
27	221	Low	Male	0	-2	-1	0	2
28	253	Low	Male	0	-2	-1	0	2
29	120	Low	Male	0	-2	-1	0	2
30	146	Low	Male	0	-2	-1	0	2

Figure 17.4 shows the SPSS output from the multiple regression with the data layout given in Figure 17.3. As noted earlier, the five ANOVA hypotheses tested with this multiple regression are described in Table 17.2 (H_{01}, H_{02}, H_{03}, H_{04}, and H_{05}). The omnibus test in the **ANOVA** table in Figure 17.4 shows that the group differences targeted with these five null hypotheses account for a statistically significant proportion of the variance in the dependent variable (reading scores), $F(5, 24) = 3.90$, $p = .01$. Specifically, $R^2 = .448$ (**Model Summary** table) indicates that 44.8 percent of the variance in reading is attributed to the group differences specified in H_{01}, H_{02}, H_{03}, H_{04}, and H_{05}. Furthermore, the results in the **Coefficients** table indicate statistical significance for the regression coefficients of three contrast-coded predictors, X_2, X_3, and X_5, at the .05 level. This implies that we can reject the null hypotheses tested by these predictors; that is,

(a) reject H_{02}: $\frac{\mu_{1A} + \mu_{2A}}{2} - \mu_{3A} = 0$,

(b) reject H_{03}: $\mu_{1B} - \mu_{2B} = 0$, and

(c) reject H_{05}: "There is no interaction between the differences defined in H_{02} and H_{03}."

Figure 17.4 *SPSS output from the multiple regression model in Figure 17.3*

Model Summary

Model	R	R Square	Adjusted R Square	Std. Error of the Estimate
1	.669[a]	.448	.333	52.956

a. Predictors: (Constant), X5, X4, X3, X2, X1

ANOVA[b]

Model		Sum of Squares	df	Mean Square	F	Sig.
1	Regression	54652.667	5	10930.533	3.898	.010[a]
	Residual	67303.200	24	2804.300		
	Total	121955.9	29			

a. Predictors: (Constant), X5, X4, X3, X2, X1

Coefficients[a]

Model		Unstandardized Coefficients		Standardized Coefficients	t	Sig.
		B	Std. Error	Beta		
1	(Constant)	197.733	9.668		20.452	.000
	X1	14.250	11.841	.182	1.203	.241
	X2	16.517	6.837	.366	2.416	.024
	X3	24.667	9.668	.387	2.551	.018
	X4	1.750	11.841	.022	.148	.884
	X5	16.283	6.837	.361	2.382	.026

a. Dependent Variable: Reading

Recall that in this example factor A is socio-economic status (high, middle, low) and factor B is gender (male, female). As we reject H_{02}: $(\mu_{1A} + \mu_{2A})/2 - \mu_{3A} = 0$, and given the positive sign of the regression coefficient for the contrast-coded predictor X_2 ($b_2 = 16.517$), we can say that the average reading performance of students with high and middle socio-economic status is *higher* than that of students with low socio-economic status. At the same time, the failure to reject H_{01}: $\mu_{1A} - \mu_{2A} = 0$ implies that the groups with high and middle socio-economic status *do not differ* in reading. Further, we reject H_{03}: $\mu_{1B} - \mu_{2B} = 0$. Given the positive sign of the regression coefficient for the contrast-coded predictor X_3 ($b_3 = 24.667$), we can say that females did better than males in reading.

The regression coefficient of the predictor X_4, which is the interaction product of X_1 and X_3, is not statistically significant ($p = .884$). Therefore, we fail to reject H_{04}. Given that X_1 is used to test H_{01}: $\mu_{1A} - \mu_{2A} = 0$ [the difference between high and middle SES groups] and X_3 is used to test H_{03}: $\mu_{1B} - \mu_{2B} = 0$ [the difference between males and females], the lack of an X_1X_3 interaction implies that the difference in H_{01} is the same for the groups compared in H_{03}. In other words, the reading difference between the students with high and middle socio-economic status is the same for males and females.

On the other hand, the regression coefficient of the predictor X_5, which is the interaction product of X_2 and X_3, *is* statistically significant ($p = .026$). Thus, we reject H_{05}. Given that X_2 is used to test H_{02}: $(\mu_{1A} + \mu_{2A})/2 - \mu_{3A} = 0$, [the difference between the average score of the groups with high and middle SES versus the score of the low SES group] and X_3 is designed to test H_{03}: $\mu_{1B} - \mu_{2B} = 0$ [the difference between males and females], the presence of an X_2X_3 interaction implies that the difference in H_{02} is *not* the same for the groups compared in H_{03}. In other words, the difference between the average score of the groups with high and middle SES versus the score of the low SES group is not the same for males and females.

We can examine the interactions X_1X_3 and X_2X_3 differently by presenting the relationship between the predicted values of the dependent variable (Y = reading score) and the values of the contrast-coded predictor X_3 (1 = female, -1 = male) as a function of the values of X_1 (1 = high SES, -1 = low SES) and X_2 (1 = high or middle SES, -2 = low SES). To do so, we start with the multiple regression equation for predicting Y from the contrast-coded predictors:

$$\hat{Y} = 14.25X_1 + 16.52X_2 + 24.67X_3 + 1.75X_4 + 16.28X_5 + 197.73,$$

where the regression coefficients (rounded to the nearest hundredth) are provided in Figure 17.4 (**Coefficients** table). By replacing in this equation $X_4 = X_1X_3$ and $X_5 = X_2X_3$, and with simple regrouping of terms, we obtain:

$$\begin{aligned}\hat{Y} &= 14.25X_1 + 16.52X_2 + 24.67X_3 + 1.75X_1X_3 + 16.28X_2X_3 + 197.73\\ &= (1.75X_1 + 16.28X_2 + 24.67)X_3 + (14.25X_1 + 16.52X_2 + 197.73),\end{aligned}$$

thus representing the relationship between $\hat{Y}$ and X_3 as a simple linear regression equation. Then, if we denote the slope (the first term in parentheses) by B and the intercept (the second term in parentheses) by A, the simple linear regression for predicting Y from X_3 becomes

$$\hat{Y} = BX_3 + A, \tag{17.9}$$

where: $B = 1.75X_1 + 16.28X_2 + 24.67$ and $A = 14.25X_1 + 16.52X_2 + 197.73$.

Thus, the slope of the simple linear relationship between $\hat{Y}$ and the contrast-coded predictor X_3 (1 = female, −1 = male) depends on the values of the contrast-coded predictors X_1 and X_2. As the product X_1X_3 is not statistically significant (p = .884 for X_4), we turn our attention to the statistically significant product X_2X_3 (p = .026 for X_5). Specifically, we will interpret the interaction product X_2X_3 in terms of changes in the predicted slope ($B = 1.75X_1 + 16.28X_2 + 24.67$) across the values of X_2 (1 = high or middle SES, −2 = low SES). The coefficient of X_2 in this equation for the slope (16.28) indicates the change in the slope, B, related to change in X_2 (assuming no change in X_1). Thus, when $X_2 = 1$, the slope is expected to increase by 16.28 units. However, when $X_2 = -2$, the slope decreases by 32.56 units [(−2) x 16.28 = −32.56.] This indicates that changes in X_3 are more important when $X_2 = 1$ than when $X_2 = -2$. That is, gender (X_3) plays a more important role in the reading performance of students with high or middle socioeconomic status ($X_2 = 1$) than for students with low economic status ($X_2 = -2$).

Let us now replace $X_1 = 0$ and $X_2 = 0$ in the expressions for the slope, B, and intercept, A, in Equation 17.9. As X_1 and X_2 are contrast-coded predictors and the ANOVA design in this example is balanced (equal observations in each cell), the average values of X_1 and X_2 are zero. With $X_1 = 0$ and $X_2 = 0$, we obtain $B = 24.67$ and $A = 197.73$, so the simple linear relationship between the predicted reading score ($\hat{Y}$) and gender (X_3) in Equation 17.9 takes on the form

$$\hat{Y} = 24.67X_3 + 197.73. \tag{17.10}$$

The slope in Equation 17.10 ($B = 24.67$) indicates that a one-unit increase in X_3 produces a 24.67 units increase in $\hat{Y}$. Thus, a two-unit increase in the coding values for X_3, from $X_3 = -1$ (male) to $X_3 = 1$ (female), will produce an increase of 49.34 units [2 x 24.67 = 49.34]. In other words, the predicted reading score for females is *higher* than that for males by 49.34 units (on the reading test scale) when the contrast-coded predictors X_1 and X_2 are fixed to their average values (zero). This is depicted in Figure 17.5, where 197.73 is the *grand mean* (obtained for $X_1 = X_2 = X_3 = 0$).

Figure 17.5 *Simple linear relationship between predicted reading scores ($\hat{Y}$) and X_3 (1 = female, −1 = male) for $X_1 = 0$ and $X_2 = 0$*

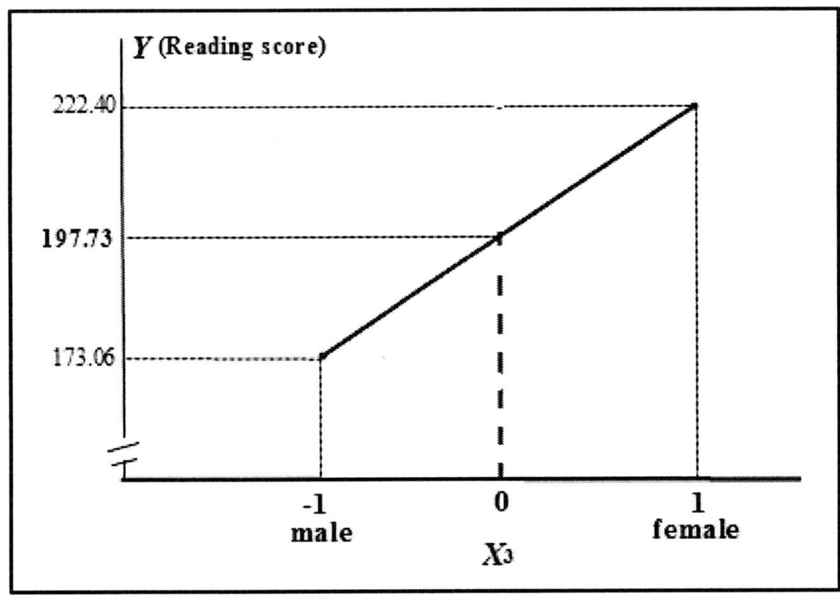

The logic of orthogonal contrast-coding for two-factor ANOVA carries over into ANOVA with three or more factors. For (A x B x C) ANOVA, for example, where factor A has three levels, factor B two levels, and factor C two levels, the coding scheme is shown in Table 17.4.

Table 17.4 *Orthogonal contrast coding for 3 x 2 x 2 ANOVA with three factors (A, B, and C)*

Null hypothesis	**Contrast-coded predictor**
H_{01}: $\mu_{1A} = \mu_{2A}$	X_1: **1 −1 0**
H_{02}: $\frac{\mu_{1A} + \mu_{2A}}{2} = \mu_{3A}$	X_2: **1 1 −2**
H_{03}: $\mu_{1B} = \mu_{2B}$	X_3: **1 −1**
H_{04}: $\mu_{1C} = \mu_{2C}$	X_4: **1 −1**
H_{05}: There is no interaction between the differences defined by H_{01} ($\mu_{1A} - \mu_{2A}$) and H_{03} ($\mu_{1B} - \mu_{2B} = 0$).	$X_5 = X_1X_3$: **(1 −1 0)(1 −1)** = **1 −1 −1 1 0 0**
H_{06}: There is no interaction between the differences defined by H_{02} $\left(\frac{\mu_{1A} + \mu_{2A}}{2} - \mu_{3A} = 0\right)$ and H_{03} ($\mu_{1B} - \mu_{2B} = 0$).	$X_6 = X_2X_3$: **(1 1 −2)(1 −1)** = **1 −1 1 −1 −2 2**
H_{07}: There is no interaction between the differences defined by H_{01} ($\mu_{1A} - \mu_{2A}$) and H_{04} ($\mu_{1C} - \mu_{2C} = 0$).	$X_7 = X_1X_4$: **(1 −1 0)(1 −1)** = **1 −1 −1 1 0 0**
H_{08}: There is no interaction between the differences defined by H_{02} $\left(\frac{\mu_{1A} + \mu_{2A}}{2} - \mu_{3A} = 0\right)$ and H_{04} ($\mu_{1C} - \mu_{2C} = 0$).	$X_8 = X_2X_4$: **(1 1 −2)(1 −1)** = **1 −1 1 −1 −2 2**
H_{09}: There is no interaction between the differences defined by H_{03} ($\mu_{1B} - \mu_{2B} = 0$) and H_{04} ($\mu_{1C} - \mu_{2C} = 0$).	$X_9 = X_3X_4$: **(1 −1)(1 −1)** = **1 −1 −1 1**
$H_{0,10}$: The interaction (if any) tested by H_{05} does not change across the levels of factor C.	$X_{10} = X_1X_3X_4$ = (1 −1 0)(1 −1)(1 −1) = **1 −1 −1 1 0 0 −1 1 1 −1 0 0**
$H_{0,11}$: The interaction (if any) tested by H_{06} does not change across the levels of factor C.	$X_{11} = X_2X_3X_4$ = (1 1 −2)(1 −1)(1 −1) = **1 −1 1 −1 −2 2 −1 1 −1 1 2 −2**

Note. More details on this topic can be found, for example, in Judd & McClelland (1989).

17.3 Summary

This chapter discusses the use of a multiple regression with orthogonal contrast-coded predictors for one-factor ANOVA and two-factor ANOVA. The presented methods and interpretations are readily extendable to cases of ANOVA with three or more factors.

• For an ANOVA (or *t*-test) with two groups, we employ a simple liner regression with a contrast-coded predictor X (1 −1) to test H_0: $\mu_1 - \mu_2 = 0$. If the regression coefficient for X (b) is statistically significant, we reject H_0 [for the value of b, see Equation 17.1.]

• A **contrast,** Ψ, among K population means is a linear combination of the means ($\Psi = c_1\mu_1 + c_2\mu_2 + \cdots + c_K\mu_K$), where the sum of coefficients is zero ($c_1 + c_2 + \cdots + c_K = 0$). To use a multiple regression for an ANOVA with K groups, it is necessary to employ $K - 1$ contrast codes.

• Two contrasts are considered **orthogonal** to each other when the sum of the paired products of their coefficients equals zero. For example, the contrast codes (1 −1 0) and (1 1 −2) are orthogonal to each other: (1)(1) + (−1)(1) + (0)(−2) = 1 – 1 + 0 = 0.

• A set of contrast-coded predictors is referred to as an **orthogonal set of predictors** if any two predictors in this set are orthogonal to each other.

• The regression coefficient for a contrast-coded predictor equals the ratio of the corresponding contrast to the sum of squared coding values of the contrast [see Equations 17.6, 17.7, and 17.8.]

• Contrast-coded predictors in a multiple regression for an unbalanced ANOVA design (with an unequal number of observations across cells) are *not* independent, even when the contrast codes are defined as orthogonal (see NOTE [17.1]).

• A typical set of contrast-coded predictors for a one-factor ANOVA with three groups is shown in Table 17.1.

• A typical set of contrast-coded predictors for a (3 x 2) ANOVA is shown in Table 17.2.

17.4 Study Questions

1. How many contrast coded-predictors are needed in a multiple regression for a one-factor ANOVA with four groups?

2. Provide two orthogonal contrast-coded predictors, X_1 and X_2, to test the following two hypotheses in a one-factor ANOVA with three groups:

$$H_{01}: \mu_2 = \mu_3 \text{ and } H_{02}: \mu_1 = \frac{\mu_2 + \mu_3}{2}.$$

3. Which of the following pairs of contrast-coded predictors are orthogonal to each other:

   (A) X_1: 0 1 −1 and X_2: 2 −1 −1,
   (B) X_1: 1 −1 0 and X_2: 2 −1 −1,
   (C) X_1: 2 1 −1 and X_2: 0 −1 1,
   (D) All of the above.

4. The sample means in a one-factor ANOVA with three groups are $\bar{Y}_1 = 10$, $\bar{Y}_2 = 7$, and $\bar{Y}_3 = 8$. Compute the estimates of the regression coefficients, b_1 and b_2, of the contrast-coded predictors using a multiple regression to test the following two null hypotheses:

$$H_{01}: \mu_1 = \mu_3 \text{ and } H_{02}: \frac{\mu_1 + \mu_3}{2} = \mu_2.$$

[*Hint*: see Equation 17.8]

5. Use SPSS to conduct a multiple regression to test H_{01}: $\mu_1 = \mu_2$ and H_{02}: $\frac{\mu_1 + \mu_2}{2} = \mu_3$ for the data provided in Figure 14.2 (Chapter 14) and interpret the results. [*Hint*: see Example 17.1].

6. Use SPSS to conduct a multiple regression to test the null hypotheses defined in Table 17.2, with factor A = *Ethnicity* and factor B = *Gender*, for the data in Figure 15.1 (Chapter 15). Interpret the results following the format of discussion provided in Example 17.2 (pp. 287-289).

CHAPTER 18

ANOVA WITH RANDOM FACTORS

In Chapters 14 and 15 we discussed conducting an ANOVA with factors such as gender, ethnicity, type of treatment, etc. Such factors are called **fixed factors** because the number of their levels is naturally "fixed." For example, gender levels (male, female) are naturally fixed and, therefore, it does not make sense to consider them as randomly selected from a large pool of gender levels. The same holds for ethnicity, teaching method, drug type, and so forth. In contrast, a factor with levels that can be randomly selected from a large pool of existing levels for this factor is called a **random factor**. For example, if five teachers are randomly selected in an ANOVA to examine the performance of their students on a math test, "Teacher" would be considered a random factor. In two-factor ANOVAs, it may happen that one factor is fixed and the other factor is random, or both factors are random [the case in which both factors are fixed was already addressed in Chapter 15]. While the primary goal when conducting an ANOVA with fixed factors is to test for main and interaction effects, the key question related to a random factor is whether the results can be generalized (e.g., is the students' achievement generalizable to a population of teachers and/or schools?). In this chapter, the presentation of ANOVA with random factor(s) is limited to basic models with a focus on their conceptual understanding, SPSS aided applications, and interpretations.

18.1 ANOVA with One Random Factor

18.1.1 Random Effects

Suppose a researcher wants to know to what degree differences among students' scores on a math test can be attributed to differences among math teachers. Figure 18.1 presents hypothetical data for an ANOVA in which five math teachers (T_1, T_2, T_3, T_4, T_5) were randomly selected from the population of math teachers in a school area of interest. The math test scores of six randomly-selected students per teacher are used in this analysis. Thus, *teacher* is a random factor with five levels ($K = 5$) and six observations in each level ($n = 6$).

Technically, the random-factor ANOVA is the same as the fixed-factor ANOVA, so the computations of the teacher *effects*, between-teacher variance (*mean-squares between*, MS_B) and within-teacher variance (*mean-squares within*, MS_W) for the data in Figure 18.1 are based on the procedures and formulas described in Chapter 14 (Section 14.3). The main difference is that the effects produced by the levels of a random factor are **random effects** (i.e., they vary across random selections of factor levels), whereas those produced by the levels of a fixed factor are **fixed effects**. Random effects are denoted here $a_k = \mu_k - \mu_\bullet$ to distinguish from the notation of fixed effects introduced in Chapter 14, $\alpha_k = \mu_k - \mu_\bullet$. The sample estimates of the teacher random effects, $\hat{a}_k$ ($k = 1, 2, 3, 4, 5$), are shown in Figure 18.1 (right panel). Just like with the fixed ANOVA model (see Equation 14.16), the random ANOVA model assumes that any score, Y_{ik}, is a sum of the grand mean, $\mu_\bullet$, the random effect a_k, and the residual of the score ($\varepsilon_{ik} = Y_{ik} - \mu_k$):

$$Y_{ik} = \mu_\bullet + a_k + \varepsilon_{ik}. \quad \textbf{(18.1)}$$

Figure 18.1 *Students' math scores across five teachers and random effects of teachers*

T_1	T_2	T_3	T_4	T_5
35	21	41	24	35
28	26	40	29	28
39	32	46	34	42
46	30	50	32	47
35	31	42	36	41
28	25	39	38	37
$\bar{Y}_1 = 35.17$	$\bar{Y}_2 = 27.50$	$\bar{Y}_3 = 43.00$	$\bar{Y}_4 = 32.17$	$\bar{Y}_5 = 38.33$
$\bar{Y}_\bullet = 35.23$				

Estimates of *random effects* of teachers:

$\hat{a}_1 = \bar{Y}_1 - \bar{Y}_\bullet = -0.06$

$\hat{a}_2 = \bar{Y}_2 - \bar{Y}_\bullet = -7.73$

$\hat{a}_3 = \bar{Y}_3 - \bar{Y}_\bullet = 7.77$

$\hat{a}_4 = \bar{Y}_4 - \bar{Y}_\bullet = -3.06$

$\hat{a}_5 = \bar{Y}_5 - \bar{Y}_\bullet = 3.10$

18.1.2 Assumptions of the Random-factor ANOVA

The linear model for the random-factor ANOVA in Equation 18.1 holds under the following two assumptions:

1. The random effects, a_k's, are independent and follow a normal distribution with a mean of zero and variance σ_a^2.
2. The error terms of individual scores ($\varepsilon_{ik} = Y_{ik} - \mu_k$) are independent and follow a normal distribution with a mean of zero and variance σ_ε^2 [*population error variance*].

The second assumption is, in fact, an equivalent form of the *homogeneity of variance assumption* [which is also required with the fixed-factor ANOVA]. The first assumption, required only with the random-factor ANOVA, means that the population means of the levels of the random factor, μ_k's, are normally distributed around the grand mean, $\mu_\bullet$, with a variance of σ_a^2.

18.1.3 Expected Mean Square (Within and Between) in the Random-factor ANOVA

As known from the presentation of the fixed-factor ANOVA in Chapter 14, the within-groups variance, referred to as *mean square within* (MS_W), represents an unbiased estimate of the population error variance, σ_ε^2. This means that the theoretical mean of MS_W, obtained from an infinite number of independent replications of the study sampling under the same conditions, equals σ_ε^2. In other words, **the expected value of MS_W is σ_ε^2**, or

$$E(MS_W) = \sigma_\varepsilon^2. \tag{18.2}$$

Equation 18.3, the derivation of which is beyond the scope of this book, represents the expected value of the between-groups variance (*mean square between*, MS_B) as a sum of the population error variance, σ_ε^2, and the variance of random effects, σ_a^2, multiplied by the number of observations for each effect, n [in a balanced ANOVA design]. That is,

$$E(MS_B) = n\sigma_a^2 + \sigma_\varepsilon^2. \tag{18.3}$$

Solving for σ_a^2 from Equations 18.2 and 18.3, we obtain

$$\sigma_a^2 = \frac{E(MS_B) - E(MS_W)}{n}. \tag{18.4}$$

18.1.4 The Primary Question in a Random-factor ANOVA

As noted earlier, testing for main effects of random factors in ANOVA is meaningless. For example, it makes no sense to compare the mean scores of five teachers, since the results will clearly vary across different random samples of five teachers. Instead, the question to ask is, "How much of the variance in the dependent variable (e.g. students' math scores) is attributable to differences among teachers?" As the differences among teachers are reflected in the variance of their effects, σ_a^2, the estimation of this variance is the central task of the random-factor ANOVA. An estimate of σ_a^2 is obtained directly from Equation 18.4 by using MS_W and MS_B instead of their (unknown) expected values, $E(MS_W)$ and $E(MS_B)$, respectively. That is,

$$\hat{\sigma}_a^2 = \frac{MS_B - MS_W}{n}. \quad \textbf{(18.5)}$$

As the computation of MS_W and MS_B is the same for both fixed-factor and random-factor ANOVAs, we can use Equations 14.9 and 14.11 [or just use SPSS to conduct an ANOVA regardless of whether the factor is fixed or random]. Then, replacing MS_W and MS_B with their values in Equation 18.5, we obtain an estimate of the random effect variance, $\hat{\sigma}_a^2$.

Typically, the magnitude of $\hat{\sigma}_a^2$ is evaluated in comparison with MS_W, which represents an estimate of the population error variance ($MS_W = \hat{\sigma}_\varepsilon^2$). Specifically, the ratio $\hat{\sigma}_a^2/\hat{\sigma}_\varepsilon^2$ shows how many times the variance associated with the random factor is greater (or smaller) than the variance among the scores within the levels of this factor. In the example of teachers as a random factor, this ratio will tell us how many times the variance among teachers is greater (or smaller) than the variance in math scores among students who have the same teacher. Put another way, the ratio $\hat{\sigma}_a^2/\hat{\sigma}_\varepsilon^2$ indicates how many times the differences among levels of the random factor are greater (or smaller) than differences that may occur by chance ($\hat{\sigma}_\varepsilon^2$).

EXAMPLE 18.1. This example illustrates how to calculate and interpret the ratio $\hat{\sigma}_a^2/\hat{\sigma}_\varepsilon^2$ using the data in Figure 18.1, where the random factor (teacher) is represented by five levels (T_1, ..., T_5) and the dependent variable is students' math scores. The SPSS entry of these data is shown in Figure 18.2 (left panel). [For the time being ignore the variable **Method** as it will be used in an example provided later in this chapter.] Now, using SPSS to conduct an ANOVA (as shown in Example 14.2) we obtain the output provided in Figure 18.2 (right panel). As noted earlier, in SPSS it does not matter if the variable **Teacher** is used as a fixed factor or random factor for the purposes of computing MS_B and MS_W.

The mean square values in the SPSS output (right upper panel) are $MS_B = 208.717$ and $MS_W = 30.260$. Given that MS_W is an estimate of the population error variance, $\hat{\sigma}_\varepsilon^2 = 30.260$. As also shown in Figure 18.2 (right lower panel), the estimate of the variance associated with the teacher factor is $\hat{\sigma}_a^2 = 29.74$. The computation is based on Equation 18.5, with six observations per teacher ($n = 6$). The ratio of interest for the random-factor ANOVA in this example is close to 1 ($\hat{\sigma}_a^2/\hat{\sigma}_\varepsilon^2 = 0.98$). This indicates that the variance associated with the random factor (Teacher) is as large as the variance due to random differences among the scores of students that have the same teacher. Thus, the variation among teachers should not be a concern as it does not exceed the variation that may occur by chance with the data in this example.

NOTE [18.1] If, due to sampling error, the estimate of the variance for the random factor is negative ($\hat{\sigma}_a^2 < 0$), set this estimate to zero ($\hat{\sigma}_a^2 = 0$) as a variance can never be negative.

Figure 18.2 *SPSS for intermediate computations in estimating the variance of the random factor (Teacher), $\hat{\sigma}_a^2$, and its comparison to the estimate of the population error variance, $\hat{\sigma}_\varepsilon^2$.*

EXAMPLE_18_1_2.sav [DataSet

File Edit View Data Transform Analy

30 :

	SCORE	Teacher	Method
1	35	1	1
2	28	1	1
3	39	1	2
4	46	1	2
5	35	1	3
6	28	1	3
7	21	2	1
8	26	2	1
9	32	2	2
10	30	2	2
11	31	2	3
12	25	2	3
13	41	3	1
14	40	3	1
15	46	3	2
16	50	3	2
17	42	3	3
18	39	3	3
19	24	4	1
20	29	4	1
21	34	4	2
22	32	4	2
23	36	4	3
24	38	4	3
25	35	5	1
26	28	5	1
27	42	5	2
28	47	5	2
29	41	5	3
30	37	5	3

Tests of Between-Subjects Effects

Dependent Variable: SCORE

Source	Type III Sum of Squares	df	Mean Square	F	Sig.
Corrected Model	834.867[a]	4	208.717	6.897	.001
Intercept	37241.633	1	37241.633	1230.722	.000
Teacher	834.867	4	208.717	6.897	.001
Error	756.500	25	30.260		
Total	38833.000	30			
Corrected Total	1591.367	29			

a. R Squared = .525 (Adjusted R Squared = .449)

MSw

MSB

$$\hat{\sigma}_\varepsilon^2 = \text{MS}_\text{W} = 30.26$$

$$\hat{\sigma}_a^2 = \frac{\text{MS}_\text{B} - \text{MS}_\text{W}}{n} = \frac{208.717 - 30.260}{6} = 29.74$$

$$\hat{\sigma}_a^2 / \hat{\sigma}_\varepsilon^2 = 29.74/30.26 = 0.98$$

It is important to note that the very small number of observations per teacher ($n = 6$) was used to facilitate the illustration with this example, but in a real study such an analysis would require a larger sample. Formally, the F-statistic for **Teacher** with the SPSS output in Figure 18.2 indicates there are statistically significant differences among the score means of the five teachers, $F(4, 25) = 6.897$, $p = .001$. That is, we can reject the null hypothesis H_0: $\sigma_a^2 = 0$, where σ_a^2 is the population variance associated with differences among teachers. Again, this result must be interpreted with great caution given the very small sample size. In real studies, H_0: $\sigma_a^2 = 0$ might be of some interest, but the computation of $\hat{\sigma}_a^2$ and its comparison to $\hat{\sigma}_\varepsilon^2$ (through the ratio $\hat{\sigma}_a^2/\hat{\sigma}_\varepsilon^2$) must be the primary goal in addressing the main question: How much of the variance in the dependent variable is attributable to differences among levels of the random factor?

18.2 Two-factor Mixed-Effects ANOVA Model

18.2.1 The Concept of a Mixed-effects Model

ANOVA models with fixed factors are referred to as **fixed-effects models**, whereas ANOVA models with random factors are referred to as **random-effects models**. ANOVA models that involve both fixed and random factor(s) are called **mixed-effects models**. This section deals with a mixed-effect model that involves one fixed factor and one random factor. An illustration of such a model is provided with the ANOVA data in Figure 18.2, but now all three variables are included — **SCORE** (math scores as a dependent variable), **Teacher** (independent random factor), and **Method** (independent fixed factor). The fixed factor (Method) has three levels that represent three methods of teaching math (say, M_1, M_2, and M_3). Each of the three methods is independently used by each teacher with two students. The two-way data layout for this model presented in Figure 18.3.

Figure 18.3 *Data layout for a two-factor (Method x Teacher) mixed model ANOVA*

	Teacher					
Method	T_1	T_2	T_3	T_4	T_5	
M_1	35, 28	21, 26	41, 40	24, 29	35, 28	$\bar{Y}_{1\bullet} = 30.70$
M_2	39, 46	32, 30	46, 50	34, 32	42, 47	$\bar{Y}_{2\bullet} = 39.80$
M_3	35, 28	31, 25	42, 39	36, 38	41, 37	$\bar{Y}_{3\bullet} = 35.20$
	$\bar{Y}_{\bullet 1} = 35.17$	$\bar{Y}_{\bullet 2} = 27.50$	$\bar{Y}_{\bullet 3} = 43.00$	$\bar{Y}_{\bullet 4} = 32.17$	$\bar{Y}_{\bullet 5} = 38.33$	$\bar{Y}_{\bullet\bullet} = 35.23$

In addition to the five random effects of teachers, a_1, a_2, …, a_5 (see their estimates in Figure 18.1), there are also three fixed effects of methods (denoted, say, β_1, β_2, and β_3) and 15 interaction terms, denoted here as βa_{jk}, where index j indicates the method (j = 1, 2, 3) and index k indicates the teacher (k = 1, 2, …, 5). The interaction terms are random, as they involve levels of the random factor (teacher). The formulas for the effects are the same as those provided with the two-fixed factors ANOVA in Chapter 15 (Equations 15.1-15.7). For example, the estimate of the effect of the first method (M_1) is $\hat{\beta}_1 = \bar{Y}_{1\bullet} - \bar{Y}_{\bullet\bullet} = 30.70 - 35.23 = -4.53$, whereas the estimate of the interaction term of the cell for the second method and fourth teacher (M_2, T_4) is: $\beta a_{24} = \bar{Y}_{24} - \bar{Y}_{2\bullet} - \bar{Y}_{\bullet 4} + \bar{Y}_{\bullet\bullet} = 33 - 39.80 - 32.17 + 35.23 = -3.74$ [$\bar{Y}_{24} = 33$ is the cell mean].

For the population, the variance of random teacher effects is σ_a^2, the variance of fixed method effects is σ_β^2, and the variance of random interaction terms is $\sigma_{\beta a}^2$. The null hypotheses that are testable in this case are:

1. **Fixed main effect for method,** H_{01}: $\mu_{1\bullet} = \mu_{2\bullet} = \mu_{3\bullet}$ [or, $\sum \beta_j^2 = 0$; (j = 1, 2, 3).]
2. **Random main effect for teacher,** H_{02}: $\sigma_a^2 = 0$.
3. **Random interaction effect,** H_{03}: $\sigma_{\beta a}^2 = 0$.

Our main interest in this example lies in testing H_{01} for the fixed main effect of method. The information related to random effects is useful in making decisions about how generalizable the fixed main effect of method is to the population of teachers. In general, this is a guiding principle for asking the right question(s) in mixed-effects ANOVA models: The focus is on the *fixed effects*, while the information about random factors is used to make decisions about the generalizability of the fixed effects to the population levels of the random factors. In addition to testing H_{02} and H_{03} for the random effects, it is even more useful to estimate the variances of the random effects (σ_a^2 and $\sigma_{\beta a}^2$) and to compare them with the estimate of population within-cells variance (σ_ε^2).

NOTE [18.2] The main tasks in a two-factor mixed ANOVA model are to (a) test the null hypothesis for the fixed main effect, H_{01}, (b) compute $\hat{\sigma}_a^2$, $\hat{\sigma}_{\beta a}^2$, and $\hat{\sigma}_\varepsilon^2$ [MS_W], (c) compute the ratio $\hat{\sigma}_a^2/\hat{\sigma}_\varepsilon^2$ to evaluate how much of the variance in the dependent variable is attributable to random main effects (differences among levels of the random factor), and (d) compute the ratio $\hat{\sigma}_{\beta a}^2/\hat{\sigma}_\varepsilon^2$ to evaluate how much of the variance in the dependent variable is attributable to random interaction effects. Thus, the focus is on the fixed main effect, while the random effects are used to evaluate the generalizability of the fixed main effect to the population levels of the random factor.

18.2.2 Assumptions of the Two-factor Mixed ANOVA Model

In the two-factor mixed ANOVA model, let Y_{ijk} denote the score of person *i* from level *j* of the fixed factor and level *k* of the random factor. The linear model for Y_{ijk} in this case is

$$Y_{ijk} = \mu_{\bullet\bullet} + \beta_j + a_k + \beta a_{jk} + \varepsilon_{ijk}, \qquad \textbf{(18.6)}$$

where $\mu_{\bullet\bullet}$ is the grand mean, β_j is the fixed effect of level *j* of the fixed factor, a_k is the random effect of level *k* of the random factor, βa_{jk} is the interaction term for the cell (*j*, *k*), and ε_{ijk} is the within-cell error term of the score Y_{ijk} ($\varepsilon_{ijk} = Y_{ijk} - \mu_{jk}$). The assumption of the two-factor mixed ANOVA model, are:

1. The random main effects, $a_k = \mu_{\bullet k} - \mu_{\bullet\bullet}$, are normally distributed with a mean of zero and a variance of σ_a^2.
2. The random interaction effects, $\beta a_{jk} = \mu_{jk} - (\beta_j + a_k + \mu_{\bullet\bullet})$, are normally distributed with a mean of zero and a variance of $\sigma_{\beta a}^2$.
3. The random error terms, $\varepsilon_{ijk} = Y_{ijk} - \mu_{jk}$, are normally distributed with a mean of zero and a variance of σ_ε^2.
4. The variance of the score differences between any two levels of the fixed factor remains the same — assumption of *sphericity*.

The assumption of sphericity is necessary when testing the null hypothesis for the fixed main effect, H_{01}. A sufficient condition for this assumption to be met is that *all levels of the fixed factor have the same variance and the correlations between any two levels are equal*. This sufficient condition can be easier to check and, then (a) if it holds, then sphericity will exist, or (b) if it does not hold, sphericity may or may not exist, so additional verification would be necessary.

When the sphericity is not in place, the *F*-test for the main fixed effect becomes somewhat "liberal" — that is, makes it unduly easier to reject H_{01} (e.g., see Glass & Hopkins, p. 547).

Clearly, then, when H_{01} is not rejected, there is no need to check for the sphericity assumption. Indeed, if H_{01} is not rejected with a liberal F-test (when the sphericity assumption is violated), it will be even more difficult to reject H_{01} with the less liberal actual F-test (when sphericity exists). If, however, H_{01} is rejected with a liberal F-test (when the sphericity assumption is violated), additional information is needed to make a valid decision about H_{01}. This is achieved by adjusting the degrees of freedom for the F-test. Specifically, both the degrees of freedom for the numerator (df_1) and the denominator (df_2) are multiplied by a constant, ε, referred to as the "epsilon multiplier" (Huynh & Feldt, 1979). In general, the probability of Type I error in decisions about the fixed main effect in mixed ANOVA is rarely inflated by the lack of sphericity (e.g., Collier, Baker, Mandeville, & Hays, 1967). Therefore, more details on the assumption of sphericity are provided in the discussion of repeated-measures ANOVA where this assumption plays more central role (see Chapter 19).

18.2.3 Expected Mean Square (Within and Between) in the Two-factor Mixed ANOVA

The meaning of *expected mean square within*, E(MS_W), and *expected mean square between*, E(MS_B), was explained in Section 18.1.3 (see Equations 18.2 and 18.3). In the case of a two-factor mixed ANOVA model, there are four sources of variation — fixed main effect (β_j), random main effect (a_k), random interaction effect (βa_{jk}), and error terms (ε_{ijk}). The variances of these effects are σ_β^2, σ_a^2, $\sigma_{\beta a}^2$, and σ_ε^2, respectively. Let's denote the expected mean squares for these sources in the context of the (Method x Teacher) ANOVA model shown in Figure 18.3 as follows: E(MS_M) — Method, E(MS_T) — Teacher, E(MS_{MT}) — Method x Teacher interaction, and E(MS_W) — within-cells error. The equations for these expected mean squares, the derivation of which is beyond the scope of this book, are:

$$E(MS_M) = (nK)\sigma_\beta^2 + (n)\sigma_{\beta a}^2 + \sigma_\varepsilon^2 \quad \textbf{(18.7)}$$

$$E(MS_T) = (nJ)\sigma_a^2 + \sigma_\varepsilon^2 \quad \textbf{(18.8)}$$

$$E(MS_{MT}) = (n)\sigma_{\beta a}^2 + \sigma_\varepsilon^2 \quad \textbf{(18.9)}$$

$$E(MS_W) = \sigma_\varepsilon^2, \quad \textbf{(18.10)}$$

where J is the number of levels with the fixed factor, Method ($J = 3$), K is the number of levels with the random factor, Teacher ($K = 5$), and n is the number of observations per cell ($n = 2$).

In the above equations, the coefficient (in parentheses) of the variance for a given effect shows the number of observations used for the estimation of this effect. For example, the coefficient of σ_β^2 in Equation 18.7 ($nK = 10$) shows the number of observations that produce a given fixed effect for the data in Figure 18.3 [10 observations per method across all teachers]. Likewise, the coefficient of σ_a^2 in Equation 18.8 ($nJ = 6$) equals the number of observations that produce a given random effect [six observation per teacher across all methods]. Further, n shows the number of observations within a cell that produce any interaction term ($n = 2$).

Note that the residual term for E(MS_M) is $(n)\sigma_{\beta a}^2 + \sigma_\varepsilon^2$. Indeed, when the null hypothesis for the fixed main effect (H_{01}: $\sum \beta_j^2 = 0$) is true, the first component in the right-hand side of Equation 18.7 becomes zero and the remaining part, $(n)\sigma^2_{\beta a} + \sigma^2_{\varepsilon}$, is the residual. Note also that this residual is exactly E(MS_{MT}). The implication of this is that the F-ratio for testing H_{01} is

$$F_M = \frac{MS_M}{MS_{MT}}. \quad \textbf{(18.11)}$$

That is, the denominator in the F-ratio for the fixed main effect of Method (F_M) is now the mean square of the interaction (Method x Teacher). Recall that when the two factors are fixed, the denominator of the F-ratio is MS_W (see Equations 15.22 and 15.23).

Conversely, Equations 18.8 – 18.10 show that σ^2_{ε} is the residual term for both the E(MS_T) and E(MS_{MT}). Therefore, the F-ratios for the two random effects in this case are

$$F_T = \frac{MS_T}{MS_W} \text{ and } F_{MT} = \frac{MS_{MT}}{MS_W}. \quad \textbf{(18.12)}$$

While F_M is used in testing the fixed main effect (H_{01}: $\mu_{1\bullet} = \mu_{2\bullet} = \mu_{3\bullet}$), which is of primary interest with the two-factor ANOVA, F_T and F_{MT} are used in testing hypotheses of lesser interest, H_{02}: $\sigma^2_a = 0$ and H_{03}: $\sigma^2_{\beta a} = 0$, respectively. Regarding the random effects, it might be more useful to compute $\hat{\sigma}^2_a$ and $\hat{\sigma}^2_{\beta a}$ and then to compare them to $\hat{\sigma}^2_{\varepsilon}$ through the ratios $\hat{\sigma}^2_a/\hat{\sigma}^2_{\varepsilon}$ and $\hat{\sigma}^2_{\beta a}/\hat{\sigma}^2_{\varepsilon}$. The formulas for the computation of $\hat{\sigma}^2_a$ and $\hat{\sigma}^2_{\beta a}$ are derived directly from Equations 18.8 and 18.9, respectively, taking into account that $\hat{\sigma}^2_{\varepsilon} = MS_W$. Using simple algebra, we obtain:

$$\hat{\sigma}^2_a = \frac{MS_T - MS_W}{nJ}, \quad \textbf{(18.13)}$$

$$\hat{\sigma}^2_{\beta a} = \frac{MS_{MT} - MS_W}{n}. \quad \textbf{(18.14)}$$

EXAMPLE 18.2. This example illustrates the SPSS procedure for a two-factor mixed ANOVA using the data in Figure 18.2 [see also Figure 18.3]. The dependent variable is **SCORE** (students' math scores), the fixed factor is **Method** (M_1, M_2, M_3), and the random factor is **Teacher** (T_1, T_2, T_3, T_4, T_5). SPSS provides an option to specify fixed and random factors, so we are going to use this option to avoid manual computation of the F-ratio for the fixed main effect (Equation 18.11). The SPSS steps for the purposes of this example are:

1. Click **Analyze**, click **General Linear Model**, and click **Univariate**.
2. Click **SCORE**, and click ▶ to move it into the box **Dependent Variable**.
3. Click **Method**, and click ▶ to move it into the box **Fixed Factor(s)**.
4. Click **Teacher**, and click ▶ to move it into the box **Random Factor(s)**.
5. Click **Options** and then check the boxes **Descriptive statistics, Estimates of effect size**, and **Homogeneity tests.**
6. Click **Continue**.
7. Click **OK**.

Figure 18.4 provides the table **Tests of Between-Subjects Effects**, which is of central importance to the purposes of this example. With two observations per cell in (n = 2), SPSS did not report results for the Levene's test for homogeneity of variance. The result of main interest is the F-test for the fixed main effect of Method. As we specified **Treatment** as a random factor when we conducted the test in SPSS (see Step 4), the F-ratio for Method in the SPSS output is computed using Equation 18.11. As this F-ratio is statistically significant, $F(2, 8) = 10.23$, $p = .006$, we reject the null hypothesis for the fixed main effect of Method. Thus, at least two of the methods (M_1, M_2, and M_3) yield different means in math scores for the population of students. [Due to the small sample size, post-hoc results are not reported here, but related comments are provided in the next section.]

The F-test for the random factor Teacher suggests that there are statistically significant differences among the mean scores of the five teachers. This result, however, is of little interest given the random nature of this factor. Rather, we want to estimate the variance of the random sources using Equations 18.13 and 18.14. Given that $MS_T = 208.717$, $MS_{MT} = 20.242$, and $MS_W = 12.033$, $J = 3$, $K = 5$t, and $n = 2$, we obtain:

$$\hat{\sigma}_a^2 = \frac{MS_T - MS_W}{nJ} = \frac{208.717 - 12.033}{(2)(3)} = 32.78.$$

$$\hat{\sigma}_{\beta a}^2 = \frac{MS_{MT} - MS_W}{n} = \frac{20.242 - 12.033}{2} = 4.10.$$

The ratio $\hat{\sigma}_a^2/\hat{\sigma}_\varepsilon^2 = 32.78/12.033 = 2.72$ indicates that the variance among teachers is 2.72 times larger than the variance within teachers. On the other hand, the ratio $\hat{\sigma}_{\beta a}^2/\hat{\sigma}_\varepsilon^2 = 4.10/12.033 = 0.34$ shows that the variance component for the (method x teacher) interaction is about one third of the variance within teachers. Thus, we can say that the differential effect of teachers on students' math performance across the three methods of teaching is negligible. To summarize, a relatively large variation among teachers, but no differential effects of teachers across methods, must be a concern for those interested in generalizing the teaching method effect to the population of teachers.

Figure 18.4 *Selected SPSS output for the (Method x Teacher) two-factor mixed ANOVA*

Tests of Between-Subjects Effects

Dependent Variable: SCORE

Source		Type III Sum of Squares	df	Mean Square	F	Sig.	Partial Eta Squared
Intercept	Hypothesis	37241.633	1	37241.633	178.432	.000	.978
	Error	834.867	4	208.717[a]			
Method	Hypothesis	414.067	2	207.033	10.228	.006	.719
	Error	161.933	8	20.242[b]			
Teacher	Hypothesis	834.867	4	208.717	10.311	.003	.838
	Error	161.933	8	20.242[b]			
Method * Teacher	Hypothesis	161.933	8	20.242	1.682	.183	.473
	Error	180.500	15	12.033[c]			

a. MS(Teacher)

b. MS(Method * Teacher)

c. MS(Error)

MS_T MS_W MS_{MT} $F_M = 10.23, p = .006$

18.2.4 Effect Size of Mean Differences among Levels of the Fixed Factor

We can compute the effect size of the mean differences among the levels of the fixed factor in a two-factor mixed ANOVA by adjusting Formula 14.31 (in Chapter 14) to take into account that the residual in the *F*-ratio for the fixed factor is the mean square of the interaction between the two factors (*not* MS_W). In the context of Example 18.2, we replace MS_W in Formula 14.31 with the mean square of the interaction (Method x Teacher), MS_{MT}, thus obtaining the following formula for the effect size of mean differences among levels of the fixed factor (Method):

$$d_{i,j} = \frac{|\bar{Y}_{i\bullet} - \bar{Y}_{j\bullet}|}{\sqrt{MS_{MT}}}, \qquad \textbf{(18.15)}$$

where $\bar{Y}_{i\bullet}$ and $\bar{Y}_{j\bullet}$ are the sample means of the two compared levels, *i* and *j*, of the fixed factor.

Thus, given that $MS_{MT} = 20.242$ (see Figure 18.4) and given the sample means for the levels of the fixed factor in Figure 18.3, we can compute the effect size of the differences among the three methods (M_1, M_2, and M_3) using Formula 18.15 as follows:

$$d_{1,2} = \frac{|\bar{Y}_{1\bullet} - \bar{Y}_{2\bullet}|}{\sqrt{MS_{MT}}} = \frac{|30.70 - 39.80|}{\sqrt{20.242}} = \frac{|-9.10|}{\sqrt{20.242}} = \frac{9.10}{4.50} = 2.02,$$

$$d_{1,3} = \frac{|\bar{Y}_{1\bullet} - \bar{Y}_{3\bullet}|}{\sqrt{MS_{MT}}} = \frac{|30.70 - 35.20|}{\sqrt{20.242}} = \frac{|-4.50|}{\sqrt{20.242}} = \frac{4.50}{4.50} = 1.00, \text{ and}$$

$$d_{2,3} = \frac{|\bar{Y}_{2\bullet} - \bar{Y}_{3\bullet}|}{\sqrt{MS_{MT}}} = \frac{|39.80 - 35.20|}{\sqrt{20.242}} = \frac{|4.60|}{\sqrt{20.242}} = \frac{4.60}{4.50} = 1.02.$$

The purpose of these computations is purely illustrative. Given the hypothetical nature of the data and the extremely small sample size, it does not make sense to interpret the magnitude of the [unrealistically large] effect sizes in this example.

NOTE [18.3] The logic behind replacing MS_W with the mean square for the interaction, MS_{MT}, applies also to post-hoc tests for multiple comparisons among levels of the fixed factor. Take, for example, the **studentized range statistic** in the Tukey post-hoc test provided in Chapter 14 (Equation 14.20):

$$q_1 = \frac{\bar{Y}_1 - \bar{Y}_K}{s_{\bar{Y}}},$$

where $s_{\bar{Y}}$, the *standard error of the mean* for the dependent variable, *Y*, is computed as follows:

$$s_{\bar{Y}} = \sqrt{\frac{MS_W}{n}}.$$

To use this statistic for the levels of the fixed factor in a two-factor mixed ANOVA model, it would be necessary to replace MS_W with MS_{MT} in the formula for $s_{\bar{Y}}$. That is, $s_{\bar{Y}} = \sqrt{\frac{MS_{MT}}{n}}$.

18.2.5 Generalizations with the Two-factor Mixed ANOVA

This section discusses the fact that, in general, the F-test for the fixed factor in a two-factor mixed ANOVA is less powerful than the F-test for this factor when both factors are treated as fixed. This is due to a smaller number of degrees of freedom for the denominator in the F-ratio for the fixed factor with the mixed ANOVA [fewer degrees of freedom in the denominator of the F-ratio yields a larger F-critical value thus making it more difficult to reject the null hypothesis]. For our (Method x Teacher) mixed ANOVA, for example, the F-ratio for the fixed factor (Method) is $F(2, 8) = 10.23$, $p = .006$ (see Figure 18.4). When both factors (Method and Teacher) were treated as fixed, however, the F-ratio for Method, reported in the SPSS output [not shown here], was $F(2, 15) = 17.205$, $p = .000$. Although both are statistically significant in this case, the p-value for F-test with the mixed ANOVA ($p = .006$) is larger than that for the F-test when both factors are fixed ($p = .000$) because the degrees of freedom for the denominator in the former (8) are less than the degrees of freedom for the denominator in the latter (15).

Thus, **it does not make sense to expect statistical significance for the fixed factor in a mixed ANOVA model if this factor is not statistically significant when all factors are treated as fixed.** As Glass and Hopkins (1996) state "if one cannot generalize method effects implemented by the teachers in the study (the only teachers on whom data are available), to a different sample of students how can one safely generalize method effects to the population of teachers? Such implausible results must be type-I errors" (p. 557).

Based on this logic, Glass and Hopkins (1996) recommend the so-called *incremental generalization strategy* (Hopkins, 1983), according to which the first step in a mixed ANOVA would be to treat all factors as fixed. This step would allow the researcher to assess whether the fixed-factor effects are generalizable to the population of subjects (e.g., students). If the findings *are* significant, the next step is to "free" the random factor from being treated as fixed. The results from this second step would allow to assess whether the findings are generalizable to the population levels of the random factor (e.g., teachers).

In the case of two or more random factors in a mixed ANOVA model, the sequence of steps with the incremental generalization strategy continues by "freeing" the random factors (one at a time) from being treated as fixed. This allows the researcher to gradually assess the generalizability of results about the fixed factor(s) to the population levels of each random factor (e.g., teachers, schools, districts, etc.).

18.3 Summary

• ANOVA models that involve both fixed and random factor(s) are called **mixed-effects models.**

• With mixed-effects models the interest lies in the determining effects of the fixed factor(s) using the information obtained about the random factor(s) to assess the generalizability of the findings to the population levels of the random factor(s).

• The linear model for the random-factor ANOVA (Equation 18.1) holds under two assumptions: 1. The random effects, a_k's, are independent and follow a normal distribution with a mean of zero and variance σ_a^2, and 2. The error terms of individual scores (ε_{ik} = Y_{ik} - μ_k) are independent and follow a normal distribution with a mean of zero and variance σ_ε^2 [*population error variance.*]

• The main question of interest regarding the random factor in a two-factor mixed ANOVA is, How much of the variance in the dependent variable is attributable to differences among levels of the random factor (e.g., teachers)? To address this question, it is necessary to estimate the variances of the random effects (see Equations 18.13 and 18.14).

• The denominator in the *F*-ratio for the fixed factor in a two-factor mixed ANOVA is the mean square for the interaction between the two factors (not MS_W) — e.g., Equation 18.11.

• To compute the effect size of the mean differences among the levels of the fixed factor in a two-factor mixed ANOVA, it is necessary to replace MS_W with the mean square of the interaction between the two factors — see Equation 18.15. The same holds for the computation of post-hoc test statistics that involve MS_W (e.g., Tukey) — see NOTE [18.3].

• The *F*-test for the fixed factor(s) in a mixed-effects ANOVA is less powerful than the *F*-test for this factor when all factors are treated as fixed. This is due to the loss of degrees of freedom in the denominator of the former compared to the number of degrees of freedom in the denominator of the latter. The positive trade-off of this is that the random factors in a mixed-effects ANOVA provide information to assess the generalizability of the findings related to the fixed factor.

• According to the *incremental generalization strategy* (Hopkins, 1983), the first step in a two-factor mixed ANOVA should be to treat both factors as fixed. This step would allow the researcher to assess whether the fixed-factor effects are generalizable to the population of subjects (e.g., students). If the findings are significant, the next step is to "free" the random factor from being treated as fixed. This would allow the researcher to assess whether the findings are generalizable to the population levels of the random factor (e.g., teachers).

• When there are two or more random factors in a mixed ANOVA model, the sequence of steps with the incremental generalization strategy continues with "freeing" the random factors (one at a time) from being treated as fixed. This allows the researcher to gradually assess the generalizability of results about the fixed factor(s) to the population levels of each random factor (e.g., teachers, schools, districts, etc.).

18.4 Study Questions

1. Which ANOVA models are referred to as mixed-effects ANOVA models?
2. What is the main question of interest in a two-factor mixed ANOVA model?
3. What are the assumptions with the one-random factor ANOVA?
4. What are the assumptions with the two-factor mixed ANOVA?
5. In a two-factor mixed ANOVA, the assumption of *sphericity* is necessary when

   A. testing the null hypothesis for the fixed main effect
   B. testing the null hypothesis for the random effects
   C. comparing the estimates of variance components
   D. None of the above.

6. What is the sufficient condition for sphericity to exist?
7. What is the value of the ε-multiplier when sphericity exists?
8. In a two-factor mixed ANOVA, MS_W is an estimate of which variance?

   A. $\hat{\sigma}_a^2$; **B.** $\hat{\sigma}_{\beta a}^2$; **C.** $\hat{\sigma}_\beta^2$; **D.** $\hat{\sigma}_\varepsilon^2$; **E.** None of the above.

9. A two-factor mixed ANOVA model is used to study students' attitudes toward school math and science. There is a fixed factor *Ethnicity* (Caucasian, African-American, Hispanic, Asian, Other) and a random factor *School* (with 10 schools randomly selected from the school system in a large urban area).. This is a balanced ANOVA design with a total sample of 800 randomly selected students. Given the mean square values for Ethnicity ($MS_E = 380$), School ($MS_S = 420$), Ethnicity x School interaction ($MS_{ES} = 80$), and error ($MS_W = 20$), compute (a) the *F*-ratio for the main effect of Ethnicity, (b) the estimate of the variance for school effects, $\hat{\sigma}_s^2$, and (c) the estimate of the variance for Ethnicity x School interaction terms, $\hat{\sigma}_{es}^2$. [*Hint*: see Formulas 18.11, 18.13, and 18.14.]
10. In a two-factor mixed ANOVA, is it appropriate to use the Tukey post-hoc test option in SPSS when the main effect of the fixed factor is statistically significant? (Why?).
11. A balanced two-factor ANOVA design is used to examine the effect of three methods of counseling on students' motivation to learn. The data are provided with the SPSS file **CH18_Q11.sav** [available on http://cehd.gmu.edu/book/dimitrov]. The dependent variable is **SCORE** (motivation score) and the two factors are **counselor** and **method**. The data consist of 60 observations that come from the three methods of counseling and 10 randomly selected school counselors, with the motivation scores of two randomly selected students within each cell (same counselor and same method) [10 x 3 x 2 = 60]. The SPSS output provided here is from a two-factor ANOVA in which both factors (counselor and method) were treated as fixed factors.

Tests of Between-Subjects Effects

Dependent Variable: SCORE

Source	Type III Sum of Squares	df	Mean Square	F	Sig.
Corrected Model	2713.733[a]	29	93.577	6.748	.000
Intercept	70452.267	1	70452.267	5080.692	.000
method	605.033	2	302.517	21.816	.000
counselor	1795.733	9	199.526	14.389	.000
method * counselor	312.967	18	17.387	1.254	.284
Error	416.000	30	13.867		
Total	73582.000	60			
Corrected Total	3129.733	59			

a. R Squared = .867 (Adjusted R Squared = .739)

Given the results from this first step in the *incremental generalization strategy* (see Section 18.2.5), complete the second step by (a) computing the F-ratio for method, treating counselor as a random factor [see Equation 18.11], (b) estimating the variance components for the random sources [see Equations 18.13 and 18.14], and (c) interpreting the results. After the completion of this step, through manual computations for tasks (a) and (b), use SPSS with the data set **CH18_Q11.sav** for a two-factor mixed ANOVA, as described in Example 18.2.

CHAPTER 19

REPEATED-MEASURES ANOVA

ANOVA designs in which the subjects are measured repeatedly on the variable(s) of interest are called **repeated-measures designs** [or *split-plot* designs.] For example, when the repeated measurements are taken at different time points, the repeated-measures factor is *time*. An example of this is when the effect of an experimental medication is measured at different time points during the day (e.g., morning, noon, and evening). If, however, the repeated measures come from different dosages of a medication, the repeated-measures factor would be *dosage*. In developmental studies, the repeated-measures factor is *age* (e.g., when the cognitive skills of children are measured across different age levels). An experimental study that involves trials (e.g., recognition of patterns) would have *trials* as the repeated-measures factor. The repeated-measures factor is called also the **within-subjects factor**. Of course, instead of subjects, the observational units in a repeated-measures design can be, for example, schools [this often occurs with evaluation studies in the field of education].

Studies that involve repeated measurements across numerous (three or more) time points are referred to also as **longitudinal studies**. For example, the National Education Longitudinal Study of 1988 (NELS:88) is a longitudinal study in which a nationally representative sample of eighth-graders were first surveyed in the spring of 1988 and then a sample of these respondents were resurveyed in four follow-ups in 1990, 1992, 1994, and 2000 [information, data, and results from this study are available at http://nces.ed.gov/surveys/NELS88].

19.1 A Simple Repeated-Measures ANOVA

19.1.1 Univariate Repeated-measures Analysis

A *simple repeated-measures ANOVA* is used to analyze repeated-measures for a single group of subjects (or other units of observation). It is also referred to as a *single-group repeated measures* (or *one-way repeated-measures*) ANOVA. The repeated-measures factor (e.g., time, age, trials, etc.) is treated as a fixed factor while the subjects represent a random factor. The main questions in this type of ANOVA relate to the significance of the repeated-measures factor and how generalizable the results are to the population of subjects. Thus, the simple repeated-measures ANOVA represents a two-factor mixed ANOVA, with the repeated–measures factor being a fixed factor and the subjects being a random factor. If we denote subjects by *S* and the repeated-measures factor by *T* (*time*), the score of any subject, *s*, at time point *t*, Y_{st}, can be represented as

$$Y_{st} = \mu_{\bullet\bullet} + \beta_t + a_s + \beta a_{ts} + \varepsilon_{ts}, \qquad \textbf{(19.1)}$$

where $\mu_{\bullet\bullet}$ is the grand mean, β_t is the fixed (repeated-measures) effect, a_s is the random (subjects) effect, βa_{ts} is the (time-by-subjects) interaction effect, and ε_{ts} is the error term.

The variances of the effects in Equation 19.1 are denoted as follows: σ_t^2 [variance of β_t], σ_s^2 [variance of a_s], and $\sigma_{ts,e}^2$ — the variance of (βa_{ts} + ε_{ts}) together. Note that, when subjects are treated as levels of a random factor, there is only one observation per cell (*n* = 1), Y_{st}, which also serves as the cell mean (i.e., $Y_{st} = \bar{Y}_{st}$). Thus, the within-cell error terms cannot be estimated ($\varepsilon_{ts} = Y_{st} - \bar{Y}_{st} = 0$). This does not mean that there is no within-cells error for the population of observations that may hypothetically occur if the same subjects, *s*, were measured independently and repeatedly at the same time point, *t* — it just means that this error cannot be estimated when there is only one observation per cell ($n = 1$). Therefore, the interaction term of the cell and the within-cell error are "lumped" together ($\beta\alpha_{ts} + \varepsilon_{ts}$), with $\sigma^2_{ts,e}$ denoting the resulting variance.

When the purpose of a study is to investigate the effects of a treatment over time, an important advantage of observing the same subjects repeatedly, rather than observing different subjects at different time points, is that the subjects serve as their own controls. This reduces the error variance and thus increases the power of the test. Specifically, when different subjects are measured at different time points, part of the error variance (MS$_W$) is due to differences among subjects. With the repeated-measures design, however, this part of the error variance is "removed," thus increasing the power of the test. This is illustrated in Figure 19.1. To facilitate the computations, a small sample of fictitious integer numbers is used. This is the familiar two-way data layout with a two-factor ANOVA (e.g., see Figure 15.1).

Figure 19.1 *Repeated-measures across three time points*

	Time			
Subject	T_1	T_2	T_3	
S_1	1	2	9	$\bar{Y}_{1\bullet} = 4$
S_2	0	2	1	$\bar{Y}_{2\bullet} = 1$
S_3	10	20	30	$\bar{Y}_{3\bullet} = 20$
S_4	5	0	4	$\bar{Y}_{4\bullet} = 3$
	$\bar{Y}_{\bullet 1} = 4$	$\bar{Y}_{\bullet 2} = 6$	$\bar{Y}_{\bullet 3} = 11$	$\bar{Y}_{\bullet\bullet} = 7$

The error variance for the ANOVA data in Figure 19.1 is computed here (a) assuming that different subjects are measured at each time point [a *completely randomized design*] and (b) the same subjects are measured repeatedly across the time points [a *repeated-measures design*]. In either case, the significance of the fixed factor (Time) is of primary interest, but the purpose here is to illustrate that the error variance with the repeated-measures design is smaller than that with the completely randomized design. These two cases are discussed in more detail below.

1. The **completely randomized design** here is the familiar one-factor ANOVA presented in Chapter 14. Thus, the *F*-test for significance of the main effect of Time is $F = \text{MS}_T/\text{MS}_W$, where MS$_T$ is the between-time (between-columns) variance and MS$_W$ is the within-time (within-columns) variance. Taking into account that each column in Figure 19.1 ($\bar{Y}_{\bullet t}$), is based on four observations, the *between-time sum of squares*, SS$_T$, *is computed* as follows:

$$\text{SS}_T = 4\Sigma(\bar{Y}_{\bullet t} - \bar{Y}_{\bullet\bullet})^2 = (4)[(4-7)^2 + (6-7)^2 + (11-7)^2] = (4)(9+1+16) = (4)(26) = 104.$$

The *within-time sum of squares* (SS$_W$) is the sum of the within-columns deviations from the mean. That is,

$$\begin{aligned}\mathrm{SS_W} &= \sum\sum(Y_{st} - \bar{Y}_{\bullet t})^2 \\ &= (1-4)^2 + (0-4)^2 + (10-4)^2 + (5-4)^2 \\ &+ (2-6)^2 + (2-6)^2 + (20-6)^2 + (0-6)^2 \\ &+ (9-11)^2 + (1-11)^2 + (30-11)^2 + (4-11)^2 \\ &= (9+16+36+1) + (16+16+196+36) + (4+100+361+49) \\ &= 62 + 264 + 514 = 840.\end{aligned}$$

Given that there are three time points ($T = 3$), the degrees of freedom for SS_T are $\mathrm{T} - 1 = 3 - 1 = 2$ and $\mathrm{MS}_T = \mathrm{SS}_T/(T - 1) = 104/2 = 52$. With four observations per column ($n = 4$), the degrees of freedom for $\mathrm{SS_W}$ are $T(n - 1) = (3)(4 - 1) = 9$. Thus, $\mathrm{MS_W} = \mathrm{SS_W}/T(n - 1) = 840/9 = 93.33$. The F-ratio for the main effect of Time is then $F = \mathrm{MS}_T/\mathrm{MS_W} = 52/93.33 = 0.56$. In this case this F-ratio is not statistically significant because it does not exceed the F-critical value with degrees of freedom 2 and 9 at the .05 level ($F_{\mathrm{c.v.}} = 4.26$).

2. Under the **repeated-measures design** (when the same subjects are measured over time), part of the error variance under the one-factor ANOVA model ($\mathrm{SS_W} = 840$) is due to differences among subjects. This part, called the *sum of squares between subjects* ($\mathrm{SS_{BS}}$), is computed here by taking into account that the mean score for any subject is based on three observations:

$$\begin{aligned}\mathrm{SS_{BS}} = 3\sum(\bar{Y}_{s\bullet} - \bar{Y}_{\bullet\bullet})^2 &= (3)[(4-7)^2 + (1-7)^2 + (20-7)^2 + (3-7)^2] \\ &= (3)(9 + 36 + 169 + 16) = (3)(230) = 690.\end{aligned}$$

By subtracting $\mathrm{SS_{BS}}$ from $\mathrm{SS_W}$, we obtain the reduced error variability, referred to here as the *sum of squares residual* ($\mathrm{SS_{RES}}$), for the repeated-measures design:

$$\mathrm{SS_{RES}} = \mathrm{SS_W} - \mathrm{SS_{BS}}. \qquad \textbf{(19.2)}$$

In this example, $\mathrm{SS_{RES}} = \mathrm{SS_W} - \mathrm{SS_{BS}} = 840 - 690 = 150$. Given Equation 19.2, the degrees of freedom for $\mathrm{SS_{WS}}$ can be obtained by subtracting the degrees of freedom for $\mathrm{SS_{BS}}$ from the degrees of freedom for $\mathrm{SS_W}$. With T denoting the number of time points and S, the number of subjects, we have: $df_{\mathrm{RES}} = df_{\mathrm{W}} - df_{\mathrm{BS}} = T(S - 1) - (S - 1)$. After removing the parentheses and using a bit of simple algebra, we can see that

$$df_{\mathrm{RES}} = (T - 1)(S - 1). \qquad \textbf{(19.3)}$$

Thus, $df_{\mathrm{RES}} = (T - 1)(S - 1) = (3 - 1)(4 - 1) = (2)(3) = 6$. The *mean square residual* is then computed as follows: $\mathrm{MS_{RES}} = \mathrm{SS_{RES}}/df_{\mathrm{RES}} = 150/6 = 25$. So, under the repeated-measures design, the F-ratio for the main effect of Time is

$$F_T = \frac{\mathrm{MS}_T}{\mathrm{MS_{RES}}}. \qquad \textbf{(19.4)}$$

Here, with $\mathrm{MS}_T = 52$ and $\mathrm{MS_{RES}} = 25$, we have: $F = 52/25 = 2.08$. Again, this F-ratio is not statistically significant, as it does not exceed the F-critical value with degrees of freedom 2 and 6 at the .05 level ($F_{\mathrm{c.v.}} = 5.14$). Note, however, that it is much larger than the F-ratio obtained under the one-factor ANOVA using the same data ($F = 0.56$). This is because the error variance under the repeated-measures ANOVA ($\mathrm{MS_{RES}} = 25$) is much smaller than its counterpart under the one-factor ANOVA ($\mathrm{MS_W} = 93.33$).

In general, Equation 19.2 shows that the error variability under the repeated-measures design (SS_{RES}) is *always smaller* than that obtained with a completely randomized design (SS_W), giving higher power to the *F*-test under the repeated-measures ANOVA.

NOTE [19.1] If the repeated-measures design is treated as a two-factor mixed ANOVA, with Subjects as the random factor and Time as the fixed factor, Equation 18.11 (Chapter 18, Section 18.2.3) shows that the mean square of the (Subject x Time) interaction with this design ($MS_{S \times T}$) is, in fact, MS_{RES} for the *F*-test with the repeated-measures ANOVA (see Equation 19.4). Thus,

$$F_T = \frac{MS_T}{MS_{RES}} = \frac{MS_T}{MS_{S \times T}} \quad \textbf{(19.5)}$$

Keep in mind, however, that in this case the interaction term (*S* x *T*) is "lumped" together with the within-cell error because there is only one observation within each cell in a repeated-measures design.

19.1.2 Assumptions in Repeated-measures ANOVA

The null hypothesis of interest in repeated-measures ANOVA is about the main effect of the repeated-measures factor. With *K* levels of a repeated-measure factor (e.g., *K* time points), the *F*-statistic in Equation 19.5 is used to test the hypothesis for the main effect of this factor:

$$H_0: \mu_{T_1} = \mu_{T_2} = \ldots = \mu_{T_K} \quad \textbf{(19.6)}$$

There are four assumptions for testing this null hypothesis in a repeated-measures ANOVA: *normality*, *homogeneity of variance*, *independence of observations*, and *sphericity*. The first three assumptions were discussed in Chapters 14 and 15. The assumption of **sphericity** was introduced in Chapter 18 —it means that the population variances of the differences for all pairs of the levels of the repeated-measures factor are equal. It has been proven that sphericity exists if two conditions, referred to as **compound symmetry**, are in place: (a) the variances of all levels of the repeated-measures factor are equal and (b) the correlations between any two levels of the repeated-measures factor are equal. Compound symmetry is a sufficient (albeit not *necessary*) condition for sphericity. The condition of compound symmetry is *stronger* than that of sphericity, but it might be easier to test in some situations. For the data in Figure 19.1, sphericity is defined by

$$\sigma^2_{T_1-T_2} = \sigma^2_{T_1-T_3} = \sigma^2_{T_2-T_3}.$$

Compound symmetry, which guarantees sphericity, is met in this case if (a) $\sigma^2_{T_1} = \sigma^2_{T_2} = \sigma^2_{T_3}$ and (b) $\rho_{12} = \rho_{13} = \rho_{23}$.

When the sphericity assumption is *not* met, the *F*-test for the repeated-measures factor becomes somewhat "liberal" — that is, it makes it unduly easier to reject the null hypothesis, H_0. When H_0 is not rejected, there is no need to check whether the sphericity assumption holds. Indeed, if H_0 is not rejected with a liberal *F*-test (when the sphericity assumption is violated), we cannot expect that it would be rejected with the less liberal *F*-test that results when the sphericity assumption is in place.

If, however, H_0 is rejected with a liberal *F*-test (the sphericity assumption is violated), additional information is needed to make a valid decision about H_0. This is achieved by adjusting the degrees of freedom for the F-ratio in Equation 19.5. Specifically, both the degrees of freedom for the numerator (df_1) and for the denominator (df_2) should be multiplied by a constant, ε, referred to as an "epsilon multiplier" (Huynh & Feldt, 1979). The values of the ε-multiplier are always greater than 0, but smaller or equal to 1 ($0 < \varepsilon \leq 1$), with $\varepsilon = 1$ indicating that sphericity exists. The lowest value of ε, indicating the largest possible departure from sphericity, is $\varepsilon = 1/(K - 1)$, where K is the number of fixed levels. For example, with five levels in the fixed factor ($K = 5$), we have $1/(5 - 1) = 0.25$, so $0.25 \leq \varepsilon \leq 1$. If, for example, $\varepsilon = 0.5$ and the degrees of freedom with a liberal F-test (when sphericity does not exist) are $df_1 = 4$ and $df_2 = 60$, the adjusted degrees of freedom are: $df_1^* = (\varepsilon)(df_1) = (0.5)(4) = 2$ and $df_2^* = (\varepsilon)(df_2) = (0.5)(60) = 30$. The ε-estimate with the Huynh-Feldt correction for the degrees of freedom, $df_1 = T - 1$ and $df_2 = (T - 1)(S - 1)$, is provided in SPSS and other statistical packages.

NOTE [19.2] When there are only two repeated measures (e.g., two time points or two trials), the condition of compound symmetry and, thus, the assumption of sphericity will be met.

19.1.3 The Multivariate Test for Repeated-measures ANOVA

The repeated-measures ANOVA can also be addressed through *multivariate analysis of variance* (MANOVA), which deals with testing hypotheses that involve two or more dependent variables, taking into account possible correlations among them. For example, consider the null hypothesis in (19.6) with four repeated measures (say, Y_1, Y_2, Y_3, and Y_4):

$$H_0\text{: } \mu_1 = \mu_2 = \mu_3 = \mu_4.$$

This hypothesis can also be represented as H_0: $\mu_1 - \mu_2 = 0$, $\mu_2 - \mu_3 = 0$, and $\mu_3 - \mu_4 = 0$. Given this, the MANOVA approach to testing H_0 is based on the analysis of variables that represent the differences between adjacent repeated measures: $Y_1 - Y_2$, $Y_2 - Y_3$, and $Y_3 - Y_4$.

Among the several MANOVA statistics available for testing H_0, the most widely used is **Wilk's Λ**, where Λ (the capital Greek letter "lambda") equals the ratio "within-group variability to total variability." In matrix algebra notations, this ratio is represented as

$$\Lambda = \frac{|\mathbf{W}|}{|\mathbf{T}|}, \tag{19.7}$$

where the numerator, $|\mathbf{W}|$, is a number (determinant) for the multivariate analog to the "within" variability in univariate ANOVA, whereas the denominator, $|\mathbf{T}|$, is a number (determinant) for the multivariate analog to the "total" (between + within) variability in univariate ANOVA. Two approximations of the sampling distribution of Λ, commonly used in MANOVA are (a) the Bartlett's chi-square (χ^2) distribution and (b) the Rao's F-distribution. Generally, the χ^2-test and the F-test lead to the same decision on H_0, but the F-test [which is reported in SPSS] works better with relatively small samples. Ideally, $\Lambda = 0$ occurs when $|\mathbf{W}| = 0$ — that is, when the "within" (or "error") variance is zero. Conversely, the worst-case scenario is when $\boldsymbol{\Lambda} = 1$ because it occurs when $|\mathbf{W}| = |\mathbf{T}|$ (that is, the total variance is "error" variance). Given this, Λ can be viewed as an *effect size*. Just keep in mind that the closer Wilk's Λ is to zero, the larger the effect size. Equivalently, the effect size measured by Λ can be represented as a **multivariate eta squared** ($\text{m}\eta^2$) index of effect size:

$$\text{m}\eta^2 = 1 - \Lambda \tag{19.8}$$

As can be seen, $m\eta^2$ is the multivariate analog to the omnibus effect size "eta squared" (η^2) discussed in Chapter 14 (see Equation 14.33).

19.1.4 Univariate or Multivariate Approach to Repeated-measures ANOVA?

Previous studies provide extensive discussions on the properties and relative power of the univariate and multivariate approaches to repeated-measures ANOVA (e.g., Davidson, 1972; Maxwell & Delaney, 1990; O'Brien & Kaiser, 1985). An advantage of the MANOVA approach is that it does not require the assumption of sphericity [but, of course, it keeps the assumptions of multivariate normality, homogeneity of variance, and independent observations]. However, Stevens (2002) noted that "In terms of controlling for Type I error, there is no real basis for preferring the multivariate approach because use of the modified tests (i.e., multiplying the degrees of freedom by $\hat{\epsilon}$) yields an 'honest' error rate. The choice then involves a question of power. If sphericity holds, then the univariate approach is more powerful" (p. 509). Note that $\hat{\epsilon}$ is the estimate of the "epsilon multiplier" (see Section 19.1.2). A recommended guideline is that if $\hat{\epsilon}$ is .75 or higher ($\hat{\epsilon} \geq .75$), the univariate approach to repeated-measures ANOVA is the method of choice (Glass & Hopkins, 1996).

19.1.5 SPSS for the Simple Repeated-measures ANOVA

The SPSS output for a simple repeated-measures ANOVA provides both multivariate and univariate test results. Along with Wilk's Λ [denoted in SPSS **Wilks' Lambda**], three other multivariate tests are reported — Pillai's Trace, Hottelling's Trace, and Roy's Largest Root. In the case of a simple repeated-measures ANOVA, all four multivariate tests must yield the same result, but we will interpret Wilk's Λ, primarily for the effect-size information provided by Λ (or by the multivariate "eta squared": $m\eta^2 = 1 - \Lambda$).

If Wilk's Λ is statistically significant, we reject H$_0$: $\mu_{T_1} = \mu_{T_2} = \ldots = \mu_{T_K}$. In this case we can skip the SPSS tables that relate to the univariate approach to repeated-measures ANOVA — **Mauchley's Test of Sphericity** and **Tests of Within-Subjects Effects**. This is because (a) the multivariate tests for the repeated-measures ANOVA do not require sphericity and (b) if H_0 is rejected with the multivariate test, there must be even stronger evidence for rejecting H_0 with the (generally more powerful) univariate test.

If Wilk's Λ is not statistically significant, then we must examine the two univariate tables: **Mauchley's Test of Sphericity** and **Tests of Within-Subjects Effects,** which includes the standard univariate ANOVA (labeled *Sphericity Assumed*) and two alternative univariate tests (labeled *Greenhouse-Geisser* and *Huynh-Feldt*, respectively). First, recall that the assumption of sphericity is met *if* the $\hat{\epsilon}$-value (labeled *Epsilon* in the **Mauchley's Test of Sphericity** table) equals 1.00. If this is the case, the decision on H_0 must be based on the F-test under *Sphericity Assumed* in the **Tests of Within-Subjects Effects** table. However, if sphericity does not exist (*Epsilon* is smaller than 1), the decision on H_0 must be based on the alternative tests: Greenhouse-Geisser and Huynh-Feldt (which is usually preferred). Typically, these two alternative tests lead to the same decision on H_0, although their p-values are generally not equal. This is because the Greenhouse-Geisser method tends to underestimate ϵ, especially when ϵ is close to 1, whereas the Huynh-Feldt method tends to overestimate ϵ (Maxwell & Delaney, 1990). Taking this into account, Stevens (2002) recommended using the average of the ϵ-values reported under these two methods as the estimate of ϵ.

Multiple comparisons among repeated measures are also available in SPSS through the use of six options for different "contrasts." For example, the contrast labeled **Simple** can be used to compare all repeated measures to either the first or the last measure ("reference category"). Another contrast, labeled **Repeated**, is used to compare adjacent categories (repeated measures) — each category, except for the first, is compared to the one that precedes it. When the repeated measures are equally spaced (e.g., at equal time intervals), the option for polynomial contrasts (**Polynomial**) can be very useful in testing for linear effect, quadratic effect, cubic effect, etc.

EXAMPLE 19.1 The purpose of this example is to illustrate the use of SPSS to conduct a simple repeated-measures ANOVA. The repeated measures are task performance scores of five subjects under three successive experimental conditions — **normal**, **penalty**, and **reward.** These conditions represent three levels of a repeated-measures factor labeled **CONDITION**. The data are provided in Figure 19.2. The question of interest is whether the conditions of penalty and reward make a difference in task performance compared to the "normal" condition (neither penalty nor reward is given when the task is performed). This question requires the use of the SPSS contrast option labeled **Simple**, with the first condition (*normal*) being the "reference category." Of course, multiple comparisons will be interpreted if the omnibus (multivariate and/or univariate) test for repeated-measures ANOVA is statistically significant. To use SPSS for this analysis, follow the steps described in Figure 19.2 (right panel).

Figure 19.2 *SPSS for repeated-measures ANOVA — data and processing steps*

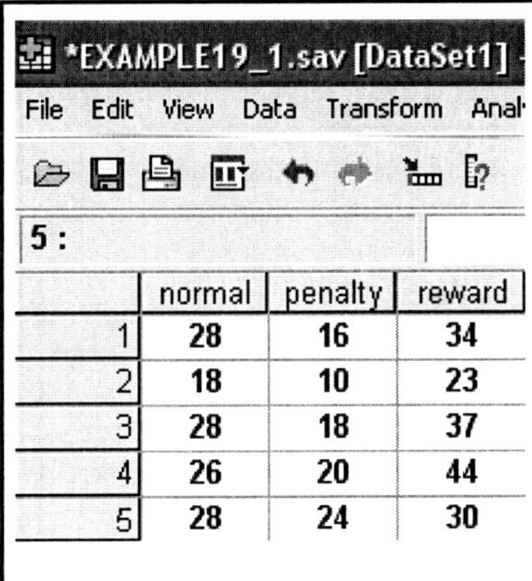

	normal	penalty	reward
1	28	16	34
2	18	10	23
3	28	18	37
4	26	20	44
5	28	24	30

1. Click **Analyze**, click **General Linear Model**, and click **Repeated Measures.**
2. In the dialog box **Repeated Measures Define Factor(s)** do the following: type **CONDITION** [or other label for the repeated-measures factor] in the **Within-Subject Factor Name** box, type **3** in the box **Number of Levels**, click **Add,** and click **Define.**
3. In the dialog box **Repeated Measures**, hold down the Ctrl key and click on **normal**, **penalty**, and **reward.** Then click ▶ to move them into the box **Within-Subjects Variables**.
4. Click **Options**.
5. Check the boxes for **Descriptive Statistics** and **Estimates of effect size**.
6. Click **Continue**.
7. Click **Contrasts** [bottom of the **Repeated Measures** box].
8. In the drop-down menu, select **Simple**, and click **Change**.
9. Click **Plots**, click **CONDITION**, and click ▶ to move it into the box **Horizontal Axis**. Then click **Add**.
10. Click **Continue**.
11. Click **OK**.

The SPSS output is provided in Figure 19.3 (omnibus tests) and Figure 19.4 (multiple comparisons). The means and standard deviations (not shown in the figures) are provided by the levels of the repeated-measures factor, **normal** ($M = 25.60$, $SD = 4.34$), **penalty** ($M = 17.60$, $SD = 5.18$), and **reward** ($M = 33.60$, $SD = 7.83$). In Figure 19.3, the results from the multivariate tests indicate a statistically significant effect of the repeated-measures factor — conditions of task performance (normal, penalty, and reward), at the .05 level. Specifically, Wilk's $\Lambda = .09$, $F(2, 3) = 15.53$, $p = .026$, $m\eta^2 = .91$. With the simple repeated-measures ANOVA, the "partial eta squared" reported in the **Multivariate Tests** table is the *multiple eta squared* ($m\eta^2 = 1 - \Lambda$).

Figure 19.3 *Selected SPSS output for a simple repeated-measures ANOVA — multivariate and univariate omnibus tests for the data in Figure 19.2*

Multivariate Tests

Effect		Value	F	Hypothesis df	Error df	Sig.	Partial Eta Squared
CONDITION	Pillai's Trace	.912	15.530[a]	2.000	3.000	.026	.912
	Wilks' Lambda	.088	15.530[a]	2.000	3.000	.026	.912
	Hotelling's Trace	10.354	15.530[a]	2.000	3.000	.026	.912
	Roy's Largest Root	10.354	15.530[a]	2.000	3.000	.026	.912

a. Exact statistic

Mauchly's Test of Sphericity

Measure: MEASURE_1

Within Subjects Effect	Mauchly's W	Approx. Chi-Square	df	Sig.	Epsilon		
					Greenhouse-Geisser	Huynh-Feldt	Lower-bound
CONDITION	.509	2.026	2	.363	.671	.885	.500

Tests of Within-Subjects Effects

Measure: MEASURE_1

Source		Type III Sum of Squares	df	Mean Square	F	Sig.
CONDITION	Sphericity Assumed	640.000	2	320.000	20.426	.001
	Greenhouse-Geisser	640.000	1.341	477.139	20.426	.004
	Huynh-Feldt	640.000	1.770	361.521	20.426	.001
	Lower-bound	640.000	1.000	640.000	20.426	.011
Error(CONDITION)	Sphericity Assumed	125.333	8	15.667		
	Greenhouse-Geisser	125.333	5.365	23.360		
	Huynh-Feldt	125.333	7.081	17.699		
	Lower-bound	125.333	4.000	31.333		

As noted earlier, given that Wilk's lambda is statistically significant, we can omit the univariate tables (**Mauchley's Test of Sphericity** and **Tests of Within-Subjects Effects**). Nonetheless, for illustration, key results provided in these tables are discussed here. First, key results in the table **Mauchley's Test of Sphericity** are the *epsilon* estimates ($\hat{\epsilon}$) of Greenhouse-Geisser ($\hat{\epsilon} = .671$) and Huynh-Feldt ($\hat{\epsilon} = .885$), with the latter being usually recommended. [If needed, the average of these two estimates, $\hat{\epsilon} = .778$, can be used as a more balanced estimate of ϵ.] As expected, the univariate test results (**Tests of Within-Subjects Effects** table) also indicate a statistically significant effect of the repeated-measures factor. Specifically, the *F*-test with the

Huynh-Feldt correction for degrees of freedom is statistically significant at the .05 level, $F(2, 7) = 20.43$, $p = .001$. [The corrected degrees of freedom for the F-ratio, rounded here to the nearest integer, are 1.77 and 7.081 for the numerator and denominator, respectively.]

Figure 19.4 *Selected SPSS output for a simple repeated-measures ANOVA — multiple comparisons and profile plot for the data in Figure 19.2*

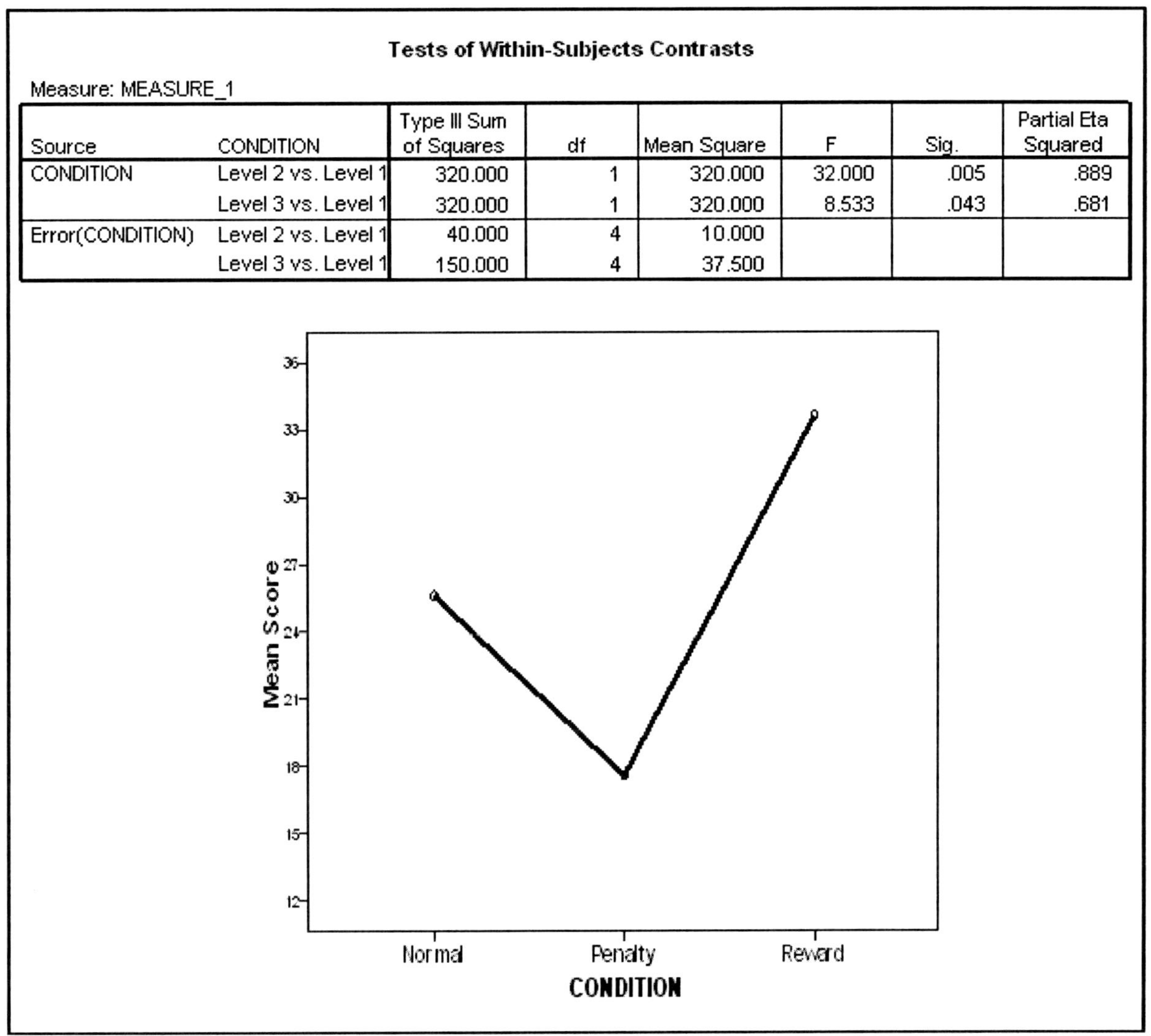

Tests of Within-Subjects Contrasts

Measure: MEASURE_1

Source	CONDITION	Type III Sum of Squares	df	Mean Square	F	Sig.	Partial Eta Squared
CONDITION	Level 2 vs. Level 1	320.000	1	320.000	32.000	.005	.889
	Level 3 vs. Level 1	320.000	1	320.000	8.533	.043	.681
Error(CONDITION)	Level 2 vs. Level 1	40.000	4	10.000			
	Level 3 vs. Level 1	150.000	4	37.500			

Figure 19.4 shows the SPSS output for the two comparisons of interest in this example (*penalty* versus *normal* and *reward* versus *normal*) along with the profile plot of the repeated measures. As can be seen, the contrast "Level 2 vs. Level 1" (*penalty* versus *normal*) is statistically significant, $F(1, 4) = 32.00$, $p = .005$, $p\eta^2 = .89$. This indicates that the task performance under the "control" condition (normal, $M = 25.60$, $SD = 4.34$) has dropped significantly under the condition of penalty ($M = 17.60$, $SD = 5.18$). The contrast "Level 3 vs. Level 1" (*reward* versus *normal*) is also statistically significant at the .05 level, $F(1, 4) = 8.53$, $p = .043$, $p\eta^2 = .68$, thus indicating that the task performance under the condition of reward ($M = 33.60$, $SD = 7.83$) is significantly higher than that under the control condition (normal, $M = 25.60$, $SD = 4.34$). The changes across conditions of repeated measures (normal, penalty, and reward) are depicted with

the profile plot in Figure 19.4. As a clarification regarding the effect size of these changes, the *partial eta squared* (pη^2) for a specific contrast shows its contribution to explaining the total (generalized) variance *after controlling for the effect(s) of the other contrast(s)*. Thus, pη^2 for a contrast is different from the omnibus effect size measure provided with the multivariate test (*multivariate eta squared*, mη^2).

19.2 Repeated-Measures ANOVA with one Between-Subjects Factor

As shown in the previous section, the main purpose to conduct a simple repeated-measures ANOVA is to determine the **within-subjects effects** — that is, the effects associated with the repeated-measures factor. However, in addition to within-subjects effects, part of the total (generalized) variance of the repeated-measures can be attributed to **between-subjects effects** — that is, the effects associated with between-subjects factors such as gender, ethnicity, anxiety level, etc. If the researcher wants to know both within-subjects and between-subjects effects, repeated-measures designs with one or more between-subjects factors are employed, and both the within-subjects and between-subjects factors are considered fixed.

This section illustrates how to use SPSS to conduct and interpret the results from a repeated-measures ANOVA with one between-subjects factor. The theoretical framework of this design, known also a **split-plot** design, is an extension of the simple repeated-measures design that takes into account the differences among the levels of the between-subjects factor.

EXAMPLE 19.2 The data for the repeated-measures ANOVA with one between-subjects factor in this example are shown in Figure 19.5. They are available with the file **Anxiety 2.sav** in the standard set of files provided with the SPSS software (recent and older versions). The data consists of the repeated measures of 12 subjects on four sets of tasks, called *trials* [named trial1, trial2, trial3, and trial4]. The scores represent the number of errors in task performance. Also, the subjects are grouped by the levels of two between-subjects factors: **anxiety** and **tension**. Each of these two factors has two levels, denoted 1 and 2 (1 = low, 2 = high). In this example **anxiety** is considered a between-subjects factor. [The case with **tension** as the between-subjects factor is assigned as a study question at the end of this chapter.] The question of interest here is: **"Does the task performance of the subjects improve throughout their repeated trials and does their anxiety level affect the task performance?"**

To use SPSS, we follow the steps described in Figure 19.2, with the following changes:

(a) the name of the repeated-measures factor now is **TRIAL** with four levels — **trial1**, **trial2**, **trial3**, and **trial4**,

(b) insert the following new step between steps 3 and 4 in Figure 19.2: Click **anxiety**, and click ▶ to move it to the **Between-Subjects Factor(s)** box,

(c) in step 8, select the contrast **Repeated** [to compare adjacent trials], and

(d) in step 9, move **TRIAL** to **Horizontal Axis** box and move **anxiety** to the **Separate Lines** box.

The SPSS output for the omnibus tests is provided in Figure 19.6, and the multiple comparisons (with the Repeated contrast) and the profile plot are presented in Figure 19.7. The descriptive statistics, not shown in the figures, are provided in APA style with Table 19.1.

Figure 19.5 *SPSS data file* ***Anxiety 2.sav***

*Anxiety 2.sav [DataSet1] - SPSS Data Editor

File Edit View Data Transform Analyze Graphs Utilities Add-ons Window Help

12 :

	subject	anxiety	tension	trial1	trial2	trial3	trial4
1	1	1	1	18	14	12	6
2	2	1	1	19	12	8	4
3	3	1	1	14	10	6	2
4	4	1	2	16	12	10	4
5	5	1	2	12	8	6	2
6	6	1	2	18	10	5	1
7	7	2	1	16	10	8	4
8	8	2	1	18	8	4	1
9	9	2	1	16	12	6	2
10	10	2	2	19	16	10	8
11	11	2	2	16	14	10	9
12	12	2	2	16	12	8	8

In Figure 19.6, the results from the multivariate tests indicate a statistically significant effect of the within-subjects factor (trial). Specifically, Wilk's $\Lambda = .04$, $F(3, 8) = 64.85$, $p < .001$, $m\eta^2 = .96$ [$m\eta^2 = 1 - \Lambda$]. However, there is no statistically significant interaction between the within-subjects factor (trial) and the between-subjects factor (anxiety), Wilk's $\Lambda = .52$, $F(3, 8) = 2.45$, $p = .14$, $m\eta^2 = .48$. This indicates that the within-subjects effects, which were found to be significant, *do not change* across the levels of the between-subjects factor. In other words, the difference between the mean scores in any two trials remains the same across the two anxiety groups. These findings are supported by the univariate test results (**Tests of Within-Subjects Effects** table). Specifically, the Huynh-Feldt *epsilon* estimate is smaller than 1 ($\hat{\epsilon} = .70$) thus indicating that the sphericity assumption is not met. Taking this into account, we use the *F*-test with the Huynh-Feldt correction for the degrees of freedom [in APA-style reports, the corrected degrees of freedom are rounded to the nearest integer]. Again, the results indicate that there is statistical significance for the within-subjects factor, $F(2, 21) = 128.63$, $p < .001$, $p\eta^2 = .93$, but not for the (trial x anxiety) interaction, $F(2, 21) = 1.09$, $p = .36$, $p\eta^2 = .10$. Additionally, the results from the tests of between-subjects effects in Figure 19.6 indicate that there is no statistically-significant effect of the between-subjects factor (anxiety), $F(1, 10) = 0.59$, $p = .46$, $p\eta^2 = .06$. That is, the mean scores of the two anxiety groups across all trials are equal. We can conclude that the membership of the subjects in different anxiety groups, as defined by the data, does not make any difference in their task performance across the repeated trials.

In Figure 19.7, the *F*-tests for repeated contrasts indicate that, for all three pairs, the differences between adjacent trials *are* statistically significant ($p < .001$). The (trial x anxiety) interaction is not statistically significant for the first two contrasts, trial 1 versus trial 2 ($p = .82$) and trial 2 versus trial 3 ($p = .18$), but it is statistically significant for the third contrast, trial 3 versus trial 4, $F(1, 10) = 8.75$, $p = .014$, $p\eta^2 = .47$. Given these results and that a lower score (fewer errors) means better task performance, the profile plot shows that the subjects improve their task performance over the trials and that their anxiety classification does not make any difference in this regard, except for a slightly better performance of the second anxiety group in the last trial.

Figure 19.6 *Selected SPSS output for a repeated-measures ANOVA with one between-subjects factor (TRIAL) — multivariate and univariate omnibus tests with the data in Figure 19.5*

Multivariate Tests

Effect		Value	F	Hypothesis df	Error df	Sig.	Partial Eta Squared
TRIAL	Pillai's Trace	.961	64.854[a]	3.000	8.000	.000	.961
	Wilks' Lambda	.039	64.854[a]	3.000	8.000	.000	.961
	Hotelling's Trace	24.320	64.854[a]	3.000	8.000	.000	.961
	Roy's Largest Root	24.320	64.854[a]	3.000	8.000	.000	.961
TRIAL * anxiety	Pillai's Trace	.479	2.451[a]	3.000	8.000	.138	.479
	Wilks' Lambda	.521	2.451[a]	3.000	8.000	.138	.479
	Hotelling's Trace	.919	2.451[a]	3.000	8.000	.138	.479
	Roy's Largest Root	.919	2.451[a]	3.000	8.000	.138	.479

Mauchly's Test of Sphericity

Measure: MEASURE_1

Within Subjects Effect	Mauchly's W	Approx. Chi-Square	df	Sig.	Epsilon		
					Greenhouse-Geisser	Huynh-Feldt	Lower-bound
TRIAL	.283	11.011	5	.053	.544	.701	.333

Tests of Within-Subjects Effects

Measure: MEASURE_1

Source		Type III Sum of Squares	df	Mean Square	F	Sig.	Partial Eta Squared
TRIAL	Sphericity Assumed	991.500	3	330.500	128.627	.000	.928
	Greenhouse-Geisser	991.500	1.632	607.468	128.627	.000	.928
	Huynh-Feldt	991.500	2.102	471.773	128.627	.000	.928
	Lower-bound	991.500	1.000	991.500	128.627	.000	.928
TRIAL * anxiety	Sphericity Assumed	8.417	3	2.806	1.092	.368	.098
	Greenhouse-Geisser	8.417	1.632	5.157	1.092	.346	.098
	Huynh-Feldt	8.417	2.102	4.005	1.092	.357	.098
	Lower-bound	8.417	1.000	8.417	1.092	.321	.098
Error(TRIAL)	Sphericity Assumed	77.083	30	2.569			
	Greenhouse-Geisser	77.083	16.322	4.723			
	Huynh-Feldt	77.083	21.016	3.668			
	Lower-bound	77.083	10.000	7.708			

Tests of Between-Subjects Effects

Measure: MEASURE_1

Transformed Variable: Average

Source	Type III Sum of Squares	df	Mean Square	F	Sig.	Partial Eta Squared
Intercept	1200.000	1	1200.000	280.839	.000	.966
anxiety	2.521	1	2.521	.590	.460	.056
Error	42.729	10	4.273			

Figure 19.7 *Selected SPSS output for a repeated-measures ANOVA with one between-subjects factor (TRIAL) — multiple comparisons and profile plot for the data in Figure 19.5*

Tests of Within-Subjects Contrasts

Measure: MEASURE_1

Source	TRIAL	Type III Sum of Squares	df	Mean Square	F	Sig.	Partial Eta Squared
TRIAL	Level 1 vs. Level 2	300.000	1	300.000	52.023	.000	.839
	Level 2 vs. Level 3	168.750	1	168.750	83.678	.000	.893
	Level 3 vs. Level 4	147.000	1	147.000	78.750	.000	.887
TRIAL * anxiety	Level 1 vs. Level 2	.333	1	.333	.058	.815	.006
	Level 2 vs. Level 3	4.083	1	4.083	2.025	.185	.168
	Level 3 vs. Level 4	16.333	1	16.333	8.750	.014	.467
Error(TRIAL)	Level 1 vs. Level 2	57.667	10	5.767			
	Level 2 vs. Level 3	20.167	10	2.017			
	Level 3 vs. Level 4	18.667	10	1.867			

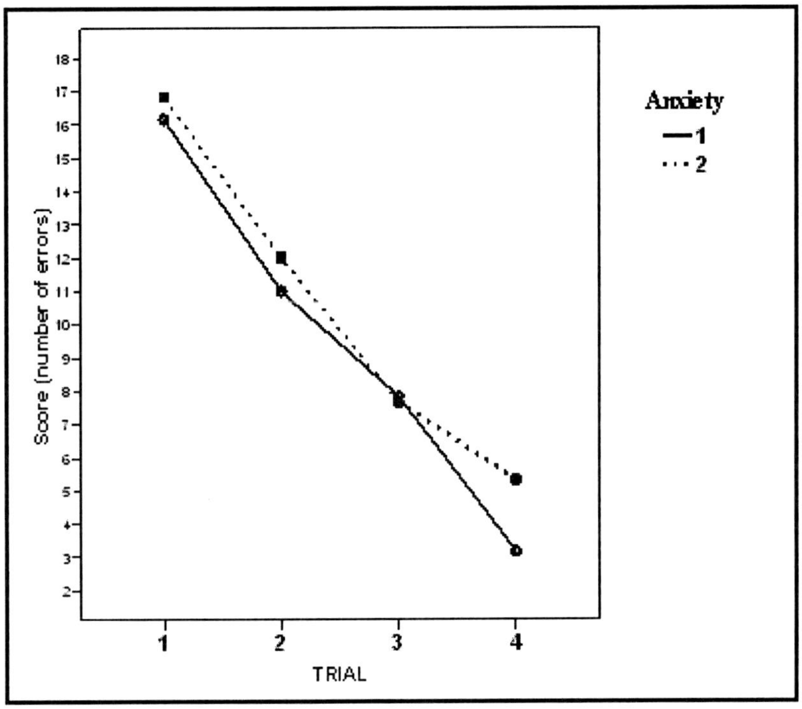

The results from the repeated-measures ANOVA in this example are also summarized in Tables 19.1, 19.2, and 19.3 in accordance with APA style for ANOVA tables. Table 19.1 shows the means and standard deviations for task performance scores (number of errors). Table 19.2 presents the results from the univariate omnibus test, with the Huynh-Feldt correction for degrees of freedom [the omnibus multivariate test, Wilk's Λ, is reported in the text]. Table 19.3 presents the results obtained by using the SPSS contrast option for multiple comparisons between adjacent levels of the within-subjects factor (trial). The *partial eta squared* ($p\eta^2$) for the effect size of a contrast indicates the proportion of the total variance accounted for by the difference between adjacent trials for this contrast controlling for the effects of the other contrasts.

Table 19.1

Means and Standard Deviations for Task Performance Scores by Repeated Trials and Anxiety Groups (1 and 2)

Trial	Anxiety 1[a]		Anxiety 2[a]		Total[b]	
	M	*SD*	*M*	*SD*	*M*	*SD*
Trial 1	16.17	2.71	16.83	1.33	16.50	2.07
Trial 2	11.00	2.10	12.00	2.83	11.50	2.43
Trial 3	7.83	2.71	7.67	2.34	7.75	2.42
Trial 4	3.17	1.84	5.33	3.44	4.25	2.86

[a] $n = 6$. [b] $n = 12$.

Table 19.2

Analysis of Variance for Repeated Measures on Task Performance

Source	*df*	*F*	$p\eta^2$	*P*
		Between subjects		
Anxiety (A)	1	0.59	.06	.46
S within-group error	10	(4.27)		
		Within subjects		
Trials (T)	2	128.63***	.93	.00
T X A	3	1.09	.10	.36
T X S within-group error	2	(3.67)		

Note. Values enclosed in parentheses represent mean square errors.

S = subjects.

***$p < .001$.

Table 19.3

Multiple Comparisons Between Adjacent Trials in a Repeated-Measures Design

Source	*Contrast*	*df*	*F*	*p*η2	*P*
Trial (T)					
	Trial 1 versus Trial 2	1	52.02***	.84	.00
	Trial 2 versus Trial 3	1	83.68***	.89	.00
	Trial 3 versus Trial 4	1	78.75***	.89	.00
T x Anxiety					
	Trial 1 versus Trial 2	1	0.06	.01	.82
	Trial 2 versus Trial 3	1	2.02	.17	.18
	Trial 3 versus Trial 4	1	8.75	.47	.01
T x S within-group error					
	Trial 1 versus Trial 2	10	(5.77)		
	Trial 2 versus Trial 3	10	(2.02)		
	Trial 3 versus Trial 4	10	(1.87)		

Note. Values enclosed in parentheses represent mean square errors. S = subjects.
$^{*}p < .05.$ $^{***}p < .001.$

19.3 Caution with Repeated-Measures ANOVA for Pretest-Posttest Data

The repeated measures ANOVA has been used in published studies to analyze pretest-posttest data with one between-subjects (treatment) factor and one within-subjects (pretest-posttest) factor. Previous research, however, has demonstrated that the results provided by the repeated measures ANOVA for pretest-posttest data can be misleading (e.g., Jennings, 1988; Huck & McLean, 1975). Specifically, the *F* test for the treatment main effect, which is of primary interest, is very conservative because the pretest scores are not affected by the treatment. Also, a very little known fact is that the *F* statistic for the interaction between the treatment factor and the pretest-posttest factor is *identical* to the *F* statistic for the treatment main effect in a one-way ANOVA on gain scores (Huck & McLean, 1975). Thus, when conducting a repeated measures ANOVA with pretest-posttest data, the *interaction F* ratio, not the main effect *F* ratio, must be used for testing the treatment main effect. Empirical evidence of this is provided in the next example.

EXAMPLE 19.3 The pretest-posttest data in Figure 19.8 are analyzed in this example by conducting (a) an ANOVA on gain score (**Gain**) and (b) a repeated-measures ANOVA with the pretest and posttest data treated as repeated measures at two time points. In both cases, the grouping variable (**Group**) is the between-subjects factor. The three levels of the between-subjects factor (coded 1, 2, and 3) are treatment conditions in a pretest-posttest experimental design. An APA-style summary of the results is provided in Table 19.4.

Figure 19.8 *Pretest-posttest data*

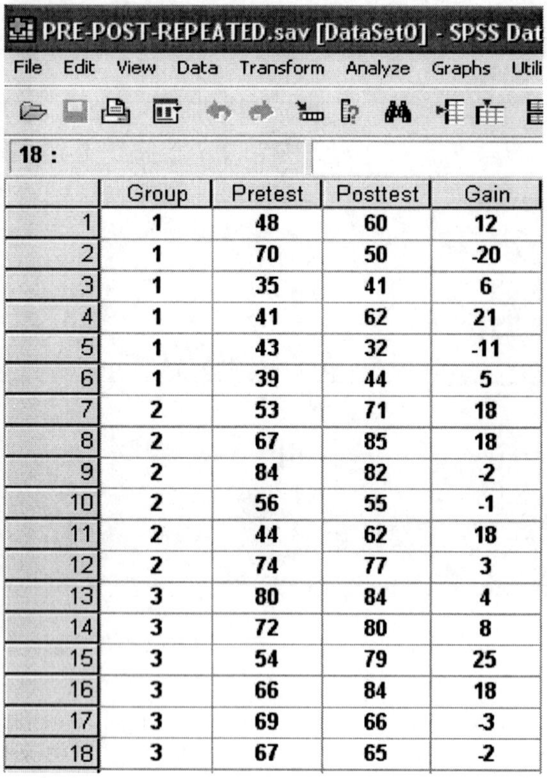

PRE-POST-REPEATED.sav [DataSet0] - SPSS Dat

File Edit View Data Transform Analyze Graphs Utili

18 :

	Group	Pretest	Posttest	Gain
1	1	48	60	12
2	1	70	50	-20
3	1	35	41	6
4	1	41	62	21
5	1	43	32	-11
6	1	39	44	5
7	2	53	71	18
8	2	67	85	18
9	2	84	82	-2
10	2	56	55	-1
11	2	44	62	18
12	2	74	77	3
13	3	80	84	4
14	3	72	80	8
15	3	54	79	25
16	3	66	84	18
17	3	69	66	-3
18	3	67	65	-2

Table 19.4

ANOVA on Gain Score and Repeated-measures ANOVA for Pretest-Posttest Data

Model Source	*df*	*F*	$p\eta^2$	*p*
ANOVA on gain score				
			Between subjects	
Group (G)	2	**0.56**	.07	.58
S within-group error	15			
Repeated-measures ANOVA				
			Between subjects	
Group (G)	2	**11.34****	.60	.00
S within-group error	15	(75.47)		
			Within subjects	
Time (T	1	5.04*	.25	.04
T x G	2	**0.56**	.07	.58
T x S within-group error	15	(188.27)		

Note. Values enclosed in parentheses represent mean square errors. S = subjects.
$^{*}p < .05.$ $^{***}p < .001.$

Table 19.4 shows the results from both the ANOVA on gain scores and the repeated measures ANOVA with one between subjects factor (Group) and one within subjects factor, Time (pretest-posttest) [the F-values of interest are shown in bold]. As the highlighted parts in Table 19.4 show, the F-test result for the treatment factor (Group) with the ANOVA on gain score is *identical* to the F-test result for Group x Time interaction with the repeated-measures design: $F(2, 15) = 0.56, p = .58, p\eta^2 = .07$. While this result clearly indicates the lack of statistical significance for the between-subjects factor, the F-test result for this factor under the repeated measures ANOVA is different and statistically significant, $F(2, 15) = 11.34, p < 0.001, p\eta^2 = .60$, thus leading to a false rejection of the null hypothesis for main effect of the between-subjects factor (Group).

NOTE [19.3] When a repeated-measures ANOVA with one between-subjects factor is used with pretest-posttest data, the significance of the main effect of the between-subjects factor is indicated by the F-test for the interaction between this factor and the within-subjects (repeated-measures) factor. To avoid confusion and potential mistakes in this regard, one can directly use a one-way ANOVA on gain scores and/or ANCOVA with the pretest scores as a covariate.

19.4 Summary

• ANOVA designs in which the subjects are measured repeatedly on the dependent variable are called **repeated-measures designs.** When the repeated measurements take place across different time points, the repeated-measures factor is *time*. Other typical examples of between-subjects factors are *trials*, *conditions*, etc.

• The **repeated-measures factor,** also called the **within-subjects factor**, is treated as a *fixed* factor.

• The main question to address with a simple repeated-measures ANOVA is whether the repeated measures factor is statistically significant. Specific differences among the levels of this factor are usually tested through the use of contrasts [options are available with SPSS and other major statistical packages].

• In repeated-measures ANOVA, the subjects serve as their own controls. This reduces the error variance and thus increases the power of the test. Specifically, the error variability under repeated-measures ANOVA (SS_{RES}) is always smaller than the error variability under the regular one-factor ANOVA (SS_W) because a certain part of the latter is due to between-subjects variation (MS_{BS}). After removing this part, we have $SS_{RES} = SS_W - SS_{BS}$ which proves that SS_{RES} is smaller than SS_W ($SS_{RES} < SS_W$).

•There are four assumptions a in repeated-measures ANOVA — *normality, homogeneity of variance, independence of the observations*, and *sphericity*. **Sphericity** is defined by equal variances of the differences between any two levels of the repeated-measures factor for all possible pairs of levels. A sufficient condition for sphericity to exist is the so-called **compound symmetry** condition: the same variance for all levels and same correlation for all pairs of levels of the repeated-measures factor.

• When the sphericity assumption is not met, the F-test for the repeated-measures factor becomes somewhat "liberal." That is, it makes it unduly easier to reject the null hypothesis. This is "corrected" by multiplying the degrees of freedom for the F-test by a constant, ϵ, referred to as the "epsilon multiplier." When there are only two repeated measures, the sphericity assumption is met [i.e., there is no need of testing for sphericity].

• A repeated-measures ANOVA with one-between subjects factor is used to address questions that target both *within-subjects effects* and *between-subjects effects*. Here both the within- subjects factor and the between-subjects factor are considered fixed.

• Along with the univariate approach, there is a multivariate approach to repeated-measures ANOVA. An advantage of the multivariate approach is that it does not require the assumption of sphericity.

• The multivariate omnibus test statistic Wilk's Λ represents the ratio "within-group variability to total variability" ($\Lambda = |W|/|T|$). A measure of multivariate effect size, referred to as *multivariate eta squared* ($m\eta^2$), is defined as follows: $m\eta^2 = 1 - \Lambda$.

• The univariate and multivariate approaches to repeated-measures ANOVA do not differ in controlling for Type I error. However, if the sphericity assumption holds, the univariate approach is more powerful. [When the epsilon multiplier is .75 or higher ($\hat{\epsilon} \geq .75$), the univariate approach to repeated-measures ANOVA is recommended as the method of choice.]

• When a repeated-measures ANOVA with one between-subjects factor is conducted with pretest-posttest data, the significance of the main effect of the between-subjects factor is indicated by the F-test for the *interaction* between this factor and the within-subjects (repeated-measures) factor. To avoid confusion and potential mistakes in this regard, a better practice is to directly conduct a one-way ANOVA on gain scores and/or an ANCOVA with the pretest scores as a covariate.

19.5 Study Questions

1. Five science teachers participated in a six-month professional development program offered in their school. To evaluate the effectiveness of this program, four students from each teacher's class of students were randomly selected and their satisfaction with the teacher's work was measured three times during the school year – prior to the beginning of the professional development program, three months later, and one month after the program has ended. If a repeated-measures ANOVA is used to analyze the data, answer the following questions:
   a. What is the dependent variable?
   b. What is the within-subjects factor?
   c. What are the subjects — teachers or students?
   d. Is there a between-subjects factor?
   e. How many observations are there?
2. If the *compound symmetry* condition (equal variances of the repeated measures and equal correlations for all pairs of repeated measures) is not met, does this mean that sphericity does not exist? Explain.
3. If the repeated-measures factor has only two levels, is it necessary to test for the sphericity assumption? Explain.

4. If the Huynh-Feldt estimate of the *epsilon* multiplier equals 1.00 ($\hat{\varepsilon} = 1.00$), what does this mean for the assumption of sphericity?
5. What is a split-plot design?
6. In Section 19.1.1 we used the data in Figure 19.1 to compare the error variance obtained through (a) a regular one-factor ANOVA, with Time as a fixed factor (MS_W), and (b) a simple repeated-measures ANOVA, with Time as a within-subjects factor (MS_{RES}). The SPSS output provided here below is from a regular two-factor ANOVA, with fixed factors Subject and Time, using the same data.

Tests of Between-Subjects Effects

Dependent Variable: Score

Source	Type III Sum of Squares	df	Mean Square	F	Sig.
Corrected Model	944.000[a]	11	85.818	.	.
Intercept	588.000	1	588.000	.	.
Subject	690.000	3	230.000	.	.
Time	104.000	2	52.000	.	.
Subject * Time	150.000	6	25.000	.	.
Error	.000	0	.		
Total	1532.000	12			
Corrected Total	944.000	11			

a. R Squared = 1.000 (Adjusted R Squared = .)

Based on the results in the SPSS output for the two-factor (Subject x Time) ANOVA, answer the following questions:

a. Why is the estimate of the within-cell variance with this ANOVA design (MS_W) "missing" (.) in the SPSS output? [This will explain why the *F*-values and their *p*-values are also "missing."]
b. Compute the *F*-ratio to test for the effect of factor Time, treated as a repeated-measures factor, and make a decision about the statistical significance of this effect by comparing the computed *F*-ratio to the appropriate *F*-critical value. (*Hint*: see NOTE [19.1])

7. Replicate the analysis in Example 19.2, with the same SPSS data file (**Anxiety 2.sav**), but this time use Tension (instead of Anxiety) as the between-subjects factor. In addition to the discussion of the results provided by the SPSS output, tabulate these results in APA style as shown in Tables 19.1, 19.2, and 19.3.
8. Figure 19.9 provided here below shows the repeated measures on a short-term memory test across three time points (morning, noon, evening) for children with low, medium, and high ability level in math. Given this information perform the following:

8.1 Use SPSS for a repeated measures ANOVA with Time (morning, noon, evening) as a within-subjects factor and Ability (low, medium, high) as a between-subjects factor and interpret the results.

8.2 Use the appropriate contrast option in SPSS to compare the children's test performance at noon and evening versus their morning performance.

8.3 Use the Tukey post-hoc test (if necessary) for the between-subjects multiple comparisons.

8.4 Report the results in APA style (as shown in Tables 19.1, 19.2, and 19.3).

Figure 19.9 *Repeated measures on a short-term memory test across three time points (morning, noon, evening) for children at low, medium, and high ability level in math*

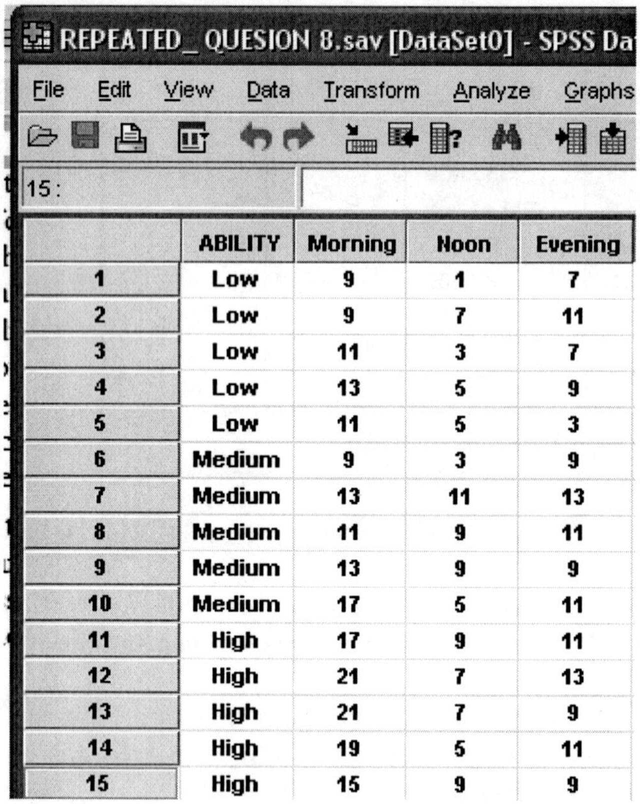

REPEATED_ QUESION 8.sav [DataSet0] - SPSS Da

File Edit View Data Transform Analyze Graphs

15 :

	ABILITY	Morning	Noon	Evening
1	Low	9	1	7
2	Low	9	7	11
3	Low	11	3	7
4	Low	13	5	9
5	Low	11	5	3
6	Medium	9	3	9
7	Medium	13	11	13
8	Medium	11	9	11
9	Medium	13	9	9
10	Medium	17	5	11
11	High	17	9	11
12	High	21	7	13
13	High	21	7	9
14	High	19	5	11
15	High	15	9	9

MULTIVARIATE DATA ANALYSIS

CHAPTER 20

LOGISTIC REGRESSION

In Chapter 13 we used *multiple linear regression* to predict one continuous dependent variable from a set of continuous and/or dichotomous predictors. There are, however, situations in which the dependent variable is categorical and, therefore, a multiple regression is not applicable. A statistical method referred to as **logistic regression** allows one to predict the chances that a subject with given scores on a set of (continuous or categorical) predictors belongs to a specific category of the dependent variable. In educational research, the questions of interest often relate to predicting various categorical outcomes in the areas of academic achievement, behavior, attitude, etc. (e.g., *pass a proficiency test, graduate from high school*). When the dependent variable is a binary (dichotomous) variable, the logistic regression is referred to as a **binary logistic regression**. When the dependent variable has more than two categories, this is called a **multinomial logistic regression**. If the categories are ranked in some (increasing or decreasing) order, the logistic regression is referred to as an **ordinal logistic regression.** In this chapter we discuss only binary logistic regression, with focus on its conceptual understanding, SPSS aided applications, and interpretation of the results. Therefore, to simplify the terminology, logistic regression in this chapter refers only to binary logistic regression unless otherwise specified.

20.1 The Concept of Logistic Regression

The binary values of the dependent variable in a logistic regression are 1 and 0, with 1 indicating the outcome of interest, called **success**, and 0 indicating the alternative outcome, called **failure**. For example, there are two possible outcomes when students take a proficiency test in math: pass or fail. If the goal is to predict the probability that a student will "pass" the test, given the student's gender, GPA, and teacher-assigned grade in math, we can use a logistic regression with a binary dependent variable Y (1 = pass, 0 = fail) and three predictors: X_1 = gender (say, 0 = male, 1 = female), X_2 = GPA, and X_3 = teacher-assigned math grade. In this case, "success" ($Y = 1$) is to pass the exam. Then the purpose is to predict the *probability of success* [or, $P(Y = 1)$ which denotes the probability that the "event" $Y = 1$ (pass) will occur]. Before going further, however, we will clarify some key terms and concepts related to logistic regression.

20.1.1 Probability, Odds, and Odds Ratio

Probability. When tossing a die, the probability that an "even number will show" is .5 (i.e., 50% chances). This is because there are 3 outcomes (2, 4, and 6) that favor the event of interest (even number) out of 6 outcomes in total (1, 2, 3, 4, 5, and 6). Thus, P(even number) = 3/6 = .5. In general, the probability that an event A will occur is defined by the ratio

$$P(A) = \frac{m}{n}, \qquad \textbf{(20.1)}$$

where m = number of outcomes that favor the event A and n = number of all possible outcomes.

Suppose that 90 students (of which 50 are females and 40 are males) took a proficiency test and the results showed that 40 females and 30 males passed the exam. As 40 out of 50 females passed, the probability for a female student to pass is 40/50 = .80. Likewise, as 30 out of 40 males pass, the probability for a male student to pass is 30/40 = .75. Thus, the probability of success for females and males are P(pass, if female) = .80 and P(pass, if male) = .75, respectively.

Odds. If P denotes the probability for an event to occur (*success*), the difference 1 – P is the probability of the opposite event (*failure*). The ratio of the probability for success to the probability of failure is called the odds for success; that is,

$$\textbf{Odds}\text{ (success)} = \frac{Probability\ of\ success}{Probability\ of\ failure} = \frac{P}{1-P} \qquad \textbf{(20.2)}$$

In the above example, the odds for success (pass the exam) are as follows:

$$\text{Odds } (success, \text{ if female}) = \frac{.80}{1-.80} = \frac{.80}{.20} = 4$$

$$\text{Odds } (success, \text{ if male}) = \frac{.75}{1-.75} = \frac{.75}{.25} = 3$$

The odds of 4 for females show that the probability of success is 4 times greater than the probability of failure. Thus, we can say that "the odds are 4 to 1 (or 4:1)" that a female student will pass the exam. Likewise, the odds are 3 to 1 (or 3:1) that a male student will pass the exam.

Odds ratio (OR). Given the odds for females and males for *success* (in this case, to pass an exam), the odds ratio (OR) for success is

$$\text{OR} = \frac{\text{Odds } (success, \text{ if female})}{\text{Odds } (success, \text{ if male})} = \frac{4}{3} = 1.33. \qquad \textbf{(20.3)}$$

Thus, the odds for a female to pass the proficiency exam are 1.33 times greater than for a male.

The computation and interpretation of the odds ratio is straightforward when the data are presented in a 2 x 2 table. For example, the pass/fail data for females and males can be presented in a 2 x 2 table as follows:

	Female	Male
Pass	40	30
Fail	10	10

Given that the outcome of interest (success) is "pass the exam," the odds of success for each gender category are given by the "pass/fail" ratio. Thus, the odds of success for females are 40/10, whereas for males they are 30/10. The odds ratio is then

$$\text{Odds ratio} = \frac{40/10}{30/10} = \frac{4}{3} = 1.33.$$

20.1.2 The Logistic Model

As indicated earlier, the values of the dependent variable in a logistic regression are 1 and 0, with $Y = 1$ denoting the outcome of interest (*success*) (e.g., to pass an exam, get admitted to a graduate program, etc.). The main goal is to predict the probability of success, $P(Y = 1)$, from a set of predictors, say, $X_1, X_2, \ldots, X_K$. The idea is then to obtain a combination of these predictors that yields the best prediction of $P(Y = 1)$. It is assumed that the general form of such a "combination" of predictors is linear; that is,

$$\mathbf{X} = B_1X_1 + B_2X_2 + \ldots + B_KX_K + A. \quad \textbf{(20.4)}$$

Just like the regression coefficients in a multiple regression produce the best prediction of Y values in terms of *smallest total error* [sum of squared errors], the regression coefficients in Equation 20.1 ($B_1, B_2, \ldots, B_K$, and the constant A) are estimated to produce the best prediction of the probability of success, $P(Y = 1)$. This is achieved by linking the linear combination of the predictors, denoted by the bold $\mathbf{X}$, to the probability $P(Y = 1)$ through a mathematical relationship between $\mathbf{X}$ and Y referred to as a **logistic function**. The analytic form of this function is

$$P(Y = 1) = \frac{e^{\mathbf{X}}}{1 + e^{\mathbf{X}}}, \quad \textbf{(20.5)}$$

where $\boldsymbol{e}$ is the mathematical constant $\boldsymbol{e} = \mathbf{2.718}$ (rounded to the nearest thousandth), and e^{X} is the *exponential function*. Te logistic function in Equation 20.5 is shown in Figure 20.1.

Figure 20.1 *Logistic regression for predicting P(Y = 1) from* ***X***

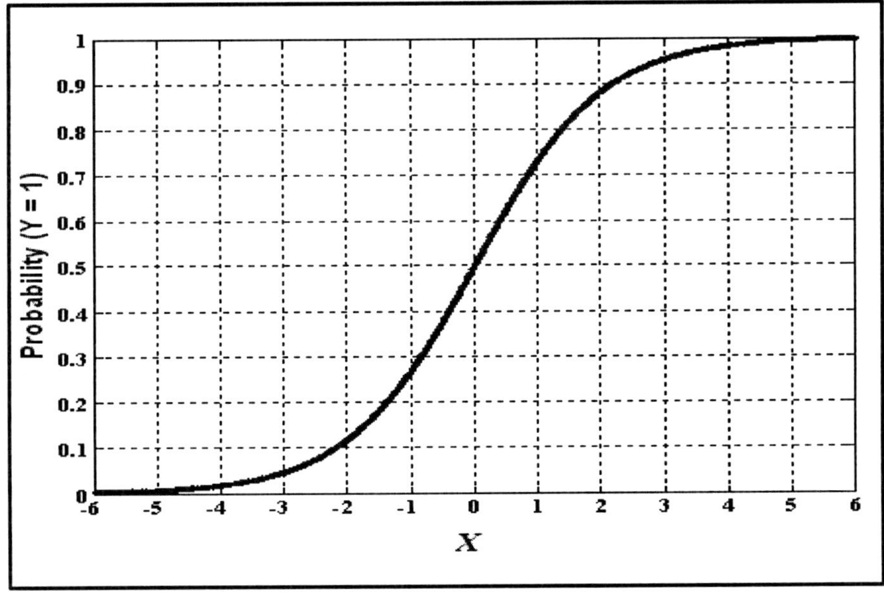

As can be seen, $X = 0$ yields $P(Y = 1) = .5$. Thus, for a person with the average composite score ($\mathbf{X} = 0$) the predicted probability of success is .5 (i.e., 50% chances of success). Indeed, by replacing $\mathbf{X}$ with 0 in Equation 20.5, we obtain

$$P(Y = 1) = \frac{e^0}{1 + e^0} = \frac{1}{1 + 1} = \frac{1}{2} = 0.5.$$

Thus, for $X = 0$ the odds are: P/(1 – P) = .50/(1 – .50) = .50/.50 = 1/1 (or, 1:1). However, if $X >$ 0, then $P(Y = 1) > .5$. That is, subjects with a composite score above the average ($X > 0$) have more than 50% chances of success. Conversely, if $X < 0$, then $P(Y = 1) < .5$, which indicates that subjects with a composite score below the average ($X < 0$) have less than 50% chances of success [recall that "success" is the binary outcome of interest].

In general, given the observations for an initial sample of subjects on both the dependent variable ($Y = 1$ or 0) and the predictors ($X_1, X_2, \ldots, X_K$), the coefficients in the linear combination of predictors in Equation 20.4 ($B_1, B_2, \ldots, B_K$, and A) are estimated to produce the best "fit" to the probability of "success" ($Y = 1$) using the logistic function in Equation 20.5. The statistical method for this estimation is called the **maximum likelihood** (ML). Testing the logistic regression model for data fit and statistical significance of the prediction is critical for the validity of the results and their interpretation.

20.1.3 Logit Form of the Logistic Regression Model

It is important to our work here to note first that the inverse function of e^X is ln(X) — the *natural logarithm* (logarithm to base ***e***: $\log_e X$). Mathematically, the inverse relationship between e^X and ln(X) means that $\ln(e^X) = X$. For example, $\ln(e^2) = 2$, $\ln(e^{-5}) = -5$, $\ln(e^X) = X$, etc.; [recall that ***e*** is the mathematical constant 2.718...].

Given that $P(Y = 1)$, or just P, is the *probability for success*, odds = P/(1 – P) represent the *odds for success*. By replacing P with its logistic expression in Equation 20.5 and using some simple algebra, we obtain

$$\textbf{odds} = \frac{P}{1-P} = \frac{\frac{e^X}{1+e^X}}{1-\frac{e^X}{1+e^X}} = \frac{\frac{e^X}{1+e^X}}{\frac{1+e^X-e^X}{1+e^X}} = \frac{\frac{e^X}{1+e^X}}{\frac{1}{1+e^X}} = \frac{e^X}{1} = e^X.$$

Thus,

$$\textbf{odds} = \frac{P}{1-P} = e^X. \qquad \textbf{(20.6)}$$

Then, taking the natural logarithm on both sides of Equation 20.6, we obtain:

$$\ln(\textbf{odds}) = \ln\left(\frac{P}{1-P}\right) = \ln\,(e^X) = X. \qquad \textbf{(20.7)}$$

The natural logarithm of the odds for success, *ln*(**odds**), is called the **logit** of the probability for success, P. Thus, taking into account that $X = B_1X_1 + B_2X_2 + \ldots + B_KX_K + A$ (see Equation 20.4), we use Equation 20.7 to present the so-called **logit form of the logistic regression model**:

$$\text{logit } P(Y=1) = \ln\left(\frac{P}{1-P}\right) = B_1X_1 + B_2X_2 + \ldots + B_K X_K + A \qquad \textbf{(20.8)}$$

20.1.4 Interpretation of the Regression Coefficients

The logit form of the logistic regression model (Equation 20.8) is particularly useful for the interpretation of the regression coefficients ($B_1, B_2, \ldots, B_K$, and A). To illustrate this, suppose that a logistic regression with two predictors, X_1 = gender (0 = male, 1 = female) and X_2 = GPA, is used to predict the probability for students to pass a proficiency exam. That is, the goal is to predict $P(Y = 1)$, where $Y = 1$ indicates *success* (pass the exam) and $Y = 0$ indicates *failure* (fail the exam). Using the logit form of this logistic regression model (Equation 20.8), with the short notation logit P for logit $P(Y = 1)$, we have:

$$\text{logit P} = B_1(gender) + B_2(\text{GPA}) + \text{A}. \qquad \textbf{(20.9)}$$

Let also P_f and P_m denote the probability of success for females and males, respectively. To interpret the regression coefficient B_1, we replace the predictor *gender* in Equation 20.9 with its values 1 and 0, for any fixed value of the other predictor, GPA (i.e., GPA remains the same). Thus, for females (*gender* = 1) we obtain

$$\text{logit } P_f = B_1(1) + B_2(\text{GPA}) + A = B_1 + B_2(\text{GPA}) + A,$$

whereas for males (*gender* = 0) we have:

$$\text{logit } P_m = B_1(0) + B_2(\text{GPA}) + A = B_2(\text{GPA}) + A,$$

Now, by subtracting the logits for males and females, we obtain

$\text{logit } P_f - \text{logit } P_m = B_1 + B_2(\text{GPA}) + A - B_2(\text{GPA}) - A = B_1$; that is,

$$B_1 = \text{logit } P_f - \text{logit } P_m \qquad \textbf{(20.10)}$$

Thus, given the gender coding (0 = male, 1 = female), the regression coefficient for gender, B_1, represents the change in the logit that would result from a "one unit change" in gender when the other predictor, GPA, is fixed.

An even more useful interpretation of B_1 can be reached by taking the exponent of B_1, that is, e^{B_1}, denoted also as $exp(B_1)$. Specifically, it can be easily shown that $exp(B_1)$ equals the *odds ratio* (OR) of females to males. That is, using the definition in Equation 20.3, it can be seen that

$$exp(B_1) = \frac{\text{Odds }(success,\ \text{if female})}{\text{Odds }(success,\ \text{if male})}. \qquad \textbf{(20.11)}$$

For example, if $B_1 = 1$, $exp(B_1) = exp(1) = e^1 = e = 2.718$ (or, 2.72 if rounded to the nearest hundredth). Thus, given Equation 20.11, we have

$$\frac{\text{Odds }(success,\ \text{if female})}{\text{Odds }(success,\ \text{if male})} = 2.72.$$

The interpretation of this odds ratio is straightforward: **For students with the same GPA, the odds for females to pass the exam are 2.72 times higher than for males.** [Note that $exp(B_1)$ compares the *odds*, not the probabilities, for success of females against males.]

Similarly, it can be seen that the regression coefficient B_2 (for GPA) represents the change in the logit that would result from a "one unit change" in GPA for subject of the same gender. The analog of Equation 20.10 in this case is

$$B_2 = \text{logit } P_1 - \text{logit } P_0, \qquad \textbf{(20.12)}$$

where P_1 and P_0 denote the probability of success for any two students that differ by one unit in GPA but that are either both males or both females (i.e., *gender* is fixed). For example if GPA_1 and GPA_0 denote two GPAs that differ by one unit (e.g., $GPA_1 = 4.00$ and $GPA_0 = 3.00$), then P_1 and P_0 denote the probability of success for the (same-gender) students with grade-point average GPA_1 and GPA_0, respectively. If we replace consecutively, say GPA = 4 and GPA = 3, in Equation 20.9 and then subtract the resulting expressions we will obtain: logit P_1 − logit $P_0 = B_2$.

As with B_1, an alternative interpretation of B_2 is obtained by taking its exponent, $exp(B_2)$. The analog of Equation 20.11 in this case is

$$exp(B_2) = \frac{\text{Odds}\,(success,\ \text{if}\,\text{GPA}_1)}{\text{Odds}\,(success,\ \text{if}\,\text{GPA}_0\,)}. \quad \textbf{(20.13)}$$

For example, if $B_2 = 0.5$, then $exp(B_2) = exp(0.5) = 1.65$. This indicates that for every one-unit increase in GPA, with gender being the same, the odds for success (passing the exam) would increase 1.65 times.

Regarding the interpretations of the constant A in the logistic regression model (e.g., see Equation 20.8), it can be seen directly that, if $X_1 = X_2 = \ldots = X_K = 0$, then A = logit P(Y = 1). We can say, then, that **the constant *A* indicates the natural logarithm of the odds that would result for a logistic model without any predictors at all**. Such a model is referred to also as a **baseline model** (or *background model*).

20.2 Tests and Interpretations of Logistic Regression Results

The discussion in this section is supported by illustrations using results from SPSS output tables for the SPSS data file **EXAMPLE_20_1.sav** [available at the companion website http://cehd.gmu.edu/book/dimitrov]. The data consist of 69 observations obtained in a study about the prediction of student retention from parental support, peer pressure, gender, and ethnicity.

20.2.1 Goodness-of-fit Test

Full model versus baseline model. A meaningful first question to ask in the analysis of logistic regression results is whether all predictors together contribute to the prediction of the outcome of interest (*success*). Recall that the prediction model that includes only the constant, A, and no predictors at all is referred to as the **baseline model**. The model with the constant and all predictors is called the **full model**. For any model, a **log-likelihood (LL)** is defined by the following summation across all individual observations ($i = 1, 2, \ldots, n$):

$$\text{log-likelihood} = \sum\left[Y_i ln(\hat{Y}_i) + (1 - Y_i) ln(1 - \hat{Y}_i)\right], \quad \textbf{(20.14)}$$

where Y_i is the actual outcome (1 or 0) for subject i and $\hat{Y}_i$ is the predicted probability for this outcome [*ln* stands for *natural logarithm*.]

The difference between two models (baseline versus full) in terms of predictive power is tested for statistical significance by a chi-square statistic which is approximately equal to the difference between the log-likelihoods (LLs) of the two models multiplied by "negative 2" (-2). When applied to the difference between the baseline model and the full model, this chi-square (χ^2) statistic is:

$$\chi^2 = -2[\mathbf{LL}(\text{baseline model}) - \mathbf{LL}(\text{full model})], \quad \mathbf{(20.15)}$$

or, equivalently,

$$\chi^2 = 2[\mathbf{LL}(\text{full model}) - \mathbf{LL}(\text{baseline model})]. \quad \mathbf{(20.16)}$$

The degrees of freedom (*df*) for this χ^2-test equal the difference between the degrees of freedom for the full model and the degrees of freedom for the baseline model. For a full model with K predictors, there are $K + 1$ degrees of freedom (one for each predictor and one for the constant). For the baseline model, $df = 1$ (only for the constant). Thus, the degrees of freedom for χ^2 in Equation 20.15 are: $df = (K + 1) - 1 = K$ (i.e., the number of predictors with the full model).

A statistically significant chi-square would indicate statistical significance for the full logistic regression model (at the specified level of significance, α). The SPSS output for this chi-square test is reported in the table **Omnibus Tests of Model Coefficients.** This table is provided below for an example in which student retention in a school program ($Y = 1$: retained) is predicted from survey scores on *parental support*, *peer pressure*, and *gender* (1 = female, 0 = male) using the data in **EXAMPLE_20_1.sav** [at this point *Ethnicity* is not used as a predictor]. The results for **Model** shown below, indicate that the prediction of student retention from parental support, peer pressure, and gender is statistically significant, $\chi^2(3) = 19.66, p < .001$.

Omnibus Tests of Model Coefficients

		Chi-square	df	Sig.
Step 1	Step	19.660	3	.000
	Block	19.660	3	.000
	Model	19.660	3	.000

$\chi^2(3) = 19.66, p < .001$

20.2.2 Hosmer-Lemeshow Goodness-of-fit Test

Recall the assumption in multiple regression that the actual and predicted scores are linearly related (i.e., there is a statistically significant multiple correlation). The analog of this assumption in logistic regression is that there is a linear relationship between the weighted combination of the predictor variables ($B_1X_1 + B_2X_2 + \ldots + B_KX_K + A$) and the *natural log of the odds* [*ln*(odds)] for the outcome variable ($Y = 1$) — see Equation 20.8. This assumption is tested by the **Hosmer-Lemeshow goodness-of-fit test**. In this test, the subjects are first arranged in order by their predicted probability, $P(Y = 1)$, and then divided into ten groups (*deciles*). The lowest group (lowest *decile*) is defined by $P(Y = 1) < .1$, whereas the highest group (highest *decile*) is for subjects with $P(Y = 1) > .9$. Each of these groups is then divided into two groups based on the actual Y score (1 or 0). This results in a 2 x 10 contingency table and the expected frequencies for each cell are obtained from the logistic model. A good "fit" between observed and expected frequencies is indicated by a non-significant chi-square statistic [see Chapter 12, Section 12.3, for the goodness-of-fit test].

The SPSS table for the Hosmer-Lemeshow test shown here is for the logistic regression of student retention from parental support, peer pressure, and gender **[EXAMPLE_20_1.sav].** The 2 x 10 contingency table is also provided. The results show that the chi-square statistic is non-significant, $\chi^2(8) = 4.71$, $p = .79$, thus indicating a good data fit for the logistic regression model in this case.

Hosmer and Lemeshow Test

Step	Chi-square	df	Sig.
1	4.714	8	.788

Contingency Table for Hosmer and Lemeshow Test

		Retained = NO		Retained = YES		
		Observed	Expected	Observed	Expected	Total
Step 1	1	6	5.479	1	1.521	7
	2	5	4.356	2	2.644	7
	3	2	2.897	5	4.103	7
	4	2	2.416	6	5.584	8
	5	1	1.456	5	4.544	6
	6	1	1.243	6	5.757	7
	7	1	.884	6	6.116	7
	8	1	.639	6	6.361	7
	9	0	.404	7	6.596	7
	10	1	.227	5	5.773	6

20.2.3 Test for Significance of Predictor Variables

Among several tests that have been developed to test for significance of individual predictor variables, the simplest and most widely used is the **Wald test.** The Wald test statistic is obtained by dividing the squared logistic regression coefficient by its squared standard error and, therefore, it is actually a **chi-square** (χ^2) statistic. The SPSS table **Variables in the Equation** (see below) includes the Wald test for individual predictor variables and is presented here for the example predicting student retention from parental support, peer pressure, and gender **[EXAMPLE_20_1.sav].**

The Wald test results show that there are two statistically significant regression coefficients: $B_1 = 0.618$ (for parental support), $\chi^2(1) = 11.16$, $p = .001$, and $B_2 = -0.494$ (for peer pressure), $\chi^2(1) = 8.01$, $p = .005$. Interpreting the exponents of these coefficients, Exp(B), we can say that (a) Exp(B) = 1.855 for B_1 indicates that the odds for retention increase 1.855 times when the parental support score increases by one unit, for students with the same peer pressure score and same gender; and (b) Exp(B) = 0.610 for B_2 indicates that the odds for retention decrease by a factor of 0.610 when the peer pressure score increases by one unit, for students with the same score on parental support and same gender [in this case Exp(B) < 1 because the regression coefficient is negative, $B_2 = -0.494$]. As illustrated later in this chapter, SPSS also provides a 95% confidence interval for Exp(B).

Variables in the Equation							
		B	S.E.	Wald	Df	Sig.	Exp(B)
Step 1	Parental_support	.618	.185	11.162	1	.001	1.855
	Peer_pressure	-.494	.174	8.012	1	.005	.610
	Gender	.407	1.087	.140	1	.708	1.502
	Constant	.205	.933	.048	1	.826	1.227

20.2.4 Effect Size Information with Logistic Regression

R^2-like measures of effect size. An analog to R^2 in multiple regression is the R^2-like measure for logistic regression developed by Cox and Snell (1989). This measure, denoted R^2_{CS}, is based on a log-likelihood difference and takes into account the sample size, *n*.

$$R^2_{CS} = 1 - exp\left[\left(\frac{-2}{n}\right)\left[\text{LL(full model)} - \text{LL(baseline model)}\right]\right]. \qquad \textbf{(20.17)}$$

As R^2_{CS} is always smaller than 1, Nagelkerke (1991) proposed an adjustment to R^2_{CS}, denoted R^2_N, with which a value of 1 could be reached. Both R^2_{CS} and R^2_N are provided in SPSS, along with the **-2log likelihood** value for the full model, that is, −2LL(full model).

It is important to emphasize that none of the R^2 measures that have been proposed for logistic regression (R^2_{CS}, R^2_N, and others) is a direct analog to R^2 in multiple regression, and, thus, cannot be interpreted as the "proportion of variance in *Y* accounted for by all predictors." This is because the variance in a binary variable ($Y = 1$ or 0) depends on the frequency distribution of that variable, so R^2 measures for logistic regressions with different frequency distributions of their dependent variable cannot be compared directly. In addition, the R^2 measures in a logistic regression are not in concert with goodness-of-fit measures. It may happen, for example, that the Nagelkerke R^2_N is relatively high when the goodness-of-fit is not even acceptable in a logistic regression model. Therefore, R^2 values in logistic regression must be reported as "R^2-like" measures — not as an actual proportion of variance in the dependent variable, *Y*, attributed to all predictors together.

The SPSS **Model Summary** table provided here below also relates to the logistic regression model predicting retention from parental support, peer pressure, and gender [using the data **EXAMPLE_20_1.sav]**. Both R^2_{CS} (.248) and R^2_N (.354) are reported, but the Nagelkerke R^2 is preferred. As already noted, the (−2)Log likelihood value for the full model, −2LL(full model) = 63.419 is also reported. This value is used, for example, to compare two logistic regression models [analogous to the comparison of full versus restricted model in multiple regression – see Chapter 13, Section 13.2].

Model Summary			
Step	-2 Log likelihood	Cox & Snell R Square	Nagelkerke R Square
1	63.419[a]	.248	.354

Some sources (e.g., Tabachnick & Fidell, 2007) suggest that an option for binary logistic regression models is to calculate R^2 directly from the actual Y values (1 or 0) and their predicted probabilities, which may be saved as resulting data from the logistic regression in SPSS or other statistical packages. Or, alternately, one could take the η^2(eta-squared) measure of effect size obtained from an ANOVA using the predicted Y scores (probabilities) as the dependent variable and the actual Y scores (1 or 0) as a grouping variable (fixed factor) — see Chapter 14 (Equation 14.33).

Odds ratios as effect size measures. As illustrated in Section 20.1.4, the odds ratio for a predictor indicates how many times the odds for *success* ($Y = 1$) would change with a one-unit change in that predictor, controlling for all other predictors. Thus, the odds ratio can be viewed as a measure of a (partial) effect-size ["partial" because of the control over the other predictors] — e.g., see Equations 20.11 and 20.13. It is desirable, however, to report each odds ratio with its confidence interval limits [SPSS provides such confidence intervals on request].

NOTE [20.1] Keep in mind that the odds ratio for a predictor is provided by the exponent of its regression coefficient, *exp*(*B*), whereas the regression coefficient, *B*, is the natural logarithm of the odds ratio. That is,

$$B = ln(\text{odds ratio}) \text{ and } exp(B) = \text{odds ratio}. \qquad \textbf{(20.18)}$$

Meta-analysis of odds ratios can provide very useful information for their accuracy and generalizability as long as the necessary assumptions for such analysis are taken into account. For example, Chinn (2000) converted the odds ratio to Cohen's d measure of effect size for a dichotomous predictor by dividing the regression coefficient, B, by 1.81:

$$d = B/1.81, \qquad \textbf{(20.19)}$$

where the denominator (1.81) is the standard deviation of the standard logistic distribution, $\pi/\sqrt{3}$ = 1.81 (rounded to the nearest hundredth) and, as noted previously, $B = ln(\text{odds ratio})$. This is for cases in which the dichotomous predictor (e.g., 1 = high blood pressure, 0 = low blood pressure) is obtained by dichotomizing a normally distributed continuous variable (e.g., blood pressure) through the use of cutting points. Under this condition, one may also consider converting the effect size, d, obtained via Equation 20.19, into another Cohen's measure of effect size, eta-squared (η^2) (Cohen, 1988), as follows: $\eta^2 = d^2/(d^2 + 4)$; (e.g., Tabachnick & Fidell, 2007).

20.2.5 Classification Table

The **Classification Table** in a binary logistic model is a 2 x 2 table. The rows contain the frequency of the observed values and the columns contain the frequency of the predicted values of the binary dependent variable. The classification table provided here is from the SPSS output for the logistic regression predicting student retention from parental support, peer pressure, and gender [data in **EXAMPLE_20_1.sav**]. In this table, *success* ($Y = 1$) is denoted "YES" and the opposite "event" (Y = 0) is denoted "NO."

Classification Table

Observed			Predicted		
			Retained		
			NO	YES	Percentage Correct
Step 1	Retained	NO	11	9	55.0
		YES	3	46	93.9
		Overall Percentage			82.6

The classification table does not provide information for goodness-of-fit testing because, instead of taking into account the predicted *Y* values (1 or 0) obtained by the logistic regression, this table uses binary (1 or 0) predictions based on a cutting score (.5). However, a model in which most predictions, true or false, are close to the .5 cutting score does not fit the data as well as a model in which the predicted scores cluster around either 1 or 0. Therefore, the classification table results play a primarily descriptive role. Some key concepts concerning the classification table are:

- **Hit rate** — the proportion of correct predictions (the number of correct predictions divided by sample size). In our example, *hit rate* = .826 [or 82.6% correct classifications].
- **Sensitivity** — the proportion of correct predictions in the reference category of the dependent variable ($Y = 1$). In our example, the correct predictions in the reference category (YES) are 46 out of 54 observations in this category, so *sensitivity* = 46/54 = .85 [or 85%].
- **Specificity** — the proportion of correct prediction in the opposite category (Y = 0). In our example, the correct predictions in the opposite category (NO) are 11 out of 14 observations in this category, so *specificity* = 11/14 = .786 [or 78.6%].
- **False positive rate** — the number of cases when an actual $Y = 0$ is predicted $Y = 1$, as a proportion of all cases in which $Y = 0$. In our example, there are 9 cases in which actual "NO" values were predicted "YES," and there are 20 actual "NO" values, so the *false positive rate* = 9/20 = .45 [or 45%].
- **False negative rate** — the number of cases when an actual $Y = 1$ is predicted $Y = 0$, as a proportion of all cases in which $Y = 1$. In our example, there are 3 cases in which actual "YES" values were predicted "NO," and there are 49 actual "YES" values, so the *false negative rate* = 3/49 = .061 [or 6.1%].

20.3 Coding Categorical Predictors

When a predictor is a dichotomous categorical variable (e.g., gender), the recommended coding values are 0 and 1, with 1 being used for the "reference" category — the category against which the opposite category will be compared. For example, if the predictor is gender and we want to know how females compare to males on the outcome of interest ($Y = 1$, for *success*), we should use the coding: 0 = female, 1 = male. Any coding in which the higher coding value is assigned to males (e.g., 1 = female, 2 = male) will achieve the same purpose. Coding gender as character "f" and "m" also works, since "f" precedes "m" when sorting, but 0 and 1 coding is preferable.

Dummy coding. When a categorical predictor has more than two categories, there are different coding schemes that serve different interpretation purposes. The simplest way is to use dummy coding [which is the **Indicator** option in SPSS]. If the predictor has K categories, the dummy coding will "generate" $K - 1$ predictors. For example, suppose a predictor variable *Ethnicity* has three categories (1 = Caucasian, 2 = African-America, and 3 = Hispanic) and the first category (Caucasian) is designated as the reference category. In this case ($K = 3$), there will be two "internal" predictors for *Ethnicity*, say, labeled **Ethnic_1** and **Ethnic_2.** The dummy coding scheme is shown in Figure 20.2. The cases in the reference category (Caucasian) are coded 0 for all internal predictors. Thus, the two internal predictors (Ethnic_1 and Ethnic_2) are developed to compare the reference category (Caucasian) against the other two categories — African-American and Hispanic, respectively. The logic of dummy coding in this case carries over the cases of categorical predictors with more than three categories.

Figure 20.2 *Dummy coding for a predictor Variable (ethnicity) with three categories where Caucasian is the reference category*

	Ethnic_1	**Ethnic_2**
Caucasian	**0**	**0**
African-American	1	0
Hispanic	0	1

SPSS coding options. Seven coding schemes based on contrasts (see Chapter 14, Section 14.2.2.1) are available with logistic regression in SPSS. Two of them (Indicator and Simple) provide the dummy coding illustrated in Figure 20.2. The SPSS "Help" description of the coding contrasts for logistic regression is as follows:

- **Indicator**. Contrasts indicate the presence or absence of category membership. The reference category is represented in the contrast matrix as a row of zeros.
- **Simple**. Each category of the predictor variable (except the reference category) is compared to the reference category.
- **Helmert**. Each category of the predictor variable except the last category is compared to the average effect of subsequent categories.

- **Difference**. Each category of the predictor variable except the first category is compared to the average effect of previous categories. Also known as "reverse Helmert contrasts."
- **Repeated**. Each category of the predictor variable except the first category is compared to the category that precedes it.
- **Polynomial**. Orthogonal polynomial contrasts. Categories are assumed to be equally spaced. Polynomial contrasts are available for numeric variables only.
- **Deviation**. Each category of the predictor variable except the reference category is compared to the overall effect.

Figure 20.3 shows the SPSS dialog box for a logistic regression with options for contrast coding of categorical predictors. In this case, Ethnicity (Caucasian, African-American, Hispanic) is coded under the option **Indicator** thus generating the dummy coding in Figure 20.2 with two internal predictors for ethnicity [labeled in SPSS as **Ethnicity(1)** and **Ethnicity(2)**]. The SPSS steps, output, and interpretation of results with this example are provided in the next section.

Figure 20.3 *SPSS dialog box for contrast coding of categorical predictors*

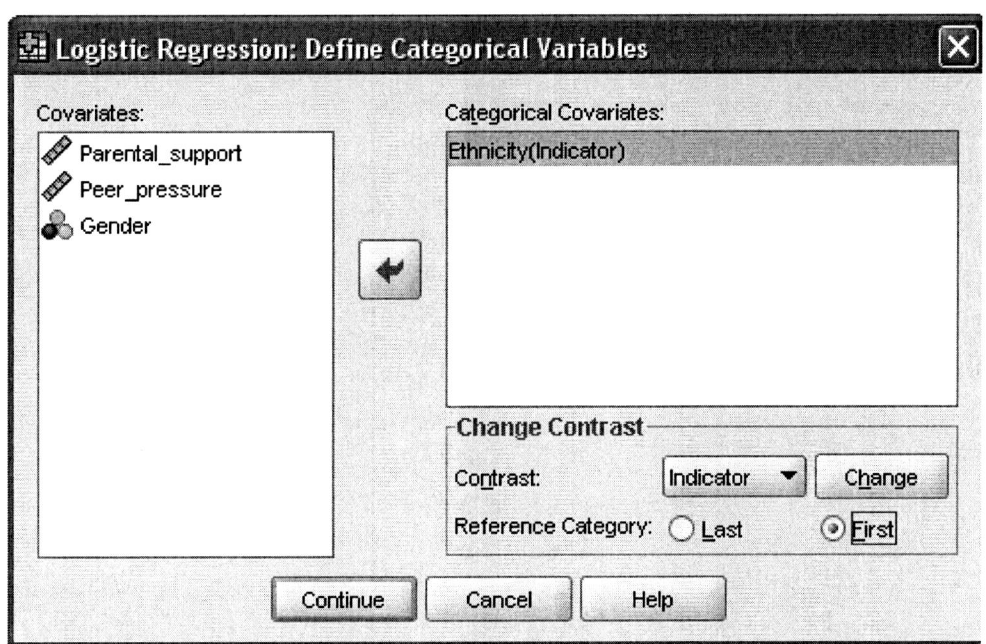

Note. Under **Deviation**, **Simple**, or **Indicator**, select either *First* or *Last* as the reference category. Then click *Change* to finalize the selection of the method.

20.4 Using SPSS for Binary Logistic Regression

SPSS provides options for *binary* logistic regression, *multinomial* logistic regression (more than two categories in the dependent variable), and *ordinal* logistic regression (ordered categories in the dependent variable). As noted earlier, this chapter discusses only binary logistic regression.

EXAMPLE 20.1 This example illustrates how to use SPSS to conduct a binary logistic regression using the data file **EXAMPLE_20_1.sav** [at http://cehd.gmu.edu/book/dimitrov]. The data consist of 69 observations obtained in a study about the prediction of student retention from parental support, peer pressure, gender, and ethnicity. Some tables from the SPSS output for a logistic regression using three predictors (parental support, peer pressure, and gender) were provided for the purposes of illustration in the previous sections of this chapter. In this example, ethnicity is added to the set of predictors, so four predictors are used to predict student retention in a school program: parental support, peer pressure, gender (0 = male, 1 = female), and ethnicity (1 = Caucasian, 2 = African-American, and 3 = Hispanic). The SPSS names of the variables, with the first 14 (out of 69) observations are shown in Figure 20.4. As Ethnicity has three categories, dummy coding will be employed, with the first category (Caucasian) used as a reference category (see Figures 20.2 and 20.3). In this way, there will be five predictors in the logistic regression, **Parental_support**, **Peer_pressure**, **Gender**, **Ethnicity(1)**, and **Ethnicity(2).**

Figure 20.4 *SPSS data file EXAMPLE_20_1.sav*
[shown are the first 14 out of 69 observations]

*EXAMPLE 20_1.sav [DataSet1] - SPSS Data Editor

File Edit View Data Transform Analyze Graphs Utilities Add-ons

20 :

	Parental_support	Peer_pressure	Gender	Ethnicity	Retention
1	7	2	0	1	1
2	4	6	0	3	0
3	5	4	1	1	1
4	4	4	1	1	1
5	1	4	1	1	0
6	7	3	0	1	1
7	5	6	0	1	0
8	2	5	0	2	0
9	1	4	0	3	0
10	6	5	0	1	1
11	4	4	0	3	1
12	6	2	0	2	1
13	2	7	0	3	1
14	1	4	0	2	0

The SPSS steps for the logistic regression in this example are:

1. Click **Analyze**, click **Regression**, and click **Binary Logistic**.
2. Click **Retention**, and click ► to move it to the **Dependent** box. Holding the CTRL key, select **Parental_support**, **Peer_pressure**, **Gender**, and **Ethnicity**, and then click ► to move them to the box **Covariates**.
3. Click **Categorical** [this will bring down the dialog box shown in Figure 20.3], then click **Ethnicity**, and click ► to move it to the box **Categorical Covariates**.

4. As shown in Figure 20.3, the contrast **Indicator** [which we need] is shown as a default option, so just select the *Reference Category* **First** [which is Caucasian in our data], and then click **Change** [to finalize the selection of **Indicator** as a contrast coding for Ethnicity].
5. Click **Continue**.
6. Click **Options**, and then check the box **Hosmer-Lemeshow goodness-of-fit**, and check the box **CI for exp(B)** [this is to provide 95% confidence intervals for the odds ratios of the predictors].
7. Click **Continue**.
8. Click **OK**.

The SPSS output with the main tables is provided with Figure 20.5. The results are tested for statistical significance at the .05 level. The outcome of interest (success) is *student retention* (YES). As can be seen from the results, the chi-square for Model in the table **Omnibus Tests of Model Coefficients** is statistically significant, $\chi^2(5) = 30.65$, $p < .001$, thus indicating that parental support, peer pressure, gender, and ethnicity do predict student retention. There is also a good data fit to the model, as indicated by the nonsignificant Hosmer-Lemeshow statistic, $\chi^2(8) = 5.91$, $p = .66$. For space considerations, the contingency table for the Hosmer-Lemeshow test is not provided in Figure 20.5, but it depicts the expected trend that, in the case of a good data fit, (a) the grouping frequencies for the reference category (YES) increase from the lowest to highest deciles and, conversely, (b) the grouping frequencies for the opposite category (NO) decrease from the lowest to highest deciles [although less pronounced, this trend can be seen in the contingency table in Section 20.2.2].

The Nagelkerke R^2 value is .512 ($R_N^2 = .512$) thus indicating a relatively high explanatory effect in the prediction of student retention from all four predictors together, keeping in mind that this is a *R^2-like* measure, not a direct analog of the coefficient of multiple determination in multiple regression, R^2.

The descriptive information provided in the **Classification Table** indicates a relatively good *hit rate* (84.1%). The *sensitivity* in this prediction (proportion of correct predictions in the reference category) is also relatively high, 45/(45 + 7) = 45/52 = .865 [i.e., 86.5%], whereas the *specificity* (proportion of correct predictions in the opposite category) is somewhat lower, 13/(13 + 4) = 13/17 = .765 [i.e., 76.5%]. Further, the *false positive rate* is 7/(13 + 7) = 7/20 = .35 [i.e., 35%], whereas the *false negative rate* is 4/(4 + 45) = 4/49 = .082 [i.e., 8.2%].

The results from the Wald test in the **Variables in the Equation** table [not shown in Figure 20.5, but summarized in Table 20.1] indicate statistical significance for the regression coefficients of parental support ($p = .001$), peer pressure ($p = .009$), and ethnicity ($p = .017$), but not for gender ($p = .304$). Regarding ethnicity, however, it is also evident that the second contrast, Ethnicity(2), is statistically significant ($p = .004$), whereas the first one, Ethnicity(1), is not ($p = .322$). Given the coding scheme in the table **Categorical Variables Coding**, we can say that there is a statistically significant difference in the odds for student retention between the Caucasian and Hispanic groups, but not between the Caucasian and African-American groups, when controlling for all other effects.

As already noted, the **Variables in the Equation** table is not shown in Figure 20.5 for space consideration, but the odds ratios, Exp(B), reported in the this table are provided as the entries of thc column labeled **Odds Ratios** in Table 20.1. The 95 percent confidence intervals for the odds ratios are also provided with Table 20.1.

Figure 20.5 *SPSS output for logistic regression [data in EXAMPLE_20_1.sav]*

Categorical Variables Codings

		Frequency	Parameter coding (1)	(2)
Ethnicity	Caucasion	30	.000	.000
	Hispanic	11	1.000	.000
	African-American	28	.000	1.000

Block 1: Method = Enter

Omnibus Tests of Model Coefficients

		Chi-square	df	Sig.
Step 1	Step	30.647	5	.000
	Block	30.647	5	.000
	Model	30.647	5	.000

Model Summary

Step	-2 Log likelihood	Cox & Snell R Square	Nagelkerke R Square
1	52.432[a]	.359	.512

Hosmer and Lemeshow Test

Step	Chi-square	df	Sig.
1	5.911	8	.657

Classification Table[a]

	Observed		Predicted Retention: NO	YES	Percentage Correct
Step 1	Retention	NO	13	7	65.0
		YES	4	45	91.8
		Overall Percentage			84.1

a. The cut value is .500

In Table 20.1, the value of the odds ratio for parental support, Exp(B) = 2.14, indicates that the odds for student retention increase by a factor of 2.14 (i.e., about two times) for a one-unit increase in parental support, when controlling for all other predictors. Conversely, Exp(B) = 0.60 for peer pressure indicates that the odds for student retention are multiplied by a factor of 0.60 (i.e., they decrease) for a one-unit increase in peer pressure, when controlling for all other predictors. Further, Exp(B) = 14.54 for the internal predictor Ethnicity(2) indicates that the retention odds for Hispanic students are about 14.5 times higher than those for Caucasian students, with all other factors for these students being equal (parental support, peer pressure, and gender).

However, this effect must be interpreted with great caution given its very large confidence interval (from 2.31 to 91.56, at the 95% level of confidence). In contrast, the estimates of the odds ratio effects for parental support and peer pressure are more stable, given the relatively small range of their confidence intervals. As indicated earlier, reporting confidence intervals of effects is important to the evaluation of their accuracy and generalizability.

An APA-style summary of the results provided in the SPSS table **Variables in the Equation** is presented in Table 20.1. Note that the standard errors of the regression coefficients, *SE*(*B*), are not reported in this table. This is because the Wald chi-square (χ^2) is the ratio of the squared regression coefficient to its squared standard error, that is: $\chi^2 = [B/SE(B)]^2$. Therefore, given the regression coefficient, *B*, and its Wald χ^2, the standard error of *B* can be obtained directly as follows: $SE(B) = \sqrt{B^2/\chi^2}$. For parental support, for example, $SE(B) = \sqrt{0.76^2/11.92} = 0.22$.

Table 20.1

Logistic Regression Analysis of Student Retention as a Function of Parental Support, Peer Pressure, Gender, and Ethnicity: Students Retained in School vs. Students who Dropped from School

				95% Confidence Interval for Odds Ratio	
Variables	B	Wald χ^2	Odds Ratio	Lower	Upper
Parental support	0.76	11.92**	2.14	1.39	3.31
Peer pressure	−0.51	6.84**	0.60	0.41	0.88
Gender	1.43	1.06	4.18	0.27	63.82
Ethnicity					
Caucasian vs. Afr.-American	1.00	0.98	2.72	0.38	19.77
Caucasian vs. Hispanic	2.68	8.13**	14.54	2.31	91.56
(Constant)	−1.44	1.46			

Note: Wald ($df = 1$).

** $p < .01$.

20.5 Comparison of Full and Restricted Models

The logic behind comparing full and restricted models in multiple regression (see Chapter 13, Section 13.2) carries over into comparisons of full and restricted models in logistic regression as well. If a specific logistic regression model is treated as a full model, a restricted model is obtained by eliminating (removing) one or more predictors from the full model. In general, when predictors are removed from a logistic regression model, its chi-square (χ^2) decreases. If the difference between the chi-square values for the full model (χ^2_{Full}) and the restricted model (χ^2_{Restr}) is not statistically significant, then the two models do not differ in terms of their contribution to the prediction of the outcome of interest ($Y = 1$). In this event, the more parsimonious restricted model should be used.

EXAMPLE 20.2 In Example 20.1, the chi-square for the logistic regression model with four predictors (parental support, peer presser, gender, and ethnicity) was found to be statistically significant, $\chi^2(5) = 30.65$, $p < .001$. In Section 20.2.1, the chi-square for the logistic regression model with three predictors (parental support, peer presser, and gender), using the same data, was also statistically significant, $\chi^2(3) = 19.66$, $p < .001$. Clearly, the latter model is obtained from the former by removing one predictor (Ethnicity). Thus, the four-predictor model can be considered a full model and the three-predictor model a restricted model. The chi-square difference between the two models is $\Delta\chi^2 = \chi^2_{\text{Full}} - \chi^2_{\text{Restr}} = 30.65 - 19.66 = 10.99$, and the difference in their degrees of freedom is $\Delta df = df_{\text{Full}} - df_{\text{Restr}} = 5 - 3 = 2$. With two degrees of freedom, the critical χ^2-value at the .05 level is 5.99 (see Table A-3). As the chi-square difference ($\Delta\chi^2 = 10.99$) *exceeds* the critical χ^2-value (5.99), there is a statistically significant difference between the full and restricted models in predicting the outcome of interest (student retention). Thus, the elimination of ethnicity as a predictor from the full logistic regression model is associated with a statistically significant decrease in the predictive contribution of this model. Given this, it is better to use the full (four-predictor) model.

20.6 Selection of Predictors in Logistic Regression

The selection of predictors in logistic regression is guided by the principles and procedures that hold for the selection of predictors in multiple regression (see Chapter 13, Section 13.9). It is desirable that the criteria to select the "best" set of predictors are specified *before* conducting a regression analysis. Particular efforts should be made to guard against **specification errors**; that is, errors which occur when relevant predictors are omitted or irrelevant predictors are included into the regression equation.

In **direct logistic regression**, all predictors enter the regression model simultaneously. As illustrated in Example 20.2, this method allows for testing for the omnibus significance of the model with all predictors, as well as for the unique contribution of each predictor, controlling for the effect of the other predictors.

Just like with multiple regression, methods of **forward** selection, **backward** selection, or **stepwise** combinations of both, are available in logistic regression as well. Of course, the problems associated with these methods in multiple regression remain when they are used in logistic regression. A major drawback of forward selection, for example, is that once a given predictor enters the equation, it stays in the equation even though it might lose its initial importance when new predictors are added to the equation. The methods of stepwise (forward, backward, or mixed) selection can be useful in comparative replication studies, preliminary screening, or generating hypotheses at initial stages of research.

In **blockwise selection,** predictors are grouped in ordered "blocks" based on theoretical or empirical considerations. First, a stepwise selection is conducted for the predictors in the first block. Then, a stepwise selection is conducted with the other blocks, one at a time, using the predictors that have survived the immediately preceding stepwise selection.

In **hierarchical selection**, intact blocks (meaningful units) of predictors are *forced* into the logistic regression equation, one at a time, to determine their specific contribution to the prediction of the outcome of interest (*success*). The statistical significance of the contribution of each block is tested by the *chi-square difference* ($\Delta\chi^2$) test described in the previous section for the comparison of full and restricted models. Also, forcing some blocks (e.g., treatment variables) into the equation and conducting blockwise selection on others is a useful combination in many research applications of logistic regression.

20.7 Assumptions in Logistic Regression

Unlike in multiple regression, **logistic regression does not assume** (a) a linear relationship between the dependent and independent variables, (b) normal distributions of the predictor variables, or (c) equal variances of the predictor variables within groups. Instead, **logistic regression assumes** a linear relationship between the weighted combination of the predictor variables ($B_1X_1 + B_2X_2 + \ldots + B_KX_K + A$) and the *natural log of the odds* [*ln*(odds)] for the outcome variable ($Y = 1$) — see Equation 20.8. As stated in Section 20.2.2, this assumption is tested by the Hosmer-Lemeshow goodness-of-fit test. **Logistic regression also assumes** that the observations are independent of each other [recall that this assumption holds in multiple regression and analysis of variance as well].

Like in multiple regression, the accuracy of prediction with a logistic regression is negatively affected by the presence of *multicollinearity* and/or *outliers*. Multicollinearity among categorical predictors can be detected by using the appropriate frequency analysis of contingency tables. However, when deleting redundant predictors to reduce multicollinearity, caution is needed to avoid specification errors that may occur with the deletion of predictors that are substantively important.

20.8 Summary

• **Logistic regression** is a statistical method that allows one to predict the chances that a subject with given scores on a set of (continuous or categorical) predictors belongs to a specific category of the dependent variable.

• When the dependent variable is a binary categorical variable, the logistic regression is referred to as a **binary logistic regression**. When the dependent variable has more than two categories, this is the case of a **multinomial logistic regression**. If the categories are ranked, the logistic regression is referred to as an **ordinal logistic regression.**

• With a binary logistic regression, the two categories of the dependent variable, Y, are coded 1 and 0, with $Y = 1$ indicating the category of interest referred to as *success*.

• The **probability that an event, A, will occur** is defined as a ratio, P(A) = m/n, where m is the number of outcomes that favor the event A and n is number of all possible outcomes. If P is the probability for an event to occur (*success*), 1 – P is the probability of the opposite event (*failure*). The ratio of the probability of success to the probability of failure is called the *odds* for success, **odds** = P/(1 – P).

• **The odds ratio** (**OR**) is the ratio of the odds for an event to occur in one group to the odds of this event occurring in another group. The two groups can be based on treatment (e.g., control, experimental), gender (males, females), blood pressure (low, high), etc.

• The notation e^X, or *exp*(*X*), stands for the exponential function, where $e = 2.718\ldots$ is a mathematical constant.

• The notation *ln*(*X*) stands for the *natural logarithm* of *X* (logarithm to base **e**: $\log_e X$). The mathematical relationship between e^X and *ln*(*X*) is inverse; that is: $\ln(e^X) = X$.

• The main purpose of using logistic regression is to predict the probability of *success*, $P(Y = 1)$, from a set predictors, $X_1, X_2, \ldots, X_K$. The combination of predictors that yields the best prediction of $P(Y = 1)$ is denoted $\mathbf{X} = B_1X_1 + B_2X_2 + \ldots + B_KX_K + A$ [**X** is a *composite score*].

• Under the **logistic regression model**, the probability for success is predicted from the composite score, **X**, as follows: $P(Y = 1) = e^X/(1 + e^X)$.

• The natural logarithm of the odds for success, *ln*(**odds**), is called the **logit** of the probability for success, P.

• The **logit form of the logistic regression** is: $ln(\textbf{odds}) = B_1X_1 + B_2X_2 + \ldots + B_KX_K + A$.

• The **regression coefficient** B_k for a predictor X_k represents the **change in the logit**, *ln*(**odds**), that would result from a "one unit change" in X_k when the other predictors are fixed.

• The **exponent of a regression coefficient** B_k **equals the odds ratio** [$exp(B_k) = \textbf{OR}$] for any two subjects that differ by one-unit on the predictor, X_k, but that have the same scores on all other predictors. This is the basis for interpreting regression coefficients in a binary logistic regression.

• The prediction model that includes only the constant, *A*, and no predictors at all is called a **baseline model**. The model with the constant and all predictors is called the **full model.**

• The test for statistical significance of the prediction with a (full) logistic regression model is a **chi-square test** for the difference between the likelihoods of the full and baseline models [see Equations 20.15 and 20.16].

• The **Hosmer-Lemeshow goodness-of-fit test** is for the logistic regression assumption of the existence of a linear relationship between the composite score ($\mathbf{X} = B_1X_1 + B_2X_2 + \ldots + B_KX_K + A$) and the *natural log of the odds* [*ln*(odds)] for the outcome of interest ($Y = 1$).

• The significance of individual predictors is tested by the **Wald test,** which is based on a *chi-square statistic* obtained by dividing the squared logistic regression coefficient by its squared standard error: $\chi^2 = [B/SE(B)]^2$.

• The Nagelkerke R^2 (and other R^2-like measures) for logistic regression is a "proxy," but not a direct analog, to R^2 in multiple regression and thus cannot be interpreted as the actual proportion of variance in *Y* accounted for by all predictors.

• The **classification table** [in the SPSS output for logistic regression] does not provide information for goodness-of-fit testing because, instead of taking into account the predicted *Y* values (1 or 0) obtained by the logistic regression, it uses binary (1 or 0) predictions based on a cutting score (.50).

• Key concepts with the classification table are (a) **hit rate** — the proportion of correct predictions, (b) **sensitivity** — the proportion of correct predictions in the reference category of the dependent variable ($Y = 1$), (c) **specificity** — the proportion of correct prediction in the opposite category ($Y = 0$), (d) **false positive rate** — the number of cases when an actual $Y = 0$ is predicted $Y = 1$, as a proportion of all cases in which $Y = 0$, and (e) **false negative rate** — the number of cases when an actual $Y = 1$ is predicted $Y = 0$, as a proportion of all cases in which $Y = 1$.

• Recommended coding values for a binary predictor are 0 and 1 (e.g., 0 = male, 1 = female), with 1 being the reference category against which the other category (0) is compared.

• **Dummy coding** is used for categorical predictors with more than two categories. For a predictor with *K* categories, the dummy coding generates $K - 1$ internal predictors. The values of the reference category, against which all other categories are compared, equal zero in all K – 1 internal predictors (e.g., see Figure 20.2). In SPSS, such dummy coding is provided by two (out of seven) options of coding contrasts, denoted **Indicator** and **Simple**.

• The contrast **coding procedures available in SPSS for logistic regression are (a) Indicator** — contrasts indicate the presence or absence of category membership, where the reference category is represented in the contrast matrix as a row of zeros, (b) **Simple** — each category of the predictor variable (except the reference category) is compared to the reference category, (c) **Helmert** — each category of the predictor variable except the last category is compared to the average effect of subsequent categories, (d) **Difference** — each category of the predictor variable except the first category is compared to the average effect of previous categories, (e) **Repeated** — each category of the predictor variable except the first category is compared to the category that precedes it, (f) **Polynomial** — orthogonal polynomial contrasts, where the categories are assumed to be equally spaced; [available for numeric variables only], and (g) **Deviation** — each category of the predictor variable except the reference category is compared to the overall effect.

20.9 Study Questions

1. If a logistic regression is used to predict college admission from high school GPA, SAT, and gender, (a) What is the dependent variable, *Y*?; (b) What is the appropriate coding for *Y*?; and (c) What would be the coding for gender if the goal were to see how females compare to males?
2. Which of the contrast coding procedures available in SPSS compares each category of the predictor variable (except the reference category) to the reference category?
3. If the categorical variable *parent education* (lower than high school, high school, bachelor, and graduate) is a predictor in a logistic regression, provide the dummy coding scheme for this predictor with "graduate" level of education used as the reference category [*Hint*: see Figure 20.2].
4. The graduation records for a random sample of 150 students show that 40 out of 62 students from low-income families and 75 out of 85 students from middle-class families graduated from high school. Given this information, (a) tabulate the results in a 2 x 2 table, and (b) calculate the odds ratio (OR) to compare the odds for high school graduation of students from middle-class families versus students from low-income families.
5. In a logistic regression for the prediction of substance abuse by teenagers, the regression coefficient for one of the predictors, *school attendance* (1 = YES, 0 = NO), is $B = -0.69$. Compute the odds ratio for this predictor and interpret its value [suppose *B* is statistically significant].

6. Replicate the analysis in Example 20.1, using Hispanic as the reference category in the coding for Ethnicity. Interpret the results and provide a summary table in APA style as shown in Table 20.1.

7. Consider the SPSS data file **Employee data.sav** shown in Figure 6.5 (Chapter 6) [these data are available with the SPSS package]. Using SPSS, employ a logistic regression analysis to predict **minority status** (1 = YES, 0 = NO) of the employees from the variables named **gender** (m = male, f = female), **educ** (years of education), and **salary** (current salary). Interpret the results and provide a summary table in APA style as shown in Table 20.1. [*Note*: When interpreting the odds ratio for gender, take into account that "f" precedes "m" which is treated in SPSS as 0 = female, 1 = male].

8. Extend the logistic regression model for the prediction of minority status, described in the previous question, by including an additional predictor: the categorical variable named **jobcat** which has three employment categories (1 = Clerical, 2 = Custodial, and 3 = Manager). Use dummy coding (**Indicator** in SPSS) for this predictor, with Manager as the reference category. Again, interpret the results and provide a summary table in APA style as shown in Table 20.1.

9. Consider the logistic regression model described in question 7 as a *restricted model* for the prediction of minority status from three predictors and the logistic model with question 8, as a full model for the prediction of minority status from four predictors. Compare the full and restricted models, given that the chi-square test provides $\chi^2(5) = 42.496$, $p < .0001$, with the full model and $\chi^2(3) = 37.32$, $p < .0001$, with the restricted model [*Hint*: use the chi-square difference ($\Delta\chi^2$) test — see Example 20.2].

CHAPTER 21

MULTIVARIATE ANALYSIS OF VARIANCE

Multivariate analysis of variance (MANOVA) is used when a researcher wants to investigate difference among two or more groups on a set of two or more dependent variables. For example, MANOVA would be the method of choice if the research question seeks to determine whether high school students from three types of residential areas (urban, suburban, and rural) differ in their responses to survey questions about attitudes toward school, motivation to learn, plans to attend college, homework completion, academic achievement (GPA), and SAT scores. In this case, the MANOVA would have one independent variable (fixed factor) with three levels: type of residential area; and six dependent variables: attitude toward school, motivation to learn, planning to attend college, homework completion, GPA, and SAT.

21.1 The Concept of MANOVA

Suppose that three ethnic groups of students are compared on a single dependent variable, Y. In this case, we can use a univariate analysis of variance (ANOVA) to test the null hypothesis for this group comparison:

$$H_0\text{: } \mu_1 = \mu_2 = \mu_3. \qquad \textbf{(21.1)}$$

As we know from Chapter 14, this null hypothesis is tested with the ratio $F = \text{MS}_\text{B}/\text{MS}_\text{W}$, where MS_B (*mean squares between*) is the between-groups variance, and MS_W (*mean squares within*) is the within-group variance.

Suppose now that the three ethnic groups are compared on two dependent variables, Y_1 and Y_2. The null hypothesis in this case is that the three population means are equal on both Y_1 ($\mu_{11} = \mu_{12} = \mu_{13}$) and Y_2($\mu_{21} = \mu_{22} = \mu_{23}$), where the first part of the subscript indicates the dependent variable, and its second part indicates the group. In matrix algebra notations, this multivariate null hypothesis translates into "the population mean vectors are equal":

$$H_0\text{: } \begin{pmatrix}\mu_{11}\\ \mu_{21}\end{pmatrix} = \begin{pmatrix}\mu_{12}\\ \mu_{22}\end{pmatrix} = \begin{pmatrix}\mu_{13}\\ \mu_{23}\end{pmatrix}. \qquad \textbf{(21.2)}$$

Among the several MANOVA statistics available for testing H_0, the most widely used is **Wilk's Λ**, where Λ (the capital Greek letter "lambda") equals the ratio "within-group variability to total variability." As already described in Chapter 19 (Section 19.1.3), the matrix algebra notation of this ratio is $\Lambda = |\mathbf{W}|/|\mathbf{T}|$, where $|\mathbf{W}|$ is a number (determinant) for the multivariate analog to the "within" variability in univariate ANOVA, and the denominator, $|\mathbf{T}|$, is a number (determinant) for the multivariate analog to the "total" (between + within) variability in univariate ANOVA. Recall that Λ can be viewed as an *effect size*, keeping in mind that the closer Wilk's Λ is to zero, the larger the effect size will be. Also, $m\eta^2 = 1 - \Lambda$ (*multivariate eta squared*) represents a measure of the *omnibus effect size* in MANOVA.

21.2 MANOVA versus Separate ANOVAs

It is important to emphasize from the beginning that MANOVA takes into account the correlations among dependent variables, while such correlations are ignored when multiple ANOVAs are used to compare the groups on each variable separately. Also, contrary to a frequently-manifested misconception, a statistically significant Wilk's Λ does *not* necessarily mean that the groups differ on (one or more) separate dependent variables. Rather, it indicates that the groups differ on *at least one linear combination of the dependent variables*. With m dependent variables, $Y_1, Y_2, \ldots, Y_m$, the general form of such a linear combination is

$$\boldsymbol{D} = a_1Y_1 + a_2Y_2 + \ldots + a_mY_m, \tag{21.3}$$

where the coefficients $a_1, a_2, \ldots, a_m$ are correlation-type "weights" for the contribution of each dependent variable to the "composite" ***D***. The meaning of ***D*** as a *linear function* of the dependent variables is defined by the collective meaning of the dependent variables with the highest significant weights in ***D***. It may happen that some (or all) linear functions, ***Ds***, are defined primarily by a single dependent variable, but generally this is not the case [more details on the nature and use of linear functions in MANOVA are provided in Section 21.6].

Additionally, Wilk's Λ does not provide information about the overall Type I error rate produced by conducting separate ANOVAs. It may happen that Wilk's Λ is statistically significant, yet none of the univariate ANOVA tests is statistically significant. Conversely, a statistically non-significant Wilk's Λ may be followed by a statistically significant result for some univariate ANOVA tests. *Thus, conducting MANOVA as a preliminary step to using univariate ANOVAs is unnecessary and in some cases can be misleading.* However, this matter is still commonly misunderstood in applications of MANOVA in behavioral research. Indeed, MANOVA and separate ANOVAs address different research questions and provide different information about the data and their interpretation. The choice between conducting a MANOVA or separate ANOVAs should be guided by the nature of the research question(s). Moreover, the results from the omnibus MANOVA may suggest the investigation of additional (more refined) research questions that involve the employment of other statistical methods (e.g., discriminant analysis, *t*-tests, etc.).

21.3 When to Use Separate ANOVAs?

It is appropriate to conduct separate ANOVAs when the research question aims to identify the dependent variables on which the compared groups differ. Here are two typical situations in which it is appropriate to conduct separate ANOVAs:

1. When the dependent variables are conceptually independent of one another — for example, when one variable is parental support, another variable is critical thinking, and a third variable is motivation of middle school students. As it is not expected that some linear composite of unrelated dependent variables will "emerge" to separate the groups, it is not necessary to use MANOVA in this case.
2. When the goal is to examine relationships between the independent variable (e.g., treatment conditions) and individual dependent variables, either for exploratory purposes or to compare results with previous studies on such relationships.

As noted earlier, it is a common misconception that if the omnibus MANOVA statistic(s) (e.g., Wilk's Λ) indicate statistical significance, this will maintain the overall probability of type I error with univariate ANOVAs at the adopted level of significance (e.g., $\alpha = .05$). As this is not the case, instead of following a significant MANOVA, one can maintain the overall (familywise) for univariate ANOVAs by conducting each of them at a lower level than α. Specifically, using the Bonferroni adjustment, one should use for each ANOVA a level of significance equal to α/k, where k is the number of univariate ANOVAs. For example, for the comparison of groups on five dependent variables ($k = 5$), each separate ANOVA should be tested at the level of significance .01 (i.e., .05/5) to maintain the overall level of significance at .05. Also, keep in mind that the correlations among dependent variables are ignored with univariate ANOVAs which leads to analysis and interpretation of redundant information.

21.4 When to Use MANOVA?

Comparing groups on separate dependent variables by conducting multiple ANOVAs does not allow for addressing broader and more insightful questions involving relationships among dependent variables. Such questions can be answered by using MANOVA. For example, MANOVA will allow a researcher to addresses questions related to (a) which subsets of dependent variables (if any) serve to separate groups, (b) what are the underlying constructs for such subsets (i.e., what constructs "emerge" as linear combinations of the dependent variables), and (c) what is the relative contribution of individual dependent variables to group separation.

A significant omnibus MANOVA (i.e. a statistically significant *Wilk's lambda*) means that the compared groups differ on some linear combination(s) of the dependent variables. Such linear combinations are referred to as **linear discriminant functions** (***LDF*s**). Thus, each *LDF* is a latent construct that "emerges" from relationships among dependent variables and discriminates (separates) the groups. With K groups and m dependent variables, the number of possible *LDF*s is the smaller number of ($K - 1$) and m. For example, when four groups ($K = 4$) are compared on six dependent variables ($m = 6$), there are three possible *LDF*s because 3 is the smaller number of $K - 1 = 3$ and $m = 6$. As another example, with four groups and two dependent variables, there are two possible *LDF*s [2 is the smaller number of $K - 1 = 3$ and $m = 2$]. Information about the *LDF*s and how they discriminate (separate) the groups is provided by a discriminant analysis following a statistically significant *Wilk's lambda.*

As a point of comparison, note that (a) the predicted Y score ($\hat{Y}$) in multiple regression is a linear combination of the predictor variables, $\hat{Y} = b_1X_1 + b_2X_2 + \ldots + b_mX_m$, that maximally correlates with the observed Y score ($r_{Y\hat{Y}}$ = max); (b) the composite score in logistic regression is a linear combination of the predictor variables, $\boldsymbol{X} = B_1X_1 + B_2X_2 + \ldots + B_mX_m$, that maximizes the accuracy of the predicted probability for the outcome of interest ($Y = 1$); and (c) the linear discriminant function (*LDF*) in discriminant analysis is a linear combination of the dependent variables, $LDF = a_1Y_1 + a_2Y_2 + \ldots + a_mY_m$ (see Equation 21.3), which maximally discriminates (separates) the groups.

21.5 Assumptions in MANOVA

The assumptions in MANOVA are multivariate analogs to the assumptions in ANOVA:

1. The subjects are randomly sampled from the target population.
2. The observations are statistically independent of one another.
3. The dependent variables follow a multivariate normal distribution within each group.
4. All groups have the same variance on each dependent variable.
5. The correlations between any two dependent variables are the same in all groups.

Violations of any of the first two assumptions are particularly damaging to the validity of the MANOVA results. The violation of the second assumption may occur, for example, when the participants in a treatment condition work in small groups and interact with each other. Although MANOVA is relatively robust to violation of the last three assumptions, caution is necessary. The third assumption is difficult to test, but for practical purposes one can test the normality of each dependent variable in each group separately (e.g., using the Q-Q plot test in SPSS). The violation of normality has little effect on the type I error rates, but serious departures from normality may reduce the statistical power of the MANOVA test statistics (e.g., *Wilk's lambda*).

Taken together, the last two assumptions are equivalent to the assumption that all groups have the same within-group population covariance matrix. A test for homogeneity of covariance matrices, referred to as **Box's M**, is available with SPSS (and other major statistical packages). Box's M, however, is not dependable when the assumption of multivariate normality is not met. The assumption of homogeneity of covariance matrices (assumptions 4 and 5 together) is met relatively well when the MANOVA design is balanced (i.e., the groups have equal sample size), but this is not the case with sharply unequal group sizes. Specifically, the omnibus MANOVA test becomes (a) "liberal" (makes it unduly easy to reject the null hypothesis) when larger sample sizes are associated with smaller variances, and (b) "conservative" (makes it unduly difficult to reject the null hypothesis) when larger sample sizes are associated with larger variances. One way to deal with this problem is to use an appropriate transformation of the original scores on the dependent variables. For example, if the scores on a given dependent variable are proportions, the group variances on this variable can be stabilized by using the "square root" transformation (i.e., replacing each score with its square root value).

21.6 MANOVA with Discriminant Analysis

As already noted, a statistically significant *Wilk's lambda* for the omnibus MANOVA test indicates that there is *at least one* linear combination of the dependent variables, referred to as a linear discriminant function (*LDF*), that maximally separates the groups. The *LDF*s maximize the "between- to within-group variability" ratio, **B/W**, where **B** and **W** represent the multivariate analogs of univariate ANOVA's *sum of squares between* (SS_B) and *sum of squares within* (SS_W), respectively. As **B** is a measure of the differential effect of the grouping variable (e.g., treatment conditions), the larger the **B/W** ratio, the greater the group separation.

The *LDF*s are determined in decreasing order according to their contribution to the separation of the groups. They are *orthogonal* (uncorrelated) because, after a specific *LDF* is determined, its contribution to the group separation is "partialled out," so the next (less contributing) *LDF* is the one that maximizes the remaining **B/W** ratio. At each step, an *LDF* is tested for statistical significance by a chi-square statistic, with degrees of freedom equal to $(m - d)(K - d - 1)$, where K = the number of groups, m = the number of dependent variables, and d = the number of statistically significant *LDF*s determined in the previous steps.

EXAMPLE 21.1 This example illustrates how to conduct a MANOVA and discriminant analysis using SPSS. The data consist of 835 observations representing the scores of high school students on a science test following an experiment in teaching science. Three groups of students were randomly assigned to two experimental variations using computer simulations ($\mathbf{E_1}$ and $\mathbf{E_2}$) to teach science and to a traditional science teaching method (**Control**). There are five variables (Y_1, Y_2, Y_3, Y_4, and Y_5) that represent the students' scores on five groups of test questions measuring different aspects of science knowledge and skills: Y_1 = **terminology** (knowledge of science terms), Y_2 = **application** (application of rules and principles), Y_3 = **definitions** (knowledge of definitions and principles), Y_4 = **problem identification** (pursue different strategies for identifying problems), and Y_5 = **causal inferences** (establish cause-and-effect relationships). The three treatment groups (E_1, E_2, and Control) consisted of 272, 337, and 226 participants, respectively. The SPSS file, named **EXAMPLE 21_1.sav**, is available at http://cehd.gmu.edu/book/dimitrov.

The **research question** seeks to determine whether the treatment conditions (E_1, E_2, and Control) produce differences in the students' performance on the set of science knowledge and skills (terminology, application, definitions, problem identification, and inferences). The relative contribution of each of these variables to the separation of the treatment groups is also of interest. The Pearson correlations for all pairs of the five variables were statistically significant ($p < .01$) and varied from .12 to .36. Thus, given the research question and the existence of linear relationships among the five variables of interest, we will conduct MANOVA with **treatment** (E_1, E_2, and Control) as the independent variable and five dependent variables (Y_1 = *terminology*, Y_2 = *application*, Y_3 = *definitions*, Y_4 = *problem identification*, and Y_5 = *causal inferences*).

The SPSS syntax for MANOVA, followed by a discriminant analysis and then by post-hoc comparisons of the groups on separate dependent variables, is provided in Figure 21.1. The **bold** text does not change in the SPSS syntax because this text contains the SPSS instructions required to conduct the desired procedures. The names of the grouping variable (treatment) and the five dependent variables (Y_1, Y_2, Y_3, Y_4, and Y_5), on the other hand, are not in bold because this information changes across cases. These names should be typed in the SPSS syntax in exactly the same way as they appear as variable names in the SPSS file (**EXAMPLE 21_1.sav.** The five dependent variables are named Y_1, Y_2, Y_3, Y_4, and Y_5 and labeled *terminology*, *application*, *definitions*, *problem identification*, and *causal inferences*, respectively [the labels are not used with the syntax – see Figure 21.1]. To run the SPSS syntax in Figure 21.1, follow the steps:

1. In the SPSS Data Editor, click **File**, click **New**, and click **Syntax**.
2. In the SPSS Syntax Editor, type the syntax in Figure 21.
3. In the SPSS Syntax Editor, click **Run**, and click **All**.

Figure 21.1 *SPSS syntax for MANOVA, discriminant analysis, and post-hoc pairwise comparisons of three groups on five dependent variables*

```
=====================================================
MANOVA Y1 TO Y5 BY treatment(1,3)
   /PRINT CELLINFO(MEANS) HOMOGENEITY (COCHRAN, BOXM).

DISCRIMINANT GROUPS = treatment(1, 3)
  /VARIABLES = Y1 TO Y5
  /METHOD = WILKS/FIN=0/FOUT=0
  /STATISTICS = FPAIR
  /PLOT = COMBINED.

  T-TEST GROUPS = treatment(1,2)
    /VARIABLES = Y1 TO Y5.

  T-TEST GROUPS = treatment(1,3)
    /VARIABLES = Y1 TO Y5.

  T-TEST GROUPS = treatment(2,3)
    /VARIABLES = Y1 TO Y5.
=====================================================
```

> **NOTE [21.1]** It would be useful to save the SPSS syntax in Figure 21.1 and, when used with different data, keep the text in bold and change only the names of the independent and dependent variables as they appear in the SPSS data file. Once you have the syntax file saved, open the SPSS data file and then open the syntax file: In the SPSS Data Editor, click **File**, click **Open**, and click **Syntax**.

For space considerations, the SPSS output from the MANOVA procedure (the first two syntax lines) is not provided here, but the results are as follows. First, *Wilk's lambda* ($\Lambda = .53$) was statistically significant, $F(10, 1654) = 61.80$, $p < .001$. At this point, we can only conclude that there is a statistically significant difference between *at least two* groups on some linear combination(s) of the five dependent variables. The normality assumption, which is important primarily for the correctness of Box's M statistic, was supported to a large extent by the normal Q-Q plot test for each dependent variable separately [the normal Q-Q plot test is described in Chapter 7, Section 7.1.5]. The Box's M (35.65) was statistically non-significant, $\chi^2(30) = 35.34$, $p = .231$, thus indicating that the assumption of equal variance-covariance matrices is met.
The next step is to determine *which* linear combinations of the dependent variables separate the treatment groups. The SPSS output for the discriminant analysis, produced by the second independent "block" of syntax lines (3-7) in Figure 21.1, is provided in Figure 21.2. As three groups are being compared on a set of five dependent variables, there are two possible linear discriminant functions (*LDF*s); [Why?]. The results from the **Eigenvalues** table show that the first linear discriminant function (LDF_1) accounts for 65.9 percent of the total variance for the set of five dependent variables across the three groups. The remaining 34.1 percent is accounted for by the second linear discriminant function (LDF_2); [the *LDF*s are *orthogonal* (uncorrelated) and ordered from most to least important to the separation of the groups.] As the linear discriminant functions are orthogonal, the sum of their contributions to accounting for the total variance equals 100 percent. The lack of "overlap" between the linear discriminant functions facilitates their interpretation both statistically and substantively.

The results from the **Wilk's Lambda** table indicate that the first linear discriminant function (LDF_1) is statistically significant, $\Lambda = .53$, $\chi^2(10) = 520.75$, $p < .001$. The second linear discriminant function (LDF_2) is also statistically significant, $\Lambda = .80$, $\chi^2(4) = 188.37$, $p < .001$.

The examination of the **Structure Matrix** table clearly shows that the dependent variables Y_3 and Y_1 correlate with LDF_1, whereas Y_5, Y_2, and Y_4 correlate with LDF_2 [the variables are ordered by the decreasing magnitude of their correlations with the *LDF* that they define].

The table **Standardized Canonical Discriminant Function Coefficients** provides information about possible redundancy among variables that define a specific linear discriminant function (*LDF*). In this case, Y_3 and Y_1 define LDF_1, but comparison of their standardized coefficients in this table shows that the meaning of LDF_1 is defined primarily by Y_3 because its standardized coefficient (.980) is much higher than that for Y_1 (-.136). Given that Y_3 stands for *definitions* (knowledge of definitions and principles), we can label LDF_1 as **content knowledge**.
Likewise, Y_5, Y_2, and Y_4 correlate with LDF_2, but their standardized coefficients are .837, .021, and -.282, respectively. This shows that the meaning of LDF_2 is defined primarily by Y_5 and Y_4, whereas Y_2 provides some redundant information. Given that Y_5 = *causal inferences* (establish cause-and-effect relationships) and Y_4 = *problem identification* (pursue different strategies for identifying problems), we can label LDF_2 as **problem solving skills**. Thus, two dimensions "emerged" as linear combinations of the dependent variables that provide the best separation of the treatment groups: LDF_1 = **content knowledge** and LDF_2 = **problem solving skills**.

Figure 21.2 *SPSS output with the discriminant analysis of three groups on five variables*

Eigenvalues

Function	Eigenvalue	% of Variance	Cumulative %	Canonical Correlation
1	.493[a]	65.9	65.9	.574
2	.255[a]	34.1	100.0	.451

a. First 2 canonical discriminant functions were used in the analysis.

Wilks' Lambda

Test of Function(s)	Wilks' Lambda	Chi-square	df	Sig.
1 through 2	.534	520.751	10	.000
2	.797	188.368	4	.000

Standardized Canonical Discriminant Function Coefficients

	Function	
	1	2
Y1 = terminology	-.136	-.233
Y2 = application	-.163	.021
Y3 = definitions	.980	.502
Y4 = problem identification	.124	-.282
Y5 = causal inferences	-.739	.837

Structure Matrix

	Function	
	1	2
Y3 = definitions	.676*	.668
Y1 = terminology	-.091*	.060
Y5 = causal inferences	-.399	.850*
Y2 = application	-.120	.212*
Y4 = problem identification	.086	.132*

*. Largest absolute correlation between each variable and any discriminant function

Functions at Group Centroids

	Function	
treatment	1	2
E1	-.910	.312
E2	.740	.303
Control	-.009	-.827

The group means, called "group centroids," are provided in the **Functions at Group Centroids** table in Figure 21.2. Their graphical representation is shown in Figure 21.3. The omnibus null hypothesis in MANOVA states that the group centroids are equal for the study population (see Equation 21.2). As Figure 21.3 shows, however, the three groups are separated by two aspects of student performance on the science test: *content knowledge* and *problem solving skills.* On content knowledge, the strongest separation is between the two experimental groups in favor of the second experimental group. The two experimental groups do not differ on problem solving skills, but they both exceed the control group in this regard.

Figure 21.3 *Group centroids for three groups (E_1, E_2, Control) separated by two linear discriminant functions, LDF_1 = content knowledge and LDF_2 = problem solving skills*

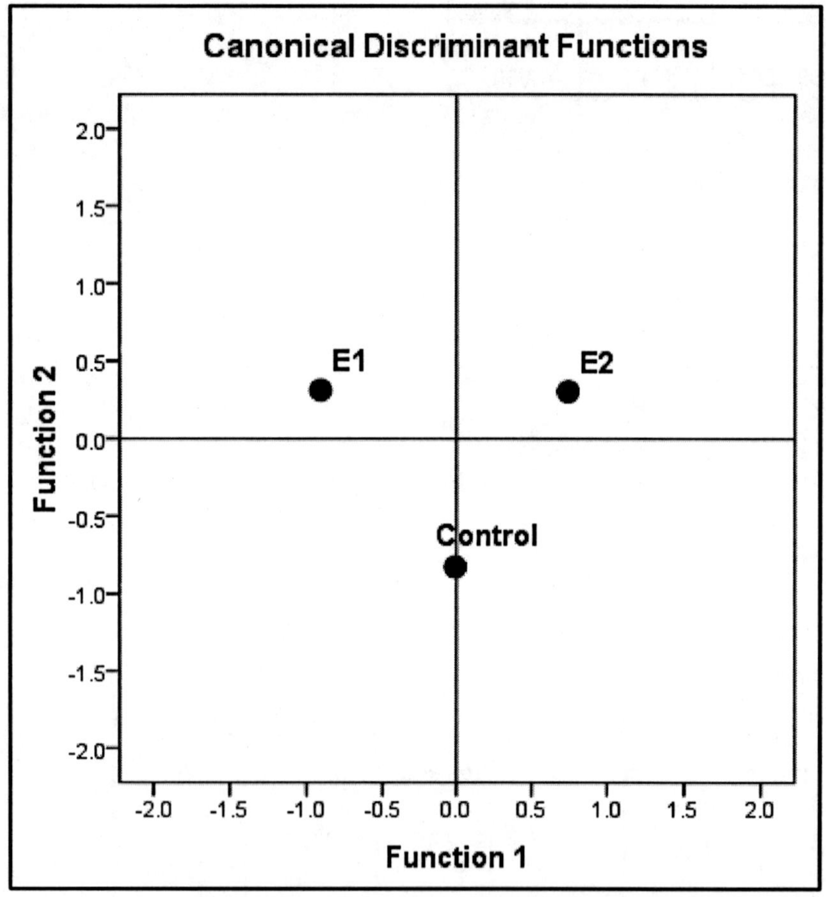

The relative importance of each dependent variable to the group separation, which is also of interest to the research question, is determined by the magnitude of its "*F*-to-remove" statistic. For a given dependent variable, this statistic indicates by how much the separation of the groups would decrease if this variable were deleted. Thus, the larger the *F*-to-remove statistic, the more important the dependent variable is to the separation of the groups. Although provided in the SPSS output, the *F*-to-remove statistics are not shown in Figure 21.2 for space consideration. Instead, they are summarized in Table 21.1 (APA format) along with the results from the **Structure Matrix** and **Standardized Canonical Discriminant Function Coefficients** tables.

The F-to-remove statistics for Y_3 (173.04) and Y_5 (132.87) are much greater than those of the other variables. Thus, Y_3 (knowledge of definitions and principles) and Y_5 (establish cause-and-effect relationships) are the most important contributors to the separation of the treatment groups. Note that these two variables are the key representatives of the two dimensions of group separation (*LDFs*): *content knowledge* and *problem solving skills*, respectively.

Table 21.1
Statistics for Five Variables of Science Test Performance Related to Two Linear Discriminant Functions — LDF_1 (Content Knowledge) and LDF_2 (Problem Solving Skills)

Variables	Correlation coefficients		Standardized coefficients		F-to-remove
	LDF_1	LDF_2	LDF_1	LDF_2	
Y_1 (terminology)	0.09*	0.06	−0.14	−0.23	6.06
Y_2 (application)	−0.12	0.21*	−0.16	0.02	3.43
Y_3 (definitions and principles)	0.68*	0.67	0.98	0.50	173.04
Y_4 (problem identification)	0.09	0.13*	0.12	−0.28	7.02
Y_5 (causal inferences)	−0.40	0.85*	−0.74	0.84	132.87

The SPSS output for pairwise group comparisons on each dependent variable [requested by the T-TEST syntax in Figure 21.1, but not shown here] indicated that (a) group E_1 did better than the E_2 and Control groups on Y_2 (application) and Y_5 (inferences), and (b) group E_2 did better than group E_1 on Y_3 (definitions and principles) and better than the Control group on Y_3 (definitions and principles), Y_4(problem identification), and Y_5 (causal inferences).

21.7 MANOVA with Planned Comparisons

Instead of pairwise comparisons, a question of interest in MANOVA may relate to comparisons that researchers have planned in advance. In addition to the information provided by the discriminant analysis in MANOVA, such questions can address theoretical or empirical expectations about group differences. This can be achieved by testing contrasts that reflect the group differences of interest. Contrasts for group comparisons in univariate ANOVA were presented in Chapters 14, 15, and 17. Now, let's take another look at the difference between orthogonal and nonorthogonal contrasts. Suppose that the null hypotheses in comparing four groups are:

$$H_{01}: \frac{\mu_1 + \mu_2 + \mu_3}{3} = \mu_4,\ H_{02}: \frac{\mu_1 + \mu_2}{2} = \mu_3, \text{ and } H_{03}: \mu_1 = \mu_2. \quad \textbf{(21.4)}$$

Representing H_{01} in contrast form, H_{01}: $\mu_1 + \mu_2 + \mu_3 - 3\mu_4 = 0$, the coefficients for the group means provide the coding of the contrast for this hypothesis, Ψ_1: 1 1 1 −3. Likewise, the contrast form of the second null hypothesis, H_{02}: $\mu_1 + \mu_2 - 2\mu_3 = 0$, provides the contrast, Ψ_2: 1 1 −2 0. Finally, presenting the third null hypothesis in the form H_{03}: $\mu_1 - \mu_2 = 0$, provides the coding of its contrast, Ψ_3: 1 −1 0 0. As can be seen, the sum of the products of the coefficients for any contrasts equals zero — e.g., $\Psi_1\,\Psi_2 = (1)(1) + (1)(1) + (1)(-2) + (-3)(0) = 1 + 1 - 2 + 0 = 0$. [Check also that $\Psi_1\,\Psi_3 = 0$ and $\Psi_2\,\Psi_3 = 0$.] This indicates that the contrasts Ψ_1, Ψ_2, and Ψ_3 will be **orthogonal** if they are used with a balanced MANOVA design.

The advantage of using orthogonal contrasts in MANOVA is analogous to that of using orthogonal predictors in multiple regression analysis: the total contribution of each contrast to the multivariate between-groups variability is *unique* (i.e., not confounded by the contribution of other contrasts). Correlated contrasts may occur when (a) the sum of the products of the coefficients does not equal zero, or (b) the MANOVA design is not balanced (i.e., the compared groups do not have equal sample sizes) even when the contrast codes are defined as orthogonal. With correlated contrasts, the unique contribution of each contrast is obtained by removing (partialling out) its correlation with the other contrasts. This section provides examples of the SPSS syntax needed to conduct MANOVA with both uncorrelated and correlated contrasts.

EXAMPLE 21.2 This example illustrates how to conduct a MANOVA with uncorrelated contrasts using SPSS syntax. Specifically, the contrasts Ψ_1, Ψ_2, and Ψ_3 for the null hypotheses in (21.4) are tested for statistical significance on a set of two dependent variables, Y_1 and Y_2, for the 24 observations in Figure 21.4, where the levels of the independent variable are four ethnic groups (say, E_1, E_2, E_3, and E_4). The three contrasts are uncorrelated because (a) any two of them are orthogonal to each other, and (b) the MANOVA design is balanced [in this case, $n = 6$]. The SPSS syntax for MANOVA with the contrasts Ψ_1, Ψ_2, and Ψ_3 is provided in Figure 21.4. Recall that in the SPSS syntax the notations of the grouping variable ("ethnicity") and the dependent variables (Y1 and Y2) should match the names given to these variables in the SPSS Data Editor. The coefficients for the contrasts are enclosed in parentheses after SPECIAL in the subcommand CONTRAST, where the first four 1's indicate that there are four groups in this case, followed by the coding of the contrasts Ψ_1, Ψ_2, and Ψ_3, respectively. The elements in the SPSS syntax given in **bold** are not case sensitive and do not change when used with different dependent variables and groups. What may change are the coding coefficients and notations for the dependent and grouping variables. Note that in the subcommand DESIGN the notations ethnicity(1), ethnicity(2), ethnicity(3) stand for the contrasts Ψ_1, Ψ_2, and Ψ_3, respectively (not for the first three ethnic groups).

For space considerations, the selected SPSS output in Figure 21.5 provides only the results related to the first contrast (Ψ_1), indicated by the notation "EFFECT .. ETHNICITY(1)." The Box's M statistic was non-significant, M = 11.71, $\chi^2(9) = 9.60$, $p = .384$, thus indicating that the multivariate assumption of equal variance-covariance matrices is met. As shown in Figure 21.5, the *Wilk's lambda* for Ψ_1 is statistically significant, $\Lambda = .53$, $F(2, 19) = 8.51$, $p = .002$. Given that Ψ_1 represents H_{01}: $\mu_1 + \mu_2 + \mu_3 - 3\mu_4 = 0$ [i.e., H_{01}: $(\mu_1 + \mu_2 + \mu_3)/3 = \mu_4$], this means that the average effect of the first three ethnic groups (E_1, E_2, and E_3) is different from the effect of the fourth ethnic group (E_4) on the set of two dependent variables (Y_1 and Y_2). Further, the results from the univariate *F*-tests indicate that the first contrast, Ψ_1, is statistically significant for Y_1, $F(1, 20) = 7.92$, $p = .011$, as well as for Y_2, $F(1, 20) = 15.44$, $p = .001$. Thus, the average effect of the first three ethnic groups (E_1, E_2, and E_3) is different from the effect of the fourth ethnic group (E_4) on each dependent variable taken separately.

The results for the contrast Ψ_2 (not shown here) indicated that (a) *Wilk's lambda* was statistically significant, $\Lambda = .35$, $F(2, 19) = 17.89$, $p < .001$, (b) Ψ_2 was statistically significant on Y_1, $F(1, 20) = 15.84$, $p = .001$, and Y_2, $F(1, 20) = 33.00$, $p < .001$. Given that Ψ_2 represents the second null hypothesis, H_{02}: $\mu_1 + \mu_2 - 2\mu_3 = 0$ [i.e., H_{02}: $(\mu_1 + \mu_2)/2 = \mu_3$], these results show that the average effect of the first two ethnic groups (E_1 and E_2) is different from that of the third ethnic group (E_3) on the set of two dependent variables, Y_1 and Y_2, as well as on each of them taken separately. The results for the contrast Ψ_3 (also not shown) indicated that (a) *Wilk's lambda* was not statistically significant, $\Lambda = .98$, $F(2, 19) = 0.20$, $p = .819$. As can be expected, Ψ_3

was not statistically significant either on Y_1, $F(1, 20) = 0.02$, $p = .874$, or on Y_2, $F(1, 20) = 0.42$, $p = .524$. Given that Ψ_3 represents the null hypothesis H_{03}: $\mu_1 - \mu_2 = 0$ [i.e., H_{03}: $\mu_1 = \mu_2$], these results indicate that the first two ethnic groups (E_1 and E_2) do not differ either on the set of two dependent variables, Y_1 and Y_2, or on each of them taken separately.

Figure 21.4 *SPSS data and syntax for three orthogonal contrasts with a balanced MANOVA for four ethnic groups and two dependent variables (Y_1, Y_2).*

==

*EXAMPLE_21_2.sav [Data

File Edit View Data Trans

12:

	ethnicity	Y1	Y2
1	1	20	14
2	1	19	12
3	1	14	11
4	1	16	12
5	1	12	8
6	1	18	10
7	2	16	11
8	2	18	8
9	2	16	12
10	2	19	16
11	2	16	14
12	2	16	12
13	3	12	6
14	3	8	9
15	3	6	2
16	3	10	4
17	3	16	2
18	3	5	1
19	4	18	4
20	4	4	1
21	4	6	2
22	4	11	8
23	4	10	7
24	4	8	3

```
MANOVA Y1, Y2 BY ethnicity(1, 4)
 /CONTRAST(ethnicity) = SPECIAL(1 1 1 1  1 1 1 -3  1 1 -2 0  1 -1 0 0)
 /PARTITION(ethnicity)
 /DESIGN = ethnicity(1), ethnicity(2), ethnicity(3)
 /PRINT CELLINFO(MEANS) HOMOGENEITY(COCHRAN, BOXM).
```

==

Note: The data is available with the SPSS data file named **EXAMPLE_21_2.sav** at the web site for this book [http://cehd.gmu.edu/book/dimitrov].

Figure 21.5 *Selected SPSS output for the multivariate and univariate significance of the contrast representing the null hypothesis H_{01}: $(\mu_1 + \mu_2 + \mu_3)/3 = \mu_4$.*

```
EFFECT .. ETHNICITY(1)
Multivariate Tests of Significance (S = 1, M = 0, N = 8 1/2)

Test Name          Value        Exact F      Hypoth. DF        Error DF        Sig. of F

Pillais           .47263        8.51385            2.00           19.00             .002
Hotellings        .89620        8.51385            2.00           19.00             .002
Wilks             .52737        8.51385            2.00           19.00             .002
Roys              .47263
Note.. F statistics are exact.

- - - - - - - - - - - - - - - - - - - - - - - - - - - - - - - - - - - - - - - - - - - - -
EFFECT .. ETHNICITY(1) (Cont.)
Univariate F-tests with (1,20) D. F.

Variable      Hypoth. SS      Error SS     Hypoth. MS        Error MS            F      Sig. of F

Y1             102.72222     259.33333      102.72222        12.96667      7.92202           .011
Y2             110.01389     142.50000      110.01389         7.12500     15.44055           .001
```

Note. Information on the effect size of the multivariate and univariate tests can be obtained by extending the subcommand PRINT in the MANOVA syntax as follows:
/PRINT = CELLINFO(MEANS) SIGNIF(EFSIZE) HOMOGENEITY (COCHRAN, BOXM).

As noted above, the contrasts Ψ_1, Ψ_2, and Ψ_3 in Example 21.2 are **uncorrelated** because any two of them are *orthogonal* [the sum of the products of their coefficients equals zero] and the MANOVA design is *balanced* [there are equal sample sizes for all groups: $n_1 = n_2 = n_3 = n_4 = 6$]. The next example illustrates the use of SPSS for MANOVA with correlated contrasts.

EXAMPLE 21.3 The data in this example consist of 474 observations for four groups randomly assigned to four middle school math teaching methods: two experimental conditions and two control conditions. The SPSS data file named **EXAMPLE 21_3.sav** is available at the website for this book [http://cehd.gmu.edu/book/dimitrov]. The four groups are assessed on two dependent variables, Y_1 = *application* and Y_2 = *evaluation* in math problems. The Pearson correlation between Y_1 and Y_2 is statistically significant, $r = .88$, $p < .001$. In the SPSS file, the independent variable is named **method**, with its four levels labeled EXP_1, EXP_2, CTRL_1, and CTRL_2, respectively. The dependent variables are named **Y1** and **Y2** and labeled *application* and *evaluation*, respectively [there is also a variable **gender** which is not used in this example]. The null hypotheses of interest here are:

$$H_{04}: \frac{\mu_1 + \mu_2}{2} = \frac{\mu_3 + \mu_4}{2}, \; H_{05}: \mu_1 = \mu_2, \text{ and } H_{06}: \mu_3 = \mu_4. \quad \textbf{(21.5)}$$

These null hypotheses are denoted H_{04}, H_{05}, and H_{06} to distinguish them from H_{01}, H_{02}, and H_{03} addressed in the previous example. Following the familiar procedure, H_{04}, H_{05}, and H_{06} can be presented in a contrast form as follows: H_{04}: $\Psi_4 = 0$, H_{05}: $\Psi_5 = 0$, and H_{06}: $\Psi_6 = 0$, where the new contrasts are $\Psi_4 = \mu_1 + \mu_2 - \mu_3 - \mu_4$, $\Psi_5 = \mu_1 - \mu_2$, and $\Psi_6 = \mu_3 - \mu_4$. The coefficients of these contrasts provide their coding: (1 1 −1 −1) for Ψ_4, (1 −1 0 0) for Ψ_5, and (0 0 1 −1) for Ψ_6.

As can be seen, Ψ_4, Ψ_5, and Ψ_6 represent a set of orthogonal contrasts because any two of them are orthogonal to each other. For example, the sum of the products of the coefficients for Ψ_4 and Ψ_5 is zero: $(1)(1) + (1)(-1) + (-1)(0) + (-1)(0) = 1 - 1 + 0 + 0 = 0$. [You can check also that $\Psi_4\Psi_6 = 0$ and $\Psi_5\Psi_6 = 0$.] However, although Ψ_4, Ψ_5, and Ψ_6 are defined as orthogonal, they are **correlated** contrasts because the sample sizes for the groups are not equal ($n_1 = 53$, $n_2 = 190$, $n_3 = 122$, and $n_4 = 109$). Therefore, to determine the unique contribution of a contrast (Ψ_4, Ψ_5, or Ψ_6), we need to remove (partial out) its correlation with the other two contrasts. In SPSS, this can be achieved with the syntax provided in Figure 21.6.

Figure 21.6 *SPSS syntax for MANOVA with planned correlated contrasts for the comparison of four ethnic groups on a set of two dependent variables, Y_1 and Y_2.*

```
==========================================================================
MANOVA Y1, Y2 BY method(1,4)
  /METHOD = SEQUENTIAL
  /CONTRAST(method) = SPECIAL(1 1 1 1  1 1 -1 -1  1 -1 0 0  0 0 1 -1)
  /PARTITION(method)
  /DESIGN = method(1), method(2), method(3)
  / DESIGN = method(2), method(3), method(1)
  / DESIGN = method(3), method(1), method(2)
  / PRINT CELLINFO(MEANS) SIGNIF(EFSIZE) HOMOGENEITY(COCHRAN, BOXM).
==========================================================================
```

With the subcommand METHOD = SEQUENTIAL, each contrast is adjusted only for all contrasts to the left of it in any DESIGN subcommand that follows. The coefficients for the contrasts are enclosed in parentheses after SPECIAL in the subcommand CONTRAST, where the first four 1's indicate that there are four groups in this case, followed by the coding of the contrasts Ψ_4, Ψ_5, and Ψ_6, respectively. In the DESIGN subcommand, method(1), method(2), and method(3) stand for the contrasts in the order they are specified in the command CONTRAST (i.e., Ψ_4, Ψ_5, and Ψ_6, respectively). The purpose of using three DESIGN subcommands in this syntax is to adjust each contrast for its correlation with any other contrast. Figure 21.7 shows the results produced by the second subcommand, /DESIGN = method(2), method(3), method(1), where the contrast method(1) = Ψ_4 is adjusted for its correlation with the contrasts to the left of it, method(3) = Ψ_6 and method(2) = Ψ_5.

The results show that the unique contribution of Ψ_4 is statistically significant (a) on the set of two dependent variables, as indicated by the multivariate *Wilk's lambda* test, $\Lambda = .56$, $F(2, 468) = 186.34$, $p < .001$; and (b) on each dependent variable separately, as indicated by the univariate F-test for Y_1, $F(1, 469) = 341.34$, $p < .001$, and Y_2, $F(1, 469) = 233.52$, $p < .001$. Given that the contrast Ψ_4 represents H_{04}: $(\mu_1 + \mu_2)/2 = (\mu_3 + \mu_4)/2$, this means that the average of the first two groups (experimental conditions) differs from the average of the third and fourth groups (control conditions) on the set of two dependent variables and on each of them separately.

The results for Ψ_5 (not shown here) indicate that this contrast is not statistically significant on the set of two variables, $\Lambda = .99$, $F(2, 468) = 0.53$, $p = .586$. Thus, given that Ψ_5 represents H_{05}: $\mu_1 = \mu_2$, the two experimental groups do not differ on the set of two dependent variables. These groups do not differ on each variable separately either, as Ψ_5 is not statistically significant either on Y_1, $F(1, 469) = 0.90$, $p = .343$, or on Y_2, $F(1, 469) = 0.04$, $p = .835$.

Finally, the results for Ψ_6 (also not shown here) indicate that this contrast is statistically significant on the set of two dependent variables, $\Lambda = .57$, $F(2, 468) = 177.05$, $p < .001$, as well as on each of them separately, as indicated by the univariate F-test for Y_1, $F(1, 469) = 310.67$, $p < .001$, and Y_2, $F(1, 469) = 243.08$, $p < .001$. Thus, given that Ψ_6 represents H_{06}: $\mu_3 = \mu_4$, the two control groups differ on the set of two dependent variables and on each of them separately.

The results presented in this example should be interpreted with caution as the Box's M test was statistically significant, $\chi^2(9) = 674.60$, $p < .001$, thus indicating that the multivariate assumptions of equal variance-covariance matrices is *not* met in this case. Although MANOVA is relatively robust to violations of this assumption, additional analyses (e.g., using appropriate data transformations) can be employed to ensure validity of the results.

Figure 21.7 *Selected SPSS output for the multivariate and univariate significance of the contrast representing the null hypothesis H_{04}: $(\mu_1 + \mu_2)/2 = (\mu_3 + \mu_4)/2$.*

EFFECT .. METHOD(1)
Multivariate Tests of Significance (S = 1, M = 0, N = 233)

Test Name	Value	Exact F	Hypoth. DF	Error DF	Sig. of F
Pillais	.44331	186.34371	2.00	468.00	.000
Hotellings	.79634	186.34371	2.00	468.00	.000
Wilks	.55669	186.34371	2.00	468.00	.000
Roys	.44331				

Note.. F statistics are exact.

EFFECT .. METHOD(1) (Cont.)
Univariate F-tests with (1,469) D. F.

Variable	Hypoth. SS	Error SS	Hypoth. MS	Error MS	F	Sig. of F
Y1	347.90617	478.02673	347.90617	1.01925	341.33655	.000
Y2	70.41833	141.42823	70.41833	.30155	233.51913	.000

21.8 Sample Size in MANOVA

Determining an appropriate sample size with MANOVA applications is not a simple matter, as it involves the consideration of factors such as the number of groups, the number of dependent variables, the effect size, the power of the test, and the level of statistical significance established (e.g., $\alpha = .05$ or .01). Using too many dependent variables is not recommended because the power of the test tends to decrease when the number of dependent variables increases, meaning that larger sample sizes would be needed in order to maintain a desired level of test power. Also, small differences on a large number of dependent variables that do not play a strong substantive role may obscure differences on fewer, yet substantively important, dependent variables. Further, problems related to the reliability of scores on the dependent variables may accumulate when the number of such variables increases. All this implies that researchers may consider reducing an initially large number of dependent variables by selecting only those that are expected to have important theoretical or empirical roles in the research questions at hand. In cases when the initial pool of available dependent variables represents items on an instrument (e.g., test or survey), it might be better to use subscales of the instrument, thus obtaining fewer, yet more meaningful, dependent variables. If such subscales are not defined *a priori*, they can be identified by the means of factor analysis which is discussed in the next chapter.

Tables that are designed to assist researchers to determine the appropriate sample size in MANOVA applications are provided, for example, in Stevens (2002) for a pre-specified number of groups, number of dependent variables, effect size, test power, and level of statistical significance (α). Briefly, for studies with three to five groups, rough estimates of the sample size needed to maintain a power of .70, at the .05 level of significance, is (a) $n \cong 16$, with a very large effect size; (b) $n \cong 31$, with a large effect size; (c) $n \cong 54$, with a medium effect size; and (d) $n \cong 120$, with a small effect size. Recall that the univariate effect size (*ES*) shows the amount (in standard deviation units) of separation between the population means (see Chapter 14, Section 14.8). According to guidelines proposed by Cohen (1988), an effect size close to .20 is *small*, an effect size close to .50 is *medium*, and an effect size close to .80 is *large*.

21.9 Summary

- **Multivariate analysis of variance (MANOVA)** is used to address research questions related to group differences on a set of (two or more) dependent variables, taking into account possible correlations among them.
- A statistically significant omnibus MANOVA test (e.g., *Wilk's lambda*), does not necessarily protect against an inflated type I error rate in follow-ups with univariate ANOVAs.
- Separate ANOVAs, with a Bonferroni adjustment of the level of significance, can be used when the dependent variables are conceptually independent of one another, for exploratory purposes, or when comparing results with previous studies. Keep in mind that separate ANOVAs do not take into account correlations among the dependent variables.
- MANOVA is appropriate when a researcher wants to investigate questions about group differences on linear composites of dependent variables. A linear composite, referred to also as a *linear discriminant function* (*LDF*), represents a weighted sum of the dependent variables.
- An *LDF* is interpreted as a latent variable (construct, dimension) which is defined by the meaning of those original variables that have high weights (correlations) on the construct, excluding the variables that provide redundant information.
- The linear discriminant functions (*LDF*s) are determined in decreasing order according to their contribution to the group separation. The *LDF*s are uncorrelated, since after an *LDF* is determined, its contribution to the group is "partialled out" (removed).
- The omnibus null hypothesis in MANOVA states that the group centroids are equal for the study population. A statistically significant *Wilk's lambda* for the omnibus MANOVA test indicates that *at least one* construct (*LDF*) has emerged as a linear combination of dependent variables that maximally separates the groups. A subsequent discriminant analysis is needed to test the *LDF*s for statistical significance, define them substantively, and determine their role in separating the groups.
- With K groups compared on m dependent variables, the number of possible *LDF*s is the smaller number of $(K - 1)$ and m.
- Information about the relative contribution of a dependent variable to the separation of the compared groups is provided by the *F-to-remove* statistic, which indicates the impact of this dependent variable (if deleted) on the decrease of group separation. The larger the *F-to-remove* statistic, the more important is the dependent variable.
- Another perspective in MANOVA relates to group comparisons planned a priori by the researchers. The *contrasts* associated with such comparisons may be *uncorrelated* (i.e., orthogonal contrasts with a balanced MANOVA) or *correlated.*

• Uncorrelated contrasts are preferable, as their total contribution to group separation is unique (i.e., not confounded by the contribution of the other contrasts).

• When the contrasts correlate, the unique contribution of each contrast is determined after adjusting this contrast for its correlation with the other contrasts.

21.10 Study Questions

1 What is the purpose of MANOVA?

2 What does the omnibus null hypothesis in MANOVA state?

3 Does a statistically significant omnibus MANOVA test guard against inflated type I error rate in univariate ANOVAs?

4 What does a statistically significant *Wilk's lambda* indicate?

5 Is it possible that there are group differences on the set of dependent variables, but no group differences on individual dependent variables?

6 What is a *linear discriminant function* (*LDF*)?

7 How many *LDF*s are possible with the comparison of five groups on three dependent variables?

8 Is it possible that some *LDF*s are correlated ?

9 What is the purpose of using contrasts to test null hypotheses with MANOVA?

10 When are two contrasts orthogonal?

11 When do correlated contrasts occur?

12 What is the advantage of using uncorrelated contrasts in MANOVA?

13 Using the SPSS data file **EXAMPLE_21_1.sav** [http://cehd.gmu.edu/book/dimitrov], test the following MANOVA null hypotheses for the comparison of the three treatment groups (E_1, E_2, and Control) on the set of five independent variables (Y_1,Y_2, Y_3, Y_4, Y_5) using the appropriate contrast coding:

$$H_{01}: (\mu_1 + \mu_2)/2 = \mu_3 \text{ and } H_{02}: \mu_1 = \mu_2$$

[*Hint*: Adapt the SPSS syntax with correlated contrasts for the case of three groups with two contrasts. You will need two **DESIGN** subcommands in this case.]

14 Using the SPSS data file **QUESTION_21_14.sav** [http://cehd.gmu.edu/book/dimitrov], perform a MANOVA with a subsequent discriminant analysis following Example 21.1. The independent variable in this case is **socioeconomic status (SES)** defined with three levels (1 = high, 2 = middle, 3 = low). There are four dependent variables [named **Y1**, **Y2**, **Y3**, and **Y4**] that represent the scores [on a 5-point scale] of 758 high school students on *academic performance* (**Y1**), *attitude toward school* (**Y2**), *proficiency test performance* (**Y3**), and *motivation* (**Y4**).

CHAPTER 22

EXPLORATORY FACTOR ANALYSIS

Researchers in education and related fields often try to simplify and explain the complexity of variables and relationships among them by determining a smaller number of constructs (factors) that underlie such relationships. This task involves the application of statistical procedures known as *factor analysis*. Recall that when discussing multiple regression or MANOVA, factor analysis was recommended to reduce the number of predictor variables, thus reducing multicollinearity, or to reduce the number of initially available dependent variables. Factor analysis plays a key role in validation of instruments such as tests, questionnaires, or inventories in education and related fields. For example, Erford, Balcolm, and Moore-Thomas (2007) used factor analysis to examine the underlying structure of a 40-item teacher and parent rating scale called the *Screening Test for Emotional Problems* (STEP). In general, **factor analysis** is used to determine (a) how many factors underlie a set of variables, (b) which variables form which factor, (c) the correlations between individual variables and factors, (d) the correlations (if any) among factors, and (e) what proportion of the variance in the variables is accounted for by the factors. An **exploratory factor analysis** is used when researchers do not have enough information to hypothesize how many factors underlie the set of observable variables and which variables form which factor.

22.1 Correlated Variables and Underlying Factors

Let's examine the correlation matrix in Figure 22.1 [the sample of 30 observations for the four variables is provided in Example 22.1]. As can be seen, there is a statistically significant correlation between X_1 and X_2, $r_{12} = .644$, $p < .001$, as well as between X_3 and X_4, $r_{34} = .660$, $p < .001$, but none of the variables in the (X_1, X_2) pair correlates with a variable in the (X_3, X_4) pair.

Figure 22.1 *SPSS output for Pearson correlations among four variables*

Correlations

		X1	X2	X3	X4
X1	Pearson Correlation	1.000	.644**	-.241	-.173
	Sig. (2-tailed)		.000	.200	.362
	N	30.000	30	30	30
X2	Pearson Correlation	.644**	1.000	-.039	-.178
	Sig. (2-tailed)	.000		.839	.348
	N	30	30.000	30	30
X3	Pearson Correlation	-.241	-.039	1.000	.660**
	Sig. (2-tailed)	.200	.839		.000
	N	30	30	30.000	30
X4	Pearson Correlation	-.173	-.178	.660**	1.000
	Sig. (2-tailed)	.362	.348	.000	
	N	30	30	30	30.000

**. Correlation is significant at the 0.01 level (2-tailed).

The correlation between the variables X_3 and X_4 (.660) indicates that they have something in common — a factor, denoted here F_1, that accounts for some part of their variance. Likewise, the correlation between X_1 and X_2 (.644) suggests that they relate to a second factor, F_2, accounting for some part of their variance. As X_3 and X_4 do not correlate with X_1 and X_2, we can expect that the two factors, F_1 and F_2, are uncorrelated (orthogonal) — see Figure 22.2.

The labeling of a factor depends on the meaning of the variables that correlate with this factor. In this case, the correlation matrix in Figure 22.1 is produced by the scores of 30 children on *spelling* (X_1), *reading* (X_2), *coloring* (X_3), and *cutting* (X_4), on a 5-point scale. Thus, given that factor F_1 correlates with X_3 and X_4, this factor can be labeled "motor skills," whereas factor F_2 can be labeled "verbal skills" because it correlates with X_1 and X_2.

Figure 22.2 *Four variables and two orthogonal factors*

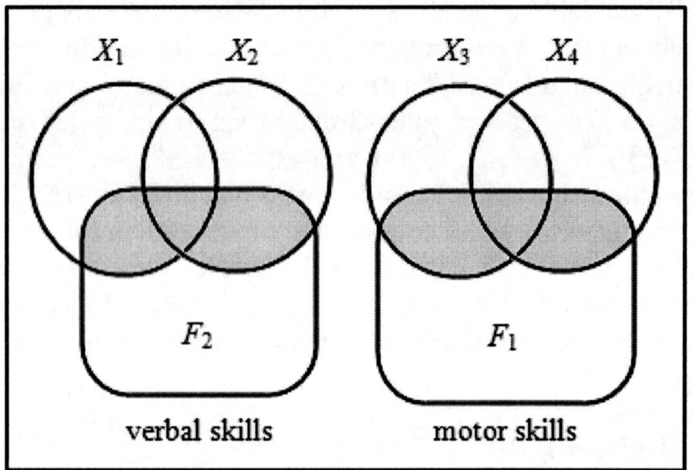

With a small number of variables, the examination of the correlation matrix may provide general information about factors that underlie these correlations. However, situations in which there are just a few variables and a "clean" underlying structure of orthogonal (uncorrelated) factors are exceptions in educational research. Whatever the case, more accurate and valid information about the factorial structure of a set of variables can be obtained through factor analysis.

22.2 Basic Concepts in Exploratory Factor Analysis

An **exploratory factor analysis (EFA)** is typically used when researchers do not have enough theoretical or empirical information to hypothesize how many factors underlie the set of observable variables and which variables form which factor. An EFA defines factors through a mathematical procedure that usually maximizes the total variance in the observed variables accounted for by the factors. There are several types of EFA procedures, each with different assumptions and yielding somewhat different results.

Under the commonly used **principal factor methods** in the EFA, the first factor to be extracted from the correlation matrix of observed variables is a *weighted linear combination* of all observed variables that produces the *highest squared correlation* between the variables and the factor. The second factor maximizes the variance extracted from the residual correlation matrix obtained after removing the effect of the first factor. Therefore, the second factor is orthogonal to (uncorrelated with) the first factor. Then, the third factor maximizes the variance extracted from the residual correlation matrix after removing the effect of the first two factors. Thus, the third factor is orthogonal to the first two factors. This process continues until all factors that meet a prespecified statistical criterion are extracted. Any two factors are orthogonal to one another because the extraction of any factor is based on the residualized correlation matrix, after removing the effects of all preceding factors.

Suppose there are two factors (F_1 and F_2) that underlie a set of four variables, X_1, X_2, X_3, and X_4. Under the so-called **full component model** (see Table 22.1), the score of an individual (i) on any variable (X_m) is reproduced with the equation

$$X_{im} = w_{m1}F_{1i} + w_{m2}F_{2i}, \quad \textbf{(22.1)}$$

where w_{m1} and w_{m2} are the "weights" for variable X_m on the factors F_1 and F_2, respectively, whereas F_{1i} and F_{2i} are the scores of individual i on F_1 and F_2, respectively; (m = 1, 2, 3, 4). In the general case of k factors (components), the equation for the full component model is

$$X_{im} = w_{m1}F_{1i} + w_{m2}F_{2i} + \ldots + w_{mk}F_{ki}. \quad \textbf{(22.2)}$$

Typically, the smaller components are dismissed as due to inaccuracy of the model's data fit for a particular sample. Thus, **truncated components** are the usual form of a component analysis.

Table 22.1 *Full component model with four variables and two factors*

	Factor	
Variable	F_1	F_2
X_1	w_{11}	w_{12}
X_2	w_{21}	w_{22}
X_3	w_{31}	w_{32}
X_4	w_{41}	w_{42}

In another model, referred to as the **common factor model**, an additional term, $w_{mu}U_{im}$, is added to Equation 22.1 to reflect the assumption that there is a "unique" factor (U_m) for each variable, X_m. The extended form of Equation 22.2 under the common factor model is

$$X_{im} = w_{m1}F_{1i} + w_{m2}F_{2i} + \ldots + w_{mk}F_{ki} + w_{mu}U_{im}. \quad \textbf{(22.3)}$$

Table 22.2 shows the common factor model with four variables and two common factors. The weights for an observed variable (w_{m1}, w_{m2}, ..., w_{mk}) are called **pattern coefficients**, whereas the correlations between a factor and the observed variables are referred to as **structure coefficients** for that factor. The pattern coefficients are also referred to as "factor coefficients," or "factor *loadings,*" although both terms are occasionally used to refer to the structure coefficients as well. The structure coefficients are used to determine which variables form which factors, thus allowing the researchers to interpret and label the factors. When factors are orthogonal (uncorrelated), the pattern coefficients equal the structure coefficients.

Table 22.2 *Common factor model with four variables and two common factors*

	Common factors		Unique factors			
Variable	F_1	F_2	U_1	U_2	U_3	U_4
X_1	w_{11}	w_{12}	w_{1u_1}	0	0	0
X_2	w_{21}	w_{22}	0	w_{2u_2}	0	0
X_3	w_{31}	w_{32}	0	0	w_{3u_3}	0
X_4	w_{41}	w_{42}	0	0	0	w_{4u_4}

22.3 Communalities and Eigenvalues

The proportion of the variance in a given variable which is accounted for by the common factors is called **communality** of this variable. The communality of a variable, X_m, is denoted h_m^2 [thus, h_1^2 is the communality of X_1, h_2^2 is the communality of X_2, and so on]. Suppose that the two common factors in Table 22.2 are correlated, and r_{12} is their Pearson correlation coefficient. It is known that the communality h_m^2 in this case is

$$h_m^2 = \frac{w_{m1}^2 + w_{m2}^2 + 2w_{m1}w_{m2}r_{12}}{\sigma_m^2}, \tag{22.4}$$

where σ_m^2 is the variance of the variable, X_m ; ($m = 1, 2, 3, 4$).

When the scores are presented in standard form (z-scores), which is typically the case in factor analysis, then $\sigma_m^2 = 1$. In this case, Equation 22.4 becomes

$$h_m^2 = w_{m1}^2 + w_{m2}^2 + 2w_{m1}w_{m2}r_{12} \tag{22.5}$$

Further simplification is obtained when the two factors are orthogonal ($r_{12} = 0$) and the observed scores on the variables are standardized ($\sigma_m^2 = 1$):

$$h_m^2 = w_{m1}^2 + w_{m2}^2. \tag{22.6}$$

The **eigenvalue** of a factor equals the *sum of squared loadings* (SSL) for this factor. Thus, the eigenvalue of a factor indicates the proportion of the total variance for all variables that is accounted for by this factor. For the case of four variables and two factors in Table 22.2, for example, the eigenvalue of F_1 and F_2, denoted λ_1 and λ_2, respectively, are:

$$\lambda_1 = w_{11}^2 + w_{21}^2 + w_{31}^2 + w_{41}^2 \text{ and} \tag{22.7}$$

$$\lambda_2 = w_{12}^2 + w_{22}^2 + w_{32}^2 + w_{42}^2. \tag{22.8}$$

The shaded area in Figure 22.3 (left panel) represents the *communality* for variable X_1 (i.e., the proportion of the variance in X_1 accounted for by the two factors, F_1 and F_2), whereas the shaded area in the right panel represents the *eigenvalue* for factor F_1 [it is assumed that two correlated factors, F_1 and F_2, underlie the set of four variables, X_1, X_2, X_3, and X_4].

Figure 22.3 *Graphical representation of the communality for a variable (X_1) and the eigenvalue for a factor (F_1) in the case of four variables and two correlated factors*

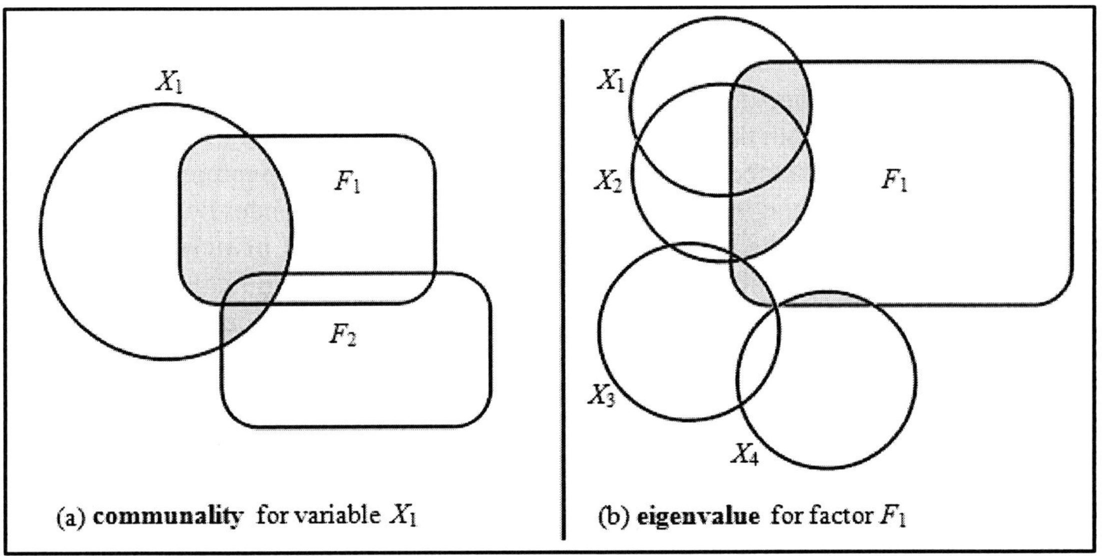

22.4 The Principle Factor Method of Extracting Factors

Let **R** denote the correlation matrix of v variables ($X_1, X_2, \ldots, X_v$) [**R** is symmetric — e.g., see Figure 22.1]. Also, let **P** denote the matrix of pattern coefficients for the v variables and k underlying factors ($F_1, F_2, \ldots, F_k$). For the case of four variables and two factors in Table 22.2, for example, **P** will be the (4 x 2) matrix of pattern coefficients [the unique factor loading are not included in **P**]. Further, let **P**′denote the *transposed* matrix of **P** — that is, **P**′ is obtained by changing the roles of rows and columns in matrix **P** [e.g., for a (4 x 2) factor pattern matrix, the transposed matrix will be a (2 x 4) matrix].

When the factors ($F_1, F_2, \ldots, F_k$) are orthogonal, it has been shown that the correlation matrix **R** can be "decomposed" into the product of the factor pattern matrix and its transposed matrix:

$$\mathbf{R} = \mathbf{PP'} \qquad \textbf{(22.9)}$$

Equation 22.9 is referred to as the *fundamental equation of factor analysis.* When the factors are not orthogonal, Equation 22.9 is extended to take into account the correlations among them and the unique factor loadings (e.g., Table 22.2, right panel). The resulting matrix algebra equation and related technical transformations are beyond the scope of this book (e.g., Gorsuch, 1983).

Solutions of the matrix algebra equation 22.9 are obtained by using methods referred to as the **principle factor method.** Under this method, the solution for the first factor for a set of v variables ($X_1, X_2, \ldots, X_v$) represents a vector of v factor loadings ($w_{11}, w_{21}, \ldots, w_{v1}$) so that the linear combination $w_{11}X_1 + w_{21}X_2 + \ldots + w_{v1}X_v$ maximally correlates with the factor. Thus, the first factor accounts for the maximum possible amount of the variance extracted from the correlation matrix **R**. The sum of squared factor loadings for the first factor, F_1, is called the *eigenvalue* for this factor (λ_1) — e.g., see Equation 22.7 for the case of four variables.

After the first factor is extracted, its effect is removed from the correlation matrix **R**, so a residualized correlation matrix is produced. The solution of factor loadings for the second factor (w_{12}, w_{22}, ..., w_{v2}) is obtained so that this factor maximizes the amount of variance extracted from the residualized correlation matrix. Thus, the second factor is uncorrelated with the first factor. The sum of squared factor loadings for the second factor, F_2, is called the *eigenvalue* for this factor (λ_2) — e.g., see Equation 22.8 for the case of four variables. Then a third factor is extracted so that it is uncorrelated with the first two factors, and so on.

The correlation matrix obtained from the extracted factors is the **reproduced correlation matrix**. The principle factor method minimizes the sum of squared differences between the original and reproduced correlations. The principle factor method is called (a) **principal component analysis (PCA)**, when it is used under the full component factor model (Equation 22.2), or (b) **principle factor analysis (PFA)**, when used under the common factor model (Equation 22.3). As already described, the principle factor method produces orthogonal factors and does not work directly when correlated factors are expected. Therefore, the initial orthogonal solutions obtained under the principle factor method are "rotated" to produce more interpretable solutions.

22.5 Rotation of Factors

Factors extracted with the initial orthogonal solutions under the principle factor method are usually difficult to interpret. To address this problem, the initial factors are "rotated" to more desirable positions. A rotated factor represents a linear combination of the initial factors and is much easier to interpret. In fact, the rotated factors explain the same amount of the total variance of the observed variables, but they divide it up in a way that facilitates their interpretation. To illustrate this, let us examine Figure 22.4, which provides the initial extraction of two orthogonal factors, F_1 and F_2, from the correlation matrix in Figure 22.1. The two tables in Figure 22.4 come from the SPSS output for an exploratory factor analysis of 30 observations on four variables provided in Example 22.1 (page 377). As the two factors are orthogonal, the factor loadings in each table are both pattern coefficients *and* structure coefficients (correlations between variables and factors). The results in the two tables in Figure 22.4 are graphically represented in Figure 22.5.

As can be seen, the initial solutions for the two factors are difficult to interpret, as they do not provide a clear picture of which variables relate to which factor. For example, the initial "coordinates" of the variable X_1 are −.732 on F_1 and .529 on F_2 (w_{11}= −.732 and w_{12}= .529). After an orthogonal rotation of the two factors (i.e., keeping their initial orthogonal relationship), the new coordinates of X_1 are -.160 (on F_1^*) and .889 (on F_2^*), thus clearly indicating that the first variable, X_1, correlates with the second factor, F_2 (or F_2^* after the rotation). The same holds true for the other three variables, so the rotated solutions clearly indicate that (a) the first factor is defined by the variables X_3 (*coloring*) and X_4 (*cutting*), so this factor can be labeled "motor skills," and (b) the second factor is defined by the variables X_2 (*reading*) and X_1 (*spelling*), so this factor is labeled "reading skills."

The factor loadings for the two rotated factors (Figure 22.4, right panel) reveal a factor structure which is close to what is known as a *simple structure***.** Specifically, a factor has a **simple structure** when (a) each variable has at least one zero loading; (b) each factor has a set of linearly independent variables whose factor loadings are zero; (c) for every pair of factors, there are variables whose loadings are zero for one factor but not for the other; (d) for every pair of factors, a large proportion of the variables have zero loadings on both factors whenever more than about four factors are extracted; and (e) for every pair of factors, there is only a small number of variables with nonzero loadings on both (Thurstone, 1947).

Figure 22.4 *Initial and rotated extraction of two orthogonal factors from four variables*

Component Matrix[a]

	Component	
	1	2
X1_spelling	-.732	.529
X4_cutting	.725	.539
X3_coloring	.700	.593
X2_reading	-.646	.648

Extraction Method: Principal Component Analysis.
a. 2 components extracted.

Initially extracted factors (components)

Rotated Component Matrix[a]

	Component	
	1	2
X3_coloring	.916	-.058
X4_cutting	.896	-.114
X2_reading	-.017	.915
X1_spelling	-.160	.889

Extraction Method: Principal Component Analysis.
Rotation Method: Varimax with Kaiser Normalization.
a. Rotation converged in 3 iterations.

Rotated factors (components)

Figure 22.5 Initial factors, F_1 and F_2, and their rotated counterparts, F_1^* and F_2^*.

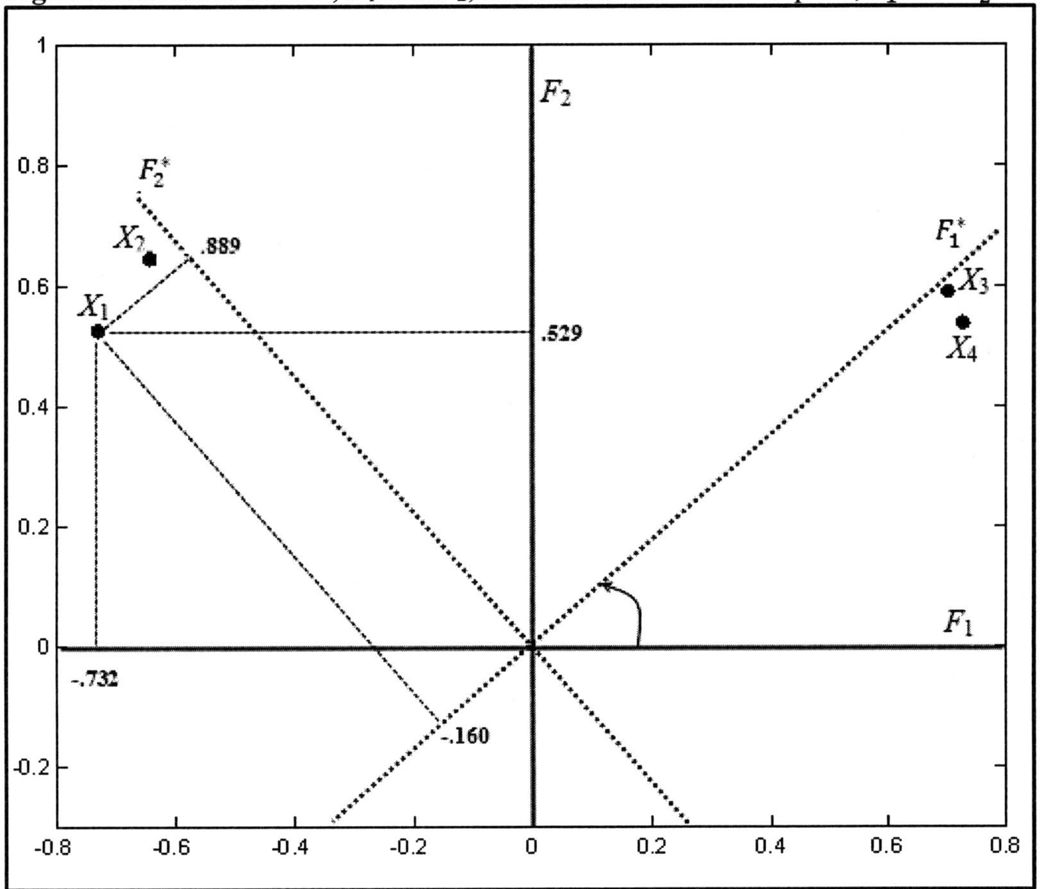

The criteria for a simple structure are used as guiding principles in most approaches to rotation of factors. With a frequently used rotation, called **varimax**, the variance of the squared factor loadings across all factors is maximized. The rotation position which maximizes the variance across all factors is referred to as the *varimax solution*. Keep in mind, however, that the varimax rotation is inappropriate when there is a tendency that a single general factor underlies the set of observable variables. For example, it is inappropriate to apply varimax to test items with high internal consistency (e.g., indicated by a high Cronbach's alpha coefficient) because high internal consistency means that there is one general factor underlying the test items.

When correlated factors are expected, an **oblique rotation** should be used instead. With an oblique rotation, the angles between the factors are no longer orthogonal when represented geometrically. Such rotation is appropriate when the correlations among factors are minor to moderate in magnitude. The main approaches to an oblique rotation [available in SPSS] are the following:

- **Quartimax** rotation minimizes the sum of the crossproducts of the squared variable loadings. This rotation method is not very helpful to exploratory research goals, as it often yields to a general factor with which most variables correlate to a high or moderate degree.
- **Equimax** rotation compromises between Varimax and Quartimax criteria.
- **Direct oblimin** rotation produces higher eigenvalues but diminishes the interpretability of the factors.
- **Promax** rotation uses the initial orthogonal solution (e.g., obtained via varimax) as a basis for producing an ideal oblique solution. An improved solution using promax versus an orthogonal solution is indicated when (a) the moderate and low loadings with promax are lower than in the orthogonal solution and (b) the high loadings in the orthogonal solution remain relatively high with promax. Decreasing factor loadings is obtained in promax by raising them to a higher power. In SPSS, the power index with promax, denoted $\boldsymbol{k}$, is set to four ($\boldsymbol{k} = 4$), but one can vary the power in a search for the simplest structure with the least correlation among factors.

22.6 Determining the Number of Factors

In typical applications of exploratory factor analysis (EFA) researchers do not have enough theoretical or empirical information to hypothesize how many factors underlie the set of observable variables. This naturally gives rise to the question about the proper number of factors to be extracted from the correlation matrix. The statistical translation of this question is whether there is a statistically significant variance left in the residual correlation matrix after a certain number of factors have been extracted. Recall that the *residual correlation matrix* is obtained as a difference between the original correlation matrix and the correlation matrix reproduced by the extracted factors (see Equation 22.2). If the residual correlation matrix is statistically significant, then the search for additional factor(s) continues. If not, the proper number of factors has been found and the extraction of factors terminates.

22.6.1 "Eigenvalues of one or higher" Criterion

A quick first step in determining the number of factors is to examine the eigenvalues obtained with a principal components extraction. A factor with an eigenvalue smaller than 1 is not considered as important because the variance that each standardized variable contributes to a principal component extraction equals 1. This is the basis for the "eigenvalues of one or higher" criterion for determining the number of factors. This approach is known as the **root ≥ 1 criterion** [the eigenvalues are referred to also as *characteristic roots* — mathematical solutions in extracting factors.] The "root ≥ 1" criterion works relatively well when the number of variables, v, is 40 or smaller ($v \leq 40$) and the sample size is large. In this case, a rule of thumb is that the number of factors is expected to be between the number of variables divided by 5 and the number of variables divided by 3 (i.e., from $v/5$ to $v/3$). For example, a principle component extraction with 30 variables is expected to produce between 6 and 10 factors [$v/5 = 30/5 = 6$ and $v/3 = 30/3 = 10$]. In other situations, the "root ≥ 1" (eigenvalues of one or higher) criterion tends to overestimate the number of factors.

22.6.2 Scree Test

A reasonably accurate approach to determining the number of factors is the so-called **scree test** (Cattell, 1966). This test involves plotting the eigenvalues in descending order of their magnitude against their factor numbers and determining where they level off. The "elbow" — the break between the steep slope and the leveling-off indicates the number of factors. The term "scree" is taken from the geological description of the rubble at the bottom of a mountain.

Figure 22.6 shows the scree plot provided with the SPSS output for a principal component analysis of 11 variables. The scree plot indicates that there are two factors that underlie the set of 11 variables. This decision is also supported by the "root ≥ 1" criterion, as the eigenvalues of these two factors are greater than 1. Keep in mind, however, that the scree plot approach to selecting the number of factors involves a certain amount of subjective judgment.

Figure 22.6 *Scree plot for the principal component analysis of 11 variables*

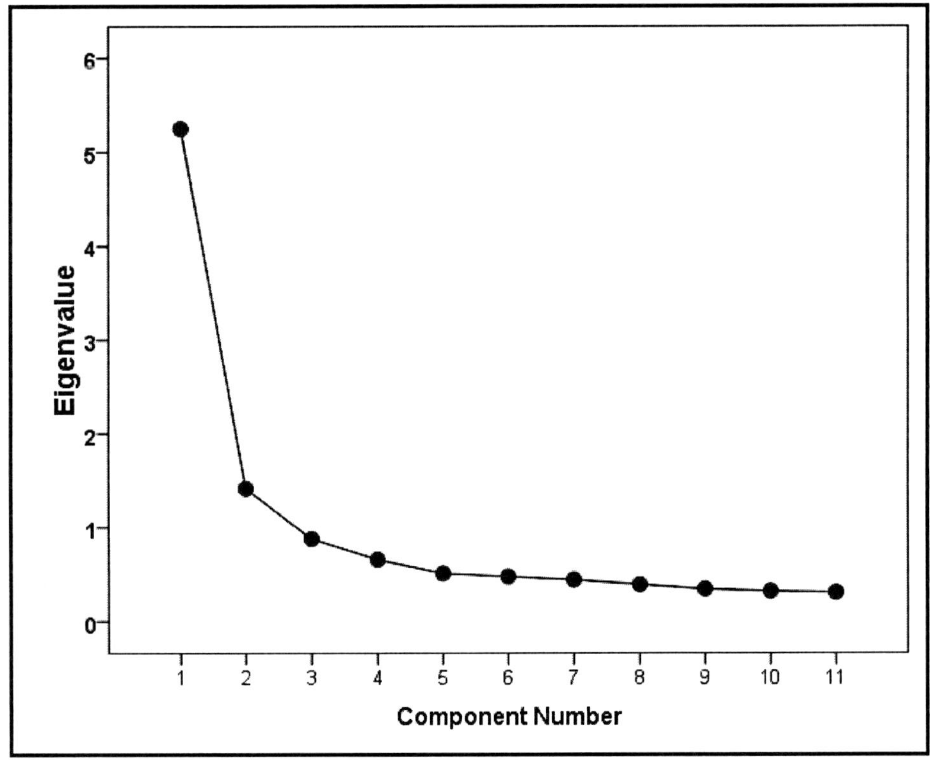

22.6.3 Parallel Analysis

A major limitation of the criterion for retaining factors with eigenvalues larger than 1, is that it tends to overestimate the number of factors due to sampling error. In an attempt to overcome this limitation, Horn (1965) proposed an approach to retaining factors referred to as **parallel analysis (PA)**. The logic behind PA is that the eigenvalues of meaningful factors that underlie a set of variables should be larger than the eigenvalues of "parallel" factors derived from random data sets with the same sample size and number of variables as the original data set.

The PA can be described as a stepwise procedure under which (a) a data set with the same sample size and number of variables as the real data set is randomly generated, (b) the eigenvalues of all factors extracted from the random data under the principle component analysis are computed and "stored," (c) these two steps are repeated a sufficiently large number of times (e.g. >1000), and (d) the eigenvalues obtained from all random data sets are then averaged and compared to the eigenvalues obtained from the real data set. Specifically, the first real eigenvalue is compared to the first average random eigenvalue, the second real eigenvalue is compared to the second average random eigenvalue, and so on. Factors corresponding to the real eigenvalues that are greater than the parallel average random eigenvalues are retained. Actual eigenvalues less than or equal to the parallel average random eigenvalues are considered to be a result of sampling error. Glorfeld (1995) suggested that, instead of using the *mean* of the random eigenvalues, it is better to use their upper percentiles (e.g., the 95th percentile) to determine whether the real eigenvalues are larger than what could be expected by chance.

Table 22.3 provides the real eigenvalues obtained via the PCA option in SPSS, as well as the *mean* and the 95th percentile of simulated eigenvalue distributions obtained via the O'Conner (2000) procedure for parallel analysis (http://people.ok.ubc.ca/brioconn/nfactors/nfactors.html). The SPSS data file (1028 observations on 11 items), named EXAMPLE_23_1, is available at the web site for the book (http://cehd.gmu.edu/dimitrov/book). These data, used also to produce the scree plot in Figure 22.6, are described in more details in the next chapter (see, Example 23.1). As can be seen, the *real* eigenvalues for the first two factors (5.295 and 1.410) exceed both the mean and the 95th percentile of the random eigenvalues thus suggesting that two factors (F_1 and F_2) should be retained. This is consistent with the two-factor solution suggested by the scree plot in Figure 22.6, but such consistency is not always the case.

Table 22.3 *Parallel analysis with 11 variables and 1028 observations*

FACTOR	Real eigenvalues	Random eigenvalues *Mean*	Random eigenvalues 95th percentile
F_1	5.295	1.151	1.185
F_2	1.410	1.108	1.131
F_3	0.883	1.078	1.101
F_4	0.643	1.049	1.067
F_5	0.498	1.023	1.041
F_6	0.483	0.998	1.017
F_7	0.448	0.973	0.994
F_8	0.379	0.948	0.966
F_9	0.337	0.920	0.939
F_{10}	0.316	0.892	0.913
F_{11}	0.309	0.859	0.884

22.7 Using SPSS for Exploratory Factor Analysis

SPSS provides procedures for exploratory factor analysis with options for orthogonal rotation (varimax) and oblique rotations (quartimax, equimax, direct oblimin, and promax) described in Section 22.1.4. In this section, Example 22.1 illustrates how to use SPSS to conduct an exploratory factor analysis with orthogonal rotation.

EXAMPLE 22.1 The data in this example represent the scores of 30 children on *spelling* (X_1), *reading* (X_2), *coloring* (X_3), and *cutting* (X_4), on a 5-point scale. The correlation matrix for these data is provided with Figure 22.1, with a discussion of two factors that seem to underlie the set of four variables. This correlation matrix is used now for a principle component analysis.

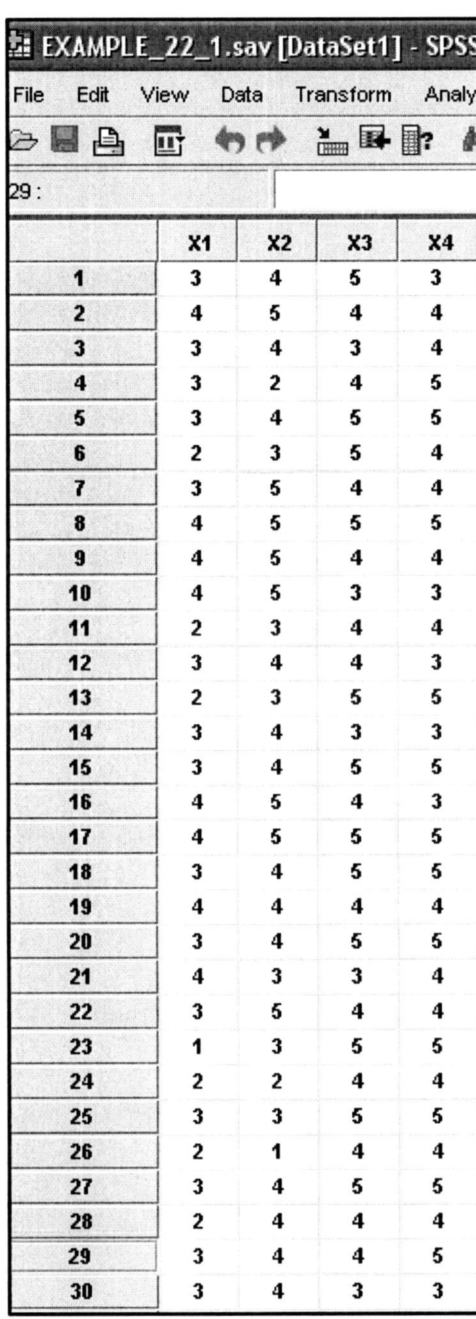

	X1	X2	X3	X4
1	3	4	5	3
2	4	5	4	4
3	3	4	3	4
4	3	2	4	5
5	3	4	5	5
6	2	3	5	4
7	3	5	4	4
8	4	5	5	5
9	4	5	4	4
10	4	5	3	3
11	2	3	4	4
12	3	4	4	3
13	2	3	5	5
14	3	4	3	3
15	3	4	5	5
16	4	5	4	3
17	4	5	5	5
18	3	4	5	5
19	4	4	4	4
20	3	4	5	5
21	4	3	3	4
22	3	5	4	4
23	1	3	5	5
24	2	2	4	4
25	3	3	5	5
26	2	1	4	4
27	3	4	5	5
28	2	4	4	4
29	3	4	4	5
30	3	4	3	3

To use SPSS for principle component analysis with varimax orthogonal rotation, follow the steps:

1. Click **Analyze**, click **Data Reduction**, and click **Factor**.
2. While holding the *Ctrl* key down, click on **X1_spelling**, **X2_reading**, **X3_coloring**, and **X4_cutting**, and then click ▶ to move them to the box **Variables**.
3. Click **Extraction**.
4. In the dialog box *Factor Analysis: Extraction*, select **Principle Component** [which appears as a first option for *Method*], and check **Scree plot** in the *Display* panel [**Unrotated factor solution** is checked by default in SPSS.] Click **Continue,** and then click **Rotation**.
5. Select **Varimax,** and then click **Continue**.
6. Click **Options** and check the **Sorted by size** box in the panel *Coefficient Display Format.*
7. Click **Continue**, and then click **Scores**.
8. In the dialog box *Factor Analysis: Factor Scores*, check the box **Save as variables**, and then select **Bartlett** [recommended here for the computation of factor scores].
9. Click **Continue**.
10. Click **OK**.

Note: The main tables from the resulting SPSS output are provided in Figure 22.7 (see also, Figures 22.4 and 22.5).

Figure 22.7 *Principle component analysis with varimax rotation for four observed variables*

Total Variance Explained

Component	Initial Eigenvalues			Extraction Sums of Squared Loadings			Rotation Sums of Squared Loading		
	Total	% of Variance	Cumulative %	Total	% of Variance	Cumulative %	Total	% of Variance	Cumula
1	1.970	49.247	49.247	1.970	49.247	49.247	1.668	41.711	4
2	1.343	33.568	82.815	1.343	33.568	82.815	1.644	41.104	8
3	.446	11.155	93.970						
4	.241	6.030	100.000						

Extraction Method: Principal Component Analysis.

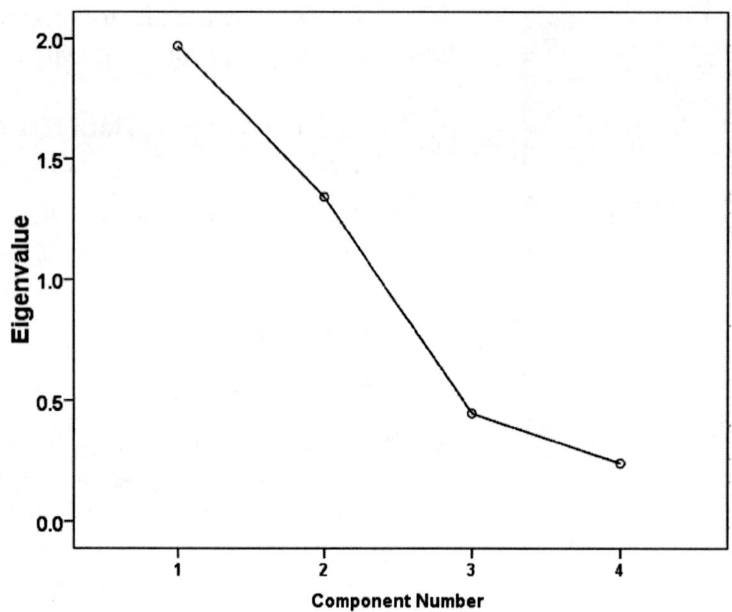

Component Matrix[a]

	Component	
	1	2
X1_spelling	-.732	.529
X4_cutting	.725	.539
X3_coloring	.700	.593
X2_reading	-.646	.648

Extraction Method: Principal Component Analysis.

a. 2 components extracted.

Initially extracted factors (components)

Rotated Component Matrix[a]

	Component	
	1	2
X3_coloring	.916	-.058
X4_cutting	.896	-.114
X2_reading	-.017	.915
X1_spelling	-.160	.889

Extraction Method: Principal Component Analysis.
Rotation Method: Varimax with Kaiser Normalization.

a. Rotation converged in 3 iterations.

Rotated factors (components)

The results in the SPSS output is accompanied here with some technical comments to enhance their understanding. First, the results indicate that two factors (components) were extracted using the principle component analysis with varimax rotation. As the factors are orthogonal, the factor loadings represent both pattern coefficients *and* structure coefficients. That is, the **Component Matrix** and **Rotated Component Matrix** tables in Figure 22.7 represent both the *factor pattern* and the *factor structure* matrices obtained before and after the varimax rotation, respectively. The initial eigenvalues in the **Total Variance Explained** table (1.970 and 1.343) are computed from the factor loadings provided in the **Component Matrix** table using Equations 22.7 and 22.8, respectively. To illustrate, using Equation 22.7, the eigenvalue for the first factor is $\lambda_1 = (-.732)^2 + (.725)^2 + (.700)^2 + (-.646)^2 = 1.97$. Likewise, using Equation 22.8, the eigenvalue for the second factor is: $\lambda_2 = (.529)^2 + (.539)^2 + (.593)^2 + (.648)^2 = 1.34$.

Note also that the sum of all eigenvalues equals the number of variables (1.970 + 1.343 + 0.446 + 0.241 = 4). As this is always true when the variable scores are standardized, the ratio of an eigenvalue for a factor to the number of variables indicates the proportion of the total variance accounted for by this factor [recall that the variance of a standardized variable equals 1, so with four variables we have: 1 + 1 + 1 + 1 = 4]. Here, the first factor accounts for 49.25 percent of the total variance, which is obtained by dividing the eigenvalue for this factor by the number of variables: 1.970/4 = 0.4925 [or 49.25%]. Likewise, the second factor accounts for 32.57 percent of the total variance, which is obtained by dividing the eigenvalue for this factor by the number of variables: 1.343/4 = 0.3357 [or 33.57%]. The two factors together account for 82.82 percent of the total variance. Note that this amount remains the same after the factor rotation, but it is differently distributed across the two factors — namely, 41.71 percent and 41.10 percent is attributed to the first and second rotated factors, respectively.

Regarding the proper number of factors to be retained, both the "root ≥ 1 criterion" and the scree test clearly indicate the presence of two factors. This is supported also by the parallel analysis results provided in Table 22.4. Given the "clean" structure of the two factors revealed by the factor loadings, we can see that the 95th percentile for the random eigenvalues works better than the average eigenvalue in support of retaining two factors [the real eigenvalues for F_3 and F_4 are larger than the average random eigenvalues, but still smaller than the 95th percentile]. This is because the 95th percentile for the random eigenvalues guards better against the sampling error which can be relatively large in this case due to the small sample size ($n = 30$).

Table 22.4 *Parallel analysis with four variables and 30 observations*

FACTOR	**Real eigenvalues**	**Random eigenvalues**	
		Average	95th percentile
F_1	1.970	1.435	1.665
F_2	1.343	1.108	1.260
F_3	0.446	0.863	0.992
F_4	0.241	0.594	0.754

As the interpretation of the factor loadings was provided in Section 22.1.4 (see Figures 22.4 and 22.5), it is not repeated here. The first factor was labeled "motor skills," as it correlates with the variables X_3 (*coloring*) and X_4 (*cutting*), whereas the second factor was labeled "reading skills," as it correlates with the variables X_2 (*reading*) and X_1 (*spelling*).

The communality estimates for each variable are provided in the SPSS output, but they are not shown in Figure 22.7 for space considerations. Under the initial full model (i.e., before the extraction of factors), all communalities equal 1 because all the variance in each variable is fully explained by all factors (see Equation 22.2). In the SPSS communality chart, the column with these communalities (all equal to 1) is labeled "Initial." The communalities obtained after the principle component extraction are called *final communalities*. The column with the final communalities is labeled "Extraction." The final communalities are obtained by summing the squared factor loadings — "horizontally" by rows for each variable in either the **Component Matrix** or the **Rotated Component Matrix** [the rotation of factors does not change the amount of variance that they account for by in the variance of each variable]. Thus, using Equation 22.6 with the factor loadings provided in the **Rotated Component Matrix**, the final communality values for the four variables are:

$$h_3^2 = w_{31}^2 + w_{32}^2 = (0.916)^2 + (-0.058)^2 = 0.842,$$
$$h_4^2 = w_{41}^2 + w_{42}^2 = (0.896)^2 + (-0.114)^2 = 0.816,$$
$$h_2^2 = w_{21}^2 + w_{22}^2 = (-0.017)^2 + (0.915)^2 = 0.838, \text{ and}$$
$$h_1^2 = w_{11}^2 + w_{12}^2 = (-0.160)^2 + (0.889)^2 = 0.816.$$

Thus, the two common factors (**motor skills** and **reading skills**) account for 84.2% of the variance in X_3 (*coloring*), 81.6% of the variance in X_4 (*cutting*), 83.8% in the variance of X_2 (*reading*), and 81.6% in the variance of X_1 (*spelling*). [*Check*: the sum of the communalities (0.842 + 0.816 + 0.838 + 0.816 = 3.312) equals the sum of the squared loadings for the two rotated factors in the **Total Variance Explained** table]. The ratio of this sum, called **trace**, to the total number of variables represents the proportion of the total variance in all variables accounted for by the extracted factors. In this case, there are four variables ($v = 4$), so the ratio is computed as follows: **trace/*v*** = 3.312/4 = 0.828. [This ratio yields the 82.815 "cumulative %" reported in the **Total Variance Explained** table in Figure 22.7.] Table 22.5 presents the estimates of factor loadings and communalities (rounded to the nearest hundred, as required in APA-style reports). The bold numbers are the dominating factor loadings for each factor.

As requested in Step 8 from the list of SPSS steps provided in Example 22.1, the children's scores on each of the two factors appear as two new variables, named **FAC1** and **FAC2**, in the SPSS data sheet [of course, these new variables can be renamed as desired]. The factor scores **(FAC1** and **FAC2)** are provided in a standard form (*mean* = 0, *standard deviation* = 1). They can be used in subsequent analysis (e.g., as predictors in a multiple regression analysis). A linear transformation of the scores (e.g., to present them on a T-scale: $\mu = 50$, $\sigma = 10$) is also an option.

Table 22.5 *Principle component analysis of four variables*

	Factor		
Variable	Motor skills	Reading skills	Communality, h^2
Coloring	**.92**	−.06	0.84
Cutting	**.90**	−.11	0.82
Reading	−.08	**.92**	0.84
Spelling	−.16	**.89**	0.82

22.8 Summary

• **Factor analysis** is used to determine (a) how many factors underlie a set of variables, (b) which variables form which factor, (c) the correlations between individual variables and factors, (d) the correlations (if any) among factors, (e) what proportion of the variance in the variables is accounted for by the factors.

• An **exploratory factor analysis** is used when researchers do not have enough theoretical or empirical information to hypothesize how many factors underlie the set of observable variables and which variables form which factor.

• Under the **principal factor method** in the EFA, the first factor to be extracted from the correlation matrix of the observed variables is a weighted linear combination of all observed variables that produces the highest squared correlation between the variables and the factor. The second factor maximizes the variance extracted from the residual correlation matrix obtained after removing the effect of the first factor, and so on. The extracted factors are orthogonal.

• Under the **full component model**, the score of an individual (i) on any variable (X_m) is reproduced with no error from the factors (see Equation 22.2).

• Under the **common factor model**, an additional term, $w_{mu}U_{im}$, reflects the assumption that there is a "unique" factor (U_m) for each variable, X_m (see Equation 22.3).

• The principle factor method is called (a) **principal component analysis (PCA)** when it is used under the full component model and (b) **principle factor analysis** (PFA) when it is used under the common factor model.

• The **communality** of a variable (h^2) represents the proportion of the variance in this variable accounted for by the common factors (see Equations 22.4, 22.5, and 22.6).

• Factors extracted with the initial orthogonal solutions under the principle factor method are usually difficult to interpret and are, therefore, "rotated" to more desirable positions.

• A factor has a **simple structure** when (a) each variable has at least one zero loading, (b) each factor has a set of linearly independent variables whose factor loadings are zero, (c) for every pair of factors, there are variables whose loadings are zero for one factor but not for the other, (d) for every pair of factors, a large proportion of the variables have zero loadings on both factors whenever more than about four factors are extracted, and (e) for every pair of factors, there is only a small number of variables with nonzero loadings on both. The criteria for a simple structure are used as guiding principles in most approaches to rotation of factors.

• With the orthogonal rotation **varimax**, the variance of the squared factor loadings across all factors is maximized. The rotation position which maximizes the variance across all factors is referred to as the *varimax solution*. The varimax rotation is inappropriate when there is a tendency for a single general factor to underlie the set of observable variables.

• When minor to moderate correlations among the factors are expected, an **oblique rotation** should be used. With an oblique rotation, the angles between the factors are no longer orthogonal when represented geometrically. The main oblique rotations [available in SPSS] are *quartimax*, *equimax*, *direct oblimin*, and *promax*.

• The rotated factors explain the same amount of the total variance of the observed variables as the initially extracted factors, but they divide it up in a way that facilitates their interpretation. Thus, the communality for a variable remains unchanged with the factor rotation.

• The **eigenvalue** for a factor (λ) indicates the proportion of the total variance in all variables accounted for by this factor. The eigenvalue equals the sum of squared loadings for the factor obtained with the initial extraction of the factor (i.e., prior to its rotation).

• Commonly used tests for determining the proper number of factors are (a) the criterion "**root ≥ 1**" (eigenvalues of one or higher) — a factor with an eigenvalue smaller than 1 is not considered as important because the variance that each standardized variable contributes to a principal component extraction equals 1, (b) the **scree test** — plotting the eigenvalues in descending order of their magnitude against their factor numbers and determining where they level off, and (c) **parallel analysis** — the eigenvalues of meaningful factors that underlie a set of variables should be larger than the eigenvalues of "parallel" factors derived from random data sets with the same sample size and number of variables as the original data set.

22.9 Study Questions

1. What is the general purpose of factor analysis?

2. When is an exploratory factor analysis used?

3. What is the difference between the full component and the common factor models?

4. What is the difference between the factor pattern and factor structure coefficients?

5. Are the factor patter matrix and the factor structure matrix ever identical?

6. What does the communality for a variable indicate?

7. What does the eigenvalue for a factor indicate?

8. Is it appropriate to apply varimax rotation when the data come from a test with high internal consistency reliability? [Why?]

9. What is the logic behind the method of parallel analysis for determining the appropriate number of factors?

10. The rotation position which maximizes the variance across all factors is referred to as

A. simple structure
B. oblique rotation
C. varimax solution
D. direct oblimin
E. none of the above

11. Provided below are the factor loadings for two factors extracted by a principle component analysis with varimax rotation for seven variables. The variables represent seven survey questions (Q1, Q2, Q3, Q4, Q5, Q6, and Q7) scored on a 5-point scale.

Component Matrix

	Component	
	1	2
Q5	.813	.217
Q1	.728	.290
Q4	.723	.317
Q7	-.714	.420
Q3	.704	.305
Q6	-.636	.535
Q2	-.403	.475

Rotated Component Matrix

	Component	
	1	2
Q5	.792	-.287
Q4	.775	-.153
Q1	.763	-.178
Q3	.752	-.152
Q6	-.217	.802
Q7	-.347	.752
Q2	-.060	.620

Given this information, answer the following questions:

a. Compute the eigenvalue for each factor [show work].

b. Compute the communality for each variable [show work].

c. Calculate what percent of the total variance in all seven variables is accounted for by each of the two common factors.

d. Calculate what percent of the total variance in all seven variables is accounted for by the two common factors together.

e. Compare the sum of the eigenvalues to the sum of seven communalities.

f. Make a decision on the proper number of factors based on (a) the "**root ≥ 1**" criterion, (b) **scree test** [see Figure 22.8], and (c) **parallel analysis** [see Table 22.6].

Figure 22.8 *Scree plot for principle component analysis with seven variables*

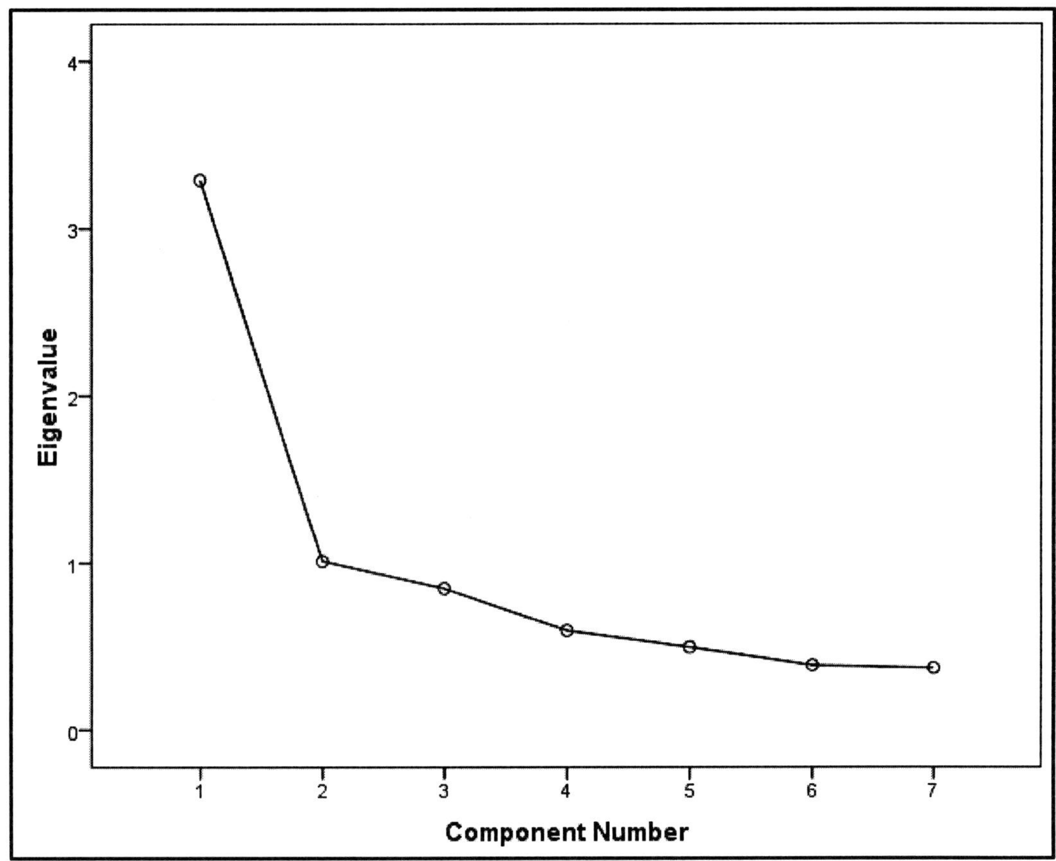

Table 22.6 *Parallel analysis with 616 observations on seven variables*

FACTOR	**Real eigenvalues**	**Random eigenvalues** Average	95th percentile
F_1	3.288	1.149	1.200
F_2	1.011	1.087	1.124
F_3	0.848	1.042	1.071
F_4	0.597	1.000	1.031
F_5	0.497	0.955	0.979
F_6	0.388	0.908	0.942
F_7	0.371	0.857	0.897

12. The SPSS data file **QUESTION_23_14-EFA.sav** [which is provided on the website for this book, http://cehd.gmu.edu/book/dimitrov] contains a categorical variable, **gender,** and the scores of 461 students on nine survey items **(X1, X2, …, X9)**. Ignoring gender, (a) use SPSS for an exploratory factor analysis with varimax rotation with the nine items, (b) determine the number of factors using the "root ≥ 1" , scree plot, and parallel analysis, and (c) interpret the results. [To conduct the parallel analysis, use the SPSS syntax named "parallel.sps" from the web site with computer programs for the O'Conner (2000) procedure for parallel analysis: http://people.ok.ubc.ca/brioconn/nfactors/nfactors.html]

CHAPTER 23

CONFIRMATORY FACTOR ANALYSIS

As discussed in Chapter 22, an **exploratory factor analysis (EFA)** is typically used when a researcher does not have enough theoretical and/or empirical information to hypothesize how many factors underlie the set of observable variables and which variables form which factor. In contrast, a **confirmatory factor analysis (CFA)** is employed when the goal is to test the validity of a hypothesized model of factors and their relationships to a set of observed variables. In both the EFA and CFA the factors represent *unobservable* variables, called **latent variables** or **constructs**, whereas the observed variables are referred to as **indicators** of such latent variables (constructs). *Factors, latent variables,* and *constructs* are synonymously used in this chapter. The set of factors and indicators associated with them define the **factorial structure** underlying the set of observable variables.

Factor analysis (EFA, CFA, or both) is widely used and plays a key role in the process of development and validation of instruments for assessment in education, counseling, psychology, and other social and behavioral fields. Validity studies which employ factor analysis are widely represented, for example, in professional journals such as *Educational and Psychological Measurement, Measurement and Evaluation in Counseling and Development, Developmental Psychology, Journal of Personality Assessment, Journal of Clinical Psychology, Psychological Assessment,* and others. Theoretical and technical aspects of factor analysis are addressed, for example, in professional journals such as *Structural Equation Modeling, Multivariate Behavioral Research,* and *Journal of Educational and Behavioral Statistics.*

23.1 Differences between EFA and CFA Models

The basic features of confirmatory factor analysis (CFA) are better understood in comparison with their counterparts in exploratory factor analysis (EFA). The main conceptual difference is that EFA is a *data-driven* approach to "discovering" unknown factorial structures, whereas CFA is a *theory-driven* approach to "confirming" hypothesized factorial structures. Listed below are some specific differences between EFA and CFA, the first two of which are depicted in Figure 23.1 for the general case of two common factors underlying a set of five variables. It is assumed that the first factor, F_1, is identified through its correlations with the observed variables, X_1, X_2, and X_3, whereas the second factor, F_2, correlates primarily with X_4 and X_5. Although both the EFA (left panel) and CFA (right panel) are common factor models, they have the following differences:

1. Under the EFA model, all observed variables (indicators) are assumed to correlate with all factors, whereas the under CFA model the correlations between factors and indicators are limited (restricted) to previously-hypothesized relationships among them. For example, under the EFA model, the indicator X_1 is predicted from both F_1 and F_2, so $X_1 = w_{11}F_1 + w_{12}F_1 + e_1$, where the standardized regression coefficients, w_{11} and w_{12} are the pattern coefficients for X_1, and e_1 is the error term in the prediction of X_1. Under the CFA model, it is hypothesized that X_1 is predicted *only* from F_1, so $X_1 = \lambda_{11}F_1 + e_1$. Thus, the

regression coefficient of F_2 for the prediction of X_1 is fixed to zero ($\lambda_{12} = 0$). The equations for the prediction of all five indicators from the two common factors, F_1 and F_2, under the EFA and CFA models are provided with Figure 23.1 (lower panel).

2. The EFA model assumes that all common factors are either correlated or uncorrelated. In contrast, CFA allows a researcher to specify in advance only those correlations among factors that are considered substantively meaningful. Although this point is not explicitly depicted in Figure 23.1, as there are only two factors, the two-way arrow connecting F_1 and F_2 indicates that the correlation between them is hypothesized *a priori* and will be tested for significance in the CFA model.

3. While the EFA model assumes no correlations between errors associated with indicators, the CFA model allows for testing hypotheses about the presence of such correlations. In Figure 23.1, the two-way arrow connecting the errors associated with the indicators X_1 and X_4 means that it is expected these two error terms will correlate. Typically, correlations between errors are expected when, for the most part, these errors have common sources — for example, when the indicators are test items (questions) that relate to the same reading passage, same figure, etc.

Figure 23.1 EFA and CFA models for two common factors and five variables

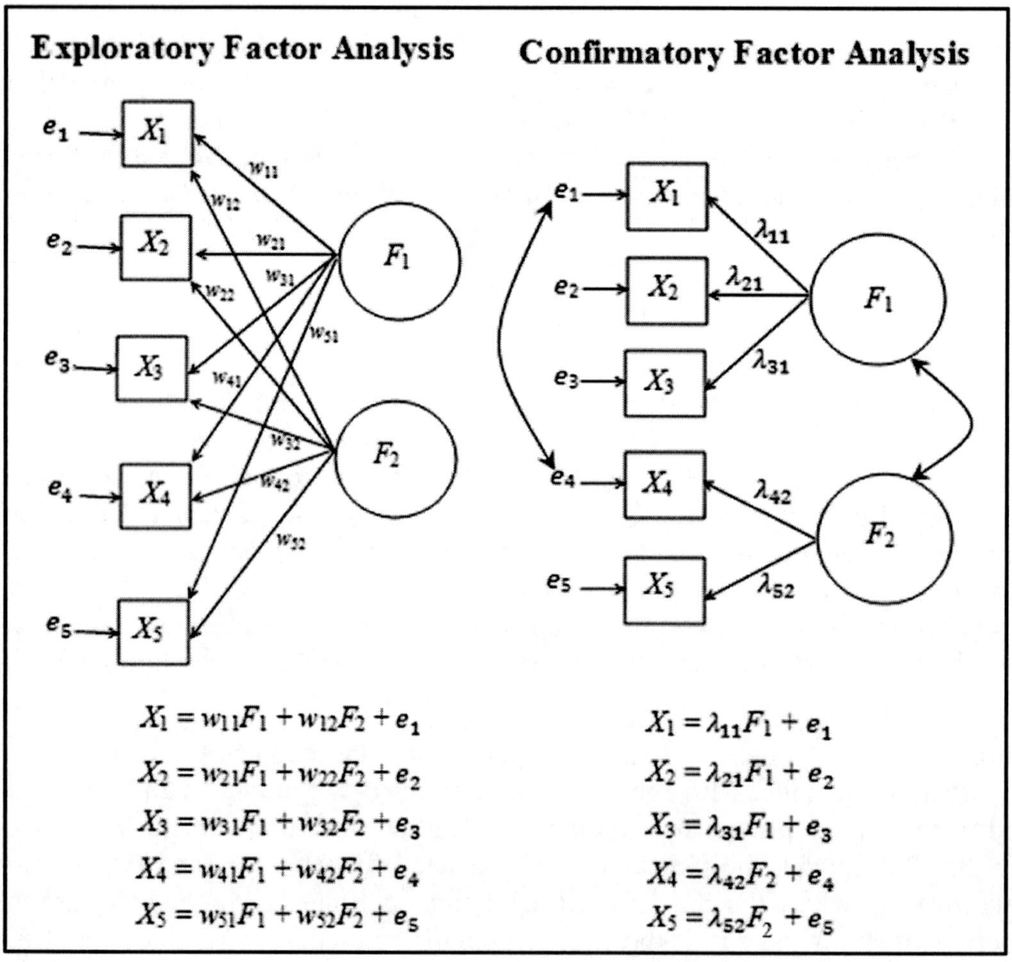

4. Unlike the EFA model, CFA allows for testing hypotheses about (a) equal factor loadings, (b) equal factor variances, (c) equal error variances, (d) validity of the factorial structure with data across different populations or across time points (e.g., with pretest-posttest data), and (e) comparison of alternative ("rival") factorial structures for a set of indicators — a procedure of critical importance to validation of constructs.

5. There are situations in factorial validations of assessment instruments when it is not clear whether some factors have substantive meaning or are simply due to statistical artifacts stemming from (a) positively and negatively worded items — with positively worded items loading on one factor and negatively worded items on another, (b) different methods of measurement — e.g. , multiple-choice items and open-ended items, or (c) differential item difficulty — e.g., with easy test items loading on one factor and difficult test items on another. Problems of this kind cannot be solved in EFA, whereas they can be efficiently addressed with testing procedures in the framework of CFA.

23.2 Basic Steps for CFA

23.2.1 Specification of the CFA Model

The first step in CFA is to specify a hypothesized CFA model based on theoretical and/or empirical knowledge about constructs (factors) of interest and relationships among them. This includes specification of how many factors are expected, which factors relate to which observed variables (indicators), which factors (if any) are expected to correlate, which errors (if any) are expected to correlate, which factor loadings (if any) should be held equal, etc. It is very helpful to present CFA models as path diagrams, where (a) circles (or ellipses) depict unobservable factors, referred to also as latent variables or constructs, (b) a one-way (single-headed) arrow from a factor to an indicator means that the indicator is influenced by the factor [statistically, the indicator is predicted from the factor], (c) a curved two-way (double-headed) arrow connecting two factors (or two error terms) represents a correlation between them, and (d) an error term (*e*), with a short one-way arrow ending at an indicator represents the error (residual) in the prediction of the indicator from a factor. Such path diagram is illustrated in Figure 23.1 (upper right panel).

If it is hypothesized that a given factor does not relate to some indicators, the factor loadings (regression coefficients) in the prediction of these indicators from the factor are fixed to zero. In Figure 23.1, for example, the lack of one-way arrows from F_1 to X_4 and X_5 indicates that $\lambda_{41} = \lambda_{51} = 0$. Likewise, the lack of one-way arrows from F_2 to X_1, X_2, and X_3 indicates that $\lambda_{12} = \lambda_{22} = \lambda_{32} = 0$. Further, for any given factor, the measurement scale of one specific indicator is selected to represent the metric of this factor. This indicator, called the **reference indicator** for the factor, is specified by fixing its loading to 1. For the CFA model in Figure 23.1, for example, if X_1 is selected as a reference indicator for factor F_1, then the factor loading for X_1 must be fixed to 1 (i.e., $\lambda_{11} = 1$). In this way, the latent factor F_1 will be measured on the scale for X_1. Likewise, if X_5 is the reference indicator for F_2, then $\lambda_{52} = 1$. With this, the latent factor F_2 will be measured on the same scale as X_5. By assigning a value of 1 to the factor loadings for X_1 and X_5, the remaining three factor loadings (λ_{21}, λ_{31}, and λ_{42}) will be estimated "freely." The selection of a reference indicator is based on its statistical and substantive representativeness for the respective hypothesized factor. For example, one can select reference indicators based on information obtained from a preliminary exploratory factor analysis with a separate independent sample [speaking of which, it is *not appropriate* to conduct EFA and CFA using the same data.]

23.2.2 Evaluation of the CFA Model Adequacy

Typically, CFA models are tested for data "fit" using maximum likelihood tests within the framework of *structural equation modeling* (SEM). When a CFA model is tested for data fit, the factor loadings are estimated to minimize the discrepancy between the sample covariance matrix for the observed variables, **S**, and the population covariance matrix implied by the model, **Σ** [that is, **S** – **Σ** = minimum]. The function describing such discrepancy is denoted F(**S, Σ**). The smallest (minimal) value of this function, denoted F_{min}, is used as a measure of the difference (residual) between **S** and **Σ**.

Statistical assumptions. Testing for CFA data fit is valid under the SEM *assumption of multivariate normality*; that is, (a) the distribution of each observed variable is normal, (b) the joint distributions for all combinations of observed variables are normal, and (c) all bivariate scatter plots are linear and homoscedastic (all conditional distributions have equal variances). Violations of this assumption can cause distortion of the goodness-of-fit statistics (Hu, Bentler, & Kano, 1992; Curran, West, & Finch, 1996) and inflation of the type I error rate in testing factor loadings, correlations, and other model parameters for statistical significance (Kline, 1998). Slight deviations of the data from multivariate normality are handled relatively well by major SEM programs such as LISREL (Jöreskog & Sörbom, 1996), EQS (Bentler, 2005), and M*plus* (Muthén & Muthén, 2006).

Goodness-of-fit indices. Numerous inferential and descriptive fit indices have been developed to assist the evaluation of goodness-of-fit of a CFA model as a whole. Typically, the evaluation of model fit is based on an inferential goodness-of-fit index, called the **chi-square value**, in combination with several descriptive indices. The chi-square value is, in fact, the test statistic $T = (N - 1)F_{min}$, where N is the sample size and F_{min} is the computed minimal difference (residual) between the covariance matrices **S** and **Σ** obtained with the actual sample data and implied for the population by the model, respectively. When the CFA model fits the data, this T statistic approaches a central chi-square distribution; hence, the name "chi-square value." The degrees of freedom for the chi-square distribution of T are computed as $df = v(v + 1)/2 - p$, where v is the number of observed variables and p is the number of model parameters (factor loadings, variances, and covariances) to be estimated. Thus, evidence of data fit is provided when the chi-square value is *not* statistically significant (i.e., when its p-value is larger than the adopted level of significance — e.g., $p > .05$). However, when the sample size, n, increases, the T statistic also increases, thus yielding smaller p-values and, therefore, an artificial tendency to reject the model fit. Alternatively, an artificial tendency to support the model fit occurs with small samples, as T tends to remain small and thus its p-value remains large. Thus, the chi-square value alone does not provide sufficiently valid evidence for the presence (or lack) of model fit (e.g., see Bentler & Bonnett, 1980; Raykov & Marcoulides, 2006). Other goodness-of-fit indices must also be examined in the evaluation of CFA model fit. The following descriptive indices of model fit are commonly reported in empirical studies:

- *Goodness- of- fit index* (GFI). This index (similar to R^2 in multiple regression) tends to represent the proportion of the variance and covariance accounted for by the CFA model. A GFI value higher than .95 (GFI > .95) is considered an indication of a reasonable model fit (Hu & Bentler, 1999). The same holds for its adjusted-for-population value (AGFI). In general, the GFI must be above .90 (GFI > .90) to be interpreted as "somewhat acceptable" for model fit.
- "*Chi-square to degrees of freedom*" ratio (χ^2/df). When the ratio obtained by dividing the chi-square value to its degrees of freedom is smaller than 2.00 ($\chi^2/df < 2$), this indicates an acceptable model fit (Bollen, 1989).

- *Comparative fit index* (CFI; Bentler, 1990). Generally, speaking the CFI indicates the ratio of improvement from a *null* model to the hypothesized CFA model [the null model is defined as model with zero variances and covariances]. A CFI greater than .93 (CFI > .93) is considered as evidence of a good model fit (Hu & Bentler, 1999). The following criteria are also used for (a) unacceptable fit: CFI < .85, (b) mediocre fit: CFI between .85 and .89, (c) acceptable fit: CFI between .90 and .95, (d) close fit: CFI between .95 and .99, and (e) exact fit: CFI = 1.00.
- *Standardized root mean square residual* (SRMR). This index represents the standardized difference between the observed covariance and the covariance implied by the model. Logically, a value of zero indicates perfect fit. A value less than .08 (SRMR < .08) is considered to indicate a good model fit. Keep in mind, however, that this index tends to get smaller as the sample size increases and as the number of parameters in the model increases.
- *Root mean square error of approximation* (RMSEA, Steiger, 1990). This fit index is estimated with the following formula:

$$\text{RMSEA} = \sqrt{\frac{\chi^2/df - 1}{N-1}}, \qquad \textbf{(23.1)}$$

where N is the sample size and df = degrees of freedom for the model [i.e., $df = v(v + 1)/2 - p$, with v = number of observed variables and p = number of model parameters]. When χ^2 is smaller than the degrees of freedom for the model ($\chi^2 < df$), the RMSEA is set to zero. An RMSEA of .05 or less (RMSEA ≤ .05) indicates a good model fit (Browne & Cudeck, 1983). Conversely, models with RMSEA of .10 or higher have a poor fit. A 90 percent confidence interval for the RMSEA is also used in fit evaluations. An excellent model fit is indicated when the lower value of the interval is close to (or includes) zero and its upper value is smaller than .08. Keep in mind, however, that the RMSEA can be misleading when the degrees of freedom (df) are small and the sample size (N) is not large. For example, with $\chi^2 = 3.25$, $df = 2$, and $N = 51$ in Formulas 23.1, we obtain RMSEA = 0.11 [thus indicating a poor fit].
- The *Akaike information criterion* (AIC, Akaike, 1987). This index is very useful in cross-validations and comparing alternative ("rival") CFA models that use the same indicators. The AIC takes into account both the measure of fit and model complexity. It measures the degree to which a hypothesized CFA model is expected to replicate in another sample taken from the same population. When two models are compared, the model with the smaller AIC value is preferred.

Modification indices. If the initially hypothesized model does not fit, an immediate task is to determine which parameters in the model are misspecified. A parameter is considered specified when it is statistically significant [the estimate of the parameter divided by its standard error must exceed the z-critical value of 1.96, at the .05 level of significance]. In Figure 23.1, for example, the absence of a path (one-way arrow) from factor F_2 to the indicator X_3 represents a constraint in the sense that the loading of X_3 on F_2 is fixed to 0 (i.e., $\lambda_{32} = 0$). If a parameter is "freed" from its constraint (if any), the chi-square value for the model will decrease by a certain amount measured by the so-called **modification index** (MI). Thus, the MI value for a parameter gives the expected drop in the model chi-square value if this parameter is freely estimated (e.g., Byrne, 2001; Jöreskog & Sörbom, 1989).

It is known that a single change (e.g., freeing one factor loading) can affect the estimates of parameters in the model (e.g., Jöreskog & Sörbom, 1989). Therefore, if there are several parameters with statistically significant MIs, they should be freed *one at a time*, starting with the parameter which has the largest MI. It should be emphasized, however, that changes suggested by modification indices must be made *only* if they allow for substantive interpretations in the framework of the theory behind the initial model and its possible modifications. Also, models that result from such changes must be cross-validated (i.e., tested with another sample) before final decisions related to model fit are made.

MI values are reported with major statistical programs for structural equation modeling such as LISREL (Jöreskog & Sörbom, 1996), EQS (Bentler, 2000), M*plus* (Muthén & Muthén, 2006), and AMOS (Arbuckle, 1995). In EQS, the MIs are referred to as *Lagrange multiplier statistics*. The CFA examples provided here (and later, in Chapter 24) are based on analyses in the framework of SEM conducted using M*plus* (Muthén & Muthén, 2006). However, discussion of M*plus* or other computer programs for SEM is beyond the scope of this book. The focus is on CFA specification, evaluation, and interpretation of the results [more information in this regard is provided with the online addendum to SEM at http://cehd.gmu.edu/book/dimitrov].

Cross-validation. If there is no sufficient theoretical and/or empirical information to start directly with a hypothesized CFA model, an exploratory factor analysis (EFA) can be employed first to help in specifying such model. Then, a CFA must be conducted with an *independent sample* to test the hypothesized model. If the initially available sample is large enough, it can be randomly split into two subsamples to be used with the EFA and CFA, respectively.

EXAMPLE 23.1 The purpose of this example is to illustrate how to conduct a CFA in the statistical validation of two constructs: **psychosocial distress** and **successful coping** for a population of people with multiple sclerosis. The data were taken from an existing data pool produced through the Employment Preparation Survey Project funded by the National Multiple Sclerosis Society (Dimitrov, 2006; Roessler, Rumrill, & Hennessey, 2001). They are available in SPSS format [http://cehd.gmu.edu/book/dimitrov]. The data file, named **EXAMPLE_23_1.sav**, contains 1028 observations on a variable named GROUP [not used in this example] and eleven survey items, named **Item_1, Item_2**, …, **Item_11**, which were hypothesized to tap into the two constructs of interest. As the CFA was performed using the computer program M*plus* (Muthén & Muthén, 2006), the SPSS data file was converted into ASCII.dat format [the M*plus* syntax for a CFA model with this data file is provided with Figure 23.4].

The CFA in this example represents the *measurement* part of a SEM model discussed in Chapter 24 for the comparison of people with multiple sclerosis, grouped by their typical course of illness (*relapsing* versus *progressive*), on the constructs of interest: *psychosocial distress* and *successful coping*. The hypothesized model is provided in Table 23.1 and depicted in Figure 23.2. *Psychosocial distress* relates to six items and *successful coping* relates to five items of the Employment Preparation Survey. Item 6 is the reference indicator for *psychosocial distress* (factor loading fixed to 1.00), thus indicating that the scale of Item 6 is selected as a scale of *psychosocial distress*. Likewise, Item 9 is the reference indicator for successful coping, thus indicating that the scale of this item is selected as a scale of *successful coping*. The choice of Item 6 and Item 9 as reference indicators was based on their high factor loadings obtained with a preliminary exploratory factor analysis (with Promax rotation for correlated factors) and their substantive relation to the hypothesized constructs.

It is also hypothesized that *psychosocial distress* and *successful coping* are (negatively) correlated. With the sample data, the Cronbach's alpha coefficient of internal consistency reliability for the items associated with *psychosocial distress* and *successful coping* was 0.88 and 0.81, respectively.

Table 23.1 *Initial model of two hypothesized constructs (psychosocial distress and successful coping) underlying eleven survey items for people with multiple sclerosis*

Construct	Survey item
	In the last month, how often have you…
Psychosocial distress	
Item 1	been upset because of something that happened unexpectedly?
Item 2	felt that you were unable to control the important things in life?
Item 3	felt nervous and distressed?
Item 4	been angered because of things that happened outside of your control?
Item 5	found that you cannot cope with all the things you had to do
Item 6	felt difficulties were piling up so high that you could not overcome them?
Successful coping	
Item 7	felt that things were going your way?
Item 8	dealt successfully with irritating life hassles?
Item 9	felt confident about your ability to handle your personal problems?
Item 10	been able to control irritations in your life?
Item 11	felt that you were effectively coping with important changes that were occurring in your life?

The goodness-of-fit statistics [obtained with M*plus*] indicate an acceptable model fit according to the criteria discussed earlier in this section: CFI = .96, SRMR = .036, and RMSEA = .068, with a 90 percent confidence interval from .060 to .076; that is, 90% CI = (.060, .076). The chi-square value was statistically significant, $\chi^2(43) = 247.93, p < .001$. However, given the sensitivity of the chi-square value to sample size, its statistical significance with the data in this case (N = 1028) should not be taken as a definite inferential evidence of poor data fit.

In Figure 23.2, the numbers associated with the one-way arrows from the two constructs to their indicators are the unstandardized factor loadings; [recall that the observed scores on each indicator are on a 5-point survey scale]. All factor loadings are statistically significant ($p < .001$) thus providing evidence of fit at the level of individual parameters of the model. As all parameter estimates in Figure 23.2 are unstandardized, the coefficient associated with the two-way arrow connecting **Psychosocial distress** and **Successful coping** (−0.46) is an estimate of the covariance between the two constructs. This negative coefficient is statistically significant ($p < .001$), so there is a negative linear relationship between *psychosocial distress* and *successful coping*.

The examination of the modification indices (MIs) with values greater than 10 [reported in the M*plus* output, but not shown here] suggested that there is a potential cross-loading for four items. Specifically, (a) items 1 and 6, related to *psychosocial distress*, were likely related to *successful coping* as well, and (b) items 7 and 8, related to *successful coping* were likely related to *psychosocial distress* as well. We will drop these four items from the model (by fixing their loadings zero) in an attempt to obtain a model with less indicators, yet providing better fit for its own data. The primary purpose of doing this here is to highlight some technical and methodological aspects related to such modifications in CFA [deleting indicators from the initial CFA model].

Figure 23.2 *Initial model of two hypothesized constructs (psychosocial distress and successful coping) underlying 11 survey items for people with multiple sclerosis*

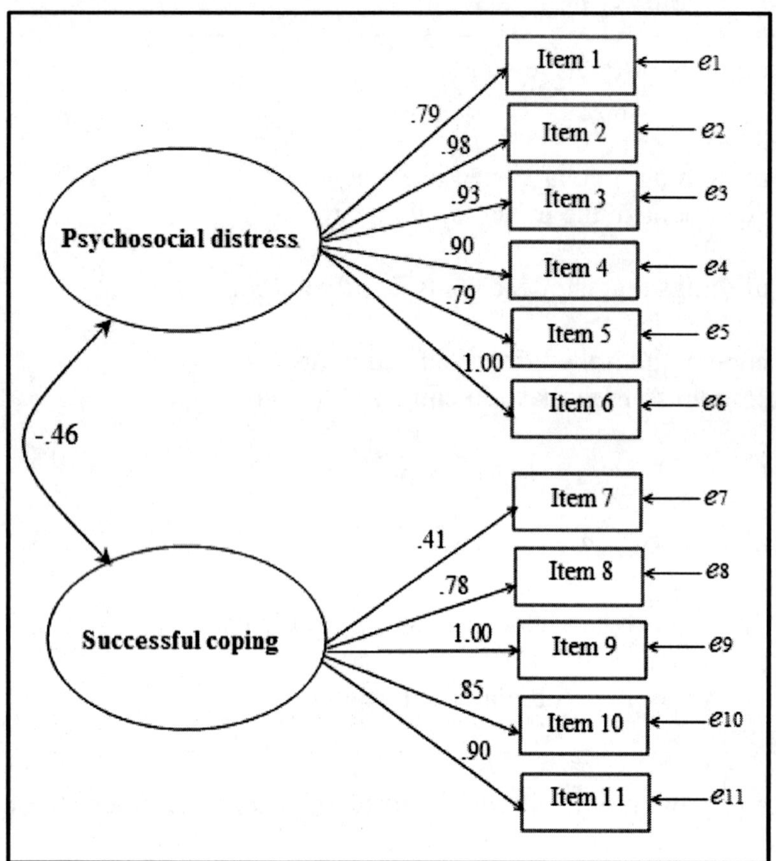

The 7-item model obtained from the initial 11-item model (after deleting the cross-loading items 1, 6, 7, and 8) is referred to here as a "reduced" model (see Figure 23.3). The goodness-of-fit indices for the two models are summarized in Table 23.2. The results indicate that, relatively speaking, the reduced model provides better data fit for its own data. As the two model use different sets of indicators, it is not accurate to say that the reduced model represents an improvement over the initial model (see NOTE [23.1]). The working term "reduced model" used here does not mean that this is a restricted version of the initial model in the sense of "full versus restricted" nested models — such models occur with imposing restrictions in the initial model (e.g., equal factor loadings), but keeping the same indicators. For illustration purposes, we will proceed with the reduced model taking into account its reasonable data fit and assuming that its seven items (indicators) represent well the substance of the two hypothesized constructs.

NOTE [23.1] When "reducing" an initial CFA model by deleting some of its indicators [fixing their factor loadings to zero], the resulting reduced model is NOT nested within the initial model because the two models have different data structure. Hence, **it is not correct to compare the two models using the chi-square difference test for nested models. Neither is it appropriate to compare them using the Akaike information criterion (AIC).**

Table 23.2 *Goodness-of-fit indices with the 11-item initial model and 7-item reduced model*

Model	χ^2	*df*	CFI	SRMR	RMSEA	90% CI for RMSEA	
						Lower	Upper
Initial	247.93	43	.96	.036	.068	.060	.076
Reduced	28.50	13	.99	.014	.034	.017	.051

Figure 23.3 *Reduced model of two hypothesized constructs underlying 7 survey items for people with multiple sclerosis*

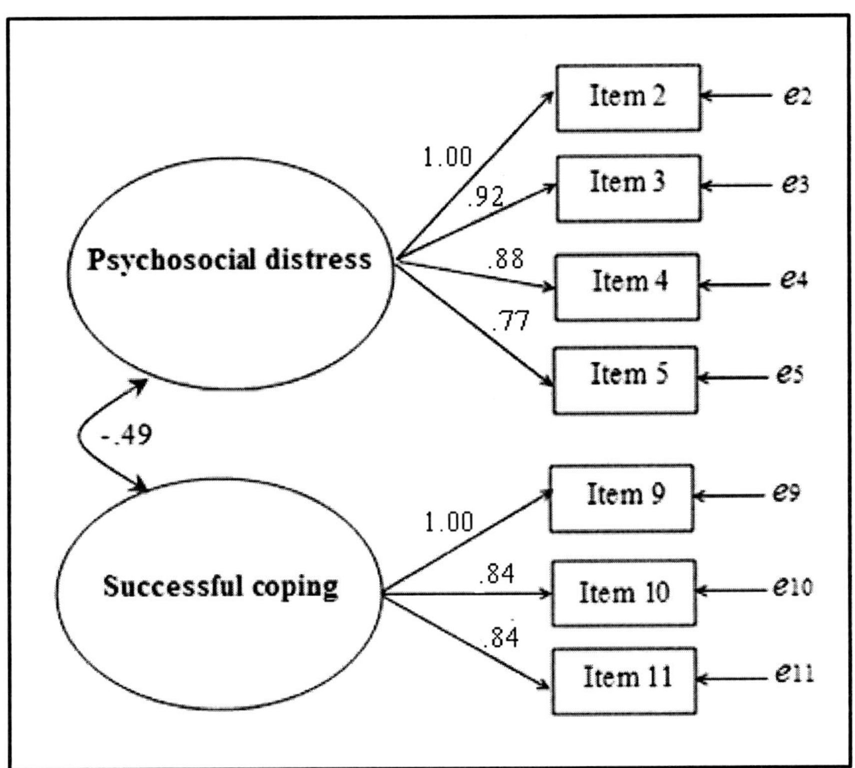

Just like in regression analysis, the unstandardized loadings are more useful for *interpretations*, whereas the standardized loadings (Table 23.3) indicate the relative *importance* of indicators in defining the construct to which they relate in the hypothesized model. Also, as each indicator is "predicted" from a single predictor [the underlying construct], the standardized factor loading for the predictor equals its correlation with the construct. Hence, the squared value of the standardized loading indicates the proportion of the variance in the indicator explained (accounted for) by the construct. For example, Item 2 has the strongest correlation (.80) with *psychosocial distress*. The squared value of this correlation is $(.80)^2 = .64$, thus indicating that 64 percent of the variance in Item 2 is explained by the variability in *psychosocial distress*. Likewise, the squared loading of Item 9 is $(.85)^2 = .7225$, which indicates that 72.25 percent of the variance in Item 9 is explained by the variability in *successful coping*.

Table 23.3 *Standardized factor loadings and proportion of variance explained in indicators with the restricted model*

Construct/Indicator	Factor loading	Percent variance explained
Psychosocial distress		
Item 2	.80	64.00
Item 3	.75	56.25
Item 4	.71	50.41
Item 5	.64	40.96
Successful coping		
Item 9	.85	72.25
Item 10	.76	57.76
Item 11	.77	59.29

Figure 23.4 provides the M*plus* syntax for the CFA with the reduced model depicted in Figure 23.3. For simplicity in syntax notations, X1, …, X11 denote Item 1, …, Item 11, respectively. The USEVARIABLES syntax line indicates the variables used with the reduced model: X2-X5 (from X2 to X5) and X9-X11 (from X9 to X11). The variable **group** [not used in this example] stands for two groups of people with multiple sclerosis classified by typical course of illness (*relapsing* versus *progressive*). This variable is used in Chapter 24. In the M*plus* syntax, the data file **EXAMPLE_23_1.dat** is obtained by saving the SPSS file **EXAMPLE_23_1.sav** [http://cehd.gmu.edu/book/dimitrov] in ASCII.dat format.

Figure 23.4 *Mplus syntax for the CFA with the reduced model*

```
==============================================
TITLE: EXAMPLE 23.1— CFA (7-item reduced model);
DATA: FILE IS "C:\EXAMPLE_23_1.dat";
VARIABLE: NAMES ARE group X1-X11;
          USEVARIABLES ARE  X2-X5  X9-X11;
ANALYSIS: TYPE IS GENERAL;
          ESTIMATOR IS ML;
          ITERATIONS = 1000;
          CONVERGENCE = 0.00005;
OUTPUT: MODINDICES  STANDARDIZED;
MODEL:  DISTRESS  BY  X2  X3  X4  X5;
        COPING  BY  X9  X10  X11;
        DISTRESS  WITH  COPING;
==============================================
```

23.3 Summary

• Confirmatory factor analysis (CFA) is conducted when the goal is to test the validity of a hypothesized model of factors and their relationships with a set of observed variables. In this model, the researcher specifies the number of latent factors (constructs) and which factor relates to which indicators based on information from previous theoretical and/or empirical research.

• Main differences between EFA and CFA models:

- Under the EFA model, all observed variables (indicators) are assumed to correlate with all factors, whereas the under CFA model the correlations between factors and indicators are restricted to previously hypothesized relationships among them.
- The EFA model assumes that all common factors are either correlated or uncorrelated, whereas the CFA model allows the researcher to specify in advance only those correlations among factors that are considered substantively meaningful.
- While the EFA model assumes no correlations between errors associated with indicators, the CFA model allows for testing of such correlations.
- Unlike the EFA model, CFA allows for testing hypotheses about (a) equal factor loadings, (b) equal factor variances, (c) equal error variances, (d) validity of the factorial structure with data across different populations or across time points (e.g., with pretest-posttest data), and (e) comparison of alternative (rival) factorial structures for a set of indicators.
- Unlike the EFA model, CFA can address problems related to factors due to statistical artifacts stemming from positively and negatively worded items, different methods of measurement, or differential item difficulty.

• When a CFA model is tested for data fit, the factor loadings are estimated to minimize the difference between the sample covariance matrix for the observed variables, **S**, and the population covariance matrix implied by the model, **Σ** (i.e., **S** – **Σ** = minimum).

• The specification of a CFA model includes specification of how many factors are expected, which factors relate to which observed variables (indicators), which factors (if any) are expected to correlate, which errors (if any) are expected to correlate, which factor loadings (if any) should be held equal, etc.

• The evaluation of model fit in CFA includes testing for the assumption of multivariate normality, computation of goodness-of-fit indices, testing of model parameters (factor loading, correlations, etc.) for statistical significance, possible adjustments in the hypothesized model based on modification indices (MIs), and cross-validation.

• Violations of the assumption of multivariate normality can cause distortion of the goodness-of-fit statistics and inflation of the type I error rate in testing for statistical significance of factor loadings, correlations, and other model parameters. Slight deviations from multivariate normality are handled by major SEM programs such as LISREL, EQS, M*plus*, and AMOS.

• A good model fit is evidenced by the following criteria for descriptive goodness-of-fit indices: GFI > .95, $\chi^2/df < 2$, CFI > .93, SRMR < .08, and RMSEA ≤ .05, with a 90 percent confidence interval from a value close to (or including) zero to a value smaller than .08. The chi-square value provides an inferential evidence of good model fit when its p-value is larger than the prespecified level of significance (typically, $\alpha = .05$). Thus, a nonsignificant chi-square value ($p > .05$) is desired for a good model fit. However, taking into account the sensitivity of the chi-square value to sample size, a statistically significant chi-square value should not be taken as a definite inferential evidence of misfit.

• The *Akaike information criterion* (AIC) index is particularly useful in cross-validations and comparing alternative (rival) CFA models that use the same set of indicators. When two rival models are compared, the model with smaller AIC value is preferred.

• The *modification index* (MI) value for a parameter indicates the expected drop in the model chi-square value if this parameter is freely estimated. A common rule of thumb is that MI values greater than 10 merit close consideration [e.g., in M*plus* outputs]. If there are several parameters with MI "red flags," they should be freed one at a time, starting with the largest MI. Changes suggested by modification indices must be made only if they allow for substantive interpretations in the framework of the theory behind the model.

• If there is no sufficient theoretical and/or empirical information to start directly with a hypothesized CFA model, a cross-validation procedure can be employed: an exploratory factor analysis (EFA) is used first to help in specifying a hypothesized model and then a CFA is used to test the model *using a different sample.* If the initially available sample is large enough, it can be randomly split in two subsamples for the EFA and CFA, respectively.

• The squared value of the standardized factor loading of an indicator indicates the proportion of variance in this indicator accounted for by the factor (construct) related the indicator.

• When "reducing" an initial CFA model by deleting some of its indicators [fixing their factor loadings to zero], the resulting reduced model is NOT nested within the initial model because the two models have different data structure. Hence, it is not correct to compare the two models using the chi-square difference test for nested models. Neither is it appropriate to compare them using the Akaike information criterion (AIC).

Study Questions

1. When is confirmatory factor analysis (CFA) appropriate?
2. The CFA assumes that all factors are either correlated or uncorrelated. (True or False?)
3. Correlated errors can be tested with both EFA and CFA models. (True or False?)
4. What does the specification of a CFA model involve?
5. What does the F_{min} value indicate?
6. What are the consequences of violating the assumption of multivariate normality?
7. Interpret a *p*-value of, say, .12 ($p = .12$) reported with the chi-square value for model fit.
8. What are the cutting values of the following goodness-of-fit indices that indicate a good model fit: GFI, χ^2/df, CFI, SRMR, and RMSEA, with a 90 percent confidence interval?
9. Should a statistically significant chi-square (χ^2) value be taken as a definite inferential evidence of poor model fit? (Explain).
10. Given the AIC values of two rival models, which model should be preferred?
11. What does the value of the modification index (MI) for a parameter indicate?
12. What would be an appropriate procedure to use when there is no sufficient theoretical and/or empirical information to start directly with a hypothesized CFA model?
13. Given that the factor loading associated with the regression path (one-way arrow) from a factor to an indicator is .70, what percent of the variance in the indicator is accounted for by the variability in the factor?

14. Table 23.4 describes nine items from a survey for middle school students. As there was insufficient preliminary information on the number of underlying factors and their relationship to the survey items, a cross-validation procedure was conducted in three steps. First, the random sample of survey respondents was randomly divided into two samples. After deleting a few cases with missing data, this resulted in Sample 1 with 461 observations ($n_1 = 461$) and Sample 2 with 439 observations ($n_2 = 439$). The data for these two samples are available as SPSS files named **QUESTION23-14-EFA.sav** and **QUESTION23-14-CFA.sav**, respectively [http://cehd.gmu.edu/book/dimitov]. Each file contains a categorical variable **gender** [not used for the analyses for this question] and nine survey items on a 5-point scale, named **X1**, …, **X9**. Second, using SPSS, an exploratory factor analysis (EFA) with varimax rotation was performed with the data for Sample 1 [**QUESTION23-14-EFA.sav**]. The rotated component matrix provided in the SPSS output is given in Figure 23.5. Third, using the factors identified with the factor matrix in Figure 23.5, a confirmatory factor analysis (CFA) was employed using the SPSS file **QUESTION23-14-CFA.sav** converted into an ASCII data file for use in M*plus* applications. The results are summarized in Table 23.5.

Given this information, answer the following questions:

a. Using the EFA results in Figure 23.5, specify a hypothesized model for CFA analysis and provide the path diagram of this model [e.g., see Figures 23.2 and 23.3]. Label the factors based on the description of their indicators in Table 23.4.

b. Using the CFA results in Table 23.5, assign the factor loadings values to the one-way arrow in the path diagram of the hypothesized model.

c. Using the CFA results in Table 23.5, interpret the goodness-of-fit indices and complete the column labeled *Percent of variance explained* in this table.

d. Using the SPSS data file **QUESTION23-14-EFA.sav**, perform the EFA on your own, summarize the results (just like in Table 22.5), provide the scree plot, and summarize the results from a parallel analysis (just like in Table 22.4) using a syntax for parallel analysis [http://flash.lakeheadu.ca/~boconno2/nfactors.html].

Table 23.4 *Nine items from a survey for middle schools students*

Item #	Description
X1	Ignore problems at school
X2	Refuse to talk about problems when asked
X3	Ask questions in class when don't understand something
X4	Volunteer to participate in classroom activities
X5	Trying to help other students when asked
X6	Express opinions in front of classmates
X7	Share problems in school with parents
X8	Express opinion when disagree with parents
X9	Ask parents for help with homework assignments

Figure 23.5 *EFA with nine survey items*

Rotated Component Matrix

	Component		
	1	2	3
X5	.867	.123	-.138
X3	.801	.199	-.215
X6	.721	.202	-.076
X4	.721	.199	-.331
X8	.188	.806	-.116
X7	.204	.782	-.057
X9	.129	.708	-.152
X1	-.168	-.123	.866
X2	-.262	-.151	.821

Extraction Method: Principal Component Analysis.
Rotation Method: Varimax with Kaiser Normalization.

Table 23.5 *Standardized factor loadings, proportion of variance in the indicator explained by the factor [to be completed] and goodness-of-fit indices for the three-factor model*

Construct/Indicator	Factor loading	Percent variance explained	Goodness-of-fit indices
Factor 1			
X5 [Item 5]	.85		$\chi^2(24) = 18.08$, $p = .80$
X3 [Item 3]	.81		CFI = 1.00
X6 [Item 6]	.76		SRMR = .014
X4 [Item 4]	.61		RMSEA = .00, with
Factor 2			90% CI = (.00, .026)
X8 [Item 8]	.79		
X7 [Item 7]	.78		
X9 [Item 9]	.61		
Factor 3			
X1 [Item 1]	.81		
X2 [Item 2]	.84		

CHAPTER 24

ELEMENTS OF STRUCTURAL EQUATION MODELING

Confirmatory factory analysis (CFA) deals with validation of constructs (latent variables, factors) and their measurement through hypothesized relations between the constructs and observable variables (indicators). Thus, CFA validates **measurement relations** between latent variables and observable indicators. The main question of interest in most research situations, however, is to hypothesize *causal relations* among latent variables based on previous theoretical and/or empirical studies and to test such relations for statistical significance. The hypothesized causal relations are called **structural relations** among latent variables. A statistical technique, known as **structural equation modeling** (SEM), allows for testing and estimating hypothesized causal relations among observable variables, latent variables, and/or a mixture of both. Typically, SEM integrates (a) a *measurement part* — CFA for validation and measurement of latent variables, and (b) a *structural part* — causal relations among latent and observable variables.

SEM will be the method of choice, for example, when it is hypothesized that motivation plays a mediation role in the impact of socio-economic status on academic achievement. If all variables are interpreted as observable variables, this question can be addressed in the framework of path analysis — a special type of SEM based on the employment of multiple regression analyses. In this case, the SEM contains a structural part for causal relations among observed variables [socio-economic status → motivation → academic achievement]. If, however, some (or all) variables are latent variables measured by multiple indicators, the SEM model will add a measurement part (e.g., a CFA component for measuring *motivation* through multiple indicators). Although typical SEM applications involve latent variables with multiple indicators, models of path analysis, which involve one indicator for each variable, can be useful in some research situations and facilitate the understanding of concepts, ideas, and procedures in SEM.

24.1 Path Analysis

Path analysis was developed as a statistical method of determining direct and indirect effects in hypothesized causal relations among variables (Wright, 1934). As Pedhazur (1982) noted, "path analysis is *not* intended to discover causes but to shed light on the tenability of the causal models a researcher formulates base on prior knowledge and theoretical considerations" (p. 768).

To introduce basic concepts in path analysis, consider the data provided in Figure 24.1 (left panel), where *PI* = *Principal Isolation*, *TPD* = *Teacher Professional Development*, and *SAP* = *Student Academic Performance* [see also Example 11.3]. The scores are based on a random sample of 20 schools in a large urban area. The *PI* scores come from a survey on principals; feelings of isolation, with higher scores indicating a higher level of professional isolation perceived by a school principal. The *TPD* scores come from a teacher survey, with higher scores indicating a higher level of school support for the professional development of teachers in a given school. The *SAP* scores represent an overall evaluation of the academic performance of the students in the school. Professional isolation of a school principal is defined as a lack of (or insufficient) communication with teachers about their professional development and related issues.

Figure 24.1 *Data on three variables (PI, TPD, and SAP) and path diagram of hypothesized causal relations among them [mediated cause]*

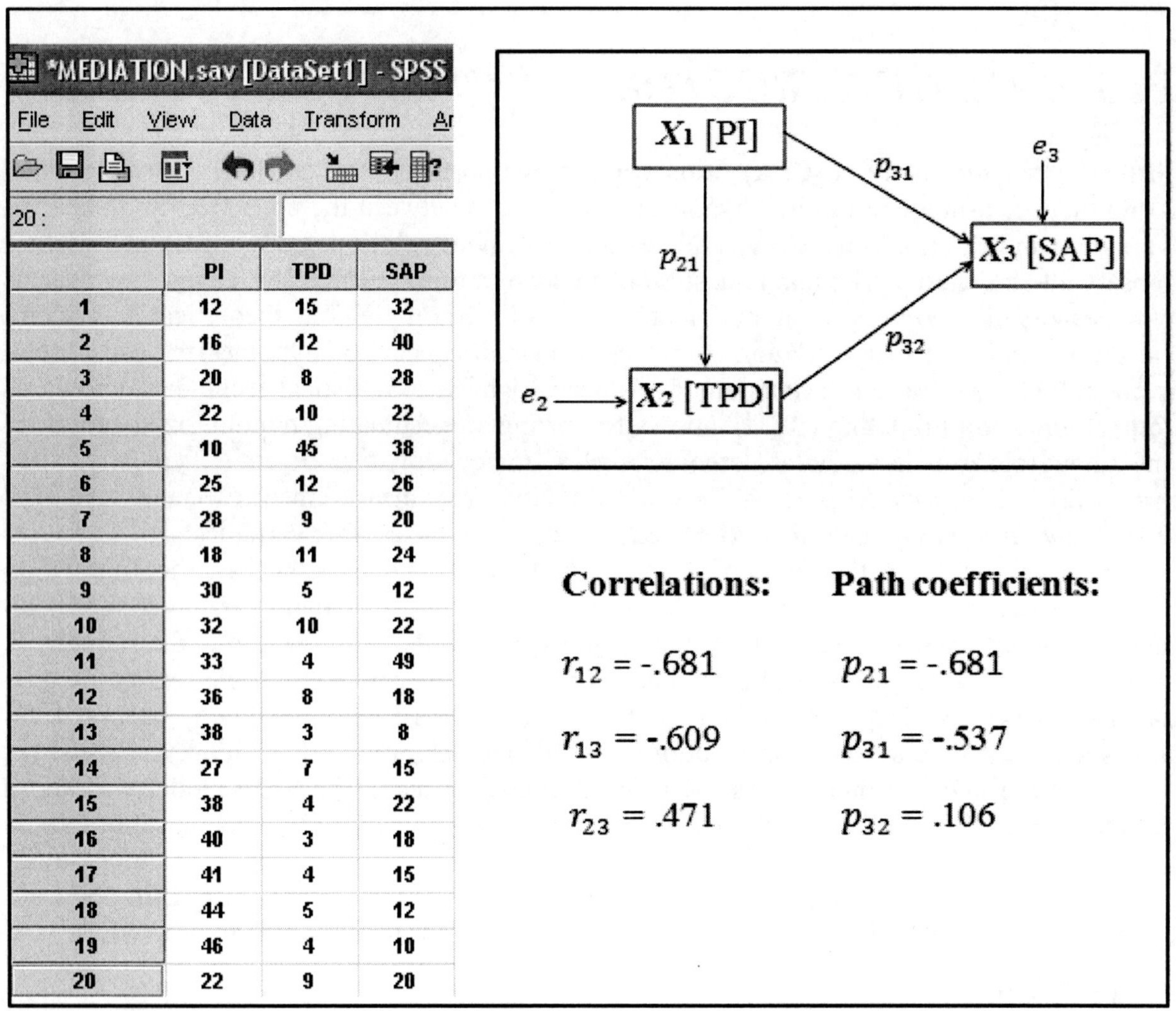

	PI	TPD	SAP
1	12	15	32
2	16	12	40
3	20	8	28
4	22	10	22
5	10	45	38
6	25	12	26
7	28	9	20
8	18	11	24
9	30	5	12
10	32	10	22
11	33	4	49
12	36	8	18
13	38	3	8
14	27	7	15
15	38	4	22
16	40	3	18
17	41	4	15
18	44	5	12
19	46	4	10
20	22	9	20

24.1.1 Path Coefficients

Consider now the hypothesized causal relations depicted in the path diagram in Figure 24.1 (upper right panel). For convenience, the following variable notations are also used: X_1 = PI, X_2 = TDP, and X_3 = SAP. The Pearson correlations between the variables are also provided in Figure 24.1 (lower right panel). The path (one-way arrow) from X_1 to X_2 indicates that X_1 has a causal impact on X_2 (or, X_1 affects X_2). The path coefficient assigned to this path, p_{21}, represents the standardized regression coefficient resulting from a simple linear regression for the prediction of X_2 from X_1, whereas e_2 denotes the error term in this prediction. That is, if z_1 and z_2 represent the standard (z-) scores for X_1 and X_2, respectively, we have:

$$z_2 = p_{21}z_1 + e_2. \quad \textbf{(24.1)}$$

Likewise, the path coefficients p_{31} and p_{32} represent the standardized regression coefficients in the multiple regression equation for the prediction of X_3 from X_1 and X_2. That is

$$z_3 = p_{31}z_1 + p_{32}z_2 + e_3. \quad \textbf{(24.2)}$$

To compute p_{21}, we use SPSS for a simple linear regression to predict X_2 from X_1. That is, we predict *teacher professional development* (TPD) from *principal isolation* (PI) with the data of 20 observations in Figure 24.1. The standardized regression coefficient ("Beta") provided in the SPSS output [not shown here] equals $-.681$. That is, $p_{21} = -.681$. To compute p_{31} and p_{32}, we use SPSS for a multiple regression predicting X_3 from X_1 and X_2. That is, *student academic performance* (SAP) is predicted from both the *principal isolation* (PI) and *teacher professional development* (TPD). The standardized regression coefficients provided in the SPSS output [not shown here] are $-.537$ and .106, respectively. That is, $p_{31} = -.537$ and $p_{32} = .106$. [**Check**: obtain these results on your own using SPSS to run the two regression analyses described here using the data in Figure 24.1.] The path coefficients p_{21}, p_{31}, and p_{32} are shown in Figure 24.1.

The path models presented in this chapter are **recursive path models** — models in which the causal relations are unidirectional (there are no causal "loops"). A path coefficient indicates the **direct effect** of a variable hypothesized as a cause of another variable. The sign (positive or negative) of the path coefficient indicates the direction (positive or negative) of the linear relationship between the two variables. Thus, $p_{21} = -.681$ shows the direct effect of X_1 (*principal isolation*) on X_2 (*teacher professional development*). The negative sign of the path coefficient ($-.681$) indicates that there is a negative linear relationship (negative correlation) between the two variables. Likewise, $p_{31} = -.537$ shows the direct effect of X_1 on X_3, whereas $p_{32} = .106$ shows the direct effect of X_2 on X_3. [The positive sign of p_{32} indicates a positive correlation between *teacher professional development* and *student academic performance*.] Note that $p_{21} \neq p_{12}$. These two path coefficients cannot coexist in a recursive causal model because p_{21} indicates the effect of X_1 on X_2, whereas p_{12} would indicate the effect of X_2 on X_1, thus yielding a causal "loop" which is not allowed with recursive path models. Likewise, $p_{31} \neq p_{13}$ and $p_{32} \neq p_{23}$.

Let R^2 be the coefficient of multiple determination in a linear regression prediction of a given dependent variable in a causal model. As known from multiple regression analysis, R^2 indicates the proportion of the variance in the dependent variable explained (accounted for) by its predictors (see Equation 13.3). Thus, $1 - R^2$ indicate the residual (unexplained) proportion of the variance in the dependent variable. In the context of a path diagram, this means that the residual path coefficient, associated with the path from the error term (residual) to the dependent variable, equals $\sqrt{1 - R^2}$. For the path model in Figure 24.1, the SPSS regression of X_2 on X_1 produced a coefficient of multiple determination $R^2_{2.1} = .464$ [this equals the squared path coefficient p_{21} as the regression of X_2 on X_1 is a simple linear regression: $R^2_{2.1} = r^2_{12} = p^2_{21} = (-.681)^2 = .464$] . Thus, the residual path coefficient for X_2, associated with the path from e_2 to X_2, can be computed as follows: $p_{2,e2} = \sqrt{1 - R^2_{2.1}} = \sqrt{1 - .464^2} = .886$. Likewise, the SPSS regression of X_3 on X_1 and X_2 produced $R^2_{3.12} = .377$. Thus, the residual path coefficient associated with the path from e_3 to X_3 equals: $p_{3,e3} = \sqrt{1 - R^2_{3.12}} = \sqrt{1 - .377^2} = .926$. To simplify the path diagram in Figure 24.1, the residual path coefficients, $p_{2,e2}$ and $p_{3,e3}$, are not shown. [**Check**: obtain $R^2_{2.1} = .464$ and $R^2_{3.12} = .377$ on your own with the respective two regression analyses using the data in Figure 24.1.]

24.1.2 Exogenous and Endogenous Variables

A variable involved in a causal model is called an **exogenous variable** if the variance of this variable is not explained by the variance of other variables in the model. That is, an exogenous variable is not *caused* by another variable in the model. Graphically, there are no paths (one-way arrows) ending at an exogenous variable in the path diagram of the model. On the other hand, a variable involved in a causal model is called an **endogenous variable** if the variance of this variable is explained by the variance of other variables in the model. That is, an endogenous variable is *caused* by one or more variables in the model. In this case, there is at least one path (one-way arrow) ending at the endogenous variable in the graphic representation of the model. In the causal model depicted by the path diagram in Figure 24.1 (right panel), there are one exogenous variable (X_1) and two endogenous variables (X_2 and X_3).

In a causal model, an exogenous variable is *always* an independent variable in its relationship with other variables in the model. In contrast, an endogenous variable can be an independent variable in its relations with some variables and a dependent variable in regard to other variables in the model. For the path diagram in Figure 24.1, the exogenous variable X_1 represents an independent variable in its relationships with X_2 and X_3 (i.e., X_1 is a "predictor" of X_2 and X_3). The endogenous variable X_3 is a dependent variable in its relationships with X_1 and X_2 (i.e., X_3 is predicted from X_1 and X_2). The endogenous variable X_2, however is (a) a dependent variable in its relationship with X_1 and (b) an independent variable in its relationship with X_3.

24.1.3 Assumptions

As mentioned above the path models presented in this chapter are **recursive path models** — models in which the causal relations are unidirectional (i.e., there are no causal "loops"). The application of such models is based on the following main assumptions:

1. The relations among variables in the model are linear, additive, and causal (e.g., Equations 24.1 and 24.2 represent linear and additive relations among the variables in the causal model depicted in Figure 24.1).
2. The residual (error term) of an endogenous variable does not correlate with the variables that precede this variable in the model. This also implies that the residuals are not correlated among themselves. That is, there are no two-way arrows (to depict correlations) that connect (a) an endogenous variable to other variables or (b) any two residuals in the model.
3. The variables are measured on an interval scale.
4. The variables are measured without error.

24.1.4 Decomposition of Correlation Coefficients

The correlation between two endogenous variables or between an exogenous and an endogenous variable in a causal model can be decomposed into components that involve path coefficients and (possibly) correlations between exogenous variables. In general, there are four types of components in the decomposition of a correlation beween two variables, say X_1 and X_2, in a causal model: (a) a **direct effect** — one of the variables has a causal effect on the other, (b) an **indirect effect** — X_1 causes X_2 through the mediation of a third variable, (c) **spuriousness** — a third variable is a common cause of X_1 and X_2, and (d) **unexplained covariation** — both X_1 and X_2 are exogenous and the correlation between them is not explained by the model.

To illustrate this, consider again the causal model depicted in Figure 24.1. Assuming that the variables are standardized (i.e., using z-scores), the correlation between any two variables can be represented as the mean of the products of their z-score (see Equation 10.4). Thus, the correlation between X_1 and X_2 is

$$r_{12}=\frac{1}{N}\sum z_1 z_2\,, \tag{24.3}$$

where N is the sample size. Given Equation 24.1, we replace z_2 in Equation 24.3 with $z_2 = p_{21}z_1 + e_2$, thus obtaining

$$r_{12} = \frac{1}{N}\sum z_1 z_2 = \frac{1}{N}\sum z_1(p_{21}z_1 + e_2) = p_{21}\frac{\sum z_1^2}{N} + \frac{\sum z_1 e_2}{N} = p_{21}(1) + 0 = p_{21}.$$

In this analytic derivation we use the rule that (a) the variance of z-scores equals 1, $\frac{\sum z_1^2}{N} = 1$, and (b) the correlation between the error term e_2 and X_1 is zero, $\frac{\sum z_1 e_2}{N} = 0$ [see assumption 2 in the previous section]. Thus, the correlation between X_1 and X_2 equals p_{21}, which represents the direct effect of X_1 on X_2:

$$r_{12} = p_{21} \qquad \textbf{(24.4)}$$

In fact, Equation 24.4 represents a known fact that the standardized regression coefficient in a simple linear regression equals the correlation between the dependent variable (X_2) and the predictor (X_1). That is: Beta = $p_{21} = r_{12}$.

Consider now the correlation between X_2 and X_3 taking into account Equation 24.2:

$$r_{23} = \frac{1}{N}\sum z_2 z_3 = \frac{1}{N}\sum z_2(p_{31}z_1 + p_{32}z_2 + e_3) = p_{31}\frac{\sum z_1 z_2}{N} + p_{32}\frac{\sum z_2^2}{N} + \frac{\sum z_2 e_3}{N}$$

$$= p_{31}r_{12} + p_{32}(1) + 0 = p_{31}p_{21} + p_{32}.$$

In this analytic derivation we use the rule that (a) the variance of z-scores equals 1, $\frac{\sum z_2^2}{N} = 1$, (b) the correlation between the error term e_3 and X_2 is zero, $\frac{\sum z_2 e_3}{N} = 0$, and (c) $r_{12} = p_{21}$. Thus, the correlation between X_2 and X_3 is decomposed into the following two components:

$$r_{23} = p_{32} + p_{31}p_{21}. \qquad \textbf{(24.5)}$$

Finally, consider the correlation between X_1 and X_3, using again Equation 24.2:

$$r_{13} = \frac{1}{N}\sum z_1 z_3 = \frac{1}{N}\sum z_1(p_{31}z_1 + p_{32}z_2 + e_3) = p_{31}\frac{\sum z_1^2}{N} + p_{32}\frac{\sum z_1 z_2}{N} + \frac{\sum z_1 e_3}{N}$$

$$= p_{31}(1) + p_{32}r_{12} + 0 = p_{31} + p_{32}p_{21}.$$

As with the previous derivation, we use that $\frac{\sum z_1^2}{N} = 1$, $\frac{\sum z_1 e_3}{N} = 0$, and $r_{12} = p_{21}$. Thus, the correlation between X_1 and X_3 is decomposed into the following two components:

$$r_{13} = p_{31} + p_{32}p_{21}. \qquad \textbf{(24.6)}$$

In summary, the decomposition of correlations for the causal model in Figure 24.1 is

1. $r_{12} = p_{21}$, indicating that r_{12} represents the **direct effect** of X_1 on X_2 (p_{21}).
2. $r_{13} = p_{31} + p_{31}p_{21}$, indicating that r_{23}can be decomposed into two parts: p_{31} — the **direct effect** of X_1 on X_3, and $p_{32}p_{21}$ — the **indirect effect** of X_1 on X_3 via X_2.

3. $r_{23} = p_{32} + p_{31}p_{21}$, indicating that r_{23} can be decomposed into two parts: p_{32}— the **direct effect** of X_2 on X_3, and $p_{31}p_{21}$— a **spurious part** of the correlation between X_2 and X_3 due to the fact that they share a *common cause* (X_1) [see Section 11.1].

24.1.5 Testing the Causal Model for Data Fit

24.1.5.1 Just-identified models. A recursive model is called a **just-identified model** when any two variables are either correlated (if both exogenous) or causally related (if at least one is endogenous) and the assumptions described in Section 24.1.3 are met. With a just-identified model, the number of equations that relate correlations between the variables in the model to path coefficients equals the number of the path coefficients. For example, the model in Figure 24.1 is just-identified. Indeed, as can be seen from the path diagram, any two variables are causally related [this model does not include correlations between exogenous variables]. Also, there are three equations (24.4, 24.5, and 24.6) that relate the three correlations (r_{12}, r_{13}, and r_{23}) to the three path coefficients (p_{21}, p_{31}, and p_{32}) in this model. Thus, if the correlations are known and the path coefficients are unknown parameters for the model, Equations 24.4, 24.5, and 24.6 will provide an exact solution for these parameters because the number of equations equals the number of unknown parameters. Therefore, *the correlation coefficients will always be exactly reproduced by the path coefficients in a just-identified model.* In other words, any just-identified model will have a perfect data fit regardless of its substantive merit. To illustrate this for the model in Figure 24.1, we perform the following computations using Equations 24.4, 24.5, and 24.6 with the correlation coefficients and the path coefficients provided in Figure 24.1. Recall that the correlations were computed directly from the data in Figure 24.1 (left panel), whereas the path coefficients were obtained through the use of two regression analyses described in Section 24.1.1. Specifically, we have:

(a) actual $r_{12} = -.681$ and reproduced $r_{12} = p_{21} = -.681$,
(b) actual $r_{13} = -.609$ and reproduced $r_{13} = p_{31} + p_{32}p_{21} = -.537 + (.106)(-.681) = -.609$,
(c) actual $r_{23} = .471$ and reproduced $r_{23} = p_{32} + p_{31}p_{21} = .106 + (-.537)(-.681) = .471$.

Figure 24.2 *A just-identified causal model*

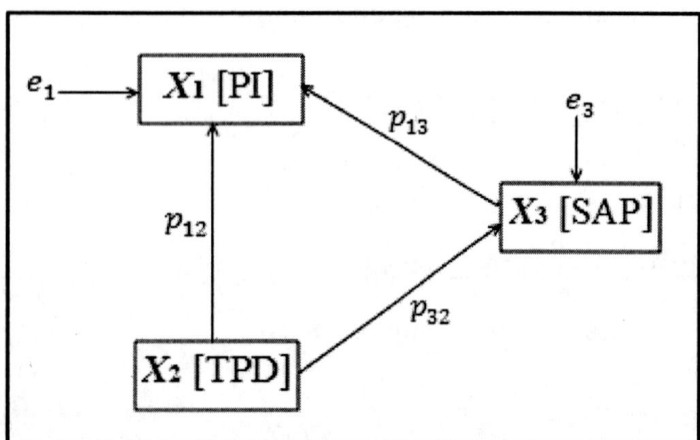

Thus, the actual correlations between the variables in the just-identified model in Figure 24.1 are perfectly reproduced by the model-implied decomposition of these correlations. Similarly, it can be seen that this is true for the just-identified causal model in Figure 24.2 with the same data [the performance of this task is left as a study question at the end of this chapter].

In general, if the actual correlation matrix **R** is reproduced in a just-identified model, this has *no implication* for the validity of this model. Of course, hypothesizing that all variables are interconnected (in a just-identified model) is not likely to occur in thoughtful causal modeling.

24.1.5.2 Overidentified models. Consider now the causal model in Figure 24.3 in which it is hypothesized that *principal isolation* (X_1) affects *student academic performance* (X_3) only through the mediation role of *teacher professional development* (X_2) — that is, PI affects TDP which in turn affects SAP. Clearly, this is not a just-identified model since not all variables are interrelated; specifically, there is no causal connection between X_1 and X_3. Thus, there are three known correlations (r_{12}, r_{13}, and r_{23}) and only two unknown path coefficients ($p_{21}$and p_{32}) in this model. This "overidentification" allows for a possible discrepancy between the actual correlations and those reproduced by the model-implied equations. In general, an **overidentified causal model** exists when the number of known elements (correlations) exceeds the number of unknown parameters (path coefficients).

Figure 24.3 *An overidentified model*

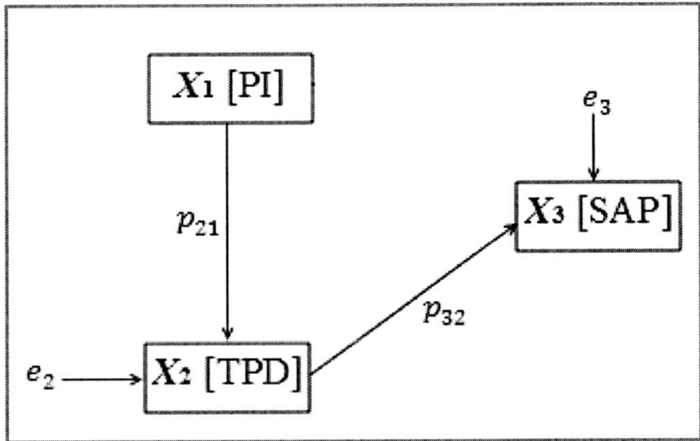

In the overidentified model in Figure 24.3, X_2 is predicted from X_1 and X_3 is predicted from X_2, so the standard (z-) scores of X_2 and X_3 can be represented as follows:

$$z_2 = p_{21}z_1 + e_2 \quad \textbf{(24.7)}$$

$$z_3 = p_{32}z_2 + e_3. \quad \textbf{(24.8)}$$

As equation 24.7 is based on a simple linear regression for the prediction of X_2 from X_1, the standardized regression coefficient in this regression (p_{21}) equals the correlation between X_1 and X_2, that is: $r_{12} = p_{21} = -.681$ (see the value of r_{12} in Figure 24.1). Likewise, the standardized regression coefficient in the simple linear regression for predicting X_3 from X_2 (p_{32}) equals the correlation between X_2 and X_3, that is: $r_{23} = p_{32} = .471$ (see the value of r_{23} in Figure 24.1). [**Check**: using SPSS to run a simple regression using the data in Figure 24.1, predict X_2 from X_1 to verify that the standardized regression coefficient is Beta = −.681, and then predict X_3 from X_2 to verify that the standardized regression coefficient is Beta = .471.] Thus, there is no problem reproducing the actual correlations $r_{12} = -.681$ and $r_{23} = .471$ with their model-implied relations ($r_{12} = p_{21}$ and $r_{23} = p_{32}$). The question now is whether the actual correlation between X_1 and X_3, $r_{13} = -.609$ (given in Figure 24.1), will be reproduced by its model-implied decomposition:

$$r_{13} = \frac{1}{N}\sum z_1 z_3 = \frac{1}{N}\sum z_1(p_{32}z_2 + e_3) = p_{32}\frac{\sum z_1 z_2}{N} + \frac{\sum z_1 e_3}{N} = p_{32}r_{12} + 0 = p_{32}r_{12}.$$

Thus, $r_{13} = p_{32}r_{12}$ [or, $r_{13} = p_{32}p_{21}$] = (.471)(−.681) = −.321. As the actual correlation between X_1 and X_3 (−.609) is not reproduced by its model-implied decomposition (−.321), the causal model is not consistent with the data.

Yet another example of an overidentified causal model with the same three variables is depicted in Figure 24.4. It is hypothesized that *principal isolation* (X_1) and *teacher professional development* (X_2) are correlated [connected by a two-way arrow], with only the latter (X_2) having a causal effect on *student academic performance* (X_3).

Figure 24.4 *An overidentified model with correlated exogenous variables (X_1 and X_2)*

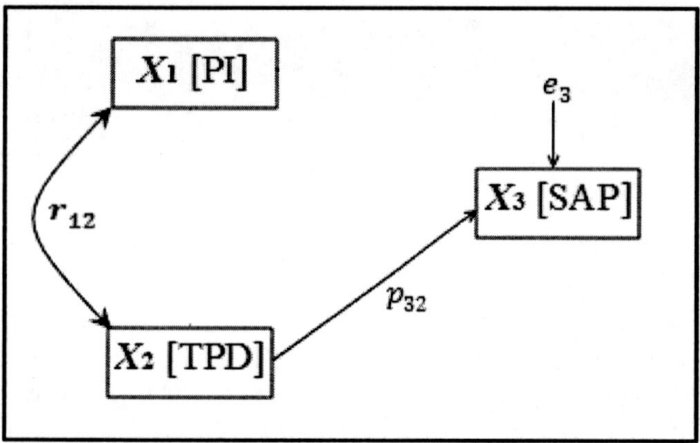

As with the model in Figure 24.3, $z_3 = p_{32}z_2 + e_3$ and $r_{23} = p_{32} = .471$. As also shown in the previous model, the decomposition of the correlation between X_1 and X_3 is: $r_{13} = p_{32}r_{12}$. However, while in the previous model $r_{12} = p_{21}$, this is not the case in the new model because there is no causal effect of X_1 on X_2 in Figure 24.4. The only component of r_{13} in this case ($p_{32}r_{12}$) is unanalyzed due to the correlation between X_1 and X_2. The actual correlation between X_1 and X_2 is $r_{13} = -.609$, whereas its model-implied decomposition is $r_{13} = p_{32}r_{12} =$ (.471)(−.681) = −.321. Thus, with both models (Figures 24.3 and 24.4) the model-implied correlation between X_1 and X_3 is the same ($r_{13} = -.321$), but “off-target” in reproducing the actual correlation (−.609).

NOTE [24.1] When a causal model is not consistent with the data, this is an evidence that the model is not valid. If, however, the model is consistent with the data, this does not necessarily mean that the model *is* valid, because some ‘rival” models can be equally effective in reproducing the actual correlations among the variables in the model. In such cases, the decision about adopting a specific causal model must be based on *substantive considerations* inferred from previous theoretical and/or empirical research.

EXAMPLE 24.1 The purpose of this example is to illustrate the employment of a path analysis given correlations among the variables involved in a causal model. Because the original observations (scores) are not available in this example, the path coefficients cannot be estimated by using regression analyses [as we did in the previous sections using the data in Figure 24.1]. Instead, their estimation is illustrated through the use of correlation decompositions, and then the complete analysis is conducted using the computer program M*plus* (Muthén & Muthén, 2006). Along with providing estimates of path coefficients and their statistical significance, M*plus* provides goodness-of-fit indices for model fit in the framework of structural equation modeling (SEM) — *chi-square* value, CFI, SRMR, and RMSEA (with a 90 percent confidence interval). Descriptions and interpretations of these indices were provided in Chapter 23 (Section 23.2.2).

The causal model in Figure 24.5 represents a restricted (overidentified) version of a just-identified model used by Slone and Hancock (2008) to study the influence of teacher efficacy on career indecision of pre-service teachers and the mediation role of career self-efficacy in this process Although the purpose of this example is pedagogical, not to replicate or discuss the original study (Slone & Hancock, 2008), it must be reiterated that any just-identified model is not useful in model validations as it provides a perfect data fit regardless of its substantive merit.

Figure 24.5 *An overidentified causal model of career indecision*

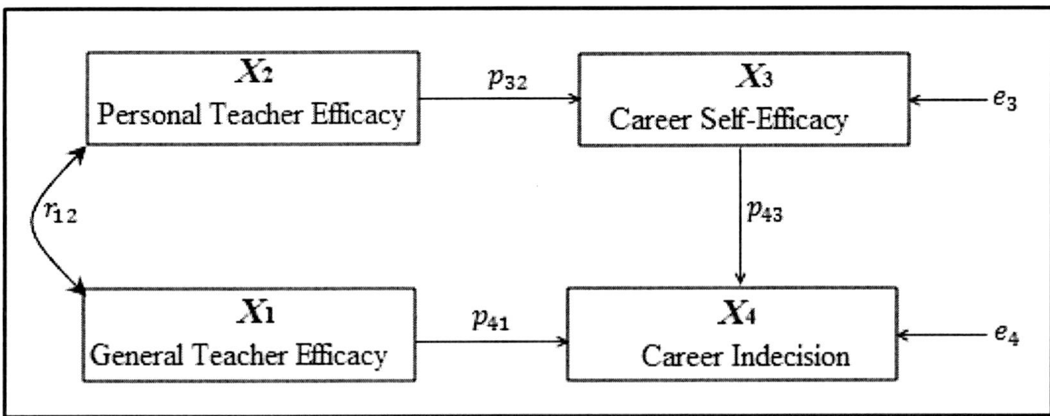

The correlations among the variables X_1 (general teacher efficacy), X_2 (personal teacher efficacy), X_3 (career self-efficacy), and X_4 (career indecision), as provided by the original study (Slone & Hancock, 2008) are given in Table 24.1. The path coefficients reported in the original study are useless here, since they were obtained for a just-identified model using multiple regressions with sample data [not available for this example]. Theoretically, the standard (z-) scores of the two endogenous variables in Figure 24.5 (X_3 and X_4) can be presented as follows:

$$z_3 = p_{32}z_2 + e_3 \quad \textbf{(24.9)}$$

$$z_4 = p_{41}z_1 + p_{43}z_3 + e_4. \quad \textbf{(24.10)}$$

Table 24.1 *Correlations among the variables in the causal model*

Variable	X_1	X_2	X_3	X_4
General teacher efficacy (X_1)	1.00			
Personal teacher efficacy (X_2)	.197	1.00		
Career self-efficacy X_3)	.067	.156	1.00	
Career indecision (X_4)	−.340	−.150	−.385	1.00

Note. $N = 305$.

Although estimates of the path coefficients for the model in Figure 24.5 and goodness-of-fit information are obtained in this example using M*plus*, the model-implied decompositions of the correlations are provided before that for illustration and additional practice. First, the correlation between X_2 and X_3 (r_{23}) equals the path coefficient p_{32} because it represents the standardized regression coefficient in a simple linear regression for the prediction of X_3 from X_2, that is: $r_{23} = p_{32} = .156$ (see Table 24.1). To simplify the decompositions of correlations that follow next, we ignore the error term in Equations 24.9 and 24.10 because they always produce zero correlations with other variables (see assumption 2 in Section 24.1.3). So, we are going to use $z_3 = p_{32}z_2$ and $z_4 = p_{41}z_1 + p_{43}z_3$. With this, the correlation between X_1 and X_4 can be decomposed as follows:

$$r_{14} = \frac{1}{N}\sum z_1 z_4 = \frac{1}{N}\sum z_1(p_{41}z_1 + p_{43}z_3) = p_{41}\frac{\sum z_1^2}{N} + p_{43}\frac{\sum z_1 z_3}{N}$$

$$= p_{41}(1) + p_{43}\frac{\sum z_1(p_{32}z_2)}{N} = p_{41} + p_{43}p_{32}\frac{\sum z_1 z_2}{N} = p_{41} + p_{43}p_{32}r_{12}.$$

In this case, then, r_{14} has two components — a *direct effect* (p_{41}) and *unexplained covariation* ($p_{43}p_{32}r_{12}$):

$$r_{14} = p_{41} + p_{43}p_{32}r_{12}. \quad \textbf{(24.11)}$$

Likewise, the correlation between X_3 and X_4 can be decomposed as follows:

$$r_{34} = \frac{1}{N}\sum z_3 z_4 = \frac{1}{N}\sum z_3\,(p_{41}z_1 + p_{43}z_3) = p_{41}\frac{\sum z_1 z_3}{N} + p_{43}\frac{\sum z_3^2}{N}$$

$$= p_{41}\frac{\sum z_1(p_{32}z_2)}{N} + p_{43}(1) = p_{41}p_{32}\frac{\sum z_1 z_2}{N} + p_{43} = p_{41}p_{32}r_{12} + p_{43}.$$

Here, r_{34} also has two components — a *direct effect* (p_{43}) and *unexplained covariation* ($p_{41}p_{32}r_{12}$):

$$r_{34} = p_{43} + p_{41}p_{32}r_{12}. \quad \textbf{(24.12)}$$

The unexplained covariation (unanalyzed component) in Equations 24.11 and 24.12 is due to correlated causes (X_1 and X_2).

Further, the correlation between X_2 and X_4 can be decomposed as follows:

$$r_{24} = \frac{1}{N}\sum z_2 z_4 = \frac{1}{N}\sum z_2\,(p_{41}z_1 + p_{43}z_3) = p_{41}\frac{\sum z_1 z_2}{N} + p_{43}\frac{\sum z_2 z_3}{N}$$

$$= p_{41}r_{12} + p_{43}\frac{\sum z_2(p_{32}z_2)}{N} = p_{41}r_{12} + p_{43}p_{32}\frac{\sum z_2^2}{N} = p_{41}r_{12} + p_{43}p_{32}(1)$$

$$= p_{41}r_{12} + p_{43}p_{32},$$

that is, r_{24} is decomposed to an *indirect effect* ($p_{43}p_{32}$) and *unexplained covariation* ($p_{41}r_{12}$):

$$r_{24} = p_{43}p_{32} + p_{41}r_{12} \quad \textbf{(24.13)}$$

By replacing in Equation 24.11: $r_{14} = -.340$, $r_{12} = .197$, and $p_{32} = .156$ (= r_{23}), we obtain an equation with two unknown parameters (p_{41} and p_{43}):

$$-.340 = p_{41} + (.156)(.197)\, p_{43} \tag{24.14}$$

Likewise, replacing in Equation 24.12: $r_{34} = -.385$, $r_{12} = .197$, and $p_{32} = .156$, we obtain another equation with the same two unknown parameters (p_{41} and p_{43}):

$$-.385 = p_{43} + (.156)(.197) p_{41}. \tag{24.15}$$

Without going into technical details, solving Equations 24.14 and 24.15 for the two unknown parameters yields the following estimates (rounded to the nearest hundredth):

$$p_{41} = -.32 \text{ and } p_{43} = -.37.$$

As shown next, the same estimates, along with their standard errors and *p*-values for statistical significance, are provided with the M*plus* output for the model in Figure 24.5 using the correlation matrix in Table 24.1. The M*plus* syntax for this analysis is shown in Figure 24.6. The data file, named **EX24_1.dat**, is an ASCII.dat file with the correlation matrix [in a triangular format as seen in Table 24.1]. The number of observations, 305, is specified in the M*plus* syntax.

Figure 24.6 *Mplus syntax for path analysis based on a correlation matrix and number of observations*

```
TITLE: PATH ANALYSIS

DATA:
   FILE IS "C:\EX24_1.dat";
   TYPE IS CORRELATION;
   NGROUPS = 1;
   NOBSERVATIONS = 305;

VARIABLE:
   NAMES ARE X1-X4;
   USEVARIABLES ARE X1-X4;

ANALYSIS:
  TYPE IS GENERAL; ESTIMATOR IS ML;
  ITERATIONS = 1000; CONVERGENCE = 0.00005;

OUTPUT:  STANDARDIZED;

MODEL:   X3 ON X1 X2;
         X4 ON X1 X2 X3;
```

The M*plus* output provides goodness-of-fit indices for model fit. A non-significant *chi-square* value, $\chi^2(2) = 0.84$, $p = .66$, indicates that the causal model in Figure 24.5 is consistent with the data. This is supported also by the goodness-of-fit indices CFI = 1.00 [CFI > .95 is requested], SRMR = .016 [SRMR < .083 is requested], and RMSEA = .00 and 95%CI = (.00, .09) [RMSEA ≤ .05 is requested]. A selected part of the M*plus* output, with estimates of model parameters (path coefficients and residual variances), is provided in Figure 24.7.

Figure 24.7 *Selected Mplus output for path analysis (syntax in Figure 24.6)*

```
STANDARDIZED MODEL RESULTS
                                                        Two-Tailed
                    Estimate       S.E.  Est./S.E.     P-Value

X3       ON
    X2                 0.156      0.056      2.792       0.005

X4       ON
    X1                -0.317      0.048     -6.637       0.000
    X3                -0.365      0.047     -7.795       0.000

Residual Variances
    X3                 0.976      0.017     55.974       0.000
    X4                 0.759      0.042     18.267       0.000
```

The estimate for "X3 ON X2" in the M*plus* output (0.156) is the path coefficient that corresponds to the arrow from X_2 to X_3 in Figure 24.5. That is, p_{32} = .156. The standard error for this estimate of p_{32} is S.E. = 0.056. The ratio "Est./S.E." (estimate to standard error), referred to also as a *critical ratio* (CR), indicates statistical significance when it exceeds 1.96 [the z-critical value for $\alpha = .05$]. The *p*-value associated with the CR is also reported. Thus, p_{32} = .156 is statistically significant ($p = .005$). Likewise, we can see that $p_{41} = -.317$ and $p_{43} = -.365$ are both statistically significant ($p < .001$). Note that the M*plus* estimates of p_{32}, p_{41}, and p_{43} are the same as those that we obtained earlier via manual decomposition of correlations. Figure 24.7 also provides the residual variance in X_3 predicted from X_2 (0.976) and the residual variance in X_4 predicted from X_1 and X_3 (0.759).

In summary, the causal model in Figure 24.5 is consistent with the data so we **fail to disconfirm** the hypothesized causal relations in this model. The influence of general teacher efficacy on career indecision is a negative direct effect ($p_{41} = -.317$). That is, higher general teacher efficacy leads to lower career indecision. Additionally, the influence of personal teacher efficacy on career indecision is a negative indirect effect: $p_{43}p_{32} = (-.365)(.156) = -.057$ (see Equation 24.13). In this case, higher personal teacher efficacy leads to higher career self-efficacy which in turn produces lower career indecision. In general, the *total effect* is the sum of direct and indirect effects (TE = DE + IE). In this case, however, the total effect of general teacher efficacy on career indecision consists only of a direct effect, whereas the total effect of personal teacher efficacy on career indecision consists only of an indirect effect.

24.2 Elements of Structural Equation Modeling

24.2.1 Upgrading Path Analysis Models to Typical SEM Models

The confirmatory factor analysis (CFA) presented in Chapter 23 and the path analysis presented here both fall within the framework of structural equation modeling (SEM). However, while CFA deals with measurement relations between latent variables (constructs) and their observable indicators, path analysis deals with structural relations among observable variables. For example, the model in Figure 24.5 involves *structural* relations, but there is no *measurement* part, since all variables are interpreted as observable variables. In fact, the four variables in this model (general teacher efficacy, personal teacher efficacy, career self-efficacy, and career indecision) are *constructs*, but in the original study (Slone & Hancock, 2008) they are taken as observable variables measured by the total scores on (a) 16 items on a Teacher Efficacy Scale (Gibson & Dembo, 1984), (b) four items on a Career Self-Efficacy Scale (Wulff & Steitz, 1996), and (c) 19 items on a Career Decision Scale (Osipow, 1980). A typical SEM-type development of this model, on the other hand, would include *both* the structural relations depicted in Figure 24.5 and the measurement relations between the four constructs and their indicators (scale items) — e.g., see Figure 24.8. Major advantages of the SEM model in Figure 24.8 over its path analytic version in Figure 24.5 are that (a) the scores on each construct are "error free" (true scores) and (b) the SEM results remain stable across studies where the constructs are measured by different, yet valid, scales.

Figure 24.8 *Hypothetical SEM model for career indecision of pre-service teachers*

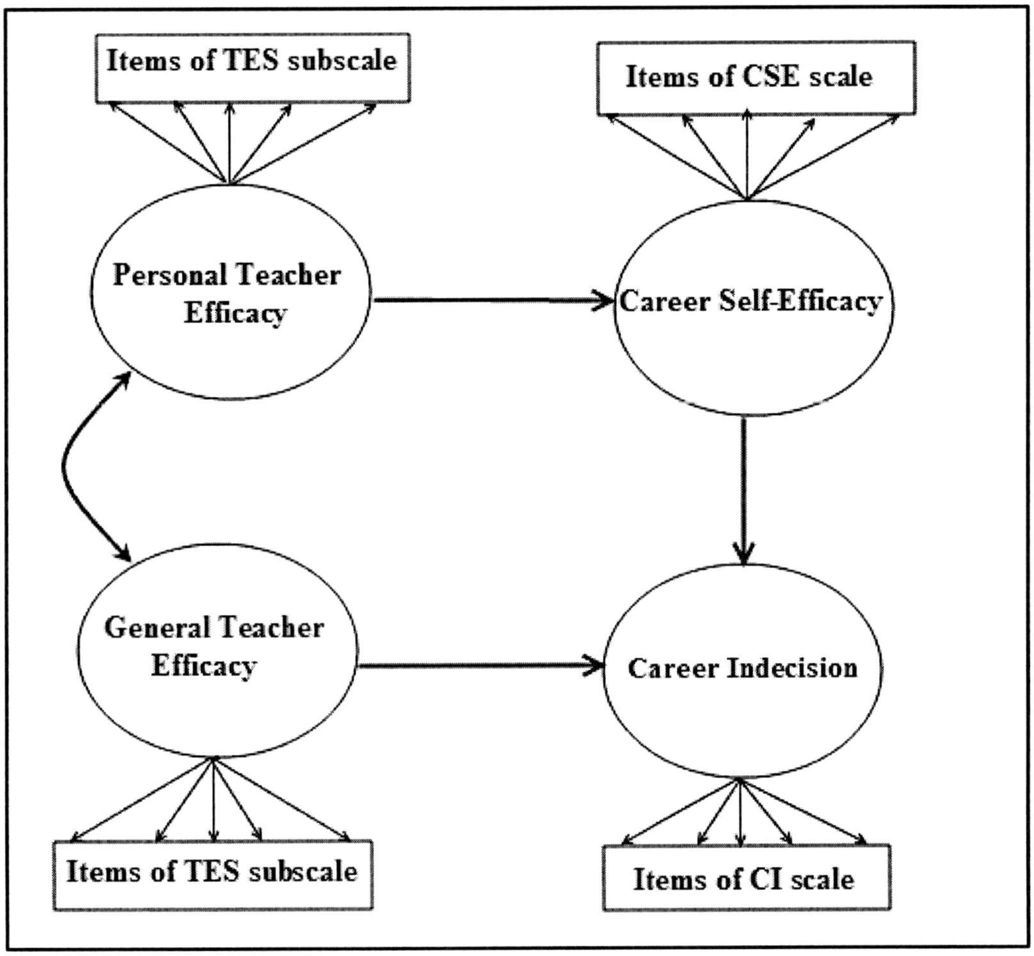

Items of TES subscale
Items of CSE scale
Personal Teacher Efficacy
Career Self-Efficacy
General Teacher Efficacy
Career Indecision
Items of TES subscale
Items of CI scale

24.2.2 Comparing Groups on Latent Variables

24.2.2.1 SEM versus MANOVA. The complexity of relationships between variables in educational settings can be efficiently investigated using multivariate methods of statistical analysis. Testing for group mean differences on a set of observed variables typically requires the use of multivariate analysis of variance (MANOVA) or structural equation modeling (SEM). MANOVA is more appropriate when groups are compared on constructs which "emerge" as a linear composite of the observed variables; that is, when the observed variables represent causal agents of the construct. An example of such an *emergent variable system* is when groups of people categorized by disability type are separated by "stress" – a construct caused by observed dependent variables such as demands of the workplace and relationship with family members. Methodological principles of using MANOVA were discussed in Chapter 21.

SEM is more appropriate with a *latent variable system* in which the construct (latent variable) has a causal influence on the observed variables. For example, "self-esteem" is a construct that may underlie the responses of injured workers on specific questionnaire items during a rehabilitation process. An important feature of the SEM methods is that, unlike MANOVA, they provide error-free measures of the latent variables (constructs, factors, subscales) by eliminating the random error of measurement for the observed variables (e.g., questionnaire items) associated with the latent variable(s). A frequently-occurring scenario in educational research in which SEM can be efficiently employed with a latent variable system is when groups of people are compared on subscales of an instrument (e.g., questionnaire or survey). For example, in a study on prevention of abuse in a workgroup context (Mangione & Mangione, 2001), male and female workers were compared on three subscales of a survey on stressful factors in the workplace: *Hostility* (e.g., "been embarrassed or insulted in front of others"), *Harassment* (e.g., "experienced unwanted sexual advances"), and *Negativity* (e.g., not been praised for your work"). In another study (Beron & Farkas, 2004), students were grouped by age (ages 5-10 and 11-17), social class, gender, and race (non-Hispanic White and African-American) and then compared on three latent variables (constructs): basic cognitive skills, reading skills, and advanced reading skills, with basic cognitive skills acting as a mediator for the group differences on reading skills and advanced reading skills.

In these (and numerous other) examples of SEM in behavioral studies, the subscales of an instrument represent latent variables (factors, constructs) that *underlie* the persons' responses on the items of this instrument. Hereafter, the terms *latent variable*, *construct*, *factor*, and *subscale* will be used interchangeably. While SEM provides an excellent framework for the comparison of group means on latent variables, traditional statistical methods such as *t*-tests, analysis of variance, and analysis of covariance are still predominantly employed in educational research.

24.2.2.2 Factorial invariance across groups. Typically, research applications of SEM involve comparisons of groups on latent variables (factors, constructs). For example, there is strong evidence that self-regulation is positively related to student academic achievement (Kornell & Metcalfe, 2006; Zimmerman & Kitsantas, 2005). As *self-efficacy*, *metacognitive self-regulation*, and *attributions* are constructs that underlie the phases of the self-regulation process (Zimmerman, 1989), researchers in educational psychology are interested in investigating differences in these constructs across groups by gender, socio-economic status, ethnicity, and other grouping variables. As another example, the constructs of *psychosocial distress* and *successful coping* are compared later in this section across two groups of people with multiple sclerosis based on their typical course of illness: (a) *relapsing* — relapsing-remitting or chronic relapsing illness, and (b) *progressive* — secondary progressive or primary progressive illness.

A central question to be addressed prior to comparing groups on constructs is whether the constructs have the same *meaning* for each group. In SEM terminology, this is a question of testing for factorial invariance across groups. In general, **factorial invariance** across groups occurs when there are (a) *invariant factor loadings* — the factor-loading regression paths are the same for each group, (b) *invariant intercepts* — the intercepts in regressing indicators to factors are equal across groups, (c) *invariant factor variances and covariances* — the variances of the factors (constructs) and the covariances among them are equal across groups, and (d) *invariant residual variances* — the variances of the residuals (errors) in regressing indicators to factors are equal across groups. The first two conditions (invariant factor loadings and invariant intercepts) are also called conditions of **measurement invariance**. In measurement parlance, the lack of measurement invariance indicates the presence of *item bias* (or *differential item functioning*). For example, students from different groups that have equal verbal ability may perform differently on some items in a verbal ability test because of, say, offensive language in these items that may affect students who belong to a particular group (e.g., Holland & Wainer, 1993).

As a prerequisite to testing for factorial invariance, it is necessary to identify a baseline model, which is estimated for each group separately. The most parsimonious, yet substantively most meaningful and best fitting model to the data for a group is referred to as **baseline model** for this group (e.g., Byrne, Shavelson, & Muthén, 1989). Testing for factorial invariance is conducted then by using the chi-square square test for the difference ($\Delta\chi^2$) between two "nested" models — a model with "invariance assumed"($\chi^2_{\text{Invariance}}$) and a model with "no invariance assumed" ($\chi^2_{\text{No invariance}}$). The invariance of the parameters being tested (e.g., factor loadings) is confirmed when the chi-square difference ($\Delta\chi^2 = \chi^2_{\text{Invariance}} - \chi^2_{\text{No invariance}}$) is *not* statistically significant at the prespecified level of significance (e.g., $\alpha = .05$). Specifically, a logical sequence of nested models are ordered in an increasingly restrictive fashion, and the $\Delta\chi^2$ test is conducted at each step to test for invariance across two groups:

- **Model 0**: The baseline model is fit in the two groups together allowing all parameters (factor loadings, intercepts, variances/covariances, and residual variances) to be free — that is, no invariance of the parameters across the two groups is assumed.
- **Model 1**: The baseline model is fit in the two groups together, with the factor loadings held equal across the groups. As Model 1 is nested within Model 0, the chi-square difference for the two models ($\Delta\chi^2_{\text{M1-M0}}$) is used to test for invariance of the factor loadings.
- **Model 2**: The baseline model is fit in the two groups together, with the factor loadings and intercepts held equal across the groups. As Model 2 is nested within Model 1, the chi-square difference for the two models ($\Delta\chi^2_{\text{M2-M1}}$) is used to test for invariance of the intercepts.
- **Model 3**: The baseline model is fit in the two groups together, with the factor loadings, intercepts, and factor variances and covariances held equal across the groups. As Model 3 is nested within Model 2, the chi-square difference for the two models ($\Delta\chi^2_{\text{M3-M2}}$) is used to test for invariance of the factor variances and covariances.
- **Model 4**: The baseline model is fit in the two groups together, with the factor loadings, intercepts, and residual variances held equal across the groups. As Model 4 is nested within Model 2, the chi-square difference for the two models ($\Delta\chi^2_{\text{M4-M2}}$) is used to test for invariance of the factor variances and covariances; [note that Model 4 is nested within Model 2, not within Model 3].

24.2.2.3 Partial measurement invariance. As noted earlier, *measurement invariance* across groups exists when the factor loadings and intercepts are invariant across the groups. Specifically, a non-significant chi-square difference between Model 1 and Model 0 ($\Delta\chi^2_{\text{M1-M0}}$) indicates invariant factor loadings and non-significant chi-square difference between Model 2 and Model 1 ($\Delta\chi^2_{\text{M2-M1}}$) indicates invariant slopes. There are situations, however, in which there is no perfect measurement invariance, but neither is there evidence of complete inequality of factor loadings or intercepts. This situation is termed **partial measurement invariance.** As previous research shows, given the stringent nature of the hypotheses for invariance, the invariance is a matter of degree estimated by the proportion of parameters that are invariant (e.g., Byrne, Shavelson, & Muthén, 1989).

Suppose that that the factor loadings are invariant across two groups (i.e., $\Delta\chi^2_{M1-M0}$ is not statistically significant), but $\Delta\chi^2_{M2-M1}$ *is* statistically significant, thus indicating that the intercepts are not invariant (i.e., not all intercepts are equal) across the two groups. To determine the degree of partial measurement invariance in this case, Model 2 must be modified by setting some intercepts "free" (non invariant) across the two groups. Which intercepts to start freeing depends on the values of their modification indices reported for Model 2 by the SEM software being used (e.g., Mplus, AMOS, EQS, or LISREL). The **modification index (MI)** for a parameter gives the *expected drop in the model's chi-square value if this parameter is freely estimated* (see Section 23.2.2). The MI for one parameter is statistically significant if it exceeds 3.84 (the chi-square value with $df = 1$). If there are several parameters with statistically significant MIs, they should be freed *one at a time*, starting with the parameter which has the largest MI. In general, there is no fixed rule as to what degree of partial invariance is acceptable. Less than 20 percent freed parameters seems acceptable in practical applications, but it is up to researchers to decide, as long as the observed degree of invariance is reported with the results (e.g., Byrne, Shavelson, & Muthén, 1989; Levine, Kaplan, Kripke, et al., 2003).

The presence of measurement invariance (or partial measurement invariance) is critical for practical comparisons of groups on latent variables (factors, constructs). The assumption of invariant factor variances and covariances is analogous to the assumption of homogeneous variance-covariance matrices in MANOVA. As indicated earlier, this assumption is met when the chi-square difference between Model 3 and Model 2 ($\Delta\chi^2_{M3-M2}$) is non-significant. Testing for invariant residual (error) variances is not of practical interest in comparing groups on constructs. Moreover, testing for the invariance of error parameters represents an overly restrictive test of the data (e.g., Bentler, 2004; Byrne, 1988).

24.2.2.4 Structured means modeling. With the assumption of measurement invariance across groups met, the door is open for comparison of the group means on the latent variables of interest. There are two major approaches to addressing this task in the context of SEM: *structured means modeling* and *group code (MIMIC) modeling*. **Structured means modeling (SMM)** is applied with models that contain intercepts for the purpose of estimating group means on a construct. To illustrate SMM, Figure 24.9 depicts the comparison of gender groups (say, 0 = males, 1 = females) on the construct *motivation* measured by three indicators (Y_1, Y_2, and Y_3).

In Figure 24.9, the notations with small Greek letters are: η (*eta*) for the construct; λ_k (*lambda*, with a subscript *k*) for the factor loadings representing the impact of the construct η on the indicator Y_k (or, the unstandardized regression coefficient in the prediction of Y_k from η), τ_k (tau, with a subscript *k*) for the intercept in the prediction of Y_k from η, ; and ε_k (*epsilon*, with a subscript *k*) for the residual in Y_k (i.e., the variability in the indicator Y_k not explained by η).

Suppose that the model in Figure 24.9 is a baseline model that holds for both groups (males and females) and the assumption of measurement invariance across the two groups is met; that is, the factor loadings (λ_2 and λ_3) and the intercepts (τ_1, τ_2, and τ_3) are equal across the two groups. The intercept for an indicator shows the predicted value on this indicator for subjects with a score of zero on the construct ($\eta = 0$). The first factor loading is set to 1 ($\lambda_1 = 1$) to indicate that Y_1 is the reference indicator for the construct η (i.e., η and Y_1 are measured on the same scale).

Figure 24.9 *Structured means model (SMM) for group differences on motivation measured by* Y_1, Y_2, and Y_3

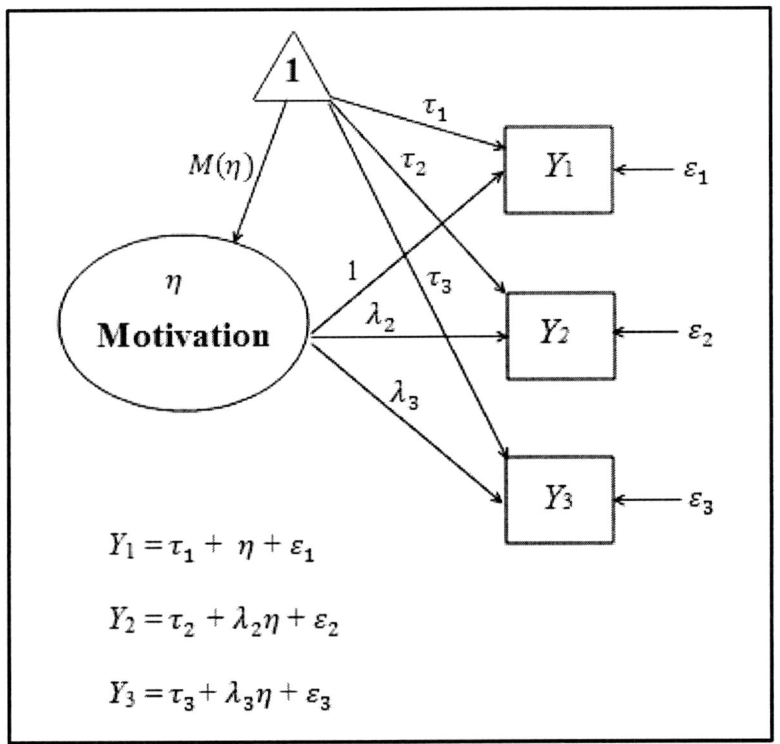

The three equations in Figure 24.9 represent the linear relationships between *Y*-scores and η-scores with this model. In general, the symbolic matrix form of these equations is

$$\mathbf{Y} = \boldsymbol{\tau} + \boldsymbol{\Lambda\eta} + \boldsymbol{\varepsilon}, \qquad \textbf{(24.16)}$$

where the matrices are the following vectors: $\mathbf{Y} = [Y_1, Y_2, Y_3]$, $\boldsymbol{\tau} = [\tau_1, \tau_2, \tau_3]$, $\boldsymbol{\Lambda} = [1, \lambda_2, \lambda_3]$, and $\boldsymbol{\varepsilon} = [\varepsilon_1, \varepsilon_2, \varepsilon_3]$. It is assumed that the vector $\boldsymbol{\tau}$ is multiplied by a unit vector, $\mathbf{1} = [1, 1, 1]$, depicted by the notation **1** in the triangle in Figure 24.9.

Thus, the $\boldsymbol{\tau}$ values (τ_1, τ_2, and τ_3) are viewed as paths to the indicators (Y_1, Y_2, and Y_3) from a unit-constant *pseudovariable* on which all subjects have a score of 1 (e.g., Hancock, 2004). The relationship between the mean *Y*-scores and the mean η-scores, denoted here $M(Y)$ and $M(\eta)$, respectively, is based on Equation 24.16. Taking into account that the mean of a residual is zero [$M(\varepsilon_1) = M(\varepsilon_2) = M(\varepsilon_3) = 0$], we have:

$$M(Y_1) = \tau_1 + M(\eta) \qquad \textbf{(24.17)}$$
$$M(Y_2) = \tau_2 + \lambda_2 M(\eta) \qquad \textbf{(24.18)}$$
$$M(Y_3) = \tau_3 + \lambda_3\, M(\eta) \qquad \textbf{(24.19)}$$

Equations 24.17, 24.18, and 24.19 represent the **mean structure**, which is estimated in SMM analyses along with the **covariance structure** represented by the following equations:

$$\text{VAR}(Y_1) = \text{VAR}(\eta) + \text{VAR}(\varepsilon_1) \quad \textbf{(24.20)}$$
$$\text{VAR}(Y_2) = \lambda_2^2\, \text{VAR}(\eta) + \text{VAR}(\varepsilon_2) \quad \textbf{(24.21)}$$
$$\text{VAR}(Y_3) = \lambda_3^2\, \text{VAR}(\eta) + \text{VAR}(\varepsilon_3) \quad \textbf{(24.22)}$$
$$\text{COV}(Y_1, Y_2) = \lambda_2 \text{VAR}(\eta) \quad \textbf{(24.23)}$$
$$\text{COV}(Y_1, Y_3) = \lambda_3 \text{VAR}(\eta) \quad \textbf{(24.24)}$$
$$\text{COV}(Y_2, Y_3) = \lambda_2 \lambda_3\, \text{VAR}(\eta) \quad \textbf{(24.25)}$$

In the above six equations (24.20–24.25), the notations VAR and COV stand for *variance* and *covariance*, respectively. These equations are obtained from those given in Figure 24.9 by applying the basic properites of variances and covariances for the sum of variables and the product of variables and constants (λ_2 and λ_3) — see Chapter 6, Sections 6.2.3.4.

To estimate the difference between the two group means on the construct, η, one of the groups is chosen to serve as a reference group and its mean on the construct is fixed to zero. With this, the construct mean of the other group represents the difference between the construct means of the two groups, assuming that the factor loadings (λ_k) and the intercept (τ_k) do not change in value across the two groups [hence, SMM works under the assumption of measurement invariance]. For example, if the gender group coded by zero (0 = males) represents the reference group, the mean of this group on the construct is fixed to zero, $M_0(\eta) = 0$. Thus, if $M_1(\eta)$ is the mean of the other group on the construct, the difference between the two means is $M_1(\eta) - M_0(\eta) = M_1(\eta) - 0 = M_1(\eta)$.

The nine model-implied equations given here above — three mean structure equations (22.17–22.19) and six covariance structure equations (24.20–24.25) generate 18 equations for the two populations from which the two compared groups are being randomly selected. Under the assumption of measurement invariance, the factor loadings and intercepts are the same for the populations, so there only 14 unknown parameters to estimate with these 18 equations, namely, 2 factor loadings (λ_2 and λ_3), 3 intercepts (τ_1, τ_2, and τ_3), 6 residual (error) variances (3 per population), 2 factor variances (1 per population), and 1 factor mean, $M_1(\eta)$. [Recall that the mean of the reference group is fixed to zero.] It follows, then, that this model has 4 degrees of freedom (18 – 14 = 4). In the framework of maximum likelihood estimation, the parameters are selected to minimize the discrepancy between observed and model-implied variances-covariance matrices and vectors of means on the set of indicators (e.g., Bollen, 1989; Hancock, 2004).

If the goodness-of-fit statistics (e.g., chi-square value, CFI, SRMR, and RMSEA) provide evidence of a satisfactory data-model fit, a simple z-test is used to test the estimated construct mean of the nonreference group, $\widehat{M}_1(\eta)$, for statistical significance: $z = \widehat{M}_1(\eta)/\text{SE}[\widehat{M}_1(\eta)]$, where $\text{SE}[\widehat{M}_1(\eta)]$ is the standard error of the mean for this group. In fact, this is a test for statistical significance of the difference between the two groups, since the mean of the other (reference) group is fixed to zero, $M_0(\eta) = 0$.

As shown in Hancock (2001), the effect size of the difference between the two groups on the construct of interest, η, can be estimated as follows

$$\hat{d} = \frac{|\widehat{M}_1(\eta)|}{\sqrt{\widehat{VAR}(\eta)}}, \quad \textbf{(24.26)}$$

where $\widehat{VAR}(\eta)$ is the poolled (weighted) variance of the estimates of the consrtuct variances for the two groups (see Chapter 6, Formula 6.6). The value of this effect size measure, $\hat{d}$, indicates the group separation in terms of latent standard deviations on the construct of interest.

24.2.2.5 Group-code (MIMIC) modeling. Just like a *t*-test, the SMM method presented in the previous section keeps the data from the two groups *separate*. In contrast, the **group-code modeling** presented in this section keeps the data from the two groups *together* and is based on the idea of using dummy coding in regression analysis for group comparisons. The construct of interest is regressed on a dummy variable, *X*, which assumes values of 0 and 1. Thus, all subjects in one group are assigned a "score" of 0 on *X* [we may refer to this group as the reference group], whereas all subjects in the other group are assigned a "score" of 1 on *X*. The logic behind using group coding in regression analysis for the purposes of group comparisons is discussed in Chapter 17 (e.g., see Figure 17.1 for two groups coded −1 and 1, respectively). To specify that the group comparison is within the framework of structural equation modeling, the group-code modeling is called **Multiple-Indicator, Multiple-Cause (MIMIC) Modeling**. The MIMIC translation of the SMM modeling in Figure 24.9 is depicted in Figure 24.10.

Figure 24.10 *MIMIC modeling for gender differences on Motivation*

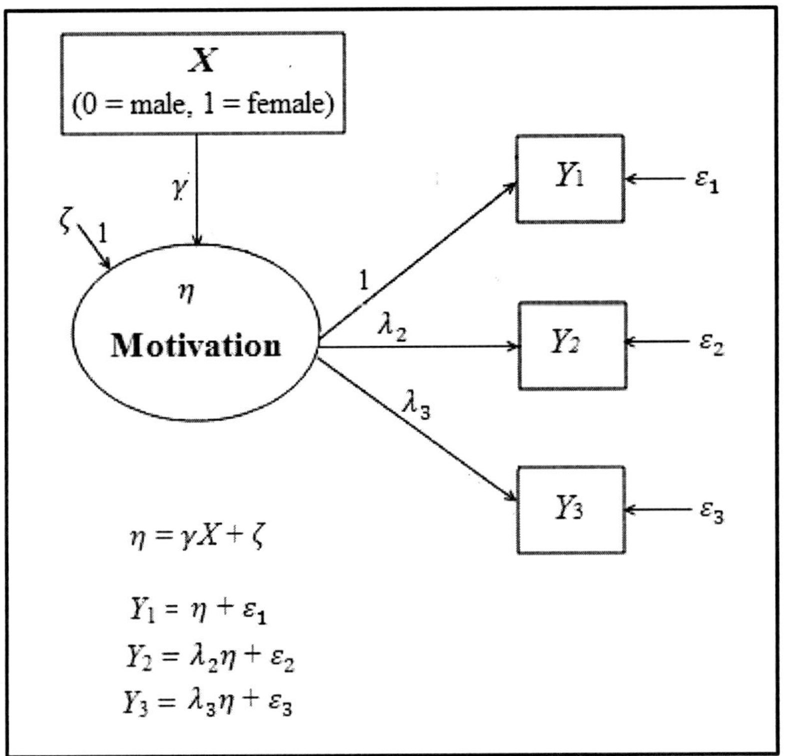

The structural part of the MIMIC model is presented by the regression of the construct, η, on the dummy variable, *X*, with coding values of 0 and 1 (0 = male and 1 = female):

$$\eta = \gamma X + \zeta, \quad \textbf{(24.27)}$$

where γ (*gamma*) is the regression coefficient, representing the impact of the dummy variable *X* on the construct η, and ζ(*dzeta*) is the residual in η (i.e., the part in η which is not explained by gender differences). The variance of this residual, VAR(ζ), is called *disturbance variance*. There is no intercept in Equation 24.27 because all variables, including the dummy variable *X*, are treated as if there were presented as deviation scores (i.e., differences between the scores and their mean). Recall that the sum (or mean) of deviation scores is zero.

Clearly, of central interest is the statistical significance of the structural coefficient γ and its magnitude (effect size). A statistically significant positive γ would indicate that the group coded 1 (females) score *higher* on motivation compared to the reference group (0 = males). As with the SMM method, a simple z-test is used to test γ for statistical significance:

$$z = \frac{\hat{\gamma}}{SE(\hat{\gamma})}, \tag{24.28}$$

where $\hat{\gamma}$ is the model estimate of γ and $SE(\hat{\gamma})$ is its standard error.

The standardized effect size of the difference between the means of the two groups on the construct of interest (η) is estimated as follows (Hancock, 2001):

$$\hat{d} = \frac{|\hat{\gamma}|}{\sqrt{\widehat{VAR}(\zeta)}}, \tag{24.29}$$

where $\widehat{VAR}(\zeta)$ is the variance of the residual (ζ) — i.e., the variance of the construct (η) which is not explained by the group differences. That is, $\widehat{VAR}(\zeta)$ represents an estimate of a pooled within-group variance. Thus, the effect size estimate, $\hat{d}$, shows how many latent standard deviations separate the means of the two groups on the construct of interest (η).

NOTE [24.2] Theoretically, MIMIC modeling is based on stronger assumptions than structured means modeling (SMM). Indeed, while SMM requires only measurement invariance (equal factor loadings and equal intercepts across the two groups), MIMIC modeling keeps the data from the two groups together, thus assuming invariance of the factor loadings, intercepts, factor variances and covariances, and residual variances.

As previous research shows that testing for the invariance of residual variances (error variance parameters) represents an *overly restrictive* test of the data (e.g., Bentler, 2004; Byrne, 1988), practical applications of MIMIC modeling require testing for invariance of factor loadings, intercepts, and factor variances and covariances. The logic of such testing is described with Models 0, 1, 2, and 3 for invariance testing in Section 24.2.2.2.

As the construct (η) is regressed on a dummy variable (X), the MIMIC estimation of model parameters is based only on equations for the *variance-covariance structure*. For the MIMIC model in Figure 24.10, for example, there are 10 variance-covariance equations:

$$\begin{aligned}
&\text{VAR}(Y_1) = \text{VAR}(\eta) + \text{VAR}(\varepsilon_1)\\
&\text{VAR}(Y_2) = \lambda_2^2\text{VAR}(\eta) + \text{VAR}(\varepsilon_2)\\
&\text{VAR}(Y_3) = \lambda_3^2\text{VAR}(\eta) + \text{VAR}(\varepsilon_3)\\
&\text{VAR}(X) = \text{VAR}(X)\\
&\text{COV}(Y_1, Y_2) = \lambda_2\text{VAR}(\eta)\\
&\text{COV}(Y_1, Y_3) = \lambda_3\text{VAR}(\eta)\\
&\text{COV}(Y_2, Y_3) = \lambda_2\lambda_3\text{VAR}(\eta)
\end{aligned}$$

$COV(X, Y_1) = \gamma VAR(X)$
$COV(X, Y_2) = \gamma\lambda_2 VAR(X)$
$COV(X, Y_3) = \gamma\lambda_3 VAR(X)$

In the above 10 equations, $VAR(\eta) = \gamma^2 VAR(X) + VAR(\zeta)$, which is obtained from Equation 24.27 using the rules for variances described in Chapter 6, Section 6.2.3.4 [the same rules are used to obtain the above 10 equations from those provided in Figure 24.10]. Thus, there are 10 equations to estimate 8 unknown parameters: 1 structural path coefficient (γ), 2 factor loadings (λ_2 and λ_3), 1 variable variance [VAR(X)], 1 disturbance variance [$VAR(\zeta)$], and 3 residual variances for the indicators [$VAR(\varepsilon_1)$, $VAR(\varepsilon_2)$, and $VAR(\varepsilon_3)$]. With 10 equations available for the estimation of 8 unknown parameters, there are 2 degrees of freedom (10 – 8 = 2) for the MIMIC model in Figure 24.10. In the framework of maximum likelihood estimation, the eight unknown parameters are selected to minimize the difference between the 10 actual variances and covariances produced by the 4 observed variables (X, Y_1, Y_2, Y_3, and Y_4) and their counterparts implied by the model.

EXAMPLE 24.2 The purpose of this example is to illustrate the employment of MIMIC modeling with a preliminary testing for its assumptions of invariant factor loadings, invariant intercepts, and invariant factor variances and covariances. Specifically, using the data described in Example 23.1, two groups of people with multiple sclerosis are compared on two constructs: **psychosocial distress** (PD) and **successful coping** (SC). The two groups were formed based on their typical course of illness, namely (a) *relapsing* (relapsing or relapsing-remitting), or (b) *progressive* (secondary progressive or primary progressive). These two groups are referred to hereafter as **relapsing illness group** (n = 669) and **progressive illness group** (n = 359). The SPSS data file **EXAMPLE_23_1.sav** [available at http://cehd.gmu.edu/book/dimitrov] contains 1028 observations for the two groups on a variable GROUP (0 = relapsing, 1 = progressive) and eleven survey items (**Item_1**, **Item_2**, ..., **Item_11**) initially hypothesized to tap into the two constructs of interest. These items are described in Chapter 23 (Table 23.1).

In fact, the 7-item model, referred to as "reduced" model in Chapter 23 (see Figure 23.3) is used here as a baseline model and tested for invariance across the two groups prior to comparing these groups on the two latent variables (constructs): psychosocial distress and successful coping. A reasonable data fit of this model for the two groups together is indicated by the fit indices reported in Chapter 23 (Table 23.2). Here, a confirmatory factor analysis (CFA) was conducted first with the baseline model for each of the two groups separately. The results, provided by the M*plus* output for this analysis, indicate a very good model fit for each group (Table 24.2).

Table 24.2 *Goodness-of-fit indices by two groups (relapsing, progressive)*

						90% CI for RMSEA	
Group	χ^2	*df*	CFI	SRMR	RMSEA	Lower	Upper
Relapsing	16.165[a]	13	1.00	.013	.019	.000	.045
Progressive	24.200[b]	13	.99	.024	.049	.015	.079

[a] p = .240; (N = 669). [b] p = .029; (N = 359).

The standardized factor loadings for the baseline model are provided in Table 24.3.

Table 24.3 *Standardized factor loadings and standard errors by groups*

	Group (Course of illness)	
Construct/Indicator	Relapsing	Progressive
Psychosocial distress		
Item 2	.82 (.02)	.75 (.03)
Item 3	.76 (.02)	.75 (.03)
Item 4	.74 (.02)	.65 (.04)
Item 5	.65 (.03)	.61 (.04)
Successful coping		
Item 9	.88 (.02)	.80 (.03)
Item 10	.76 (.02)	.76 (.03)
Item 11	.76 (.02)	.78 (.03)

Notes. 1. Standard errors of factor loadings are given in parentheses.
2. The correlation between the two constructs is −.51 and −.45 for the relapsing and progressive illness group, respectively.

Testing for invariance of factor loadings, intercepts, and variances/covariances across the two groups was conducted according to the procedures described in Section 24.2.2.2. The results provided by the M*plus* output are summarized in Table 24.4

Table 24.4 *Testing for the invariance of factor loadings, intercepts, and variances and covariances across two groups (relapsing and progressive)*

Model	χ^2	*df*	$\Delta\chi^2$	Δdf	χ^2 critical value[a]
Model 0	40.365	26			
Model 1	44.258	31	3.893	5	11.07
Model 2	56.749	36	12.491*	5	11.07
Model 2P	48.201	35	3.943	4	9.49
Model 3	49.847	37	1.646	2	5.99

Note. **Model 0**: Non invariant slopes and intercepts.
Model 1: Invariant slopes, non invariant intercepts.
Model 2: Invariant slopes and invariant intercepts.
Model 2P: Partial measurement invariance — invariant slopes and invariant intercepts except for a “free” intercept for Item 3.
Model 3: Partial measurement invariance and invariant variances and covariances.

[a] α = .05 level of significance. * $p < .05$.

As can be seen, the chi-square difference between Model 1 and Model 0 ($\Delta\chi^2_{M1-M0}$) not statistically significant, $\Delta\chi^2(5) = 3.893$, $p > .05$, thus indicating invariance of the factor loadings across the two groups. However, the chi-square difference between Model 2 and Model 1 ($\Delta\chi^2_{M2-M1}$) *was* statistically significant, $\Delta\chi^2(5) = 12.491$, $p < .05$, thus indicating the lack of complete invariance of the intercepts across the two groups. The examination of the modification indices (MI) in this case showed that the there were two modification indices "signaled" by M*plus* [as having a chi-square greater than the critical value of 3.84 for *df* = 1] — namely, MI = 7.29 for Item 2 and MI = 8.47 for Item 3 (both in the relapsing illness group). Following the recommendation of "freeing" one parameter at a time, starting with the largest MI, Model 2 was modified by "freeing" the intercept for Item 3 (i.e., allowing the intercept for Item 3 to have different estimates across the two groups). With this, the chi-square value for Model 2 dropped from 56.749 to 48.201 (this "modified" model was named Model 2P in Table 24.3). The chi-square difference between Model 2P and Model 1 was no longer statistically significant, $\Delta\chi^2(4) = 3.943$, $p > .05$. This provides evidence of *partial measurement invariance* in the baseline model (in Figure 23.3) across the two groups, with invariant factor loadings and invariant intercepts except for the intercept of one indicator (Item 3).

Once there is an acceptable level of partial measurement variance, we proceed with testing for invariance of the factor variances and covariances. Model 3 was obtained from Model 2P by restricting the variances of the two constructs and the covariance between them to be equal in the two groups. The chi-square difference between Model 3 and Model 2P was not statistically significant, $\Delta\chi^2(2) = 1.646$, $p > .05$, thus indicating that the assumption of invariant variances and covariances across the two groups is also met.

The door is now open to proceed with the MIMIC model comparing the two groups of people with multiple sclerosis on the constructs of interest (psychosocial distress and successful coping). The path diagram of this model is provided in Figure 24.11. The goodness-of-fit indices indicated that, despite the statistically significant chi-square value ($\chi^2(17) = 31.91$, $p = .015$), there is a satisfactory data-model fit: CFI = .995 [with CFI > .95 requested], SRMR = .016 [with SRMR < .08 requested], RMSEA = .029 [with RMSEA ≤ .05 requested], and 90 percent confidence interval for RMSEA = (.013, .045).

In Figure 24.11, the factor loadings are standardized, so their squared values indicate the proportion of the variance in the indicator accounted for by the variability in the construct. For example, the factor loading for Item 2 is .80, so its squared value, $(.80)^2 = .64$ indicates that 64 percent of the variance in Item 2 ("unable to control important things in life") is explained by variability in psychosocial distress. As the structural coefficients in Figure 24.11 are also standardized, the statistically significant coefficient associated with the two-way arrow connecting **Psychosocial distress** and **Successful coping** represents an estimate of the correlation between these two constructs ($r = -.68$, $p < .001$).

Still in Figure 24.11, the structural coefficient with the path from **GROUP** to **Psychosocial distress** (.04) is not statistically significant, thus indicating that the two groups (relapsing illness and progressive illness) do *not* differ on psychosocial distress. An exception in this regard is the statistically significant structural coefficient for the direct effect of **GROUP** on **Item 3** [recall that the intercepts for Item 3 were found to be *not* equal across the two groups in testing for measurement invariance]. Since the estimate of this direct effect (−.07) is negative and statistically significant ($p < .05$), given the coding of the two groups (0 = relapsing, 1 = progressive), we can conclude that the progressive illness group performed slightly lower than expected on Item 3 ("In the last month, how often you felt nervous and distressed?").

Figure 24.11 *MIMIC model for group differences on two constructs*

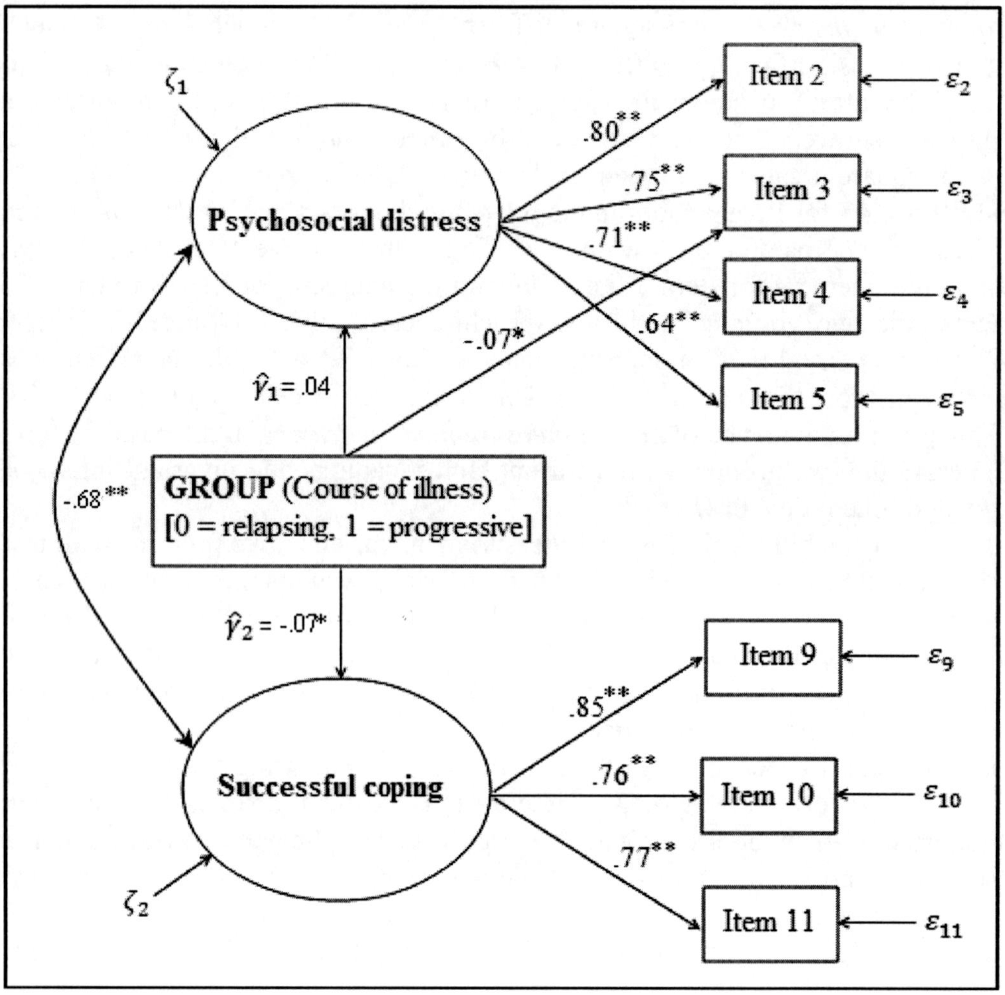

* $p < .05$. ** $p < .001$.

The standardized structural coefficient for the path from **GROUP** to **Successful coping** (-0.07) is also statistically significant ($p < .05$), thus indicating that the two groups differ on successful coping. Given the group coding (0 = relapsing, 1 = progressive), the negative sign of this coefficient shows that the progressive illness group scores lower than the relapsing illness group on successful coping. An estimate of the effect size of the mean group difference on successful coping is now computed using Formula 24.29 with the unstandardized value of the coefficient $\hat{\gamma}_2$ (-0.12) and the residual variance for successful coping, $\widehat{VAR}(\zeta_2) = 0.66$, both provided with the M*plus* output [not shown here for space consideration]:

$$\hat{d} = \frac{|\hat{\gamma}|}{\sqrt{\widehat{VAR}(\zeta)}} = \frac{|-0.12|}{\sqrt{0.66}} = \frac{0.12}{0.8124} = 0.15.$$

Thus, there is a relatively small effect size ($\hat{d} = 0.15$) for the difference in successful coping for people with a progressive course of multiple sclerosis compared to people with a relapsing course of multiple sclerosis.

24.3 Summary

• **Structural equation modeling** (SEM) is a statistical technique that allows for testing and estimating hypothesized causal relations among observable variables, latent variables, or a mixture of both. Typically, SEM integrates (a) a *measurement part* — CFA for validation and measurement of latent variables, and (b) a *structural part* — causal relations among latent and observable variables.

• **Path analysis** is a statistical method of determining direct and indirect effects in hypothesized causal relations among observable variables. It represents SEM limited to causal relations among observable variables.

• Path models in which the causal relations are unidirectional (i.e., there are no causal "loops") are called **recursive path models**.

• A **path coefficient** in a path model indicates the *direct effect* of a variable hypothesized as a cause of another variable.

• A variable involved in a causal model is called an **exogenous variable** if its variance is not explained by the variance of other variables in the model. That is, an exogenous variable is not caused by another variable in the model.

• A variable involved in a causal model is called an **endogenous variable** if its variance is explained by the variance of other variables in the model. That is, an endogenous variable is caused by one or more variables in the model.

• The **assumptions** in recursive path models are that (a) the relations among variables in the model are linear, additive, and causal, (b) the residual (error) of an endogenous variable does not correlate with the variables that precede this variable in the model [this implies that the residuals are not correlated among themselves], (c) the variables are measured on an interval scale, and (d) the variables are measured without error.

• The correlation between two variables (say, X_1 and X_2) in a causal model can be decomposed into components that may include (a) a **direct effect** — one of the variables has a causal effect on the other, (b) an **indirect effect** — X_1 causes X_2 through the mediation of a third variable, (c) **spuriousness** — a third variable is a common cause of X_1 and X_2, and (d) **unexplained covariation** — both X_1 and X_2 are exogenous and the correlation between them is not explained by the model. The sum of the direct effect and indirect effect is called **total effect**.

• A recursive model is called a **just-identified model** when any two variables are either correlated (if both exogenous) or causally related (if at least one is endogenous) and the model assumptions are met.

• The actual correlations between the observed variables in a just-identified model are perfectly reproduced by the model-implied decomposition of these correlations. Therefore, if the actual correlation matrix **R** is reproduced in a just-identified model, this has *no implication* for the validity of this model.

• An **overidentified causal model** exists when the number of known elements (correlations) exceeds the number of unknown parameters (path coefficients). Overidentified models are desirable when establishing the validity of causal models.

• A structural equation modeling (SEM) model typically includes both structural *and* measurement parts — that is, causal relations that involve latent variables (factors, constructs) measured by multiple indicators.

• Major advantages of typical SEM models over path analytic models are that (a) the scores on each construct in the SEM model are "error free" (true scores), and (b) the SEM results remain stable across studies where the constructs are measured by different, yet valid, scales.

• In testing for group mean differences on a set of observed variables, MANOVA is more appropriate when the groups are compared on constructs which "emerge" as a linear composite of the observed variables (i.e., the observed variables represent causal agents of the construct). In contrast, SEM is more appropriate with a *latent variable system* in which the construct (latent variable) has a causal influence on the observed variables.

• **Factorial invariance** across groups is defined by (a) *invariant factor loadings* — the factor-loading regression paths are the same for each group, (b) *invariant intercepts* — the intercepts in regressing indicators to factors are equal across groups, (c) *invariant factor variances and covariances* — the variances of the factors (constructs) and the covariances among them are equal across groups, and (d) *invariant residual variances* — the variances of the residuals (errors) in regressing indicators to factors are equal across groups. The first two conditions (invariant factor loadings and invariant intercepts) define **measurement invariance.**

• As a prerequisite to testing for factorial invariance, it is necessary to identify a baseline model, which is estimated for each group separately. [The most parsimonious, yet substantively most meaningful and best fitting model to the data for a group is referred to as the **baseline model** for this group.]

• Testing for factorial invariance is performed by using the chi-square square test for the difference ($\Delta\chi^2$) between two nested models — a model with "invariance assumed"($\chi^2_{\text{Invariance}}$) and a model with "no invariance assumed" ($\chi^2_{\text{No invariance}}$). The invariance of the parameters being tested is confirmed when the chi-square difference is not statistically significant at the prespecified level of significance (e.g., $\alpha = .05$).

• **Partial measurement invariance** is defined as a situation in which there is no perfect measurement invariance, but neither is there evidence of complete inequality of factor loadings or intercepts.

• The lack of invariance for a parameter (e.g., factor loading or intercept) is "signaled" by its modification index (MI). [In M*plus*, for example, MIs with a chi-square larger than 3.84 (the critical chi-square value with $df = 1$) are reported.] Such a parameter must be "freed" from the constraint of being invariant across groups and before continuing to test for partial invariance. If there is a "red flag" (i.e., high MI) for two or more parameters, they should be freed starting with the one that has the largest MI.

• **Structured means modeling (SMM)** is applied with models that contain intercepts for the purpose of estimating group means on a construct. SMM assumes *measurement invariance* (i.e., invariant factor loadings and invariant intercepts). Just like a *t*-test, the SMM keeps the data from the two groups separate. The maximum likelihood estimation of model parameters under SMM is based on equations of the *mean structure* (e.g., Equations 24.17, 24.18, and 24.19) and *variance-covariance structure* (e.g., Equations 24.20–24.25).

• **Multiple-Indicator, Multiple-Cause (MIMIC) Modeling** keeps the data from the two groups together and is analogous to the method of using dummy coding in regression analysis for group comparisons. The MIMIC estimation of model parameters is based only on equations for the *variance-covariance structure.*

• MIMIC modeling is based on stronger assumptions than structured means modeling (SMM). SMM requires only measurement invariance (equal factor loadings and equal intercepts across the two groups), whereas MIMIC modeling requires invariance of the factor loadings, intercepts, factor variances and covariances, and residual variances.

24.4 Study Questions

1. What is structural equation modeling (SEM)?
2. What is path analysis?
3. What is a recursive path model?
4. What is the difference between *exogenous* and *endogenous* variables in a causal model?
5. What are the assumptions in a recursive path model?
6. What does a path coefficient in a path model represent?
7. When does *spuriousness* occur in the correlation between two variables?
8. If *e* is a residual (error) term in a causal path model and z is the standard score of a variable in this model, (a) what does $\frac{\sum z^2}{N}$ mean and what is its value? and (b) what does $\frac{\sum ez}{N}$ mean and what is its value?
9. Reproduce the correlation coefficients for the just-identified model in Figure 24.2 using the values for these coefficients in Figure 24.1 [$r_{12} = -.681$, $r_{13} = -.609$, and $r_{23} = .471$]
10. Given the correlation matrix in Table 24.1 and the causal path model depicted here below, (a) compute the model-implied correlation between X_1 and X_4, assuming that $p_{31} = .07$, $p_{32} = .150$, and $p_{43} = -.37$, and (b) compute the total effect of X_2 on X_4.

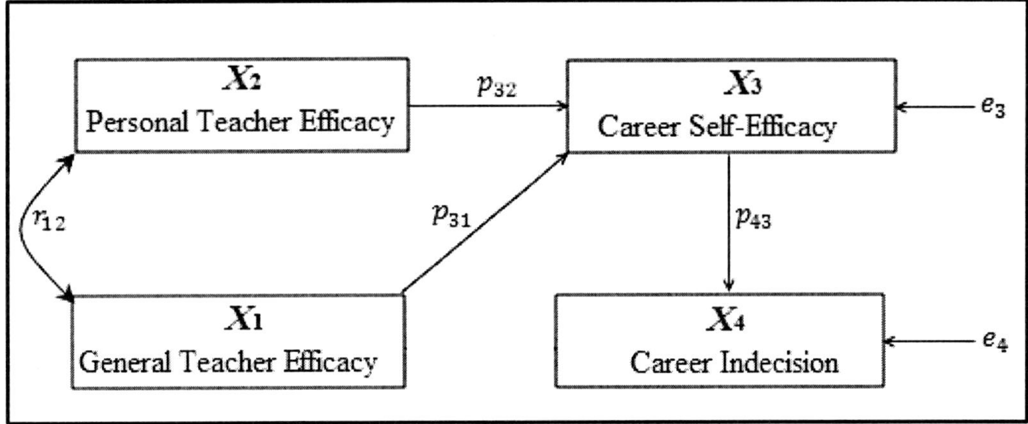

11. In testing for group mean differences on a set of observed variables, (a) when is MANOVA appropriate?, (b) when is SEM appropriate?, and (c) what is the advantage of the SEM approach over MANOVA?
12. What is a *baseline model* for comparing groups on latent variables (constructs)?
13. What is *factorial invariance* across groups?
14. What is *measurement invariance* across groups?
15. What is *partial measurement invariance*?
16. When the modification indices (MIs) indicate that several parameters (e.g., intercepts) are not invariant across two groups, what approach is recommended to modify the model?
17. What is the approach to testing for factorial invariance?

18. Which model parameters are assumed invariant under the structured means method (SMM) for group comparison on latent variables?

19. Which model parameters are assumed invariant under the MIMIC modeling in comparing groups on latent variables? [Which assumption can be ignored as being too stringent?]

20. Although the structure coefficient $\hat{\gamma}_1$(= .04) in Figure 24.11 is not statistically significant, compute the effect size ($\hat{d}$) of the mean group difference on psychosocial distress, given that the disturbance variance for this construct is VAR(ζ_1) = 0.77.

REFERENCES

Aiken, L S., & West, S. G. (1991). *Multiple regression: Testing and interpreting interactions.* Thousand Oaks, CA: Sage.

Akaike, H. (1987). Factor analysis and AIC. *Psychometrika, 52*, 317-332.

Arbuckle, J. L. (1995). *Amos user's guide*. Chicago: Smallwaters.

Asher, H. B. (1976). *Causal modeling*. University Paper series on Quantitative Applications in the Social Sciences, 07-003. Beverly Hills, CA: Sage Publications.

Bentler, P. M. (1990). Comparative fit indexes in structural models. *Psychological Bulletin, 107,* 238–246.

Bentler, P. M. (2000/2004). *EQS 6: Structural equation program manual.* Encino, CA: Multivariate Software.

Bentler, P. M., & Bonnett, D. (1980). Significance tests and goodness of fit in the analysis of covariance structures. *Psychological Bulletin, 88*, 588-606.

Beron, K. J., & Farkas, G. (2004). Oral Language and Reading Success: A Structural Equation Modeling Approach. *Structural Equation Modeling, 11(1)*, 110-131.

Bollen, K. A. (1989). *Structural equations with latent variables*. New York: Wiley.

Browne, M. W., & Cudeck, R. (1993). Alternative ways of assessing model fit. In K. A. Bollen & J. S. Long (Eds.), *Testing structural equation models* (pp. 136–162). Newbury Park, CA: Sage.

Byrne, B. M. (1988). The Self Description Questionnaire III: Testing for equivalent factorial validity across ability. *Educational and Psychological Measurement, 48,* 397–406.

Byrne, B. M. (2001). *Structural Equation Modeling with AMOS: Basic Concepts, Applications and Programming*, Mahwah, NJ: Lawrence Erlbaum.

Byrne, B. M. (2004). Testing for Multigroup Invariance Using AMOS Graphics: A Road Less Traveled. *Structural Equation Modeling, 11(2)*, 272-300.

Byrne, B. M., & Shavelson, R. J. (1986). On the structure of adolescent self-concept. *Journal of Educational Psychology, 78,* 474–481.

Byrne, B. M., Shavelson, R. J., & Muthén, B. (1989). Testing for the equivalence of factor covariance and mean structures: The issue of partial measurement invariance. *Psychological Bulletin, 105,* 456–466.

Campbell & Stanley (1963). *Experimental and quasi-experimental designs for research.* Chicago: Rand McNally.

Cattell, R. B. (1966). The scree test for the number of factors. *Multivariate Behavioral Research, 1,* 245-276.

Cohen, J. (1988). *Statistical power analysis for the behavioral sciences* (2nd ed.). Lawrence Erlbaum, Hillsdale, NJ.

Cohen, J. (1960). A coefficient of agreement for nominal scales. *Educational and Psychological Measurement, 20*, 37-46.

Cohen, J., & Cohen, P. (1983). *Applied multiple regression/correlation analysis for the behavioral sciences* (2nd ed.). Hillsdale, NJ: Lawrence Erlbaum.

Cohen, P. A., Kulik, J. A., & Kulik, C. C. (1982). Educational outcomes of tutoring: A meta-analysis of findings. *American Educational Research Journal, 19(2)*, 237-248.

Collier, R. O., Jr., Baker, F. B., Mandeville, G. K., & Hays, H. T. (1967). Estimates of test size for several tests procedures based on conventional ratios in the repeated measures design. *Psychometrika, 32*, 339-354.

Cook, R. D. (1977). Detection of influential observations in linear regression. *Technometrics, 19*, 15-18.

Cook, T. D., & Campbell, D. T. (1979). *Quasi-experimentation: Design and analysis issues for field settings*. Chicago: Rand McNally.

Cox, D. R., & Snell, D. J. (1989). *The analysis of binary data* (2nd ed.). London: Chapman and Hall.

Cronbach, L. J. (1982). *Designing evaluations of educational and social programs*. San Francisco: Jossey-Bass.

Cronbach, L. J. (1971). Test validation. In R. L. Thorndike (ed.), *Educational measurement* (2nd ed.). Washington, DC: American Council on Education.

Cronbach, L. J (1951). Coefficient alpha and the internal structure of a test. *Psychometrika, 16*, 297-334.

Cronbach, L. J., & Gleser, G. C. (1965). *Psychological tests and personnel decisions* (2nd ed.). Urbana: University of Illinois Press.

Cronbach, L. J. & Furby, L. (1970). How should we measure change - or should we? *Psychological Bulletin, 74*, 68–80.

Cronbach, L. J., & Meehl, P. E. (1955). Construct validity in psychological tests. *Psychological Bulletin, 52,* 281-302.

Curran, P. J.,West, S. G., & Finch, J. F. (1996). The robustness of test statistics to nonnormality and specification error in confirmatory factor analysis. *Psychological Methods, 1,* 16–29.

Davidson, M. L. (1972). Univariate versus multivariate tests in repeated measures experiments. *Psychological Bulletin, 77*, 446-452.

Dimitrov, D. M. (2006) Comparing groups on latent variables: A structural equation modeling approach. *WORK: A Journal of Prevention, Assessment & Rehabilitation, 26*, 429-436.

Enright, M. S. (1996). The relationship between disability status, career beliefs, and career indecision. *Rehabilitation Counseling Bulletin, 40(2)*, 134-152.

Erford, B.T. (1993). *Manual for the Disruptive Behavior Rating Scale*. East Aurora, NY: Slosson Educational Publications.

Erford, B. T., Balcom, L., & Moore-Thomas, C. (2007). The *Screening Test for Emotional Problems* (*STEP*): Studies of reliability and validity. *Measurement and Evaluation in Counseling and Development, 39*, 209-225.

Finn, J. D., Fulton, B. D., Zaharias, J. B., & Nye, B. A. (1989/92). Carry-over effects of small classes. *The Peabody Journal, 67(1)*.

Gay, L. R., & Airasian, P. (2000). *Educational research: Competencies for analysis and application* (6th ed.). Upper Saddle River, NJ: Prentice-Hall.

Gibson, S., & Dembo, M. (1984). Teacher efficacy: A construct validation. Journal of *Educational Psychology, 76(4)*, 569-582.

Glass, G. V. (1976). Primary, secondary, and meta-analysis of research. *Educational Researcher, 5,* 3-8.

Glass, G. V. (1977). Integrating findings: The meta-analysis of research. In L. Shulman (Ed.), *Review of research in education*. Itasca, IL: Peacock.

Glass, G. V., & Hopkins, K. D. (1996). *Statistical methods in education and psychology* (3rd ed.) Needham Heights, MA: Allyn and Bacon.

Glass, G. V., McGaw, B., & Smith, M. L. (1981). *Meta-analysis in social research*. Beverly Hills: Sage.

Glass, G. V., Peckham, P. D., & Sanders, J. R. (1972). Consequences of failure to meet assumptions underlying the fixed-effects analysis of variance and covariance. *Review of Educational Research, 42*, 237-288.

Glorfeld, L. W. (1995). An improvement on Horn's parallel analysis methodology for selecting the correct number of factors to retain. *Educational and Psychological Measurement, 55(3),* 377-393.

Gorsuch, R. L. (1983) *Factor analysis* (2nd ed.) Hillsdale, NJ: Lawrence Erlbaum.

Grossman, J., & Mackenzie, F. J. (2005). The randomized controlled trial: gold standard, or merely standard? *Perspectives in Biology and Medicine, 48(4)*, 516-534.

Hancock, G. R. (2001). Effect size, power, and sample size determination for structured means modeling and MIMIC approaches to between-groups hypothesized testing of means on a single latent construct. *Psychometrika, 66*, 373-388.

Hancock, G. R. (2004). Experimental, quasi-experimental, and nonexperimental design and analysis with latent variables. In D. Kaplan (Ed.), *The SAGE handbook of quantitative methodology for the social sciences* (pp. 317-334). Thousand Oaks, CA: Sage.

Hays, W. L. (1963). *Statistics for psychologists*. New York: Holt, Rinehart & Winston.

Hedges, L. V. (1981). Distribution theory for Glass' estimator of effect size and related estimators. *Journal of Educational Statistics, 6*, 107-128.

Hinkle, D. E., & Oliver, J. D. (1983). How large the sample part be? A question with no simple answer? Or .... *Educational and Psychological Measurement, 43*, 1051-1060.

Holland, P. W., & Wainer, H. (1993). *Differential Item Functioning*, Hillsdale, NJ: Erlbaum.

Hollander, M. and Wolfe, D. A. (1973). *Nonparametric statistical methods*, New York: Wiley.

Hopkins, K. D. (1983). A strategy for analyzing ANOVA designs having one or more random factors. *Educational and Psychological Measurement, 43*, 107-113.

Hu, L.T., & Bentler, P. M. (1999). Cutoff criteria for fit indexes in covariance structure analysis: Conventional criteria versus new alternatives. *Structural Equation Modeling, 6,* 1–55.

Hu, L. T., Bentler, P. M., & Kano, Y. (1992). Can test statistics in covariance structure analysis be trusted? *Psychological Bulletin, 112,* 351–362.

Huck, S. W., & McLean, R. A. (1975). Using a repeated measures ANOVA to analyze data from pretest-posttest design: A potentially confusing task, *Psychological Bulletin* **82**, 511–518.

Hunter, J. E., Schmidt, F. L., & Jackson, G. B. (1982). *Meta analysis: Cumulating research findings across studies*. Beverly Hills: Sage Publications.

Huynh, H., & Feldt, L. S. (1976). Estimation of the Box correction for degrees of freedom in randomized block and split-plot designs. Journal of Educational Statistics, *1*, 29-82.

Jennings, E. (1988). Models for pretest-posttest data: repeated measures ANOVA revisited, *Journal of Educational Statistics* **13,** 273–280.

Jöreskog, K. G., & Sörbom, D. (1989/1996). *LISREL 8: User's reference guide.* Chicago: Scientific Software.

Kane, M. T. (2001). Current concerns in validity theory. *Journal of Educational Measurement, 38*, 319-342.

Kelley, T. L. (1939). The selection of upper and lower groups for the validation of test items. *Journal of Educational Psychology, 30*, 17-24.

Kerlinger, F. N. (1986). *Foundations of behavioral research.* New York: Holt.

Kline, R. B. (1998). *Principles and practice of structural equation modeling.* New York: Guildwood.

Kornell, N., & Metcalfe, J. (2006). Study efficacy and the region of proximal learning framework. *Journal of Experimental Psychology: Learning, Memory, and Cognition, 32*(3), 609-622.

Kreber, C. (2001) Learning Experientially through case studies? A Conceptual analysis. *Teaching in Higher Education, 6(2)*, 217-228.

Kulik, J. A., Kulik, C. C., & Cohen, P. A. (1979). A meta-analysis of outcome studies of Keller's personalized system of instruction. *American Psychologist, 34*, 307-318.

Levine, D. W., Kaplan, R. M., Kripke, D. F., Bowen, D. J., Naughton, M. J., & Shumaker, S. A. (2003). Factor structure and measurement invariance of the women's health initiative insomnia rating scale, *Psychological Assessment 15*, 123–136.

Linn, L. & Slindle, J. A. (1977). The determination of the significance of change between pre- and posttesting periods, *Review of Educational Research*, *47*, 121–150.

Mangione, L. L., & Mangione, T. W. (2001). Work group context and the experience of abuse: An opportunity for prevention, *WORK*: *A Journal of Prevention, Assessment & Rehabilitation, 16 , 259–267.*

Maxwell, J. (2004). Causal explanation, qualitative research, and scientific inquiry in education *Educational Researcher, 33(2)*, 3-11.

Maxwell, S., & Delaney, H. (1990). *Designing experiments and analyzing data*. Belmont, CA: Wadsworth.

McNemar, Q. (1969). *Psychological statistics* (4th ed.). New York: Wiley.

Mellenbergh, G. J. (1999). A note on simple gain score precision. *Applied Psychological Measurement, 23*, 87-89.

Messick, S. (1989). Validity. In R. L. Linn (Ed.), *Educational Measurement* (3rd ed., pp. 13-103).

Messick, S. (1995). Validity of psychological assessment: Validation of inferences from persons' responses and performances as scientific inquiry into score meaning. *American Psychologist, 50*, 741-749.

Mosteller, F. (1995). The "Tennessee study of class size in the early school grades. *The Future of Children: Critical Issues for Children and Youths, 5(2)*, 113-127.

Muthén, L., & Muthén, B. O. (2006). *MPLUS user's guide*. Los Angeles: Muthén & Muthén.

Nagelkerke, N. J. D. (1991). A note on general definition of the coefficient of determination. *Biometrika, 78*, 691-692.

Nunnally, J. C., & Bernstein, I. H. (1994). *Psychometric theory* (3rd ed.). New-York: McGraw-Hill.

Nash, R. (2005). Explanation and quantification in educational research: the arguments of critical and scientific realism. *British Educational Research Journal, 31(2)*, 185-204.

O'Brien, R., & Kaiser, M. (1985). MANOVA method for analyzing repeated-measures designs: An extensive primer. *Psychological Bulletin, 97*, 316-333.

O'Connor, B. P. (2000). SPSS and SAS programs for determining the number of components using parallel analysis and Velicer's MAP test. *Behavior Research Methods, Instrumentation, and Computers, 32*, 396-402.

Osipow, S. H. (1980). *Manual for the career decision scale*. Columbus, OH: Marathon Consulting and Press.

Overall, J. E., & Woodward, J. A. (1975). Unreliability of difference scores: A paradox for measurement of change, *Psychological Bulletin, 82*, 85–86.

Pedhazur, E. J. (1982). *Multiple regression in behavioral research: Explanation and prediction.* (2nd edition). Fort Worth, TX: Holt, Rinehart and Winston, Inc.

Pedhazur, E. J. (1997). *Multiple regression in behavioral research: Explanation and Prediction* (3rd ed.). Wadsworth: Thompson Learning.

Raykov, T., & Marcoulides, G. A. (2006) *A first course in structural equation modeling* (2nd ed.). Mahwah, NJ; Lawrence Erlbaum.

Rosenbaum, P. R., & Rubin, D. B. (1983). The central role of the propensity score in observational studies for causal effects. *Biometrika, 70(1)*, 41-55.

Rosenberg, M. (1965). *Society and the adolescent self image.* Princeton, NJ: Princeton University Press.

Roessler, R., Rumrill, P., & Hennessey, M. (2001). *Employment Concerns of People with Multiple Sclerosis: Building a National Employment Agenda*, National Multiple Sclerosis Society, New York.

Rogosa, D., Brandt, D., & Zimowski, M. (1982). A growth curve approach to the measurement of change, *Psychological Bulletin*, *92*, 726–748.

Rubin, D. B. (1974). Estimating causal effects of treatments in randomized and nonrandomized studies. *Journal of Educational Psychology, 66*, 688-701.

Slone, M. B., & Hancock, M. D. (2008). Teacher efficacy and career indecision among pre-service teachers: A model of direct and indirect effects. *Mid-Western Educational Researcher, 21(2)*, 24-29.

Stevens, J. P. (2002). *Applied multivariate statistics for the social sciences* (4th ed.). Mahwah, NJ: Lawrence Erlbaum.

Suldo, S. M., Shaunessy, E., & Hardesty, R. (2008). Relationships among stress, coping, and mental health in high-achieving high school students. *Psychology in the Schools, 45(4)*, 273-290.

Tabachnick, B. G., & Fidell, L. S. (2007). *Using multivariate statistics* (5th ed.). Boston, MA: Pearson Education, Inc.

Thurstone, L. L. (1947). *Multiple factor analysis*. Chicago: University of Chicago Press.

West, C. K., & Anderson, T. H. (1976). The question of preponderant causation in teacher expectancy research. *Review of Educational Research, 46(4)*, 613-630.

Westby, C. E. (1994). The effects of culture on genre, structure and style of oral and written texts. In G. P. Wallach & K. G. Butler (Eds.), *Language learning disabilities.* (pp. 152–196). New York: Macmillan.

Wood, T., Cobb, P., & Yaekel, E. (1991). Change in teaching mathematics: A case study. *American Educational Research Journal, 28*, 587-616.

Wright, S. (1934). The method of path coefficients. *Annals of Mathematical Statistics, 5*, 161-215.

Wulff, M. B., & Steitz, J. A. (1996). A measure of career self-efficacy. *Journal of Perceptual and Motor Skills, 82*, 240-242.

Yin, R. K. (1993). *Applications of case study research.* Newbury Park, CA: Sage.

Zimmerman, B.J. (2000). Attainment of self-regulation: A social cognitive perspective. In M. Boekaerts, P.R. Pintrich, & M. Zeidner (Eds.), *Handbook of self-regulation* (pp. 13-39). San Diego, CA: Academic Press.

Zimmerman, B., & Kitsantas, A. (2005). The hidden dimension of personal competence: Self-regulated learning and practice. In A. J. Elliot, & C. S. Dweck (Eds.), *Handbook of Competence and Motivation* (pp. 509-526). New York: Guilford Publications.

Zimmerman, D. W, & Williams, R. H. (1982). Gain scores in research can be highly reliable. *Journal of Educational Measurement, 9*, 149-154.

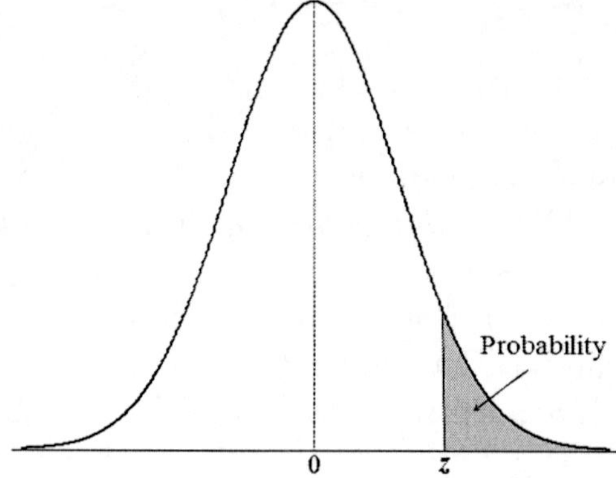

Table A-1 *Standard normal distribution: z- scores and upper-tail probabilities*

Z	0.00	0.01	0.02	0.03	0.04	0.05	0.06	0.07	0.08	0.09
0.00	**.500**	**.496**	**.492**	**.488**	**.484**	**.480**	**.476**	**.472**	**.468**	**.464**
0.10	.460	.456	.452	.448	.444	.440	.436	.433	.429	.425
0.20	.421	.417	.413	.409	.405	.401	.397	.394	.390	.386
0.30	.382	.378	.375	.371	.367	.363	.359	.356	.352	.348
0.40	.345	.341	.337	.334	.330	.326	.323	.319	.316	.312
0.50	**.309**	**.305**	**.302**	**.298**	**.295**	**.291**	**.288**	**.284**	**.281**	**.278**
0.60	.274	.271	.268	.264	.261	.258	.255	.251	.248	.245
0.70	.242	.239	.236	.233	.230	.227	.224	.221	.218	.215
0.80	.212	.209	.206	.203	.201	.198	.195	.192	.189	.187
0.90	.184	.181	.179	.176	.174	.171	.169	.166	.164	.161
1.00	**.159**	**.156**	**.154**	**.152**	**.149**	**.147**	**.145**	**.142**	**.140**	**.138**
1.10	.136	.134	.131	.129	.127	.125	.123	.121	.119	.117
1.20	.115	.113	.111	.109	.108	.106	.104	.102	.100	.099
1.30	.097	.095	.093	.092	.090	.089	.087	.085	.084	.082
1.40	.081	.079	.078	.076	.075	.074	.072	.071	.069	.068
1.50	**.067**	**.066**	**.064**	**.063**	**.062**	**.061**	**.059**	**.058**	**.057**	**.056**
1.60	.055	.054	.053	.052	.051	.050	.049	.048	.047	.046
1.70	.045	.044	.043	.042	.041	.040	.039	.038	.038	.037
1.80	.036	.035	.034	.034	.033	.032	.031	.031	.030	.029
1.90	.029	.028	.027	.027	.026	.026	.025	.024	.024	.023
2.00	**.023**	**.022**	**.022**	**.021**	**.021**	**.020**	**.020**	**.019**	**.019**	**.018**
2.10	.018	.017	.017	.017	.016	.016	.015	.015	.015	.014
2.20	.014	.014	.013	.013	.013	.012	.012	.012	.011	.011
2.30	.011	.010	.010	.010	.010	.009	.009	.009	.009	.008
2.40	.008	.008	.008	.008	.007	.007	.007	.007	.007	.006
2.50	**.006**	**.006**	**.006**	**.006**	**.006**	**.005**	**.005**	**.005**	**.005**	**.005**
2.60	.005	.005	.004	.004	.004	.004	.004	.004	.004	.004
2.70	.004	.003	.003	.003	.003	.003	.003	.003	.003	.003
2.80	.003	.003	.002	.002	.002	.002	.002	.002	.002	.002
2.90	.002	.002	.002	.002	.002	.002	.002	.002	.001	.001
3.00	**.001**	**.001**	**.001**	**.001**	**.001**	**.001**	**.001**	**.001**	**.001**	**.001**
3.10	.001	.001	.001	.001	.001	.001	.001	.001	.001	.001
3.20	.001	.001	.001	.001	.001	.001	.001	.001	.001	.001
3.30	.001	.001	.001	.000	.000	.000	.000	.000	.000	.000
3.40	.000	.000	.000	.000	.000	.000	.000	.000	.000	.000
3.50	**.000**	**.000**	**.000**	**.000**	**.000**	**.000**	**.000**	**.000**	**.000**	**.000**

Note. As an example, when $z = 1.96$, the upper tail probability is $p = .025$.

Table A-2 *Critical values of the Student's t-distribution*

Degrees of freedom	α (one-sided test)				
	.10	.05	.025	.01	.005
	α (two-sided test)				
	.20	.10	.05	.02	.01
1	3.078	6.314	12.706	31.821	63.657
2	1.886	2.920	4.303	6.965	9.925
3	1.638	2.353	3.182	4.541	5.841
4	1.533	2.132	2.776	3.747	4.604
5	1.476	2.015	2.571	3.365	4.032
6	1.440	1.943	2.447	3.143	3.707
7	1.415	1.895	2.365	2.998	3.499
8	1.397	1.860	2.306	2.896	3.355
9	1.383	1.833	2.262	2.821	3.250
10	1.372	1.812	2.228	2.764	3.169
11	1.363	1.796	2.201	2.718	3.106
12	1.356	1.782	2.179	2.681	3.055
13	1.350	1.771	2.160	2.650	3.012
14	1.345	1.761	2.145	2.624	2.977
15	1.341	1.753	2.131	2.602	2.947
16	1.337	1.746	2.120	2.583	2.921
17	1.333	1.740	2.110	2.567	2.898
18	1.330	1.734	2.101	2.552	2.878
19	1.328	1.729	2.093	2.539	2.861
20	1.325	1.725	2.086	2.528	2.845
21	1.323	1.721	2.080	2.518	2.831
22	1.321	1.717	2.074	2.508	2.819
23	1.319	1.714	2.069	2.500	2.807
24	1.318	1.711	2.064	2.492	2.797
25	1.316	1.708	2.060	2.485	2.787
26	1.315	1.706	2.056	2.479	2.779
27	1.314	1.703	2.052	2.473	2.771
28	1.313	1.701	2.048	2.467	2.763
29	1.311	1.699	2.045	2.462	2.756
30	1.310	1.697	2.042	2.457	2.750
31	1.309	1.696	2.040	2.453	2.744
32	1.309	1.694	2.037	2.449	2.738
33	1.308	1.692	2.035	2.445	2.733
34	1.307	1.691	2.032	2.441	2.728
35	1.306	1.690	2.030	2.438	2.724
36	1.306	1.688	2.028	2.434	2.719
37	1.305	1.687	2.026	2.431	2.715
38	1.304	1.686	2.024	2.429	2.712
39	1.304	1.685	2.023	2.426	2.708
40	1.303	1.684	2.021	2.423	2.704
50	1.299	1.676	2.009	2.403	2.678
60	1.296	1.671	2.000	2.390	2.660
70	1.294	1.667	1.994	2.381	2.648
80	1.292	1.664	1.990	2.374	2.639
90	1.291	1.662	1.987	2.368	2.632
100	1.290	1.660	1.984	2.364	2.626
∞	1.282	1.645	1.960	2.326	2.576

Table A-3 *Critical values of the chi-square distribution (α = .05 and α = .01 upper tail)*

df	α = .05	α = .01
1	3.84	6.64
2	5.99	9.21
3	7.82	11.35
4	9.49	13.28
5	11.07	15.09
6	12.59	16.81
7	14.07	18.48
8	15.51	20.09
9	16.92	21.67
10	18.31	23.21
11	19.68	24.73
12	21.03	26.22
13	22.36	27.69
14	23.69	29.14
15	25.00	30.58
16	26.30	32.00
17	27.59	33.41
18	28.87	34.81
19	30.14	36.19
20	31.41	37.57
21	32.67	38.93
22	33.92	40.29
23	35.17	41.64
24	36.42	42.98
25	37.65	44.31
26	38.89	45.64
27	40.11	46.96
28	41.34	48.28
29	42.56	49.59
30	43.77	50.89
31	44.99	52.19
32	46.19	53.49
33	47.40	54.78
34	48.60	56.06
35	49.80	57.34
36	51.00	58.62
37	52.19	59.89
38	53.38	61.16
39	54.57	62.43
40	55.76	63.69
41	56.94	64.95
42	58.12	66.21
43	59.30	67.46
44	60.48	68.71
45	61.66	69.96
46	62.83	71.20
47	64.00	72.44
48	65.17	73.68
49	66.34	74.92
50	67.51	76.15
51	68.67	77.39
52	69.83	78.62
53	70.99	79.84
54	72.15	81.07
55	73.31	82.29
56	74.47	83.52
57	75.62	84.73
58	76.78	85.95
59	77.93	87.17
60	79.08	88.38
61	80.23	89.59
62	81.38	90.80
63	82.53	92.01
64	83.68	93.22
65	84.82	94.42
66	85.97	95.63
67	87.11	96.83
68	88.25	98.03
69	89.39	99.23
70	90.53	100.42
71	91.67	101.62
72	92.81	102.82
73	93.95	104.01
74	95.08	105.20
75	96.22	106.39
76	97.35	107.58
77	98.49	108.77
78	99.62	109.96
79	100.75	111.15
80	101.88	112.33
81	103.01	113.51
82	104.14	114.70
83	105.27	115.88
84	106.40	117.06
85	107.52	118.24
86	108.65	119.41
87	109.77	120.59
88	110.90	121.77
89	112.02	122.94
90	113.15	124.12
91	114.27	125.29
92	115.39	126.46
93	116.51	127.63
94	117.63	128.80
95	118.75	129.97
96	119.87	131.14
97	120.99	132.31
98	122.11	133.47
99	123.23	134.64
100	124.34	135.81

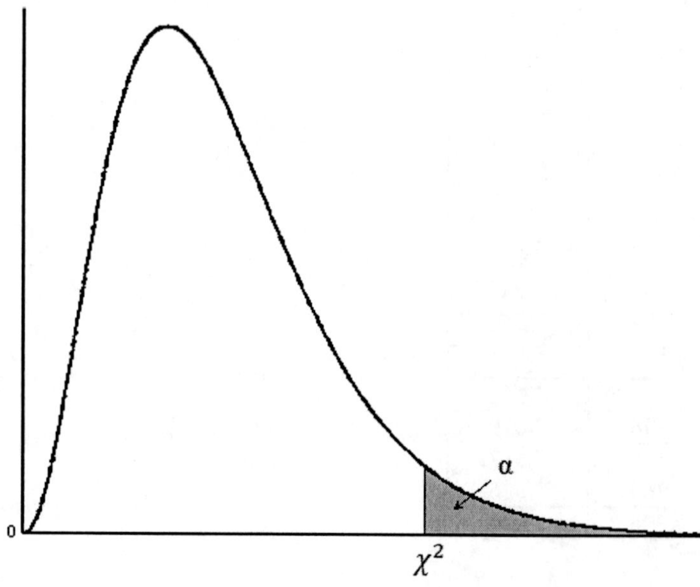

Example:
For α = .05 and *df* = 30,
the chi-square critical value is
$\chi^2 = 43.77$.

Table A-4 *Critical values of the F- distribution (α = .05 upper tail)*

α = .05	***Degrees of freedom for numerator (df_1)***									
df_2	**1**	**2**	**3**	**4**	**5**	**6**	**7**	**8**	**9**	**10**
1	161.45	199.50	215.71	224.58	230.16	233.99	236.77	238.88	240.54	241.88
2	18.51	19.00	19.16	19.25	19.30	19.33	19.35	19.37	19.39	19.40
3	10.13	9.55	9.28	9.12	9.01	8.94	8.89	8.85	8.81	8.79
4	7.71	6.94	6.59	6.39	6.26	6.16	6.09	6.04	6.00	5.96
5	6.61	5.79	5.41	5.19	5.05	4.95	4.88	4.82	4.77	4.74
6	5.99	5.14	4.76	4.53	4.39	4.28	4.21	4.15	4.10	4.06
7	5.59	4.74	4.35	4.12	3.97	3.87	3.79	3.73	3.68	3.64
8	5.32	4.46	4.07	3.84	3.69	3.58	3.50	3.44	3.39	3.35
9	5.12	4.26	3.86	3.63	3.48	3.37	3.29	3.23	3.18	3.14
10	4.97	4.10	3.71	3.48	3.33	3.22	3.14	3.07	3.02	2.98
11	4.84	3.98	3.59	3.36	3.20	3.10	3.01	2.95	2.90	2.85
12	4.75	3.89	3.49	3.26	3.11	3.00	2.91	2.85	2.80	2.75
13	4.67	3.81	3.41	3.18	3.03	2.92	2.83	2.77	2.71	2.67
14	4.60	3.74	3.34	3.11	2.96	2.85	2.76	2.70	2.65	2.60
15	4.54	3.68	3.29	3.06	2.90	2.79	2.71	2.64	2.59	2.54
16	4.49	3.63	3.24	3.01	2.85	2.74	2.66	2.59	2.54	2.49
17	4.45	3.59	3.20	2.97	2.81	2.70	2.61	2.55	2.49	2.45
18	4.41	3.56	3.16	2.93	2.77	2.66	2.58	2.51	2.46	2.41
19	4.38	3.52	3.13	2.90	2.74	2.63	2.54	2.48	2.42	2.38
20	4.35	3.49	3.10	2.87	2.71	2.60	2.51	2.45	2.39	2.35
21	4.33	3.47	3.07	2.84	2.69	2.57	2.49	2.42	2.37	2.32
22	4.30	3.44	3.05	2.82	2.66	2.55	2.46	2.40	2.34	2.30
23	4.28	3.42	3.03	2.80	2.64	2.53	2.44	2.38	2.32	2.28
24	4.26	3.40	3.01	2.78	2.62	2.51	2.42	2.36	2.30	2.26
25	4.24	3.39	2.99	2.76	2.60	2.49	2.41	2.34	2.28	2.24
26	4.23	3.37	2.98	2.74	2.59	2.47	2.39	2.32	2.27	2.22
27	4.21	3.35	2.96	2.73	2.57	2.46	2.37	2.31	2.25	2.20
28	4.20	3.34	2.95	2.71	2.56	2.45	2.36	2.29	2.24	2.19
29	4.18	3.33	2.93	2.70	2.55	2.43	2.35	2.28	2.22	2.18
30	4.17	3.32	2.92	2.69	2.53	2.42	2.33	2.27	2.21	2.17
35	4.12	3.27	2.87	2.64	2.49	2.37	2.29	2.22	2.16	2.11
40	4.09	3.23	2.84	2.61	2.45	2.34	2.25	2.18	2.12	2.08
50	4.03	3.18	2.79	2.56	2.40	2.29	2.20	2.13	2.07	2.03
60	4.00	3.15	2.76	2.53	2.37	2.25	2.17	2.10	2.04	1.99
70	3.98	3.13	2.74	2.50	2.35	2.23	2.14	2.07	2.02	1.97
80	3.96	3.11	2.72	2.49	2.33	2.21	2.13	2.06	2.00	1.95
100	3.94	3.09	2.70	2.46	2.31	2.19	2.10	2.03	1.98	1.93
150	3.90	3.06	2.66	2.43	2.27	2.16	2.07	2.00	1.94	1.89
300	3.87	3.03	2.63	2.40	2.24	2.13	2.04	1.97	1.91	1.86
1000	3.85	3.00	2.61	2.38	2.22	2.11	2.02	1.95	1.89	1.84

Note. ***df_2*** = degrees of freedom for denominator.

Table A-4 (continued)

α = .05	*Degrees of freedom for numerator* (df_1)									
df_2	**11**	**12**	**13**	**14**	**15**	**16**	**17**	**18**	**19**	**20**
1	243.98	243.91	244.69	245.36	245.95	246.46	246.92	247.32	247.69	248.02
2	19.41	19.41	19.42	19.42	19.43	19.43	19.44	19.44	19.44	19.45
3	8.76	8.75	8.73	8.72	8.70	8.69	8.68	8.68	8.67	8.66
4	5.94	5.91	5.89	5.87	5.86	5.84	5.83	5.82	5.81	5.80
5	4.70	4.68	4.66	4.64	4.62	4.60	4.59	4.58	4.57	4.56
6	4.03	4.00	3.98	3.96	3.94	3.92	3.91	3.90	3.88	3.87
7	3.60	3.58	3.55	3.53	3.51	3.49	3.48	3.47	3.46	3.45
8	3.31	3.28	3.26	3.24	3.22	3.20	3.19	3.17	3.16	3.15
9	3.10	3.07	3.05	3.03	3.01	2.99	2.97	2.96	2.95	2.94
10	2.94	2.91	2.89	2.87	2.85	2.83	2.81	2.80	2.79	2.77
11	2.82	2.79	2.76	2.74	2.72	2.70	2.69	2.67	2.66	2.65
12	2.72	2.69	2.66	2.64	2.62	2.60	2.58	2.57	2.56	2.54
13	2.64	2.60	2.58	2.55	2.53	2.52	2.50	2.48	2.47	2.46
14	2.57	2.53	2.51	2.48	2.46	2.45	2.43	2.41	2.40	2.39
15	2.51	2.48	2.45	2.42	2.40	2.39	2.37	2.35	2.34	2.33
16	2.46	2.43	2.40	2.37	2.35	2.33	2.32	2.30	2.29	2.28
17	2.41	2.38	2.35	2.33	2.31	2.29	2.27	2.26	2.24	2.23
18	2.37	2.34	2.31	2.29	2.27	2.25	2.23	2.22	2.20	2.19
19	2.34	2.31	2.28	2.26	2.23	2.22	2.20	2.18	2.17	2.16
20	2.31	2.28	2.25	2.23	2.20	2.18	2.17	2.15	2.14	2.12
21	2.28	2.25	2.22	2.20	2.18	2.16	2.14	2.12	2.11	2.10
22	2.26	2.23	2.20	2.17	2.15	2.13	2.11	2.10	2.08	2.07
23	2.24	2.20	2.18	2.15	2.13	2.11	2.09	2.08	2.06	2.05
24	2.22	2.18	2.16	2.13	2.11	2.09	2.07	2.05	2.04	2.03
25	2.20	2.17	2.14	2.11	2.09	2.07	2.05	2.04	2.02	2.01
26	2.18	2.15	2.12	2.09	2.07	2.05	2.03	2.02	2.00	1.99
27	2.17	2.13	2.10	2.08	2.06	2.04	2.02	2.00	1.99	1.97
28	2.15	2.12	2.09	2.06	2.04	2.02	2.00	1.99	1.97	1.96
29	2.14	2.10	2.08	2.05	2.03	2.01	1.99	1.97	1.96	1.95
30	2.13	2.09	2.06	2.04	2.02	2.00	1.98	1.96	1.95	1.93
35	2.08	2.04	2.01	1.99	1.96	1.94	1.92	1.91	1.89	1.88
40	2.04	2.00	1.97	1.95	1.92	1.90	1.89	1.87	1.85	1.84
50	1.99	1.95	1.92	1.90	1.87	1.85	1.83	1.81	1.80	1.78
60	1.95	1.92	1.89	1.86	1.84	1.82	1.80	1.78	1.76	1.75
70	1.93	1.89	1.86	1.84	1.81	1.79	1.77	1.75	1.74	1.72
80	1.91	1.88	1.85	1.82	1.79	1.77	1.75	1.73	1.72	1.70
100	1.89	1.85	1.82	1.79	1.77	1.75	1.73	1.71	1.69	1.68
150	1.85	1.82	1.78	1.76	1.73	1.71	1.69	1.67	1.67	1.64
300	1.82	1.78	1.75	1.72	1.70	1.68	1.66	1.64	1.62	1.60
1000	1.80	1.76	1.73	1.70	1.68	1.65	1.63	1.61	1.60	1.58

Note. df_2 = degrees of freedom for denominator.

Table A-4 (continued)

α = .05	*Degrees of freedom for numerator* (df_1)									
df_2	**21**	**22**	**23**	**24**	**25**	**26**	**27**	**28**	**29**	**30**
1	248.32	248.57	248.82	249.07	249.25	249.44	249.62	249.81	249.94	250.12
2	19.45	19.45	19.45	19.45	19.46	19.46	19.46	19.46	19.46	19.46
3	8.65	8.65	8.64	8.64	8.63	8.63	8.63	8.62	8.62	8.62
4	5.79	5.79	5.78	5.77	5.77	5.76	5.76	5.75	5.75	5.75
5	4.55	4.54	4.53	4.53	4.52	4.52	4.51	4.50	4.50	4.50
6	3.86	3.86	3.85	3.84	3.83	3.83	3.82	3.82	3.81	3.81
7	3.43	3.43	3.42	3.41	3.40	3.40	3.39	3.39	3.38	3.38
8	3.14	3.13	3.12	3.12	3.11	3.10	3.1	3.09	3.08	3.08
9	2.93	2.92	2.91	2.90	2.89	2.89	2.88	2.87	2.87	2.86
10	2.76	2.75	2.75	2.74	2.73	2.72	2.72	2.71	2.70	2.70
11	2.64	2.63	2.62	2.61	2.60	2.59	2.59	2.58	2.58	2.57
12	2.53	2.52	2.51	2.51	2.50	2.49	2.48	2.48	2.47	2.47
13	2.45	2.44	2.43	2.42	2.41	2.41	2.40	2.39	2.39	2.38
14	2.38	2.37	2.36	2.35	2.34	2.33	2.33	2.32	2.31	2.31
15	2.32	2.31	2.3	2.29	2.28	2.27	2.27	2.26	2.25	2.25
16	2.26	2.25	2.24	2.24	2.23	2.22	2.21	2.21	2.20	2.19
17	2.22	2.21	2.20	2.19	2.18	2.17	2.17	2.16	2.15	2.15
18	2.18	2.17	2.16	2.15	2.14	2.13	2.13	2.12	2.11	2.11
19	2.14	2.13	2.12	2.11	2.11	2.10	2.09	2.08	2.08	2.07
20	2.11	2.10	2.09	2.08	2.07	2.07	2.06	2.05	2.05	2.04
21	2.08	2.07	2.06	2.05	2.05	2.04	2.03	2.02	2.02	2.01
22	2.06	2.05	2.04	2.03	2.02	2.01	2.00	2.00	1.99	1.98
23	2.04	2.02	2.01	2.01	2.00	1.99	1.98	1.97	1.97	1.96
24	2.01	2.00	1.99	1.98	1.97	1.97	1.96	1.95	1.95	1.94
25	2.00	1.98	1.97	1.96	1.96	1.95	1.94	1.93	1.93	1.92
26	1.98	1.97	1.96	1.95	1.94	1.93	1.92	1.91	1.91	1.90
27	1.96	1.95	1.94	1.93	1.92	1.91	1.90	1.90	1.89	1.88
28	1.95	1.93	1.92	1.91	1.91	1.90	1.89	1.88	1.88	1.87
29	1.93	1.92	1.91	1.90	1.89	1.88	1.88	1.87	1.86	1.85
30	1.92	1.91	1.90	1.89	1.88	1.87	1.86	1.85	1.85	1.84
35	1.87	1.85	1.84	1.83	1.82	1.82	1.81	1.80	1.79	1.79
40	1.83	1.81	1.80	1.79	1.78	1.77	1.77	1.76	1.75	1.74
50	1.77	1.76	1.75	1.74	1.73	1.72	1.71	1.70	1.69	1.69
60	1.73	1.72	1.71	1.70	1.69	1.68	1.67	1.66	1.66	1.65
70	1.71	1.70	1.68	1.67	1.66	1.65	1.65	1.64	1.63	1.62
80	1.69	1.68	1.67	1.65	1.64	1.63	1.63	1.62	1.61	1.60
100	1.66	1.65	1.64	1.63	1.62	1.61	1.60	1.59	1.58	1.57
150	1.63	1.61	1.60	1.59	1.58	1.57	1.56	1.55	1.54	1.54
300	1.59	1.58	1.57	1.55	1.54	1.53	1.52	1.51	1.51	1.50
1000	1.57	1.55	1.54	1.53	1.52	1.51	1.50	1.49	1.48	1.47

Note. df_2 = degrees of freedom for denominator.

Table A-4 (continued)

α = .05	*Degrees of freedom for numerator* (df_1)									
df_2	**31**	**32**	**33**	**34**	**35**	**36**	**37**	**38**	**39**	**40**
1	250.25	250.38	250.50	250.56	250.69	250.82	250.88	250.88	251.07	251.13
2	19.46	19.46	19.46	19.47	19.47	19.47	19.47	19.47	19.47	19.47
3	8.61	8.61	8.61	8.61	8.60	8.60	8.60	8.60	8.60	8.59
4	5.74	5.74	5.74	5.73	5.73	5.73	5.72	5.72	5.72	5.72
5	4.49	4.49	4.48	4.48	4.48	4.47	4.47	4.47	4.47	4.46
6	3.80	3.8	3.8	3.79	3.79	3.79	3.78	3.78	3.78	3.77
7	3.37	3.37	3.36	3.36	3.36	3.35	3.35	3.35	3.34	3.34
8	3.07	3.07	3.07	3.06	3.06	3.06	3.05	3.05	3.05	3.04
9	2.86	2.85	2.85	2.85	2.84	2.84	2.84	2.83	2.83	2.83
10	2.69	2.69	2.69	2.68	2.68	2.67	2.67	2.67	2.66	2.66
11	2.57	2.56	2.56	2.55	2.55	2.54	2.54	2.54	2.53	2.53
12	2.46	2.46	2.45	2.45	2.44	2.44	2.44	2.43	2.43	2.43
13	2.38	2.37	2.37	2.36	2.36	2.35	2.35	2.35	2.34	2.34
14	2.30	2.30	2.29	2.29	2.28	2.28	2.28	2.27	2.27	2.27
15	2.24	2.24	2.23	2.23	2.22	2.22	2.21	2.21	2.21	2.20
16	2.19	2.18	2.18	2.17	2.17	2.17	2.16	2.16	2.15	2.15
17	2.14	2.14	2.13	2.13	2.12	2.12	2.11	2.11	2.11	2.10
18	2.10	2.10	2.09	2.09	2.08	2.08	2.07	2.07	2.07	2.06
19	2.07	2.06	2.06	2.05	2.05	2.04	2.04	2.03	2.03	2.03
20	2.03	2.03	2.02	2.02	2.01	2.01	2.01	2.00	2.00	1.99
21	2.00	2.00	1.99	1.99	1.98	1.98	1.98	1.97	1.97	1.96
22	1.98	1.97	1.97	1.96	1.96	1.95	1.95	1.95	1.94	1.94
23	1.95	1.95	1.94	1.94	1.93	1.93	1.93	1.92	1.92	1.91
24	1.93	1.93	1.92	1.92	1.91	1.91	1.90	1.90	1.90	1.89
25	1.91	1.91	1.9	1.90	1.89	1.89	1.88	1.88	1.88	1.87
26	1.89	1.89	1.88	1.88	1.87	1.87	1.87	1.86	1.86	1.85
27	1.88	1.87	1.87	1.86	1.86	1.85	1.85	1.84	1.84	1.84
28	1.86	1.86	1.85	1.85	1.84	1.84	1.83	1.83	1.82	1.82
29	1.85	1.84	1.84	1.83	1.83	1.82	1.82	1.81	1.81	1.81
30	1.83	1.83	1.82	1.82	1.81	1.81	1.80	1.80	1.80	1.79
35	1.78	1.77	1.77	1.76	1.76	1.75	1.75	1.74	1.74	1.74
40	1.74	1.73	1.73	1.72	1.72	1.71	1.71	1.70	1.70	1.69
50	1.68	1.67	1.67	1.66	1.66	1.65	1.65	1.64	1.64	1.63
60	1.64	1.64	1.63	1.62	1.62	1.61	1.61	1.60	1.60	1.59
70	1.62	1.61	1.60	1.60	1.59	1.59	1.58	1.58	1.57	1.57
80	1.59	1.59	1.58	1.58	1.57	1.56	1.56	1.55	1.55	1.54
100	1.57	1.56	1.55	1.55	1.54	1.54	1.53	1.52	1.52	1.52
150	1.53	1.52	1.51	1.51	1.50	1.50	1.49	1.49	1.48	1.48
300	1.49	1.48	1.48	1.47	1.46	1.46	1.45	1.45	1.44	1.43
1000	1.46	1.46	1.45	1.44	1.43	1.43	1.42	1.42	1.41	1.41

Note. df_2 = degrees of freedom for denominator.

Table A-4 (continued)

α = .05	*Degrees of freedom for numerator* (df_1)									
df_2	45	50	60	70	80	100	120	150	300	1000
1	251.51	251.76	252.21	252.52	252.72	253.04	253.23	253.48	253.87	254.19
2	19.47	19.48	19.48	19.48	19.48	19.48	19.49	19.49	19.49	19.49
3	8.59	8.58	8.57	8.57	8.56	8.55	8.55	8.54	8.54	8.53
4	5.71	5.70	5.69	5.68	5.67	5.66	5.66	5.65	5.64	5.63
5	4.45	4.44	4.43	4.42	4.41	4.41	4.40	4.39	4.38	4.37
6	3.76	3.75	3.74	3.73	3.72	3.71	3.70	3.70	3.68	3.67
7	3.33	3.32	3.30	3.29	3.29	3.27	3.27	3.26	3.24	3.23
8	3.03	3.02	3.01	2.99	2.99	2.97	2.97	2.96	2.94	2.93
9	2.81	2.80	2.79	2.78	2.77	2.76	2.75	2.74	2.72	2.71
10	2.65	2.64	2.62	2.61	2.60	2.59	2.58	2.57	2.55	2.54
11	2.52	2.51	2.49	2.48	2.47	2.46	2.45	2.44	2.42	2.41
12	2.41	2.40	2.38	2.37	2.36	2.35	2.34	2.33	2.31	2.30
13	2.33	2.31	2.30	2.28	2.27	2.26	2.25	2.24	2.23	2.21
14	2.25	2.24	2.22	2.21	2.20	2.19	2.18	2.17	2.15	2.14
15	2.19	2.18	2.16	2.15	2.14	2.12	2.11	2.10	2.09	2.07
16	2.14	2.12	2.11	2.09	2.08	2.07	2.06	2.05	2.03	2.02
17	2.09	2.08	2.06	2.05	2.03	2.02	2.01	2.00	1.98	1.97
18	2.05	2.04	2.02	2.00	1.99	1.98	1.97	1.96	1.94	1.92
19	2.01	2.00	1.98	1.97	1.96	1.94	1.93	1.92	1.90	1.88
20	1.98	1.97	1.95	1.93	1.92	1.91	1.90	1.89	1.86	1.85
21	1.95	1.94	1.92	1.90	1.89	1.88	1.87	1.86	1.83	1.82
22	1.92	1.91	1.89	1.88	1.86	1.85	1.84	1.83	1.81	1.79
23	1.90	1.88	1.86	1.85	1.84	1.82	1.81	1.8	1.78	1.76
24	1.88	1.86	1.84	1.83	1.82	1.80	1.79	1.78	1.76	1.74
25	1.86	1.84	1.82	1.81	1.80	1.78	1.77	1.76	1.73	1.72
26	1.84	1.82	1.80	1.79	1.78	1.76	1.75	1.74	1.71	1.70
27	1.82	1.81	1.79	1.77	1.76	1.74	1.73	1.72	1.70	1.68
28	1.80	1.79	1.77	1.75	1.74	1.73	1.71	1.70	1.68	1.66
29	1.79	1.77	1.75	1.74	1.73	1.71	1.70	1.69	1.66	1.65
30	1.77	1.76	1.74	1.72	1.71	1.70	1.68	1.67	1.65	1.63
35	1.72	1.70	1.68	1.66	1.65	1.63	1.62	1.61	1.58	1.57
40	1.67	1.66	1.64	1.62	1.61	1.59	1.58	1.56	1.54	1.52
50	1.61	1.60	1.58	1.56	1.54	1.52	1.51	1.50	1.47	1.45
60	1.57	1.56	1.53	1.52	1.50	1.48	1.47	1.45	1.42	1.40
70	1.55	1.53	1.50	1.49	1.47	1.45	1.44	1.42	1.39	1.36
80	1.52	1.51	1.48	1.46	1.45	1.43	1.41	1.39	1.36	1.34
100	1.49	1.48	1.45	1.43	1.41	1.39	1.38	1.36	1.32	1.30
150	1.45	1.44	1.41	1.39	1.37	1.34	1.33	1.31	1.27	1.24
300	1.41	1.39	1.36	1.34	1.32	1.30	1.28	1.26	1.21	1.17
1000	1.38	1.36	1.33	1.31	1.29	1.26	1.24	1.22	1.16	1.11

Note. df_2 = degrees of freedom for denominator.

Table A-5 *Critical U-values of the Mann-Whitney distribution* (***α* = .025** *and* ***α* = .05**)

		n_2																	
n_1	α	**3**	**4**	**5**	**6**	**7**	**8**	**9**	**10**	**11**	**12**	**13**	**14**	**15**	**16**	**17**	**18**	**19**	**20**
3	.025	0	0	1	2	2	3	3	4	4	5	5	6	6	7	7	8	8	9
	.05	1	1	2	3	3	4	5	5	6	6	7	8	8	9	10	10	11	12
4	.025	0	1	2	3	4	5	5	6	7	8	9	10	11	12	12	13	14	15
	.05	1	2	3	4	5	6	7	8	9	10	11	12	13	15	16	17	18	19
5	.025	1	2	3	4	6	7	8	9	10	12	13	14	15	16	18	19	20	21
	.05	2	3	5	6	7	9	10	12	13	14	16	17	19	20	21	23	24	26
6	.025	2	3	4	6	7	9	11	12	14	15	17	18	20	22	23	25	26	28
	.05	3	4	6	8	9	11	13	15	17	18	20	22	24	26	27	29	31	33
7	.025	2	4	6	7	9	11	13	15	17	19	21	23	25	27	29	31	33	35
	.05	3	5	7	9	12	14	16	18	20	22	25	27	29	31	34	36	38	40
8	.025	3	5	7	9	11	14	16	18	20	23	25	27	30	32	35	37	39	42
	.05	4	6	9	11	14	16	19	21	24	27	29	32	34	37	40	42	45	48
9	.025	3	5	8	11	13	16	18	21	24	27	29	32	35	38	40	43	46	49
	.05	5	7	10	13	16	19	22	25	28	31	34	37	40	43	46	49	52	55
10	.025	4	6	9	12	15	18	21	24	27	30	34	37	40	43	46	49	53	56
	.05	5	8	12	15	18	21	25	28	32	35	38	42	45	49	52	56	59	63
11	.025	4	7	10	14	17	20	24	27	31	34	38	41	45	48	52	56	59	63
	.05	6	9	13	17	20	24	28	32	35	39	43	47	51	55	58	62	66	70
12	.025	5	8	12	15	19	23	27	30	34	38	42	46	50	54	58	62	66	70
	.05	6	10	14	18	22	27	31	35	39	43	48	52	56	61	65	69	73	78
13	.025	5	9	13	17	21	25	29	34	38	42	46	51	55	60	64	68	73	77
	.05	7	11	16	20	25	29	34	38	43	48	52	57	62	66	71	76	81	85
14	.025	6	10	14	18	23	27	32	37	41	46	51	56	60	65	70	75	79	84
	.05	8	12	17	22	27	32	37	42	47	52	57	62	67	72	78	83	88	93
15	.025	6	11	15	20	25	30	35	40	45	50	55	60	65	71	76	81	86	91
	.05	8	13	19	24	29	34	40	45	51	56	62	67	73	78	84	89	95	101
16	.025	7	12	16	22	27	32	38	43	48	54	60	65	71	76	82	87	93	99
	.05	9	15	20	26	31	37	43	49	55	61	66	72	78	84	90	96	102	108
17	.025	7	12	18	23	29	35	40	46	52	58	64	70	76	82	88	94	100	106
	.05	10	16	21	27	34	40	46	52	58	65	71	78	84	90	97	103	110	116
18	.025	8	13	19	25	31	37	43	49	56	62	68	75	81	87	94	100	107	113
	.05	10	17	23	29	36	42	49	56	62	69	76	83	89	96	103	110	117	124
19	.025	8	14	20	26	33	39	46	53	59	66	73	79	86	93	100	107	114	120
	.05	11	18	24	31	38	45	52	59	66	73	81	88	95	102	110	117	124	131
20	.025	9	15	21	28	35	42	49	56	63	70	77	84	91	99	106	113	120	128
	.05	12	19	26	33	40	48	55	63	70	78	85	93	101	108	116	124	131	139

Source: Verdooren, L. R. (1963). Extended tables of critical values for Wilcoxon's test statistic. *Biometrika, 50*(1/2), 177-186.

Note. To reject the null hypothesis at the level of significance α, the *critical value* of *U* provided in this table must be *greater* than the computed value of *U* (the smaller number of U_1 and U_2 — see Formulas 12.1 and 12.2, respectively, in Chapter 12). Keep in mind that (a) α = .025 is used for one-sided test with α = .025 or two-sided test with α = .05, and (b) α = .05 is used for one-sided test with α = .05 or two-sided test with α = .10.

Table A-6 *Critical T-values for the Wilcoxon matched-pairs signed-ranks test*

n	α (*one-sided test*)		
	.025	**.01**	**.005**
	α (*two-sided test*)		
	.05	**.02**	**.01**
7	2	0	—
8	4	2	0
9	6	3	2
10	8	5	3
11	11	7	5
12	14	10	7
13	17	13	10
14	21	16	13
15	25	20	16
16	30	24	20
17	35	28	23
18	40	33	28
19	46	38	32
20	52	43	38
21	59	49	43
22	66	56	49
23	73	62	55
24	81	69	61
25	89	77	68

Source: Wilcoxon, F. & Wilcox, R. A. (1964) *Some rapid approximate statistical procedures* (rev. ed.). Pearl River, NY: Lederie Laboratories.

Note. To reject the null hypothesis at the level of significance α, the *critical value* of T provided in this table must be *greater* than the computed value of T.

Author Index

Subject Index